Real-Life
Sociology

Real-Life Sociology

Sociology

A Canadian Approach

Anabel Quan-Haase

Lorne Tepperman

OXFORD

UNIVERSITY PRESS

OXFORD
UNIVERSITY PRESS

Oxford University Press is a department of the University of Oxford.
It furthers the University's objective of excellence in research, scholarship,
and education by publishing worldwide. Oxford is a registered trade mark of
Oxford University Press in the UK and in certain other countries.

Published in Canada by
Oxford University Press
8 Sampson Mews, Suite 204,
Don Mills, Ontario M3C 0H5 Canada

www.oupcanada.com

Library and Archives Canada Cataloguing in Publication
Quan-Haase, Anabel, author
Real-life sociology : a Canadian approach / Anabel Quan-Haase and
Lorne Tepperman.

Includes bibliographical references and index.
Issued in print and electronic formats.
ISBN 978-0-19-902469-8 (softcover).–ISBN 978-0-19-902476-6 (PDF)

1. Sociology–Textbooks. 2. Sociology–Canada–Textbooks.
3. Canada–Social conditions–21st century. 4. Textbooks. I. Tepperman,
Lorne, 1943-, author II. Title.

HM586.Q35 2018   301.0971   C2017-906142-9
                                          C2017-906143-7

Cover image: Neil Webb/Getty Images
Cover design: Laurie McGregor
Interior design: Laurie McGregor

Oxford University Press is committed to our environment.
Wherever possible, our books are printed on paper which comes from
responsible sources.

Printed and bound in the United States of America
1 2 3 4 — 21 20 19 18

Brief Contents

Contents

3   Cultures as Ways of Seeing Reality   57

6 · Economic Inequality and Class Exploitation   129

7 · Gender Inequality and Gender Domination   161

8   Racialization and the Construction of Social Marginality   183

11   Experiences in Schools and Formal Education   265

12   Work and the Economy in Real Life   293

13   The Power of Religious Ideas and Institutions   319

16 Social Movements and Collective Action   391

Preface

The job of any textbook is to invigorate an old field (or discipline), giving it new life. If successful, the present book does this by highlighting ways that the field— cultivated over centuries in various ways, for a variety of historical reasons—can help us better understand the present day, and perhaps even the future.

In *Real-Life Sociology*, we have tried to show how the present-day world has been shaped by rapid developments in science and technology, and how, in turn, social forces have brought science and technology to fruition. As we will see, science and technology have flourished at particular times and places, but never as much as today. As a result, many aspects of daily life—how we play, work, and learn—have been transformed by technological innovation—by computers, the internet and social media, modern medicine, space age modes of transportation, and household appliances that would have been unimaginable only a century ago, to name a few of these "miracles."

Sociologists are becoming increasingly aware of the rapid scientific and technological transformations that are unfolding. This provides a unique opportunity for understanding and predicting how all of these technological marvels will affect our personal lives, institutions, and social norms. Sociologists are developing new methodologies to study how people communicate and interact in a world mediated by mobile phones, social media, and online communities. This is an exciting time, as many new questions surface and new ways of looking at the social world emerge. But it is also a time of post-truth, unprecedented forms of alienation and inequality, and rapid transformations in many domains of life.

Futurologist Alvin Toffler said in the 1970s that we were all at risk of suffering "future shock"— the result of a speeded up pace of life and unparalleled social change. There is some evidence Toffler was right: for example, we see high and growing rates of anxiety, depression, and addiction in many parts of the world, especially among our young people. In some part, these issues are a response to the stress produced by change and uncertainty. Yet humanity has always struggled—and will continue to struggle—with rapid social change. It is our hope that this book, which sets some of the most newsworthy and important social changes in a sociological context, will help students overcome "future shock" by adapting to the future as it unfolds.

So, with that thought in mind, we hope our readers find this "real-life approach" to present-day society exhilarating and useful. Let us know what you think.

Acknowledgments

It takes a village to raise a child and a community of helpers to write a book as wide-ranging as this one.

At the University of Toronto, a variety of undergraduate researchers helped Professor Tepperman research, write, and edit this book. These excellent research assistants included Ivana Avramov, Teodora (Teddy) Avramov, Gary Guinness, Richard Kennedy, Darya (Dasha) Kuznetsova, Ashley Ramnaraine, Jacqueline Wing Yang Siu, Sylvia Urbanik, Alice Wang, and Jiaqi Wang. They were headed up by the amazing Zoe Sebastien, who has now gone on to an MA program in philosophy with a SSHRC grant in hand and can be expected to do great things in the future. Thanks go to all of our undergraduate helpers for their insights and efforts. At Western University, Professor Quan-Haase benefitted greatly from the help of students Isioma Elueze, Chandell Gosse, Kelsang Legden, Ryan James Mack, Victoria O'Meara, Abdul Malik Sulley, and Carly Williams.

We were also helped by a number of anonymous reviewers who provided wonderful and instrumental suggestions for improvement at various stages of development. Big thanks go, then, to our reviewers

- Alexa Carson, Humber College;
- Rita Hamoline, University of Saskatchewan;
- Alicia Horton, University of the Fraser Valley, Kwantlen Polytechnic University, and Douglas College;
- Susan Miller, University of Manitoba;
- Lina Samuel, McMaster University;
- Ondine Park, MacEwan University and University of Alberta;
- Sonia Perna, SAIT Polytechnic;
- Katarzyna Rukszto, Sheridan College;
- Li Zong, University of Saskatchewan;

as well as several who chose to remain anonymous.

Last and certainly not least, we want to thank the marvelous people at Oxford University Press who supported our work throughout with great dedication. They include Darcey Pepper, who, as former acquisitions editor, helped us launch the project; Amy Gordon, our developmental editor, who provided a steady flow of good humour and countless invaluable suggestions. Amy made our job genuinely enjoyable, even at times when we were struggling. So, thank you, Amy. Joanne Muzak, our copy editor, was extraordinarily thorough and helpful; it was a particular pleasure experiencing her professionalism.

We also thank our colleagues at the University of Toronto and Western University for their input and support. Finally, we thank our parents, who through their hard work made generational upward mobility, and in that way the writing of this book, a reality.

Anabel Quan-Haase
Western University

Lorne Tepperman
University of Toronto

Introducing . . . *Real-Life Sociology*

Society shapes our everyday lives in ways we often cannot see unless we exercise our sociological imaginations. It is our hope that *Real-Life Sociology* will not only teach you to engage your sociological imagination, but will also help you understand why this skill is so important, particularly in today's globalized and technology-driven world.

In preparing this new book, we had one paramount goal: to produce the most relatable, comprehensive, and dynamic introduction to sociology available to Canadian students. We hope that as you browse through the pages that follow, you will see why we believe *Real-Life Sociology* is the most exciting and innovative textbook available to Canadian sociology students today.

(p. 2005). In 2017 the federal government allocated $3.4 billion in spending for infrastructure, health, and education in Indigenous communities (CBC News, 2017). Even as the internet functions as a source of inequality, it has helped Indigenous people put forward the crises they face, connect with allies, and push governments into providing better infrastructure and services. See Chapter 16 for more on Indigenous communities using the internet to gain media coverage, political leverage, and access to resources.

Homelessness

In recent decades, Canadian cities have experienced a housing crisis in line with exponential increases in real estate prices. This crisis has further intensified the lack of affordable housing in cities, creating an increase in homelessness.

Most affected by this trend are low-income people and families, because they are usually renters and not homeowners. This fact makes them vulnerable to fluctuations in rental demand and rental price. For them, even small increases in rental prices can mean being forced onto the streets and into shelters. How many people are homeless in Canada in a given year is impossible to know exactly; indeed, the numbers of homeless people seem to vary from day to day. However, estimates suggest that Canada's homeless population numbers between 200,000 and 300,000 people (see Figure 6.5).

These numbers don't tell the full story, as an estimated 50,000 Canadians are described as "**hidden homeless**"—people without homes who stay with friends or family temporarily. Many homeless people temporarily or more permanently stay in shelters, where and when they are available. Emergency shelters provide immediate, short-term accommodation to homeless people, with residents being expected to leave the facilities each morning. Other shelters provide longer-term homes for specific populations, such as for homeless youth or women and their children who are victims of family violence. We discuss family violence and victimization in Chapter 7.

hidden homeless people without homes who stay with friends or family temporarily rather than in shelters or in public spaces.

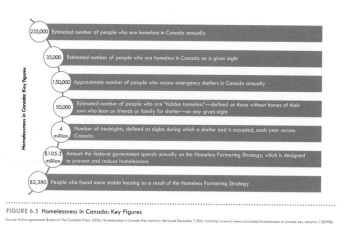

FIGURE 6.5 Homelessness in Canada: Key Figures

Source: Author generated. Based on The Canadian Press. (2016). Homelessness in Canada: Key statistics. Retrieved December 7, 2016, from http://www.ctvnews.ca/canada/homelessness-in-canada-key-statistics-1.2819986

What Makes This a One-of-a-Kind Textbook

A Canadian Textbook for Twenty-first Century Canadian Students

Written by Canadians for Canadians, *Real-Life Sociology* highlights the realities of Canadian society as it exists today: it uses recent major events with sociological drivers and effects— such as #NoMoreStolenSisters, the Syrian refugee crisis, the Trudeau cabinet, and many more—to illustrate sociological concepts.

drawn into these jobs. They must seek their labour on a day-to-day basis and live without the comforts of permanent employment.

Non-standard work is the fastest-growing type of employment in high-income countries today. The rise in non-standard work arrangements, such as part-time work, has even affected full-time workers. With fewer full-time jobs, more is expected of full-time workers. Many are forced to work longer hours, often unpaid, to compensate for the shortage of workers on site (Jackson, Baldwin, Robinson, & Wiggins, 2000). So, while some workers today are unemployed or fear unemployment, others are underemployed—working well below their skill and training level—while others still are overemployed. This leads to less solidarity and more inequality among workers.

The "Feminization" of Work

One feature of all non-standard work is that it tends to be "precarious"—uncontrollable and unpredictable. In Canada, 39.1 percent of employed women hold "precarious jobs" (Law Commission of Ontario, 2009). Precarious jobs have one or more of the following features: part-time employment, self-employment, fixed-term work, temporary work, on-call work, homework, and telecommuting. What they have in common is that they are not "standard" types of jobs, typified by full-time work by one particular employer.

A United Way report by Wayne Lewchuk et al. (2015; see also Lewchuk et al., 2016) on precarious employment in the Greater Toronto and Hamilton area, *The Precarity Penalty*, shows that standard employment relationships (i.e., non-precarious employment) have continued to decline in the last few years; and today, men and women are almost equally likely to hold precarious (i.e., non-standard) jobs, at a rate of roughly 50 per cent (see Figure 12.3). According to these same data, non-standard jobs have been increasing even more rapidly for men than for women. The decline in non-standard employment is more rapid for racialized workers than for white workers, and it is particularly marked for racialized men (Lewchuk et al., 2015).

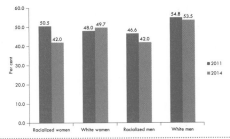

FIGURE 12.3 Percentage of Workers of Each Type employed in "Standard Work Relationship," by Sex and Racialization, GTHA 2011 and 2014

Source: Adapted from www.unitedwaytyr.com/document.doc?id=307 p. 28.

An Intersectional Approach

While the chapters in *Real-Life Sociology* are organized according to the traditional separation of gender, racialization, and class, the concept of intersectionality has been implemented throughout the book. Students will better understand the intersections of racialization, gender, gender presentation, citizenship status, Indigeneity, sexuality, disability, and class when discussing topics such as the wage gap, suicide statistics, educational attainment, social mobility, and status symbols.

Coverage of Technology and the Digital Society

In addition to Anabel Quan-Haase's expertise on the social changes led by information and communication technologies, every chapter includes powerful and accessible case studies and examples that show how technology and digital media are changing our everyday lives—and who these changes are leaving behind.

Introduction

From a sociological perspective, the systematic study of global inequality goes back only about 250 years. Adam Smith (1776), the founder of economics, was motivated to find an explanation for global inequality when he wrote the first classic work in economics, *The Wealth of Nations*. Why are some nations wealthy and powerful while others are not? Smith concluded the answer was specialization and trade, which allowed educated, trained individuals engaged in economic exchanges to maximize their well-being. Similarly, one of sociology's founders, Émile Durkheim (1892/1933), made a pitch for specialization and cooperation in his classic work *The Division of Labour* just over a century later. A highly specialized workforce that coordinates toward a common goal has an edge: this insight proved central to the functionalist approach in sociology to modernization and global inequality during the last hundred years. Today, a specialized workforce is one that is innovative and highly specialized. Box 9.1 shows the many advantages of technological innovations to health outcomes.

Think Globally

9.1 | Science, Technological Progress, and the Alarming Longevity Gap

Around the world, we see differences in individuals' and social groups' access to health care and advances in medical technology. These variations have profound effects on a person's health and are related to the length of time a newborn baby is expected to live. While a child born in Japan can expect to live for over 80 years (allowing for a slight difference in the life expectancies of males and females), a child born in Malawi can expect to live for about 51 years (WHO, 2016b, 2017). There is no biological or genetic reason for these striking differences in health and life expectancy. These global variations in life expectancy result from social and economic inequalities. When we look at health across the life course, it is shocking to see that many of the health problems and death risks are experienced by children under the age of five. In Canada, similar health risks also exist for specific social groups. For example, Inuit and First Nations children on isolated reserves are at a much higher risk of death before age five than other Canadian children (CIHR, 2008).

Canada is contributing, in various ways, to reducing national and global health inequalities. For example, expertise developed in Canada is shared with other nations to support their health initiatives. The Canadian Institutes for Health Research (CIHR, 2008) has identified global health research as a priority area and is supporting research that addresses the health challenges of low- and middle-income countries around the world. As well, CIHR is helping to build research capacity in these countries through education and technology transfer, so they are better able to meet their own health challenges.

The world is vibrating with active, creative people who are using what they have at hand to make their lives better and compete in an unequal global economy.

Time to reflect

In what ways has your own health benefitted from being in Canada? In what ways has the Canadian system let you down?

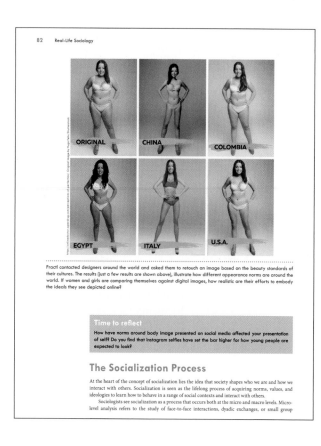

82   Real-Life Sociology

ORIGINAL   CHINA   COLOMBIA

EGYPT   ITALY   U.S.A.

Fractl contacted designers around the world and asked them to retouch an image based on the beauty standards of their cultures. The results (just a few results are shown above), illustrate how different appearance norms are around the world. If women and girls are comparing themselves against digital images, how realistic are their efforts to embody the ideals they see depicted online?

Time to reflect
How have norms around body image presented on social media affected your presentation of self? Do you find that Instagram selfies have set the bar higher for how young people are expected to look?

The Socialization Process

At the heart of the concept of socialization lies the idea that society shapes who we are and how we interact with others. Socialization is seen as the lifelong process of acquiring norms, values, and ideologies to learn how to behave in a range of social contexts and interact with others.
Sociologists see socialization as a process that occurs both at the micro and macro levels. Micro-level analysis refers to the study of face-to-face interactions, dyadic exchanges, or small group

A Visual, Thought-Provoking Presentation

Students are encouraged on every page to adopt a sociological imagination in order to see the sociology in everyday life. Carefully chosen photos and captions, provocative Time to Reflect questions, and end-of-chapter review questions invite readers to apply theory to their everyday lives.

Case Studies and Compelling Viewpoints

In addition to the Time to Reflect boxes, *Real-Life Sociology* features five other types of boxes that illustrate sociological concepts by highlighting issues, events, and ideas at the centre of contemporary life.

Think Globally

Think Globally boxes apply a global perspective to the concepts in the chapter, either comparing Canada with the world or bringing up key issues in other countries that illustrate the chapter concepts.

Theory in Everyday Life

Theory in Everyday Life boxes introduce theories and theorists and apply their work to the real world.

Sociology 2.0

Sociology 2.0 boxes outline contemporary examples as case studies that are relevant for students, particularly related to science and technology.

Digital Divide

Digital Divide boxes discuss inequality in a digital and technology-driven age, relating the concepts in the chapter to modern inequality.

Spotlight On

Spotlight On.... boxes illustrate key sociological concepts with relatable, familiar examples.

Online Resources

Real-Life Sociology is part of a comprehensive package of learning and teaching tools that includes resources for both students and instructors.

Dashboard: OUP's Learning Management System platform

Dashboard is a text-specific integrated learning system that offers quality content and tools to track student progress in an intuitive, web-based learning environment. It features a streamlined interface that connects students and lecturers with the functions used most frequently, simplifying the learning experience to save time and put student progress first.

 Throughout the book you may notice this icon in the margins; this will let you know that additional material on this topic is available on Dashboard ™.

In addition to the functionality of Dashboard as a platform, *Dashboard for Real-Life Sociology* includes the following content:

- Integrated e-book
- Test bank
- Chapter summaries
- Key terms lists
- Interactive flash cards for students
- Self-grading quizzes for students
- Student activities
- Case studies with suggested answers
- Sociology-related RSS newsfeed

Dashboard for Real-Life Sociology is available through your OUP sales representative, or visit dashboard.oup.com.

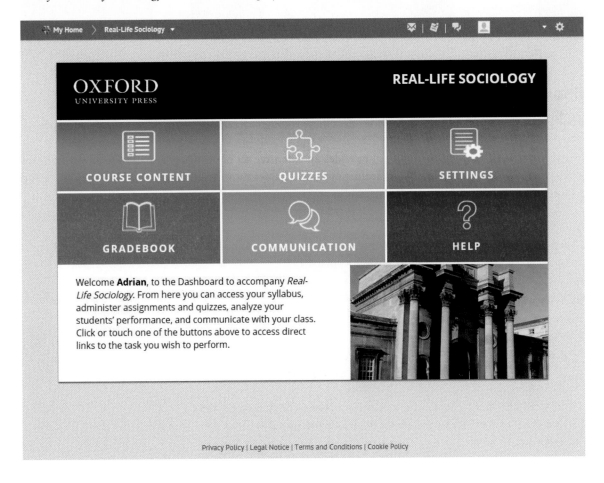

OUP Canada's Sociology Streaming Video Library

Over 20 award-winning feature films and documentaries of various lengths (feature-length, short films, and clips) are available online as streaming video for instructors to either show in the classroom or assign to students to watch at home. An accompanying video guide contains summaries, suggested clips, discussion questions, and related activities so that instructors can easily integrate videos into their course lectures, assignments, and class discussions. Access to this collection is free for instructors who have assigned this book for their course. For access, speak to your OUP sales representative, or visit www.oupcanada.com/SocVideos.

Click on the link to download the Video Viewing Guide for all 23 videos of the Sociology Collection (PDF).

Additional Material for Instructors

In addition to the above materials, OUP Canada offers these resources free to all instructors using the textbook:

- A comprehensive instructor's manual provides an extensive set of pedagogical tools and suggestions for every chapter, including a sample syllabus, lecture outlines, chapter summaries, suggested in-class activities, suggested teaching aids, cumulative assignments, and essay questions.
- Classroom-ready PowerPoint slides summarize key points from each chapter and incorporate graphics and tables drawn straight from the text.
- An extensive Test Generator enables instructors to sort, edit, import, and distribute a bank of questions in multiple-choice, true–false, and short-answer formats.

Talk to your sales representative, or visit www.oupcanada.com/QuanHaase&Tepperman for access to these materials.

Additional Material for Students

The Student Study Guide includes chapter overviews and summaries, lists of learning objectives and key terms, critical thinking questions, recommended readings, and recommended online resources to help you review the textbook and classroom material and to take concepts further.

Visit www.oupcanada.com/QuanHaase&Tepperman for access to student materials.

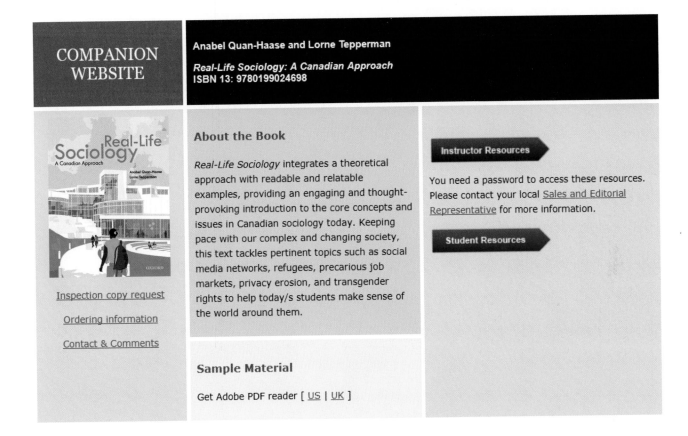

COMPANION WEBSITE

Anabel Quan-Haase and Lorne Tepperman

Real-Life Sociology: A Canadian Approach
ISBN 13: 9780199024698

Inspection copy request

Ordering information

Contact & Comments

About the Book

Real-Life Sociology integrates a theoretical approach with readable and relatable examples, providing an engaging and thought-provoking introduction to the core concepts and issues in Canadian sociology today. Keeping pace with our complex and changing society, this text tackles pertinent topics such as social media networks, refugees, precarious job markets, privacy erosion, and transgender rights to help today/s students make sense of the world around them.

Sample Material

Get Adobe PDF reader [US | UK]

Instructor Resources

You need a password to access these resources. Please contact your local Sales and Editorial Representative for more information.

Student Resources

Real-Life Sociology

1 Inspiring the Sociological Imagination

Learning Objectives

In this chapter, you will:

> See how sociology forms a picture of society

> Learn about the history and development of sociology as a social scientific discipline

> Be introduced to three key processes in sociology

> Gain an introduction to four main approaches of sociological analysis

> Understand how sociology can improve your skills necessary for employment

◀ Neil Webb/Getty Images

Introduction

The summer of 2015 saw an interesting example of the continued conflict between technology and society. It involved the outing of 30 million clients of Ashley Madison, a website established by a Toronto entrepreneur to help people cheat (sexually) on their spouses. Hackers whose identities remain unknown got inside the Ashley Madison servers, stole personal information about the customers of this service, and published it online, where anyone could see it. The consequences were immediate and widespread: they included shock and fear among the millions of people who had been "outed," a fall in the corporate value of Ashley Madison stock, and the resignation of the company's founder.

What happened, sociologically speaking? First, the company founder used a new technology—the internet—to violate traditional moral and religious values around marital fidelity. Then, hackers used the same new technology to punish the company founder and users, and reassert traditional moral and religious values.

Dashboard

Case study

Time to reflect

Do you think public shaming on the internet is a fair consequence to violating social expectations and values? Whether or not you agree or disagree with this tactic, reflect on why and how it is effective as you continue to read this chapter and the rest of the book.

Members of the public continue to debate the rights and wrongs of these events: for example, do people have a right to privacy if they are using the internet to violate traditional norms of fidelity? But that debate isn't new. People have been debating the unexpected and unintended uses of science and technology since at least the beginning of the Industrial Revolution, around 1776. In the last 250 years, science and technology have brought humanity great benefits: a higher material standard of living through mass production, for example. They have also brought humanity new worries: environmental pollution and global warming; systematicity in mass killing (e.g., the concentration camp); and increased social inequality, to name just a few. Many people wonder whether new developments, for example, in digital entertainment like YouTube, will fall into the first category (i.e., benefits to society) or the second (i.e., detriments to society).

Science, Technology, and the Sociological Imagination

Before we can proceed, we need to clarify a few key concepts: especially, sociological imagination, science, and technology.

C. Wright Mills and the Sociological Imagination

sociological imagination the ability to perceive the underlying societal causes of individual experiences and issues; and to think outside the accepted wisdom and common routines of daily life.

Today, every sociologist understands the importance of a "**sociological imagination**." The great American sociologist C. Wright Mills (1955) defined sociological imagination as a "vivid awareness of the relationship between personal experience and the wider society" (p. 5). Sociological imagination is not a theory but an outlook that tries to steer us away from thinking routinely about our everyday lives.

Mills (1959) wrote that the sociological imagination is an ability to connect large and small, fast changing and slow changing, parts of social life. It makes us aware of the relation between people and the wider society. It helps us to look at our personal experiences in a different, more objective way. It forces us to ask how our lives are shaped by the larger social context in which we live. Finally, the sociological imagination helps us see society as the result of millions of people working out their personal lives.

To simplify, we could say that using the sociological imagination means applying imaginative thought to the asking and answering of sociological questions. What does this mean? Well, for example, the sociological imagination helps us understand that individuals actions not only have social consequences, they also have social causes. Usually, we do what we are told to do, or have learned to do. Often, our actions are the product of (invisible) **norms** and **values**; such invisible norms and values exist in every society at all times, though they change over time. Equally, our actions take place within a particular social context that allows us only some choices and not others. The things we do affect other people and, in that way, they shape the society we live in and subtly contribute to social change.

The sociological imagination is also a learned capacity to shift from one way of thinking to another—to pull away from the immediate situation and think from an alternative point of view. Often we can do this only by rejecting everyday knowledge and "common sense." In short, applying the sociological imagination requires us to break free from personal experiences and habits, if only for a while.

In principle, this approach to understanding should lead sociologists to empathize with disadvantaged people and pursue social justice. Mills felt that a lack of sociological imagination could make people apathetic—that is, lacking in willingness to study and solve social problems. Without a sociological imagination, they might lose their ability to respond appropriately to human tragedies and injustices, or to criticize their political leaders. They might wilfully lash out at disadvantaged or blameless people and avoid engagement with the people most in need of help, because they—the sociologically deprived—did not correctly understand their own role in society, or the reasons why bad things happen to good people.

In studying sociology, you will find many opportunities to use your sociological imagination. Some would say that the sociological imagination is the application of critical thinking skills to social issues, and we see some merit in that argument; however, the sociological imagination is more than that. It is a way of thinking about society as a tapestry of individual lives interacting and evolving over time. So, though the sociological imagination is challenging, we think it will make the world come alive for you and help you to see your life in new, more interesting, and provocative ways.

How Sociology Relates to Science and Technology

By **science**, a term we will use repeatedly in this book, we mean an approach to knowledge of the natural and social world that relies on the systematic analysis of empirical evidence—that is, evidence we collect through our senses (especially, our eyes and ears.) Also, we mean the body of knowledge that accumulates through the use of this scientific method. By **technology**, we mean the object or material instruments developed to serve a particular, practical purpose. From this standpoint, technology includes everything from a simple penknife to a nuclear reactor to an app. However, sociologists mean more than that by the term *technology*.

Sociologists since Max Weber have viewed technology within the framework of applied rationality. In his writings, Weber shows repeatedly how a desire to rationalize society leads to significant changes in the domains of law, business, science, commerce, and other human activities. The rise to dominance of technology and technological solutions to human problems points to the growth of a human preoccupation with efficiency and effectiveness. And as sociologist Michel Foucault points out, it has also suited a growing preoccupation with the need for individuals to exercise systematic self-monitoring and self-control, the essence of what he calls "governmentality." We will have much more to say about Weber and Foucault, rationalization, governmentality, and a host of other related topics in the course of this book.

Of course, not all scientific theories yield technological uses; and not all technology requires a great deal of scientific theorizing. Much has been developed through practical, hit-and-miss experimentation. However, in the modern industrial world, the most socially transformative technologies—television, computers, plastics, and modern medicines, to name a few—have grown out of scientific research, theory, and application. In fact, some people believe that technological change is the source

norms the rules or expectations of behaviour people consider acceptable in their group or society. People who do not follow these norms may be shunned, punished, or ridiculed. Norms, like values, vary from one society to another and change over time.

values shared understanding of what a group or society deems good, right, and desirable; a way of viewing the world and attaching positive or negative sentiments.

science the systematic study of the structure and behaviour of the physical and natural world through observation and experiment. Science, from a sociological standpoint, is a communal system of organized doubt and skepticism that aims to refine theories through the collection and use of empirical data.

technology objects developed to serve a particular (e.g., social, political, cultural, or personal) purpose.

of all important social change. This idea is usually called technological determinism. In this book, we do not take this position. Instead, we will argue that there is a complex interplay between science, technology, and society that needs careful examination. And this book will provide such an examination. Moreover, we do not argue that the influence on society of science and technology has been wholly beneficial. As we will see, from environmental issues to warfare and mass extermination to mindless consumerism (and so on), both science and technology have created new troubling social problems, while solving many others.

Time to reflect

Think of a technological invention that has happened during your lifetime, and how it has changed social expectations. For example, before smartphones, we did not expect people to check their social media throughout the day. How has that expectation changed the kinds of social pressure you experience on any given day?

There are entire university programs that study the history of science and technology, so it is impossible to do justice to this topic in a few paragraphs. In short, sociology is one way of studying human life on planet Earth: how societies resemble and differ from one another, how people co-operate to achieve their goals and how they conflict, and how our major organizations and institutions operate. If this description sounds unclear or overly ambitious, wait until you have finished reading this book before deciding what sociology is actually about.

Why is sociology well positioned to study social change resulting from science and technology? There has always been a strong connection between scientific discovery, technological change, and social change. Repeatedly, societies have had to catch up with scientific and technological advances: to adjust themselves to new risks, dangers, and moral uncertainties. With the development of industrial technology, societies have also had to reorganize themselves—create new kinds of families, workplaces, and governments, for example. And that is where the study of sociology got its start. Just as there has been technology for millennia, there has been some form of sociology. In an important way, Herodotus (484–425 BC)—the so-called founder of history—can be considered an early sociologist. Similarly, some may view the great North African thinker Ibn Khaldun (AD 1332–1406) as the first sociologist. However, most sociologists will tell you that the modern study of sociology began over two centuries ago during the Enlightenment.

Time to reflect

As you'll see below, the accepted history of sociology in most North American and European schools is that it emerged from a prolonged debate between tradition and the so-called Enlightenment. Think about what the word *enlightened* means, and how it places certain (white European) people in superior opposition to the rest of history, and to the rest of the world. In what way does calling Ibn Khaldun a seminal thinker in the field of sociology disrupt this story, and why might that be threatening to some people?

The Age of Enlightenment (roughly 1650 to 1850) was an important era in philosophical, intellectual, scientific, and cultural life in the Global North. The Enlightenment promoted secular (that is, non-religious) institutions, rule of law, free economic markets, and mass literacy. Enlightenment thinkers opposed arbitrary political power, religious superstition, and the traditional hierarchies (i.e., monarchy, aristocracy, and clergy). Enlightenment thinking also emphasized science.

In the early nineteenth century, armed with Enlightenment thinking and its effects of traditional social life, sociologists began to formulate a science of society. With the use of evidence-based theories, many believed that people would be able to build better societies in the future. These aspirations are evident in the thinking of sociology's three founding figures: Émile Durkheim, Karl Marx, and Max Weber.

Also evident in the thinking of sociology's founders was a concern about the dangers of industrialism, capitalism, and "modernity." On this score, Durkheim wrote about the dangers of "anomie," Marx about the problems of "alienation" and "exploitation," and Weber about what he called the "iron cage" of bureaucratic modernity, for example. Later generations of sociologists wrote at length about the fragmentation of community, the loss of faith, the undermining of stable authority, the social and psychological effects of disorganization, and so on. Beyond that, many sociologists called attention to the persistent significance of non-scientific and non-technological elements in social life—for example, the persistence of religion, ethnic loyalties, family ties, and community sentiments.

As American social theorist Talcott Parsons famously showed in his first important book, *The Structure of Social Action* (1937), a central contribution of the founding European sociologists was the discovery of the "non-rational." Though science and technology promoted rational, evidence-based thinking, leading some (like English social theorists Herbert Spencer and H.G. Wells and, in France, Saint-Simon, Comte, Fourier, and Proudhon) to imagine a nineteenth-century leap in social evolution, non-rational elements of social life persisted. As Durkheim showed, religious ritual and social connectedness remained important for human survival; and as Weber showed, religious belief and political legitimacy remained important for orderly change. And while Marx might criticize religion for being an opiate of the uninformed masses, he recognized its political importance. Later Marxists, especially those in the Frankfurt School, would pay a great deal of attention to the social and political importance of non-rational ideologies, beliefs, and everyday practices (such as consumer fetishism.)

Yet we cannot deny the importance of science and technology for the development of sociology. As Max Weber might say, there was an *elective affinity*—a deep compatibility of goals and purposes— between technological change and the rise of sociology. Both technology and sociology sought to improve or better understand the everyday lives of ordinary people, through scientific investigation and the systematic application of knowledge.

Aside from this basic compatibility, there was also a causal connection between the two. Sociology, like any art or science, cannot prosper under general conditions of poverty and despair; by increasing prosperity, science and technology provided the necessary conditions for the growth of universities and, within them, the growth of academic sociology.

In turn, sociology embraced this opportunity. Throughout the golden age of technology (1870 to 1940) following the Enlightenment, sociology investigated ways to solve the social problems associated with economic modernization and political change. Max Weber wrote about the rise of science, Durkheim about the rise of modern industry, and Marx about the socially disruptive role of technology in work relations.

It would be wrong to credit the rise and growth of sociology entirely to Enlightenment thinking. Sociology also has deep roots in the humanities, such as social and moral philosophy, and history. It also has roots in counter-Enlightenment thinking, in the writings of people who saw flaws and weaknesses in the Enlightenment project, despaired of a wholesale rejection of tradition, and argued in favour of pre-industrial, pre-scientific, and religious values. Writers such as these despaired of the loss of community, authority, custom, ritual, and the personal certainties that went with these social certainties. (For a discussion of these traditional concerns and their role in the evolution of sociology, you might read books by the sociologist Robert Nisbet that include *The Quest for Community* [2014] and *The Sociological Tradition* [1993].)

It would also be wrong to imagine that European white men dominated sociology from the beginning. Many other early sociologists—some of them women and some of them racialized people—played an important role in the founding of sociology. For example, Harriet Martineau (see Box 1.4) wrote insightfully about household labour and on how to conduct research on problems of social life. W.E.B. Du Bois wrote significant work on the consequences of slavery and racial discrimination in American society. Dorothy E. Smith, a prominent Canadian sociologist, wrote about how one's place in society affects how one sees that society (see Chapter 2). Frantz Fanon, the great North African thinker and psychoanalyst, wrote about the ways that colonial subjugation affects a person's self-image and world view.

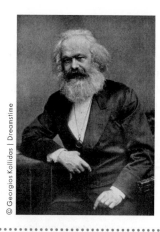

Keystone Pictures USA/Alamy Stock Photo

© Georgios Kollidas | Dreamstime

Pictorial Press Ltd/Alamy Stock Photo

Chronicle/Alamy Stock Photo

Here are the key founders of sociology: from left to right, Weber, Marx, and Durkheim. Martineau (far right), an important early influence, is less often read today, despite important sociological insights. What do the three founders appear to have in common? Do you think this commonality influenced the way sociology developed in its first hundred years—which topics sociology studied and how it studied them, for example?

Dashboard

Interactive activity

In Canada, the Critical Ethnicity and Anti-Racism research cluster of the Canadian Sociological Association recently posted the photos of five important African Canadian sociologists: Drs Daniel G. Hill, Wilson Head, Althea Prince, Agnes Calliste, and George S. Dei. The first two of these were important activists in the fight for racial equality—Dr Hill as first director of the Ontario Human Rights Commission and Dr Head as founder and head of the Urban Alliance for Race Relations. Photos of these important sociologists can be found on the Canadian Sociological Association website.

So, as students of social life, we need to understand this fundamental connection between sociology, science, and technology. This book aims to clarify and affirm that old connection in the present-day context of computers, biogenetics, and space travel.

Time to reflect

What had you heard about sociology before you started taking this course? Had you heard that it was difficult or easy, interesting or boring, theoretical or commonsensical? Have any of your ideas about this changed yet?

Theory in Everyday Life

1.1 | Émile Durkheim

Émile Durkheim was born in 1858 in France. Instead of becoming a rabbi like his father, Durkheim pursued an academic career. His doctoral thesis *The Division of Labor in Society* was written in 1893 and was followed by *Suicide* in 1897.

In many ways, Durkheim wrote *Suicide* (1897/1951) to set up sociology as a recognized academic discipline.

His approach in *Suicide* was based on what he called "the sociological method," founded on the principle that "social facts must be studied as things, as realities external to the individual." Durkheim showed that existing, non-sociological explanations of suicide were inadequate. He reasoned that if suicide is strictly a symptom of insanity, then it should have no social patterning, since presumably insanity has no social patterning. (Sociologists have since found that this assumption is wrong.) Further, insanity does not always lead to suicide, suggesting that other factors influence a person's decision to commit suicide. Here, Durkheim noted that the Jewish community had the highest rate of mental illness but lowest rate of suicide.

Then, Durkheim discussed the "social causes and sociological types of suicide." He noted that individuals may commit suicide when they are isolated or excluded from the social group to which they belong, or when its bonds are weakened by excessive individualism. In support of his theory, he showed that Protestants, with a weaker religious community than Catholics, had higher rates of suicide. (This has also since been called into question by sociologists.) Along similar lines, Durkheim also found that married people had lower rates of suicide than single or divorced people.

Durkheim also wrote about "the suicides produced by any sudden social shock or disturbance, such as that due to economic disturbance." Here Durkheim took the example of a financial crisis. People did not commit suicide merely because they were poor but because, through impoverishment, they had been subjected to "a painful process of social readjustment" where many of their social standards were disturbed.

In short, he showed that social isolation and rapid social change can have life-and-death outcomes for members of society.

Time to reflect

Durkheim distrusted explanations of suicide that relied on evidence provided in suicide notes or family accounts of the death. Would you find Durkheim's research more or less persuasive if he had incorporated this kind of evidence?

Theory in Everyday Life

1.2 | Karl Marx

Karl Marx was born in 1818 to well-off parents in Prussia. In 1843 he married and moved to Paris, where he met Friedrich Engels. They both joined the Communist League and in 1848 published the *Manifesto of the Communist Party* (also known as *The Communist Manifesto*). A short burst of revolutionary activity across Europe was eventually unsuccessful, and Marx and Engels moved to London. Marx's views continued to win him both admiration and persecution for the rest his life.

In the *Manifesto of the Communist Party*, Marx and Engels proclaimed the certain collapse of the capitalist system of production and thus the end to social inequality and social strife. They showed how the capitalist system of production continually splits society into two opposing classes, the bourgeoisie and the proletariat:

"By bourgeoisie is meant the class of modern capitalists, owners of the means of social production and employers of wage labour. By proletariat, the class of modern wage labourers who, having no means of production of their own, are reduced to selling their labour power in order to live" (Marx & Engels, 1848/2002, p. 3) This antagonism, they predicted, would result in the downfall of the bourgeoisie and the end of all class conflict.

The *Manifesto* is generally critiqued on two major points: its materialist conception of history, and its prophetic ability. This materialistic interpretation of history and society has been consistently challenged by historians and sociologists—starting with Max Weber, whom we will discuss shortly. On its prophetic ability, the continued existence of class conflict speaks for itself.

Time to reflect

Has class conflict or struggle played a part of your family history? Does Marx's emphasis on class as the basis of social conflict resonate with you? Why or why not?

Theory in Everyday Life

1.3 | Max Weber

Max Weber was born in Erfurt, Germany, the son of a wealthy and worldly businessman/politician, and a mother who had been raised in strict Calvinist orthodoxy. Weber enrolled at the Heidelberg University in 1882, interrupting his studies after two years to do his year of required military service.

He did his most important work after 1903. Weber's major works span a variety of topics: politics, science, religion, law, formal organization, and economics, among others. His most famous work is the book *The Protestant* *Ethic and the Spirit of Capitalism*, in which he argues that religion was one of the reasons the economies of the West and the East developed differently. This concept is discussed further in Chapter 3.

General Economic History is Weber's final work and brings together all his distinctive interpretations of economic life and change. This book is his most thorough and easily grasped collection of ideas about rationalization and its connection to modernity.

Time to reflect

Do you think your religious values (whether or not you belong to an organized religion) have affected your economic aspirations and goals? What do you think has been a greater influence on your life and your goals for the future, your family's religion, or your family's social class?

Theory in Everyday Life

1.4 | A (Somewhat Unheralded) Early Sociologist: Harriet Martineau

Harriet Martineau was born in England in 1802 to a wealthy textile manufacturer. Raised in a Unitarian household, her mother enforced strict feminine behaviours such as sewing (and hiding any skill at scholarship). In 1829 her father's business failed and Harriet stepped in to keep her family afloat by publishing articles. In 1837 she wrote the treatise *Society in America* after a two-year stay in the United States. In it, she wrote about the relations between politics, economics, morals, and social life, and was fiercely critical of the social injustices women, slaves, and the working poor commonly experienced. In this and other work, she emphasized the importance of examining political, religious, and social institutions in the study of inequality.

Some credit Martineau with writing the first book on sociological research methodology, *How to Observe Morals and Manners* (1838), in which she details her approach to observational research. In it, she suggests that research must be conducted by trained observers, and must be guided by appropriate ends—similar to the critical theory perspective today, which asserts the pursuit of knowledge is inherently political.

Martineau's final important contribution to sociology was her translation of Auguste Comte's *Philosophy Positive* (1853). She not only translated this major work—Comte is credited with coining the term *sociology*—but condensed it and made it much more readable. It was said that Comte himself stopped reading his own version, and would refer to Martineau's translation instead (Hamlin, 2016). Unfortunately, after her death, her influence ended and she was largely forgotten, until the 1990s, when sociologists rediscovered her work. She is now considered one of the early important figures of sociology.

Time to reflect

Why do you think Martineau's work lacked attention from the academic community for so long? What makes her more appealing to a twenty-first-century audience?

Basic Concepts of Sociology

Sociology is characterized as a distinctive discipline by its subject matter, its basic concepts, and its approaches. The biggest difference between sociology and the other social sciences is its subject matter, which is usually described as a study of the interrelationships among individuals and groups.

Concepts—the tools of thought and argument—are the key to understanding any field, including sociology. Social structure is a key concept in sociology and you will soon see why.

Social structure is any enduring, predictable pattern of social relations among people in society. There is a lot of debate about how social structure works, but this much is clear: social structure is important because it constrains and shapes people's behaviour. First, it limits people's actions in a way that is dictated by the situation and, in that sense, it constrains them. People with very different personalities and lifestyles, for example, all behave similarly when they are sitting in a church.

Second, social structure causes the same people to act in very different ways at different times; in that way, it is transformative. So, for example, the black-robed judges who behave so decorously in their courtrooms may behave just like you or I—loudly, crudely, and aggressively—at a hotly contested baseball game.

Equally important for the study of sociology is the study of *culture*. As we will see in Chapter 3, culture is the lens of values and beliefs through which we view reality. Cultures differ widely across time and space; for this reason, it is rarely useful to speak about "human nature." Nor is it useful to speak about better and worse cultures, or "primitive" and "highly civilized" culture. Sociology, indeed all the social sciences, requires a high degree of cultural relativism: an acceptance of human diversity and conflicting values.

We all learn our culture and the social structure into which we are born through socialization—a topic we will discuss at length in Chapter 4. For human babies, the most fundamental transformation of all occurs in childhood, as we internalize the norms, values, attitudes, and beliefs that are a part of our society. Note that these assumptions about social structure are precisely opposite to the assumptions that underlie genetics research and psychology. According to those fields, people don't change much from one situation to another, and they are fundamentally different from one another in unbridgeable ways. Sociologists have a different approach to social behaviour.

Consider the sociological approach to suicide we mentioned earlier—an example we will consider repeatedly in this book because of its association with Durkheim. Some might think that suicide, which is intensely personal, would not be socially structured—that is, subject to social influences. Yet Durkheim showed that suicide *is* socially structured. For example, divorced people (especially, men) without children are much more suicide-prone than married people (especially, women) with children. This observation might lead a sociologist to ask, what is the **constraining power** of marriage and parenthood? And what is the **transformative power** of divorce? Moreover, focusing on the social element of suicide gives us the ability to better predict rates of suicidal behaviour than does focusing on the personal, psychological aspect.

In the abstract, these ideas about social structure may sound difficult, but in practice they are familiar and simple. Consider the relationship between a doctor and a patient—the topic of a classic analysis by the sociologist Talcott Parsons (1951). When you visit a doctor for a check-up, you take along very specific expectations. You expect him or her to act in a serious, concerned, and knowledgeable manner. The doctor also expects you, as a patient, to show concern for your health, pay attention to the diagnosis, and follow the professional advice you receive.

How do we know that people really have such expectations and that these expectations are enduring and predictable? We can often see otherwise invisible expectations by taking note of the social

social structure any enduring, predictable pattern of social relations among people in society that constrains and shapes people's behaviour.

Dashboard

Flash cards can help you learn key terms

constraining power the ability of a social institution to control people's behaviour and increase their obedience to social norms.

transformative power the tendency of social institutions and social experiences to radically change people's routine behaviour.

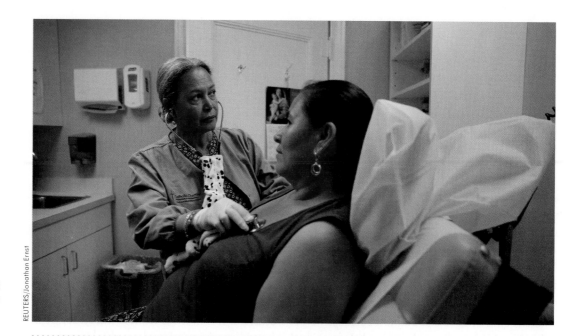

REUTERS/Jonathan Ernst

There is an unspoken social bond between doctor and patient—a set of expectations on each side about what is proper or improper behaviour. What behaviours are proper and improper for the doctor? For the patient? How is each punished for breaking the rules?

dyad a two-person set of people who interact and communicate with each other.

society a group of people who occupy a particular territorial area, feel themselves to constitute (or are viewed as) a unified and distinct entity, and in many respects, share a common set of assumptions about reality.

social institution one kind of social structure governed by established or standardizing patterns of rule-governed behaviour. Social institutions include the family, education, religious, economic, and political structures.

social relationship a pattern of ongoing contact and communication between two or more people that follows an expected pattern.

status the relative rank that an individual holds, with attendant rights, duties, and lifestyle, in a social hierarchy based upon honour or prestige.

role a set of connected behaviours, rights, obligations, beliefs, and norms as conceptualized by people in a social situation.

disturbance caused by their violation. If we violate doctor–patient expectations, both the doctor and patient alike will feel uncomfortable, even upset or disoriented. One or the other may even end the doctor–patient relationship.

Sociologists have found that what we learn about one social relationship—for example, the doctor–patient relationship—can help us understand other, different social relationships. Sociology is fascinated by the similarities and differences between relationships. It is also fascinated by the structures they form when fitted together. What we learn about conformity, power, persuasion, exclusion, belief, and engagement in one relationship often applies to many others. This willingness to generalize is one of sociology's most distinctive features.

Sociology is interested in all social structures—two-position (or **dyadic**) relationships like doctors and patients, all the way up to total societies and global empires. Social structure, you will remember, is any enduring, predictable pattern of social relations among people in society. **Society** in this sense is the basic large-scale human group. Members of a society interact with one another and share a common geographic territory. To some degree, they also share a common culture and sense of collective existence, and they take part in social institutions together.

A **social institution** is one kind of social structure, made up of a number of **social relationships**—stable patterns of meaningful orientations to one another. Typically, people use institutions to achieve their intended goals, such as schools for students, or hospitals for patients. Within a social institution, people participate in one or more social relationship, such as the relationships between doctor and patient, doctor and hospital administrator, and doctor and his or her child.

Statuses are socially defined positions that determine how the individual should relate to other people (such as their mutual rights and responsibilities) and with whom the individual will interact. Being a parent or a patient or a doctor defines one's status in an institution. **Roles**, also called social roles, are patterns of interaction with others. Being a doctor is a status, while acting like a doctor is a role performance. Role expectations are shared ideas about how people, regardless of personal characteristics, should carry out the duties attached to a particular status.

Each of us participates in social life in terms of the statuses and roles we have adopted or have been assigned. Being a "student," for example, carries with it a lot of learned behaviour patterns, expectations, and motives. Most of us learn to be students in elementary school. Once that role is learned, we retain expectations of what it means to be a student and how to do whatever it is that students do. We also develop expectations about teachers and how and why teachers do whatever it is that they do.

For an individual, being a student does not mean carrying out some impersonal set of duties, obligations, or expectations. We are all individuals, and we experience and act out our roles and statuses in our own particular ways. Yet, despite this, classroom behaviour is still largely predictable. Sociologically speaking, one class of students is like another. Though we have seen a great many important changes in the past hundred years, it is remarkable how slowly social structures change from year to year, and how little they vary from one place to another—for example, between Dartmouth, Nova Scotia, and Richmond, British Columbia—as we shall see repeatedly in this book.

There are many reasons that social relationships are enduring and stable. We learn to value stable relationships. Often, we lack the knowledge or courage to change our relationships. Sometimes those in power develop a strong investment in the way things are and stand to lose something if they change, and so they encourage us to meet the expectations of others. These reasons, and many others we shall discuss, help to maintain the social relationships of the society in which we live.

At the same time, social roles and relationships don't just exist: they are enacted through interaction and negotiation. By **interaction** we mean the processes and manner in which social actors—people trying to meet each other's expectations—relate to each other, especially in face-to-face encounters. It includes a wide variety of forms of communication, such as words, body language, attentiveness (or inattentiveness), and what some sociologists have called "face-work." By **negotiation** we mean all of the ways people try to make sense of one another, and to one another: for example, by conferring, bargaining, making arrangements, compromising, and reaching agreements. Though often hidden or masked by habit, processes of interaction and negotiation are what make role and relationships work. They are the mechanisms underlying social structure.

interaction a pattern exchange of information, support, and/or emotions between at least two people in a social setting.

negotiation a type of interaction whose goal is to define the expectations or boundaries of a relationship.

Time to reflect

Think about how you have managed your interactions and negotiations throughout the day today. Did you listen attentively to a professor? Did you try to determine whether you and your classmates will become friends? How much attention did you pay to these casual, day-to-day interactions and negotiations at the time?

Knowing What We Know

Present-day sociology concerns itself not only with knowing the social world, but also with examining how we know what we know. For sociologists in the empirical (especially, quantitative) tradition, the goal of sociological research is to propose and examine models of reality—commonly known as theories. As scientists, we seek the best available theory when we ask, "what happens if xyz is true?" For other sociologists, especially those who do qualitative and historical analysis, the goal of sociological research is to propose and examine explanations of reality. In both instances, sociologists approach the subject of study with caution and skepticism.

Overall, the process of research is typically as follows: we develop new concepts, measure new relationships between them, develop plausible new explanations of the observed relations, derive new hypotheses, collect new data, and so on. This process will be explained in more detail in Chapter 2.

To sociologists, the use of "common sense" to understand the world is not enough. Common sense knowledge often consists of nothing more than beliefs and ideas that people take for granted. A failure to question their beliefs often leads people to form incomplete and inaccurate explanations of the world. Instead, sociologists use research to seek scientifically sound explanations—explanations based on empirical evidence. The process they follow is commonly called the "research process" (see Chapter 2).

Sociologists note that social circumstances largely control the outcomes of people's lives. One such circumstance is unequal opportunity, the result of being born into a particular social class. Usually, unequal opportunity passes down from one generation to the next: people born into wealthier families tend to stay wealthy, and people born into poor families tend to stay poor. Differences

Spotlight On

1.5 | The Social Determinants of Health

Social scientists have now spent many decades studying the effects of various social, economic, and political factors—together commonly referred to as the social determinants of health—on population health outcomes (Raphael, 2009). The first of the Whitehall Studies, a classic study in public health conducted over 10 years beginning in 1967, examined data on 18,000 British civil servants and found that position in the civil service hierarchy was a powerful predictor of a person's health and longevity (people lower down the hierarchy lived shorter, less healthy lives.) Since then, there has been a lot of research that confirms the hypothesis that social inequality undermines people's health (e.g., Marmot, 2005; Wilkinson & Marmot, 2003). For a detailed discussion of the Whitehall Studies, see Marmot et al., 1991; Marmot, 1993; Marmot et al., 1995.

Taking this further, research in sociology and public health has shown that in societies where there is greater inequality, everyone's health (both in the highest and lowest classes) is worse than in countries with

lower inequality. In short, inequality is bad for people's health, even if they do not suffer from poverty. We discuss the social determinants of health in more depth in Chapter 6.

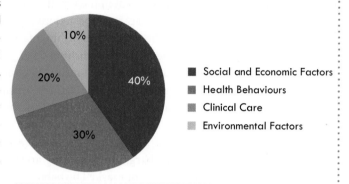

FIGURE 1.1 Determinants of Health, by Weighting

Source: Adapted from Booske, B., Athens, J., Kindig, D., Park, H., & Remington, P. (2010). Different perspectives for assigning weights to determinants of health (County health rankings working paper, University of Wisconsin, Population Health Institute). Retrieved from www.countyhealthrankings.org/sites/default/files/differentPerspectivesForAssigningWeightsToDeterminantsOfHealth.pdf

in opportunities and life experiences are rarely a simple result of higher intelligence, harder work, better values, or other personal characteristics. However, common sense tends to encourage people to make conclusions based on these individual traits, mostly because the larger social circumstances are invisible (or much more difficult to see) in everyday life. For another example, see Box 1.5.

Time to reflect

Try to come up with a list of three or four "invisible" social factors that influence how you behave and the choices you make. What social penalties would you have to pay to break out of these constraints on your choice?

In short, common sense is likely to misinform us about society. The central goal of sociologists is to replace such faulty common-sense reasoning with empirical evidence and scientific explanation. Each sociologist does this by conducting unbiased research, and by combining this knowledge with the knowledge of other sociologists' research. Through careful data collection and analysis, sociologists give us evidence-based theories about reality. They provide interesting new insights into our motives, actions, relationships, and possible future lives. Sociology does not provide indisputable theories that make accurate predictions with great regularity, but it does better than common sense. In this respect, it ranks roughly with climatological analyses (e.g., weather forecasts) and economic analyses (e.g., stock market forecasts) as a source of insight and future planning.

This is not to say that sociologists ignore "common sense" interpretations of reality, for the simple reason that these interpretations are often the reasons why people act the ways they do in social situations. This is merely to say that sociologists need to put themselves outside common sense interpretations and view them as objects of study.

Ways of Looking at Sociology

Over the years, scholars have broken up the field of sociology in a variety of ways. Today, many sociologists highlight five schools of thought (also called "approaches" or "paradigms") and we will highlight them repeatedly in this book; they are called conflict theory, feminist theory, functional theory (or functionalism), symbolic interactionism, and postmodernism.

These approaches differ in several main ways, as we will see in the course of the book. One of these approaches, feminist sociology—perhaps the most progressive and groundbreaking sociological approach today—is largely a fusion of the other four approaches. To conflict theory, feminist sociology brings new insights on inequality—especially, gender inequality. To symbolic interactionism, it brings new insights on social constructionism and qualitative methodology. To postmodernism, it brings new insights on intersectionality and deconstruction. Finally, to functionalism, it brings new insights on social forms and subcultures. In this book, we will look at all five approaches and see how they each illuminate the digital society's main issues. **Postmodern approaches**, which are especially relevant to discussions of modern media and technology, are spread throughout each chapter.

postmodern(ism) a style of thinking or school of thought in social science and humanities that denies the validity of universal, sweeping statements about the world or groups of people within the world, and analyzes the motives behind such statements and the consequences of people's believing them.

Conflict Theory

Conflict theory—whether it focuses on class, gender, sexual orientation, or something else—is centrally concerned with the unequal distribution of power and the domination of one group by another. Conflict theorists view society as a collection of groups that constantly struggle with each other to dominate society and its institutions, or at least, to achieve equal access.

Conflict theory draws its inspiration from two of sociology's founders, Marx and Weber. Marx proposed that social conflict comes from the economic disparity between social classes. Members of the working class or proletariat, being powerless, feel alienated from the processes and products of their work. Given its emphasis on economic inequality, the Marxist solution to social problems is to end class differences. We will have much more to say about the theories of Marx in later chapters of this book.

Time to reflect

Now that you have read more on the topic, reconsider the questions earlier about Marx's emphasis on class as the basis of social conflict, and whether you think your family's class or religion have had more of an impact on your life. Have either of your answers changed?

Unlike Marx, Weber did not focus just on class. Instead, he included all conflicts between contending status groups—for example, between people of different nationalities, religions, and racialized or ethnic groups. These groups fight for power in society and use a range of social mechanisms to get power and keep it.

Among conflict theorists, proponents of Marx and Weber differ on the importance of cultural ideas in social conflict and change. Weber proposed that ideas—including religious ideas and economic ideas—can be transformative forces in human history. By contrast, Marx proposed that economic relations—not ideas—shape society. According to Marx, capitalist economic relations give rise to a characteristic idea-system, including a dominant ideology, which justifies capitalism and keeps capitalism functioning through a neo-liberal consumer culture. In other words, economic relations are the basis of all social relations, and culture (including religion, art, and other ideas) is the product of economic relations.

In the past century, Marxism has shifted its focus from economic relations to include other sources of domination as well, including ideas. This shift affirms Weber's ideas about culture. Marxist theorists who are familiar with the work of Weber propose that consumer culture keeps capitalism going. However, like Weber they recognize the role of other factors as well—especially, the role of the state. Increasingly, they also recognize the importance of religions, ideologies, mass media, and intellectuals.

One thousand protestors were arrested at the height of the G20 riots in Toronto in 2010. The police and security forces were widely thought to have exceeded the limits of their proper authority in controlling the protest. Have you ever participated in a social protest?

John Porter and the Vertical Mosaic

A non-Marxist version of conflict theory is evident in the work of esteemed Canadian sociologist John Porter (1921–1979), author of the classic work *The Vertical Mosaic* (1965/2015). The work of Canadian sociologist John Porter is instructive, for it shows us how societies create and control conflict, despite systemic inequalities.

The Vertical Mosaic examines the unequal opportunities that different ethnic groups face in Canadian society. It is considered a landmark study because it put to rest many common misconceptions about Canada as a classless society. Contrary to popular myth, Canadian society is class-based, a *vertical* hierarchy of classes defined by wealth and power. However, unlike (for example) the United States, where immigrants are encouraged to give up their ethnic traditions and assimilate quickly into American life, Canada is also a cultural *mosaic* of unassimilated ethnic groups preserving their customs and heritage.

Porter noted that Canada was socially stratified by the unassimilated cultures, with economic power in the hands of a small elite group promoting and protecting one another's interests. Porter also found inequalities in the patterns of ethnic division and ethnic loyalty that separated immigrants from non-immigrants, and WASPs (white Anglo-Saxon Protestants) from non-WASPs. Indigenous people—reportedly the most disadvantaged in Canada—had the least power and influence. These cultural groups held different positions in the class-based hierarchy. In that sense, Canada is a vertical mosaic.

Porter concluded that in Canada, ethnic differences reproduce class differences in social inequality and set limits to social mobility, the opportunity to improve one's class fortunes (more on social mobility in Chapter 4).

The Vertical Mosaic was widely influential in its day. After its publication in 1965, it became instantly popular and set off 20 years of sociological research on power, mobility, ethnicity, and immigration in Canada. A great many other books and papers focused on upper-class membership in

Canada, including Wallace Clements's *The Canadian Corporate Elite: An Analysis of Economic Power* (1975) and Dennis Olsen's *The State Elite* (1980). Many of these later works showed that elites were gaining increased power in society, and using this power to promote the success of those within their social group. In other words, the problem Porter diagnosed was getting worse, not better.

Today, Porter's book remains a landmark in Canadian sociology. By challenging previous misconceptions, Porter led sociologists and policy makers to develop new ideas about Canadian society (Helmes-Hayes, 1998). Additionally, Porter's support for a more open, more accessible educational system influenced a huge expansion of post-secondary education in Canada. As a post-secondary student, you, like millions of other Canadians, have probably benefitted from Porter's call for educational expansion.

However, most sociologists would say the findings of *The Vertical Mosaic* are dated, since Porter's data came from the 1950s. More recent analyses show that today, non-Charter *ethnic* origins are no obstacle to educational and occupational advancement, though *racial* minorities continue to suffer a disadvantage (Darden, 2004). See more on this in Chapter 8. And for an interesting selection of work by current Canadian sociologists, ranging from Canada Research Chairs to top graduate students, you should look over the 67 short pieces in *Reading Sociology* (Albanese, Tepperman, and Alexander, 2017).

The Frankfurt School: Culture + Politics = Ideology

Porter's shift away from a strict focus on economic relations affirms the importance of Weber's ideas about politics and culture. The Frankfurt School of sociologists provides another example of the melding of Marxist and Weberian ideas. These "critical theorists," including Max Horkheimer, Theodor Adorno, Herbert Marcuse, and Walter Benjamin, all focused on the analysis of capitalist ideology, mass consumerism, and especially popular entertainment, which they noted is useful in diverting the masses from feeling exploited and alienated. Collectively, these theorists viewed culture as a means that powerful social groups use to maintain their dominance in ongoing class conflict.

In the late twentieth century, conflict theory built on the work of Ralf Dahrendorf, Lewis Coser, and Randall Collins. Dahrendorf's most influential work on social inequality is *Class and Class Conflict in Industrial Society*, published in 1959. Like Marxism, he characterized modern society as being in a constant state of change and conflict. In this way of thinking, coercion—forcing someone to do something—holds society together, not shared norms and values. Like Weber, Dahrendorf focused on the role of authority in society. But Dahrendorf noted that people in positions of authority have the potential to turn into "conflict groups"—that is, groups actively pursuing their own interests—and their actions can lead to changes in the society. These may be actions by conscious economic classes, elite authority groups, or mobilized "status groups" (as Weber called them).

Lewis Coser, another twentieth-century conflict theorist, applied Durkheimian ideas to conflict. Coser noted that, more often than not, conflict has social functions, which is why conflict is universal and never-ending. Under many conditions, groups can remain locked in conflict for long periods of time without any changes, thus maintaining the status quo. Equally, long-term conflicts produce alliances between groups and clarify the boundaries between contenders. In this way, conflict may promote communication and co-operation, maintaining social order so long as people—even enemies—are talking to each other. Coser was the first sociologist to show that conflict could increase social solidarity. You may note the overlap between this theory and functionalism once you read about the functionalist approach below.

Finally, Randall Collins, in a book aptly titled *Conflict Sociology* (1974), asserted,

> For conflict theory, the basic insight is that human beings are sociable but conflict-prone animals . . . The basic argument, then, has three strands: that men live in self-constructed subjective worlds; that others pull many of the strings that control one's subjective experience; and that there are frequent conflicts over control. Life is basically a struggle for status in which no one can afford to be oblivious to the power of others around him. (pp. 56–61)

In recent years, sociologists have developed more modern iterations of conflict and critical theory, such as queer theory and critical race theory. Space does not permit a discussion of these important theories here, though they will come up at other points in the book.

Functional Theory

Functional theory views society as a set of interconnected parts that work together to preserve the overall stability and efficiency of the whole. Rather than exploring how parts of society clash, such as in conflict theory, functionalism assumes that each part plays a necessary and complementary role, just like the organs and parts of a human body. Examples of different parts of society include families, schools, religious institutions, the economy, and government. Society apparently needs each of these parts to function. Otherwise, we would not find these institutions in every known society.

Sociologist Robert Merton made key contributions to the development of the functionalist approach. In his classic work *Social Theory and Social Structure* (1957), he proposed the important idea that all social institutions perform both manifest and latent functions. Manifest functions are intended and easily recognized; latent functions are unintended and often hidden. For example, formal education is a social institution with a manifest function of providing students with the knowledge, skills, and cultural values that will help them to work effectively in society. Both the school and its participants—students, teachers, parents, and others—formally recognize these goals.

However, formal education also has latent functions: it works as a regular "babysitter" for young children, and as a "matchmaker" for older high school and university students by letting them meet and mingle with potential lovers or marriage partners. Interestingly, these latent functions are as important to society as the manifest functions, though people don't often admit their importance. When did you last hear school administrators, students, or parents admit that public school is largely a daycare service?

Manifest and latent functions are important because they help us understand how every social institution has a purpose. Moreover, the institutional functions also influence one another. For example, changes in family life, such as increasing divorce and single parenthood, often have important, unconscious, and unintended consequences for work and education, such as the introduction of full-day kindergarten programs.

luckybusiness/123RF

One of the key latent functions of education is to bring young people with common interests together for a chance to find potential partners. Which do you think were the more valuable lessons from high school: those you learned inside or outside the classroom?

Functionalists see social problems as the failure of institutions to adapt during rapid social and economic shifts. According to this view, industrialization and urbanization in North America caused a sharp increase in social disorganization. In turn, this led to an increase in crime, mental illness, addiction, and domestic violence. Thinking about these issues more than a century ago, Durkheim introduced the term *anomie*, or "normlessness," to describe how social norms weaken in periods of rapid social change (see, e.g., 1933/1964). From the functionalist perspective, a good way to deal with social problems is to strengthen social norms and increase social integration by bolstering traditional institutions—supporting family life, community life, and religious life, for example.

Symbolic Interactionism

Functional theory, feminist theory, and conflict theory all focus on large elements of society, such as social institutions and major demographic groups. In contrast, *symbolic interactionism* focuses on small-group interactions. Said another way, symbolic interactionists focus on how people interact with one another, and the meanings, definitions, and interpretations behind these interactions.

Symbolic interactionists study how people use symbols—purely conventional objects used to represent concepts and things—when they communicate. So, for example, the word *banana* is a symbol for the fruit we call a banana; but you can't peel and eat the word. Likewise, a red maple leaf is the symbol for "Canada" and a swastika is the symbol for Nazism. Because of what they represent, they can excite strong positive or negative emotions, even though these shapes outside of their cultural and historical context are innocuous.

It is through face-to-face, symbol-using interaction that people "construct" reality together. Through these interactions, people interpret and change the culture of everyday life. Therefore, culture is fluid, not static. Ordinary people change society every single day, in ways so slight they are often hard to see (Blumer, 1986). Yet, as we see in Box 1.6 below, people are constantly inventing and reinventing themselves online and elsewhere.

Sociology 2.0

1.6 | Online Gaming Communities and Symbolic Interactionism

Symbolic interactionism studies how people interact with each other and the selves that develop through these interactions. Online games and video games can help people develop and negotiate their senses of self by participating in alternative realities created and shared with other players.

In Massively Multiplayer Online Role-Playing Games (MMORPGs), internet users can choose to play as one of a variety of characters or customize a character themselves. For some, playing an online game is like a "fresh start," enabling the creation of an identity that is removed from a "physical identity." Games such as *Second Life*, *Everquest*, and *World of Warcraft* offer a safe space in which players can try out different versions of themselves. For this reason, MIT researcher Amy Bruckman (1992) calls these game-spaces "identity workshops." Similarly, professor of American culture

Lisa Nakamura (1995) refers to these online gaming spaces as opportunities for "identity tourism"; they are spaces where users can take "mini-vacations" from their real life identities.

Nick Yee (Yee & Bailenson, 2007), a psychologist who specializes in the digital world, coined the term *the Proteus effect* to describe the ways in which avatars, or digital representations in online gaming, can come to affect the offline "daily lives" of game users. In one study, Yee asked users to choose between two pictures of individuals for online dating. He found that users who played with more attractive characters played more confidently and picked the more attractive partners. This suggested that acting more confidently in the digital world can improve a person's self-confidence and self-esteem in the real world (D'Anastasio, 2015; Yee & Bailenson, 2007).

Time to reflect

Do you think that groups who form around video games are as "real," "meaningful," or personally important as groups that form in other ways—for example, around team sports or musicians? What has been your own experience with the people who play video games and their social involvements?

The goal of *social constructionism* is to examine how people interact to create a shared social reality. In *The Social Construction of Reality* (1966), Peter Berger and Thomas Luckmann propose that *all* knowledge—including the most taken-for-granted knowledge of everyday life—is a social construct. According to this approach, any idea, however natural or obvious it may seem to the people who accept it, is just an invention of a particular group, culture, or society. Is Canada undergoing an economic recession, as one political party tells us, or is the economy sound? Are Canadians in danger of attack by terrorists, as one faction says, or are we safe from such danger? As sociologists, we need to understand how (and why) some claims become widely accepted as "true," while others do not.

One approach, which grows out of the early twentieth-century work of George Herbert Mead, is about how societies perpetuate rules. Mead (1934) wrote that children learn to be social creatures through interaction with others, following a shared system of rules and symbols that allows them to share meanings. With shared meanings, they can play together, perform complementary roles, and become a part of the social group. For Mead, this ability to co-operate is the basis of all social order. Shared rules and meanings make social interaction possible, and interaction allows people to work together and influence one another. Social life, for Mead, is thus the sharing of rules and meanings—that is, the co-operative (social) construction of reality.

A generation later, Erving Goffman (1959) proposed that we can think of society as a theatre in which people compose and perform social scripts together. Social life, according to Goffman, is little more than a set of scripted, directed performances. It is inside our social roles that we find and express (or hide and protect) our true identity. From this *dramaturgical* standpoint, scripted social roles are merely specific versions of the rules and meanings we all need for social interaction.

For social constructionists, the central sociological questions must be, who makes the rules, roles, meanings, scripts, and beliefs that dominate our social interactions? How do the powerful use their power to construct a "reality" that obliges us to behave in certain ways? Specifically, what strategies of claims-making and moral entrepreneurship bring about—that is, construct—the social order that constrains us all?

People in power can create social rules (consider the example in Box 1.7). However, official rules are often ignored, unless they are supported by widespread agreement, enforced, and

Think Globally

1.7 | Learning to Queue as a Form of Civility

We tend to take for granted certain patterns of everyday behaviour, such as lining up at a bus stop and waiting our turn. Yet cultures vary in the emphasis they place on types of behaviour we consider common civility; and indeed, civility itself is something that arises only through dedicated political effort (see, for example, Elias, 1978).

In the lead up to the 2008 Beijing Olympics, the Chinese government sought to "civilize" the inhabitants of Beijing through monthly queue practising days. Zhang Huiguang, director of the Capital Ethic Development Office, explained that the purpose of Queuing Day was to encourage people to wait in line whenever there were more than two people. On the 11th of each month in the

100 days leading up to National Day (October 1), 4,500 orange-vested volunteers descended on the city's bus stops and subway stations to oversee queuing practice in Beijing. Why the eleventh day? Because the two orderly ones in "11" model the practice of lining up patiently. A survey indicated that 85 per cent of transit stops with volunteers formed lines, though the same survey also found that only 30 per cent of stops without volunteers queued ("Beijing Institutes Queuing Day," 2007).

Nonetheless, Shu Xiaofeng, director of the Capital Ethic Development office, believed that the city's population of 17.5 million could be taught to follow these new rules of etiquette. A "civilization index" created by Renmin University supports his assertion. In its study of urban behaviour, the university found a significant decrease in queue jumping, as well as spitting, littering, and shirt rolling (some Beijing men have the habit of rolling up the bottom of their shirts on hot days.) (MacKinnon, 2009).

In 2005 the "civilization index" rated Beijinger behaviour at 65.21 out of 100; by 2009, this number had gone up 82.68, indicating great overall improvement. Queuing Day is partly responsible for this index upgrade, but fines for unbecoming behaviour, such as a 50 Yuan (US$6.45) fine for spitting, have also helped to enforce better etiquette. As a symbolic interactionist would point out, producing a change in the public behaviour of Beijingers required creating a new set of symbols and shared understandings around "civility," as well as enforcing these new practices while they became habitual (Reynolds, 2008).

Time to reflect

Is the assumption that the North American practice of lining up is "more civilized" and therefore better behaviour an objective truth, or is it a socially constructed assumption?

perpetuated through everyday interaction, also known as interpersonal negotiations. These negotiations may be formal and direct, such as a contract drafted between a union and an employer. However, most negotiated agreements are less visible and less conscious: the result of informal communication. This communication may be verbal, or it can consist of gestures, body language, and even material symbols like clothing. When people deviate from these formal or informal agreements, they are often labelled in a way that indicates their deviance (e.g., bully, slut, criminal, freak).

This sociological approach, known as *labelling*, eliminates the assumption of wrongdoing present in theories of personal dysfunction or mental illness. Instead, it asks us to consider, who is accusing whom? What do they accuse them of doing? Under what circumstances are these accusations accepted as truthful and damning by (at least some) others? Labelling often has long lasting and harmful consequences for people who are labelled deviant. It can even result in "secondary deviation," which is deviant behaviour caused by people thinking they are fated or doomed to break the rules, and encourages association with other rule-breakers in deviant subcultures. Later in the book, we will discuss a classic symbolic interactionist study on the role of stigma as a form of social control.

Feminist Theory

Earlier, we mentioned that feminist sociology can be viewed as a fusion of earlier sociological approaches, as well as a source of important new ideas. But note that there are several versions of feminist theory in sociology, including liberal feminism, socialist feminism, radical feminism, eco-feminism, and others. Throughout this book, we will explore the differences between these various perspectives. Here, though, it is important to note one important thing they all have in common: all feminism focuses on gender inequality, or relations of dominance and subordination between men and women.

Feminists are particularly interested in how gender inequality makes women's lives different from men's. They note that women often act out a role that men have defined, which shapes their most important social activities at home, at work, and in the public domain. This fact also forces women to acquiesce in their own domination, since they risk exclusion and even violence if they do not. Thus, rejection of the female role is far more costly—even dangerous—to women than is men's rejection of the male role (though feminists also note the harmful effect that the male role can have on men).

The first wave of the feminist movement occurred between the mid-nineteenth century and the early twentieth century, culminating in women gaining the right to vote in many Western countries. The second wave, between roughly 1960 and 1980, focused on issues like housework, equal pay for work of equal values, and the right to birth control. In the last few decades, the focus of feminist scholarship has shifted, coming to stress the diversity of women's experience as members of different nations, classes, and racialized and ethnic groups. Following from this, contemporary feminists are especially interested in intersectionality—the interaction of gender with other social characteristics such as class and racialization, to produce particular combinations of disadvantage (e.g., the particular problems of black men, lesbians living in poverty, or Muslim immigrant women).

A common theme across the many types of feminism is the view that the subordination of women is not a result of biological determinism—the idea that men's and women's biological differences justify their separate social roles and responsibilities—but of socioeconomic and ideological factors. Feminists differ in thinking about how they might achieve change, but they are all committed to erasing women's continued social inequality. As well, despite important differences between women due to class, ethnic identity, age, and other social factors, there is general agreement among feminists that

- all personal life has a political dimension (or, as C. Wright Mills [1956] has written, personal troubles are the private side of public issues);
- both the public and private spheres of life are gendered (that is, unequal for men and women);
- despite differences among women, women's social experience routinely differs from men's;
- patriarchy—or male control—structures the way most societies work; and
- because of routinely different experiences and differences in power, women and men view the world differently.

So, for example, men and women typically have different views about divorce, since men and women experience divorce differently. For men, divorce usually means a brief drop in the standard of living, if any decline at all, a huge drop in parenting responsibilities, and reduction in social support. For women, it usually means a dramatic, long-term loss in income and an increase in parental responsibilities, since mothers usually keep custody of their children (see, for example, Amato, 2000; Wallerstein & Blakeslee, 2004).

The cultural effects of gendering are just as evident, and just as harmful, as the social and economic effects because they attack people's self-esteem. Consider the problem created by highly gendered video games and misogynistic gamers (Box 1.8).

Digital Divide

1.8 | #Gamergate

As mentioned, feminist scholars are interested in how gender inequality shapes the different lived experiences of men and women. A new area of feminist interest is exploring what gender inequality looks like online, and, specifically, in gaming communities.

Feminists and academics commonly criticize the gaming industry on the grounds that its portrayals of women, minority groups, and violence are socially harmful. In 2014 the online movement responded with #Gamergate, which was started by gamers who wanted to protest against "outsiders" (usually academics and feminists) who they felt were threatening gamer culture (Hathaway, 2014).

This set off new conflicts between the gamer community and outsiders. In 2014 Zoe Quinn's new game *Depression Quest* received positive reviews from review magazine *Kotaku*. Shortly afterwards, her ex-boyfriend, Eron Gjoni, alleged that Quinn had solicited these reviews by having affairs with multiple game journalists. The response of #Gamergate was terrifying: Quinn was doxxed—her personal information, including her phone number and address, were released publicly online—and she was later forced from her home by anonymous death threats (Stuart, 2014).

Around the same time, Anita Sarkeesian, a Canadian American feminist known for her YouTube channel *Feminist Frequency*, began to point out the stereotypical ways that women are portrayed in video games. Sarkeesian's work was meant to teach people to be critical consumers of new entertainment and technology. In response, #Gamergate targeted her with doxxing and death threats. Critics of #Gamergate conclude that the movement's vitriolic response to these women is a reflection of the "toxicity within gaming" that Sarkeesian critiques, as well as "tech culture" (Collins, 2014). What do you think?

Time to reflect

Now that you've read about some of the mainstream, foundational theories of sociology, reflect on how you relate to each of them. Which do you think best reflects your current world view? Did any theory surprise you, or get you thinking about connections you might otherwise not have made?

Sociological Theories Today

In higher-level sociology courses, you will get more opportunity to explore sociological theory and sociological theorists than we can provide in this introductory book. However, it will be helpful to understand a few things about sociological theory, whether we view it in terms of the history of the discipline, key theorists, the "sociological imagination," or "a "sociological lens" on society.

Sociological theory is always changing and developing, just like theory in every other scientific discipline. That fact is evident in Figure 1.2, which displays the frequency with which different published sociological articles are cited by professional sociologists in sociological journals, as counted using citation data in the Web of Science database.

We note several important things from this figure. First and most important, there is relatively little carry-over from one decade to the next in which articles sociologists cite most often. That is because, with each decade, new discoveries are made, new theories are put forward, and new perspectives are applied to old problems. Second, we note that, for the most part, even the most commonly cited articles are cited only hundreds of times in a decade, not thousands of times. That tells us that sociology is a diverse and fragmented discipline, in which different sociologists take different approaches to different, or sometimes the same, problems.

Third, if you read the titles of these most-often-cited papers, you will discover that few, if any, explicitly describe their approach as functionalist, conflict, symbolic interactionist, or feminist. That is because, when real sociologists do real research, they apply a variety of useful theoretical approaches. Most sociological theories in actual use cross the simplified boundaries (or classifications) we have imposed in this chapter.

You will also notice that only a handful of sociological journals have published these most-often-cited articles. These are the journals with the greatest impact on the field of sociology worldwide. They show us the direction sociological theory is going, and they move the discipline powerfully in certain directions. That said, within each subfield of sociology—whether the sociology of families, culture, crime, or religion, for example—there are also key influential journals that play an important part in the theoretical development of these subfields.

In short, if we define " real-life sociology" as the theories that living sociologists produce when they do their research, we see that sociology is constantly changing. We also see that sociological theory is fragmented into subfields, yet there is a community of sociologists who read and cite one another's work. It is that ever-changing body of widely read work that we try to capture in this book.

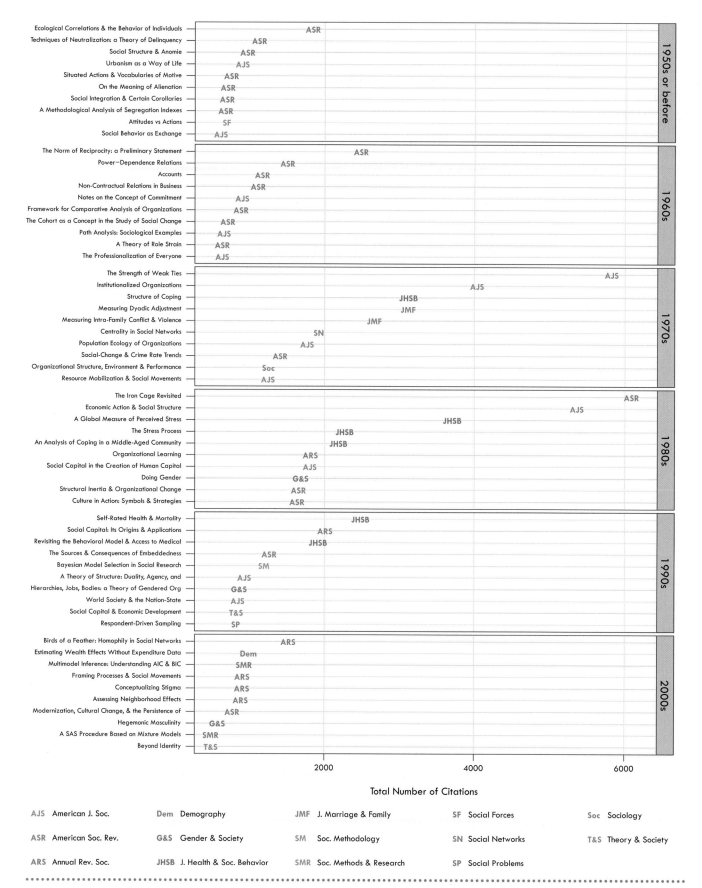

FIGURE 1.2 The 10 Most Often Cited Journal Articles in Each Decade

Source: Retrieved from https://kieranhealy.org/blog/archives/2014/11/15/top-ten-by-decade/

Skills Gained from Studying Sociology

As you will discover, there are many good reasons to study sociology. Most of you reading this book will not become professional sociologists, or even sociology majors, but you stand to gain from studying sociology nonetheless.

On the intellectual side, sociology students learn to integrate the findings of other social science disciplines, such as economics, political science, psychology, and history, in the study of a wide variety of pressing issues. They also learn to view the world in ways that combine diverse sociological perspectives. Sociology provides a rich and varied picture of how the social world works. Most important of all, exercising one's sociological imagination is a means of exercising one's critical thinking skills. We have all heard that, today, every aspect of our lives—as students, workers, family members, media consumers, and voters, to mention a few domains—requires critical thinking, a careful examination of evidence in decision-making. There is nothing that prepares us better for such critical thinking than a well developed sociological imagination.

Sociological insight is important too, as it prepares us for the world of work. In a 2015 *New York Times* article titled "Why What You Learned in Preschool Is Crucial at Work" Claire Miller notes that

> skills like cooperation, empathy and flexibility have become increasingly vital in modern-day work. Occupations that require strong social skills have grown much more than others since 1980, according to new research. And the only occupations that have shown consistent wage growth since 2000 require both cognitive and social skills.

This means that, today, you need to understand (at least a little) technology, science, and statistics; you need to know how to read and write effectively; and you need to know how social groups, institutions, and policies work. And sociology helps on all of these dimensions.

For many employers, the skill set you bring with you is more important than the specific field your degree is in. So, whatever your major, sociology provides you with a skill set that makes you a valuable asset for any organization. Skills you will gain in any good sociology course include the following:

- research capabilities;
- cross-cultural awareness and understanding;
- problem solving and critical thinking skills;
- communication, reading, and writing skills; and
- recognition of trends and patterns.

To sum up, sociology students develop valuable skills. These are the type of employable skills that are highly valued by employers in both the private and public sector; they also provide a solid base for people entering graduate studies in a range of disciplines.

As Figure 1.3 shows, graduates of sociology programs themselves take these useful skills into a wide variety of fields.

Time to reflect

How might knowledge of sociology be useful for someone who is preparing to be a medical doctor or nurse? An economist? A computer scientist? An author? A biologist? How might sociology be useful for your own career of choice?

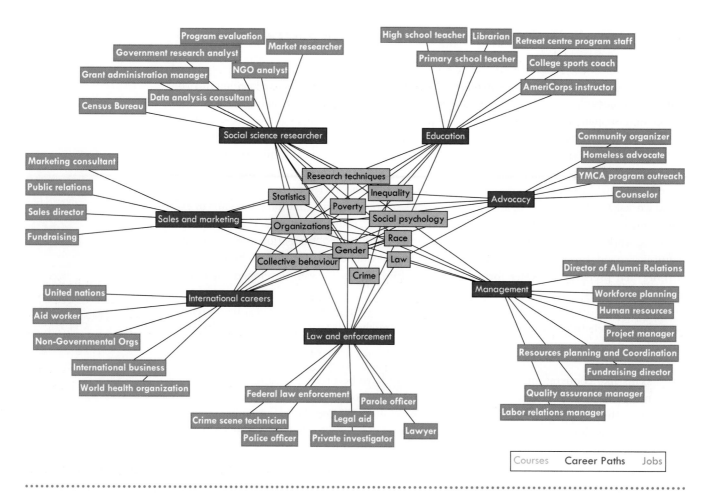

FIGURE 1.3 Sociology: From Courses to Careers

Source: Retrieved from https://s-media-cache-ak0.pinimg.com/736x/91/45/6b/91456be5e29c659a629dae557edf4818.jpg

Conclusions

In this introductory chapter, we learned that sociology is the systematic study of social institutions, societies, inequality, and different types of people, relationships, and groups. The sociological imagination is a way of viewing and interpreting the world that helps us understand our own society and others as well. As we saw, sociology developed during the Enlightenment and reactions against the Enlightenment, a time of turmoil and rapid social change. Sociology has always been oriented toward problem solving—to finding better ways of living together, and to finding and correcting the roots of violence and injustice. Sociology believes that while everyone has agency and free will, everyone is also constrained and manipulated. As sociologists, we want to understand our constraints.

We have identified four main approaches to sociological thinking.

Conflict theory assumes that conflict and change are universal. In *The Communist Manifesto*, Marx and Engels noted that in every society there is a division between economic classes. A generation later, Max Weber expanded Marx's insight to include non-economic conflict and conflict between non-economic groups.

Feminist theory, for its part, highlights the importance of gendered differences and inequalities in our society. The way a woman experiences the world is different from the way a man experiences it, and this structured difference must be taken into account whenever sociologists study society, no matter the particular topic they are studying.

Functionalism rests on the assumption that society is a cohesive social system—a set of interconnected parts that are in equilibrium. Sudden change is disruptive to this equilibrium and causes significant change. In this way, population growth, urbanization, and industrialization can pose problems for social cohesion.

For symbolic interactionists, society is a product of face-to-face interactions between people using symbols. In *The Social Construction of Reality*, Peter Berger and Thomas Luckmann (1966) make clear that the purpose of sociology is to help people understand how they cooperate to organize and interpret everyday life. In the interactionist perspective, people respond to others, and their actions, based on a shared understanding of norms and meanings.

Questions for Critical Thought

1. How would the four sociological approaches give you different insights into the experience of being an undergraduate student? Are these insights compatible or in conflict with one another?

2. Why are people more likely to commit suicide during periods of rapid change? Do you think there would be a similar connection between social change and homicide?

3. In what ways can conflict in society be constructive? Does it become more constructive, the more conflict there is?

4. Why do people have trouble understanding their own (and other people's) everyday lives? How does sociology overcome this difficulty?

5. Describe how studying sociology will improve your skills and knowledge needed for your future career of choice.

Take it Further: Recommended Readings

Kenneth Allan, *The Social Lens: An Invitation to Social and Sociological Theory* (Thousand Oaks, CA: Pine Forge Press, 2007). The goal of this book is to provide a comprehensive introduction to both classical and contemporary social theory. It outlines different approaches to sociology and describes the scholars behind these approaches.

Cristina Bicchieri, *The Grammar of Society: The Nature and Dynamics of Social Norms* (Cambridge: Cambridge University Press, 2006). The goal of this text is to explain social norms. It considers how and why social norms emerge, evolve and survive.

Paul Blackledge, *Reflections on the Marxist Theory of History* (Manchester, UK: Manchester University Press, 2006).

This book outlines Marxist theory's transition, from Europe in the nineteenth century, to the Soviet Union in the twentieth, to its relevance in modern sociology.

David Cheal, *Dimensions of Sociological Theory* (New York: Palgrave Macmillan, 2005). This is a clear and reader-friendly discussion of five key sociological debates.

Anthony Thomson, *The Making of Social Theory: Order, Reason, and Desire*, 2nd ed. (Toronto: Oxford University Press, 2010). This book chronicles the development of classic sociological theories within a historical social context to give students an understanding of the social conditions behind sociological thinking.

Take it Further: Recommended Online Resources

The Broadbent Institute
www.broadbentinstitute.ca

Canada without Poverty
www.cwp-csp.ca

Centre for Social Justice
www.socialjustice.org

Inequality for All **(film)**
http://inequalityforall.com/

Tri-Council Policy Statement: Ethical Conduct for Research Involving Humans
www.pre.ethics.gc.ca/eng/policy-politique/initiatives/ tcps2-eptc2/Default

More resources available on  Dashboard

2 Measuring the Real World Sociologically

Learning Objectives

In this chapter, you will:

❯ Learn how to design a research study from its inception to execution, including the write up and dissemination of findings

❯ Evaluate different methodological approaches and weigh their strengths and weaknesses in relation to a study

❯ Consider in depth the ethical dimensions relevant to setting up a research study

❯ Consider how inequalities and power imbalances influence how we conduct research and gain insights

❯ Trace changes related to developments in science and technology in how sociologists conduct research

Introduction

Sociologists are interested in learning about the social world; they want to understand diverse social groups, uncover trends, and describe social change and its effects on individuals, institutions, and the environment. To uncover the social world is no easy task. While careful observation is a good start for discerning what occurs around us—as when we sit in a coffee shop observing passersby—these kinds of observations may be susceptible to bias.

bias any predisposition that prevents neutral consideration of a question or idea. It can influence a researcher's interpretation of participants' responses or the interpretation of the data.

Bias refers to systematic errors in how we draw conclusions based on our observations that may lead to inaccurate or imprecise knowledge. Sociologists aim to gain insights that are trustworthy and meaningfully represent the social world.

It is only through careful observation and analysis, often over long periods, that sociologists can gain trustworthy and meaningful insights. This type of deep engagement with social phenomena and self-reflection help overcome biases and provide in-depth, analytical accounts of social reality. See Box 2.1 for an analysis of how policing is represented in the media. We'll discuss further how the police force in Canada uses new media to reinforce the idea of community policing below.

Sociologists aim to draw conclusions and build theories about social life based on systematically gathered data and close involvement with relevant social groups. Researchers must establish that the

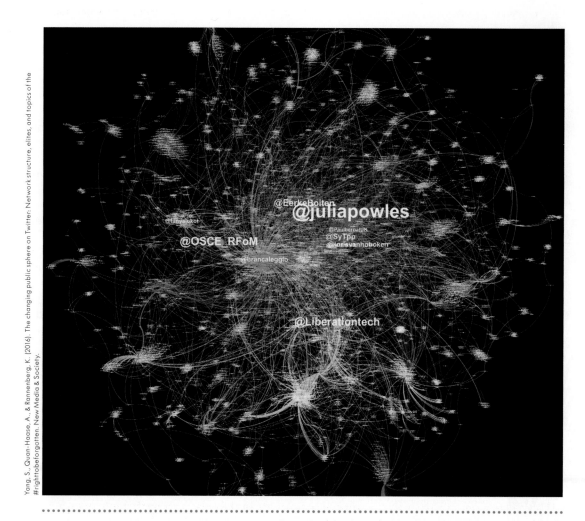

Yang, S., Quan-Haase, A., & Rannenberg, K. (2016). The changing public sphere on Twitter: Network structure, elites, and topics of the #righttobeforgotten. New Media & Society.

Big data from social media creates new opportunities for sociologists to study the social world, not only in terms of the unprecedented scale of the data, but also in terms of the unobtrusive nature of observations.

Theory in Everyday Life

2.1 | Representations of Community Policing

Human beings are not perfect creatures; sometimes we *intentionally* mask our existing realities by creating false impressions and misleading knowledge. We can easily create new realities and, by extension, new societal interactions merely by using language. We can consider the rise of community policing as a strategy used by modern police departments. Policing and police officers have not always been well regarded. Ideally, peace would be achieved by using peaceful means, but the police represent the ability of the state to use violence and force to impose the will of society upon its citizens.

Klockars (1988) suggests that community policing is primarily a *rhetorical device* (the use of language to communicate a particular message in a persuasive manner to get someone to change his or her mind). Klockars argues that community policing is a new *circumlocution* (the use of many words where a few would suffice, often in an attempt to be vague or ambiguous) used by police departments to hide the true nature of their role in society. These new circumlocutions portray policing as moving away from militarization and professionalism and towards more appealing (but still ultimately deceptive) features such as de-centralization (e.g., portrayal as "your friendly neighbourhood cop") and strategies that are more interactive with and reliant upon the community (e.g., use of "we need your help to solve crimes"). Such rhetoric distracts from their underlying mandate, which is to maintain social order, through the use of force if necessary.

Technology and mass communication provide sociologists with the opportunity to study these circumlocutions and rhetorical devices used by police departments because they are easily accessible and widely available. On television or the internet, sociologists are able to observe over long periods and thereby grasp the social realities that are actually present.

collected data and derived findings provide sufficient evidence to support their conclusions. Therefore, sociologists rely on research methods as a means to study the complexity of the social world and to critically assess and understand their own biases. Research methods can be defined as the toolset from which sociologists draw to learn about, understand, and contribute to social life. Sociologists not only use existing methods from this toolset but also develop novel methods, and reflect upon processes of knowledge creation. The use of research methods in sociological inquiry has five main goals:

1. Enumeration and description—e.g., census collection to lay out the basic characteristics of our society.
2. Prediction—e.g., much policy work that aims at determining how well one strategy of action will achieve its goal, and at what cost, compared with another potential strategy (for instance, how to get people to smoke less, eat healthier, or get more exercise). Market research and political polling are like this too. Money is invested based on these predictions, so they had better be accurate.
3. Explanation—e.g., most published work in scholarly journals is aimed at finding out how much x affects y and the likely reasons for this connection. The goal is to create theories about the world, not necessarily to influence it.
4. Debunking—e.g., showing that popular belief (myth) or common sense is wrong about something (for example, the belief that unemployed people or people on welfare simply lounge around eating junk food, rather than looking for jobs).
5. Social justice—e.g., to understand the experiences of marginalized and oppressed social groups, with the goal of achieving social change.

There are many reasons why the work of sociologists in the area of research methodology is socially relevant and closely interlinked with the well-being of individuals, institutions, and society at large. First, to develop good social policy, accurate, high-quality data is needed. We can only establish relevant social policies about welfare, policing, child care, education, health care, and the role of institutions if we can have valid and reliable information that drive these policies. Second, the work of sociologists aims to uncover, describe, and remove inequalities. Finally, sociologists describe, examine, and critique the social processes underlying the development of scientific knowledge.

The construction and dissemination of knowledge are themselves social processes that can be studied and critiqued, and are also influenced by inequalities and power imbalances. For example, Randall Collins (1998) proposed a social theory of intellectual development that traces the key patterns of intellectual networks and reveals their divisions and paths of social influence.

> ### Time to reflect
>
> Do you ever ask yourself questions about the social world around you? Have you ever noticed patterns and wondered whether they apply to society at large? In other words, are you in the habit of exercising your sociological imagination?

computational social sciences the academic subdisciplines that apply computational approaches to research.

Science and technology have always been an inherent part of how we conduct research. Advances in science and technology have provided new means for collecting, storing, analyzing, and visualizing data. Recent developments in the area of **computational social sciences** have transformed the very nature of what we understand as research. This chapter provides an overview of both traditional approaches to research and recent technological advancements that support researchers in their scholarship.

The chapter starts with an overview of the research process. Research is not a linear process; it is often a winding path, and new decisions have to be made at every turn. To show this complexity, we provide an overview of the entire research process from project conception to the write-up and dissemination of findings. Sociologists utilize a plurality of methods to study the social world, and some key methods will be introduced along with their strengths and weaknesses. The chapter ends with a discussion of the key ethical concerns that sociologists need to take into consideration when conducting any study that involves human participants.

The Process of Research

Engaging in research methods allows you to develop numerous useful research capabilities and skills ranging from the ability to design a study to being able to collect data, analyze data, interpret data and statistics, and make sense of graphs and figures. These are all relevant skills in today's data-driven society, often looked for by employers.

However, research is not a smooth path; rather, it represents a deep engagement with a topic, constant readiness for problem solving, and openness for unpredictable turns. Every research project has its own lifecycle and challenges: some projects take months while others extend over years. Figure 2.1 shows the steps that most projects follow, but it also shows how this is a non-linear, iterative learning process that may include trial and error.

Identifying an Area of Study and Formulating a Research Problem

The first step in a research project is to identify a general area of study. It is important to identify a key focus because prior to commencement of the project, a scholar needs to gain an understanding of previous studies in that area. This will help identify important research problems and formulate meaningful research questions. Three guiding principles are important in the formulation of a research question:

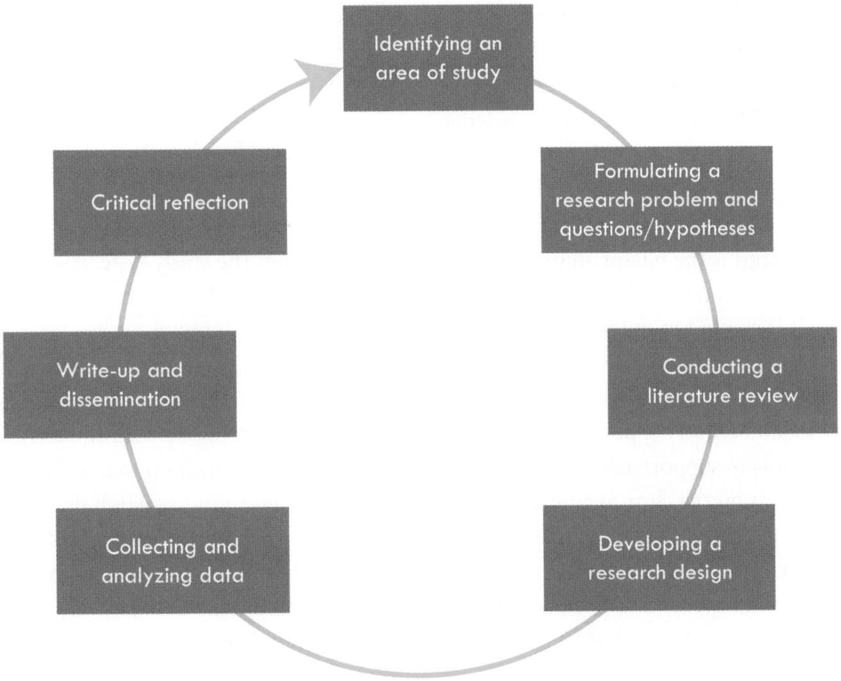

FIGURE 2.1 The Research Process
Source: Author-created.

1. Clarity: clear formulation of the research question that is easy to understand.
2. Specificity: specific formulation of the research question, evading the use of vague language and terminology.
3. Feasibility: formulation of answerable research questions that can be tackled in a single project.

Literature Review

The literature review is an essential part of every study. The goal of the literature review is to provide an overview of relevant past research, which contextualizes the study by showing what other scholars have examined on the topic.

The literature published in an area can help in the formulation of a research question in two ways. First, the literature helps to obtain a good understanding of what has been studied in the past. This knowledge then helps to identify a research gap. The research gap is critical to any sociological inquiry because it highlights where knowledge is lacking and more research is needed. It also points the researcher in the right direction, indicating which areas ought to be focused on. Second, the literature can further help formulate the significance of the study. Every research project takes time and requires resources, which means that it is particularly important to be able to formulate clearly how the study will contribute to knowledge and how it will fill a research gap. Conducting a literature review helps the researcher to distinguish his or her work from previous studies on similar topics.

Resources for a literature review can be found through the academic library catalogue, field-specific databases, and through internet search engines, such as Google Scholar. Academic libraries offer discipline-specific resources, such as databases, links to resources, and tutorials. There are also a number of social networking sites geared specifically to the research community, including Academia.edu and ResearchGate. These are similar to Facebook in that scholars create a profile, list their topics of interest, and make journal articles and chapters available to other scholars. Many scholars also keep a personal blog or web page where they post information about their current projects, key challenges encountered in the research process, and a list of publications. At the initial stages of a project, encyclopedias, reference manuals, and handbooks on a topic can also be useful to obtain a quick overview of the current state of knowledge.

Research Design

research design the blueprint of the study. It defines the study type, research question, hypotheses, variables, data collection methods, and a statistical analysis plan.

epistemology the study of the origin of knowledge and the logic of one's beliefs.

The **research design** is the blueprint or plan of the study: it defines the study type, research question, hypotheses, variables, data collection methods, and analysis plan with the aim of integrating these components. It is created to guide the researcher through the research process.

When putting together a research design, scholars need to carefully consider their **epistemological** grounding and examine criteria of research excellence, including reliability, validity, social significance, ethical considerations, and the potential contributions to knowledge. While science and technology have provided new tools to support scholarship from data collection to visualization, our ability to gain new knowledge depends on the clear formulation of a comprehensive and sound research design. A good research design is easy to follow and includes all the needed sections, integrating these in a coherent manner.

Most importantly, a good research design carefully justifies the decisions made around what data collection method is used, what population is investigated, and how the data is analyzed. Figure 2.2 provides a checklist of criteria that help develop a sound research design.

Collecting and Analyzing Data

When writing the research design, the means of data collection and analysis also need to be outlined in detail and with sufficient justification. A solid fit between the research problem, data collection, and analysis approach is essential, as different kinds of research questions require different types of data and approaches. The characteristics of a social group will also help determine the most appropriate

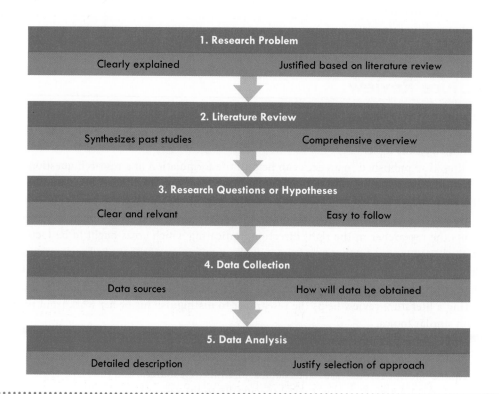

FIGURE 2.2 Checklist of Criteria for Research Design

Source: Author-generated.

method for data collection and analysis. We discuss, later in the chapter, Logan and Murdie's (2016) study of Tibetan refugees in Canada and their settlement experiences, in which the researchers used Photovoice as a data collection method, which provided a great way to show the visual experiences of the Tibetan refugees as they navigated their new home. Data collection and analysis methods are often distinguished between those relying on quantitative, qualitative, or mixed-methods approaches.

Quantitative Methods

Quantitative approaches can most easily be characterized by their reliance on numerical values obtained through surveys rather than interviews, images, videos, or other kinds of data. The kinds of data that quantitative analysis requires vary considerably and largely depend on the research question under investigation, but generally look at amounts or quantities of variables of interest (Leedy & Ormrod, 2015).

In the quantitative approach, a researcher begins with a theoretical framework established through an extensive literature review. The theoretical framework is made up of the concepts to be studied and how they relate. Based on the theoretical framework, hypotheses may be formulated and then tested using data. This is a deductive approach, whereby data is generated with the aim of testing a set of theoretically derived hypotheses. To show the trustworthiness of the research, scholars rely on two important concepts:

- **Reliability** describes the extent to which findings can be replicated and are consistent across comparable situations.
- **Validity** refers to the extent that a concept, idea, or measure represents the real world in an accurate way.

Data analysis in quantitative approaches relies largely on statistics. **Statistics** deals with large quantities of numbers and provides the mechanisms to collate, analyze, interpret, and present these numbers. Statistical data is often used to inform policy with the aim of increasing the well being and health of individuals, families, and communities. An example of the use of statistics for policy includes recording the consumption of alcohol among Canadians. About 80 per cent of Canadian adults consume alcohol (Mowat et al., 2015), and Figure 2.3 shows sales of alcoholic beverages in Canada in two

reliability the degree to which the work can be replicated. In qualitative work, reliability is often expressed in terms of trustworthiness and authenticity.

validity the extent to which findings are an accurate reflection of the social world.

statistics a branch of mathematics that concerns itself with the collection, analysis, interpretation, and representation of numerical data.

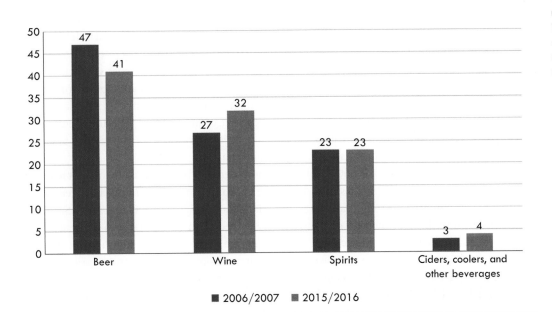

FIGURE 2.3 Proportion of Sales (in Dollars) of Alcoholic Beverages in Canada, 2006/2007 & 2015/2016

Source: Statistics Canada. Retrieved from www.statcan.gc.ca/daily-quotidien/170502/dq170502a-eng.htm

time periods: 2006/2007 and 2015/2016. The graph shows that Canadians continue to prefer beer over all other types of alcoholic beverages, but overall sales have dropped. However, there was an increase in sales of wine over the same period. While alcohol in many instances is used in moderation, alcohol consumption is associated with many harms, such as severe injuries, trauma, and aggressive behaviour (Giesbrecht et al., 2013). Interestingly, much of the societal damage resulting from alcohol use is associated with low- to high-risk drinking, not with addiction to alcohol specifically. Understanding sales of alcoholic beverages over time is important in terms of recognizing what drives people in various demographic categories to consume alcohol, as well as providing support for individuals who need to curb consumption and reduce alcohol-related harms. This insight allows for the development of effective policies that aid in changing the habits of high-risk drinkers (Babor et al., 2010; Smart & Mann, 2000).

For many families and communities, alcohol consumption has had devastating negative effects, not to mention the effects on pregnant mothers, whose infants may be born with Fetal Alcohol Spectrum Disorder (see Chapter 5 for further discussion). Quantitative analysis also reveals anomalies in the data that would otherwise go unnoticed. For example, when looking at Statistics Canada data we learn that a higher proportion of the Indigenous population in comparison to other social groups are non-drinkers (Statistics Canada, 2015).

As with revealing anomalies, statistical data may illustrate areas of interest that may otherwise be overlooked by decision makers. One noteworthy policy recommendation is the increase in alcohol pricing to deter alcohol-related harm. While at first glance this strategy may not seem particularly hard-hitting, the research demonstrates that setting a minimum price for alcohol or pricing based on alcohol content reduces alcohol consumption throughout the population (Meier, Purshouse, & Brennan, 2009; Stockwell, Auld, Zhao et al., 2012). Thus, statistics not only can help us to discover valuable information, but can lead to more effective solutions for social issues.

Qualitative Methods

Instead of relying on numbers, graphs, and mathematical models, qualitative research examines characteristics that cannot be simply reduced to numerical values (Leedy & Ormrod, 2015). Qualitative scholars recognize the complexity of social phenomena and aim to portray it in its multifaceted form with many dimensions and layers (Leedy & Ormrod, 2015).

While qualitative approaches are employed routinely across all disciplines today, sociologists Glaser and Strauss (1967) first popularized the method with the publication of their how-to book *The Discovery of Grounded Theory*. Grounded theory is a type of qualitative approach and is defined as the development of theory through in-depth data analysis. Qualitative approaches rely on different kinds of data, often making use of interviews, images (photography or digital images on social media), videos, and narratives instead of numerical values. Qualitative researchers attempt to produce rich accounts through deep engagement. Data analysis in qualitative work consists of "thick description" of social phenomena with the aim of establishing how people create and give meaning (Geertz, 1973). Luker (2008) compares the process with salsa dancing, as it is holistic, entails attention to context, and is highly concerned with questions of power and inequality.

The aim of qualitative work is not to test a hypothesis derived from existing theory but to develop new theory from data, which makes it an inductive approach. Trustworthiness and credibility of findings are accomplished through saturation and triangulation (Lincoln & Guba, 1985). **Saturation** refers to the point in time when no new insights are gained from additional data analysis (Corbin & Strauss, 2014). Qualitative researchers carefully analyze their data to establish when they have reached saturation. **Triangulation** involves comparing and contrasting data from various sources, and it allows qualitative scholars to make sense of their data.

Qualitative scholars often assign codes to their interview transcripts, images, or textual data. They also add extensive notes, a process referred to as memoing (Charmaz, 2014). For example, Schneider (2016) employed a qualitative document analysis to study what presentational strategies Canadian police are using on Twitter. The qualitative document analysis employed in the study consisted of carefully examining 105,801 tweets and placing the meaning of these tweets in a social

saturation a method used to confirm that sufficient and valuable data are collected to support the study.

triangulation a technique used by researchers to determine validity in their studies by gathering data from multiple sources. Different research methods are used with the aim of arriving at consistency across results.

London Police ON @lpsmediaoffice · 2h
Congratulations Sgt Martin! #ldnont

> **Deputy** @DarylLongworth
> Honoured 2 be on hand to c LPS Det.Paul Martin receive the Brian Young award for his efforts to prevent elder abuse.

↩   ↻ 2   ♥ 2   •••

Twitter

FIGURE 2.4 Tweets by London Police Service, @lpsmediaoffice

Source: Twitter Retrieved from https://twitter.com/lpsmediaoffice?lang=en

context (Altheide & Schneider, 2013). The study findings showed that officer tweets maintained a public professional appearance and avoided political discussions. Police are using Twitter to foster interactive communication with the public, and to establish new social relations that go beyond topics of policing. Figure 2.4 shows a tweet from the London Police Service, in which Sgt Martin is congratulated for his police work preventing elder abuse.

Time to reflect

When you imagine social research, do you think of quantitative or qualitative approaches? Has that changed as you've read this chapter?

Mixed Methods

There has been a growing interest in conducting mixed methods research because this approach combines the strengths of different data collection and analysis approaches (Johnson, Onwuegbuzie, & Turner, 2007). Generally, mixed methods is any combination of research methods.

For example, Baker et al. (2015) examined how patients in Canada and Australia evaluate the quality of interactions with their doctors by combining questionnaire responses with accounts of positive and negative experiences. The rationale for using a mixed methods design was to capture the complexity of patient-doctor interactions "since communication is a dynamic process, quantitative measures, alone, cannot capture critical elements of the communicative context or patient perspectives" (Baker et al., 2015, p. 625). Not all studies require a mixed methods approach, and Creswell (2013) states that mixed methods designs are called for when either quantitative or qualitative work alone cannot fully provide insights into a research problem and when there is one of the following needs:

- A more and diverse understanding of a single phenomenon
- To confirm quantitative findings with qualitative data
- To better contextualize quantitative instruments and measures
- To combine small scale and trend data

The merits of mixed methods studies are numerous. Data triangulation is often identified as the single most important merit and serves to determine the validity of findings. In mixed methods designs, the strengths of different approaches can be combined to obtain a more complete picture of a social phenomenon. Often the weaknesses of large-scale quantitative methods can be offset with the advantages of observations and descriptions gained from fieldwork. Similarly, statistics can add precision to narratives and accounts of participants.

Mixed methods research also has numerous challenges. First, mixed methods research is time-consuming and challenging because it draws on different methods and potentially different populations or social groups as well. Second, it also requires a scholar to have expertise in different forms of data collection, analysis, visualization, interpretation, and write-up styles. Quantitative and qualitative approaches have their distinct means of engaging with scholarship, and the researcher must be well-versed in both.

Time to reflect

Think of a project you would like to undertake, or a research question that interests you. What approach—quantitative, qualitative, or mixed—would suit your study best?

Write Up, Scholarly Communication, and Critical Reflection

The write-up of scholarly work occurs following the completion of the analysis of data. Scholars at this point often have extensive notes that help in the crafting of a document. Before scholarly work is presented at conferences or published in journal articles or books, it undergoes peer review. The aim of the peer review process is to have the work evaluated by a group of experts in the field, who can assess the merits, and provide feedback. The three most popular venues for sociologists to present their work are at the meetings of the International Sociological Association (ISA), the American Sociological Association (ASA), and the Canadian Sociological Association (CSA).

Academic venues are important for sociologists to exchange ideas, but they are not the only means by which sociologists communicate about their work. An important part of scholarly communication is disseminating work beyond the walls of academia. Scholarly communication today takes many alternative forms, from blog posts to thoughts concisely formulated in a tweet. Box 2.2 describes the field of public sociology, which concerns itself with understanding how sociology becomes relevant to the public and how sociological work can make an impact locally and globally.

Think Globally

2.2 | Call for a Global Public Sociology

Sociology is an academic discipline that studies and engages with the social world. As a result, it is natural that sociologists see engagement with the public as a key mandate of their work. Herbert Gans popularized the term *public sociology* in 1989 by stressing the critical importance of creating more linkages between the academy and the public. Public sociology is defined in terms of two means of engagement. The first is the call for sociologists to study questions that are of public relevance and directly affect people's lives (Agger, 2007). The second is for sociologists to engage with the public and disseminate their work widely.

A good example of this is the best seller *The Tipping Point* by Canadian writer Malcolm Gladwell (2000), which explains how influence is transmitted via social relations. It won the American Sociological Association's first Award for Excellence in the reporting of social issues in 2007. Global public sociology recognizes that knowledge production and use are not equally distributed across regions of the world. Sociologists working in the Global South such as San Salvador and Nigeria often have minimal access to relevant learning resources such as journal articles, books, and reports. This unequal distribution of knowledge makes it difficult for these scholars to keep up-to-date with developments in the field and to actively contribute to scholarly discourse.

Two recent initiatives are helping increase access to learning resources in these underserved regions. The first is the development of open educational resources, which are defined as educational resources such as lectures, slides, articles, and books made available online at no cost for the purposes of learning (UNESCO, 2002). The Organisation for Economic Co-operation and Development (OECD) (Orr, Rimini, & van Damme, 2015) sees open educational resources as a critical catalyst to unlock the potential of universities in nations with fewer resources by providing unlimited access to a wide range of learning resources.

Many Canadian sociologists make their work available at no cost through YouTube videos, open-access journal publications, and articles posted in university library repositories. The second key development is the use of social media as a means to reach a broad and global audience and directly engage in debate. Many sociologists have an online presence either through a personal blog, Twitter, or an Academia.edu account (Clavel et al., 2015; Rasmussen Neal, 2012).

Theoretical Approaches to Research Methods

We may think that methods are universal. But this is not the case, as methods also carry meaning about the social world. For example, consider the difference between cross-sectional and longitudinal approaches. Cross-sectional approaches look at social phenomena at one point in time and ignore change. By contrast, longitudinal approaches take into account that the social world is constantly in flux and see the study of change as critical. We will discuss next how different theories motivate the use of particular methods. (See Table 2.1 for a summary of these theories.)

Conflict Theory

Conflict theory aims to uncover and better understand inequalities in society related to access to resources, power, and privilege. A wide range of methodologies can help better understand inequalities among social groups. Marx was very aware of the inequalities that existed between workers and owners in industrial era Europe.

An important component of his theoretical work was to not only provide a more detailed picture of the hardships of workers in factories, but also to increase awareness among the workers themselves about the inequalities existent in society. Marx developed a list of 100 questions that he hoped would elicit reflection from workers and serve as a means to document the extent of worker exploitation. This list of questions became known as "A Workers' Inquiry" and represents a reflective survey that is meant to scrutinize not the abstract concept of exploitation, but rather the day-to-day experience of workers as they engage in labour. Marx employed a survey as his method to learn about the work conditions of workers and the legal frameworks that governed their work. For example, question 26 asks, "Is the employer legally bound to compensate the worker or his family in case of accident?" (Marx, 1938).

Methodologies drawing from the conflict theory perspective "position social justice as necessary for research processes as well as for research outcomes" (Brown & Strega, 2005, p. 1). Scholars working in this perspective tend to use methodologies that stress the lived experiences of marginalized social groups, without imposing the world view of the researcher. By trying to move away from pre-established notions of what knowledge is, conflict theory has sparked much reflection on the research process itself and how scholars gain knowledge. Methodologies in this tradition have three key features (Brown & Strega, 2005):

- Position of researcher: The relation that exists between the researcher, the researched, and the research topic is articulated and reflected upon. Particular attention is paid to how researchers position themselves as authority figures who can define what constitutes knowledge.
- Topic of inequality: Studies focus on marginalized social groups, the exposing of inequalities, and the mechanisms that can effect social change.
- Critical reflection: A move away from standard notions of knowledge, data, objectivity, and methodology toward deep understandings of critical, Indigenous, and anti-oppressive approaches.

Feminism

Feminism adopts methodologies that uncover inequalities among social groups in society. Large-scale studies, for example, can show imbalances in pay for men and women as will be discussed further in Chapter 7 and 12. Feminism also adopts methodologies that describe the daily experiences of marginalized social groups such as black women, Indigenous women, or transgender individuals.

Dorothy E. Smith, a Canadian sociologist, developed institutional ethnography as a means to uncover the processes, relations, and biases within an institution that shape the everyday "lived experiences" of individuals that interact with it and to counter power imbalances between social groups (see also Chapter 6). Smith's work originated from her participation in the women's movement of the 1970s and her realization of power imbalances between men and women (Campbell & Gregor, 2004). Smith sees these processes and relations as structuring social interactions in such a way that they support the dominant power structure within a society. That is, for Smith the mainstream ways of conducting research did not allow for uncovering power imbalances based on gender because these imbalances where part of the institutions and the methods being employed. To counter this, she developed institutional ethnography to investigate and explain the problems faced by individuals and groups from their standpoint. **Standpoint theory** proposes that we view the world from different social locations, depending on our ethnic background, social status, class, and other demographic characteristics that describe us. This helps understand what "standpoint" or social location women occupy in academia and how this standpoint may disadvantage them.

Smith (1990) explains that a sociologist engaged in this type of inquiry works "as an insider, as one who is a practitioner of that organization, explicating and analyzing its practices as she [he] knows and discovers them as actual practices" (p. 3). Developed from a need to understand marginalized social groups, specifically women, standpoint theory can aid in understanding various standpoints and how they affect institutions. Employing institutional ethnography, Nichols (2014) studied homeless youth services by listening to workers' experiential accounts and integrating this experiential knowledge into her analysis. In this setting, it was challenging to align institutional processes and structures with the needs of homeless youth. Through her institutional ethnography, she learned that there was an institutional need to document change in the homeless youth, as change was seen as reflecting a successful outcome, while homeless youth who failed to demonstrate change were often further marginalized and excluded. The study serves as a guide to tailor services to better meet the needs of homeless youth and to move away from simplistic measures of success.

standpoint theory
the theory that individuals view society from different social locations depending on their class, gender, and status.

> ## Time to reflect
>
> How does standpoint theory help explain the social position of researchers? In what ways can researchers' social position hinder or aid the research process? What are some of the key demographic characteristics that need to be taken into account?

Structural Functionalism

Structural functionalists examine how society is organized and the role of institutions in reinforcing social order. For instance, as will be discussed in Chapter 10, families are considered an important institution in society with family members coming together as a unified whole. The definition and composition of families are constantly under flux as society changes.

Structural functionalists often make use of large-scale survey data and analyses to quantify and understand these changes. For instance, Beaujot and Kerr (2004) examined marriage in the Canadian context and observed some changing patterns. In the 1970s, the median age at first marriage was 21 years for brides and 23 years for grooms. In 2001, the median ages were 28 and 30 years for brides and grooms, respectively. They also observed that common-law unions often delayed or replaced marriage. Drawing on data from Statistics Canada from 2002, they found that 63 per cent of first unions among women aged 20 to 29 were common-law unions instead of marriages, and these are twice as likely to end in separation than are first marriages (Beaujot & Kerr, 2007). Since 2005, when same-sex marriages were legalized in Canada, we have seen further diversity in the composition of family structures. Structural functionalists rely most commonly on quantitative data to describe changes over time to families and their compositions.

Symbolic Interactionism

Symbolic interactionism looks at the ways in which people come to understand the world around them through interactions with one another. Of particular interest to symbolic interactionists is how meaning is created and contested through social interaction and the role of symbols in meaning-making.

Even though a wide range of methods has been utilized to study social interaction, it is ethnomethodology that is most commonly associated with this approach. Garfinkel published *Studies in Ethnomethodology* in 1967, laying out the foundation for this approach by introducing key concepts, ways of understanding meaning making, and a tool set for analysis. For Garfinkel, ethnomethodology was a method that provided the tools to examine the everyday as well as the social order in which it was embedded. He focused on people's accounts of situations—that is, the explanations a person develops to explain a particular social situation.

In developing explanations, people rely upon what they perceive as everyday, "common sense" rationales. Since Garfinkel's original publication, ethnomethodology has evolved, and today it is understood as a diverse set of research techniques rather than a single approach (Maynard, 1991).

TABLE 2.1 Theoretical Approaches To Social Research

Theory	Main points
Conflict Theory	• Entails the development of methods that uncover and better understand inequalities and conflict among social groups.
	• Questions and critically examines who determines what counts as knowledge and how we establish truth.
	• Researchers do not take their role for granted, but rather critically reflect and question their own role in the research process.
Feminism	• Develops methodologies that uniquely focus on gender inequalities and their consequences.
	• Develops standpoint theory as a theory and methodology to uncover how different positions in the world influences how we see the world.
	• Standpoint theory also highlights the social location of researchers and how this impacts their knowledge production.
Structural Functionalism	• Investigates structural change over time.
	• Methodologies focus on the role of institutions and how we can measure institutional change through large-scale quantitative research or ethnographies.
Symbolic Interactionism	• Aims to develop methodologies to study the everyday and the social order imposed on it such as participant observation.
	• Focuses on uncovering the role of symbols in society and their meaning, including language.

Source: Author-generated.

Methods of Social Research

Survey Research

Interactive
activity

The goal of survey research is to gather systematic information on a topic to describe, explain, or influence a social phenomenon (Guppy & Gray, 2008). Survey research collects data through either structured interviews or questionnaires, with questionnaires being the most common of the two approaches. Survey research has three strengths that set it apart from other methods: first, questions are standardized thus reducing potential bias stemming from question wording; second, answers consist of pre-determined categories, reducing the variation in the data; and third, data from large samples can be gathered.

Survey research may be used if the aim of the study is to describe trends, establish causation, determine relationships between variables, or see the big picture of a phenomenon. For example, in the study by Beaujot and Kerr (2007) discussed above, questionnaires were utilized to determine at what age Canadians are choosing to get married. The researchers compared the average age of marriage in the 1970s with that in the 2000s to describe a changing trend. The standardization of questions facilitates the analysis of the data through statistical procedures.

Self-Administered Questionnaires

A self-administered questionnaire is designed to allow the respondent to answer a pre-written set of questions with no researcher directly involved in communicating the questions to the respondent. These can be administered on paper, by telephone (where an automated voice reads the questions and the respondent answers with a numeric keypad), or online. Since the development of online surveys, these have largely replaced traditional paper-and-pencil or telephone formats because of their versatility, ease of distribution, and additional features.

Online surveys have other advantages in comparison to traditional surveys. They overcome poor and slow response rates to mailed questionnaires (Dillman, Smyth, & Christian, 2014). Most importantly, the data accuracy is increased as the responses are directly recorded digitally and there is no need for data entry, which is prone to human error (Ilieva, Baron, & Healey, 2006). Online surveys can reach more diverse populations, potentially a global population if disseminated via social media. However, online surveys are also susceptible to problems related to data accuracy. Often participants will complete the survey several times if there is an incentive such as a prize that they could win (Ilieva et al., 2006).

census a recurring and official count of a particular population, used to systematically gather and record information about the members of the population.

Perhaps the most important survey in Canada due to its breadth of coverage is the Census of Population. The **census** is a short questionnaire that collects demographic information on all Canadians, both in Canada and abroad, to help plan services such as schooling and transportation. To gain the most accurate information possible, it is mandatory for all Canadian residents to complete the census. In the most recent census, Canadians were given the opportunity to respond to the survey online, likely due to the benefits outlined above. However, several barriers can make it particularly difficult to identify and recruit individuals from marginalized social groups for the census. Box 2.3 describes Statistics Canada's efforts to ensure full enumeration of Indigenous people in Canada, who are dispersed across large geographic regions and may see little value in completing the census.

The census consists of two parts. The first is a very brief survey covering basic information. The National Household Survey is the second part of the Census Program, and consists of a long questionnaire. It is more detailed than the first part of the census and gathers information about Canadians' demographic, social, and economic characteristics as well as information about where they live. The data collected helps with program planning and delivery in all levels of government. Table 2.2 depicts five Canadian datasets that are relevant to sociological inquiry.

Scholars need to carefully assess data accuracy prior to commencing data analysis. One successful strategy consists of combining online surveys with paper-and-pencil surveys because this strategy does not exclude individuals who are not connected to the internet (Ilieva et al., 2006). Statistics Canada combines online, paper, and telephone surveys as part of its attempt to reach as many people as possible.

Digital Divide

2.3 | Statistics Canada's Strategy for Ensuring Full Enumeration of Indigenous Communities in Canada

Statistics Canada is a governmental agency that works to produce statistical information regarding Canada's people, resources, economy, and culture. While the census is the most well-known survey produced by Statistics Canada, there are approximately 350 other surveys on health, labour markets, and digital connectivity. What makes Statistics Canada's dataset unique is the size of the sample from which they collect information. Surveys may be distributed to as many as 4.5 million households, such as the 2011 voluntary National Household Survey. Random selection of participants is used to ensure that such data is unbiased and can be generalized to the entire Canadian population.

To ensure completion of surveys, employees of Statistics Canada contact citizens via multiple means, including traditional mail surveys, phone calls, and even emails. One challenge faced by Statistics Canada is ensuring full enumeration of Canada's Indigenous population. Different strategies are used to increase accuracy, with one being the use of multiple questions to distinguish Indigenous participants. These questions cover ancestry, Indian Status, self-identification, and First Nation membership.

Additionally, all First Nations, Inuit, and northern community households were enumerated using the long-form census questionnaire in 2016, which was administered in-person by a canvasser. Indigenous peoples living off-reserve or outside northern/Inuit communities were accounted for through the same sampling structure used for the rest of the general population. By taking these measures, Statistics Canada is able to collect more accurate data on hard to reach populations, thus making the data reflective of the Canadian population as a whole.

The goal of Statistics Canada data is to provide valid and valuable information, as it is relied upon by politicians and policy makers when implementing new laws or proposing infrastructure additions. The most recent census data shows that from 2011 to 2016, the Canadian population grew 5 per cent to 35 million (Statistics Canada, 2017). It is also crucial for members of the public, as they can use it to better understand changes to their community and their country.

Researcher-Administered Questionnaires

In researcher-administered questionnaires, a trained researcher will contact respondents to ask them a set of carefully scripted questions. This form of conducting questionnaires is very common in political polling and opinion research. In this process, the telephone (or occasionally in-person) interviewer reads the respondent possible responses and asks him or her to choose the best available answer. In some cases, the interviewer asks the respondent for answers to open-ended questions—for example, to voice their concerns about the economy or identify likes and dislikes about the current

TABLE 2.2 Examples of Canadian Datasets

Name	Frequency of data collection	Sample
Census	Every 5 years	Entire population
Household Survey	Every 5 years	33% of households
Labour Force Survey	Monthly	56,000 households
Community Health Survey	Yearly	65,000 respondents
Homicide Survey	Yearly	No sample. Reports on all homicides in a given year

Source: Author-generated.

rate of immigration. Then, research assistants take these responses and "code" them—that is, put them in categories and assign numbers to these categories, for simpler data analysis. In most survey research, the researcher uses a computer to analyze the responses. Doing so increases accuracy and simplifies the use of statistical tests to find patterns.

A great deal can be said about the merits and pitfalls of survey research using human interviewers. The merits are obvious: generally, using a human interviewer increases the likelihood a sampled person will answer (all of) the survey questions, especially where the questions are sensitive and personal. Second, a human interviewer is also able to clarify questions for the respondent, if necessary. On the other hand, there are pitfalls to avoid with a human interviewer. Where human interviewers are used, they must be chosen and trained carefully, so they do not (unintentionally) influence the answers that respondents give. Certain types of interviewers are most suitable to interview certain kinds of respondents on certain types of topics (Davis, Couper, Janz, Caldwell & Resnicow, 2010). Remember, interviews are social interactions, and many respondents will answer in ways designed to exaggerate their success, popularity, intelligence, or determination.

The main disadvantage of in-person surveys is their cost. Interviewers must be paid for their time. Surveys usually require samples in the hundreds or even thousands, and we can expect a high proportion (often as low as 80 or 90 per cent for external surveys) of people contacted to refuse an interview, so a great deal of paid time is needed to complete the required number of interviews. To indicate how many individuals chose not to respond, researchers report the response rate, which is the proportion of individuals who chose to take part in the study. Sometimes, researchers reduce the cost by reducing the required sample size; but by doing so, they reduce the likelihood they will be able to draw strong, significant conclusions.

Time to reflect

Do you prefer completing a survey online, by phone, or in paper-and-pencil format? What are your reasons for preferring one format over another?

Sampling

population

the complete group of units to which the results are to be generalized. Units can be anything from individuals, animals, or objects to businesses or trips.

sample

a subset of the population of interest in a study, reducing the number of participants to a manageable size.

Survey research relies on collecting data on a specific population. The **population** describes the larger pool of individuals who all share a characteristic relevant to the study. As populations can be large, this makes it difficult to collect data from all members of a population.

To be able to draw conclusions about a population, a researcher will select a group from within the larger population; this is referred to as the **sample**. The process of selecting a sample from the population is called sampling, and different sampling strategies exist. Table 2.3 summarizes the key strategies (Given, 2008) and shows their advantages and disadvantages. The ideal sampling strategy—the stratified random sample—is very costly and researchers often take practical considerations into account to choose alternative sampling strategies. The validity of findings is a direct reflection of the soundness of the sampling strategy utilized for the formulated research question. This makes sampling one of the most critical tasks in a research project.

Survey research has many merits and allows scholars to gather large quantities of data on a population. Despite its merits, survey research also has some weaknesses. First, it does not allow participants to provide their opinions in full and reflect upon the survey questions. Often, the standardized answers may not apply to a person or may not sufficiently reflect how a person feels about an issue. Second, questionnaires reduce social reality to a pre-established set of questions/topics, ignoring the complexity of social phenomena and their transient nature. Through other methods such as ethnography scholars may go into the field without imposing a pre-set selection of topics; rather, the topics and key research questions emerge through the engagement in the field. When selecting survey research as a method, it is important to consider and weigh the strengths and weaknesses.

TABLE 2.3 Sampling Strategies and Their Advantages and Disadvantages

Sample type	Brief description	Advantages	Disadvantages
Convenience sample	Non-probability (or non-random) sampling technique where the sample is composed of participants who are easily and conveniently accessible. This strategy is useful for gaining insights on difficult to reach populations, or for gathering preliminary information before a more in-depth study.	• Easy • Cheap	• Non-random • Likely to be biased
Simple random sample	The most common form of random or probability sampling; all members of a population are equally likely to be selected as part of the sample. This allows for a non-biased representative sample of the population.	• Free of researcher bias	• Costly • Hard to get • Uneven outcome
Systematic random sample	A probability sampling strategy in which every *n*th member (where *n* is a random number) is selected to be part of the sample.	• Free of researcher bias • More even outcome	• Costly • Hard to get • May be biased by population pattern
Stratified random sample	A probability sampling strategy in which a population is divided on the basis of a particular common trait into groups (strata), then a number of participants are selected from each group.	• Free of researcher bias • More even outcome • Accurate	• Costly • Hard to get
Quota sample	A non-probability sampling strategy used to avoid bias based on specific characteristics. It selects participants for inclusion from specific subsets based on key characteristics that might otherwise not be represented in the sample if a random sample were selected.	• Easy • Cheap • Theoretically meaningful	• Not genuinely random • Intentionally biased
Cluster random sample	Based on probability sampling wherein the population is first broken down into clusters, with participants being randomly selected from each cluster. For example, a population may be segmented by geographical location, followed by participant selection from each segment.	• Easier than fully random • Cheaper than fully random • Shows regional variation	• Not genuinely random • Likely to be biased

Source: Lorne Tepperman, *Starting Points*, 2e. © Oxford University Press Canada 2011. Reprinted by permission of the publisher.

Interviews

Interviews are conversations with select individuals who belong to social groups of interest. Unlike questionnaires, interviews allow participants to provide opinions in their own words. Interviews are an ideal data collection method in projects that seek to understand a social group, garner information about people's opinions and attitudes, and aim to uncover meaning and relevance. There are two common types of interviews in sociological research: in-depth, unstructured interviews and semi-structured interviews. Bernard (2013) suggests that the choice of interview type is often guided by the nature of the research questions and needs of specific populations.

Dashboard

Video: *Out of the Question*

In-depth, unstructured interviews have little to no structure, which allows the interviewer to probe into unexpected avenues of discussion (Berg & Lune, 2014). Unstructured interviews provide the interviewer with complete freedom to take the interview into any direction. They also provide the respondents with the freedom to outline their perspective in any order. The advantage of this format is that it allows for an in-depth exploration of a topic with few external constraints imposed.

Semi-structured interviews integrate the benefits of structured interviews while also allowing the interviewer to follow new leads and prompts for clarification (Bernard, 2013). This technique provides great flexibility as it allows the researcher to explore specific topics in depth and to tailor questions in response to a participant's responses. The combination of structure provided by an interview guide and the flexibility to deviate from it if needed provides "reliable, comparable qualitative data" (Bernard, 2013, p. 182).

Semi-structured interviews are based on carefully crafted interview guides that list all important topics and points. These types of interviews are also more precise than other techniques because they include written exemplary formulations of questions that standardize the interviews and ensure they proceed efficiently. In a study of how aging Canadians integrate walking into their daily routines, researchers conducted one-on-one semi-structured interviews with 14 participants aged 65 and over (Mitra, Siva, & Kehler, 2015). They asked interviewees to bring pictures of the places in their neighbourhood where they went for walks and then used these visual representations "to inform, support and contextualize a participant's interview responses" (Mitra et al., 2015, p. 12). The study concluded that high quality and safe walking spaces encourage seniors to be more active and integrate walking into their daily lives.

Field Research

Field research simply defined is research done outside a laboratory (Palys & Atchinson, 2014). It involves careful observation of participants in their natural settings be it at schools, hospitals, or other social spaces. Data collection takes place through varied means and can include surveys, interviews, and focus groups (Sullivan, 2009).

Field research is not restrictive; rather, it aims to collect varied data types from multiple sources. This becomes a central principle of field research and helps the researcher to look at the specifics of social behaviour to then make generalizations in an inductive manner. Field research has the advantage of having high **ecological validity** because it takes place in a setting more natural than a laboratory, as it observes people in their everyday lives (Sullivan, 2009). It can also open up avenues for exploratory research because initial observations can spur additional questions and help identify new variables to examine (Sullivan, 2009).

These very same advantages can become detriments to the process because the field is unpredictable and participants can be hostile or argumentative toward the researcher (Sørnes, Hybertsen, & Browning, 2014). The closeness of the observer to the field can manifest in a subtle bias both in the researcher and the participants as preconceived notions and expectations can alter the observations (Sullivan, 2009).

ecological validity the extent to which findings can be generalized to real-life settings.

Participant Observation

Participant observation is a strategy where the researcher observes an individual, a group, or a community, in order to understand and become familiar with customs and practices as seen from the "natural habitat," or in the field (Sullivan, 2009).

What is unique about participant observation is that the observer must become a participant to get that direct access to the group or individual under study (Sullivan, 2009). The observer directly benefits from being a member as close proximity to the customs and practices under study add depth to the research. However, being completely immersed with those under observation raises problems similar to those encountered in ethnographic studies (Sullivan, 2009; also see below). For example, when participants know they are being observed, they may adjust their behaviours.

Ethnography

Ethnography involves researchers fully immersing themselves in a setting and observing participants. Ethnography distinguishes itself from other approaches because of the longer time frame and the nature of the relation between researcher and research participant. Ethnographers rely on multiple methods of data collection including field notes, interviews, and surveys to establish a personal understanding of the setting. The most important means of gaining insight is through participant observation (see above). Detailed field notes of observations and analytical notes help to create a coherent account.

Ethnographies can take years of immersion, with a scholar closely sharing the experiences of the participants being studied to understand their culture. Goffman's (2014) involvement in a low-income African American community in Chicago started when she was a sophomore and continued into her doctoral studies. A shorter example is Buffam's (2011) study at a drop-in recreational centre in Edmonton that is largely visited by Indigenous youth, which he observed for three months. The time frame will depend on the scope and nature of the research.

It is critical to consider how access will be negotiated as different social groups have different sensitivities towards being the "objects" of research. Establishing a relationship with the community and having an understanding of their cultural sensitivities is crucial for obtaining access. Trust needs to be established with key gatekeepers, in order to garner trust from the community. Exactly how involved should a scholar become in their immersion in the field? Box 2.4 describes the discussion that has emerged

Spotlight On

2.4 | Alice Goffman's Ethnographic Work in Chicago

Goffman's (2014) research topic was the impact of mass incarceration and policing on low-income African American inner-city communities (Lewis-Kraus, 2016). Goffman integrated herself for about six years into a low-income community by befriending a group of young men who were involved in criminal activity.

Goffman's unique research strategy was distinctly personal, and befriending her research participants allowed her to expose the raw perspectives of an oppressed group of people. However, studying a gang from the inside poses a number of concerns. By mainly focusing on the perspective of these young men (and giving less influence to members of the "other side," such as police officers), Goffman failed to adequately validate facts. Thus, possible rumours or myths may have become viewed as the truth (Lubet, 2015).

Furthermore, her acknowledgment of the significance of her position as a white, middle-class woman in a predominantly African American community was minimal. As she describes herself adopting various behaviours associated with this community, she obscured her role as a researcher and her sense of positionality (discussed earlier in relation to Smith's work on standpoint theory). The most controversial element of her strategy was certainly her willingness to be a passive witness or even a

co-participant in a crime that those she was studying were committing. Numerous critics were unimpressed with her inability to draw the line (Lubet, 2015).

Alice Goffman presenting a Ted Talk on her ethnographic work in Chicago.

Time to reflect

Do you think Goffman's deep involvement with her research participants was necessary to gain the trust of the community?

surrounding the involvement of Alice Goffman with those she studied and the methodological sound-ness of her approach.

Goffman's (2014) work was conducted overtly; that is, the participants had given explicit consent. Researchers can also take a covert role, where the participants are unaware of the researcher's intent and simply consider the researcher a community member. One of the disadvantages of a covert role is the deception involved, as research participants may feel betrayed once they realize they are being observed without permission.

Participatory Action Research (PAR)

Participatory action research (PAR) is considered one of the most suitable methodologies for con-ducting research with marginalized or oppressed communities or social groups. What distinguishes PAR from other approaches is that participants become collaborators in the research; that is, they help formulate research questions that are meaningful to the community and also provide input into what data will be collected and how. PAR benefits directly from the insider perspective provided by collaborators and also gains the buy-in of community members. Through the blurring of boundaries between researcher and community members and the sharing of power, participants feel involved in designing the study and empowered (LeCompte, 1995). PAR is defined not as a single method, but as a "family of practices of living inquiry" that can be quite disparate in their approach (Reason & Bradbury, 2008). PAR approaches vary precisely because of the active role of research participants in defining the research questions and design.

Researchers thus show deep immersion in the topic and genuine interest in the communities' insights and perspectives as well as the contributions they can make to the research. Ultimately, the goal of PAR is to effect social change either through increased awareness or through the implemen-tation of new social practices (Brydon-Miller, 2001; Kemmis & McTaggart, 2008). PAR does not stop with findings; the findings serve to inform policy, practice, or the communities' own perception of themselves. Kemmis and McTaggart (2008) describe the process as fluid and responsive, stressing that it is a spiral of cycles of self-reflection, including planning a change, acting and observing, reflecting on key processes and consequences, and then starting again a new cycle with re-planning.

PAR was employed to study the Aamjiwnaang First Nation Reserve, which is located in a heavily polluted area near Sarnia, Ontario. Much conflict has arisen between those living on the reserve and the Ministry of Environment, which is in charge of regulating pollution in the area. Wiebe (2016) studied Aamjiwnaang First Nations residents and their struggles through field immersion, partici-pant observation, and 35 in-depth interviews. This approach allowed her to document activities and practices on the ground as Aamjiwnaang First Nations residents cope with the ongoing impact of pollutants on their health and habitat.

Through her involvement with the community, Wiebe learned that residents speak about a rad-ical and relational form of community belonging that is simultaneously embodied and territorial. Citing Anishinabek elder Mike Plain, Wiebe provides a first-hand account of the experiences of those living in this polluted area: "I will continue to survive . . . in the midst of toxic surroundings, that touch my being . . . I will continue to survive. I still feel vibrant and full of life . . . with contamina-tions that invade my space . . . I still feel vibrant and full of life" (Wiebe, 2016, p. 29).

Photovoice

Photovoice is a method that has been used to study the experiences of individuals and social groups. As mobile technologies have become ubiquitous and taking snapshots has become a routine part of digital culture, photovoice takes advantages of the already engrained digital practice of documenting the every-day life to enrich qualitative research with additional visual data.

Photovoice is also a participatory research approach because it aims to understand the lived experiences of marginalized social groups. Cameras allow participants to take control over what stories they wish to share with researchers and how they chose to frame their stories (Rose, 2008;

AP Photo/The Abilene Reporter-News, Nellie Doneva

As part of one 2015 study on refugee integration into their new communities, children take photos to answer the question "What makes me happy?" in Abilene, Texas.

Wang, Burris, & Ping, 1996). It also gives them the opportunity to show how they see themselves and their surroundings (Rose, 2008). For example, in their study of Tibetan refugees in Canada and their settlement experiences, Logan and Murdie (2016) used photovoice to study 11 women who resided in high-rise apartments in Parkdale, a Toronto neighbourhood. To learn more about what it means for these individuals to create a new "home" in Toronto, participants were invited to take pictures of interesting things in their surroundings and inside their apartments.

Analysis of the Photovoice data identified four central concerns among these women as they settled in Toronto: their first concern was to create a comfortable house in their apartments; second, they identified places where they could connect with nature such as parks; third, it was important to them to celebrate their own culture and spirituality; and finally, they made new connections to neighbours and community services. In a photovoice project such as this study of Tibetan refugees in Toronto, the goal of the images is to encourage dialogue and discussion of key themes through the photographs (Wang et al., 1996). The photographs provide scholars with a new perspective, as they see the world from the standpoint of the participants.

When conducting a photovoice study, researchers also need to be aware of several challenges. While it is easy to take large numbers of photos with digital cameras, the analysis of those photos is complex and involved (Logan & Murdie, 2016). Photographs provide rich data with multiple meanings, making it difficult for researchers to synthesize this information into a coherent narrative that remains accurate to the original photographs and conversations about the meaning of the images for the participants.

Secondary Data Analysis

Secondary data analysis consists of the analysis and interpretation of existing data, previously collected by other scholars, produced by institutions, or created online by a global digital public. The data

TABLE 2.4 Advantages and Disadvantages of Secondary Data Analysis

Advantages	Disadvantages
Minimal cost	Takes time to familiarize with dataset
Minimal effort	Dataset is pre-established
Non-reactive	No additional data can be added
High validity	Difficult to establish quality of data
More time for data analysis and interpretation	

Source: Author-created.

can be in written or visual formats and can have been created by individuals or institutions. Diaries, letters, and photographs, for example, present first-hand accounts of events that occurred in the past and can provide direct insight into social relations and social phenomena.

Similarly, institutional documents such as government documents can provide insight into the operations of these institutions and how they relate to social life. Government documents are an important source for Canadian sociologists, as Canadian government procedures, emails of ministers, and parliamentary debates are carefully recorded and stored by Library and Archives Canada, providing a complete and accurate record for analysis. As discussed above, the use of existing datasets from Statistics Canada is also considered a type of secondary data analysis. However, secondary analysis is limited because it relies on pre-existing questions, often based on simple yes or no responses, and may not ask the questions needed to test a particular hypothesis. Table 2.4 summarizes advantages and disadvantages of secondary data analysis.

Social Media Data

What happens in an internet minute? According to Allen (2017), 3.8 million queries are posed on Google, 500 hours of video are uploaded to YouTube, 29 million messages are exchanged on WhatsApp, and 3.3 million Facebook posts are made.

User-generated content is just the tip of the iceberg, as third parties also generate copious amounts of data on users such as automatic credit ratings and location data. The massive and unprecedented generation of "big and broad data" represents a unique opportunity to learn about the social world (Quan-Haase & Sloan, 2017). Social media research has advantages over traditional research because researchers have access to vast amounts of data, often in real time. They can follow a debate as it unfolds and gain insights into public opinion, social activism, and changing political attitudes. Social media are also advantageous because the data is produced in a naturalistic setting, reducing influences from study participation such as **reactivity**. Reactivity describes changes in behaviour that result from participants knowing they are being observed.

reactivity when people who are being observed change their usual or typical behaviour because they know that they are being observed.

Analysis based on social media data also presents new challenges for researchers with data preparation and interpretation. Determining the accuracy of data is no easy task and often data sets are incomplete, lacking critical demographic information about social media users such as their real name, age, country of origin, etc. This makes meaningful analysis tedious and complex.

Many diverse approaches exist, both quantitative and qualitative, to the study of social media data (Sloan & Quan-Haase, 2017). In a study of online debate, Yang, Quan-Haase, and Rannenberg (2016) investigated how the debate unfolded on Twitter around the ruling by the European Court of Justice (2014) surrounding the right to be forgotten, which allows citizens to request personal information to be removed from a search engine's result pages. They collected 30,894 relevant tweets produced by 18,959 user accounts. By visualizing interactions on Twitter in graphs (see photo on page 30 and key topics (see Figure 2.5), the authors learned that most of the debate on Twitter concerned the effect of the ruling on Google's operations. How would Google implement the right to be

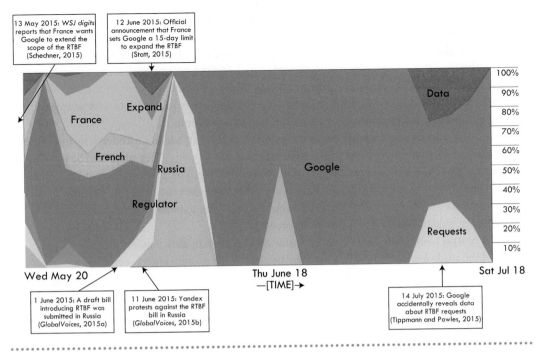

FIGURE 2.5 Trending Topics on Twitter

Source: Yang, S., Quan-Haase, A., & Rannenberg, K. (2016). The changing public sphere on Twitter: Network structure, elites, and topics of the #righttobeforgotten. *New Media & Society.* Retrieved from http://doi.org/1461444816651409

forgotten? The new ruling provides citizens with more self-determination, but also introduces new challenges to how search engines operate and the information they make available to individuals searching the web.

The Ethics of Conducting Research

Ethical standards guide the conduct of research in all disciplines because scholars aim to minimize the potentials risks to human participants associated with a study; these include physical and psychological harm.

Dashboard
Case study

Past experiences have taught us the need to carefully assess potential harm to participants. In the 1960s, Milgram (1963) conducted a series of experiments on obedience to authority figures. In his experiments, he asked a teacher (a participant in the study) to give a learner (a confederate called Mr. Wallace) electric shocks ranging from 15 volts to 450 volts, which could potentially severely hurt the participant. When participants were asked by an authority figure (in a white lab coat) to shock the learner with high levels of voltage, many of the participants followed the orders, even if they first expressed a desire not to. In reality, no shocks were given to the learner, who as a confederate was only pretending to be in pain as part of the research deception.

The series of experiments yielded famous findings, but at a very high cost to those who agreed to participate. The Milgram experiments breached the participants' trust by deceiving them into believing that they had administered a potentially dangerous electric shock to another human being. Many participants were distraught and suffered from anxiety as a consequence of their participation. Maintaining the trust of participants is essential to research; a loss of trust could jeopardize what lies at the centre of much academic work, the recruitment of participants to voluntarily participate in research studies.

Today, it is standard practice that all studies conducted at institutions of higher education in Canada involving human participants undergo careful scrutiny to guarantee the procedures follow ethical standards. A part of this process is to provide participants with a letter of information. The letter of information is always provided to participants prior to the commencement of the study and informs them about what the study is about and how the study will be conducted. In it, any potentials risks are also outlined, so as to allow participants to make an informed decision regarding their willingness to participate. The decision-making process underlying participation in a study is referred to as **informed consent**. That is, all studies need to guarantee that participants who are agreeing to partake in the study understand exactly what this participation entails.

informed consent

a process for getting permission before involving a participant in a research endeavour.

To give informed consent, potential participants must have an adequate understanding of the research topic, their role in the research, and their rights as participants. They must also be informed of the potential risks or consequences associated with participating. Voluntary participation is essential, as researchers want to avoid what is called coercion. Coercion refers to the use of measures of persuasion to convince another person to do something—in this case, to participate in the study. Coercion can consist of hidden forms of persuasion or force and threats.

Also central to ethics is debriefing. In some studies, participants may not be fully aware of the nature of the study because it would alter their behaviour. To prevent such reactivity, scholars sometimes withhold from participants information about the real purpose of the study. Following completion of the study, however, scholars are required to inform the participants of the real nature of the study and how the deception took place. The process of debriefing is critical as it helps participants understand what occurred during the study.

New opportunities for research have emerged from the massive amounts of data being generated every day by billions of internet and mobile device users. This data revolution has made it clear that sociologists need to rethink how they engage with human participants, as traditional ethical standards no longer apply to data collection via social media sites such as Twitter, Instagram, and YouTube. Box 2.5 describes a 2014 study that breached many of the ethical standards expected in research today and led to a call for further discussion around the ethics expected of research drawing from social media data (Goel, 2014).

Sociology 2.0

2.5 | The Facebook Experiment: Do Researchers Need to Ask for Consent to Study Facebook Interactions?

The Facebook Experiment has highlighted new ethical concerns emerging from the conduct of research in a digital society (Kramer, Guillory, & Hancock, 2014). As of June 2017, Facebook had 2 billion monthly active users worldwide (Fortune, 2017), with Canadians being one of the largest adopters of Facebook, with 18.6 million active users in 2017 (Statista, 2017), many of whom log into the site at least once a day. The aim of the experiments was to contest the idea that Facebook is linked to negative mental health outcomes. Past research had shown that for many social comparison was a mediating factor between Facebook use and depressive symptoms, confirming the idea that seeing Facebook friends have a good time could lead to feelings of inadequacy and low self-esteem (Steers, Wickham, & Acitelli, 2014).

The experiments ran for a week (11 January to 18 January 2012) and manipulated the amount of positive (condition 1) and negative (condition 2) emotions that users were exposed to in their news feed, without their awareness of this manipulation taking place. While the Facebook experiment challenged the link between Facebook content and negative emotions, the research community and media raised many ethical concerns related to the study design. In particular, three standard ethical research practices were violated. First, no information letter was provided to the participants informing them of the purpose and nature of the study. Second, participants did not agree to participate in the study. They were made a part by researchers unknowingly. In other words, there was no informed consent. Third, no debriefing took place about the experimental design and its intended effect after completion of the study.

The Facebook experiment has received much criticism because it ignored ethical practices that are standard in research. Vitak (2017) argues that average Facebook users who served as research participants did not know what was going on "behind the scenes" and this lack of transparency made them feel uncomfortable. This led to an outcry in the media regarding the ethical practices of big data analytics and a call for increased transparency, greater communication with research participants, and more care in the design of large-scale experiments (Sloan & Quan-Haase, 2017).

Time to reflect

How would you react if you found out that you had been a part of a large-scale study without your consent? Do you think corporations like Facebook need to be more accountable and transparent about the kind of experimental studies that take place on their site?

Research Ethics Boards (REB)

An important institution that oversees the conduct of research involving human participants is the Research Ethics Board or Ethics Review Board (often referred to as REB or ERB). The goal of an ethics review board is to make sure that a research study follows the guidelines outlined in the Tri-Council Policy Statement: Ethical Conduct for Research Involving Humans as well as other relevant regulations, policies, and guidelines. The Tri-Council Policy Statement is a joint policy developed by Canada's three leading federal research agencies and it states the agencies' ongoing commitment to the conduct of ethical research involving humans. The policy statement outlines in detail what standards research in Canada needs to follow and thereby protects Canadians from potential harms and risks.

All studies undertaken at institutions of higher education, including those that are part of a class exercise, need to be reviewed by an REB. The REB consists of experts who carefully read and evaluate a study's research design not for its scholarly merit but for its ethical soundness. All ethics protocols include the following critical components: a letter of information, informed consent, the research design, the potential risks and benefits to participants, and information about voluntary participation. The Interior Health Authority's (2017) REB in British Columbia describes its mandate this way: "The IH REB reviews proposals for research to be conducted within Interior Health by staff or physicians, or involving IH resources or people. Our purpose is to ensure that ethical and other obligations of competent research are met. In doing so, the IH REB protects the research participants, the researchers and the organization."

To provide guidelines for scholars and to help establish best practices that protect participants, including those with the greatest vulnerability in society, several reports and guidelines have been developed such as the Tri-Council Policy Statement discussed above. Guidelines serve to protect vulnerable populations such as children, pregnant women, and prisoners. Prior to embarking on any research project that involves collecting data from individuals, it is important to be familiar with the guidelines. For example, research involving Indigenous people needs to follow a set of ethical guidelines that takes the community's needs and history of oppression into account. Indigenous research "embraces the intellectual, physical, emotional and/or spiritual dimensions of knowledge in creative and interconnected relationships with people, places and the natural environment" (SSHRC, 2015).

Outlined in Chapter 9 of the Tri-Council Policy Statement, the guidelines regarding this area of research are designed to elicit sensitivity, respect for persons, concern for welfare, and community engagement. Community engagement creates interaction between researchers and their participants that "signifies a collaborative relationship between researchers and communities" (Government of Canada, Panel on Research Ethics, 2015), similar to that discussed above in PAR. Engagement of community members in the study design and execution, initiated before the study and maintained throughout, can enrich the quality of research as well as support ethical practice.

Developing strong relationships means that both parties are happy: the researchers can collect insightful information, and community members can play an active role in the cultivation of knowledge that contributes to the well-being of their community.

Conclusions

Sociologists have been at the forefront of methodological innovations not only in terms of developing new approaches to the study of social processes and social change, but also in the development of software that aids in the handling of data. As we saw earlier, Glaser and Strauss's grounded theory (1967) approach was a novel lens when first introduced for the collection, analysis, and discussion of research findings. Similarly, Smith's standpoint theory was a novel and important way of studying institutions, providing socially relevant insights. Both grounded theory and standpoint theory are examples of sociologists' contributions to methodology and have allowed sociologists to conduct new types of research. The chapter reviewed a wide range of methods from which scholars can choose. Each approach has its strengths and weaknesses, and scholars need to carefully consider which method best fits their research questions and goals.

Advances in research methodology have been closely linked to developments in science and technology. Sociologists have come to rely on technology to facilitate many aspects of the research process. Today, we see a new movement, where new technologies serve to collect and analyze data, with such examples as data collection from social media or the use of digital images for research purposes. Despite all the technological developments, the quality of research is based on good research design, because technology cannot replace good methodology. Sociologists are trained to design and conduct research that meets standards of reliability, validity, rigour, relevance, and ethics.

Questions for Critical Thought

1. What are the differences and similarities in how scholars collect and analyze data in qualitative and quantitative approaches?

2. What are the merits of mixed methods approaches? Would you advise one of your peers to conduct a mixed methods study? What considerations should they take into account before embarking on a mixed methods study?

3. What steps can be taken to increase response rates in online surveys? Do you think online surveys can collect accurate and trustworthy data?

4. How have ethical standards changed in a digital society, where massive amounts of data about users are available online?

Take it Further: Recommended Readings

B.L. Berg and H. Lune, *Qualitative Research Methods for the Social Sciences*, 8th ed. (Boston, MA: Pearson, 2014). This text explains the process of designing, collecting, and analyzing qualitative data as well as how to effectively present research findings to the scholarly community.

G.D. Bouma, R. Ling, and L. Wilkinson, *The Research Process*, 3rd ed. (Don Mills, ON: Oxford University Press, 2016). This text uses a practical approach to introduce readers to both qualitative and quantitative research methods by guiding them through the research process.

S. Brinkman and S. Kvale, *Interviews: Learning the Craft of Qualitative Research Interviews*, 3rd ed. (Thousand Oaks,

CA: Sage, 2015). This book shows how to successfully interview research participants and discusses the value of conducting interviews. It also lists the potential practical and ethical issues scholars may encounter during the interview process.

A. Bryman, E. Bell, and J.J. Teevan, *Social Research Methods*, 4th ed. (Don Mills, ON: Oxford University Press, 2016). This source introduces the reader to both qualitative and quantitative research strategies in an engaging and straightforward manner. It offers effective tips for various steps in the research process, from collecting the data to disseminating one's findings widely.

J.M. Corbin and A.L. Strauss, *Basics of Qualitative Research: Techniques and Procedures for Developing Grounded Theory*, 3rd ed. (Los Angeles, CA: Sage, 2008). This text provides useful advice to assist researchers in interpreting their collected data. It presents several approaches to coding and analyzing qualitative data.

L. Sloan and A. Quan-Haase, eds., *The Sage Handbook of Social Media Research Methods* (London: Sage, 2017). This handbook provides an overview of novel methods to harvest social media data to gain insights into social phenomena. It also contributes to reflections on methodology and ethics in social media research.

Take it Further: Recommended Online Resources

The 2016 Census
www12.statcan.gc.ca/census-recensement/2016/rt-td/population-eng.cfm

American Sociological Association
http://asanet.org/

Randall Collins, *The Sociological Eye* (blog)
http://sociological-eye.blogspot.ca/

Alice Goffman's TED Talk: How We're Priming Some Kids for College—and Others for Prison
www.ted.com/talks/alice_goffman_college_or_prison_two_destinies_one_blatant_injustice

Inter-university Consortium for Political and Social Research
www.icpsr.umich.edu/icpsrweb/landing.jsp

Statistics Canada, *The Daily*
www.statcan.gc.ca/start-debut-eng.html

Tri-Council Policy Statement: Ethical Conduct for Research Involving Humans
www.pre.ethics.gc.ca/eng/policy-politique/initiatives/tcps2-eptc2/Default

More resources available on 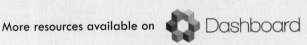 Dashboard

3

Cultures as Ways of Seeing Reality

Learning Objectives

In this chapter, you will:

> Learn to see culture as a symbolic environment in which humans live

> Consider the significance of cultural differences around the world

> Connect local and global cultures and understand how they influence each other

> Understand science and technology as subcultures as well as cultural influences

Introduction

Dashboard

Case study

Here's a problem to consider. You have just taken a job in a large engineering firm that requires you to travel around the world, consulting with clients in different countries. Your first trip is to Vietnam. You're not quite sure how to dress for dinner with Vietnamese co-workers or how to greet them; and you're not sure whether to bring a gift and, if so, what kind of gift? If you make a fool of yourself, word will get back to your boss and you may be in trouble. What should you do?

Millions of people face this problem every year, with the increase of international travel and communication, and the globalization of trade. This problem of transcultural communication also illustrates the importance, and complexity, of culture. You have heard the word *culture* hundreds of times, so you probably know—or think you know—what it means. But, in fact, it means a variety of things, and this becomes clear when we examine a diversity of sociological theories.

In Chapter 1, we noted the importance of the "non-rational" in social life: the importance of persistent religious beliefs, ethnic loyalties, political ideologies, sources of political legitimacy, and even consumer practices, often in the face of scientific evidence. None of these non-rational elements of social life are directly explainable in terms of science and technology. In fact, many of them defy science and technology because they defy rational explanation and often persist despite opposing evidence. These non-rational elements of social life (and others we will discuss) are all part of what we call *culture*, the topic of this chapter; and culture, like other aspects of society has both resisted and been transformed by science and technology.

Most important of all, culture is the repository for a society's thoughts about good and evil, purity and impurity, virtue and vice. Are the social influences of science and technology good or bad, on the whole? That is a question whose answer will be shaped by a society's culture, and it is a question whose answers have shifted continuously over time. Throughout this book, we will see

Eileen Carter/Shutterstock.com

Technology has facilitated the creation of new sites for cultural production. Millions of users of smart phones share their likes and dislikes on Instagram and Pinterest, forming new cultural tastes. Expressions of cultural preferences have become a mainstream culture in itself.

evidence that science and technology have not only influenced and challenged traditional cultural beliefs—such as beliefs about human origins, racial differences, and causes of illness—they have created new social, moral, environmental, and ethical problems that each culture will strive to understand and incorporate.

Culture is, and has been, a hotly debated concept. In general, culture is something people learn through socialization and enact in their everyday behaviour. However, opinions vary as to how many cultures there are and how to distinguish between various cultures. Theorists also have different ideas about whether culture integrates people, regulates and controls them, or both. At the very least, we can say that culture reflects the values and norms that direct the behaviour of people who belong to a particular society. By *values*, we mean all of the things that people in a society feel, think, believe, desire, and aspire to. Often, this includes what they think about good and evil, right and wrong, and so on. By **social norms**, we mean the rules that people in a society create to regulate how people behave. Some of these norms are unwritten and even unspoken, yet shared nonetheless. Others are established as laws and enforced by the criminal justice system.

social norms rules, whether written or unwritten, that people are expected to follow as members of a particular group, community, or society.

As we have said, culture is also shaped by technological developments. We will examine not only the ways science and technology shape our culture, but also how the world of science and technology develops its own culture. As a small example, consider how social media are reshaping culture in Canada and around the world, in Box 3.1.

Sociology 2.0

3.1 | Social Media Reshaping Canadian Culture

In recent years, social media have bounded into Western culture. Platforms such as Facebook, Twitter, and Instagram each boast a user base of hundreds of millions. These services, and the internet as a whole, have allowed for instant interpersonal communication forming a hyperconnected society (Quan-Haase & Wellman, 2006). They have also permitted the almost immediate sharing and accessing of cultural material such as music, videos, and written works.

Canada has been at the forefront of this technological and cultural revolution (Kemp, 2014). According to We Are Social, a London-based agency that tracks internet and social media use across the globe, Canada is the world leader in internet penetration, with 93 per cent of the population having access to the internet—well above the global average of 43 per cent. The penetration of social media is also extremely high in Canada (Kemp, 2015). For example, Canada has the fourth highest per-capita Facebook usage rate worldwide (and the highest per capita usage of countries with populations over 10 million).

These numbers suggest that Canadians have overwhelmingly embraced the internet as a means of communicating with an audience that extends well beyond their personal circle of friends and family. Canadians are hyperconnected, thanks to social networking sites with people around the globe. But perhaps we should consider whether social media are really reshaping Canadian social life, or whether they are merely permitting us to behave the same as always, just more quickly and easily.

Time to reflect

Let's think of any social group or organization as residing at the meeting point of various social and non-social factors, including culture. The Venn diagram in Figure 3.1 shows this. Do you agree that culture is as important an influence on an organization as technology, and if not, why not?

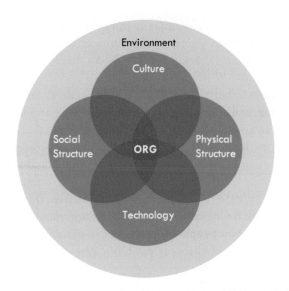

FIGURE 3.1 Venn Diagram of the Multiple Influences on a Type of Social Organization (ORG)

Source: Retrieved from http://smartbiz.nu/pages.asp?PageID=134&Base=1&MenuID=39

Cultural Universals and Cultural Relativism

ethnocentrism the tendency to use one's own culture as a basis for evaluating other cultures; also, the view that your culture is superior to other cultures.

Culture is a filter through which we view (and judge) other people's actions. People often have difficulty accepting the validity of other people's cultural values, norms, and beliefs. **Ethnocentrism** is a tendency to use one's own culture as a basis for evaluating other cultures. We can be so emotionally involved with our culture that we do not see that our own values, like other cultural traits, are merely one approach to human life. Accepting cultural variation as a fact of life and avoiding ethnocentrism are not easy matters.

After all, ethnocentrism is not merely cultural short-sightedness; it is rooted in people's upbringing and is therefore itself normal, socialized behaviour. Often people simply fail to take note of other ways of thinking. Yet, paradoxically, it is often by comparing one's own culture to another that people are able to clarify and examine their own values and behaviours. Often they realize that other societies have a more engaging—for example, more sociable, leisurely, or healthy—lifestyle than their own. Whatever the conclusion, comparing one's own culture with another one is likely to lead people to apply principles of **cultural relativism**—a willingness to understand and accept cultural practices that are different from one's own but make sense within the context of the society one is visiting.

cultural relativism the principle that a culture and its beliefs and values should be viewed from the standpoint of that culture itself, not another culture.

It is important to realize at the outset that there is not a one-to-one fit between societies and cultures. Any society—for example, Canadian society—contains many cultures and many subcultures. Likewise, any culture—for example, Western civilization or Judeo-Christian culture—may influence many societies but is not found in identical forms in any society. These facts complicate the concept of ethnocentrism, which presumes that there is a pure version of any culture.

Once we appreciate the differences between and within cultures, we can more usefully examine practices or elements that are shared by all cultures. Generations of sociologists and anthropologists, looking for cultural similarities, have identified many cultural elements that seem to be universal. For example, anthropologist George Murdock (1945) came up with an extensive list of

We all learn our culture's ideas of beauty and self-presentation throughout life, starting in infancy. Traditional Japanese ideas on this matter are very different from modern Canadian ideas, as you can see. What values do they express?

universal aspects of culture. His list includes athletic sports (organized exercise and harmless competition), bodily adornment (an indicator of status and selfhood), cooking (preparing food and eating sociably), dancing (expressing feeling through movement), funeral ceremonies (handling death and corpses), gift giving (showing gratitude and fondness), and language (giving commands and communicating views).

Sociology 2.0

3.2 | Test Your Word Knowledge

Words are the cultural building blocks we use to think and speak. No wonder, then, that in our society, a lot of the newest words come from science and technology. Which of the following list of new words and subentries added to the *Oxford English Dictionary* in 2016 do you associate with science and technology? And where do the other words come from?

Brexit
browsability
bralette
bruncheon

defang
dick pick
exampling
findability
glam-ma
hackability

hackathon
paddleboarding
soft launch
televisibility
verklempt
YouTuber

Theoretical Approaches to Culture
Conflict Theory

Recall that conflict theory focuses on dissent and opposition. Conflict theory notes that people in power often try to manipulate culture, to influence people's ideas, values, and confidence in social institutions, and, in the words of linguist and political theorist Noam Chomsky, to "manufacture consent." They do this mainly by controlling the amount and types of information people are able to access.

As noted in Chapter 1, Marx's work was a response to philosophical arguments that cultural values and ideas were the dominant factor in social organization. Marx was critical of these arguments, as they ignored or underestimated how economic relations—and especially, relations of production—shape society. Marx proposed instead that culture is shaped by the material relationships of dominance and subordination between social classes in society.

This means that every new economic order, or form of economic relations, will have a distinctive culture. Hunter-gatherer societies, which have no private land-holding, will have a different culture from feudal societies—in which most wealth is derived from agriculture and land ownership—which will have a different culture from capitalist societies—in which most wealth is derived from the sale of manufactured goods and services. In every society, the dominant class creates a dominant ideology—a system of thoughts and beliefs that justify and perpetuate the ruling class. Under capitalism, the dominant ideology is free-market liberalism, supported by a consumer culture. Marxists identify consumer culture as something that reduces social life to the seemingly impersonal, non-political exchange of marketable goods.

Under capitalism, the modern mass media play an important role (as will be discussed in Chapter 14). Since the bourgeoisie—the members of the ruling class—own most of the media, they can select which ideas the media represent. In so doing, they determine which ideas become part of public perception. Furthermore, the bourgeoisie use the mass media to transmit the ideas that they agree with, making their opinions seem legitimate and factual.

Critical race theory is an umbrella term that, like feminist theory, encompasses a variety of theories and theoretical perspectives (for an overview, see Delgado & Stefancic, 2012). Overall, however, it sees culture as a means of perpetuating dominance of the ruling white elite. So, for example, the Academy of Motion Picture Arts and Sciences's predominantly white voting membership nominates predominantly white actors, directors, and writers for Academy Awards, leading to criticisms such as #Oscarssowhite. However, the advantages enjoyed by white-skinned people go much farther than that. **White privilege** refers to the advantages and immunities that are unequally and unfairly experienced by people who are perceived and treated as "white," beyond what people racialized as "non-white" experience under similar social, political, or economic circumstances.

Critical race theorists note that people perceived as white, particularly in Western societies, enjoy advantages that those identified and treated as non-white do not experience—what researcher Peggy McIntosh (1989) calls "an invisible package of unearned assets." These include better treatment in job or housing searches, and a freedom from police targeting and harassment.

Along similar lines, feminist theorists see outdated cultural values as perpetuating misogyny, and queer theorists see them as perpetuating homophobia. Perhaps, for cultural as well as equitable reasons, this is why gays and lesbians in Canada fought so strongly for the right to marry. More will be said about these matters in Chapter 7, our chapter on gender inequality.

white privilege the advantages and immunities that are unequally and unfairly experienced by people who are perceived and treated as "white", beyond what people racialized as "non-white" experience under similar social, political, or economic circumstances.

Time to reflect

In a medium as visual as the internet, why would language differences make a difference to the accessibility of cultural ideas? What kinds of internet materials would be most likely to be language-bound and culture-bound?

Theory in Everyday Life

3.3 | Who Lives in Cyberspace?

The online world is a key source of information, social support, and commercial opportunity. The internet contains somewhere between 3.32 billion and a trillion pages; in truth, it is impossible to make a precise and accurate estimate of something so new and fast-moving.

What can sociology say about something that is effectively still in its infancy? Surprisingly, the century-old sociological theories of Georg Simmel (1950; see also Rogers, 1999) offer important insights into the virtual communities of cyberspace. This cyberworld is mainly populated by strangers. Our interactions with these strangers are predictably different from interactions with intimates in the real world. So, to understand cyberspace, we must understand how our interactions with strangers differ from our interactions with acquaintances and loved ones.

Three aspects define the social position of the stranger as described by Simmel. First, the stranger enjoys a particular combination of nearness and remoteness (or social distance) from group members. Even a stranger who is important to the functioning of the community is a cultural outsider. Second, the stranger's origins are odd and remote. With no fixed roots in the community, the stranger has the potential to wander. Finally, because of the stranger's marginality, social distance, and mobility, he or she is free to reject local values and conventions. Such a person is denied the same freedom of participation that community members enjoy. However, this gives the stranger a fresh outlook on the community and an ability to resolve disputes, if necessary. For these reasons, strangers are often met with surprising openness. "Travellers" and "tourists" are favoured categories of stranger because they are transient and, therefore, pose the least threat to the material, moral, and social basis of the community.

Simmel's insights into the role of the stranger take on a new poignancy when placed in the context of cyberspace. The insight that social distance allows for openness and clarity can be used to explain some of our online interactions with digital strangers. If you wanted to be a "stranger," how might you go about accomplishing that? What difficulties might you encounter? Would it be easier to be a stranger in the physical world, or in cyberspace?

Feminism

Feminism, in its analyses of culture, focuses on gender socialization, the process of becoming socialized to perform gender-specific roles, and on the structured performance of those roles. What is most remarkable about gender socialization is how very deep-seated it is, and how hard it is to change. This is because gender roles frame the way we see and inhabit the world and how we categorize the people we encounter.

Gender is a social and cultural construction that is learned through socialization. Even the dichotomous, or binary, character of gender is socially constructed; in many senses, sex-based characteristics range across a wide continuum that we are taught to ignore in favour of the categories of "male" and "female."

As young, pre-ideological individuals, we easily fall prey to a process that French social philosopher Louis Althusser (1918–1990) called *interpellation*. From infancy onward, we become caught up in processes that force us to accept the validity or relevance of the dominant ideology, which designates who we are and how we are to live. Often, we have no choice in this matter: if we ignore the demand to act in a way designated as proper for "people like us," we will be punished and, sooner or later, forced to adhere to these expectations.

Gender socialization is the process of learning the attitudes, thoughts, and behaviour patterns—even the emotional performances—that a culture considers appropriate for members of each sex.

People learn gender roles early in life. Infants are identified as male or female at birth. By the age of three, little boys and girls are playing separately, at different kinds of games. Already, they have learned to want different toys, enjoy different games, and avoid fraternizing openly with children of the opposite sex. In our society, notions of "masculinity" include toughness, reason, action, and violence. Conversely, "feminine" qualities include caretaking, intuition, empathy, and passivity.

emirkrasnic/pixababy.com

Dance, as a cultural activity, expresses values of grace, beauty, and vitality, but this picture of traditional dance is very different from what we would see at a Canadian high school prom. What values does this kind of dancing express?

Gender roles are no longer as rigidly or stereotypically defined as they once were. Despite these real-life changes, many mass media presentations—in movies, on television shows, and on the internet—continue to be heavily gendered. This will be discussed further in Chapter 7. It is at least partly because of the perpetuation of gender stereotypes in the mass media that women as well as men have worked to eliminate stereotyping in cyberspace. However, gendered differences in access and usage continue to hinder this change, as we see in Box 3.4.

Outside of the media, gendered socialization is both intentional and unintentional. For example, parents reinforce certain behaviour in young girls and boys according to their stereotypical expectations (into which, of course, they were also socialized), though they may not be conscious of doing so. In addition to the large role parents play in this area, feminists argue that schools socialize boys and girls differently, thereby reinforcing the different responsibilities and privileges these children will eventually grow up to enjoy. We will have more to say about this process in Chapter 11, when we consider the socialization that occurs in schools.

Functionalism

Functionalists view culture as an integral part of society. The leading twentieth-century functionalist theorist was Talcott Parsons, and many of his students went on to shape departments of sociology around the world in the mid-century. None of Parsons's students was more eminent or highly regarded than Robert Merton, whose work is still admired and taught today.

Merton, like the other functionalists, was interested in explaining how and why certain seemingly dysfunctional institutions survived. A prime example is his explanation of the survival of social inequality in twentieth-century capitalist American society. Recall that Émile Durkheim (and many early American sociologists) had expressed concern about the anomie that came with social

Digital Divide

3.4 | Gendered Internet Usage in Developing Countries

In 2015 Canadian men and women were roughly on par when it came to internet usage. Males made up 50.5 per cent of the total connected population, and females comprised 49.5 per cent of the total (Statista, 2017a). However, gender equality on the internet is not the rule in many developing countries.

Most studies assessing internet use in developing countries have found a significant gap in the rates of internet usage between men and women, with women being much less likely to use the internet than men. In the Middle East, women are thought to comprise less than 35 per cent; in Asia, 33 per cent; and, in Africa, only 18 percent (Statista, 2017b).

In a review of the literature on gender-based digital divides, Antonio and Tuffley (2014) identify four barriers women in developing countries face when it comes to the use of the internet: exclusion from technological education that would promote digital literacy; limited leisure time; restrictive social norms that prevent either access to or use of the internet; and financial constraints that prevent the purchase of digital technologies.

The lack of internet use among most women in developing countries may reinforce pre-existent gender inequalities that mark many of these nations. Low internet usage rates among women limits their access to resources that could improve their lives, such as internet-mediated educational opportunities, online job searches, and the possibility of generating income through online businesses. Overcoming the economic and social gender inequalities that persist in developing countries may require bridging the digital divide that exists between men and women in these societies. What is the best way of reducing the gendered barriers to internet use in developing societies? Would it be better to ensure that everyone has equal access to free internet and a computer, or to first attack other social and cultural barriers to gender inequality?

---

disorganization due to rapid change, social fragmentation, and social inequality under conditions of industrialization. Merton, agreeing with these earlier researchers, points out that heightened rates of suicide, mental illness, addiction, and crime are indeed features of industrial capitalist societies.

However, Merton—being a functionalist—asserts that we should view these aberrations from normality as positive "adaptations to anomie"—that is, good things, rather than bad ones—in the sense that they allow industrial, capitalist society to survive despite great inequality and injustice. While Merton acknowledged that these adaptations would have negative repercussions for those affected by and likely to experience them, he was most concerned with the health of the social system as a whole. In short, his goal was to explain how modern capitalism managed to survive, despite its many flaws.

Like Durkheim, who in his *Rules of the Sociological Method* stresses the normality of crime and its survival value to society, Merton stresses the survival value of other adaptations to anomie. In doing so, he characterizes crime as "innovation"; certain forms of mental illness, suicide, and addiction as "retreatism"; and alienated labour as "ritualism." All of these "adaptations" are latent functions—that is, unintended and non-obvious—mechanisms that maintain the survival of capitalist society in its current, unequal form. Also like Durkheim, who notes the importance of sacred rituals (and totemic or ritual objects) for maintaining social stability, Merton notes that many people in a modern society become "ritualistic," in the sense that they obey the social rules even after those rules have ceased to have any personal value or moral justification.

As we have seen, culture organizes behaviour. So, functionalist sociologists—who emphasize order—typically look to culture to explain how and why a society remains largely the same from one day to the next.

For example, functionalists would say that the high value people put on postsecondary education is a response to the need of a modern society for highly educated workers to function properly. This value on education encourages students to attend university and college, which in turn keeps these institutions running, providing jobs and input into the local economy. Once these students graduate, they supply the educated labour force that the society requires to continue to operate. Thus, culture—in the form of shared values—ensures that each part of society can carry out its respective function.

Symbolic Interactionism

For symbolic interactionists, culture comes from individual face-to-face interactions and from what people communicate to each other through these interactions.

symbol a sign whose relationship with something else also expresses a value or evokes an emotion.

Human beings are complex and creative, and they do not always follow values or norms in exactly the same ways. So, instead of thinking of culture as a set of rules, interactionists think of culture as a dictionary of words, actions, and **symbols** from which we build our conversations. For example, the importance that feminist theorists (discussed above) place on language has some of its roots in symbolic interactionism. Symbolic interactionists were the first to express interest in the interaction between an individual's interpretation of a situation, his or her use of language and action as a result of that interpretation, and subsequently how the expression of that interpretation defines what is appropriate to others in what they interpret the situation to be.

More generally, symbolic interactionism is centrally concerned with the ways humans use symbols to interact with one another, and words are (of course) symbols of things. Take the word *banana*, which stands for a fruit that is long, yellow, and pulpy inside. When we see or hear the word *banana*, we think of that fruit. (However, since the word is symbolic [not real], we are none of us in danger of slipping on the words *banana peel*.) It is a fundamental assumption of symbolic interactionism that how we name things and talk about these named things helps to organize the interactions between people, since (among other things) it organizes objects into categories such as good and bad, pure and impure, valuable and valueless, and so on.

With every interaction, we learn new ways to use culture. While the functionalists and cultural theorists believe culture controls and regulates people, symbolic interactionists believe the opposite—that *people* control and regulate culture.

TABLE 3.1 Theoretical Approaches to Culture

Theory	Main Ideas
Conflict Theory	• Culture, in the forms of ideology and religion, are used to manipulate popular opinion and ensure conformity.
Feminist Theory	• Gender inequality is almost universal.
	• This inequality is a result of patriarchal values and institutions.
	• Men and women are taught to perform different and unequal roles in our society.
Structural Functionalism	• Cultural change and uncertainty may create social disorganization and strain, and lead to deviance and crime.
Symbolic Interactionism	• Society and culture are products of continuous face-to-face interactions.
	• Socialization and labelling shape deviant identities and contribute to the formation of subcultures.
	• More generally, all subcultures (e.g., schools of thought) result from intense interactions in social networks.

Source: Author-generated.

Culture and Language

Language is the most general and most flexible form of culture, since everyone uses it and, in principle, anyone can create it (consider again the origin of some of those new words in Box 3.2). It can be used an almost infinite number of ways to communicate meanings and express identity. The more important a topic is to a society, the more words its people have to discuss it, or at least, the more flexibility they allow speakers to modify and refine their descriptions of it.

At the most basic level, language is an abstract system of sounds (speech), **signs** (written characters), and gestures (non-verbal communication) by which members of a society express their thoughts, feelings, ideas, plans, and desires. This means that language, whether spoken or written, verbal or non-verbal, is the means by which the achievements of one generation are passed on to the next. When children learn to speak the language of their culture, they learn to make the assumptions that pervade that language.

Like other signs and symbols, words carry both intended and unintended meanings. We learn both kinds of meanings as active members of a culture, as much through observation and through trial and error as by formal instruction. According to anthropologists Sapir and Whorf, language expresses our thoughts but also structures them. Stated formally and succinctly by psychologist Roger Brown, (1976), "Whorf appeared to put forward two hypotheses: 1. Structural differences between language systems will, in general, be paralleled by nonlinguistic cognitive differences, of an unspecified sort in the native speakers' two languages. 2. The structure of anyone's native language strongly influences or fully determines the world-view he will acquire as he learns the language" (p. 128). Said another way, the way in which a language is structured has significance for the way we experience the world. Different languages provide people with different conceptual tools to organize and interpret reality. This is one of many reasons why it is often difficult to completely translate the meaning of a text from one language to another, and why translations of classic works tend to change over time.

Differences in the ways members of different cultures discuss things can make communication across cultures difficult. For example, Chinese people often speak in proverbs when they discuss their norms and values. This way of thinking and talking about social life is traditionally viewed as a sign of good breeding and education. Outsiders may think that Chinese people are speaking in vague or roundabout ways when, in fact, they are stating strong views in what would seem to other Chinese people a direct manner.

How people use language is a topic of interest to many sociologists. Symbolic interactionists are interested in how individuals use (and create new) language in order to describe, and therefore characterize, the world around them. Structural functionalists are interested in the ways different subgroups, such as prisoners, develop their own language to express unique concerns and maintain group cohesion.

Feminist sociologists draw our attention to the way in which culture, through language, shapes our perception of gender norms. For feminist sociologists, **androcentric** or **sexist language** not only illustrates gender inequality in our society, it helps to perpetuate the problem. Most of the assumptions embodied in language are hidden—known but implicit or, even, unrecognized. These tacit assumptions lurk everywhere in our language. We are all accustomed to using the words *mankind*, *policeman*, *chairman*, and other words that include the word *man*. Historically, many of these words have aptly described the role in question; in the past, most police personnel and holders of chairs really were men, not women.

The view that people should switch to gender-neutral terms such as *police officer* and *chairperson* is more than a quibble. Our continued use of the masculine words implies that women are, and should be, absent from these roles. If we continue to see women who fill these roles as deviant, we end up discouraging women from seeking to do so.

signs gestures, artifacts, or words that express or meaningfully represent something other than themselves.

androcentric or sexist language language that implies male dominance or exclusivity (and female inferiority or invisibility), such as *postman*, *mankind*, or the *Rights of Man*.

Patterns of Cultural Variation

We have already noted there is tremendous cultural variety across societies. Even within a given society many subcultures develop because of generational, class, occupational, or lifestyle differences.

Subculture and Counterculture

subculture a group that shares the cultural elements of the larger society but also has its own distinctive values, beliefs, norms, style of dress, and behaviour patterns.

A **subculture** is a group that shares the cultural elements of the larger society but also has its own distinctive values, beliefs, norms, style of dress, and behaviour patterns. In the case of ethnic groups, a subculture may even have its own language. Some sociologists would dispute the very notion of subculture, saying that it implies the attribution of a lesser or secondary importance to the cultures of small groups in society. Other sociologists find the term useful because it allows them to speak about specific and bounded ways of thinking that we find in very particular social locations.

So, for example, among the many subcultures existing in our society are what social scientists call organizational cultures. All organizations have their own culture-in-miniature, complete with norms and values. In short, **organizational culture** is the values, norms, and patterns of action that characterize social relationships within a formal organization. Like every culture, it contains tacit and unconscious assumptions that underlie all group values and actions.

organizational culture the values, norms, and patterns of action that characterize social relationships within a formal organization; also, the way an organization deals with its environment. It includes norms and values that are culturally specific to the organization.

Organizational cultures are particularly important in societies like ours where organizations—especially work organizations—have become more important than most other institutions. They provide their members with solidarity, community, social relationships, and emotional satisfaction—all of which help to control their behaviour and influence their minds. At the same time, the ways people behave in organizations are influenced by the surrounding national culture. Different national cultures have different ideas about uncertainty, organization, and control. Often, these differences surface in multinational corporations and affect the ways different parts of the organization scan, select, interpret, and use information.

Organizational culture is only one type of subculture. Generally, a subculture emerges whenever a particular segment of society faces unique problems or enjoys unique privileges. Members of a subculture often share a common age, religion, ethnic heritage, belief system, occupation, interest, or hobby. Or, like prison inmates, psychiatric patients, or local hockey fans at an away game, they share exclusion from larger society.

Video: *Taqwacore*

Sorbis/Shutterstock.com

The people in this photo are wearing different clothing—some modern, some, traditional; some casual, and some more formal. It would be impossible to identify which of the people in this photo are part of a subculture until the location of the photo, and the primary cultural norms of that location, are identified.

A **counterculture** is a subculture that rejects conventional norms and values and adopts alternative or opposing ones. Such cultures are fundamentally at odds with the culture of the larger society. They are often found among younger and less advantaged members of a society. A counterculture develops among people with little reason to conform to the main culture. Such people are unlikely to get rewarded with praise, good jobs, or high incomes even if they were to conform to the main culture's rules.

In effect, a counterculture rejects conventional morality and makes deviance the new standard of behaviour. Keep in mind, though, that members of a counterculture do not reject conformity to everything, only conformity to some of the dominant values of the majority. Like a subculture, a counterculture has its own beliefs, **material culture**, and problems of cultural integration. (By material culture, we mean those aspects of a society's culture that are visible and take a material form, such as tools, books, houses, and human activities.) Members of the Hell's Angels have strict values and loyalties; anarchists follow their own norms; punk rockers have ideals; and hippies wear a particular "uniform." Like any culture, a counterculture contains contradictions between what its members say and what they do.

The distinction between subcultures and countercultures is often a subtle one. For example, sociologists have often remarked on the fact that police officers, in carrying out their professional duties, develop and practice subcultural norms of policing that are not taught in police college or endorsed in legislation. While these norms are shared and are different from the surrounding culture—hence, subcultural—we would not see them as countercultural, in the sense that they aim to defy or overthrow the existing order.

Likewise, we could characterize many hobby or sports groups as having their own subculture. Canadian sociologist Robert Stebbins (1996) has written about the subculture that has formed around barbershop quartet singing. Sociologist Michael Atkinson (2009) has written about the subculture surrounding the sport of parkour.

Often, we have trouble distinguishing a subculture from a counterculture. Is the often-studied delinquent or gang subculture merely designed to support the delinquent lifestyle of its members? Or is it a purposeful rejection of the values of the mainstream society? Sociologists disagree about this.

counterculture a subculture that rejects conventional norms and values and adopts alternative ones.

material culture the physical and technological aspects of people's lives—in short, all the physical objects that members of a culture create and use.

Spotlight On

3.5 | The Social Meaning of Gangsta Rap

A study on gangsta rap by Kubrin (2005) found that nearly 65 per cent of the songs sampled make reference to some aspect of violence and many songs were graphic in their violent depictions. It is precisely for this reason that gangsta rap is controversial and unpopular with some segments of the population. Still, rappers tell important stories through their music. Some use their street knowledge to construct first-person narratives that interpret how social and economic realities affect young black men in the context of deteriorating inner-city conditions. Other narratives may be more mythical than factual.

Regardless of their source or authenticity, rap lyrics serve specific social functions in relation to understandings of street life and violence. As Anderson (1999, cited in Kubrin) might suggest, the lyrics show how violent confrontations settle the question of "who is the toughest and who will take, or tolerate, what from whom under what circumstances" (p. 69). Rappers' lyrics delineate the rules and actively mark the border between acceptable and unacceptable behaviour. Moreover, the lyrics teach listeners how to appropriately respond in the event that rules are violated; they authorize the use of violent retaliation in certain situations and thereby prescribe violent self-help as a method of social control. As the lyrics showed, the code requires constant application and articulation with concrete events and actions in order to make the events and actions meaningful and accountable.

Time to reflect

Do you think song lyrics like those in "gangsta rap" simply document and reflect the existing "street code" or do you think they glamorize the street code and encourage more people to embrace it?

High Culture and Popular Culture

Interactive activity

Not all subcultures serve the disadvantaged or the victimized. Even though they benefit most from the way society is organized, high status people do not necessarily conform to the culture of the majority. People in the middle class, not the upper class, stand to gain most by conforming to the rules of a culture. If those in the middle class conform, they are eligible to move up the social ladder; if they do not, they risk sliding down it. People at the bottom of the social scale stand to gain least from conformity. They also have the least to lose from nonconformity: that is why they can risk forming countercultures.

As for people at the top of the social scale, they run little risk of losing their power, wealth, and position, and they stand to gain nothing by conforming to ordinary standards of behaviour. So, many members of the upper class participate in a subculture that is just as outlandish as a delinquent or punk counterculture. They love doing what the French call *épater les bourgeois*, infuriating the middle class through outlandish behaviour. This accounts for the lavish, grotesque "lifestyles of the rich and famous."

high culture high-status group preferences, tastes, and norms. Examples include fine arts, classical music, ballet, and other "highbrow" concerns.

Other high-income people take part in what is called high culture. **High culture** refers to the set of preferences, habits, tastes, values, and norms that are characteristic of, or supported by, high status groups in society. This includes fine art, classical music, ballet, and other "highbrow" concerns. Of course, wealthy people are not the only ones who attend symphony concerts, read poetry, or visit art galleries. Many people use these cultural organizations to announce to others that they, too, are "cultured"; in this way, they improve their own social status. Nevertheless, upper-class philanthropy provides much of the operating budget for these activities. Typically, wealthy and educated people sit on the boards of directors of such cultural organizations. It is to their cultural taste that these activities are directed.

And not surprisingly, high culture has historically glorified the rich. The high culture that painters, poets, and composers created for wealthy patrons before the twentieth century dignified the aristocracy's image of itself. Perhaps intentionally, high culture excludes many more people than it includes. By conveying exotic images and ignoring ordinary lives, high culture has traditionally cut ordinary people off from their own history. No wonder middle- and working-class people develop and use a culture of their own.

popular (or mass) culture the culture of ordinary people; the objects, preferences, and tastes that are widespread in a society.

Popular (or mass) culture is the culture of the masses, and includes those objects, preferences, and tastes that are widespread in a society. *Popular culture* is a blanket term for any element of culture that is distinct from the culture of high-status, subcultural, and countercultural groups. One must be careful to define it as culture for the largest number, and avoid placing an elitist judgment of "poor quality" on it. It includes both high and folk art products, so long as they maintain the individual character of the creator. For example, the comedy of Jon Stewart would be considered part of popular culture because it is widely popular, yet distinct from the comedy of, say, Chris Rock. Both comedians are popular, yet each has a distinctive style and approach to comedy. What's more, some comedy—for example, found in the works of Shakespeare, Molière, and Wilde—is also considered high art.

Like all forms of culture, popular culture varies along age, sex, and social-class lines. We see this fragmentation in market surveys that identify the viewers of different kinds of television programs: educational television versus soap operas versus sports. We find just as much fragmentation in people's tastes for leisure, dress, eating, and even living-room decoration. Among other things, this reflects the fact that there are many ways to define "culture."

At the same time, popular culture reflects the influence of high culture. For example, advertising has borrowed many images from classical oil painting (Berger, 1972). A selection of provocative borrowings can be found at various online websites celebrating the creativity of ad creators. (Search, for example, for the phrase "the best commercials that use famous works of art").

Mass media and popular culture have developed hand in hand. They both reflect the rise of enormous new audiences with money to spend. But trends in high culture reflect the growth of new audiences, too. The fine arts began to change as early as the nineteenth century with the rise of middle classes who were eager to establish their social worth by adopting the cultural taste and practices of the wealthy. The wealthy, in response, seek out new practices in an attempt to maintain their cultural distance. Eventually, the middle classes catch on to the new practices and the process repeats itself. This is one of the dynamics of cultural change.

Pictorial Press Ltd/Alamy Stock Photo

Game of Thrones was the most popular television show worldwide in 2016. Are there aspects of this series that show influence of high culture? Are there any distinctions between popular culture and high culture other than access?

Cultural Capital and Cultural Literacy

As we have just seen, culture reflects and supports the stratification system in a society. It allows powerful people to use culture—especially, high culture—to set themselves apart from others, and interact meaningfully within their restricted domain. It follows that learning the "cultural code" of the powerful would help other people establish relations with them.

The French sociologist Pierre Bourdieu (1986/2011) coined the term **cultural capital** to refer to a body of knowledge, ideas, tastes, preferences, and interpersonal skills that help people get ahead socially. Familiarity with high culture is one form of cultural capital. This familiarity helps in establishing good social relations with wealthy and powerful people. Cultural capital includes a wide variety of skills that enhance social interactions. These include knowing how to speak interestingly, what topics to discuss, how to order and eat graciously, how to play a variety of games and sports that others want to play (for example, tennis, sailing, bridge, chess, polo), and so on. In Canada and elsewhere, cultural capital also includes the ability to speak confidently and persuasively about the business world. Cultural capital affects educational attainment, job prospects, and even one's choice of marriage partners.

Few people learn these abilities in school. To learn them requires a wide variety of personal experiences, indulgent and knowledgeable parents, devoted teachers, and time and money to spare. In short, like other capital, cultural capital is not evenly distributed throughout the population. Certain people end up with more advantages because they start out with more.

Middle-class parents often try to provide their children with experiences that will give them cultural capital: ballet lessons, private schooling, trips abroad, instructional summer camps, and so on. Working-class parents, however, are rarely able to do the same. As a result, working-class children are less likely to get ahead socially than middle-class children.

Cultural capital must be distinguished from *social capital*, which has been defined in at least two ways. As the characteristic of a community, social capital refers to the networks of relationships among people who live and work in that community. As the characteristic of an individual, social capital refers to the number, diversity, and "quality" of network ties a person can call on for information or support. Often, people with a lot of cultural capital also have a lot of social capital.

Among the poorer members of society, gaining cultural literacy, not cultural capital, is often the critical issue. Unlike cultural capital, which is a luxury, cultural literacy is an absolute necessity. **Cultural literacy** is a solid knowledge of popular or mainstream culture, which contains the building

cultural capital a body of knowledge and interpersonal skills that help people get ahead socially. Cultural capital often includes learning about and participating in high culture.

cultural literacy a solid knowledge of what people "need to know" to sound educated and well-read in our society.

blocks of all communication and learning. To be culturally literate is to have enough general knowledge about the world to be able to communicate effectively with any adult member of society. It means knowing something about Shakespeare, something about the NFL, something about Donald Trump, and something about video gaming or drug culture, for example.

Historian E.D. Hirsch (1988) argues that schools ought to provide their students with such a store of cultural knowledge, instead of abstract thinking skills. A chess grandmaster, Hirsch claims, is much better than anyone else at identifying traditional game strategies and responding to them; this is what "playing chess" is. But outside a chess game—say, fixing a car, filling out an income-tax form, or preparing a meal—the grandmaster is no more capable than you or I. So, creativity and problem-solving abilities depend on concrete knowledge more than problem-solving skills.

This suggests that before people can learn anything else, they need to master a body of information. What's more, the body of information they need for everyday life is easy to identify. In North America, there is a storehouse of common knowledge—a few thousand names, dates, concepts, and expressions—to which most people refer in their thinking and communication. The vast majority of items in this storehouse date back 50 years or more. Literate people from every ethnic and racialized group, region, and social class use the cultural items in this storehouse. All of us know (or ought to know) what is meant by an Achilles heel, for example—an expression that refers to a hero in a Greek myth that dates back well over 3000 years. But it is now similarly important to be able to identify Justin Bieber, Drake, Karen Kain, and David Cronenberg.

Cultural Values and Economic Behaviour

Cultural values, whether they be from popular culture, a subculture, counterculture, or high culture, influence people's behaviour in every domain of life, and surprisingly, values from one domain (for example, religion) can influence values in another domain (for example, the economy). Sociologist Max Weber studied this phenomenon in one of the most important works of sociology, *The Protestant Ethic and the Spirit of Capitalism* (2002).

In the medieval societies of Europe, people thought that concern for worldly activities, particularly profit making through the investment of money at interest, was immoral. For people to change their economic behaviour, they had to first change their ideas about the morality of moneylending. In short, they needed to see signs of holy approval in worldly success. According to Weber, the Protestant ethic provided this force.

What Weber calls the "Protestant ethic" is a doctrine formulated by Protestant reformers like John Calvin and Martin Luther. Weber explained the change as follows: Calvinists believed that all people are predestined to go to either heaven or hell. Precisely who was going to heaven and who to hell was already decided. Because they thought salvation was predestined, Calvinists searched for a sign from God that they were among the "elect." They were inclined to see success at work as a sign of their good standing with God and of God's overall approval (Engerman, 2000). In this way, Protestantism encourages people to focus on today rather than on what happens after death.

Weber's link between religion and the economy is important for several reasons. First, it shows that both social and economic development connect to cultural change. Second, it reminds us that every society is a complex system, in which change in one part generates unexpected changes in another part. Third, it reminds us that culture is not static, nor always a hindrance to change. Cultures change too, and as they do, they cushion the psychological hardships of (or even encourage) social and economic change. Finally, and most important, Weber's work shows us that religious values can change the course of world history.

The Culture of Science

Merton's classic model of scientific thinking (1973) treats science *not* as a type of knowledge, but as a social enterprise or institution governed by social norms and cultural values, like any other institution. Merton, a functionalist discussed earlier in this chapter, proposes that science, as a set of human activities, has guiding values or cultural principles that include objectivity, free access, the universality of claims, and organized skepticism.

Time to reflect

Sociologist Robert Merton studied the rise of science and he also concluded that, like capitalism, it was connected with the rise of Protestantism. Do you agree? What do you think the connection might be?

Today, however, the everyday practice of science—especially, outside universities—falls short of the Mertonian ideal in many ways (Ziman, 2000, p. 137).

With present-day post-academic science, knowledge is often constructed according to "the commercial, political, or other social interests of the bodies that underwrite its production" (Ziman, 2000, p. 144). That is to say, such science is not disinterested, unbiased, or universalistic. So, for example, scientists are specifically hired to do research that casts doubt on the validity of research showing that smoking causes cancer, or that building casinos leads to an increase in gambling addiction.

Anti-science tactics—for example, the junk science movement—play on the inherent uncertainties in objectivity, and on the many different ways to "be scientific." Take, as an example, the competing claims about nutrition and dieting: we hear a different theory almost every week. This view takes us to the "politics of claims making"—an area of sociology called social constructionism. Here, there is no certainly right way to assess whether or not a claim is valid. According to this way of thinking, all we can do is examine how claims for validity are made and challenged, which ones succeed, and why.

Where science is concerned, the study of claims-making belongs to a specialized branch of sociology called the sociology of scientific knowledge (SSK), where researchers investigate the social nature of scientific research itself (Shapin, 1995); for a Canadian discussion of this, see Myra Hird's book, *Sociology of Science* (2011). SSK views scientific research as a form of claims-making in which individuals and groups compete to describe and explain reality in a way they find most suitable. You can see how this approach to science relates directly to symbolic interactionism, because it emphasizes that science is a social construction that arises and is maintained through human interaction. From this standpoint, science is *merely* a subculture—there is no objective "true" science, instead what is considered "good" science is merely whatever recognized scientists do when they are "doing science." This approach helps to explain the important role of scientists in legitimating social change and the reason why important discoveries are made in certain places at certain times. Consider the case of the tomato in Box 3.6.

Think Globally

3.6 | The International Success of the Tomato

From its beginnings, science has played an important part in tying the world together. Science, exploration, and trade have gone together, often with world-changing benefits. An example is the discovery and importation of plants and foodstuffs like the tomato, today a staple of Italian cuisine. Historical evidence suggests that colonists and missionaries who voyaged to Mexico brought tomato seeds back to Spain in 1519. At first, the tomato was grown for its beauty, and not widely consumed. Most Italians were hesitant to eat it, believing that it caused a variety of ailments. However, as botanists continued to study the plant, it was eventually deemed safe. New medical research led people to think that tomatoes aided the process of digestion.

Accordingly, tomatoes became more common in Italian recipes (Gentilcore, 2010).

Late in the nineteenth century, the making of pasta, tomato sauce, and sun-dried tomatoes became industrialized. Around the same time, tomatoes were beginning to be canned whole. This development led to a major shift in production and consumption. Canned tomatoes were exported to various countries, including Britain and the United States, where they were in high demand by Italian immigrants.

From the story of the tomato's conquest of Europe, and then North America, we learn that the simple fact of availability does not guarantee the adoption of a given item of food. First, the public takes into account medical and

Continued

scientific views. Second, cooks re-interpret or re-imagine the product to fit into existing tastes and practices. In this case, the tomato was blended with local ingredients (e.g., garlic and basil) and prepared to complement existing dishes (e.g., pasta and pizza). Today, we wouldn't dream of living without tomatoes.

Time to reflect

Think about the latest piece of technology you adopted, whether it was a new kind of beauty product, a new clothing fabric, a new medication, or a new app. What kind of vetting process, if any, did you go through before taking a risk on this new product?

Science, Technology, and Cultural Change

As we saw with the case of tomatoes in Box 3.6, all new discoveries, ideas, and inventions are adopted gradually, with a few brave people going first and the great majority coming later. Roger's Innovation Adoption Curve (Figure 3.2) depicts this process. At any given moment in a society, some people are far ahead of the norm in new ideas and practices, while other people are far behind it. In particular, with the rapid development of technologies such as smart phones, e-readers, and phablets, elderly people experience problems trying to keep up with digital culture (see Box 3.7).

The mass media, which we will discuss at length in Chapter 14, are an important source of **cultural integration** in the modern world and a mechanism for spreading ideas. Mass media are forms of communication that pass information to, and influence the opinions of, large audiences, without any personal contact between the senders and receivers of the information. The mass media include television, movies, newspapers, internet, and radio. As a result of new media, new means of mass cultural production such as Instagram, Twitter, and Pinterest come into place.

cultural integration the process that fits together parts of a culture—for example, ideal culture and real culture—so that they complement one another.

Time to reflect

What are the influences that affect what cultural products you consume? Do you listen to the recommendations of friends or family, look at advertisements, consult with a trusted source such as a particular commentator, try to stay current with whatever is being talked about the most, read aggregate reviews, or do you not make conscious choices about your cultural consumption?

All cultures change. Both external and internal dynamics cause them to constantly morph, reshape, progress, dissolve, and evolve. It is easy to believe that historical events—for example, wars and revolutions—help to shape a culture. What is less often noted is that scientific theories also shape

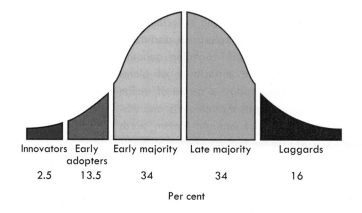

FIGURE 3.2 Adoption Curve: The Percentages Adopting a New Practice at Early, Medium, and Late Stages of Availability

Source: Retrieved from www.kentlai.com/writings/roger-adoption-curve

Digital Divide

3.7 | Including the Elderly in Today's Digital Culture

For many Canadians the internet has become a central aspect of daily life, accessed almost constantly to communicate with friends, conduct business, shop, provide entertainment, and many other things. For other Canadians, however, the internet is unimportant, used only sparingly if at all.

While an estimated 93 per cent of Canadians have easy access to the internet, internet usage rates in Canada vary significantly across demographic categories. Take the various age groups, for instance. In 2012 the internet usage rate for Canadians aged 16 to 24 was almost 99 per cent. For Canadians aged 45 to 64, however, the rate was 83.8 per cent, and for those over the age of 65 the rate was a mere 47.5 per cent (Statistics Canada, 2013). This differential internet usage proves the existence of a "digital divide"—a difference among demographic groups when it comes to accessing and using information and communications technologies.

This trend is not unique to Canada, and technologists and policy makers around the world now discuss ways to bridge the various digital divides that proliferate within and between societies. Yet Canada faces many challenges in trying to connect people who have low incomes, no digital skills, and little access to information and communication technologies equipment (Haight & Quan-Haase, 2015).

A more digitally inclusive society could benefit everyone, especially the most isolated. For example, Australian researchers (Baker et al., 2016) found that introducing elderly people to communication tools on iPads, such as photo-sharing applications, helped to alleviate feelings of isolation. Older people often suffer from social isolation, because their social networks have shrunk due to deaths, and health problems may limit their ability to seek out and interact with others. However, usability posed a challenge for the Australian study participants, who experienced difficulty interacting with the touch-screen surface of the iPad.

A similar study (Quan-Haase, Martin, & Schreurs, 2016) showed that older Canadians were interested in using technology in their everyday lives, but often needed help from their social networks. Related research by Quan-Haase, Martin, & Schreurs, 2014, looked at seniors' adoption of e-reading. It found that while seniors show an interest in e-books and e-readers, see benefits to their use, and are curious about how they function, most of them think this technology is mainly appropriate for younger generations whom they view as more tech savvy.

For these reasons, we should remember that overcoming the digital divide will require not only improved access to digital technologies, but also the fostering of digital literacy and the self-confidence to use these skills.

Time to reflect

What benefits do you think there might be for society if we were to reduce the digital divide between older and younger generations? Think not just about the benefits to the older generation, but also about the benefits from everyone getting a chance to interact with older generations online.

and change a culture. As we noted earlier, science is not "objective" but is influenced by the culture of science, and one of the things that can lead to a discovery's acceptance is when it matches up with the dominant culture's already-held beliefs.

Take the example of Charles Darwin's classic theory of evolution by natural selection. One area of knowledge to which people soon applied Darwinian thinking was economics. Even before Darwin, economic competition was common (Larson, 2006). However, after the publication of his work, Darwin's theory was used by many to justify ruthless economic competition that caused huge inequalities within Western societies during the second half of the nineteenth century and afterward (Brown, 1999, 106). Social thinkers like Herbert Spencer viewed unrestricted competition as a means to achieve social progress, by maximizing innovation and meritorious effort (Larson & Brauer, 2009; Ruse, 2000). He thought that Darwin's idea of natural competition justified limits on economic regulation, social assistance, and public health initiatives. Like the clergyman and population theorist Thomas Malthus before him, Spencer proposed that survival of the "unfit" was unnatural and, therefore, harmful to organized social life (Larson & Brauer, 2009; Brown, 2006).

> **Donald J. Trump** ✔ @realDonaldTrump · Jul 26
> ....victory and cannot be burdened with the tremendous medical costs and disruption that transgender in the military would entail. Thank you
>
> ○ 76K   ⟲ 43K   ♡ 143K   ✉

> **Donald J. Trump** ✔ @realDonaldTrump · Jul 26
> ....Transgender individuals to serve in any capacity in the U.S. Military. Our military must be focused on decisive and overwhelming......
>
> ○ 47K   ⟲ 46K   ♡ 138K   ✉

> **Donald J. Trump** ✔ @realDonaldTrump · Jul 26
> After consultation with my Generals and military experts, please be advised that the United States Government will not accept or allow......
>
> ○ 26K   ⟲ 43K   ♡ 127K   ✉

In 2017 US President Donald Trump became infamous for using his Twitter to circumvent mainstream media and "establishment" government channels in order to ensure his message remained unfiltered. In the example above, from July 2017, President Trump tweeted that transgender individuals would not be allowed to serve in the military, without an accompanying directive through proper channels. As a result, the tweet did not change military policy, but it did spark mainstream cultural conversation about transgender individuals and their rights around the world, and may prove to have longer cultural implications, particularly in the US.

While capitalists thought that Darwin's theory implied an economic struggle for natural selection, other readers of Darwin took it to imply a racial struggle. Many Darwinists imagined that human evolution would result in the victory and survival of the "most superior 'race,'" which they imagined to be a white European subgroup (Larson & Brauer, 2009, p. 189). Closely connected to this biological racism was the pseudo-science called eugenics. A set of ideas and practices originally aimed at improving livestock by controlled breeding to increase the occurrence of desirable heritable characteristics, eugenics applied to humans intended to alter genetic characteristics to prevent the decline of humanity (Paul, 2003). The belief in eugenics even spread to Canada, where compulsory sterilization of "unfit" individuals was legalized in Alberta in 1928 (repealed 1972) and in British Columbia in 1933 (repealed 1973).

What this example shows is that, since the Age of the Enlightenment, there has been a strong and growing compatibility between science, culture, and morality. It also shows that science and technology can be used for good or bad social purposes. Today, new technology that enables easy communication and rapid transportation makes the formation of a global, secular culture more plausible than ever before. Given our past experience, is this homogenization of world cultures into one single culture a good or bad thing?

Conclusions

On the one hand, culture, including science, is a society-wide phenomenon. Culture exists outside individual people, in their language, institutions, and material artifacts. In this sense, cultures are all encompassing and slow changing.

We mentioned earlier that culture has become commodified in modern societies, and certainly we can see evidence of this all around us, in pop music, television, movies, video games, and the like. However, as David Harvey warns us, this issue is far from settled, and more needs to be said. Harvey (2009) writes,

> That culture has become a commodity of some sort is undeniable. Yet there is also a widespread belief that there is something so special about certain cultural products and events (be they in the arts, theatre, music, cinema, architecture or more broadly in localized ways of life, heritage, collective memories and affective communities) as to set them apart from ordinary commodities like shirts and shoes. (p. 94)

Unlike most shirts and shoes, the main elements of a culture can outlast individuals and even generations of individuals. On the other hand, culture is inside all of us. As the symbolic interactionists remind us, culture is something we all change or reproduce every day through our activities and interactions. Culturally accepted patterns and beliefs change over time because dozens, then thousands, then millions of us change the ways we do things, including the ways we test and discover new scientific "truths."

At the beginning of this chapter, we said that culture is best understood as a symbolic environment that we all live in. However, as we looked more closely at this environment, we discovered that culture differs radically from one group to another. Though everyone using this textbook lives in the same country, to some degree we all live in different cultures. An important task for sociologists is to understand these cultures, learn how and why they are different, and come to understand how they can all co-operate and co-exist.

Questions for Critical Thought

1. How does culture relate to the social structure of society?
2. What does language tell us about culture?
3. How do the mass media shape culture?
4. How did culture change before the mass media?
5. Why do people consider art to be part of culture? Why do some people also consider science to be a part of culture or a kind of subculture? What are the similarities and differences between art and science as forms of culture?
6. What does cultural change suggest? How is it related to economic, political, and social forces? How is it related to the emergence of new technological advancements or scientific theories?
7. Do you think that a global culture is developing? If so, how will this affect the cultures and societies of the world?

Take it Further: Recommended Readings

Victoria D. Alexander, *Sociology of the Arts: Exploring Fine and Popular Forms* (Oxford: Blackwell, 2003). This is a comprehensive and sophisticated overview of the sociology of art. It outlines the theoretical perspectives and both classic and current research on art, music, literature, and popular culture.

Angela McRobbie, *The Aftermath of Feminism: Gender, Culture, and Social Change* (Los Angeles: Sage, 2009). This book provides an intersection of feminism and culture, and it lays out a theory of gender power used to analyze social and cultural phenomena in women's lives today.

Lyn Spillman, ed., *Cultural Sociology* (Malden, MA: Blackwell, 2002). This is an engaging overview of several empirical studies and theoretical works in the sociology of culture. It

is a good foundation for someone interested in exploring and learning about the field in greater depth.

Stanley Lieberson, *A Matter of Taste: How Names, Fashions, and Culture Change* (New Haven, CT: Yale University Press, 2000). This is an interesting study of how cultural taste and fashion change over time. It explores how cultural patterns shape the names parents have chosen for their children for the past two centuries.

Steve Penfold, *The Donut: A Canadian History* (Toronto: University of Toronto Press, 2008). In the hands of hockey star Tim Horton, the doughnut became an edible icon of Canadian culture: more than the national food, it came close to expressing culinary patriotism. Read how it all happened.

Take it Further: Recommended Online Resources

American Sociological Association Culture Section, Website and Newsletter
https://asaculturesection.org/

Canadian Broadcasting Corporation (CBC)
www.cbc.ca

Canadian Culture
www.canadianculture.com

Canadian Heritage
www.canadianheritage.gc.ca

National Film Board of Canada (NFB)
www.nfb.ca

United Nations Educational, Scientific and Cultural Organization (UNESCO)
www.unesco.org

More resources available on  Dashboard

4

Making Infants into Social Beings through Socialization

◀ Neil Webb/Getty Images

Introduction

socialization

the lifelong social learning a person undergoes to become a capable member of society, through social interaction with others, and in response to social pressures.

Understanding how **socialization** occurs is central to sociological thinking. While each of us is a unique individual in society with his or her own attitudes, perspectives on life, dreams and aspirations, we are all members of social groups and behave according to the norms, values, and expectations of these groups (Gecas, 2001). The processes underlying socialization help to ensure the transmission of social norms, values, and beliefs from one generation to the next. They also help us develop as unique human beings within the context of our families, schools, churches, and other institutions of socialization.

The study of socialization focuses on the institutions, mechanisms, and principles that are responsible for transmitting social norms. But society does not fully determine how we act and who we become as people. We will learn in this chapter that as individuals we also influence the socialization process and our activities and choices can impact societal norms and expectations. There is a constant interplay and tension between the transformative and constraining forces of society and the need for individual choice and freedom. Stated simply, we all make and remake society every day; but society also makes us who we are and changes us slightly from one day to the next.

Some aspects of socialization have remained unchanged over time. However, it is also true that scientific advances combined with digital technologies have transformed the socialization process in recent decades. Scientific advances have provided guidelines for parents, educators, and institutions through data and complex models of human behaviour. We will discuss how science has influenced socialization later in the chapter. Digital technologies, likewise, have come to supplement traditional

betto.rodrigues/Shutterstock.com

Today, immersive global multiplayer gaming environments represent a widespread form of socialization in society with about 19 million Canadians identifying as gamers (Entertainment Software Association of Canada, 2015). An important question arises around what social norms and values are being learned in these environments.

forms of socialization by providing alternative forms of learning and social engagement. These alternative forms of socialization have not only changed traditional forms of socialization, they have also made it more difficult for parents and educators to control their children's knowledge, attitudes, and practices. Often the term **disruptive technologies** is used to describe the transformative effect of these technologies, as they "have the potential to disrupt the status quo, alter the way people live and work, and rearrange value pools" (Manyika, et al., 2013). To illustrate how norms and values learned at home can be at odds with those learned through digital technologies we discuss the development of appearance norms in girls in Box 4.1.

disruptive technologies technologies that are responsible for transformative social change.

Box 4.1 examined how social media has emerged as a strong force in the socialization process of children and teens, shaping their sense of acceptable appearance norms. Often, these appearance norms conflict with parents' ideas about proper appearance and self-presentation. Discrepancies between parents' appearance norms and those presented via digital technologies can create tensions and elicit new areas of contestation among family members. And the learning of appearance norms is not unique to childhood: the process continues throughout the lifespan. For example, seniors face image concerns of their own as they confront societal ideals of what it means to age gracefully. In Chapter 5, we will discuss in more detail how social media help to challenge appearance norms by providing a platform for anti-appearance norm movements to mobilize around, for example hashtags such as #fatkini.

In this chapter, we will discuss the process of socialization as it occurs across the lifespan and evaluate the influence of traditional media and new media on this process. We will also examine the key institutions involved in the transmission of social norms in Western societies, stressing how technology is altering their role as agents of socialization. Socialization, in some circumstances known as acculturation, is the teaching and learning of a society's culture; what we deem "appropriate" social behaviour is defined by the cultural system in which we are immersed, be it digital or non-digital. For this reason, any factors that affect the socialization process, such as science and technology, also affect the continuity and stability of a society's culture.

Spotlight On

4.1 | Appearance Norms Influence Young Children's Sense of Self

The pressure on young people to conform to an idealized self has greatly increased. Standards about the ideal body circulate through the mass media, especially through social media. Companies selling beauty products reinforce these idealized standards and capitalize on young people's insecurities (Wachter, 2016). Young girls are encouraged to conform to appearance norms by wearing makeup, doing their nails, and wearing fashionable outfits. A particularly telling survey conducted by the Renfrew Center Foundation (2016) shows that one in five girls (aged 18 and younger) have negative feelings about their looks when they don't wear makeup. These negative feelings include self-consciousness, unattractiveness, and feeling barefaced. More than half of the girls who wear makeup started before the age of 13. Stars such as Kim Kardashian West, Taylor Swift, and Bella Thorne, who are followed by millions of fans worldwide on sites such as Instagram and Facebook, serve as role models for these young girls. Also depictions through advertisements, social media, and TV shows promote images of women wearing makeup, and the use of plastic surgery to alter a person's body image has become a new trend (BBC, 2016). The socialization of looks starts at a very young age in our digital society and continues throughout the lifespan. Parents, who traditionally were responsible for the socialization of looks, now find themselves fighting appearance norms coming from digital media. At what age should children start wearing makeup and how much makeup is age-appropriate? How about cosmetic surgery?

Fractl contacted designers around the world and asked them to retouch an image based on the beauty standards of their cultures. The results (just a few results are shown above), illustrate how different appearance norms are around the world. If women and girls are comparing themselves against digital images, how realistic are their efforts to embody the ideals they see depicted online?

Time to reflect

How have norms around body image presented on social media affected your presentation of self? Do you find that Instagram selfies have set the bar higher for how young people are expected to look?

The Socialization Process

At the heart of the concept of socialization lies the idea that society shapes who we are and how we interact with others. Socialization is seen as the lifelong process of acquiring norms, values, and ideologies to learn how to behave in a range of social contexts and interact with others.

Sociologists see socialization as a process that occurs both at the micro and macro levels. Micro-level analysis refers to the study of face-to-face interactions, dyadic exchanges, or small group dynamics that together promote the development of a person's sense of **self** and place in the social world. By contrast, macro-level analysis examines large-scale social processes including trends and changes in the functioning of social institutions (such as educational institutions). Macro-level socialization is seen as a critical process for the promotion and continuity of a society's values and norms, from one generation to the next.

Primary socialization is the first stage in the socialization process, during which children develop basic values and norms as well as ideas of the self. This takes place during an individual's early childhood in the context of the family, including the extended family. There is no set of explicit rules that needs to be followed: rather, primary socialization occurs through role modelling and encouragement on the part of primary caregivers. Consider a skill like turn-taking in conversations. Turn-taking can be straightforward when there are only two conversation partners, but it becomes more complicated as soon as three or more people are present. Small children will often interrupt because they have not fully learned the subtleties of turn-taking. Turn-taking also varies considerably across cultures. Children learn turn-taking by interacting with their families and obtaining feedback as to when they are following the society's conversational expectations. Not conforming to the expectations of turn-taking has social repercussions, as people who do not follow the norms of turn-taking are considered rude for interrupting, which leads to frustrated conversational partners and sometimes even the end of conversation.

Even primary socialization undergoes change in a modern society. Giddens (1991) notes that, in modern society, actors outside of the family unit are more involved in the process of primary socialization. Increasingly, the early socialization of children relies on science through the advice and input of experts such as paediatricians, developmental psychologists, and educators. As well, advice is no longer limited to in-person contact; even the mass media are helping disseminate expert advice through books, YouTube videos, and magazines. And within the family context, external, macro-level forces come into play, including religious beliefs, educational philosophies, and social class (Lubbers, Jaspers, & Ultee, 2009). Many social processes both at the micro and macro levels, including changes in science and technology, shape primary socialization.

Secondary socialization, by contrast, is the acquisition of knowledge and skills needed to participate in society beyond the context of the family (Lubbers et al., 2009). In secondary socialization, institutions outside the family play a dominant part and add to the values, norms, and principles already acquired during primary socialization. A wide variety of socialization agents include one's peers, institutional authority figures (such as teachers and bosses), and the mass media. Secondary socialization is how individuals learn about the norms that apply to various social settings such as school, work, among friends, and even with romantic partners. Behaviors appropriate for specific social contexts are learned and become habitual, through observation and experimentation. For example, an undergraduate student taking a sociology degree will be socialized to a specific set of study habits and will learn to communicate using key sociological terms (Klassen & Dwyer, 2016). Should the student decide to pursue a master's degree, a new set of habits and skills will need to be added, thus requiring additional secondary socialization for such a transition.

As institutions outside of the family join the socialization process, children need to also learn how to reconcile new norms and values with old ones. While some of the norms and values taught at home will be reinforced by the school system, children will be exposed at school to a much wider range of norms and values through peers, but also through teachers, books, and web resources. The opinions and beliefs learned by children from their families may be contested at school and this may lead to conflict. Lubbers et al. (2009) investigated the influence of both primary and secondary socialization on attitudes towards same-sex marriage in the Netherlands, for example. The authors focused on both the primary socialization of respondents (their parents' attitudes), their secondary socialization (their level of education and religious beliefs), and a third category called "primary-secondary socialization" (the education, religious beliefs, and behaviours of the respondents' parents).

By analyzing survey data, the authors found that parents' attitudes towards homosexuality during one's youth significantly influenced the respondents' attitudes towards same-sex marriage.

self a stable understanding of one's identity: who we are in relation to others.

primary socialization first stage in the socialization process, during which children develop basic values and norms as well as ideas of the self.

secondary socialization the acquisition of the knowledge and skills needed to participate in society beyond the context of the family.

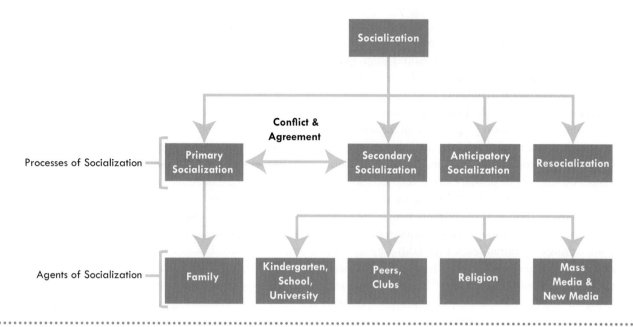

FIGURE 4.1 Processes of Socialization and Core Institutions

Source: Author-generated

The strongest factor influencing their views, however, was socialization within religious institutions. Such findings show that certain beliefs develop strongly through primary socialization and are either reinforced or reduced through strong secondary socialization, as one might experience as part of a religious group.

Figure 4.1 depicts the key processes and institutions of socialization and their relations. While primary and secondary socialization are different in nature, they will in many instances complement one another. But primary and secondary socialization may also be dissonant, creating conflict between different values, belief systems, and norms.

> ## Time to reflect
>
> Did you experience any conflict between the values, belief systems, and norms transmitted through your primary and your secondary socialization while growing up? How did you reconcile these differences?

Anticipatory Socialization and Resocialization

Two additional forms of socialization critical in a person's social development are anticipatory socialization and resocialization. **Anticipatory socialization** is associated with the process of preparing to take on a new position or social role in society. Each time we start a new phase in our lives, start a new job, take on a new responsibility, we need to learn the social norms and expectations associated with this social role.

Social roles are understood as sets of behaviours, responsibilities, and norms associated with a particular status in society. Anticipatory socialization describes the learning that occurs before we take on the role, and it typically occurs through five key sources: family, school, jobs, peers, and the media (Levine & Hoffner, 2006). This form of socialization starts early in life, with childhood, and continues into adolescence and through to early adulthood. Anticipatory socialization is displayed, for example, in the film *Legally Blonde*, when Elle Woods (Reese Witherspoon) in her admissions video essay uses legal jargon and brags about her ability to recall facts instantaneously, in hopes of showcasing her mastery of the behaviours of a typical law student. Entering law school is a big step

anticipatory socialization the process in which non-group members adopt the values and behaviours of groups that they aspire to join.

social roles a set of behaviours, responsibilities, and norms associated with a particular status in society.

for anyone, and for many students it is about developing a new identity, learning social norms, and fitting into the social context of law school. Role-playing is an important part of all anticipatory socialization, and we will elaborate on the process later in this chapter when we look at how individuals become socialized into various professions.

Resocialization is a process involving the replacement of an individual's values, beliefs, and sense of self (Gecas, 2001). There are many circumstances in life when resocialization may be necessary and even useful. For example, when an employee is promoted to a managerial position, which entails overseeing the operations of other workers in a department, this change may require additional job training, a different image, and a new set of behaviours. In this case, the resocialization process may be a welcome and voluntary change and provide a person with new challenges and job opportunities.

However, resocialization is sometimes involuntary and takes place in what Erving Goffman (1961) calls a **total institution**. A total institution is a place that is separate from society, in which its inhabitants live (sleep, eat, work, etc.) under one overarching authority. Among other things, this authority establishes and maintains a strict daily regime and oversees the continuous process of resocialization. A key goal of the total institution is to erase its inhabitants' existing values, beliefs, and overall sense of self, and to replace them with another set. Some examples of total institutions include prisons, mental hospitals, and drug rehabilitation programs as well as the military. The residential school in Canada is another example of a total institution. These schools were established after 1880 to assimilate Indigenous children into Euro-Canadian culture (Miller, 2012). Métis children for example, who are children of mixed European and Indigenous ancestry, were forced to attend residential schools often run by Catholic priests because the authorities at the time believed that "The condition of these Métis is deplorable. Large families live in one or two rooms. Children have grown up without

resocialization
a process that involves a replacement of an individual's values, beliefs, and sense of self.

total institution
a concept developed by Erving Goffman, defined as an isolated, confined social system whose main objective is to control most aspects of its participants' lives.

National Film Board of Canada. Photothèque collection/Library and Archives Canada PA048571

A classroom of the Indian Industrial School in Brandon, Manitoba, in 1946. What evidence of resocialization is visible in this photograph?

learning to read or write; some can not even speak English reasonably well. I feel that only through education can we help these people, and at the same time prevent our Métis problem from becoming more serious" (Brandt, Saskatchewan Archives Board, n.d.)

The quote above shows how the superintendent of schools, E. J. Brandt, viewed the educational needs of Métis children and the rationale he provided to the Canadian government for creating schools geared toward resocialization (Logan, 2015). Indigenous communities struggle to this day with the negative repercussions of forcing children into residential schools and the trauma this separation caused for families, community members, and individuals (Logan, 2015). Residential schools took away existing (Indigenous communities') values, social norms, and cultural beliefs, without providing Métis with a new sense of identity. It was not until 2008, that then prime minister Stephen Harper provided an apology and stated that the government had profoundly failed Indigenous peoples (CBC Digital Archives, 2008). The process of reconciliation between Indigenous people in Canada and the federal government is still ongoing and fraught with much controversy.

Socialization over the Life Course

Interactive activity

The various socialization processes discussed above occur over the course of life. At each life stage, different agents and mechanisms of socialization are at play. Socialization does not end when we become adults; rather, at various life stages different transitions need to be made and new social roles learned. Life stages are also associated with critical events. For example, adults often start a family, taking on the new role of father or mother. This experience is exciting but also has its challenges ranging from sleep deprivation to finding the right balance between work and family, and becoming an agent of primary socialization.

Sociologists generally distinguish five stages of the life course: childhood, teenager, young adult, mature adult, and old age. Each stage is associated with a set of expectations and behaviours (see Table 4.1). While some expectations must be fulfilled, others are considered desirable, and individuals who meet them are rewarded through social attention, affection, and status. Not conforming to the expectations set in each stage can lead to social consequences such as social

TABLE 4.1 Stages over the Life Course and Expectations Set by Society

Life Stage	Expectations
Childhood	· Learn symbols, including language. · Internalize family norms. · Learn rules and social roles through play.
Teenager	· Demonstrate academic achievement. · Build circle of friends outside the family. · Learn gender roles.
Young adult	· Go to college or university. · Start working. · Move out of family house.
Mature adult	· Marry. · Have children. · Increase work status.
Old age	· Stay social and active. · Live independently. · Manage health challenges.

Source: Author-generated

isolation, reprimand, and outright rejection (Tepperman & Upenieks, 2016). While biological changes do happen during these stages, the stages are predominantly culturally determined and vary greatly across cultures.

For example, in Canada, older adults enjoy living independently and having the freedom to choose what activities to engage in in their free time. By contrast, older adults in China often live with their children and help in the household and with child rearing. The meaning of aging is also constantly being redefined. Table 4.1 depicts the five stages of the life course, and provides examples of the kinds of expectations and social roles that exist for each in the Canadian context.

Theoretical Approaches to Socialization

Structural Functionalism

The structural functionalist perspective of socialization has a long history in sociology and focuses on social roles as societal building blocks dictating behaviour. For example, a doctor would act in a professional and caring manner in the context of her interactions with a sick patient. She may also wear a white coat to differentiate her attire from that of patients and signal cleanliness and professionalism. The role is predefined and the person fulfills the role by acting according to the set expectations. For structural functionalists, the learning of social roles is a critical process in socialization and helps individuals know how to engage with others, making social situations more predictable.

Functionalists give institutions a central place in the establishment and transmission of social norms and values, helping preserve a society's structure over time, and ensuring stability. From a functionalist view, this is often seen as a top-down mechanism, where individuals internalize social roles presented to them by key socialization agents. We have already listed above some of the key agents of socialization including the family, kindergarten, schools, peers, religion, and the mass media (refer to Figure 4.1).

Functionalists have examined the family as a central unit in society, where socialization and interaction take place. Because the family brings together several generations under one roof, it is considered instrumental in teaching social roles and passing along values. Parsons and other functionalist sociologists, such as Robert Bales and James Olds, were concerned with social change occurring in the 1950s and its disruptive impact on family life (Parsons & Bales, 1955/2007). Specifically, Parsons (1955/2007) examined high rates of divorce as a disruptive force. Much debate at the time saw divorce as a detriment to family values and condemned the potential negative effects it could have on the socialization of future generations.

Parson's analysis, however, disconfirmed the fear that the structure of the family was on its way out. He showed that while it was true that structural differentiation was taking place and families were undergoing social changes, nonetheless, there was no reason for alarm. His analysis of demographic data showed unequivocally that marriage rates were on the rise and the family as an institution continued to play a central role in the socialization of children. One change he observed, though, consisted of the diminishing influence of kinship structures in the form of extended families. Grandparents, aunts, uncles, and cousins were less involved in directly raising and shaping children. He noted that instead the trend was toward an increase in the participation of institutions, experts, and teachers in the socialization process of children.

This trend continues today, and much sociological debate has focused on digital technologies as potentially disruptive technologies to the family unit and its values (McKinsey & Company, 2014). Disruptive technologies as discussed above are those that not only create social change, but exercise radical change, change that is transformative in nature. Digital technologies are seen as disruptive to the functioning of the family unit because rather than family members interacting with one another, reading together, or telling stories, each family member is plugged into their own digital experience via personal devices, such as smart phones, e-readers, and tablets. A study looking at social media use among millennials (aged 19–32) found that individuals who used social media for long periods of time and frequently checked their accounts were more likely to report higher feelings of isolation than those who used it less and checked their accounts infrequently (Primack et al., 2017). While the study was able only to establish a correlation and not causation—as individuals who feel lonelier may be using social media to counter their loneliness instead of social media use leading to loneliness—it does suggest that even *social* media, meant to increase social connectedness, may not counter feelings of social isolation. This raises many questions about the effect of technology on social networks and suggests that even social technologies may be driving us apart, more than we realize.

We each basically live in our own bubble. Sherry Turkle (2011) referred to this new form of socialization as being "alone together" and contrasted it with togetherness. She sees "alone together" as having many negative repercussions for socialization and the maintenance of social relations within families. While digital technologies allow each person to watch their favourite show, read the news at their own pace, and engage in immersive global multiplayer gaming environments of their choice, these technologies do not cultivate family interaction or shared experiences that contribute to socialization and the transmission of family values and beliefs across generations (Turkle, 2011).

Time to reflect

Do you agree or disagree with Turkle's assessment that family socialization has changed from togetherness to "alone together" due to technology? Do you think that technology has disrupted family socialization?

Conflict Theory

Conflict theory is based on Marxism and aims to uncover and understand inequalities in society related to access to resources, power, and privilege. The premise is that processes of socialization are directly linked to social inequalities. Individuals who grow up in more affluent households will have access to better education, greater opportunities for learning, and more diverse forms of socialization. Class socialization maintains the status quo, making **social mobility** difficult, which is defined as the ability to move between social strata or social groups.

social mobility

a change in social status where individuals or families move from one strata to another. Movement may be vertical or horizontal, across generations or within a generation.

Pierre Bourdieu (1973) introduced the concept of *cultural capital*, defined in Chapter 3, to describe how class socialization takes place and the impact it has on a person's ability to mobilize resources, belong to social groups, and be successful in life. Cultural capital describes the sum of intangible social assets that allow an individual to claim membership in social circles, and feel a sense of belonging and acceptance (Bourdieu, 1973). Intangible social assets include formal education, knowledge of what is trendy, and understandings of appropriate behaviour and norms. An example of how cultural capital contributes to group membership constitutes hipsterism, the subculture that gained traction in the late 2000s and early 2010s, and comprised affluent or middle-class youth. To belong to the hipster subculture, a person needs to have a good understanding of indie and alternative music, to appreciate vintage fashion, and to identify as a foodie. Much has been said about distinguishing oneself culturally not only by having breadth of taste but also engaging in cultural consumption of music, art, and food (Michael, 2015; Sullivan & Katz-Gerro, 2007). Cultural capital, then, is not only having knowledge of highbrow culture, but also being knowledgeable of the latest trends and cultural products (Michael, 2015). Acquiring cultural capital is no easy task, though, as it requires investments of time and money.

Cultural capital demonstrates how the socialization process varies across social strata. More importantly, the socialization process varies not only in terms of what people learn, but also in terms of how they learn it. In a study of child socialization, Lareau (2000) investigated the socialization process of white and African American children growing up in middle-class and working-class families. She learned that boys in working-class families were given more freedom in their play and often spent time hanging out with their extended families, whereas boys who grew up in middle-class families had more structured routines, with their days filled with numerous activities ranging from art classes to engagement in sports teams to curriculum-related lessons. Lareau (2000) is cautious in linking differences in socialization during childhood directly to outcomes later in adult life. She does suggest, however, that children from middle-class families may have advantages over those growing up in working-class families because they have gained from their experiences in engaging in various activities and can more easily apply these early childhood experiences to the challenges and demands of future work settings. For Lareau (2000) some of the skills learned by middle-class children included managing a busy schedule, coordinating various events, and learning to belong in diverse social settings.

Time to reflect

Exercise your sociological imagination by considering the differences in the socialization process of children growing up in middle-class and working-class families. How might these differences create advantages or disadvantages towards a child's ability to do well later in life?

Feminism

Feminism has parallels with conflict theory in that it examines inequalities in society stemming from differences in socialization. Instead of examining class differences as does conflict theory, feminism focuses on differential forms of socialization between genders. Gender socialization refers to learning what it means to be a girl or a boy: what to wear, what activities to engage in, and how to express oneself.

Gender roles are modelled first in the home, where parents often engage in a gendered division of labour. Women are responsible for preparing meals and taking care of children, while men are considered the breadwinners, often helping around the house by taking kids to sports activities and fixing things. While these are considered traditional gender stereotypes that families are beginning to move away from (see Chapter 10), often images in school texts, media images on TV, and movies continue to reinforce these traditional roles. It is important to realize that gender roles are not universal; rather, they are social constructs that vary considerably across historical periods and cultures.

With increased migration patterns and globalization, we are also seeing challenges that arise for families in the process of gender socialization. In the case of Syrian refugees who have been displaced from their homes unwillingly, they have been forced to integrate and reconsider gender roles. Syrian refugees are struggling with how to reinforce their own cultural values, while at the same time letting their children integrate into a new society and learn new gender roles. Box 4.2 discusses the numerous challenges Syrian refugee families are negotiating as they relocate to Canada.

Feminist scholars are concerned about gendered socialization because of the repercussions it has for individuals, as it hinders women's potential for social mobility. For example, schools in Canada have been largely reformed and education is compulsory for both boys and girls.

Children of refugees from Syria would be expected to attend school in Canada regardless of their gender. Moreover, in Canada there is little gender segregation in schools today. In the past, boys and girls had to enter and exit schools through separate doors, and often were taught a different curriculum. Nonetheless, boys and girls in high school still tend to choose different subjects, and these choices then influence the kinds of careers that they can later pursue (see Chapter 7 for more detail). Careers in the sciences, such as engineering, biochemistry, and computer science, come with status and prestige as well as high-paying salaries, creating new gender gaps. But even when men and women have identical credentials and occupy the same position, women tend to earn less. Feminists see this pay gap as a clear indicator of unequal treatment

Think Globally

4.2 | Relocation and Gendered Social Scripts

Syrian citizens are escaping a conflict zone, with the country experiencing civil war since 2011. By 2017, the conflict has led to the loss of 220,000 lives and caused one of the largest refugee displacements in history, with over 5 million refugees on the move (UN Refugee Agency, 2017).

Refugees have travelled over land and sea to escape the devastation, and over 1 million refugees have sought asylum in Europe. To aid with the crises, Canada opened its borders to 25,000 Syrian refugees in 2015–2016. However, the move from Syria to Canada comes with new challenges related to socialization. These challenges are particularly stark for refugees from rural areas, who may not be familiar with Canadian lifestyles, while refugees from larger cities like Aleppo and Damascus are more familiar with Western traditions and norms. Of particular relevance is gender socialization, since in Syria women and men are socialized differently. The role of women is predefined to be in the fields, helping with maintaining the farm and/or at home making sure the children are taken care of. Also, women are not addressed directly when their husbands are present. If one needs to speak to a family, then the husband must be addressed foremost. In fact, women usually do not introduce themselves until their husbands ask them to, and they almost never say their first or last name; they refer to themselves as "the mother of (name of their eldest son)."

Marriages are pre-arranged, often at a very young age for Canadian standards (15 to 18 for women and 17 to 20 for men). The many differences between Syrian and Canadian values, norms, and traditions create enormous challenges for newcomers. The Canadian government has put various programs in place to help refugees from Syria integrate into Canadian society. Learning the language will be an important first step for initiating ties to the community and adapting to new social norms. Creating opportunities for refugees to learn about Canadian culture will be important. Many cities in Canada have centres that support newcomers to Canada and connect Canadian families to refugee families, allowing for intercultural exchange in a buddy-like system.

For example, the London Cross Cultural Learner Centre has existed since 1968 and provides a range of services to promote interactions and exchanges in informal settings, in part mirroring the Syrian culture of socialization. In Toronto, several Facebook groups emerged in 2016 and 2017 to help newcomers. Some of these groups focused on food preparation and others collected clothing, footwear, and food for Syrian newcomers.

Prime Minister Justin Trudeau welcomes refugees from Syria to Canada and new programs are put in place to aid refugees in the transition. Refugees often struggle to become familiar with new norms and traditions and develop feelings of isolation as they struggle to integrate into the community.

for men and women in the workforce. Also, women are less likely to occupy leadership positions, even in situations where they are as qualified as men to take on these roles. Prime Minister Justin Trudeau put together the first Canadian cabinet with equal representation of men and women, setting the stage for gender equality in positions of influence (Ditchburn, 2015). Chapter 7 will cover in more depth the continued need to study gendered socialization and its effects on how society functions.

The aim of feminism is to not only create greater awareness of gender roles but also question these roles and how they affect women's ability to function in society and develop a sense of self. Feminism goes beyond describing differences in social roles and advocates for social change.

Symbolic Interactionism

Symbolic interactionism concerns itself with the study of a person's self-concept and how this self-concept develops from, and guides, their interactions with others. As one of the pioneers of symbolic interactionism, Charles Horton Cooley's (1902/1964) ideas greatly influenced the discipline of sociology and how we think about socialization. His central idea was that starting from birth, humans defined themselves within the context of their socializations and over time through interactions with others developed a sense of "the self," or self-concept.

Symbolic interactionism sees socialization as a micro-phenomenon that occurs in the context of daily interaction rather than at the macro-level. Symbolic interactionists dismiss the assumptions made by structural functionalists because they see individuals as passively internalizing existing social norms and values. By contrast, symbolic interactionism focuses on how meaning is established, negotiated, and transformed through social interaction in dyads, social groups, and communities. This approach views individuals as active agents who shape the socialization process.

In Cooley's theory, social interaction serves as a feedback loop, where feedback from others is integrated back into the self and then influences future interactions. This concept of the **looking-glass self** has become integral to understanding the mechanisms involved in self-concept development. The looking-glass self has three principal elements (Cooley, 1902/1964):

1. We consider how others will see us. For example, we imagine how we will appear to others.
2. We analyze how others react to our behaviours. For example, we interpret if others accept and validate our behaviours.
3. Based on the previous two elements, we develop a self-concept around the judgments of others. For example, when others react positively to our actions, then we feel pride.

The looking-glass self presupposes that how we see ourselves largely depends on how we think others see us. Cooley's work resonates with many individuals today, as they see themselves

looking-glass self
a social psychological concept coined by Charles Horton Cooley, which states that a person's self develops from interpersonal interactions in society and observations of others.

TABLE 4.2 Theoretical Approaches to Socialization

Theory	Main Points
Structural Functionalism	· Institutions help maintain the values and norms of society.
	· The transmission of norms and values through socialization provides stability in society over time.
Conflict Theory	· Individuals' socialization experiences vary greatly by social strata.
	· The norms and behaviours we learn provide advantages and constraints in life.
Feminism	· Gendered roles and scripts are learned through various social institutions including the family, schooling, and media.
	· Gender roles provide the basis for differences in expectations placed on women and men and the opportunities they may have.
Symbolic Interactionism	· Social interactions shape the development of a person's self-concept and identity.
	· Symbols acquire meaning, which are learned in the context of social interaction.

Source: Author-generated

and others around them engaging in constant social comparison. Social pressures are particularly poignant during the teen years, but in reality, social comparison continues into adult life. In fact, digital technologies have created new means of social comparison through data and analytics. Daily, users obtain reports about how many likes their posts have received on Facebook, and how often comments were left on their Instagram posts. In this case, social media's self-presentation practices exacerbate the already existing need in individuals for social comparison. We will talk more about symbolic interactionist perspectives on socialization in the coming sections.

Time to reflect

Do you feel annoyed or hurt when no one in your network comments on or likes a picture you have posted? How does that inattention influence your self-concept?

The Self, Identity, and Social Roles

Three core concepts help explain how micro- and macro-level influences operate in relation to one another: the self, **identity**, and social roles.

The Self

identity

the unique combination of traits, values, and expressions that make people who they are.

The self is made up of information such as one's name, how one perceives oneself, one's likes and dislikes, one's personal beliefs and values, and other characteristics that make people who they are (Sedikides & Spencer, 2007). These characteristics change over the lifespan as a person is exposed to new life experiences (Anthis, 2002; McCrae & Costa, 1990).

Consider information you may have posted on Facebook or another social media site five years ago about yourself or others. Today that information may feel dated or no longer reflect your beliefs and opinions. This exercise shows how the self becomes updated as we have new experiences and integrate these into our self-concept. Higgins (1987) describes the self in terms of three core components: an actual self described by personal characteristics; an ideal self linked to how a person wishes to be, and an "ought to be" self that reflects moral values.

These three core components influence a person's behaviours and attitudes and guide everyday interactions with others. The self is often viewed as a single entity, but Coser (1975) dismissed this notion and argued that individuals have multiple selves that are expressed in different social contexts. For example, different characteristics and behaviours come to light when people interact with their peers versus when they interact with their professional network. This becomes particularly obvious when we compare information shared on Facebook versus information shared on a professional network such as LinkedIn. LinkedIn includes positive characteristics and highlights professional achievements (Utz, 2016); however, this kind of information would be seen as awkward on Facebook, where people are expected to share more fun and entertaining personal information.

Time to reflect

Do you share different kinds of information on your professional (e.g., LinkedIn, Academia.edu) and personal social networks (e.g., Facebook, Snapchat, or Instagram)? What aspects of yourself are highlighted in each context?

Similar to Coser, Goffman (1959) argues that people present different facets of themselves in various social spheres, constantly adjusting their styles of interaction and self-presentation to the expectations of social situations with the aim of fitting into distinct social groups. Specifically, he referred to the presentation of self in private space as a person's **backstage** and to the public expression of self as the **frontstage**. Goffman's theory is based on the notion that social life is about engaging in the performance of a self we wish others to see, and is geared toward **impression management**. Self-presentation is "motivated by a desire to make a favourable impression on others, or an impression that corresponds to one's ideals" (Herring & Kapidzic, 2015, p. 146). The frontstage presents a self that is more idealized and follows social norms and expectations, while the backstage presents a self that is freer from societal expectations as active impression management is not required.

Technology has affected the presentation of self in various ways. In particular, social media has changed how people present themselves, creating a new stage for performativity. Much debate has surfaced around the idea that the digital self is a distorted presentation of the "real self." The presentation of self online is certainly not a random act, as Hogan (2010) points out, but is a process of **data curation,** where users act like curators of exhibits or museums, carefully selecting pictures, information, and artifacts that are all strategically positioned to craft a unique self.

The birth of the selfie in the 2000s has also transformed the presentation of self and has led to the emergence of a new visual digital culture (Saltz, 2014). Selfies are taken in diverse social contexts ranging from celebrity selfies to political selfies to funeral selfies. Editing tools such as Adobe Photoshop and Picasa have given users more control over their appearance, which positions the selfie at the edge of immediacy and alterability (Hand, 2017). As people retake selfies of themselves with the aim of getting just the right picture, this places enormous emphasis on physical appearance, as we are subject to constant scrutiny and improvement (Hand, 2017). Drawing on Goffman's theory of performativity, the preparation and endless editing of pictures comprises the backstage, while the posting and interacting with the final product can be described as the frontstage.

backstage

when the actor is off stage and thus freed from social norms and expectations and can therefore cease performing and be his or her "true self."

frontstage

the performance of a role in relation to those around us, the audience, that follows specific social norms and expectations.

impression management

a conscious or subconscious process in which a person works to shape other peoples' perceptions of his or her self.

data curation

the processes and activities involved in managing data so that the data remains available for reuse over time or for future research purposes.

arindambanerjee/Shutterstock.com

In this photo, a protester takes a selfie before rejoining a rally protesting the Dakota Access Pipeline. Are social media posts careful curation of our frontstage personas, or are they genuine expressions of self? Are these two things mutually exclusive?

Identity

A person's identity is closely interlinked to his or her self, but what distinguishes identity is that it consists of a person's self-conception and personality, which are both shaped by membership in various social groups.

When a person is asked about his or her identity, most individuals describe who they are through the various social roles they occupy and the relations they have with others within the social groups they belong to. Examining identity is seen as critical, as our identity influences our behaviours and understandings of the world directly through the knowledge we have, the beliefs we hold, and the choices we make. Generally speaking, the goal of identity research is to gain an understanding of why individuals make the choices they do (Stryker, 2001). For example, why does a person choose to watch a show on Netflix on a Saturday evening instead of going out to a party with friends? As individuals, we are constantly making choices between alternative courses of action. Of particular relevance is the formation of in-group identities, as these often lead to the devaluation of out-groups and their points of view, creating animosity and conflict between social groups. Social roles strongly influence identity and the choices people make.

Social Roles

We discussed earlier that socialization is a complex process that takes place over the life course and consists of not only learning social norms and values but also recognizing which values and norms are of relevance in different social settings. The study of social roles and their function in society is described as role theory.

role theory
a viewpoint that considers that an individual's behaviour is guided by expectations held both by the individual and other people, which is guided by socially defined categories (e.g., mother, teacher, doctor), social learning, and experience.

Traditionally, **role theory** described social roles as pre-established by society, which then determined one's identity. Symbolic interactionism challenged this static notion of social roles (Stryker, 2001). If social roles were fully determined by society, social roles would remain unchanged and unchallenged from one generation to the next. Also, social roles would be fully determined by societal expectations with little to no input from individuals. Symbolic interactionism proposed a renewed look at identity and stated that social roles emerge in the context of everyday social interaction, thereby giving individuals more agency in how they perform various social roles and shape their own identities. According to symbolic interactionism, social roles and identities are created in the context of social interaction and filled with symbolic communication (Bailey & Yost, 2001). In this view, society continually rebuilds itself through the *reciprocal* influence of individuals taking into account one another's characteristics, and the symbolic meanings that emerge as they interact (Bailey & Yost, 2001). The central contribution of symbolic interactionism to our understanding of identity, therefore, is that neither society nor individuals alone determine social roles; rather, social roles emerge in a constant interplay of societal expectations and individuals' choices.

Types of Social Roles

Role theory has been divided into two types (Bailey & Yost, 2001):

- *Macro-level analysis of social roles.* From a macro-level analysis, social roles are part of larger social systems and are reinforced through these social systems. The macro perspective is similar to the structural functionalist approach discussed earlier in that it views social roles as helping establish continuity and integration in society. For example, social roles assure a high degree of predictability. When patients visit their family physician, a set of expectations guides the interaction. The family physician will inquire about the health status of the patient, listen carefully, and ask further follow-up questions. Someone dealing with a health-related issue, regardless of how serious it is, will be glad to encounter a social situation that is largely predictable.
- *Micro-level analysis of social roles.* The micro-level analysis makes room for individuals to exert agency. Instead of assuming that individuals simply embrace social roles as they are presented to them, the micro-level analysis sees individuals as influencing these roles by either fully embracing them or questioning them. This assumes that social roles may be incongruent with a person's self-conception and thus the person may reject the behavioural expectations associated with the role.

For sociologists, the link between macro- and micro-level social phenomena is an important subject of study. For institutions to function and people to be able to fulfill their positions within these institutions, the learning and internalization of social roles is important. At the same time, questioning social roles and their meaning is important for social change to occur. This shows that macro- and micro-level phenomena are constantly reinforcing and challenging each other.

Context of Socialization

One of the complexities of learning social roles is to also discern what role is appropriate in what social context. Coser (1975) introduced the notion of social roles to describe how we change our behaviour, adapting it seamlessly and with ease from one setting to another. Consider how you take one social role in your daily life and what this role entails. When you are at home with your family, you may take on the role of daughter or son, listen to your parents and follow the rules and norms established in their house. But when you leave your parents' home and mingle with peers, your social role is different. Your peers may have different expectations about behaviours and you will adapt your behaviour to those expectations.

Individuals are able to enact their different social roles in a way that feels natural, as the various roles come together to create a single self. Nonetheless, **role conflict** can occur in various forms. As discussed above, context is an important part of social roles, as we embrace different roles that fit with the expectations put on us. We learn to switch our language, dress code, and manners, and adopt different social scripts. New media, however, have blurred the boundaries of different social roles. Box 4.3 describes a new social phenomenon referred to as **context collapse**, where various social roles merge, clash, and possibly create conflict for individuals.

role conflict

when a person is obligated to fulfill two different positions that have clashing requirements.

context collapse

the potential that exists on social media for people, information, expectations, and norms from one context to collapse with another, and the problems that may arise.

Sociology 2.0

4.3 | Context Collapse on Social Media

Context collapse refers to how people, information, expectations, and norms from one context blend into or collapse with another (boyd, 2006; Marwick & boyd, 2011a). *Context* refers to physical environments and social roles, which include social relationships, shared and situational meanings, and societal norms and values. As we move between contexts, the expectations of others guide us through appropriate—and inappropriate—interactions and let us know which social role we should perform. In these terms, collapse refers to the overlapping of roles through the intermingling of distinct networks. There is context collapse of some degree in *all* contexts; however, some contexts are more porous and easily collapsible than others. This is apparent in digital society where much of our socializing is performed on social media.

Context collapse often refers to the expansive and imagined audiences possible online as opposed to the limited groups we interact with in face-to-face contexts (Marwick & boyd, 2011a). Popular social media such as Twitter and Facebook are very porous contexts because they collapse many contexts into one; friends, family, and co-workers converge in one network. Specialized social media such as LinkedIn is less porous as they have a more defined purpose. Since social media collapses multiple audiences into a single context and does so in an environment where many of the social cues we are used to reading are absent, the resulting setting can be challenging for users to navigate (DeGroot & Vik, 2017). Context collapse has implications in the workplace. According to Vitak, Lampe, Gray, and Ellison (2012), users of social media are cognizant of the potential negative repercussions of context collapse and have adopted strategies to mitigate those challenges.

For example, some users keep their profiles strictly private with no work contacts, or have multiple Facebook accounts for different contexts, one for friends and one for work colleagues, for instance. Another strategy is to resolve context collapse issues by espousing what Hogan (2010) describes as a lowest common denominator approach in which users consciously avoid publicly posting anything that could negatively impact their employment or relationships with co-workers.

Roles are linked to macro-level influences, as we adopt and learn norms that are part of larger social systems that we are a part of, such as the family unit, ethnic groups, religious groups, and professions. Roles are a useful tool that guide our behaviour in various social situations and allow us to fit into different social systems. At the same time, roles also limit our behaviour, as moving outside the accepted repertoire can lead to conflict and diminish belonging in a social group. Learning what the expectations are is important for fitting into society, but questioning, adapting, and rewriting social scripts are also important for society to embrace social change.

Agents of Socialization

agents of socialization
the individuals, groups, or institutions that form the social situation in which socialization takes place.

Diverse **agents of socialization** shape a person during different stages in his or her life. During primary socialization, the family and educational facilities are predominant agents, while during secondary socialization a broader and more diverse set of agents play a role, including schools, peers, and work. Agents of socialization are defined as social institutions that teach social norms, thereby exerting influence on people's sense of self and their outlook on life. These agents shape the development of the individual through various mechanisms, including the modelling of expected behaviours and social roles, and the reinforcement of values and rules through rewards and consequences.

Home and the Family

Video: *The World Before Her*

Early in life, the primary agent of socialization is the family. Infants and young children learn not only from their parents but also from their siblings, grandparents, and extended family. The transmission of norms and values occurs mainly through role modelling.

Children observe their parents as they occupy specific roles in the family, and they internalize these behavioural repertoires. At the same time, parents socialize their children through various mechanisms. Research consistently shows that parental support, guidance, and involvement are the most central mechanisms of early socialization. High levels of parental engagement benefit children's cognitive and social development and positively affect moral behaviour and self-esteem.

Parents have not always been as involved in their children's upbringing as they are today. Scientific evidence linking parental involvement with positive outcomes in children's success later in life has led to social change in attitudes toward parenting. The idea of "quality time" pervades much of the literature on parenting and encourages parents to give their undivided attention to their children with the aim of establishing a strong bond and helping them develop social and cognitive skills. This includes shared family meals and joined activities such as going for walks, watching a movie together, or taking kids to extracurricular activities. The study discussed above by Lareau (2000) listed some of the potential benefits accrued from parent commitment to getting their kids to participate in extracurricular activities. Overall, much research has shown that parental involvement helps children become well adapted to societal expectations, increases academic performance, and predicts success later in life.

Many parents consider their role in their children's upbringing as critical. Though parents do play an important role in socializing their children in the early years of development, it remains unclear as to how this influence is exerted on their children. Early theories assumed a unidirectional and strong influence of parents and family on children (see Model 1 in Figure 4.2). These theories saw children as internalizing their parents' values and norms without much questioning, and in this way recreating and perpetuating established societal standards. More recent work has demonstrated that parents not only influence their children, but children also have agency and exert influence on the parents and on the socialization process itself. The influence of children on parents' socialization has been termed **reverse socialization** to highlight the direction of influence (see Model 2 in Figure 4.2).

reverse socialization
the process by which children influence parents and help them learn or acquire some social skills; in reverse socialization, parents learn from their children.

Corsaro and Eder (1990) propose to move away from simple models that view socialization as limited to adaptation and internalization processes that are unidirectional from parent to child or

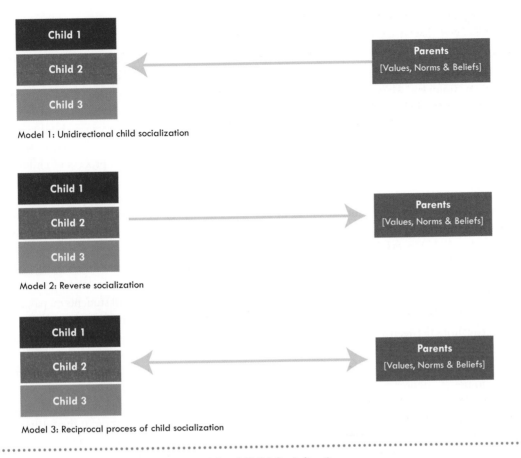

Model 1: Unidirectional child socialization

Model 2: Reverse socialization

Model 3: Reciprocal process of child socialization

FIGURE 4.2 Comparison of Three Models of Child Socialization

Source: Author-generated

from child to parent. Instead, they advocate that child socialization also includes processes of appropriation, reinvention, and reproduction. They argue that children and parents socialize neither in a top-down nor bottom-up approach. Rather, socialization occurs in shared interaction, where children and parents together co-create meaning and shape social situations. This has been referred to as a **reciprocal process** to highlight the mutual influence (Gecas, 2001) (see Model 3 in Figure 4.2).

The three models of socialization are shown in Figure 4.2. The arrows signal the type of influence that parents exert on children and children on parents. The last model shows how the influence goes both ways. When sociologists examine socialization processes they also consider birth order. While we may be inclined to think that all children growing up in the same family would experience the same kind of socialization, being the first, second, or third born has an impact on the socialization process. Parents have more time for their first-born child and tend to funnel all available resources toward her or his socialization. By contrast, parents have less time and need to divide their attention between children when their second child is born. Without intent on the part of the parents, children are socialized differently depending on where they are born in the birth order. So, when examining socialization in the family, many factors need to be taken into consideration.

reciprocal process
when both the parent and children socialize each other through their interactions; children socialize parents just as parents socialize children.

Time to reflect

Considering your own upbringing and family dynamics, which of the three models shown in Figure 4.2 resonate the most with your experience growing up? Are you the eldest or the youngest in your family? Did you find that birth order had an influence on socialization in your family? If so, in what ways?

Kindergarten and Schools

The transition to kindergarten, daycares, and preschools can be difficult, and many young children struggle to adapt to the expectations of these institutions. At home, children are socialized in a caring and supportive environment, whereas institutions of care are not tailored to individual needs and consequently are less personal. Kindergartens have rules and schedules that need to be followed to maintain social order.

As children grow up, schools become important sites of socialization because children spend a large proportion of their time there. In Canada, children spend about 6.5 hours a day in schools, interacting with peers and teachers. The role of schools in the socialization process of children is diverse. Schools help students internalize norms and expectations around educational attainment and achievement, reinforcing the need for literacy, numeracy, and knowledge acquisition. The role of schools goes well beyond educating kids, however, as they also embody social norms and expectations around socially accepted behaviours. Kids are taught to play, interact, and negotiate social relations with their peers and authority figures.

Schools have the capability to overcome and potentially reverse class inequalities. In societies like Canada where education is a public good, children from different socioeconomic backgrounds are given the opportunity to benefit equally from the education system, placing all students on par. Much research has shown though that schools often fail in their equalizing effect and indeed reinforce existing inequalities between social groups. This perspective emphasizes how social groups differentially experience school and benefit to varying degrees from schooling (Davies & Guppy, 2006).

Not all children are equally prepared for school. Students from low-income families are more likely to present poorer school readiness, which involves the ability to read and a general desire for learning. While such differences may appear subtle, they can deeply impact the students' motivation to advance academically, and their decision to pursue post-secondary education in the future. This further has long-term effects because it can reduce people's ability to obtain a job and also impacts their ability to seek employment in sectors with well-paying salaries. Thus, starting school with this disadvantage may play a role in shaping future academic decisions.

To counter differences in children's preparation to meet the demands of school, programs have been put in place to support families from low socioeconomic backgrounds. Box 4.4 demonstrates how a US program called Head Start has made a difference in the lives of families living in poverty.

Theory in Everyday Life

4.4 | Getting a Head Start for School

As children from low-income families often struggle to keep up with the curriculum, researchers have suggested that supporting families before children start school could be beneficial. The reasoning is that once children have fallen behind it is difficult to catch up with their peers. So, programs that help children get ready for school could be effective, as they would place students on par with other children from day one.

In an American study of children's kindergarten adjustment, researchers collaborated with a program called Head Start to provide home visits and supplementary learning materials to low-income families in the hopes of reducing disparities in school achievement between middle-class children and children from low-income families (Bierman et al., 2008). Each family in the experimental group was given books, learning games, and resources for study at home to supplement the literacy and social-emotional skills being taught to them in kindergarten. Children in the experimental group demonstrated higher reading achievement and were rated more positively on their social skills than those in the control groups, indicating the value of parents reinforcing early skill development occurring at school. The study suggests that supporting low-income families with supplemental resources and targeted programs can be an effective way to help prepare children for the demands of school.

College and University

Universities are also sites of socialization and help teens move into early adulthood. Similar to schools, universities not only socialize students to become learners and be ready for the work-force, but they also socialize students into becoming engaged citizens with civic skills gained through critical thinking encouraged in the classroom and participation in extracurricular activities.

Early socialization, however, not only affects the likelihood of a person's choosing to go to uni-versity, but also influences how well a person adjusts to campus life. Social class is a key predictor of educational attainment and a student's likelihood of succeeding in university. Individuals coming from working-class families continue to encounter numerous barriers to entering university. In fact, UK data shows that white boys from working-class families are the least likely to go to university (Crawford & Greaves, 2015). Research suggests that a critical barrier faced by working-class students is integrating into a seemingly middle-class culture with expectations and social norms of behaviour (Dews & Law, 1995). Students often report feeling alienated and isolated on campus, as they try to fit in with campus culture.

Lehmann (2014) has referred to the struggles of these working-class students as the "hidden injuries of class"; he elaborates, "the students need to negotiate a precarious balance between their old and new social worlds" (p. 2). Conflicting desires to remain true to their working-class identity while also wanting to assimilate to the middle-class culture is a concern that these stu-dents face, though it is often overlooked.

For example, Lehmann (2014) studied working-class students in a Canadian university and found that a select group of students do very well in university. For these students, going to university fulfilled their hopes for **upward social mobility** and also realized the educational aspirations their parents had for them. Many students viewed university as an opportunity for learning and obtaining credentials relevant for the job market. Students, however, "not only spoke about gaining new know-ledge, but also about growing personally, changing their outlooks on life, growing their repertoire of cultural capital, and developing new dispositions and tastes about a range of issues, from food to politics and their future careers" (p. 11).

University, for this group of students, was transformative. The findings suggest that despite the many barriers that exist for individuals from working-class backgrounds to enter university, a select group adapts well to the university environment and greatly benefits from the socialization oppor-tunities provided by universities. For such students, their background served as a motivator to suc-ceed, rather than a hindrance (Lehmann, 2014). In addition, the increased levels of social and cultural capital gained through the experience are also formational and further help them in the process of workplace socialization, an important topic we will discuss next.

upward social mobility
vertical social mobility into more highly regarded and higher-paying occupational positions.

The Workplace

Early on, children learn key interpersonal skills, such as bargaining, that will be important for their future work lives. By early adolescence, they will learn the perceived social value of different profes-sions, and what sorts of educational requirements and skills they might need.

In adulthood, workplaces represent central sites for socialization. In Canada, where a stan-dard workweek consists of 40 hours, most adults working full-time will spend about half of their awake time at work (Government of Canada, 2016). In fact, the 2012 National Study on Balancing Work and Caregiving shows that almost two-thirds of Canadians are spending more than 45 hours a week at work and additional time responding to emails both after work hours and weekends (Duxbury & Higgins, 2012).

Work socialization starts with an understanding of the profession and the expectations and social roles that accompany that profession. We discussed above the importance of anticipatory so-cialization as a means to prepare oneself for the expectations of a given profession. Children try out different social roles in their imaginary play, for example, pretending to be a veterinarian dressed in a white coat and with various sophisticated instruments. Once they enter the workforce as adults, workers learn their social roles as they become socialized into their profession.

The importance of adhering to norms associated with certain professions is also learned from watching popular TV shows, such as *Suits* or *Grey's Anatomy*. In the seventh season finale of *Grey's Anatomy*, Meredith Grey, a doctor and researcher at the Seattle Grace Hospital, is caught tampering with a medical trial involving Alzheimer's patients. Her motivation to transgress from the expected norms is personal because she wants to ensure her friend—Adele Webber—does not receive a placebo. When she is found out, she is fired from the Seattle Grace Hospital and her husband, Derek Shepherd, is furious at the breach of ethical standards and the potential repercussions for their medical careers. So, professional roles are performed not only through the stereotypical dress code, hierarchical roles, and behaviours, but also by demonstrating an understanding of ethical standards and expected codes of conduct.

Workplace socialization goes beyond the norms and expectations related to a specific profession. These differences can even emerge within a single industry. Some workplaces may be more traditional and have an organizational hierarchy that dictates roles and authority structures. In

Digital Divide

4.5 | Learning to Fit into the Work Culture of a Digital Global Company

A good example of a global company that has embraced a networked structure with a flat hierarchy is Google. In their book *How Google Works*, Eric Schmidt and Jonathan Rosenberg (2014) describe the work culture within Google that has allowed the company to remain innovative and has given it a competitive edge. Schmidt describes how being part of Google is not only about mastering the digital world; it is also about fitting into Google's unique work culture. He experienced the first taste of Google's work culture on his very first day of work. When he arrived at his office, it appeared to be already occupied by several software engineers. As his office was not available, Schmidt moved into a smaller office nearby, which he describes more as a closet than an office, just to find out one morning that a co-worker had moved in with him because there wasn't enough space in his own office. As he puts it, he learned that "this was not a measure-your-importance-in-square-feet kind of place" (p. 2).

Within Google, workers are given considerable leeway because the company trusts that employees have great ideas and working on these ideas can help advance Google's goal of innovation. This leeway is part of Google's work norms, as employees are given 20 per cent of their time to work on projects of their choice. Kevin Gibbs, a Google engineer, for example, developed the Google Suggest feature in his spare time. Google Suggest is the feature where you start typing a search query and it autocompletes your search after only the first few letters. For Google, maintaining a culture of innovation and promoting values that encourage creativity and divergent thinking are critical.

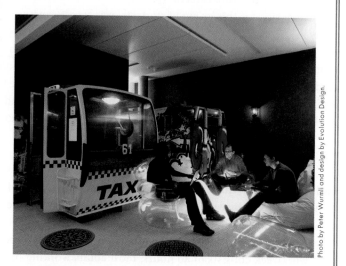

This photo is from Google's Engineering Hub in Zurich. Many young people dream of working at Google. Do you think you could fit well in Google's culture of innovation, speed, and flat hierarchy? What do you think are the challenges for a new employee of working at Google?

Source: Retrieved from www.camenzindevolution.com/Office

TABLE 4.3 Agents of Socialization

Agents	Mechanisms of socialization
Home/the family	• Transmission of family values and social norms • Learning of language and the meaning of symbols • The formation of self and identity
Kindergarten & school	• Learning of societal norms and expectations • Reinforcement of rules of socialization with peers • Learning of conformity within social settings • Anticipatory socialization
College & university	• Integration into society as an adult • Anticipatory socialization in relation to a profession • Learning about assessment frameworks and expectations of mastery
Workplace	• Learning to internalize the norms and expectations of a profession • Fitting into the culture of a workplace

Source: Author-generated

traditional work structures, the organizational chart largely dictates who communicates and reports to whom. By contrast, some workplaces have embraced new, more flexible work structures, often referred to as networked organizations, which have a flatter hierarchy and where workers are loosely connected to one another (Rainie & Wellman, 2012). Box 4.5 demonstrates Google's work culture and the socialization process that new employees undergo when they join the company.

Table 4.3 summarizes some of the key agents of socialization reviewed in this chapter and highlights key mechanisms of socialization.

Conclusions

Socialization is a process that occurs across the life course and takes place in diverse social settings. Even before children are born, socialization starts and it continues into old age. Socialization is essential for society as it guarantees the transfer of norms and values from one generation to the next through both primary and secondary socialization processes. As structural functionalists would argue, the transmission of norms through key institutions of socialization allows for stability and order.

Primary and secondary socialization may teach different norms, values, and belief systems, however, and this can lead to conflict. Parents often feel that as their children grow up, they have little control over their norms and values. Schools and peers become strong sources of socialization and children often rebel against their parents. Through this negotiation children develop a self-concept that guides their behaviours and interactions with others. While conflict between values taught at home and those learned through secondary socialization are a normal part of development, this process can be particularly challenging for immigrant and refugee families.

As we discussed with the examples of appearance norms, society can create pressures in individuals to meet almost unattainable ideals. Individuals do not simply internalize society's norms and values, however. From the perspective of symbolic interactionism, individuals engage in negotiation with the social world around them and shape their own identities. Symbolic interactionists reject an oversocialized view of the individual and give people more agency in shaping their identities. Hence, individuals constantly question and change norms and values. As a result, society constantly changes as well.

Today, science and technology have changed the institutions that influence socialization the most. New means of socialization have started to garner influence, which has opened much debate regarding how the process of socialization itself has transformed, as well as the potential negative repercussions this change has for society. Children are no longer socialized merely through family and school; they also learn from an early age about social norms through targeted children's channels such as Disney, Nickelodeon, and the Cartoon Network. Some studies estimate that children aged 10 to 14 spend as much as 8.3 hours a day online interacting with friends, consuming media content, and gaming (Pater, Miller, & Mynatt, 2015). These new forms of socialization are opening up novel questions about how socialization takes place in a digital society and the potential effect of digital media on the transfer of norms and values from one generation to the next.

Questions for Critical Thought

1. Describe the process of socialization. What complexities are involved in studying this process, and how has digital technology like Facebook and Instagram changed socialization processes?

2. Outline Cooley's main ideas of self-concept and explain the role of society in shaping a person's self-concept. What is the main criticism of Cooley's conceptualization of the self-concept?

3. Why do students coming from middle-class families do better in school than students from working-class families? Explain the various mechanisms that advantage or disadvantage students from a different social class.

4. How do people become socialized into various professions even before they start their first job?

Take it Further: Recommended Readings

P. Albanese, *Children in Canada Today*, 2nd ed. (Don Mills, ON: Oxford University Press, 2015). This book investigates the changing role of children in Canadian society and illustrates the process through which children transition through adolescence and become socially "functioning" adults.

M. Chayko, *Superconnected: The Internet, Digital Media, and Techno-Social Life* (Thousand Oaks, CA: Sage, 2016). This is a thought-provoking analysis of contemporary social life as it is shaped by the internet, social media, and mobile devices.

E. Goffman, *The Presentation of Self in Everyday Life* (Garden City, NY: Doubleday, 1959). Using the metaphor of theatrical performance, Goffman examines how individuals present themselves to others in the context of everyday life.

T. Parsons, and R.F. Bales, *Family Socialization and Interaction Processes* (Oxon: Routledge, 2007). This book describes the landmark study of small groups, with reports from a group of action theorists guided by Talcott Parsons. Parsons developed the basic framework of the theory of action from empirical observations of how people act in small groups when they are given a task.

L. Tepperman, and L. Upenieks, *Social Control* (Don Mills, ON: Oxford University Press, 2016). *Social Control* offers a clear and comprehensive introduction to the various ways in which social institutions, behaviours, and performances create social order in everyday life.

Take it Further: Recommended Online Resources

Dr. Andrew Meltzoff: Born Learning
www.youtube.com/watch?v=8aBbnz7hZsM

Contexts: The Public Face of Sociology (in association with the American Sociological Association)
https://contexts.org/

SelfieCity
http://selfiecity.net

The Society Pages
https://thesocietypages.org/#/home

Sociological Images on Pinterest by sociologist Lisa Wade and guest editors
www.pinterest.com/socimages

Toy Ads and Learning Gender
www.youtube.com/watch?v=rZn_IJoN6PI

The UN Refugee Agency: Syria Regional Refugee Response
http://data.unhcr.org/syrianrefugees/regional.php

More resources available on 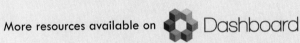 Dashboard

5

The Social Construction of Deviance and Crime

Introduction

Modern technology has made surveillance easier and more comprehensive than ever. Today, it is possible to intercept and monitor telephone calls and email in any part of the world. It is possible to hack into organizations' websites and databases, no matter how large or well-protected. It is also possible to watch people as they go about their daily business, using millions of cameras in public and private places around the world.

In short, thanks to modern technology, it is possible to monitor and therefore control people in ways we never would have imagined 50, or even 20 years ago. That's not to say that people didn't worry about the state's ability to intrude on our privacy before then. An important book published in 1949, *Nineteen Eighty-Four* by George Orwell, expressed fear of that very thing, based on what Orwell had seen and heard about life in Soviet Russia and Nazi Germany. But no one took seriously the threat of such totalitarian intrusion until computers and digital devices made round-the-clock snooping possible.

As a result, today we need to consider the issues of deviance, crime, and control in a different way than in the past. Just as computers and related devices have given rise to new kinds of deviance and crime—for example, all-caps texting, email spam, phishing, cyberbullying, and hacking—they have also given rise to new kinds of social control. What boundaries should we set around the state's power to control our behaviour through constant surveillance, while remaining mindful of the need to prevent and punish crime? And what kinds of new deviance will we take seriously enough to view as crimes?

Here, a few definitions are needed. By **deviance**, we mean any behaviour that is thought to violate a widely held *social norm*. Thus, deviance is a wide category of behaviours that includes **criminality** (i.e., the violation of criminal laws) but also includes forms of behaviour that elicit milder forms of social disapproval—for example, burping in public or wearing the "wrong" clothes to a formal dinner. Of the two, then, crime is less common than deviance, but it receives more attention because it has the power to seriously victimize people and, for this reason, is controlled by the state, through police, courts, prisons, and the like.

Not all deviant acts are visible to the public. Similarly, not all crimes are visible; and of those crimes that are visible, only a few are reported to the police. The fraction reported to the police depends on the particular crime. Most people report homicides, attempted homicides, and major property losses. On the other hand, few people report minor thefts, threats, and minor assaults. Also, there are debates about how many sexual assault cases are reported, but the number is thought to be low.

Moreover, police have considerable discretion over what cases they pursue and how they record them. This means that changes in crime statistics can have multiple causes: for example, we can have a decrease in crimes committed, in crimes reported, and in crimes recorded by the police, depending on how the statistics were measured. This variation is referred to as the crime funnel (see Figure 5.1). Sociologists study crime statistics while keeping the crime funnel in mind, and often do their own research to get more representative data.

deviance any behaviour that diverges from usual or accepted standards and, in doing so, violates social rules.

criminality behaviour that violates criminal laws.

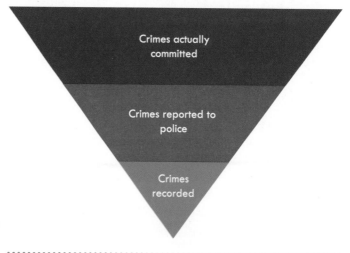

FIGURE 5.1 The Crime Funnel

Source: Author-generated.

Varieties of Deviant Behaviour

It is actually very easy to break society's rules—to become a deviant—even if you don't mean to do so. Consider appearance deviance—violating social expectations about how a person is supposed to look. These violations may include less acceptable or usual ways of dressing—for example, punk culture, tattooing, and piercing are means of deviating from conventional appearance norms. They also include obesity, anorexia, and other kinds of disapproved-of appearance.

Appearance deviations vary widely, but they have a few similar features. First, they all violate prevailing cultural standards, though cultural standards change over time and vary from one society to another. Second, they all lead to negative judgments, and sometimes even **stigmatization** and exclusion. Third, appearance deviations often give rise to deviant communities and *subcultures*, as responses to this stigmatization.

With appearance norms as with other norms, one outcome—sometimes intentional and sometimes unintentional—is the **regulation** of people's appearances and the achievement of the appearance of uniformity (as with the requirement that students wear uniforms in some schools.) However, as Michel Foucault and others have pointed out, increasingly in modern society, regulation is internalized through a process he calls **governmentality**, so that this regularity process is made a personal responsibility and a requirement for being viewed as "normal."

Clearly, there are many ways to deviate in appearance. Some kinds of appearance deviation are largely social in their origins—that is, carried out intentionally to imitate others or to indicate belonging to a particular group—while some are involuntary. Finally, some kinds of appearance deviation violate deeply held ideals about beauty or propriety, while some merely violate common, current practices.

For most of us, the mass media influences at least some of our ideas about appearances. However, appearance norms are far from realistic. To meet or even exceed these unrealistic norms, some people carry out dangerous and sometimes life-threatening strategies, such as eating disorders, skin bleaching, and cosmetic surgery.

stigmatization disgrace and marginalization because of life circumstances, or physical or social characteristics of a person that prevent them from being fully socially accepted.

regulation the process of controlling people through the creation and enforcement of social rules.

governmentality coined by Michel Foucault, the way in which the state exercises control over, or governs, its citizenry.

Video: *Miss Representation*

Women (and men) are bombarded with images that push people to conform to unrealistic beauty standards in mass media. Both physical world and digital spaces are filled with these images.

Sociology 2.0

5.1 | Challenging the Norm

Despite the ability of the internet and social media to strengthen appearance norms, creative women manage to use these platforms to show new kinds of beauty—"defining beauty on their own terms" (Porteous, 2015). One example of this is Herself.com, a website founded by *Reign* actress Caitlin Stasey (Bahadur, 2015). Stasey created Herself.com to share powerful, non-sexual images of women. The images are accompanied by personal stories about the women's histories and personal adversities (Bahadur, 2015). Stasey's goal was to create a space for women to reclaim their bodies and to be seen "through no other lens but their own" (Bahadur, 2015).

Another platform seeking to challenge appearance norms is the What's Underneath Project, a multimedia platform created in 2009 by Elisa Goodkind and Lily Mandelbaum (Southard Ospina, n.d.). The What's Underneath Project began as part of the body positivity movement. It aims to show what is "underneath all the baggage" of "social stigma" and "body hate" in a society that values rigidly held beauty ideals of nearly unattainable thinness; the message of the project is that real beauty is not what you wear, but who you are (Southard Ospina, n.d.). The platform features videos discussing issues of self-image, identity, and gender (StyleLikeU, n.d.).

One of the most powerful anti-appearance norm movements has been the #fatkini movement on Instagram and Twitter. A fatkini is a bikini made for and worn by plus-size women (Pérez, 2014). By sharing selfies on social media platforms, plus-size women have stood against society's current appearance and beauty norms for women, in this way earning the support of the online community. Placing hashtags like #losehatenotweight allows plus-size women to use social media as a forum to celebrate their bodies and "elevate the visibility" of diverse body types. The rising visibility of diverse body types has, in turn, caused retailers such as Forever 21 to create products that are suited to all body types, making bikinis for plus-size women more accessible (Pérez, 2014).

Social media are even challenging beauty norms in the modelling industry. Take the case of Canadian Winnie Harlow, born Chantelle Brown-Young. Harlow, diagnosed with vitiligo, a skin pigmentation disease, was bullied so

severely that she had to drop out of school (Jamshed, 2016). In 2011, however, she was inspired to post a YouTube video titled "Vitiligo: A Skin Condition, Not a Life Changer," and its popularity on social media brought her to the attention of top model Tyra Banks, who then invited Harlow to compete on *America's Next Top Model*. Although she did not win that contest, Harlow is now a highly sought after model and the face of Spanish fashion label Desigual (Jamshed, 2016). So, by allowing women to show themselves as they are and embrace each other's differences, social media have challenged appearance and beauty norms—allowing for more and more women to appreciate their own unique beauty.

Winnie Harlow challenged beauty norms using social media and is now a mainstream model. In what ways is Winnie Harlow an example of deviance?

Appearance norms affect everyone, but women tend to feel the effect most strongly. This is because, historically, women have been most valued (by men) for their perceived beauty and associated fertility. The scrutiny of women's adherence to appearance norms in popular magazines and blogs, for example, helps reinforce the evaluation of a woman's worth based on her appearance. These norms control women's behaviour more effectively than any written laws or regulations (e.g., school dress codes) could. In her now famous article "Visual Pleasure and Narrative Cinema," Laura Mulvey (1975) discusses how film is used to reinforce social norms of sexual desire and present women as sexual objects. Mulvey explains that in movies, women are subject to the "male gaze"—a certain camera angle or shot that makes it clear that the woman being depicted is there to be viewed as a sexual object, and as a symbol of male desire (Mulvey, 1975). The audience is forced to view the female characters from the same point of view as the other characters in the film and so the women appear as erotic objects not only to the movie characters but to the viewer as well (Mulvey, 1975). Although Mulvey's article was written in 1975, it is easy to see that the male gaze still persists in movies to this day.

Even though most people strive, most of the time, to obey appearance norms, some people cannot help but fall short. These appearance deviations show that people can become deviants—that is, they can be labelled and stigmatized and excluded as deviants —even if they do not want to be.

Sexual deviance is another type of deviance that illustrates the range of the concept of deviance. Prostitution is one example of what our society sees as sexual deviance. By calling prostitution immoral and stigmatizing people who practise it, our society clarifies the boundaries between acceptable and unacceptable behaviour. In turn, the defence of these boundaries increases **social cohesion**, as people bond over their perceived morality or immorality.

According to conflict theorists, prostitution reflects gender inequality because through the exploitation of women, men can gain income, pleasure, or both (since the vast majority of prostitutes are women who provide sex for men). Conflict theory also proposes that prostitution is usually a result of poverty. Typically, women (and occasionally men) who resort to prostitution lack access to legitimate means to earn the money they need. In many instances, prostitutes are children, teenagers, drug addicts, or vulnerable people with a history of abuse.

Survey results (Abramovich, 2005) show that both male and female sex workers are likely to have experienced high rates of physical and sexual abuse in childhood, as well as parental **substance abuse**. The result is a spread of sex work among adolescents with its attendant problems (Bamgbose, 2002). In Canada, 10 to 15 per cent of street sex workers are under the age of 18, while the average age of entry into the sex trade is between 14 and 15. However, the age of entry for Indigenous women is between 13 and 14, which indicates that social forces can impact when girls enter sex work (McClanahan, McClelland, Abram, & Teplin, 1999).

Sex work—and prostitution in particular—has long divided feminist thinking. Many feminists condemn the practice and advocate solutions to help individual women leave this way of life. As the sex industry is very exploitative, feminists have good reasons to criticize it. However, this stance does not prevent them from supporting more social rights and protections for sex workers.

But does prostitution benefit society even while it exploits a particular segment of society? Structural functional sociologist Kingsley Davis (1937) noted eighty years ago that prostitution fills the need for sexual satisfaction without imposing the socioeconomic ties of relationship and marriage. When other intimate arrangements fail or are unavailable, prostitution fills a biological (or psychological) need. The use of prostitutes is less dangerous to marriage than extramarital infidelity of the kind Ashley Madison encourages, so it persists even though it is widely disapproved of.

In Canada, prostitution itself is not illegal. In a landmark ruling in December 2013, the Supreme Court of Canada declared the then-current laws, which made it illegal to live off prostitution profits, operate a brothel, and solicit customers on the street, unconstitutional. According to the court, each of these provisions threatened the safety of prostitutes. The first prevents prostitutes from employing drivers and bodyguards, who would earn their living from the profits of prostitution. The second prevents them from working in safer indoor locations, and the third deprives them the opportunity to screen out potentially dangerous clients.

Different countries have different strategies to deal with prostitution. In the United States, both buying and selling sex is considered criminal (everywhere but Nevada, home of Las Vegas—the self-proclaimed fun and sin capital of America). In Sweden, selling sex is not a criminal offence, but buying sex is. On the other hand, in the Netherlands, buying and selling sex is legal and is regulated by the government, and there is formal registration for sex workers. Finally, in New Zealand, buying and selling sex are both legal, but there is little government regulation of the activity. So far,

sexual deviance any behaviour that involves individuals seeking erotic gratification through means a community (or its most influential citizens) considers odd, different, or unacceptable.

social cohesion the existence of bonds of trust that bind people together in a community or society, enabling co-operation and interdependence.

substance abuse excessive use of, or dependence on, an addictive substance, especially alcohol or drugs.

5.2 | Trafficking in Sex Workers

Everywhere, prostitution thrives on human suffering: poverty, war, and social dislocation, and much of global prostitution is the result of human trafficking. In India, for instance, some have estimated that as many as 50 per cent of female sex workers have ended up in that work through human trafficking (Decker et al., 2013).

The rapid growth and spread of the international sex trade is linked to several factors, including the rise in service occupations, temporary work, and corporate-fuelled consumption; an increase in labour migrations, tourism, and business travel; the connection between the information economy and the privatization of commercial consumption; and new forms of gender, sexuality, and kinship (Bernstein, 2007).

The relationship between sex workers and their clients is always unequal. And everywhere, sex work infiltrates the family life of sex workers. Whether in Uganda, India, or Mexico, many female sex workers must constantly switch between the respected role of mother and the disrespected role of prostitute. In doing so, they face society's double standard for women on a daily basis. Often, they must even hide their profession from their families to avoid punishment for breaching the ideal of female purity. As a result, they lead split lives, dividing their personalities between the mother/saint and prostitute/sinner roles and identities.

there is no clear indication of which strategy works best. That said, there is some indication that making prostitution illegal with little state oversight is likely to cause problems and dangers for the sex workers.

As a third domain of deviance, consider the "abuse" of various drugs that alter consciousness, such as alcohol, marijuana, cocaine, and heroin. These substances all change a person's mental state. Sometimes, this leads to serious health risks for the user and for others. In Canada and elsewhere, the use of legal drugs such as alcohol, tobacco, and prescription medicine is much more common and potentially more dangerous than the use of illegal drugs such as marijuana, heroin, and cocaine. Yet, our society focuses on illegal drug use as a problem while ignoring the harm done by legal drugs. This seeming irrationality reminds us that we socially construct all crime and deviance. We choose to ignore certain problems and heighten the significance of others.

Nowhere is this more obvious than in our view of drug abuse and drug addicts. In the media, people addicted to "hard" drugs are often portrayed as crazed, irrational, irresponsible, and unable to care for themselves. This is one way in which the media increases attention to illegal drug use and increases public anxiety about this matter.

moral panic a condition resulting from social concern over an issue that provokes intense feelings and fears; usually the work of moral entrepreneurs, this is often an overreaction to certain deviant or unfamiliar behaviours.

We can understand the drug debate as a form of **moral panic** about drug use. By moral panic we mean any popular controversy or dispute that provokes feelings and fears so intense they threaten the social order. Stanley Cohen, author of *Folk Devils and Moral Panics* (1972), is credited with creating the term. According to Cohen (1972) a moral panic occurs when a "condition, episode, person or group of persons emerges to become defined as a threat to societal values and interests" (p. 9) (see Figure 5.2).

Throughout history, people in power have made efforts to approve or disapprove, legalize or criminalize various kinds of drugs. These actions have rarely been a result of medical or scientific reasons alone. Usually, they have reflected prejudices against the people who customarily use these drugs. Furthermore, laws have often protected the interests of large corporations that manufacture and sell certain drugs, such as alcoholic beverages, tobacco products, and prescription drugs.

From the standpoint of deviance research, drugs and alcohol show us how important it is to understand the cultural politics that determine our laws and enforcement practices. Current ideas of what is moral or not also vary over time and place; likewise, religious and scientific claims influence what is labelled as healthy or dangerous, normal or abnormal, legal or illegal.

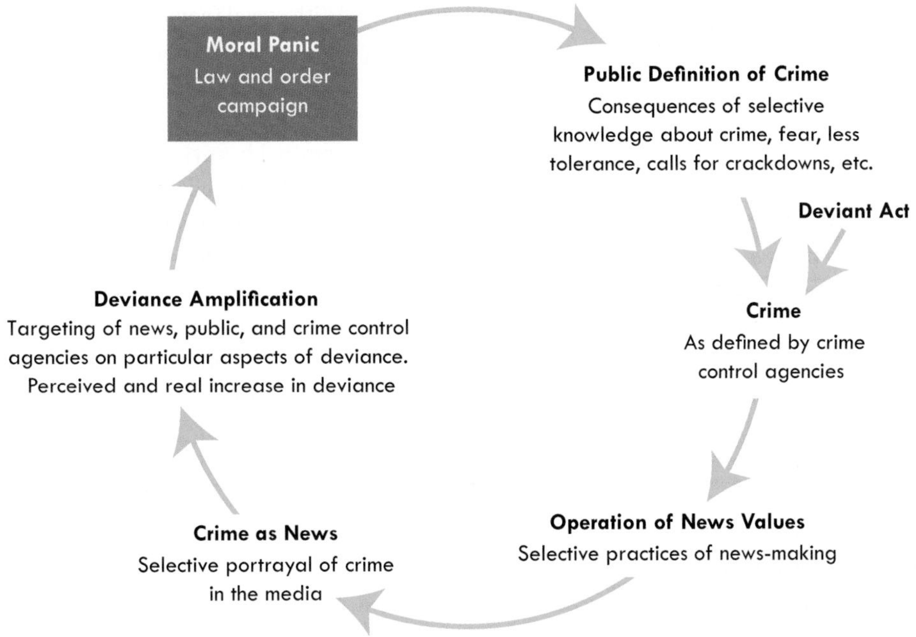

FIGURE 5.2 Creating a Moral Panic

Source: Author-generated.

Time to reflect

Have your opinions changed over time around particular deviant behaviours? Is there anything that, five years ago, you would have sworn you'd never do or want to be around, but that you do regularly now, or that your friends do that you are okay with? If so, what was it that changed your mind?

Theoretical Approaches to Deviance

In general, sociologists who study deviance and crime assume that deviance is the unusual (i.e., occasional) behaviour of normal people or the usual behaviour of normal people in deviant roles or abnormal situations. Rule-breaking may even be rational for people who lack an equal opportunity to benefit from the existing rules of society. For example, it may be perfectly rational for unemployed or marginalized people to commit property crimes.

Thus, sociological approaches to deviance and crime are different from psychological approaches, and look for answers outside the individual actors. They tend to focus on the three Cs—careers, cultures, and communities. That said, sociologists vary in their approaches to deviance and crime.

Conflict Theory

Some kinds of people and some kinds of activities are more likely to be defined as deviant or criminal, as social problems, than others. Consider the role of laws in defining and controlling crime. Laws are an important part of society but they also often support and promote social inequality. For example, corporate, commercial, and property laws best serve the interests of people with the most wealth or investments. Not surprisingly, criminal laws are also written in the interests of these people with the most to lose.

Conflict theorists propose that powerful members of society make and enforce the laws to their own advantage. Because of this, less powerful members of society must sometimes break these laws to gain their own advantage, or at least, to level the playing field. With social inequality in mind, conflict theories view rule-breaking as rational behaviour, given most people's limited opportunities and a societal goal of material success.

From this standpoint, Robert Merton's famous **strain theory** (also known as **anomie theory**) has connections to the conflict approach, since it contends that criminal behaviour—for example, theft and robbery—may result from the lack of legitimate opportunities combined with a wish for material success. This theory proposes that, given the universal (culturally learned) desire for material success, people who are denied socially acceptable opportunities will likely break the rules.

Merton urges us to think of criminal behaviour as a form of innovation—a creative adaptation to limited opportunities for legitimate success. Just as we find with criminals and other deviants, in order to innovate, there needs to be motive and opportunity. In part, opportunities and motives are socially structured, with the result that in some societies and some periods of history, a lot of innovation takes place while, in other periods and places, there is much less.

Feminist Theory

Like conflict theory, feminist theory also focuses on relations of inequality—in this case, relations of dominance and subordination between men and women. We've already discussed how deviance can be gendered (see the discussion of appearance norms earlier), so we'll consider crime here. Recent years have seen a gradual increase in documented criminal activity by women, but in terms of crime, a gender gap between men and women remains. In Canada over the past several decades, female offenders have accounted for less than 0.25 per cent of completed court cases (Mahony, 2011).

Women are less likely to commit every kind of crime, but there are also certain crimes that women are somewhat more likely to commit than men, as Table 5.1 illustrates. So, for example, women are more likely to commit fraud, simple assault, or harassing phone calls than murder, kidnapping or armed robbery.

strain theory (anomie theory) rooted in Émile Durkheim's notion of anomie and elaborated by Robert K. Merton in his typology of modes of adaptation, this theory proposes that deviant behaviour results from unequal opportunities and is a function of the gap between norms of success and access to the legitimate means of achieving them.

TABLE 5.1 Number and Rate of Youth and Adults Accused by Police, by Sex and Type of Crime (Select Crimes), 2009

Interactive activity

Criminal Code violation	Female accused (rate per 100,000)	Male accused (rate per 100,000)
Total Criminal Code violations (including traffic)	1,580.3	5,403.1
Homicide	0.4	3.3
Sexual assaults—all levels	1.7	72.7
Assault Level 3—aggravated	3.4	18.4
Assault Level 2—weapon or bodily harm	55.2	203.2
Assault Level 1	222.3	685.2
Forcible confinement, kidnapping, or abduction	2.7	28.2
Robbery	11.8	88.9
Threatening or harassing phone calls	24.7	38.1
Uttering threats	62.3	252.7
Arson	2.0	13.0
Break and enter	32.5	260.9
Theft over $5000	4.3	11.5
Theft $5000 or under	323.7	573.0
Fraud	72.5	148.4
Prostitution	9.2	11.5

Source: Adapted from Mahony, 2011, p. 184

Carlen (1990) suggests that women are more likely than men to commit property crimes, theft, and fraud because these petty crimes are reflective of their traditionally powerless status in society (see also Smart, 1991). Women who commit these crimes often grew up in hostile environments, where this powerless feeling was structurally perpetuated by the class system, patriarchy, and racism they experienced. As a result, the women who turn to these petty crimes seek to abolish their powerless feeling (Smart, 1991).

A gender gap also exists in terms of victimization. In the context of deviance and crime, the issue of victimization is of central concern among feminist sociologists. Victimization refers to the experience of being made a victim of a crime or unjust treatment such as sexism or racism. Feminist researchers examine the ways that women are targets of victimizing behaviour on multiple levels.

A woman who is the victim of sexual assault, for example, may be victimized again when she reports the crime and makes a statement to police—a process that often arouses feelings of shame and guilt, particularly if the interview is handled badly by the interviewing officer. Later, in court, she may be victimized again when she is forced to relive the experience, often in the presence of her male attacker. She may also have the crime presented in a way that makes her the subject of blame. Feminist researchers document cases in which victims are depicted as deviant (in courts and in the media, for instance) in order to diminish the gravity of the criminally deviant behaviour of which they are truly victims.

Women are more often victims of rape and sexual harassment than men. For the reasons mentioned earlier, however, many sexual assaults go unreported (Heath, Lynch, Fritch, & Wong, 2013). As well, many sexual assault cases brought to the police are dismissed as "unfounded," which means they do not count towards reported cases even though the victim tried to report the crime, Evidence suggests that as many as half of these cases should never have been designated "unfounded" at all (Doolittle, 2017).

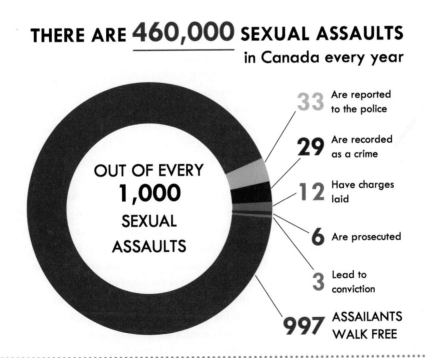

THERE ARE 460,000 SEXUAL ASSAULTS in Canada every year

OUT OF EVERY **1,000** SEXUAL ASSAULTS

33 Are reported to the police

29 Are recorded as a crime

12 Have charges laid

6 Are prosecuted

3 Lead to conviction

997 ASSAILANTS WALK FREE

As the image from the YWCA illustrates, very few sexual assaults result in a punishment of the offender. As *Globe and Mail* journalist Kirk Makin has reported, the numbers are discouraging: every 17 minutes a woman in Canada is forced to have sex; 80 per cent of all sexual assaults happen in the victims' own homes; 62 per cent of victims are physically injured in these attacks; 98 per cent of charges for sexual assault are laid for only the least severe form of assault; and on average, convicted sexual assault offenders are sentenced to only two years in jail. A majority go free.

H. Johnson, 2012. Based on research by Dr. Holly Johnson, copyright of YWCA Canada, used with permission.

Across all provinces in Canada, women are more likely to be victims of sexual offences than men. The greatest difference between male and female victims exists in Manitoba (Sinha, 2013). Even among women, however, certain groups are more likely to be targeted than others. Young women, for example, may be more likely to experience sexual violence because they are more likely to participate in recreational activities and come into contact with potential male perpetrators (Cass, 2007; Myhill & Allen, 2002). Indigenous women are also relatively more likely to experience sexual violence. In 2009 sexual assaults accounted for less than 10 per cent of crimes committed against non-Indigenous women, while they accounted for 33 per cent of violent crimes committed against Indigenous women (Brennan, 2011). In addition, women who have physical abilities or are disabled are two times more likely to be victims of sexual assault than non-disabled persons (Perreault & Brennan, 2010).

Even more unsettling about sexual harassment is the fact that, in most cases, the female victims know their attackers. According to Statistics Canada (Allen, 2016), 88 per cent of all sexual harassment and rape victims knew their attacker: 44 per cent of victims knew their attacker as an acquaintance, 38 per cent knew their attacker as a family member, and 6 per cent knew their attacker as an intimate partner. What is also troubling is the fact that as technology continues to expand, many perpetrators are using the internet and social media to meet their victims. In fact, one in five American teenagers claim they have "received an unwanted sexual solicitation via the Web" (Jessica's Law Now blog, 2011).

The problem of victimization is a central concern of feminist sociology. Since women have often been victimized by men, feminists have been especially interested in victimization and the experiences of other victimized groups. Examples of other victimized groups include poor people, racial minorities, disabled people, and people of alternative sexual orientations. Following from this, feminists have been especially interested in **intersectionality**—the interaction of gender with other victimizing social characteristics, such as class and racialized identity, to produce particular combinations of disadvantage.

Functionalism

Functionalists like Durkheim view deviance both as universal and beneficial to society. Punishments for deviance (either official state punishments such as jail time, or unofficial sanctions such as being socially ostracized) remind people of the need to obey society's rules. So, in this roundabout way, deviants encourage people to stay within moral boundaries of society. Do you agree with this view?

Durkheim also thought that people need social order and social rules; when people do not have stable, clear social rules, they suffer from what he calls "anomie." Consequences of anomie include an increase in social distress and suicide rates. According to Durkheim, the reduction of anomie is one reason why religious people are happier, and less likely to commit suicide, than non-religious people.

A more current version of the functionalist approach is control theory. Social control theorists think that people follow rules when they believe they will benefit from them—that is, they have "a stake in conformity" (Toby, 1957). This theory assumes that anyone may have deviant impulses, but for most people these impulses are not acted upon, with the result that most people do *not* break the rules, most of the time. People conform to the rules because they want and need the rewards conformity brings and fear or dislike the punishments for deviance (see Figure 5.3).

A key factor in this theory is the internalization of social norms and learning of social control. Avoidance of delinquency allows people to build strong social bonds to significant others and conventional institutions. A failure in early life to build conforming bonds and, conversely, the building of delinquent bonds may lock people into a criminal career or participation in criminal subculture. However, people may sometimes transition out of this career or cultural pattern after undergoing a key life event, such as marriage or entering the paid labour force. These events can lead to the formation of new social bonds that impose controls on behaviour and reduce the risk of further deviant behaviours.

Hirschi's *Causes of Delinquency* (1969/2002) is perhaps the most influential early statement of control theory. He reports that a child's relationship with his or her parents is the most important factor in determining his or her involvement in delinquent activities. Children who are weakly bonded to their parents are the most likely to commit delinquent acts. In general, he argues, social control works

intersectionality a theoretical approach that examines the interconnection of social categories—especially, social disadvantages—related to ethnicity, class, and gender that creates more complex, interdependent systems of oppression and disadvantage.

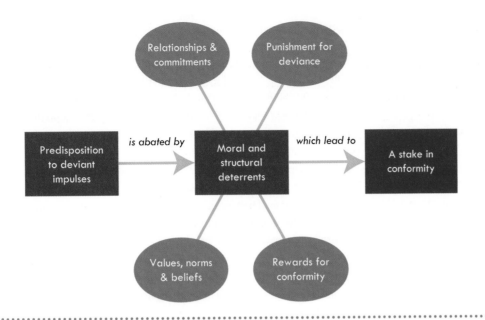

FIGURE 5.3 Social Control Theory

Source: Author-generated

through the "social bond" developed between an individual and larger society. This bond has four elements: belief (in conventional values), attachment (to others and a sensitivity to their opinions), commitment (to the social rewards of conformity), and involvement (in conventional activities).

Symbolic Interactionism

Another key concern for sociologists of deviance is why, and how, people take on a deviant identity, thus truly "becoming deviant." This question has had a great appeal for symbolic interactionists, for whom the "self"—a person's identity—is an important topic of inquiry.

Symbolic interactionists in the 1950s and 1960s started asking questions about how deviance was defined and who got to make the decisions about what was defined as deviant. These sociologists concluded that deviance was a social label that some groups use to stigmatize other groups. Labelling theory, as it came to be called, concluded that being fixed with a deviant label may increase deviant behaviour due to the label's negative impacts on one's social status, "life chances," and sense of self.

For symbolic interactionists, we learn how to participate in society while we are children. We do this through social games, coordinated roles, and anticipating and responding to the role-play of others. Sociologist Edwin Sutherland (1939) was one of the first to propose that people learn deviance—even crime—through normal processes of socialization.

Specifically, he maintained that people learn both conforming and deviant behaviour through their relationships with others. Deviance is learned through communication with, and rewards from, people who engage in deviant behaviour. We develop patterns of deviant behaviour by developing favourable definitions of deviance, in comparison to unfavourable ones. Sutherland called this differential association theory because it rests on the general principle that our behaviours will reflect the relative importance of our different associations, both deviant and conforming.

Time to reflect

What behaviours have you learned from your family? Your friends? Your community, in person or online? Do your behaviours come from one particular source more than another, or have your different associations informed your different behaviours?

TABLE 5.2 Theoretical Approaches to Deviance

Conflict Theory	• Conflicting groups promote opposing notions of "deviance" and "crime," which often results in intensified conflict. • Crime is a response to conflict, change, and inequality. • Social inequality increases the likelihood of self-interested crime.
Feminist Theory	• Feminist theory notes that female criminality is increasing, yet it remains different from male criminality. • Men are disproportionally perpetrators of violence, women are disproportionally victims of violence. • Patterns of criminal behaviour and institutional control largely reflect gendered differences in the treatment and perception of women more generally in society.
Functionalism	• Well-functioning societies require consensus, social cohesion, and social control. • Social change or inequality may create social disorganization and strain, sometimes leading to deviance and crime. • Crime strengthens social cohesion by uniting people through their shared values.
Symbolic Interactionism	• Deviance is a social accomplishment and rarely is practised solo. • Socialization and labelling shape deviant identities and subcultures. • Social problems like crime are social constructs framed by **moral entrepreneurs**.

moral entrepreneurs promoters of "morality" who use their resources as rule-makers, campaigners, and enforcers to shape public policy.

Symbolic interactionists also examine how all social problems—deviance and crime included—are constructed through social processes. In other words, social problems (e.g., crime waves) are social constructions. The social construction approach examines how certain activities or sets of events come to be defined as social problems. Only some potential problems are defined as problems, while many others are not.

Crime: A Special Case of Deviance

Case study

Sociologists study crime because it often has significant consequences for people's safety, health, and general well-being. Victims of crime often lose trust in the existing social institutions and reduce their participation in community life.

People tend to worry most about violent rule-breaking and especially violent crimes. No wonder then that, despite failing rates of homicide and other "severe" crimes, violence continues to receive extensive media coverage both as news and as entertainment. Violent crimes that do occur are most often attacks by family members or friends. It is because of media distortion that Canadians tend to think that homicide is more common than it is, and that it is most often committed by strangers.

Violent Crime

Today, the absolute numbers of violent crimes are high—1.9 million Criminal Code incidents (excluding traffic) in 2015—but the rates are lower than one or two decades ago. For example, Statistics Canada (Allen, 2016) reports that in 2015 the following trends were evident:

- For the first time in 12 years, the Crime Severity Index (CSI), which measures the volume and severity of police-reported crime in Canada, increased by 1 per cent from the previous year, due mainly to an increase in fraud, breaking and entering, robbery, and homicide.

- The overall volume and severity of violent crime, as measured by the violent CSI, increased about 6 per cent, mainly due to increases in robbery, homicide, attempted murder, and violent firearms offences.
- The homicide rate increased from about 1.45 homicides per 100,000 population in 2014 to 1.68 in 2015.
- The overall rate of Controlled Drugs and Substances Act violations continued to decline in 2015 from the previous year, due to fewer drug offences involving cannabis and cocaine.
- In contrast, the Youth Crime Severity rate and rate of youth accused of crimes continued to decrease, primarily due to the decrease in non-violent crimes such as theft.

Source: Allen, 2016

As these and other statistics show, almost all crime rates have been decreasing in the past decade and only recently have seen a small surge. For less serious crimes, we cannot be certain that variations in arrest rates, over time or from place to place, reflect variations in criminal behaviour or variations in police behaviour. For example, an increase in people being charged with a particular crime might reflect an increase in people perpetrating the crime. However, it might also simply be a result of a change in policy regarding how officers exercise their discretion regarding that particular crime—choosing to formally charge perpetrators rather than letting them go with a warning. However, more severe crimes, such as murder, robbery, and sexual assault, are subject to much less police discretion, so declines in the rate of severe crime (see Figure 5.4) are much less subject to such distortion due to variations in police discretion.

Though we do not have reliable statistics over an extended period, it seems likely that violent crime is indeed much less common today than it was a century ago (on this, see Pinker, 2011). Violence occurs when society lacks stable, accepted, non-violent means to achieve desired results. A decrease in violence means that society has non-violent means to achieve results. Therefore, as violence declines, civility increases. With civility comes the development of nation-states (see, e.g., Elias, 1978). Nation-states bring about the "rule of law" through written codes, courts, prisons, police officers, and soldiers.

Age and gender are also important factors in violent crime: young men are more likely than older men or women of any age to commit violent acts. Because of this, a society's crime rate tends to reflect changes in the proportion of young men in the population. As the proportion of young people in a

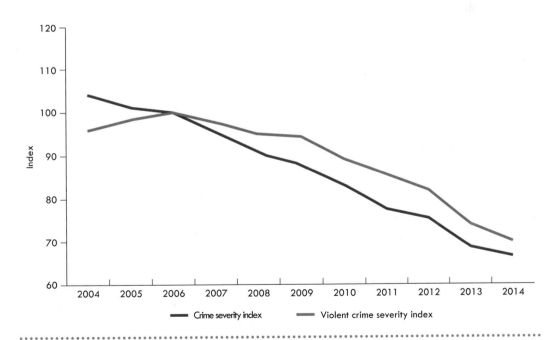

FIGURE 5.4 Police-Reported Crime Severity Indexes, 2004–2014

Note: Additional data are available on CANSIM (Table 252–0052). Crime Severity Indexes are based on Criminal Code incidents, including traffic offences, as well as other federal statute violations. The base index was set at 100 for 2006 for Canada. Populations are based upon 1 July estimates from Statistics Canada, Demography Division.

Source: Retrieved from www.statcan.gc.ca/pub/85-002-x/2015001/article/14211-eng.htm

Theory in Everyday Life

5.3 | Can Technological Entertainment Lessen Crime?

Technological development advances at a rapid pace. However, people debate whether this rapid change is beneficial for society. For example, technological innovation can inspire crime by giving rise to more tech-savvy and innovative criminals. Yet, surprisingly, despite increasing uses of information technology (and opportunities for technology-related crime), crime rates are dropping.

According to Statistics Canada (2017), crime rates have continued to drop for the past 35 years, reaching a current level lower than any seen since 1969. The significant decline in reported criminal behaviour is largely due to the decline in the size of one particular age group—youth aged 18 to 24. Using Statistics Canada data accumulated between 2009 and 2013, *Maclean's* reports 23 to 31 per cent declines in robbery, motor vehicle theft, aggravated assault, and breaking charges—all crimes usually committed by youths (indeed, male youths). Likewise, the number of charges laid for homicide has dropped by 29 per cent (McKnight, 2015).

Other criminologists explain the declining crime rates through the crime substitution hypothesis. This hypothesis proposes that other activities may be taking the place of crime. For example, some information- and communication-technology-based forms of entertainment may be taking the place of gang- and crime-related activities (McKnight, 2015). Stated simply, the enormous amount of time young people spend in cyberspace may be lessening the amount of time they have to commit crimes in "meatspace" (i.e., the physical world) (McKnight, 2015). More research will be needed to determine whether this hypothesis is accurate. It may turn out to be the case that, thanks to video games and social media, youth who might otherwise turn to crime-related activities are being kept safely occupied indoors. What do you think?

---

society shrinks through lower birth rates, the rate of violent crime can be expected to shrink as well. Thus, it should come as no surprise that, according to Statistics Canada (2017), between 2004 and 2014, the fall in serious crime mirrors the decline of the proportion of men in the population aged 15 to 35.

subculture theory the theory that certain groups or subcultures in society have values and attitudes that are conducive to deviance, crime, or violence.

Subculture theory helps to explain why arguments between young males, for example, are the most common forerunner to homicide in our own society and elsewhere. This is because young men are socialized towards identities and subcultures that encourage them to challenge each other in violent competitions for honour and respect.

This practice is most evident among inner-city youth who live according to a street code where members of the culture gain respect through violence. In these subcultures, guns symbolize respect, power, identity, and manhood. As such, they play a central role in youth violence. Youth who are regularly exposed to violence, are gang members themselves, have family members or friends who are gang members, and have peer support for violence come to view violence as "suitable" behaviour. In these subcultures, males who are not violent are, ironically, likely to be threatened with violence.

Criminologists know enough about crime to make several observations. First, there is more fear about violent crime than actual occurrence of violent crime. Second, violent crimes most often result from fights between spouses or friends. Third, some people are more likely to commit violent crimes than others—in particular, young, poor men. To some degree, this demographic link is influenced by economic and social variables. Poor young men are more likely than other people to be out of school, unemployed, and without significant social responsibilities or opportunities.

Non-Violent Crime

The goal of most non-violent crime is to get money or property, not to inflict harm. Here, we include white-collar (or suite) crime and amateur (or street) crime.

Non-violent crimes—both professional and amateur—are more common than violent crimes. As we said earlier, violent crimes often are committed against friends, acquaintances, or family members.

Think Globally

5.4 | Variations in Homicide around the World

For many reasons—economic, cultural, social, and demographic—violent crime rates vary widely from one society to another. This includes variation in the rates of homicide, which are relatively (compared to other kinds of crime) well-measured in every society. The data in Figure 5.5 shows that the United States has the highest homicide rate; there, much of the killing is attributable to an easy, relatively unregulated firearm availability. On the other hand, Canada—with fewer homicides than the United States per capita—has far more homicides than Japan and several European nations, such as Switzerland, Germany, and Sweden.

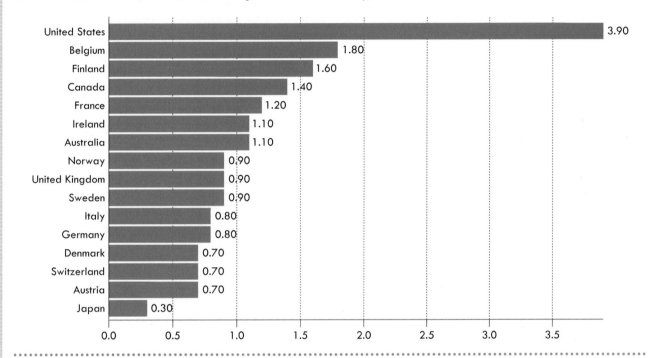

FIGURE 5.5 Rates of Homicide in Selected Countries, 2013

Source: Retrieved from http://data.worldbank.org/indicator/VC.IHR.PSRC.P5?end=2013&locations=CA-SE-US-GB-CN-JP-DE-NO-FI-BE-FR-AU-AT-IE-IT-CH-DK&start=2013&view=bar&year_high_desc=false

Time to reflect

What, besides the availability of firearms, might explain these variations between countries? Use your sociological imagination to try to list other variables that you hypothesize would correlate to gun violence by country.

Non-violent crimes, on the other hand, are more often committed against strangers. Non-violent crimes are seemingly based on a rational calculation of costs and benefit. In fact, they are ways of making a living. As in other occupations, many of these criminal activities are learned through observation, apprenticeship, and imitation.

In comparison to juvenile delinquency, violent (domestic) crime, and amateur (street) crime, professional crime—for example, a career in automobile theft or embezzlement—is well organized. At the pinnacle of organized crime are transnational criminal organizations such as the Mafia. Crimes committed by members of these criminal organizations are sometimes violent. However, most of the violence associated with organized crime is directed by professional criminals against other professional criminals. The most profitable business activities of such organizations are non-violent. Examples of

Spotlight On

5.5 | Shopping Online and Credit Card Hackers

New technology has changed the way we think about shopping. Unfortunately, however, it has also changed the way thieves think about stealing. Credit card information theft has been an issue for decades, with purse snatchers stealing people's bags and savvy criminals digging through the trash to make imprints of people's cards from carbon copies (Herron, n.d.). Online shopping, however, and companies' ability to digitally store their customers' credit card information have opened up card users to vast new threats. You may, for example, purchase an item online from an untrustworthy seller and then never receive it; do business on an unencrypted site, leaving your information available for anyone to see; or have your identity stolen by an e-commerce site and your credit card hacked afterwards (Government of Canada, 2015).

In today's digital society, identity theft and credit card hacking have become especially serious issues, as more and more criminals harness the power of new technologies for their nefarious purposes. For example, on 5 October 2015, the *Toronto Star* reported that the credit and debit card numbers of customers at seven of the Trump hotels,

including Trump International Toronto, had been stolen. It turns out that the payment systems of these hotels had been the target of hackers for nearly a year, from May 2014 to June 2015 (Associated Press, 2015).

Though we have no reports of customers' information being used by the hackers to make any purchases in this instance, generally a person's credit or debit card information can be extremely dangerous in the wrong hands. For this reason, Trump hotels made sure to let customers know that they will be doing all they can to protect everyone's identity and catch the hackers, and promised free identity protection for an entire year to all affected customers (Associated Press, 2015).

Cybercriminals and hackers are often able to stay one step ahead of new technological defences. Innovative methods of online payment, like PayPal, may make our lives easier, but they unfortunately also make the illegal activities of cybercriminals and hackers much easier as well. We must, therefore, all be very careful about the personal information we share online and with whom we share it.

these profitable activities include prostitution, gambling, drugs, money laundering, and pornography. A report commissioned by the United Nations Office on Drugs and Crime (1998) notes,

> Fuelled by advances in technology and communications, the financial infrastructure [of money laundering] has developed into a perpetually operating global system in which "megabyte money" (i.e., money in the form of symbols on computer screens) can move anywhere in the world with speed and ease. The world of offshore financial centres and bank secrecy jurisdictions is a key part of this but can also be understood as a system with distinct but complementary and reinforcing components, many of which are readily amenable to manipulation by criminals.

Some crimes are committed not by organized criminals or the poor but by prosperous business people. There are, strictly speaking, two kinds of such **white-collar crime** (also known as suite crime). First, some corporations commit crimes in their own corporate interest; this is called corporate crime. Corporate crime victimizes millions of people; it robs businesses of billions of dollars each year, and it undermines the legitimacy of public institutions. Second, some business people or professionals commit crimes in their own personal interest and often at the expense of the larger corporate body within which they work. This includes insider trading (where people use private information in illegal ways) and falsifying account books (as Canadian/British executive Conrad Black is said to have done). Usually, these frauds misrepresent a product or service. This misrepresentation allows the criminal to sell something of little or no value for a large amount of money and make a huge profit.

Today, white-collar crime has evolved into a visible global problem: it affects economies, governments, and societies around the world. Many white-collar criminals rely on offshore banking and bank secrecy to hide and launder billions of dollars stolen from people throughout the world.

white-collar crime comprises the illegal acts and misdeeds of middle-class members of the business world.

Another type of white-collar crime is bribery. Bribery is common in societies in which the state has failed to establish and enforce rights. As a result, remnants of this practice still exist in many countries that have a weak (or "failed") state. Practices of bribery vary from one society to another, depending on the state's commitment to establishing and protecting rights. There is no way to know how much money changes hands in the form of bribes. These crimes can blur the lines between corporate crime, organized crime, and political crime. Today, governments around the world are putting in more effort to fight white-collar crimes than ever before. However, far more needs to be done.

Far less spectacular than organized crime and white-collar crime are the everyday crimes we all hear about and some of us experience. Today, we call these **street crimes** because they often occur in public, in and around city streets. They include crimes such as shoplifting, vandalism, break and enter, and car theft, and they are usually carried out by amateur or part-time criminals.

Most street crimes, aside from simple assaults, are property crimes. According to *Juristat*, a publication produced by Statistics Canada that focuses on justice and public safety issues, the rate of property crimes has decreased over the past two decades, though ordinary street crime continues to be extremely common. In 2014, for example, police recorded roughly 1.1 million property crimes in Canada, compared with only 516 homicides (Boyce, 2015).

street crime crimes associated with the public and individual offenders working alone or in small groups rather than large crime structures, such as shoplifting, vandalism, break and enter, car theft, assault, and homicide.

Technology and Crime

As we increasingly become an information society, more technology crimes will occur. Police agencies will also increasingly use new technology to detect crime and pursue the offenders. For example, new methods for collecting and analyzing large data sets are helping police to predict crime before it happens, so that they better deploy officers. On the other side, major hacks allow people to steal from millions of people at once, something that was not possible before digital banks.

Globalization is another factor that intersects with technology, commerce, communication, and crime. Crimes on the internet, drug dealing, and smuggling have far-reaching, global effects. For example, a man in the United States can travel to the Philippines or Thailand to have sex with a child sex worker. Many sex

Digital Divide

5.6 | Small Businesses and Cybersecurity

In today's digital society, cybercrime has become an increasingly common issue. Many victims of cybercrime are large companies or businesses whose profits are big enough to tempt ambitious cybercriminals. However, small businesses, which lack the funds to properly protect themselves, are more often the victims of cybercrime (Viuker, 2015). What's more, according to security company Symantec, cyberattacks on small businesses increased by 300 per cent between 2011 and 2012 (Brandon, 2015).

Big companies have a lot of capital to invest in cyberdefence systems, while smaller companies do not. Indeed, some companies are so small they do not even have an IT department (Messmer, 2014). A report from McAfee found that less than 50 per cent of small and medium-sized American businesses secured their emails to prevent phishing scams, while about 90 per cent of them did not use data protection (Viuker, 2015). These businesses are essentially "sitting ducks" for hackers and cybercriminals, and these crimes can have very serious and expensive consequences (Brandon, 2015). Symantec reports that 60 per cent of small businesses go under, financially, within six months of a cyberattack (Divon, 2015).

It may be hard to take all the necessary precautions, but small businesses can do a variety of things to lessen their degree of cyber-risk. For one thing, they can make sure that employees stay away from the wrong kind of sites. They can also be careful with new vendors; sometimes a security breach can come through a third party, so small businesses should ensure that new vendors follow company security policies. Finally, small businesses can purchase cybersecurity insurance to minimize the costs to themselves if they are hacked (Viuker, 2015).

offenders do travel these great distances to commit such crimes, as global crimes are difficult to regulate with national law enforcement, and many governments do not co-operate in apprehending suspects.

It seems likely that fraud, theft, impersonation, and extortion will increase in the future, as more crime will be committed outside national jurisdictions. The current law enforcement and judicial systems alone will not be strong or flexible enough to combat transnational crime.

Time to reflect

Do you agree with the assessment above that globalization and technological change will likely continue to increase the number and success of new kinds of crime? If not, why not?

cyberspace the virtual environment in which people communicate with one another over computer networks.

cyberbullying a form of bullying or harassment using electronic forms of contact.

The growth of **cyberspace** has also had an impact on crime. **Cyberbullying** in particular has become increasingly common within adolescent populations. This form of virtual harassment produces the same harmful effects as physical bullying: violence, substance abuse, and suicidal behaviour (Litwiller & Brausch, 2013). Also, the internet enables people to sell fraudulent identities and products more easily than if they had to persuade customers face to face. Older adults in particular are most likely to become victims of the dangers of cyberspace, including spam, phishing, scams, and viruses.

This greater-than-average risk faced by older adults is mainly related to differences in education and computer use. Although older adults may use the internet regularly, they do so less than younger adults. As a result, they may lack knowledge and awareness of computer privacy threats (Grimes, Hough, Mazur, & Signorella, 2010). Of course, naive or unknowledgeable users of any age are susceptible to online identity fraud, but older adults are less likely to take action to protect themselves. Older adults are also often unaware of the potential misuses of personal data (Grimes, Hough, Mazur, & Signorella, 2010).

Many wonder how the internet community can control content without limiting free speech. Some internet providers have tried voluntary controls, asking that people not post offensive material on their sites. There have also been campaigns to censor whole categories of material. For

THE CANADIAN PRESS/Andrew Vaughan

Hundreds attended the vigil of Rehtaeh Parsons in Halifax, who took her own life after she was sexually assaulted and then bullied for months when photos of the incident were released online.

5.7 | The Study of Crimes without Victims

Are there ever crimes without victims, and if so, why are they crimes? That is the question that interests Edwin M. Schur, who wrote the classic work *Crimes without Victims: Deviant Behavior and Public Policy* (1965). In it, he proposes the **decriminalization** of "victimless crimes."

"Crimes without victims" are consensual acts by adults that break laws. One example is the selling or sharing of marijuana. In these acts, no third party is involved or evidently harmed. Therefore, no third party has a reason to complain to the police or present evidence against these rule-breakers. Usually, these acts are also hidden from public view, so police are not likely to witness them. Schur (1965) proposes that "criminal laws do not always effectively curb the behavior they proscribe," and therefore these "laws . . . are highly ineffective from the standpoint of sheer deterrence" (p. 6).

The notion of "victimless crimes" forces us to ask how, and to what degree, criminal law should be an instrument of social policy. The idea of "crimes without victims" has been essential in the legalization of homosexual acts and abortion in Canada, and it continues to play a role in discussions related to prostitution, marijuana, and other drug use.

---

example, the United States has tried several methods of state censorship, some of which have been struck down. China completely controls internet access in and out of the country.

Any censorship of the internet has the potential to prevent the debate of important ideas. Too much control also poses political dangers. Authorities already have the ability to track the messages and website addresses of individual users. In some countries, they are already doing so. The threat here is that the internet could allow those in authority to oversee (and potentially punish) people's actions, thoughts, and communications.

> **decriminalization** reflecting a change in social or moral views, the abolition of criminal penalties for a particular act.

Victimization

Victimization reminds us of the reason we have laws, police, courts, and prisons. Criminal victimization is harmful: we can identify the harm done and the people harmed. There are several theories commonly used to explain why some groups of people are more likely to be victims of crime than others. Here we will discuss the two most commonly used theories: routine activity theory and victim precipitation theory.

The most widely cited theory, **routine activity theory**, states that crime depends mainly on opportunities—in which a suitable target is placed (or places herself) in the presence of a motivated offender, without a suitable guardian—and opportunities are created by activity patterns (see Figure 5.7). Thus, victimization is a predictable result of how and where people spend their time. Mustaine and Tewksbury (2000) propose that criminal acts are also promoted by situations that involve alcohol and drug use or unsupervised interactions with violent people. As a result, individual lifestyle and social affiliations largely shape our risks of victimization (Jennings et al., 2010). Gang membership is also strongly correlated with victimization, even after controlling for demographic variables such as education, poverty, and unemployment (Taylor, Peterson, Esbensen, & Freng, 2007).

> **routine activity theory** the theory that victimization results when a vulnerable person (or "suitable target") is regularly in a dangerous place without the presence of a trusted guardian.

Hot spots, a key concept in routine activities theory, are locations where the risks of crime are especially high. Examples include downtown entertainment districts and tourist attractions. Because young people are more likely to visit hot spots, young people are at much higher risk of being victims of violent crime than older people.

Workplaces are also hot spots of victimization. A Statistics Canada report (Perreault, 2015) found that just over a quarter (27%) of all incidents of violent victimization, including physical assault, sexual assault, and robbery occur in the victim's workplace. Schools can also be hot spots for victimization. In Canadian research on bullying, Pepler, Jiang, Craig, and Connolly (2008) found 60 per cent of girls and 48 per cent of boys in Grade 1 said they had been bullied in the previous

> **hot spots** areas in a city where the risks of crime are especially high, usually because the area draws many vulnerable victims and policing is relatively light.

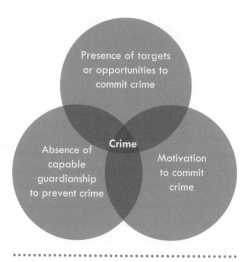

FIGURE 5.6 Routine Activity Theory

Source: Author-generated

two months, while about 27 per cent of Grade 6 students reported being the victims of cyberbullying (Holfeld & Leadbeater 2015). Another study found that 1 in 7 Canadian children between the ages of 10 and 17 were cyberbullied (Beran, Mishna, McInroy, & Shariff, 2015). Prisons, despite extensive supervision, are especially dangerous places for violent victimization. In fact, inmates of many "total institutions," including mental hospitals and nursing homes, risk victimization every day. (A total institution is any place where a large number of people live, and sometimes work, together, cut off from the larger society and subject continuously to a high degree of surveillance and supervision.)

However, not all hot spots are public places. They can be private places, too. For example, throughout Canada, family homes are "hot spots" of victimization. Often, so-called guardians are themselves the perpetrators of violence. Thanks to information and communication technology, cyberspace is a new hot spot of victimization.

Another key concept in routine activity theory is **suitable targets**. Suitable targets are people who are regularly exposed to crime or for other reasons have heightened vulnerability. The risk of violent victimization is higher among certain demographic groups, such as young Canadians (aged 15 to 24 years), people who are single, people who live in an urban area, and people who have a household income under $15,000 (Gannon & Mihorean, 2005). Risks of victimization are even higher for Indigenous people.

Three characteristics put people at risk of victimization: the victim's target vulnerability (visible physical weakness or psychological distress); target gratifiability (a feature of the victim that the attacker finds particularly appealing as a target); and target antagonism (for example, an ethnic or racial identity that may spark the attacker's hostility or resentment).

In contrast, **victim precipitation theory** proposes that people create their own risks of being victimized. Examples of creating risks include verbal provocation, body language, or wearing certain types of clothing. People may create such risk either passively or actively. Active precipitation involves attacking first or acting provocatively. Passive precipitation involves a victim unknowingly motivating the offender (for example, by being part of a group that threatens another group). This theory builds on the fact that some people are repeated victims of crime while other people rarely or never suffer victimization.

suitable target a person distinguished by particular characteristics that are likely to invite or incite victimization.

victim precipitation theory a theory that analyzes how a victim's characteristics or interactions with an offender may contribute to the crime being committed.

Time to reflect

How many decisions do you make in any given day taking the chance of becoming a victim of crime into consideration? For example, do take the time to consider your route to school, what you wear, or whether you leave your bag unattended at the library under the context of crime prevention?

Social Control and Punishment

At the beginning of the chapter, we mentioned the crime funnel, where the number of crimes committed is not reflected of the number of crimes recorded by police. A similar effect happens between crimes recorded and criminals punished. Of all recorded crimes, the police will investigate some and not others. While a portion of these criminal investigations will turn up suspects, many others will not. The police will then file charges against some of these suspects, while they will choose not to charge others. Of those charged, some will be convicted of that crime in court or submit a plea bargain while others will not. Lastly, some of these convictions will result in dispositions, or what we are calling punishments, and others will not.

A commonly accepted purpose of punishment is **deterrence**: persuading people not to commit crime by showing that if they do, they will be caught and punished. Deterrence punishments may be specific—they deter a particular criminal from crimes. They may also be "general"—they deter others from crime. In some case, they may be both. The earliest known form of deterrence was **capital punishment** (i.e., death). In 1800, England still had 220 crimes requiring capital punishment, most of which were crimes against the wealthy. Today, most industrial societies, including Canada, don't use capital punishment at all.

Among modern democracies, the United States is the only country that continues to use capital punishment. It also tortures prisoners of war. In these respects, the United States deviates from what is expected, standard, or normal among modern industrial nations. Despite the decreased popularity of the death penalty, deterrence has popular appeal, especially at times when crime is perceived to be on the rise.

A second purpose of punishment is **rehabilitation**: helping convicted criminals become law-abiding members of society. If our goal is to make society safe in the long-term, and we cannot accept the idea of execution or life imprisonment, rehabilitation is the best way to ensure our collective safety. Early rehabilitation efforts were aimed at changing the character or "disciplining the soul" of the prisoner through religion and severe personal treatments such as solitary confinement, silence, harsh personal discipline, and rigorous work schedules. Today, rehabilitation efforts focus on support and supervision from others. Support systems sometimes supply education or vocational training, help find housing, supervise probation and **parole**, or provide treatment for mental illness and substance abuse. But evidence has shown that prisons do not rehabilitate.

To discover why, researchers began to study prisons and prisoners in the early twentieth century. While doing this, sociologist Donald Clemmer (1940) developed his **prisonization theory**. It proposes that prisons degrade people, pressure them, and take away their rights. According to this theory, prisons do *not* make people more competent. On the contrary, they make people less competent by undermining their self-confidence and self-esteem.

Harsh treatment keeps the peace in prison, but it also alienates prisoners and unites them against the prison administration. Often, prisoners learn prison subculture, which leads them to become more deviant than before they went to prison. Furthermore, they gain new criminal skills, often learning to behave in even more undesirable and violent ways than they did before entering prison. After release, many return to criminal behaviour and end up back in prison. This is called **recidivism** or the revolving door. Canadian studies have shown that many offenders are repeat offenders.

However, theorist Michel Foucault (1977/2012) doubts these outcomes are either unintended or unexpected. On the contrary, he writes that the purpose of prison is to control people through surveillance and discipline, molding them into obedient, compliant people. This is achieved by breaking their resistance and their will.

Bodily discipline is an important part of this process, according to Foucault. Such discipline was first used in the military, where recruits were taught how to stand, walk, hold and fire a weapon, and so on. It soon extended to other areas such as schools, which taught students how to hold a pen, sit, eat, speak, and even think. Bodily discipline was enforced through the continual correction of slight slips and through continued testing, recording, and examination.

The other main technique of discipline was increased **surveillance**. This goal was reflected in Jeremy Bentham's prison design of the **Panopticon**—a prison where the guards can always see the prisoners, but prisoners cannot see the guards. So, the prisoners never know if they are being watched.

deterrence a legal and criminological concept that reflects the view punishment should prevent (or deter) crime by imposing significant costs on people who commit crimes.

capital punishment putting people to death as a penalty for criminal behaviour.

rehabilitation the idea that punishment should reform criminals and help them become law-abiding members of society.

parole the release of a prisoner before the completion of a sentence, on the promise of good behaviour.

prisonization (theory) the degradation of prisoners, their socialization into prison life, and their subsequent inability to function effectively outside these prison environments.

recidivism refers to prisoners who re-offend, often multiple times.

bodily discipline according to Michel Foucault, strategies of regulation that use power to reduce social agents to docile bodies, through punishment of various kinds.

surveillance close observation, especially of a suspected criminal.

Panopticon a type of institutional building designed by the English philosopher Jeremy Bentham that allows all inmates to be observed by a single watchman without the inmates knowing whether or not they are being watched. In modern societies, a form of universal, unseen surveillance.

This uncertainty leads prisoners to regulate themselves. Today, surveillance is everywhere in what Foucault calls a disciplinary society.

Prisons today are just one part of an extended framework of surveillance, recording, and domination. From the moment we are born, we are controlled, however unobtrusively, in disciplinary institutions: in hospitals, schools, workplaces, malls, public places, and prisons. Indeed, disciplinary institutions shape every stage of our lives. We internalize the rules of these institutions, and in that way, these rules provide mental discipline.

A third purpose of punishment is to repair the harm done by a crime and to "restore" the victim, the offender, and the community to a healthy state. **Restorative justice** asks offenders to take responsibility for the harm they have caused and asks victims to help determine punishments. Where possible, restorative justice also seeks to ensure that the offender compensates the victim and repairs any harm done to the community. The ultimate goal is for all community members to have confidence in public safety and the justice system. This justice approach is popular in Indigenous communities and growing elsewhere in Canadian society.

restorative justice a set of approaches to criminal punishment aimed to ensure that the criminal takes responsibility for his or her actions and that the victim, the criminal, and the community are all restored to a healthy state.

The dramatic overrepresentation of Indigenous people in Canada's jails and prisons has received scholarly attention for quite some time. As one recent report has noted, "The high rate of incarceration for Aboriginal peoples has been linked to systemic discrimination and attitudes based on racial or cultural prejudice, as well as economic and social disadvantage, substance abuse and intergenerational loss, violence and trauma" (Government of Canada, Office of the Correctional Investigator, 2013). To understand this overrepresentation we need to understand the history of Indigenous people within Canada: the generational trauma resulting from residential schooling and the 1960s scoop of Indigenous children into the mainstream foster care system; poverty and other poor conditions (housing, health, and jobs) on reserves; and choices Indigenous people face about leaving the reserve versus preserving Indigenous identity on the reserve.

This overrepresentation of Indigenous people in Canada's jails and prisons is particularly significant in some of the western provinces. Generally, Indigenous offenders are younger, less educated, less likely to be employed at the time of their admission to prison, and more likely to reoffend than non-Indigenous offenders. They also often have substance abuse problems.

Indigenous people accused of law-breaking are also treated somewhat differently than non-Indigenous people. For example, when an Indigenous person comes to trial, a Gladue report is requested. Written by a certified Gladue worker, this pre-sentencing and bail hearing report gives a the court a detailed account of the offender's life, background, community, and circumstances that brought him/her before the court. Like a non-Indigenous pre-sentence report, it cites the accused person's criminal record to assess the likelihood an offender will re-offend. Additionally and uniquely, the report will link the life story of the Indigenous offender to broader issues that have affected Indigenous life, such as the relative lack of access to services and underfunded school systems on reserve.

Indigenous people are also more likely than non-Indigenous people to be victims of crime, particularly violent crime. On-reserve crime rates are three times higher than crime rates in the rest of Canada, and on-reserve violent crime rates are eight times higher (Brzozowski, Taylor-Butts, & Johnson, 2006). (See also Chapter 6 for information on the victimization of Indigenous women.) This reminds us that imprisonment remains a form of social inequality in our society: some people are more likely than others to break the law, to be caught for doing so, and to receive severe punishment for doing so.

Conclusions

From the sociological point of view, deviance and crime are universal, natural, and normal. Therefore, sociologists look for answers to deviance *outside* of individual actors, in terms of situational factors. Typically, crime is the usual behaviour of normal people in deviant roles or abnormal situations. Sometimes, it is the behaviour of people who feel they must violate unreasonable rules to achieve equal opportunities. Crime is also a common result of deviant learning and, sometimes, of defective social connection.

Crime is a social construct and it is defined differently in different cultures. Its definition can be influenced by many factors—current ideas of morality and responsibility, religious faith, and competing scientific claims. As well, crime rates vary over time and change along with new technological developments. Indeed, though security continues to advance, cybercriminals are often able to stay a few steps ahead, stealing people's identities and taking advantage of naive internet users.

Inequality is related to crime not only when it comes to criminals, but also when it comes to victims, and the digital divide leaves those members of society who are not tech savvy vulnerable to cybercriminals like hackers and online con men. For this reason, we must work to close this digital divide and protect all members of society. Technology has changed the way in which crime is carried out and we must respond accordingly.

Questions for Critical Thought

1. Why aren't sociologists particularly interested in studying the "criminal mind?" What other factors besides the criminal mind affect the likelihood of committing a crime?

2. Which approach to crime and deviance would likely be most attentive to the problems and concerns of marginalized (minority) groups?

3. Why would a conflict theorist be interested in cybercrime? Be sure to include motivation and opportunity in your discussion.

4. What type of deviance is least well analyzed by the four main sociological frameworks we have discussed? Does this suggest other ways of analyzing crime and deviance?

5. What are the social factors that increase the amount of crime in a society? By comparison, what are the technological factors that increase the amount of crime? Which is more influential?

Take it Further: Recommended Readings

Sasha Abramsky, *American Furies: Crime, Punishment, and Vengeance in the Age of Mass Imprisonment* (Boston: Beacon Press, 2008). Abramsky examines the growth of, and violence in, American prisons.

Chester L. Britt and Michael R. Gottfredson, eds. *Control Theories of Crime and Delinquency* (New Brunswick, NJ: Transaction, 2003). In this book, contributors discuss socialization in the context of control theory and the effects that families, peers, and criminal justice have on self-control, social ties, and criminal behaviour.

John Hagan and Bill McCarthy, *Mean Streets: Youth Crime and Homelessness* (Cambridge: Cambridge University Press, 1998). Using data collected from street youth in Toronto and Vancouver, the authors ask why young people take to the streets, what dangers they encounter there, and how they manage to get off the streets.

Thomas Grisso, *Double Jeopardy: Adolescent Offenders with Mental Disorders* (Chicago: University of Chicago Press, 2004). The author considers how the juvenile justice system can best respond to the needs of children with an eye to their mental health needs.

Take it Further: Recommended Online Resources

Canadian Centre for Justice Statistics, *Juristat*
www5.statcan.gc.ca/olc-cel/olc.action?objId=85-002-X&ObjType=2&lang=en&limit=0

Canadian Centre on Substance Abuse
www.ccsa.ca/eng/Pages/default.aspx

Canadian Department of Justice
www.canada.justice.gc.ca

Statistics Canada
www.statcan.gc.ca

More resources available on  Dashboard

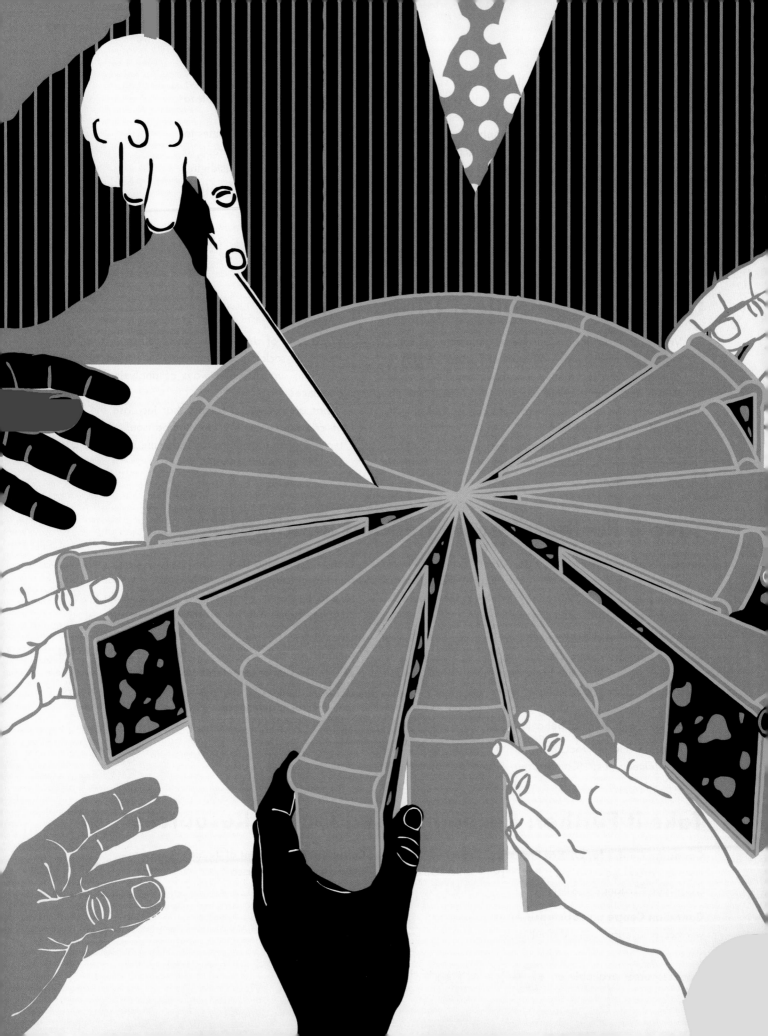

6

Economic Inequality and Class Exploitation

Learning objectives

In this chapter, you will:

> Consider to what extent Canada is a classless society with equal opportunities for social mobility

> Reflect on different measures of poverty and their strengths and weaknesses

> Learn about differences in health status across segments of Canadian society and the social determinants of health

> Learn about the challenges experienced by marginalized Canadians and discuss interventions aimed at promoting social and economic inclusion

Introduction

Alice is a typical 13-year-old girl. A lot of her time is spent on Facebook checking out pictures of her friends and writing messages. She lives in a great community, but her house and that of her neighbours is in need of major repairs. She hopes to go to university when she grows older, to fulfill "the aspirations and goals of parents, grandparents, and their extended community family" (St Germain & Dyck, 2011, p. 1). She is good at math and science and loves reading. But her school is not equipped with a library, science and technology lab, or athletic facility. Her teacher assures her it is a good idea to dream big. But she is not sure she can overcome all the challenges that lie ahead. When she is on Facebook she sees the lives of celebrities, who wear glamorous clothing and extravagant jewellery. She compares herself with these celebrities and wonders to what extent people will be accepting of her and her Indigenous background. Will it be easy to make friends? Alice symbolizes the stark social and economic disparities that continue to exist in Canada today.

Class inequality is one of the biggest problems that Canada faces. Canada has one of the highest percentages of millionaires worldwide, and this is expected to increase over the next five years (MacLeod, 2016). At the same time, the richest group of Canadians—namely, the top 20 per cent—have increased their share of the national income since the 1970s. For all other

THE CANADIAN PRESS/Jonathan Hayward

In 2016 Catherine, Duchess of Cambridge, and Prince William, Duke of Cambridge, receive a teddy bear from five-year-old Hailey Cain during a tour of Sheway, a centre that provides support for Indigenous women, during a visit to Vancouver, BC. Social media divulges millions of images daily portraying the dazzling lives of the rich and famous. Rarely are the lives of those struggling to make it in society portrayed this much; it is as if they have been erased from our digital planet.

groups, their shares have decreased. In other words, inequality in Canada has increased over time. In this chapter, we will learn about class differences and social stratification. We will also look at the many social consequences resulting from class inequality, including unemployment, poverty, poor health, and victimization in Canadian society.

Class Inequality and Social Stratification

Class as a Structuring Force

The study of social class began with the Industrial Revolution in the early nineteenth century, when the introduction of machinery fundamentally changed how work was done. It also influenced the relationship between workers and employers.

The German sociologist Karl Marx, with his friend and collaborator Friedrich Engels, took note of these changes and predicted that they would inevitably lead to class conflict. Marx argued that the new social order generated enormous tensions, as it created new and severe divisions between social groups with opposing interests. He stated that "society does not consist of individuals, but expresses the sum of interrelations, the relations within which these individuals stand" (Marx, 1939/1973, p. 265). Said another way, the class people belong to influences how they relate to others, especially to members of other classes. Marx, a careful observer of the way society was structured and the profound impact of industrialization on work, created a theoretical framework that helped thinkers grasp the significance of these changes.

Recall from Chapter 1 that at the centre of Marx's theory was the relation between those who produced goods, whom he referred to as the **proletariat** or workers, and those who owned the means of production, who were focused on maximizing profits, whom he referred to as the **bourgeoisie** or capitalists. For Marx, these were fundamentally different **classes**, whose interests were irreconcilable. The relation between these classes was one of exploitation; and it was this opposition of the interests of proletariats and bourgeoisie that created what Marx saw as the potential for **class consciousness.** This new **class system** created a hierarchy of groups, each with different opportunities, work situations, and what Max Weber would later come to call life chances (Breen, 2005; Weber, 1978). For Weber (1978), "class situation means the typical probability of procuring goods, gaining a position in life and finding inner satisfactions" (p. 302); that is, people have similar life chances if they belong to the same class because of their control of goods (such as capital) and skills (such as digital skills).

The rise of class consciousness also enabled workers to recognize their common fate: their interests were not aligned with those of their employers. Accordingly, they acted to protect themselves. The formation of unions is one important example of the ways through which workers started to protect their interests, and in doing so, they gained even more awareness of their situation. As we discussed in Chapter 2, Marx also developed the methodology of asking 100 questions to increase workers' awareness of their exploitative condition and to encourage collective action. Gradually, with this new consciousness, workers mobilized to demand higher wages, better working conditions, and more secure employment.

The concept of class has been central to much sociological work in the twentieth century. However, as times have changed, so has the meaning of class. Changes in work resulting from digital technology and new forms of capital flows have led scholars to argue that the traditional definition of class, relating to **socioeconomic status**, is "ceasing to do any useful work for sociology" (Pahl, 1989, p. 710) and requires adaptation. Even when Marx first introduced the distinction between proletariat and bourgeoisie, he recognized that other groupings existed that did not fit easily into his categorization.

Sociologists now recognize that other factors such as gender, racialization, education, and early life experiences also play significant roles in determining one's class through their effects on income levels, social connections, and life chances. They also affect one's ability to move between classes. These factors are discussed later in this chapter and in the chapters that follow.

proletariat (or working class) the social group that exchanges their labour for wages. As they do not own the means of production, they are at the mercy of the bourgeoisie (or capitalists) who own the means of production and prescribe work conditions.

bourgeoisie (or capitalists) the social group that possesses capital and thus also owns and commands the means of production.

class the division of people into social groups based on the distribution of material resources and power.

class consciousness a sense of shared identity and common interests that stem from an awareness of similar economic position, particularly relative to the economic position of others.

class system a hierarchical classification system that places individuals in relation to one another based on differences in their command of the means of production, work situations, and life chances.

socioeconomic status a method of ranking people that combines measures of wealth, authority (or power), and prestige (reputation that commands honour and respect, often irrespective of income, authority, or class position).

Social Stratification

social stratification a system of inequality that integrates class, status, and domination with other forms of differentiation, such as gender and ethnicity, to describe societal inequality.

Sociologists refer to the creation of social groups with different wealth, status, and opportunities as **social stratification**. Often, the following social classes are distinguished: the upper class, the middle class, the working class, and the lower class.

With the growth of social inequality in recent decades, the study of social stratification has gained even greater relevance and attention than in the past. Sociologists have studied the social, economic, health, and educational consequences of belonging to one class or another, and have found that social inequality has real consequences for people's lives and that of their children.

Social stratification has also been shown to have consequences for entire societies. Scholarship by Wilkinson and Picket (2010) has directly connected the well-being of societies to income inequality, showing that societies in which resources are more equally distributed are also healthier. Figure 6.1 shows this relation visually; here, we see that countries with more income equality have fewer health and social problems in all socioeconomic groups, including their high-income group. Wilkinson and Picket's (2010) work has had a profound impact on social policy, since it suggests that, in the long run, interventions aimed at reducing inequality will benefit all members of society.

Figure 6.1 shows clearly that health and social problems decrease as income equality increases—in this case, among countries in the Global North. Notice that Canada shows up in the middle of the chart. Note, finally, that most countries are scattered closely around the trend line in this diagram, showing that level of inequality is a strong predictor of health and social problems. However, the United States is an exception—its data point is practically "off the chart." This shows that other factors besides income inequality contribute to health and social problems in that country.

Time to reflect

What sociological factors, besides income inequality, might have an impact on health? Use your sociological imagination to try to list at least three other factors. Then, while reading the upcoming chapters on various dimensions of inequality, keep an eye out for coverage of health consequences.

Dashboard

Interactive activity

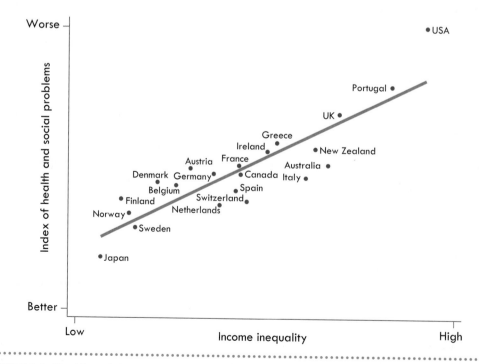

FIGURE 6.1 Health and Social Problems in Countries with High and Low Income Inequality

Source: Wilkinson, R. G., & Pickett, K. E. (2009). Income inequality and social dysfunction. *Annual Review of Sociology*, 35, 493–511.

Theoretical Approaches to Class and Inequality

Structural Functionalism

Structural functionalism is concerned with understanding how different social forms and practices contribute to the survival of society. In this way, societal institutions, organizations, and groups have a purpose, which allows society to endure in its current form, without much upheaval. In the case of social inequality, functionalists—noting that social inequality is universal—want to know what, if any, function or purpose is served by this inequality.

This has been referred to as research into the "functional necessity of stratification." Functionalist theorists have proposed that social stratification recruits and motivates individuals into key roles in the social structure (Davis & Moore, 1945). Every society has many positions and social roles to fill. For example, our society needs medical doctors, lawyers, professors, nurses, janitors, bus drivers, and so on. Some of these positions require large investments of time and money for education and preparation. To motivate people to pursue these demanding occupations, society has put a reward system in place. This system, in theory, pays high rewards to positions that are hardest to fill, since they require very specialized knowledge, skills, and often credentials. By contrast, occupations that do not require hard-to-get credentials or a specialized skill set, such as cleaning an office building or serving customers at a fast-food restaurant, will have lower status and pay, as many people can occupy these positions and so workers are more easily replaceable. To summarize their position, Davis and Moore (1945) say that "the [unequal] rewards and their distribution become part of the social order, and thus give rise to stratification" (p. 243).

Of course, reward systems are complex and can work at many levels. For example, with the expansion of the global gaming industry, worth about US$99.6 billion in 2016 (Minotti, 2016), more and more highly skilled knowledge workers are needed to write code and, through their creativity, to devise new forms of gaming. As a result, companies in the gaming industry are in constant competition with one another to recruit the best computer scientists, digital artists, and digital sound technicians.

One company that has been in the news recently is Big Viking Games, located in London, Ontario. It is considered Canada's leading HTML5 mobile game development company, producing such games as *YoWorld*, *Galatron*, and *FishWorld*. To lure the best talent, Big Viking Games provides workers with many perks if they join the company. Some of the perks include free breakfasts, lunches, snacks, on-site massage therapy, and highly competitive salaries. As a result, in 2015, Big Viking Games was recognized as one of the "Best Workplaces in Canada" by the Great Places to Work Institute.

It should be said, however, that this example also reveals the weakness of functionalist theory. The example illustrates that occupational rewards are determined by a competitive market for scarce skills and talents. It does not prove that this competition contributes to the survival or well-being of society, or that it is "socially necessary." It also ignores the fact that development of needed skills and talents in society can be driven by other factors than monetary rewards, and that talent, skill, and effort are not the only factors that determine the jobs people get in life and the rewards they earn as a result.

Time to reflect

Is it in the best interest of society that a very skilled programmer develops advertising algorithms, or would it be more beneficial for them to develop user-friendly web portals for government services online? What barriers might there be in the way of our theoretical programmer getting hired at either job (e.g., gender, immigration status, accessibility)?

Conflict Theory

The conflict theory position on poverty and inequality relies heavily on ideas first developed by Karl Marx and Friedrich Engels (1848/1955). Conflict theory rejects the structural functionalist view outlined above that all social arrangements are useful for the survival of society. On the contrary, conflict theorists argue that social inequality only serves the dominant group in society, maintaining the status quo that privileges their interests, and it may even be harmful to the survival of society as a whole. Certainly, in the views of Marx and Engels (1848/1955), class inequality tends to promote revolution and societal change.

As discussed above, Marx's theory outlines a fundamental conflict between the interests of the bourgeoisie or capitalists, who own the means of production, and the proletariats or workers, whose only option is to sell their labour (Marx & Engels, 1848/1955). The bourgeoisie exploit the labour of the working class to accumulate wealth for themselves, realizing that workers depend on their wages for survival. In this system of exploitation, machinery plays an important, non-neutral, part.

The introduction of industrial machinery into the production process during the nineteenth and twentieth centuries has led to the replacement of many skilled workers with machines or unskilled workers. For example, in the textile industry, steam-powered (then electricity-powered) machines simplified and expedited the weaving process. This mechanization allowed employers to hire non-skilled workers at lower wages, leading to an increase in unemployment among highly skilled craftspeople (Berg, 1994). The use of machinery also fundamentally changed the nature of work itself, producing alienation.

Marx identified four types of alienation in labour under capitalism, which largely came about through industrialization:

1. *alienation of the worker*: workers' separation from their "species essence" as they become integrated into an industrial system comprised of machines;
2. *alienation between workers*: in a capitalist system, labour becomes yet another commodity to be exchanged, rather than a meaningful social relationship between worker and employer;
3. *alienation of the worker from the product*: the product is commodified and mass produced, thereby ceasing to be under the worker's control; and
4. *alienation from the act of production itself*: work is perceived as a meaningless activity, with little to no intrinsic satisfactions.

Today, machines continue to reshape working conditions and alienation persists. Instead of replacing skilled workers with unskilled labourers, machines increasingly replace human workers of all skill levels (Wajcman, 2017). For example, in December 2016 Amazon introduced its new technology "Amazon Go," which promises to revolutionize shopping (Balakrishnan, 2016). At the Amazon Go store, there is no need for shoppers to stand in long checkout lines, as all items selected in the store are automatically billed to the customer's Amazon.com account as soon as they leave the store. The result of this mechanization is huge profitability: Amazon's value in 2016 was estimated at $247.6 billion, placing it among the world's top 10 retailers (Gensler, 2016).

Companies like Amazon are constantly looking for new ways to innovate to lower their costs; and doing this often means embracing automating technology that will reduce labour costs (The Canadian Press, 2017; Wajcman, 2017). Since their interests lie in profit maximization, the loss of jobs does not factor into their decision making. The result of such mechanization is increased unemployment, especially in the manufacturing and services sectors. The loss of jobs leads, in turn, to an increase in social inequalities—indeed, class polarization, with an ever-widening gap in wealth between rich and poor (Wilkinson & Pickett, 2010). The executives who run multinational corporations such as Amazon and make these decisions are, in the meantime, paid wages that are grossly out of line with the wages offered to their lower-level employees.

The consequences may be dire in the end. Marx (1939/1973) predicted that as the proletariat became aware of their exploitation, they would organize and revolt against the bourgeoisie, taking the means of production into their hands. This prediction has not come to pass, and in a sense, the opposite has happened. In country after country—consider recent national elections and plebiscites in the United States, Italy, Austria, Hungary, and the UK—large numbers of insecure and unemployed workers have voted for neo-liberal or conservative governments and/or regressive policies (Inglehart & Norris, 2016). They have made these choices instead of voting for parties and policies that favour more equitable distribution of resources and protection for the lower classes as is seen in countries such as Sweden. And in the realm of work, people are often glad to be employed in any kind of jobs available—even as hamburger flippers at McDonald's or greeters at Walmart—where salaries are low, benefits are minimal, and workers are often not unionized.

However, that is not to say there has been no protest whatsoever against the inequalities produced by capitalism and mechanization. In recent years, different kinds of movements have emerged to protest these changes, especially aimed at protesting the power of multinational corporations. One such movement is the Occupy movement, which started as a grassroots protest in New York City's Zuccotti Park on 17 September 2011. This movement spread around the world and garnered much media attention (Brickman, 2017). Occupy stands against the domination of large corporations, their unethical practices, and control over the flow of capital in such a way that it benefits a small sub-population (The Occupy Solidarity Network, n.d.).

Occupy's central slogan, "We are the 99%," reflects the movement's outrage that the current economic system favours the wealthy elite at the expense of the majority of citizens. In particular, the Occupy movement protests the unequal distribution of wealth in modern capitalist societies. Nobel Laureate Joseph Stiglitz pointed out in a recent *Vanity Fair* article that the top 1 per cent of wealthy Americans command a disproportionate share of economic capital, wealth, influence, and power (Hastings & Domegan, 2013); and French economist Thomas Piketty notes that levels of economic inequality today are as high as the levels that prevailed in Europe and North America just before the Great Depression of the 1930s (Piketty & Saez, 2003; Piketty, 2003).

Occupy has increased public awareness around the large disparities between poor and rich, and the consequences of social inequality for individuals and societies. As such, Occupy, drawing on conflict theory, reminds us that our political, economic, and legal systems are all biased in favour of the economic and social elites.

Feminism

Feminism is a distinctive perspective that focuses on gendered patterns of inequality. Central questions of interest to feminist scholars include these:

- How do our social institutions treat men and women differently, and with what effects?
- What struggles and barriers are unique to women and to their role as the non-dominant group?

Feminist sociologists also examine the intersections between various types of inequalities including class, gender, racialization, and indigeneity, at home and in the workplace. They recognize that not only is inequality impacted by gender, it is further and uniquely influenced by these other social factors.

The feminist perspective provides unique insights into employment and income distribution in Canadian society. Figure 6.2 shows the wages for men and women from 2001 to 2011 in Canada. Women in 2011 earned on average $32,000 annually, while men earned $48,000 annually, a gap of $16,000. The ratio of average women's wages to average men's wages was 62.1 per cent in 2001 and 66.7 per cent in 2011, only closing by 4.6 per cent over the 10-year period. When examining the gender wage gap among OECD countries in 2014, Canada had the seventh highest pay gap, ranking twenty-seventh out of thirty-four OECD countries examined (OECD, 2014). A 2015 United Nations Human Rights report expressed concern that the income inequality between women and men in Canada continues to persist and shows a large wage gap in comparison to other OECD countries (OHCHR, 2016).

Interactive
activity

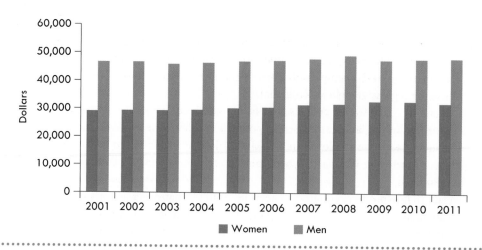

FIGURE 6.2 Wages for Men and Women from 2001 to 2011 in Canada

Source: Author-generated from Stats Can table Income Statistics Division, Statistics Canada, URL: http://www5.statcan.gc.ca/cansim/a26

According to the UN Human Rights Report (2015), what is most concerning about the pay wage gap in Canada is its disproportionate effect on vulnerable social groups that include low-income women, racialized minorities, and Indigenous women. See Chapter 7 for more on the gender wage gap in Canada.

> **Time to reflect**
>
> Some countries have tried to combat the gender wage gap by requiring all companies to publish their wage gaps online. Do you think Canada should follow suit? Would this approach address the intersectional inequalities experienced by racialized, Indigenous, and low-income women?

According to the UN Human Rights Report (2015), Canada needs to do more to guarantee that women, particularly racialized minority and Indigenous women, receive equal pay and equal treatment for their work. This gendered wage gap is particularly disproportionately high in Alberta and Nova Scotia (Jeffrey, 2015), where there seems to be the greatest need for awareness and change. Consistent legislation is needed across all provinces in both the public and private sectors to effectively eliminate the existing high level of gender-based wage discrimination.

Symbolic Interactionism

Symbolic interactionism investigates how people give meaning to social stratification and what symbols are associated with belonging to various social groups. In that sense, symbolic interactionism provides nuanced understandings of meaning-making, by examining specific subcultures and their forms of expression.

This kind of thinking is illustrated by the early work of Thorstein Veblen (1899/2009), who looked at the relation between people's consumption patterns and their expression of class differences. To clarify his thinking, Veblen introduced the concept of **conspicuous consumption**—a practice that included the purchasing of valuable goods in order to express class belonging and social status (Veblen, 1899/2009). His analysis specifically focused on how conspicuous consumption allowed upper-class families to signal their wealth and standing in society. Veblen also differentiated between the consumption patterns of women and men, showing how these patterns were a part of gender-role stereotyping. Thus, in the late nineteenth century just as today, material consumption was based on differences of class, status, and gender.

Following Veblen's work, social interactionists today study how different social classes use "status symbols" to distinguish themselves. Consider the example of smart phones. Smart phones are not only tools that perform an ever-increasing set of functions, they are also status symbols. As such,

conspicuous consumption the purchasing of valuable goods for the purpose of expressing class belonging and status.

phones are designed, marketed, and advertised in such a way that their price, capabilities, and look signal their value and, by extension, the status of the owner. Possessing the latest and greatest smart phone signals a high standing in society—or at least a high income. To some, it may also signal being what Everett Rogers (2003) has referred to as an "innovator." An innovator is someone who is always ahead of the times in their adoption of new technologies.

French sociologist Pierre Bourdieu examined the mechanisms by which people learn about the symbols that are associated with their class. He stressed that a large part of being socialized into, and belonging to, a specific class is the learning of class distinctions. According to Bourdieu, possessing the demeanor, cultural goods, or educational qualifications valued by the upper classes are all ways to increase one's **cultural capital**, which also has the potential to translate into economic benefits (Bourdieu, 1986). Belonging to a specific class includes knowing how to dress, how to speak, what to like, and how to act in various social situations. Without culturally understood class distinctions, class symbols (such as the Pink Diamond iPhone) would no longer be meaningful. But because they are culturally understood, class members can rely on these symbols to help them distinguish themselves from members of other classes, in particular from people below them in the social hierarchy.

> **cultural capital** a body of knowledge, ideas, tastes, preferences, and skills that helps people get ahead socially. Cultural capital often includes learning about and participating in high culture.

Time to reflect

What kinds of status symbols are relevant to your own peer group? When you walk around on campus, what do you notice about your fellow students (what brands of headphones they have on; what shoes they wear; their backpacks; their haircuts)? Do you make assumptions based on these appearance props?

The use of symbols, or what Goffman (1959) and Stone (1975/2009) described as appearance props, to denote class and status is so ingrained in our society that we are often unaware of how and when we learn to internalize their meaning. A diamond-encrusted Apple iPhone, a $5000 pair of jeans, or a $1000 bottle of champagne also become appearance props that represent class and status.

TABLE 6.1 Theoretical Approaches to Economic Inequality

Theory	Main points
Structural Functionalism	· Inequality and poverty serve important functions in society. · Poverty motivates people to work harder to improve their life conditions. · Rewards such as income and status motivate people to occupy certain positions.
Conflict Theory	· A structural power imbalance exists between capitalists and workers. · Workers depend on wages for survival and are therefore vulnerable to exploitation. · By exploiting workers through poor working conditions and poor pay, owners amass more wealth for themselves.
Feminism	· Class, gender, and racial inequalities interplay in "intersectionality" to explain the individualized hardships suffered by many women. · Women experience inequality differently than men. · Women's wages are rarely at par with those of their male counterparts, selling women short in the labour market.
Symbolic Interactionism	· This approach focuses on the symbols associated with different classes. · We are socialized to employ and recognize status symbols and their social meaning.

Dashboard

Case study

Digital Divide

6.1 | Disciplining Digital Play in Youth Culture

Symbolic interactionism examines how we learn and communicate the symbolic meaning of objects, and how these appearance props come to represent differences in class. The meaning of a particular technology can vary greatly from one social class or racialized group to another.

In a 2014 study, Matthew H. Rafalow used a comparative ethnographic analysis of three middle schools to reveal how class and racialization served to assign meanings differently to digital technologies for students from different backgrounds. Through interviews with teachers and students and observation of classroom interactions, Rafalow found that at one school with mostly Latino youth, students had been told that their digital expressions were irrelevant to learning. By contrast, at a second school with mostly Asian youth, students had been told their digital play was threatening their ability to succeed academically. Finally, at a third school for mostly upper-class and white youth, teachers viewed digital play as valuable, if not necessary, for day-to-day learning and achievement (Rafalow, 2014).

Thus, the perception of the same technology (and the same use of it) varied according to how teachers perceived the people *using* the technology. Teachers' shared beliefs about students and the symbolic meaning they ascribed to digital devices informed their disciplinary orientations toward digital play. In turn, these orientations determined whether the digital styles students brought to school were turned into valuable cultural capital for educational purposes, or whether they were discouraged and suppressed. Where a lot is expected of children, more flexibility is allowed around the use of this technology. This shows that an item's perceived value is affected not only by the society it appears in, but also by who is using the item and how they are perceived. In other words, factors such as racialization complicate the relationships between social status, class, and status symbols. Social inequalities can be reproduced through the symbolic meanings given to digital tools; and these implied meanings may affect children's future opportunities in the labour market. In short, the assumptions that teachers make about technology use by low-income children places these children at a disadvantage as they move through their educational career.

Is smart phone use allowed, discouraged, or actively encouraged in your classroom?

However, the importance and assumed affect of these status items can change based on how those around us perceive them—their value is not inherent (see Box 6.1).

Social Mobility

We have already discussed social stratification, the organization of society into distinct social classes: upper class, middle class, working class, and lower class. But, what does it take to switch classes? Does determination and hard work allow a person to move up the ladder? Or is it a matter of having the brain power of a genius, the right skill set, or the right social connections? Do other factors, such as racialization, gender, and indigeneity affect a person's ability to move up? *Social mobility* is the subfield of sociology that describes the process of moving from one class or occupational status to another. Sociologists give most attention to upward mobility because most people want to improve their standing. In fact, media stories—TV, movies, and newspapers—are filled with stories of upward mobility (i.e., amazing successes), but the reality is that people can also move down in status or class. The complexity of social mobility and its relevance to society has made it necessary for sociologists to study the underlying processes and identify key factors that move people up and down the social hierarchy.

Upward Mobility

As we have noted, most people in our society strive to improve their lives both economically and socially. Upward social mobility, as discussed in Chapter 4, describes the move to a higher position in the stratification hierarchy. From a societal standpoint, the rate of upward (compared to downward) mobility is a key indicator of a society's "openness" and well-being. So, it is important for policy makers to understand the conditions under which more or fewer people are upwardly mobile, and also to discern the characteristics that make people most or least mobile.

Canada, in comparison to other countries, has a high level of upward social mobility. For example, between 1993 and 2012, nine of every ten individuals in the lowest income group moved up to a higher income group (Lammam, MacIntyre, Veldhuis, & Palacios, 2016).

In Canada education is a critical influence on upward mobility, as we see at greater length later in the chapter. With good educational credentials, such as a high school diploma and post-secondary education degree, people are more likely to be upwardly mobile and less likely to be downwardly mobile. Canadians rightly consider post-secondary education—a college or university degree—to be the "path to prosperity," since investment in education often leads to higher paying jobs. Over a lifetime, small education-related benefits lead to large cumulative economic advantages, compared to people with less education.

However, Canadians have unequal opportunities to obtain an education. People whose parents do not have a university degree are less likely to go to university themselves; in fact, they have only a 26 per cent likelihood of going to university (Turcotte, 2011). In comparison, where at least one parent has a university degree, the chance that a child will obtain a university degree goes up to 56 per cent. The chance of getting a university degree is higher still for people whose parents both had received a university degree (Turcotte, 2011). These statistics show that disparities in educational attainment continue to exist in Canada, and that these disparities self-perpetuate. For more, including a more intersectional analysis on access to education, and how education affects earning potential, see Chapter 11.

Upward mobility, sociologists have learned, is governed by various mechanisms. **Exchange mobility** limits people's ability for upward mobility; that is, mobility that can only occur when an existing position becomes vacant. For example, most colleges and universities in Canada have a student association, and this association has only one president. No other student can become president of the student association until the position reopens with each new school year. This also characterizes the opportunity for mobility in all organizations that are unchanging (or even shrinking) in size, for example, most government bureaucracies and university faculties.

Structural mobility, on the other hand, is a result of structural growth through the creation of new jobs or positions, and is commonly associated with organizational or economic growth. For example, the move toward an information society, while eliminating many existing jobs, has also created many new jobs in the white-collar sector, allowing for people to occupy these jobs without displacing others, and providing new opportunities for upward mobility (Wajcman, 2017). A new elite has emerged that draws on technical expertise rather than on economic ownership (see Box 6.2).

Box 6.2 illustrates several new trends. First, technology know-how and digital skills have afforded new opportunities for social mobility. This has created new opportunities for upward mobility, but as noted earlier, it has also created more economic disparity, as many jobs in the manufacturing industry have been lost to automation. Second, it shows that social mobility applies not only to individual people but also to entire social and occupational groups. In this case, tech-savvy workers are finding employment, often in high-paying jobs, while blue-collar workers are slowly disappearing into precarious part-time work and unemployment. This decline of the traditional working class creates a

Dashboard

Video: *Circus Without Borders*

exchange mobility movement within an occupational hierarchy that can only occur when an existing position becomes vacant.

structural mobility movement within an occupational hierarchy that can occur as a result of structural growth through the creation of new jobs or positions, and that is commonly associated with organizational or economic growth.

Sociology 2.0

6.2 | A New Elite of Technological Visionaries

Famous technological visionaries include Steve Jobs, Bill Gates, and Google co-founders Larry Page and Sergey Brin. Each of these innovators had no capital to start with. Jobs and Gates did not even finish their university degrees, one because of a lack of money and the other because of a lack of interest. Page and Brin were pursuing doctoral degrees while they worked on the functionality of the Web. They had no capital and had to scramble to find some funds to set up a server in the now famous Menlo Park Garage; it was from these humble beginnings that Google began. For these four technology innovators, expertise in digital technology yielded upward mobility—all four companies were valued in the billions of dollars in 2016. The experiences of these four visionaries show that today, financiers and industrial magnates are no longer the sole commanders of the wealth of the world. Increasingly, new capital is in the hands of self-made technology giants.

Time to reflect

While all four of these people had no financial capital when they put forward their ideas, do you think their cultural capital might have helped them to become successful? What other social factors—for example, their gender, and/or the fact that they are perceived as white—might have played a factor in their successes as technology entrepreneurs?

secondary (or marginal) labour market sectors in the economy that offer low-paying jobs characterized by fewer opportunities for advancement and insecurity.

primary labour market industries that provide jobs with high wages, good opportunities for advancement, and job security.

intergenerational mobility the movement of people into positions that are higher or lower than the positions held by their parents.

intragenerational (career) mobility social mobility into positions that are higher or lower within a person's lifespan.

secondary (or marginal) labour market: a sector of the economy that offers low-paying jobs characterized by insecurity and few opportunities for advancement (Vosko, 2006). In contrast, employment in the **primary labour market** is flourishing, especially in the sectors where information and digital industries provide jobs with high wages, good opportunities for advancement, and job security. This shows that education alone is not enough for upward mobility; some educational credentials are more economically valuable than others. We talk more about the barriers to certain streams of education in Chapter 7.

Inter- and Intragenerational Mobility

We call mobility that takes place across generations **intergenerational mobility**. This is the movement of people into positions that are higher or lower than the positions held by their parents. Many immigrants to Canada work hard to provide their children with opportunities for upward economic and social mobility. For many of these immigrants, education is the most likely means of achieving mobility. As a result, Canadian data on post-secondary education show that the children of immigrants (second generation) are 11 per cent more likely to complete university than children of parents born in Canada. Likewise, General Social Survey data from 2009 show that among people aged 25 to 39, of those with at least one parent born outside Canada, 40 per cent were university graduates, compared with 29 per cent of people whose parents were both born in Canada (Turcotte, 2011).

Intergenerational mobility needs to be distinguished from **intragenerational** or **career mobility**, which describes social mobility within a person's lifespan. Consider the career mobility of Canadian singer and songwriter Justin Bieber. He started his career at 13 years of age in Stratford, Ontario, in low-income housing, when his mother started posting videos of his singing to YouTube. In 2016 Justin Bieber—among the most popular and successful male artists worldwide—had wealth estimated at US$250 million. How did Bieber rise from rags to riches, while so many other Canadians fail to do so? The study of intragenerational mobility aims to uncover the resources required to achieve such mobility. However, that's not the end of sociological interest in this topic. Sociologists also want to know how people who have achieved upward mobility assimilate economically and socially into a new class. Additionally, they want to know why Canadians are so inclined to see the Justin Bieber story as normal

Christopher Polk/Getty Images

Have you dreamed of becoming a star? Intragenerational mobility is filled with myths and ideologies around how people can achieve upward mobility. The reality is that upward mobility is hard to achieve within a single generation, and intergenerational mobility is more likely to occur.

or typical, rather than rare and almost bizarre. Part of this falls on the media, who are biased toward success stories, creating a sense that upward mobility is attainable if the right conditions are in place.

Time to reflect

In what ways does media representation of stories like Bieber's reinforce the myth of attainable social mobility? If these are the stories that people want to hear about, should media outlets be accountable for telling them?

Downward Mobility

Downward mobility is a type of vertical mobility in which people move from positions of higher pay and social status to positions of lower pay and lower status. When economies expand, people move up the ladder, but when economies contract or shift, people lose jobs or must take worse jobs (Brayne & Newman, 2013). When an individual looks for employment during a prolonged recession and is **underemployed** or unemployed for a long period, this is referred to as "scarring" (Brayne & Newman, 2013). One key problem here is that résumés with employment gaps give employers the impression of unreliability, making it more difficult for a person to get a good job. This kind of scarring can lead to long-term unemployment and downward mobility, with long-term effects on wages and career trajectories (Brayne & Newman, 2013). In other words, recessions can result in downward mobility, particularly for those in already precarious employment.

Downward mobility intersects with other dimensions of inequality, with the result that some groups are particularly prone to downward social mobility. Women, immigrants, and racialized minorities have been especially disadvantaged in these respects. As groups or social categories, they often lack access to things such as education, which enable a person to become upwardly mobile. For

downward mobility vertical social mobility into lower-regarded and paid occupational positions.

underemployment employment in a job that requires far less expertise, skill, or ability than the job-holder has to offer.

example, a key criterion for employment is work experience in Canada, which disadvantages immigrants and refugees. Additionally, language barriers and a lack of certification in Canada may contribute to prolonged unemployment and downward mobility, as newcomers see the need to take jobs that are below their educational credentials from their countries of origin. Additionally, racialized minorities are more likely to be employed in precarious jobs (see Chapter 12). Increasingly, people working in precarious labour, that is, low-paying, part-time jobs, are at a greater risk of becoming low-income Canadians even if they aren't low income already (Gaetz, Donaldson, Richter, & Gulliver, 2013).

Poverty

Many of the things people know about poverty—what it is and how it affects people and communities, for example—are based on false beliefs and erroneous suppositions (Villemez, 2001). One common belief is that poverty is self-inflicted and results from a combination of poor choices and unwillingness to work (Sharone, 2013). This belief marginalizes and unjustly brands the people in society who struggle hardest to move ahead but have the least opportunity to effect social change. They lack opportunity because they are not in positions of power or influence and their concerns go unnoticed. So understanding what poverty is turns out to be not only complex, but also highly political.

Measuring Poverty and Well-Being

The best idea of what constitutes poverty is found in the United Nations definition, which makes it clear that poverty is not only about a lack of income needed to fulfill basic needs (e.g., water, food, and clothing); it is also about the deprivation of choice, and the lack of access to important resources like health care, education, and political representation. Thus, poverty is ultimately a concept that goes well beyond basic needs and also focuses on people's human dignity.

To get at these nuanced aspects of poverty, two concepts become relevant. The first is **absolute poverty**, which revolves around not having enough income to meet basic survival needs such as water, food, shelter, and access to critical health care. The second is **relative poverty**. This describes people or families with enough income to survive but not enough to afford an average standard of living. People who are relatively poor have significantly less than the average households in their community—in other words, they experience significant inequality (Sarlo, 2007) .

Currently, there are three widely used methods to measure low income in Canada. The most common method is the **low income cut-off** (LICO), which identifies income thresholds below which a family will likely spend a larger proportion of its income on necessities than an average family of a similar size (Statistics Canada, Income Statistics Division, 2016). In other words, while a middle-income family of four might devote, say, one-fifth of its household income to housing expenses such as rent or a mortgage, a family living below the LICO might spend one-half or even three-quarters of its household income on housing expenses (and likely for a cheaper, older, and smaller apartment in a less convenient neighbourhood).

We know that one-half is a dangerously high portion because it leaves few funds available for other necessities such as food, clothing, transportation, and daycare. The LICO thresholds, based originally on 1992 consumption patterns of Canadians, are updated each year to ensure that their values are in line with the current cost of living (Murphy, Zhang, & Dionne, 2012).

A second method of measuring of low income is the **market basket measure** (MBM). The MBM calculates how much income a household requires to meet its needs, which include both subsistence needs (such as basic food and shelter) and the needs to satisfy community norms—for example, appearance norms set by the type of clothes worn in that community (Canadian Council on Social Development, 2001; Hatfield, Pyper, & Gustajtis, 2010). A number is generated, and people whose income falls below the calculated value are considered low income Canadians.

The third and final method is the **low income measure** (LIM), which calculates the low income threshold of a household as one-half of the median income of a household of the same size in a

---

absolute poverty not having enough income to meet basic survival needs such as water, food, shelter, and access to critical health care.

relative poverty having enough to meet basic survival needs, but living well below the general standard of living of a community, social group, or society.

low income cut-off (LICO) the method used to measure low income in Canada that identifies income thresholds below which a family will likely spend a larger proportion of its income on necessities than an average family of a similar size.

market basket measure (MBM) the method used to measure low income in Canada that calculates how much income a household requires to meet its needs, including subsistence needs (such as basic food and shelter) and the needs to satisfy community norms.

low income measure (LIM) the method used to measure low income in Canada that calculates the low income threshold of a household as one-half of the median income of a household of the same size in a community of a similar size.

similar-sized community (Nova Scotia, Poverty Reduction Working Group, 2008). Households with different numbers of members, in different-sized communities, will have different cut-off points. This measure counts households according to their relative poverty—in other words, not by what they can or can't afford to buy but by how much less they have than others.

There have been continuing debates about the best way to measure low income as each method of measurement leads to different conclusions about how widespread poverty is, how it is distributed, and (therefore) the best ways to reduce it. All of these refinements to the measurement process make sense, but they complicate the business of measuring, assessing, explaining, and reducing poverty. Depending on the type of measurement used, statistics about low-income Canadians may vary; one Canadian might be considered poor by one measure and not by another. So, how do these differently calculated statistics compare in their assessment of how widespread poverty is in Canada?

Not surprisingly, data from the 2011 National Household Survey reveals that the three methods of measurement produced three different sets of results (Murphy et al., 2012). In 2011, the after-tax LICO—that is, the LICO adjusted for the amount of income available to families after income taxes—revealed that 9.7 per cent of the total population in Canada 18 to 65 years of age had "low incomes"— that is, lived in poverty (Statistics Canada, 2013). In contrast, the MBM reports a poverty rate of 12.9 per cent, while the after-tax LIM shows an even higher value of 13.8 per cent (Statistics Canada, 2014). The 2016 Census stuck to the after-tax LIM and reported a low income rate of 14.2 per cent (Statistics Canada, 2017).

The three measures discussed above—LICO, MBM, and LIM—are often used for establishing poverty thresholds within Canada. These measures, however, do not provide a good way of comparing rates of poverty across countries. Because of this limitation, sociologists turn to the **Gini coefficient** (reported as a Gini ratio or as a normalized Gini index), which is the most widely used measure of income inequality for cross-country comparisons. Gini scores range from 0 to 1. A Gini score of 0 means there is total income equality in a society and a Gini score of 1 means total income inequality. As you might imagine, the Gini scores for actual societies are never 0 or 1; rather, they tend to vary between 0.2 and 0.6, for the most part.

Figure 6.3 shows changes in the Gini score in Canada from 1976 to 2010. As we can see, the Gini index dipped around 1988 to a value of 0.281, but since then it has risen to a high score of 0.32 in 2010. What this means is that since the 1980s income inequality increased in Canada, even though Canada has a high average standard of living overall (UNDP, 2015). The Gini index shows that it is important to not only look at average wealth in a society, but also how that wealth is distributed. We tend to see the highest Gini indices in countries in the Global South such as some African and South American countries, which have Gini scores of between 0.5 and 0.65. For example, the Gini score for South Africa is 0.63, for Haiti 0.60, and for Nepal 0.61 (The World Bank, 2014). Typically, poverty levels are greatest in countries with the greatest income inequality. More affluent nations in

Gini coefficient a measure of the inequality in the distribution of income among households within a country, as compared to a theoretical country of similar attributes but where everyone has the same income (where the coefficient would be 0), or where there is perfect inequality (where the coefficient would be 1).

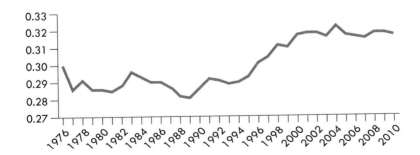

FIGURE 6.3 Income Inequality in Canada, 1976 to 2010 (Gini Coefficient Using Adjusted After-Tax Income)

Source: http://www.conferenceboard.ca/hcp/details/society/income-inequality.aspx

North America and Europe usually have less income inequality and fewer people living in poverty (McMullin, 2004).

That said, poverty is different today than it was a century or even 50 years ago. In a digital age, where much of daily life takes place online, relative poverty has taken a new meaning. People who live in poverty today—whether it is relative or absolute poverty—cannot participate in digital culture. That makes them disadvantaged in terms of getting information, applying for jobs, and benefitting from sales related to e-commerce.

Box 6.3 shows that a lack of access to digital media has many consequences for people. In a society where these media are ubiquitous, not having access can even be stigmatizing. For example, youth today stay in touch after school via text messaging and social media. This heavy reliance on digital technology may isolate young people who have little or no access to these technologies. They may be stigmatized—excluded, mocked, or ignored—by their classmates because they can't participate in the ongoing digital communication. Stigmatization can have many negative effects on people including depression and low self-esteem.

stigma disgrace and marginalization because of life circumstances or characteristics of a person, preventing that person from full social acceptance.

Indigenous Populations and Economic Challenges

Canada faces many challenges today nationally and internationally, but one of the greatest is the absolute and relative poverty of its Indigenous people. Indigenous people comprise hundreds of different nations that make up around 4 per cent of the population (Statistics Canada, 2015a). But one thing that unites them, despite different languages and cultures, is their relative disadvantage in Canadian society.

Theory in Everyday Life

6.3 | The Digital Divide, and Differential Benefits from Digital Media

People who live in absolute or relative poverty are often described as the "have nots" of society. In comparison with the "haves," they are less likely to own digital devices and have access to the internet. As our society relies more and more heavily on digital technologies for all activities, being offline has larger consequences (Quan-Haase, 2016).

For example, today, many government services have moved online, and people without internet access and skills are disadvantaged, as they cannot easily access these services. When it comes to accessing and using digital technologies, three divides have been described. The first divide, mainly studied in the 1990s, distinguished between people who had access to the internet and people who did not. This research showed that socioeconomic variables, such as education, income, and occupation, are key predictors of who can afford to be online and who cannot (Robinson et al., 2015).

The second digital divide captures differences in digital skills among various social groups, showing that a barrier to internet use is not reducible to merely having access. To prosper today, a person also has to have the skills to use the internet. Today, a third-level digital divide describes "gaps in individual capacity to translate their internet access and use into favorable offline outcomes" (van Deursen & Helsper, 2015, p. 30).

This understanding of the third-level digital divide helps us recognize how differential access to and use of the internet can amplify existing inequalities. This differential can also create real benefits for people who are online and can take full advantage of an array of informational, social, economic, and educational benefits afforded by digital media. Thus, living in either absolute or relative poverty today means not having access to the internet and lacking information resources, educational possibilities and overall participation in the digital sphere. Said another way, being poor today means not only being money-poor; it means being information-poor. Being excluded from the chief information sources of our society can have a large impact on how young people in poverty see themselves and can increase their sense of alienation and **stigma**.

Examine the benefits you have received from your use of the internet in Table 6.2. Circle yes and no responses for each question.

TABLE 6.2 Internet Outcomes Measured through Resource Mobilization

Field	Through the internet . . .	Circle	
Economic labour	I found a (better) job.	Yes	No
	I earn (more) money.	Yes	No
Economic commerce	I bought a product more cheaply than I could in the local store.	Yes	No
	I booked a cheaper vacation.	Yes	No
	I traded goods that I would not have sold otherwise.	Yes	No
Social	I have more contact with family and friends.	Yes	no
	It is easier for friends and family to get a hold of me.	Yes	No
	I made new friends whom I met later offline.	Yes	No
	I met a potential partner using online dating.	Yes	No
Political	I expressed my political opinion in online discussions.	Yes	No
	I joined a political association, union, or party.	Yes	No
	I did research to help me decide which political party to vote for.	Yes	No
Institutional governmental	I am more up-to-date with government information.	Yes	No
	I am able to contact the government.	Yes	No
	I have discovered that I am entitled to a particular benefit, subsidy, or tax advantage.	Yes	No
Institutional health	I determined the medical condition from which I was suffering.	Yes	No
	I received advice that has made me healthier.	Yes	No
	I found out where to go to be treated for a condition I suffered from.	Yes	No
Educational	I found an educational course that suits me.	Yes	No
	I attended a course that I would not have been able to take offline.	Yes	No
	I was able to do research for an assignment that I would otherwise have had to do in a library.	Yes	No
Sum		Total Yes =	
		Total No =	

Source: Adapted from van Deursen, A. J. A. M., & Helsper, E. J. (2015). The third-level digital divide: Who benefits most from being online? *Communication and Information Technologies Annual, 10,* 29–52. http://doi.org/10.1108/S2050-206020150000010002

Time to reflect

In what domain has the internet benefitted your life most? How about least? Now, consider a 12-year-old girl living in relative poverty. What do you think she would miss by not having access to the internet at home? How would this deprivation likely influence her educational outcomes and her long-term prospects in the labour market?

Indigenous populations are unique in at least two ways when it comes to socioeconomic challenges. First, a large proportion live on reserves and these reserves often lack necessary infrastructures such as roads, electricity, clean water, well-funded education, and health care services. Second, many Indigenous communities are located in remote areas and are therefore isolated from mainstream Canadian culture. The cost associated with bringing food, in particular fresh produce, to such remote communities has made it very difficult to provide adequate and affordable nourishment (Stefanovich, 2016). Food prices in many Northern communities have skyrocketed in recent years, at the same time that pollution and land development are preventing traditional hunting and fishing, creating a real food crisis on reserves. Food Secure Canada, a pan-Canadian alliance, has found that many people living in the North need to spend over half of their income on food to meet basic nutritional requirements. According to Mushkegowuk Council Grand Chief Jonathan Solomon, this puts further pressure on

Dashboard
Video:
Colonization Road

poverty line an agreed upon income at which a standard of living that is considered "acceptable" should be affordable. What is considered acceptable is not static, but varies considerably within societies, across societies, and over time.

communities that are already living under the **poverty line**. "How can people afford this? Because most of the First Nation communities have 80 to 70 per cent of unemployment and they're on social assistance" (Stefanovich, 2016).

Economic disparities are particularly evident when we compare the incomes of the Indigenous population in Canada with those of non-Indigenous Canadians (see Figure 6.4). The most recent data show that in 2010 non-Indigenous Canadians earned (on average) $27,622, while Indigenous people (including First Nations members, Métis, and Inuit people) earned $20,060, leaving an income gap of over $7,000 annually. The average earnings of First Nations people within Indigenous communities are lowest of all with an average annual income of only $17,621 (Statistics Canada, 2015c).

Further exacerbating their social and economic problems are high unemployment rates among Indigenous people, which range from 10.1 per cent in Quebec to 20.7 per cent in New Brunswick (Centre for the Study of Living Standards, 2012). Since many chronic stressors are present in these communities—such as unemployment, lack of clean drinking water, racism, poverty, poor education, unemployment, family instability, environmental degradation, and residential instability—for many Indigenous people, drugs and alcohol provide an escape and are a form of self-medication (though it's also important to note that a higher per cent of the Indigenous population are non-drinkers than the non-Indigenous population [Statistics Canada, 2015a]). The combination of stressors creates a strong barrier against social mobility. This reduced access to self-determination, along with little hope for social change, leads people to feel helpless and deters them from engaging in active coping mechanisms (King, Smith, & Gracey, 2009).

We have noted that remoteness is part of the challenge facing Indigenous populations, in terms of accessing resources, but "outside of major centres, many remote and rural First Nations remain underserved" (First Mile, n.d.; see also McMahon, O'Donnell, Smith, Walmark, & Beaton, 2011). Often this is linked to a lack of infrastructure to provide broadband or a lack of equipment and high costs. Much scholarship looking at the digital divide shows that differences in levels of connectivity linked to poor infrastructure and lack of internet-enabled devices as well as in digital literacy are further intensifying existing inequalities and creating unbalanced power relations that disadvantage people who are already marginalized (Robinson et al., 2015; Witte & Mannon, 2010). To improve connectivity, different strategies such as the First Mile program have been proposed to increase Indigenous inclusion in the networked society. According to McMahon (2014), the First Mile program is an approach that focuses on "ways that public policies, regulations, and other supports enable user communities to generate and sustain their own networked digital infrastructures"

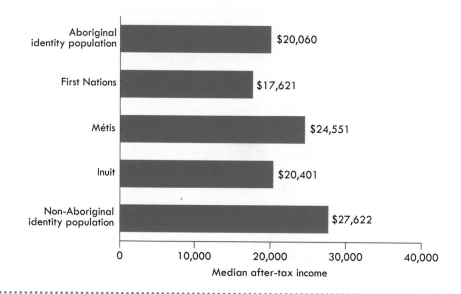

FIGURE 6.4 Median After-Tax Income in 2010 by Indigenous Identity, Population Aged 15 and Older

Source: http://www.statcan.gc.ca/pub/89-645-x/2015001/income-revenu-eng.htm

(p. 2005). In 2017 the federal government allocated $3.4 billion in spending for infrastructure, health, and education in Indigenous communities (CBC News, 2017). Even as the internet functions as a source of inequality, it has helped Indigenous people put forward the crises they face, connect with allies, and push governments into providing better infrastructure and services. See Chapter 16 for more on Indigenous communities using the internet to gain media coverage, political leverage, and access to resources.

Homelessness

In recent decades, Canadian cities have experienced a housing crisis in line with exponential increases in real estate prices. This crisis has further intensified the lack of affordable housing in cities, creating an increase in homelessness.

Most affected by this trend are low-income people and families, because they are usually renters and not homeowners. This fact makes them vulnerable to fluctuations in rental demand and rental price. For them, even small increases in rental prices can mean being forced onto the streets and into shelters. How many people are homeless in Canada in a given year is impossible to know exactly; indeed, the numbers of homeless people seem to vary from day to day. However, estimates suggest that Canada's homeless population numbers between 200,000 and 300,000 people (see Figure 6.5).

These numbers don't tell the full story, as an estimated 50,000 Canadians are described as "**hidden homeless**"—people without homes who stay with friends or family temporarily. Many homeless people temporarily or more permanently stay in shelters, where and when they are available. Emergency shelters provide immediate, short-term accommodation to homeless people, with residents being expected to leave the facilities each morning. Other shelters provide longer-term homes for specific populations, such as for homeless youth or women and their children who are victims of family violence. We discuss family violence and victimization in Chapter 7.

hidden homeless people without homes who stay with friends or family temporarily rather than in shelters or in public spaces.

FIGURE 6.5 Homelessness in Canada: Key Figures

Source: Author generated. Based on The Canadian Press. (2016). Homelessness in Canada: Key statistics. Retrieved December 7, 2016, from http://www.ctvnews.ca/canada/homelessness-in-canada-key-statistics-1.2819986

Sergei Bachlakov/Shutterstock.com

Residents of Vancouver's Eastside protest condo developments in their neighbourhood. Affordable housing is a rare commodity in Canada's largest metropolitan areas.

The homeless population is heterogeneous, comprising people from all walks of life, including single men and women, young people, families, and people with serious physical or mental health conditions. Life on the streets is dangerous, so no wonder the life expectancy of many homeless is around 39 years, which is about half the reported national average (Trypuc & Robinson, 2009). Because the streets can be dangerous, some homeless people have started to use cellphones for safety reasons as well as to stay in touch with family and services. This, however, has led to some controversy as we discuss in Box 6.4.

Food Banks

We may like to imagine that food scarcity is only a problem in the Global South and not a real issue in Canada. But the reality is that thousands of Canadians rely on food banks every day. In fact, in 2016 an estimated 863,492 people received food from food banks each month (Food Banks Canada, 2016).

Several factors have contributed to an unprecedented rise in the use of food banks. The main factor is the unstable economy, resulting in increased levels of unemployment in both mid- and low-income families. This is evident, for example, in Alberta, with the precipitous decline in the oil industry. However, regions that have seen an increase in refugees have also seen greater reliance on food banks, since 13 per cent of the people who use food banks are immigrants or refugees (CBC News, 2016).

Another contributing factor has been a spike in food prices. Food prices have gone up around 4 per cent per year—at a far faster rate than the increase in wages; and these increases have particularly affected fresh produce such as meat and eggs, making it difficult for families to afford nutritious foods (Food Banks Canada, 2016). Average salaries by contrast have only increased around 3 per cent annually, creating a real—and expanding—gap in purchasing power (Charlebois et al., 2012). Table 6.3 shows this increase in the reliance on food banks across all provinces. In particular Alberta, Saskatchewan, and Manitoba have seen large increases of up to 136 per cent, 77 per cent, and 53 per cent since 2008, respectively, putting huge pressure on food banks to meet the food needs of local communities.

Spotlight On

6.4 | Can Homeless People Afford Cellphones?

Consider the social and economic disadvantages that people who do not have internet connectivity face. People who are disconnected cannot access the news in real time, they cannot connect to social networks via Facebook, Instagram, and other social media, and they cannot access many government resources (for example, information about available services).

Often homeless people are left out of the discussion regarding internet use because many assume that if you are homeless, you have more pressing needs than internet access. Yet homeless people have interests, hobbies, a need for information, and in particular, a need for social connectivity. Precisely because they lack a permanent home, homeless people need cellphones and internet access to help them connect with the larger, dispersed world. One reason many people do not think of the homeless as needing a phone is because they think of cellphones as a status symbol, displaying wealth. Since the 2010s, however, this way of thinking has changed. Cellphones are ubiquitous today, with most Canadians relying on their phones for connectedness. Cellphone use is so popular that many young adults are already showing problematic (or addictive) use of electronic devices and cellphones (CAMH, 2016).

For homeless people, present-day cellphones, or smart phones, provide three key benefits:

- Cellphones can allow them to call for protective services, such as the police, thereby increasing their safety.
- Cellphones can help them seek and find employment and housing, since potential employers and landlords can contact them conveniently.
- Cellphones can help them coordinate essential activities, such as appointments with government services and doctors' visits.

Taken together, then, cellphones can no longer be considered a luxury item; today, they are a necessity. No wonder the UN has declared internet connectivity a human right! That's why it makes sense to promote and encourage cellphone and internet access to the Canadians who are most in need (Woolley, 2014). To achieve this, we might need to implement universal, high-quality internet access as a service paid for by our taxes—just like universal health care (and someday, perhaps, universal daycare and post-secondary education.)

The cellphone has also become integrated in entrepreneurial transactions that help homeless people. In Stockholm, homeless people can take payment through their cellphone for *Situation Stockholm*, a culture magazine sold by homeless people.

Some Canadians think that people who access food banks are homeless or otherwise unlike themselves. But this is not the case. Only 2 per cent of the people who access food banks live in shelters or on the street; 66 per cent live in rented homes, 20 per cent live in social housing, and another 8 per cent own their home (Food Banks Canada, 2016). Surprisingly, more than one-third (38 per cent) of the people helped are children and youth under 18 years of age and 40 per cent of households that receive assistance comprise families with children (see Figure 6.6). Many food bank users are highly educated as well. For example, in Toronto, more than a quarter of food bank users have completed a university degree (Food Banks Canada, 2016).

TABLE 6.3 Food Bank Use in Canada, by Province, 2008 and 2016

Province/ territory	Total assisted, 2016	Per cent children, 2016	Population, 2016	Per cent population assisted, 2016	Total assisted, 2008	Per cent Difference, 2008–2016
British Columbia	103,464	32.2	4,751,600	2.18	78,101	32.5
Alberta	37,293	39.4	4,252,900	0.88	33,580	136.1
Saskatchewan	31,395	45.2	1,150,600	2.73	17,751	76.9
Manitoba	61,914	42.9	1,318,100	4.70	40,464	53.0
Ontario	335,944	33.4	13,983,000	2.40	314,258	6.9
Quebec	171,800	34.5	8,326,100	2.06	127,536	34.7
New Brunswick	19,769	32.5	756,800	2.61	15,638	26.4
Nova Scotia	23,840	30.4	949,500	2.51	16,915	40.9
Prince Edward Island	3,370	35.5	148,600	2.27	2,892	16.5
Newfoundland & Labrador	26,366	37.5	530,100	4.97	27,260	–3.3
Territories	6,337	37.3	119,100	5.32	1,340	–
Canada	**863,492**	**38.2**	**36,286,400**	**2.38**	**675,735**	**27.8**

Source: Adapted from Food Banks Canada. (2016). *Hunger count 2016*. Mississauga, ON. Retrieved from https://www.foodbankscanada.ca/getmedia/6173994f-8a25-40d9-acdf-660a28e40f37/HungerCount_2016_final_singlepage.pdf page 6 and http://www.statcan.gc.ca/tables-tableaux/sum-som/l01/cst01/demo02a-eng.htm

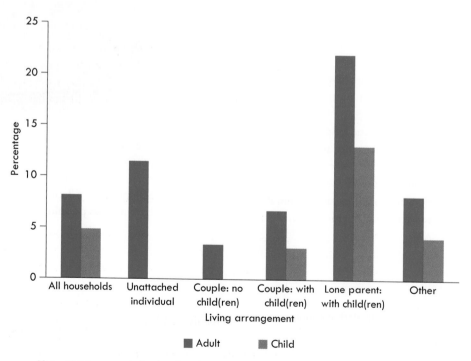

Note: Children are defined as less than 18 years old.

FIGURE 6.6 Percentage of Households with Food Insecurity (Moderate or Severe), By Living Arrangement, and Adult or Child Measure, Canada 2011–2012

Source: Statistics Canada, 2013a. http://www.statcan.gc.ca/pub/82-625-x/2013001/article/11889-eng.htm.

For many Canadian families, in particular families with children, food banks play a crucial role in supplying their nutritional needs. Thousands of volunteers across Canada help with the sorting and organizing of food at food banks. Many people don't know that as much as 38 per cent of the food provided by food banks is fresh (e.g., eggs, milk, fruit, and yogurt).

Time to reflect

Take a moment to exercise your sociological imagination. Given Canada's high economic prosperity, why might we be seeing an increase in reliance on food banks? Think about the distinction between the economic prosperity of Canada as a whole, and the economic prosperity of individuals, as well as the effects that some of the trends discussed in this chapter might have on the lives of individuals within Canada.

Social Determinants of Health

A key priority area in research on inequality is understanding health differences; and a key aspect to understanding differences in health is the study of the **social determinants of health (SDOH)**. SDOH are closely linked to differences in social class, either as a cause or consequence of class belonging, and are often found to have much greater effects on a person's health and well-being than other factors we usually consider relevant to health, such as healthy eating and maintaining an active lifestyle. For example, as seen in Figure 6.7, a Canadian's chance of surviving to 75 years of age goes up by 22.7 per cent for men and 13.9 per cent for women from the lowest to highest income group (*The Globe and Mail*, 2017).

Health is, of course, not just life expectancy but daily experience of well-being, including both physical and mental wellness. Education is one the most statistically significant determinants of health; the 2013–14 Canadian Community Health Survey found, for example, that the percentage of women who have very good or excellent self-perceived overall health varied from 48.2 per cent on average for women with less than a high school diploma, to 70.4 per cent on average for women with a bachelor's degree or higher. Perceived mental health also varied from 63.5 per cent to 76.2 per cent self-perceiving very good or excellent mental health, respectively (Bushnik, 2016).

As mentioned in Chapter 1 (Box 1.5), SDOH are estimated to account for up to 40 per cent of health outcomes, compared to health behaviours (30 per cent), clinical care (20 per cent), and environmental

social determinants of health (SDOH) the numerous social factors such as income, education, and employment security that affect a person's health and well-being.

Rene Johnston/Toronto Star via Getty Images

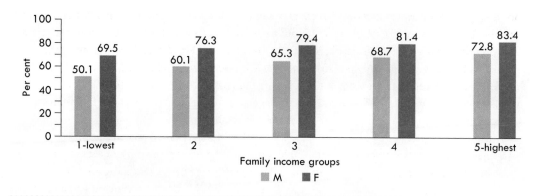

FIGURE 6.7 Probability of Survival to Age 75, by Sex

Source: Globe staff (2017, March 20). How income inequality hurts every Canadian's chance of building a better life. *The Globe and Mail*. Retrieved from http://www.the-globeandmail.com/news/national/time-to-lead/our-time-to-lead-income-inequality/article15316231/

factors (10 per cent) (Booske et al., 2010). Much of our understanding of SDOH in Canada comes from foundational work by Mikkonen and Raphael (2010), who discuss the effects of numerous factors, often interrelated, on health outcomes, including: income and income distribution, education, employment and job security, working conditions, early childhood development, food insecurity, housing, **social exclusion**, social safety net, health services, Indigenous status, gender, racialization, immigration, and disabilities.

social exclusion the inability to participate in commonly accepted activities in a given society.

To better understand how these SDOH factors are interrelated, let's take a closer look at income, employment, and education. The more educated people are, the healthier they are likely to be, as their income is likely to be higher, and they are also more likely to have access to information at home or through work about how to maintain and improve their health through workshops, expert reviews, and online websites. In other words, a person's level of education is strongly associated with other SDOH such as income, employment security, and working conditions (Mikkonen & Raphael, 2010). How much money a person makes is often considered the single most important social determinant of health. Diet, exercise, and alcohol and tobacco use vary by income, and income also has a direct impact on other social determinants such as shelter, education, and early childhood development (Mikkonen & Raphael, 2010). People who have employment not only receive a steady income from their work, but their work also gives them a structure for their daily lives; it provides social interaction, a sense of purpose, and prospects for the future. On the other hand, being unemployed leads to financial pressures and mental health issues, including stress and a higher risk of depression, anxiety, and suicide (Mikkonen & Raphael, 2010). The nature of one's work also affects health; employment security, physical conditions at work, work pace and stress, working hours, and opportunities for self-expression and individual development at work all affect a person's health and well-being. Stressful jobs can also increase the risk of both physical and mental illnesses (Mikkonen & Raphael, 2010).

Access to social and institutional supports, beyond employment and education, are also important SDOH. People who are socially excluded, marginalized, or disadvantaged often find it more difficult to secure good jobs and to access social services, including health care. As a result, they run a higher risk of poor health, and are less likely to be adequately treated when they do fall ill. The benefits, programs, and supports that protect citizens during various life changes (e.g., loss of a loved one, pregnancy, or unemployment) strengthen their social **safety net** and affect health and well-being (Mikkonen & Raphael, 2010). If a person can rely on a social safety net during life changes, then there is less likelihood of these events resulting in permanent health problems, whereas inadequate support can lead to more health problems. A significant amount of health support comes from health care services themselves. People who receive proper treatment from health professionals when they are ill or injured have better health than those who do not. Canada has a universal health care system that spreads the costs for health care across all members of society. This ensures that low-income individuals still have access to good health care, although inequalities continue to persist in terms of access to doctors, medical procedures, and quality of care.

safety net the public and private services provided to individuals with low incomes or no incomes to prevent them from falling into poverty.

Living conditions throughout our lives (and even before we are born), and our ability to access social and institutional supports, are also closely related. For example, if a pregnant woman eats a poor diet, or consumes alcohol or tobacco, this can have long-lasting detrimental health effects on her child after birth and throughout the child's life course. Research suggests that stress can also affect prenatal development (Huizink, Robles de Medina, Mulder, Visser, & Buitelaar, 2003).

Access to adequate nutrition is also crucial. As Mikkonen and Raphael (2010) put it, "people who experience food insecurity are unable to have an adequate diet in terms of its quality or quantity" (p. 26). People who experience food insecurity consume fewer servings of fruits and vegetables, milk products, and vitamins than those in food-secure households.

Another prerequisite for good health is proper shelter, in relatively clean condition, with access to plumbing and clean drinking water. Affordable housing is important, as payment for costly accommodation may leave people with less to spend on other basic needs, which can also affect their health.

Marginalized communities—including Indigenous people, women, racialized Canadians, immigrants, refugees, LGBTQ people, and people with disabilities—are affected by SDOH. In particular, Indigenous peoples in Canada experience worse health outcomes than other Canadians because of continuing income inequalities, inadequate housing and crowded living conditions, lower levels of education, higher rates of unemployment, and numerous other factors (Benoit, 2017). Although women live longer than men on average, various other gender inequalities, like access to education, unequal job opportunities, and victimization, tend to make women have poorer health outcomes than men. Racialized Canadians experience a range of hostile living circumstances that affect their health, including unemployment, lower-than-average incomes and difficulty in accessing good quality health care (Mikkonen & Raphael, 2010). The stress of daily microaggressions can aggravate health outcomes for racialized people in Canada (see Chapter 8). In addition to microaggressions such as assumptions of heterosexuality by health care professionals, LGBTQ people are also more likely to experience violent victimization, are more likely to experience discrimination at work, are more likely to be underemployed, and are more likely to be homeless than the cis-gender heterosexual majority (Mulé et al., 2009). Perceived access to social support has been shown to be positively associated with physical and mental health status (Hwang et al., 2009). Beyond any health effects related to a particular disability, the amount of perceived support available and, more importantly, the accessibility of the world around them to allow for self-sufficiency are vitally important for the health of disabled Canadians. Compared to other countries, Canada underfunds programs that provide support to people with disabilities and has also made less progress in making society accessible to our disabled citizens.

All of the above does not get into the complex intersectionalities of these marginalized communities and their SDOH. As just one example, when comparing off-reserve Indigenous women and men, one study found that after controlling for age, health behaviours, education, employment, and income, off-reserve Indigenous women were also significantly more likely than off-reserve Indigenous men to have at least one chronic health condition (Rotenberg, 2016). The important thing to note is that these intersectional inequalities exist and play a key role in individual health outcomes.

The ascendancy of neo-liberal ideologies in political discourse from the 1980s onward has brought enormous pressure to bear on governments to restrain spending on what were deemed "private" or "personal" aspects of people's lives (Raphael, 2006). Indeed, many people today think that everyone has a personal responsibility to preserve his or her own health. Though the federal and provincial governments continue to spend large amounts of money on health care, there is growing unease about the balance between public and private (or individual) responsibility in this realm. For this reason, we cannot ignore the harmful consequences of overemphasizing individual responsibility for health. Doing so decontextualizes people's real-life needs, ignores the importance of the SDOH, and indulges in victim blaming (Korp, 2008; Minkler, 1999).

Where does the neo-liberal focus on personal responsibility come from? In part, it comes from the practice of medicine itself. Underpinning these individualistic beliefs are **biomedical** and **behavioural models of health** and medicine (Raphael, 2006). From the biomedical perspective, poor health is the product of a person's physiological and genetic traits. The behavioural model likewise puts responsibility for good health on the shoulders of the individual. This theory frames bad choices, such as smoking, bad diet, or a sedentary lifestyle, as the causes of poor health, and notes that such choices are entirely within an individual's control (Baranowski et al., 2003).

biomedical model of health an approach to health that considers only physiological and genetic factors as relevant to a person's well-being.

behavioural model of health an approach to health that considers the lifestyle choices of the individual as the only factors relevant to a person's well-being.

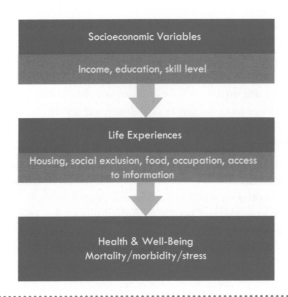

FIGURE 6.8 Example of How SDOH Affect Health and Well-Being

Source: Author generated

Because in Canada health care is paid for by the state, and the ability to pay for services is supposedly not a factor, Canadians tend to think that everyone has an equal chance of enjoying good health. But even though people of lower income use health care services the most, they have worse health outcomes than people with higher income (Atler et al., 2011). This shows that Universal health care does not negate the negative health outcomes associated with low income (Atler, Stikel, Chong, & Henry, 2011).

To address these shortcomings of the biomedical and behavioural models, researchers developed a more comprehensive **biopsychosocial** approach to health, which recognizes that a variety of emotional, mental, and physical aspects of health contribute to a person's overall well-being and a high quality of life. In addition to physiological factors, this model considers the way in which social factors influence well-being (Boudreau, Cassell, & Fuks, 2007; Strumberg & Martin, 2009). These include safe, affordable housing, social and economic integration, and a supportive social network (Yip et al., 2007; Prus, 2011). In other words, various socio-demographic factors (including sex, age, and racialization) interact to influence a person's exposure to stressors. People who are persistently subjected to discrimination, for example, are more prone to suffer anxiety, poor sleep, and even depression, both reducing their quality of life and making them more susceptible to disease. Although increasing numbers of researchers and health care professionals have adopted the biopsychosocial model, political leaders and the general public have been resistant to calls for reduced inequality as a health-promotion strategy (Gatchel, Peng, Peters, Fuchs, & Turk, 2007; Rutty & Sullivan, 2010). Among the provinces, British Columbia and Ontario have been least likely to address structural factors contributing to poor health (Gore & Kothari, 2012).

biopsychosocial model of health an approach to health that recognizes how a variety of emotional, mental, and physical aspects associated with a person's life contribute to their overall well-being.

Promoting Social and Economic Inclusion

Societies vary in terms of their success in alleviating poverty and creating greater equality among its citizens. Considering the variability that exists in poverty levels across nations (see Chapter 9), several important factors and interventions have made a real difference in low-income people's lives. Failure to do this—an inability of institutions, especially governments, to support those in need—visibly creates mistrust and anger. In the next section we discuss three approaches that address poverty and stimulate greater economic and social equality.

Child Care and Early Childhood Education

There are several reasons why child care and early childhood education are important to reducing inequality. The early years of a child's life are crucial for learning and development. As a result, children who are exposed to a rich sensory learning environment will have numerous advantages in later life. However, many low-income families cannot afford good quality child care and other early childhood education offerings. Within Canada, child-care access varies by province. For example, not only does the Quebec government subsidize child-care facilities, it directly takes a family's income into consideration when calculating payments. A family with an income of $50,545 or less will pay only $7.55 per day, per child in care (Québec, Ministère des Finances, 2016). At the highest income bracket, a family would pay only $20.70 a day per child. A second child would only cost 50 per cent of the cost for a first child in care, and there would be no additional cost for subsequent children in care. This makes it possible for families with lower incomes and several young children to afford high-quality early childhood education while seeking or holding employment. The hesitation in implementing universal child-care services throughout Canada, such as those found in Quebec, are numerous, but one reason is that some people—often, people with no children and high-income earners—oppose the use of taxpayers' money for the purposes of funding public child care and early education. Perhaps this is because they do not understand the long-term economic and cultural benefits Canada can enjoy if it implements this program nationwide.

Time to reflect

Would you support universal child care in your province, even if you never have children?

Formal Education and Credentials

A second path to greater equality is through more education. In fact, many people consider education to be the single most important equalizer in society. Education prepares people for the labour market and validates their skills and capabilities. Research shows that education levels are directly linked to finding a job, obtaining a higher wage, and maintaining employment for longer periods of time. As of 2007, people who graduated from high school had a 30 per cent higher likelihood of employment compared with those who did not graduate (Canadian Education Statistics Council, 2010). People with a completed university degree had incomes 50 per cent higher than those who only graduated from high school (Association of Universities and Colleges of Canada, 2011). The Canadian public education system ranks among the top in the world. This is due to its high-quality curriculum, which is publicly funded and free.

Data from 2012 shows that the proportion of adults aged 25 to 34 with at least a high school diploma was about 92 per cent; and this rate is considerably higher than for past generations of Canadians, and higher than in many other nations (Statistics Canada, 2015b). And the spread of education is continuing: there was also an increase from 40 per cent in 2000 to 53 per cent in 2012 in the percentage of adults aged 25 to 64 who completed their college or university degree. This places Canada in a unique position, because this is the highest rate among all OECD countries (Statistics Canada, 2015b). Still, not all Canadians have equal access to this education. We've already briefly mentioned the reduced access Indigenous communities have to education; see Chapter 11 for more on barriers to education in Canada.

Time to reflect

What motivated you to choose to pursue a post-secondary education? Were increased opportunities in the labour market a factor you took into account? How does your current educational attainment compare with the highest level of education attained in your extended family—i.e., by your parents, grandparents, uncles and aunts and cousins? Did this, consciously or subconsciously, impact your choice?

6.5 | Closing Global Inequality through Digital Education: One Laptop per Child

One Laptop per Child (OLPC) is a US non-profit organization whose mandate is to "create educational opportunities for the world's poorest children by providing each child with a rugged, low-cost, low-power, connected laptop with content and software" (OLPC, 2010). The idea behind OLPC is to empower the world's least-advantaged children by involving them in their own education and increasing their connectivity to others.

Nicholas Negroponte, the former head of MIT's Media Lab, established OLPC in 2002 following a trip to Cambodia. There, Negroponte witnessed first-hand the effect of providing children and their families with connected technologies. Understanding that two billion children in the Global South have little or no access to formal education, Negroponte aimed to use new technologies, particularly cost- and energy-efficient computers, to assist in the education of disadvantaged children by providing increased access to resources and tools available through digital sources (OLPC, 2010). The goals of OLPC are to teach computing skills through play and exploration.

One laptop per Child/Flickr

Girls in India interact with one of the OLPC prototypes, which were designed to be sturdy, environmentally friendly, and easy to use.

In many countries in the Global South, the opportunities found through public education are even more lacking, because schools there are costly or limited in availability and quality. In poor communities without public education, parents often cannot afford to send their children to school, so kids do not learn how to write, read, and do math. Often children are needed to help take care of younger siblings at home or work alongside their parents. The problem is worst for girls in patriarchal communities that limit and undervalue the roles and contributions of women. In some of the poorest countries in the world, girls have less than a 50 per cent chance of completing even primary school. But in recent years, some girls have advocated for their right to an education. Malala Yousafzai has become known worldwide for demanding the right of girls and women to become educated. Malala's commitment to women's rights and education won her the Nobel Peace Prize in 2014 at age 17, making Malala the youngest prize recipient ever (see Chapter 7). Happily, new technology has helped to open new educational opportunities for children in countries in the Global South. Box 6.5 discusses an ambitious initiative to educate children in the Global South with the aim of preparing them for a digitally based labour market.

Providing children living in the Global South with an education poses a great challenge. However, new technologies open possibilities for encouraging new forms of learning and provide access to a wealth of online resources. Still, such devices are costly. As digital technologies become more and more central to global life—to education, commerce, information access, and social connectivity—social inequalities will increase and opportunities for people lacking digital skills will decrease (Chen, Boase, & Wellman, 2002). Thus, the pervasiveness of digital technologies will create new means of learning and new opportunities for advancement, while simultaneously increasing inequality and exclusion for large numbers of citizens around the globe.

Safety Nets

A third solution to inequality has to do with safety nets. A "safety net" includes all the services—whether made available by the state or other non-profit institutions—that prevent people from falling into poverty. The most common forms of safety net services include social assistance, universal health care, homeless shelters, and food banks. In Canada, health care is publicly funded and available to all citizens (though as mentioned above, social determinants affect how easily accessible, as well as how effective, this health care is), providing perhaps the most important safety net.

A second important safety net in Canada is **social assistance**. The underlying idea of social assistance is that some members of society are unable to work; therefore, it is necessary that people who do work share part of their income with those who need it. Social assistance, however, often fails the people who receive it. Contrary to popular belief, social assistance often fails to cover basic living costs, including food expenses, clothing, and transportation. About *half* of the households accessing food banks in Canada are also recipients of social assistance (Food Banks Canada, 2016). This shows that social assistance payments are not sufficient to sustain most families. Second, social assistance programs perpetuate a spiral of inequality. Often, people living on social assistance cannot give their children the same opportunities—for example, extracurricular opportunities to study dance, art, music lessons, and sports—as people with larger and more secure incomes. This creates new inequalities that pass from one generation to the next.

> **social assistance** a program that provides money to the lowest earning and some vulnerable groups in society to enable them to meet their basic needs.

Finally, the goal of social assistance is to help people seek stable employment and end their dependence on governmental assistance. But some people who are on social assistance may not be helped in this way. For one, they feel that they are not well prepared for the workforce and will not be able to find employment. They also know that most of the jobs available to them pay low wages, and the costs of getting to and from work, and paying for daycare, will often take a big chunk of their potential paycheque—sometimes not making the transition from social assistance to working financially viable. People in this situation often feel trapped by the program that was designed to help. So, besides providing short-term social assistance, governments need to work on increasing the minimum wage and opportunities for high quality, low-cost child care to help people in seeking employment.

Food banks and shelters were discussed briefly above; they are also important safety nets, in most cases run by non-profit institutions rather than by governments. There are two important issues to consider with regards to the role of food banks in fighting poverty that we have yet to address. First, the normalization of food banks gives people the impression that the hunger crisis is taken care of, when in reality the larger problems underlying the crises are not being properly addressed (Riches, 2011). Second, this movement of responsibility from governments to "charities" has been referred to as the "de-politicization of hunger" and deflects public attention and outrage from their elected representatives (Riches & Silvasti, 2014). By creating the illusion that hunger is the domain of charity, to be taken care of by food banks, elected governments are relieved of accountability (Riches, 2011). For this problem to be solved, it is important to reframe food as a fundamental human right that needs to be available to all citizens, and is an absolute responsibility of government, not charities (Riches, 2011). Like food banks, shelters often do not have sufficient resources to take care of all the people who are in need. Many shelters rely heavily on donations and volunteer support, and have also seen their funding cut and have struggled to keep services up and running (Richmond, 2015). In both instances, governments often fail to create sufficient infrastructure and allocate enough resources to meet the obvious need. Among the long-term solutions suggested are affordable housing, subsidized care for homeless people dealing with mental health issues, and means for homeless people to train for and receive employment (Macnaughton et al., 2015).

Conclusions

This chapter has covered topics related to social inequality, social stratification, and class. All of these topics are centrally important to any understanding of sociological inquiry. They are also central to many initiatives aimed at using sociological knowledge to promote greater equality and well-being among all members of society.

The chapter has discussed the assessment of poverty and inequality by examining statistical measures of poverty. It has also examined the complex association between social inequality and outcomes such as physical and mental health, poverty, and personal well-being. In this connection, we noted the extent of poverty among different low-status groups in Canada, including Indigenous communities, homeless people, and low-income families. In doing so, we took pains to distinguish between absolute poverty—a lack of income needed to fulfill basic needs (e.g., water, food, and clothing)—and relative poverty, meaning the deprivation of choice, and the relative (or comparative) lack of income and access to resources.

Another important topic addressed in this chapter was social mobility, defined as a person's change in social status within a social hierarchy. Much of the discussion of inequality in our society tends to focus on upward mobility, often attributing economic success to individuals' achievements, talents, and perseverance. As we have seen, this is only (a very small) part of the story. In many countries in the Global North, Canada included, education has functioned as the most important equalizer, given that educational achievement typically predicts improved income and occupational status.

That said, not all Canadians have the same access to higher education, owing to the presence of class-related social barriers. These barriers operate both within and across generations, and contribute to reproducing forms of inequality in terms of health, income, and occupational status. However, more recently, as Canadian society has shifted from industrial to digital, innovation and technical skills have also emerged as important factors affecting upward mobility. As for downward mobility, while it is often absent from societal discourse, this experience is very real for many Canadians, and carries lasting harmful effects on people's lives and outlooks.

Social inequality interacts with other social determinants of health to create health outcome disparities within Canada and globally. The social determinants of health reflect a biopsychosocial perspective on health and health care, and while researchers have embraced this nuanced perspective on health, there is still intense political opposition to making policy based on this perspective. However, research continues to show that to combat health inequalities, we must reduce class and income inequality, among other things.

There are no easy solutions to the problems of social inequality and poverty. As we have seen, there are several approaches to alleviating poverty and creating greater equality in societies. Solutions include governmental social assistance programs that target low-income individuals and families, privately run food banks, and charitable housing shelters. These programs all provide important short-term solutions but do not address the underlying social and economic forces that create problems of poverty and inequality in the first place, or the mechanisms that perpetuate them.

Moreover, these programs need to be flexible, to meet the unique needs of different groups of Canadians with intersecting inequalities. Providing greater access to education relevant to the modern digital economy may, for some, come from high-quality early child-care programs, as well as primary and secondary school curricula that focus on digital skills development. For others, it may come from enrichment programs for socially at-risk students, and bridging programs for students who lack the requisite skills to transition into a university or college setting. Critically, all of these programs need to respect the specific needs and interests of targeted populations. For, though we have not discussed it in this chapter, social stratification also implies a deprivation of dignity as well as material well-being. Our programs to improve Canadian society will have to respect people's need for respect, as well as self-determination and material security.

Questions for Critical Thought

1. Is it better for Canada to be a classless society or not? Discuss from the perspectives of government, corporate society, and the general population.

2. What are the factors that make it difficult to define and measure poverty? Discuss how various definitions of poverty can serve as political tools in making decisions around resource allocation in society.

3. Discuss the benefits for families and society at large of implementing universal child-care services across Canada. Why is there such a reluctance to financially support such a program from public funds? How are universal child-care services different from other public services such as elementary education or universal health care?

4. What social groups rely on food banks in Canada? Why are food banks often described as a "Band-Aid" solution to the problem of poverty?

5. What do you think are the most relevant social determinants of health (SDOH) affecting Indigenous people in Canada today? List the most relevant SDOH and explain how they affect Indigenous women and men differently. Take into account the key ideas underlying the theory of intersectionality.

6. Describe what social assistance is and how it helps low-income Canadians. Do you see social assistance as a long-term or short-term solution to inequality?

Take it Further: Recommended Readings

M.J. Cannon and L. Sunseri, eds., *Racism, Colonialism, and Indigeneity in Canada: A Reader* (Don Mills, ON: Oxford University Press, 2011). This edited collection presents a critical analysis of the interplay of racism and colonialism and how it has affected Indigenous people. The collection is broadly focused and examines timely topics such as family compositions, the criminal justice system, gender, and relations with settler colonialists.

M. Davies and M. Ryner, eds., *Poverty and the Production of World Politics: Unprotected Workers in the Global Political Economy* (London: Palgrave Macmillan, 2006). By bringing together experts on social inequality and global poverty, this collection provides a comprehensive overview of debates related to migration, human rights, the feminization of labour markets, and the rise of the informal economy in innovative and provocative ways.

E. Grabb, J.G. Reitz, and M. Hwang, *Social Inequality in Canada: Dimensions of Disadvantage*, 6th ed. (Don Mills, ON: Oxford University Press, 2017). This is a comprehensive introductory text on social inequality in Canada and its wide-ranging impact on society. The text is unique with its focus on both persistent structural and institutional problems and potential approaches to address key issues of inequality.

D. Kendall, *Framing Class: Media Representations of Wealth and Poverty in America* (Lanham, MD: Rowman & Littlefield, 2005). Through an analysis of news reporting and television shows, the author examines how class is represented in the media. She finds biases in media representations that perpetuate negative stereotypes about working-class individuals, while glorifying the material possessions and privileged status of the wealthy.

J. Porter, *Vertical Mosaic: An Analysis of Social Class and Power in Canada* (Toronto: University of Toronto Press, 2015). This book provides one of the most compelling analyses of social class and power in Canada, showing that educational attainment and social mobility are unequally distributed.

Take it Further: Recommended Online Resources

Anniversary Project
http://theanniversaryproject.com

Bill & Melinda Gates Foundation
www.gatesfoundation.org

Covenant House
www.covenanthouse.org

Directions Youth Services
http://directionsyouthservices.ca

Food Banks Canada
www.foodbankscanada.ca

Homeless Hub
http://homelesshub.ca

Life under Mike (video)
http://vimeo.com/94704064

OECD Data, Poverty Rate
https://data.oecd.org/inequality/poverty-rate.htm

United Nations: Sustainable Development Goals
www.un.org/sustainabledevelopment/poverty

More resources available on  Dashboard

7

Gender Inequality and Gender Domination

Learning Objectives

In this chapter, you will:

> Explore the meaning of the terms *sex* and *gender* and their societal relevance

> Learn how gender shapes how we look at and experience the social world

> Examine how gender inequality affects a person's educational goals and prospects in the job market

> Critically investigate how women are the victims of violence and the factors leading toward victimization

Introduction

Research examining the use of social media sites such as Instagram and YouTube suggests that notions of femininity and masculinity may be underscored and exaggerated in these environments and are closely tied to fashion, style, celebrity, and presentations of the body as a form of aesthetics (Dobson, 2016; Zaslow, 2009). But how do we understand "feminine" and "masculine" representations? And in the age of possibilities opened up by the internet and advanced biomedical science, what does it really mean to be, or to act as, a man or woman?

gender the social construction of what men and women should be like in terms of appearance, behaviours, preferences, and social roles and expectations.

Few topics in sociology are as puzzling and controversial as the study of **gender**. Until the mid-1950s, discussions around gender were considered either unimportant or private and personal. Since then, society has seen a shift in its approach to topics of gender and hence discussions in the media are now more open, if highly polarized. A general reduction in the stigma associated with being an individual outside "typical" notions of sex and gender has allowed for greater understandings of the diversity that exists in and between sex, genders, sexual identities, and sexual orientations.

These sex and gender distinctions create a system of social difference that affect people's lives. You may not have thought of gender differences as part of a larger system of inequality. After all, being male or female is seen in our culture as an inevitable result of human biology. But, just like class or ethnic differences, gender differences disadvantage some and advantage others. For example, other things being equal, women are more likely to be poor than men. Failing to take gender into account prevents us from gaining a complete and precise picture of inequality in the Canadian context. In Canadian society, as we will discuss in this chapter, other disadvantages are often entwined with gendered disadvantages, creating unique experiences of disadvantage and discrimination.

©iStock/FatCamera

From childhood onward, we are taught what men and women are supposed to look like and be like. People who fail to follow these cultural rules are likely to suffer, though there is more flexibility today than in the past. Did you assume this child was a particular gender when you looked at this photo? What clues did you use to inform your assumption, and what cultural norms informed your guess?

This chapter will also critically examine the concept of gender and how gender influences how people experience and see the social world. Further, the chapter will highlight how **gender inequality** creates divisions in education, work, and income—sometimes explicitly and other times implicitly. Finally, we will investigate how women are often the victims of violence and the effects victimization has on their mental and psychological well-being.

gender inequality differences that exist in education, income, and other opportunities based on a person's gender or sexual orientation.

Defining *Sex* and *Gender*

How can we understand gender? Ann Oakley (2005) introduced the term *sex* to sociology—the "biological division into male and female"—and contrasted the term with *gender*, which she defined as "the parallel and socially unequal division into femininity and masculinity" (p. 13). Since Oakley's early definition of the term *gender*, it has become "extended to refer not only to individual identity and personality but also, at the symbolic level, to cultural ideals and stereotypes of masculinity and femininity and, at the structural level, to the sexual division of labour in institutions and organizations" (Scott, 2014, p. 274).

To repeat, **sex** is a biological concept. People typically present as male or female from the moment of conception and most possess unambiguous sexual organs—though some of the biological determinants of "male," "female," or other, such as chromosome configuration (e.g., XX, XY, XXY, XYY, etc.) are not visible to the naked eye. While men and women have different reproductive functions, there is little scientific proof that there are biologically based psychological or socialization differences (for example, the notion of a "maternal instinct") between males and females, and more mounting evidence that sex is less **binary** (i.e., separated into two unique and clear-cut categories) than we once thought.

Related to biological sex is gender, which refers to culturally learned notions of masculinity and femininity. By **masculinity** and **femininity**, we mean that package of qualities that people in our society expect to find in a "typical" man and a "typical" woman, respectively. Masculinity and femininity are not exclusive to either sex or gender; traits from either may be evident in those of either sex or either gender. Since societies are undergoing constant change, what constitutes masculinity and femininity also undergoes change over time and through cross-cultural interaction. Also related to this concept is **gender identity**, people's personal experience of their gender, which may or may not align with their sex, and may include or be defined along a spectrum of unique identities "in between" or outside of male and female. For example, individuals may identify as both male and female, neither male nor female, **genderqueer**, **genderfluid**, or a variety of descriptions of personal gender identity (Stryker, 2008; Brill & Kenney, 2016). Noteworthy is that unique to some Indigenous communities in Canada (and around the world) are the two-spirited individuals, people who possess mixed gender characteristics. Cameron (2005) writes that "Aboriginal sexuality was based on multiple genders, at least three, but up to six. For example, there were male, female, and not-male/not female (two-spirited)" (p. 124). These individuals may have important ceremonial or sacred roles within their communities. Finally, **sexual orientation** refers to preferences in romantic and/or sexual romantic partners and is not directly related to sex or gender orientations.

On a societal level, **gender roles** are learned patterns of behaviour existent in society as a set of expectations placed on men and women. These are present in all cultures. As we grow up and become socialized, we learn to perform, or present, particular gender roles that fit with our cultural norms and with our sense of self. In these performances, men and women are expected to embrace their gender roles completely and avoid the qualities of the opposite gender role. For example, "stereotypical" men in Canadian society are expected to control their fears and gentler emotions, and display only drive, ambition, and self-confidence; they are also expected to be rigorously heterosexual. As much as possible, they are expected to distinguish themselves from women and from gay men in their outward manner, even showing contempt for women and gay men in doing so. A "stereotypical" woman, in contrast, is expected to be demure, submissive, and

sex the biological markers of males and females.

binary anything separated into two distinct and clear-cut categories.

masculinity a social construction of gender and includes stereotypical male behaviours and attitudes such as being strong, brave, and rational.

femininity a social construction of gender and includes stereotypical behaviours and attitudes such as being emotional, caring, and nurturing.

gender identity a sense, usually beginning in infancy, of belonging to a particular gender.

genderqueer describes a person who resists gender norms, but does not seek to change their sex.

genderfluid describes a person who has a gender (or genders) that changes over time and contexts.

sexual orientation the direction of an individual's erotic impulses in terms of the gender to which they are most attracted.

gender roles the behaviours, attitudes, and markers ascribed to men and women by society.

chaste. Since gender is learned, gender roles vary from one culture to another and also change over time. For example, housework is not everywhere; nor at all times in history has it been defined as a woman's activity or considered innately demeaning. In fact, men dominated domestic service in many pre-industrial and colonial societies. Since the late nineteenth century in Canada, domestic service has been seen as exclusively "women's work"—work and activity most commonly seen as done by women—and consequently is considered demeaning for men to undertake.

It should be noted, however, that not all individuals take part in the performance of normative gender roles. As notions of gender are unstable and in transition, at least in Canada, traditional and stereotypical gender roles are equally so. That said, social norms continue to exert pressure on young men and women to behave in certain ways, with consequences for deviating from stereotypical roles ranging from shame and social stigma to physical assault.

Moreover, the degree to which a culture differentiates between males and females, and emphasizes the differences between masculinity and femininity, varies from one society to another. Generally, countries with greater degrees of gender equality (such as those in northwest Europe) differentiate less between masculinity and femininity. Not surprisingly, they also have lower levels of childbearing, meaning that women in those countries spend less of their lives bearing and raising children than North Americans and people in the Global South. Since childbearing is one of the most distinctive differences between males and females, we should not be surprised that gender differences (and inequalities) decline with drops in childbearing.

In short, gender is a social construction that varies across societies—it is, as Judith Butler (1990) says, a performance strongly influenced by patriarchy, which is defined as the structuration of society around male dominance (see Box 7.1). Gender is largely an imposed social construction, which confers more benefits on some people (in this case, certain types of men) than it does on others (namely, women and transgender people).

performativity the idea that certain social factors, such as gender, are socially constructed and then acted out using words and behaviours that have come to be associated with what it means to be, say, male or female.

Theory in Everyday Life

7.1 | The Work of Judith Butler

American feminist philosopher Judith Butler (b. 1926) has written influentially on the social construction of gender. Her work centres on the idea that gender is not innate but is derived from a narrative heavily influenced by the cultural practice of patriarchy, or male dominance. Thus, gender consists of signs imposed and internalized via the psyche.

Butler's *Gender Trouble* (1990) is the most influential of her works. In it, she deconstructs the "grand narratives" found in psychoanalysis and other fields that promote the notion that human gender is a binary—that people are either categorically male or categorically female, with no room for variance or middle ground. In opposition, she suggests that gender and identity are "free-floating"—linked not to inherent characteristics but to performativity. **Performativity** is the notion that a person's gender is continually performed, not given as a fact, and that this performance shapes an individual's sexuality (Baldick, 2008). This idea has been central to the growing field of queer theory, which emerged out of Butler's work. Queer theory holds that people's identities are not fixed and do not determine who they are (Stormhoj, 2003).

Gender does not cause performance, but performance defines gender. For Butler, the way gender, sex, and sexuality are performed is not entirely up to choice, since only certain structured possibilities of sex, gender, and sexuality are socially understood as coherent or "natural." Butler's notion of performativity thus takes the discussion of gender and sexuality beyond the physical to the realm of identity, perception, and social norms—all important aspects of the way people experience sexual behaviour (Nayak & Kehily, 2006).

Gendering and Transgendering

Advances in science and technology have transformed how we experience, portray, and talk about gender. Science and technology have helped make visible and legitimize the variety of gender identities that we find in our world today. For instance, without the help of new media, in particular YouTube channels, stories about transgender people would have remained in the shadows. One Canadian example of this is Gigi Gorgeous (see Box 7.2). The life story and ups and downs of Gigi Gorgeous are documented through her YouTube channel and a documentary (Miller & Behm-Morawitz, 2016). **Transgender** refers to people who move beyond or outside of the social norms ascribed by their culture to the gender to which they were assigned at birth (Stryker, 2008)—that is, when their sex (biological category based on chromosomal makeup, XX or XY) does not match their gender identity. In some instances, this involves identification with the opposite gender identity. In other instances, it involves inhabiting a gender space that can integrate both traditionally feminine and masculine traits.

transgender describes a discrepancy between the gender that individuals identify with and the biological sex they were identified as at birth.

Sociology 2.0

7.2 | Gigi Gorgeous

Gigi Loren Lazzarato, better known as Gigi Gorgeous, is a Canadian transgender YouTuber, model, and actress. Gigi became famous for documenting her life on YouTube, particularly through her transition from presenting as male to presenting as female. On 16 December 2013, in a YouTube video called "I Am Transgender," Gigi announced that she felt like she was indeed a woman, trapped in a male body. Gigi also drew attention when she attempted to enter the United Arab Emirates in August 2016 and was detained for "imitating a woman," which is illegal in the UAE, despite her passport stating that her gender is female. Gigi used this incident to garner support for the challenges faced by transgender people and called for equality and equal protections. While the mainstream media attempts to find its footing in accurately portraying and reporting on transgender individuals that does not rely upon stereotyping or uniquely focuses on the "salacious details" (Ryan, 2009), YouTube offers a space for transgender people to tell their own story and to have "more agency to frame

discussions" through relating their own emotions and accounts of their immediate social context (Miller & Behm-Morawitz, 2016).

Gigi Gorgeous (far left) at New York Fashion Week. Gender shapes how we look at and experience the social world.

Time to reflect

Does content from social media affect the way you think and talk about social issues? Have social media posts ever changed your mind? Do you follow anyone who posts content that stretches your sociological imagination, or challenges your world view, or do most of the people in your networks share content that fits in with what you already know and believe?

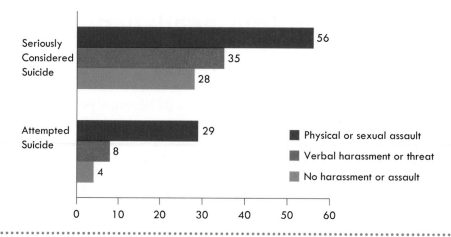

Interactive activtiy

FIGURE 7.1 Proportions of Trans Ontarians Reporting Past-Year Suicidality, by Past Experience of Transphobic Assault or Harassment, in Per Cent

Source: Bauer, G. & Scheim, A. I. (2015). *Transgender people in Ontario, Canada: Statistics to inform human rights policy.* London, ON: Trans PULSE Project. Retrieved from http://transpulseproject.ca/wp-content/uploads/2015/06/Trans-PULSE-Statistics-Relevant-for-Human-Rights-Policy-June-2015.pdf

More simply, identifying as transgender can involve a desire to move away from traditional ideas of the male and female gender binary. The procedures involved in transitioning are complex, sometimes invasive, and usually not without their risks. Such procedures vary from hormone therapy to surgical intervention to cosmetic and stylistic changes. If a transgender person decides it's right for them, advances in medicine and science allow for a complete alteration of the human body, one that is also a socially transformative process in terms of a person's perceptions of self, performativity, and lifestyle (Walters, 2015).

But there are social consequences to being transgender in Canada, and in many countries and cultures. Transgender people often report being ostracized, ridiculed, and the target of bullying, discrimination, and hate crimes. A 2015 report by the Trans PULSE Project based on the responses of Ontario transgender individuals found that of those who had been victims of physical or sexual assault, 56 per cent had seriously considered suicide and 29 per cent had attempted suicide (Bauer & Scheim, 2015). The findings presented in Figure 7.1 show that suicide rates were the highest for those who had suffered from verbal harassment, transphobic assaults, and sexual or physical abuse. This shows that suicide rates are further increased by the hardships and discrimination transgender people confront in everyday social interactions.

Many transgender people in Canada suffer from discrimination at schools, in their jobs, and at other institutions; for example, in the Trans PULSE Project they found that 13 per cent of trans Ontarians reported that they had lost a job due to their identity (Bauer & Scheim, 2015). For those transgender people who established their transgender identity as school-aged students in the United States, many (78 per cent) reported harassment and as much as 35 per cent had been physically assaulted (Grant et al., 2011).

Social change is slow. However, Bill C-279, which adds gender identity to the Canadian Human Rights Act, was passed by the Senate in June 2017 (Cossman & Katri, 2017). The bill provides transgender people further rights in terms of using washrooms, change rooms, and other public facilities that fit with their gender identity. Transgender advocates say the bill is essential to protect transgender Canadians from further discrimination and harassment.

Theoretical Approaches to Gender Inequality
Conflict Theory

Conflict theorists note that capitalism demands the low-cost social reproduction of a workforce from one generation to the next. Families are the best and most convenient way to raise new workers, and women (as mothers) provide the cheapest family labour. Mothers have the job of keeping the family earners and earners-to-be healthy—well fed, housed, and cared for emotionally—at no cost to employers.

The Marxist approach assumes that working-class men and women are on the same side, both equally victims of and exploited by the capitalist class. The theory of patriarchy—that men are the main and universal cause of women's oppression—is compatible with Marxist analyses that view working-class women as victims of both class and gender oppression (Knudson-Martin & Mahoney, 2009). Indeed, socialist feminists later interpreted Marx to suggest that should the socialist revolution come, and wealth be distributed more equally (Marx, 1904/1987), women could be liberated—at least economically (Buchanan, 2016). However, this assumes that patriarchy derives its power solely through capitalistic or economic means (Mitchell, 1971). The idea that gender inequality is intersectional, a concept further discussed below, examines how different dimensions—in this case class and gender amongst others—come together to explain inequality.

Functionalism

Functionalist theorists starting with Parsons and Bales (1955) might say that social gendering is universal and inevitable as the most effective and efficient way to carry out a society's tasks of reproduction and socialization. It may even have evolutionary survival value for the human race. A mother, by her early attachment to her child (via pregnancy and breastfeeding, for example), is well suited to raising the family's children. Since she is at home with the children anyway, the mother is also well suited to care for the household while the husband is at work outside the home. This, at least, is the skeleton of the argument.

The functionalist argument rests on the idea that "the survival of society"—rather than equality or individual rights—is a determining factor in social relations. This approach does raise many interesting questions about whether or not the supposed benefits of gender differentiation—such as a specialized division of labour between a breadwinner parent and stay-at-home parent—can be achieved without gendering or through reversed gendering: for example, can the benefits be achieved by stay-at-home fathers (or grandparents) in combination with breadwinner mothers?

Symbolic Interactionism

Symbolic interactionists, for their part, are concerned with the ways that gender differences or gender roles become gender inequalities—for example, the ways that young women become objectified and turned into sex objects. They also want to understand how the sexual double standard, which has allowed men more sexual freedom than women, has been "negotiated" so that many women go along with an agenda that benefits men more than women—for example, the view that "sexual freedom" is equal to men's free access to women. Consider Box 7.3 in which pornography is discussed in relation to the objectification of the female body through depictions filled with symbolism.

Symbolic interactionists are also interested in the social construction of gendered concepts such as femininity and masculinity, and with the role of families, schools, and the mass media in the propagation of such ideas. Answering these questions typically requires cross-national and cross-cultural comparisons, since different societies conceive of masculinity and femininity in somewhat different ways, and enforce these ideas differently as well.

Notably, all of these explanations—conflict, functionalist, and symbolic interactionist—are compatible with one another. Each focuses on a different aspect of the rise, maintenance, and decline of gender inequality. However, by far the most influential approach to studying gender issues has been the feminist approach.

Feminist Theory

Feminist theory focuses on how gender differences are socially constructed and highlights the range of inequalities that these social constructions elicit for women in a wide range of social spheres.

Spotlight On

7.3 | The Changing Nature of Pornography

Erotic and pornographic materials have existed as long as there has been mass media. Pornographic materials were present in mass-printed books in the seventeenth, eighteenth, and nineteenth centuries. Lane (2001) recounts that there have been pornographic videos since at least the 1910s; some early collections include those of sexologist Alfred Kinsey. Later in 1953, *Playboy* magazine emerged on the scene, providing men with depictions of nude women, while feature-length adult films emerged in the 1970s and proliferated on home video formats such as VHS and later DVD.

The advent of the internet drastically reshaped the production, dissemination, and consumption of pornography. As a result, perceptions of pornography and its societal function have changed, which has made pornography more widespread than ever. Pornography still retains its controversial status, as reflected in current debates about the effects of internet pornography on youth and society at large. On the one hand, Sun et al. (2016) report that internet pornography is used as a source of sexual education by youth. Unfortunately, in that role, it fails to demonstrate the consequences of potentially risky sexual behaviours and sometimes portrays unrealistic or inaccurate sexual behaviours, acting as a poor role model for maturing youth. Additionally, there are arguments that pornography commoditizes sexuality and people's bodies, in particular women's

bodies—reducing people to mere objects for consumption. Horley and Clarke (2016) argue that "the trouble with the commodification of sexuality is that sexuality can become detached from people's experiences, intentionally exploitative, and downright harmful" (p. 147). From a feminist perspective, pornography has been viewed by scholars such as Catharine MacKinnon (1987, 1993) and Gail Dines (2010) as another instance of male dominance over women as women are sometimes coerced physically, psychologically, or economically into performing, and in some cases are brutalized in the sex acts themselves. Some feminists claim that pornography can entice men to engage in violence against women.

Internet pornography has also had some beneficial effects on society. For example, in opposition to anti-porn feminists, other sex-positive feminists, such as Ellen Willis (2012), have pointed to pornography as a means of sexual liberation from society's prudish sexual norms, with the internet carrying this revolutionary force across the globe. Simon Hardy (2008) suggests that the internet has allowed for the "democratization of porn," whereby individuals have the capability to produce, star in, and distribute their own pornographic films, eroding the influence of large production companies and allowing single individuals to express their sexuality in new ways.

Time to reflect

Do you think pornography is a safe way for people to explore their sexual preferences, or do you think it encourages and perpetuates harmful behaviors and stereotypes? Do you think your gender (and subsequent socialization) influences your opinion on pornography?

There is considerable variability among feminists regarding the causes of gender inequality and these differences have resulted in a diverse set of approaches to feminism, a few of which are briefly outlined below.

Feminist theories try to describe social life and its aspects (for example, in social institutions) from a gendered perspective. One of the most important contributions of feminist sociology has been to forefront the importance of taken-for-granted everyday life assumptions and practices as a window on important social facts about the distribution of power. More recently, feminist theory has expanded its focus by also looking at inequality as related to other social groups; specifically, anti-racist/postmodern feminisms have focused on the elimination of prejudice and domination over marginalized groups, including racial and ethnic minorities and lesbian, gay, bisexual, transgender, and queer/questioning (LGBTQ) groups, as one way of ensuring that all women experience equality.

One of the most important contributions of modern feminist theory to the study of gender is the notion of **intersectionality**, an idea associated with Kimberle Crenshaw (1989). Intersectionality theory proposes we cannot assume that any dimension of inequality—gender, class, ethnicity, ability, and so on—inevitably and universally causes a particular disadvantage; nor can we predict the disadvantage suffered by a particular individual by simply adding together his or her statuses. Instead, intersectionality recognizes that particular social locations will have unique disadvantages and be uniquely marginalized.

In this model, disadvantage—including oppression, subordination, and victimization—is a result of the interaction (or intersection) of multiple types of vulnerability. Thus, gendered disadvantage is also conditional, in the sense that a woman will have a different experience of inequality depending on racialization, class, age, sexual orientation, disability, and other features associated with vulnerability. From this standpoint, it is the job of the sociologist to study particular combinations of vulnerability, in their particular social locations, to understand how and why gendered disadvantage results and is experienced.

One obvious consequence of intersectionality is that women's lives (in fact, all lives) are "individualized" so that we cannot readily make universalizing statements about oppression, or about "womanhood" as a social status. Equally, since women's lives vary so much, the shared fact of their womanhood may not be sufficient to overcome major differences in life chances associated with class, ethnicity, age, disability, and other sociologically important factors.

The idea that gendered inequality intersects with other types of disadvantage, and is therefore best studied in combination with them, also supports standpoint theory, an important theoretical approach. Because we have already discussed standpoint theory in connection with Dorothy Smith in Chapter 2, our treatment here will be brief.

Recall that standpoint theory proposes that we all view society from different social locations. In short, dominant groups—for example, white men with secure, well-paying jobs in academia—will be likely to view society in different ways from people who are subordinate, such as women, racialized minorities, and so on. Moreover, their view, or standpoint, will be privileged over other views, and will come to dominate academia and popular thinking about any topic.

Thus, accounts of reality (such as sociological theories) produced by members of the comfortable, dominant group—for example, by white, male academics—may differ substantially from most other people's experiences because their standpoint is different. This highlights the need for a type of sociology that privileges the accounts, insights, and theories of the disadvantaged.

In society, women from all walks of life have contributed to feminist thought and have helped create public awareness of women's unique struggles. Table 7.1 lists several well-known feminist icons and briefly lists their contributions to feminism.

According to feminist standpoint theory, women are in a unique situation to study and critique society because of their perspective outside of the conventional societal constructions dominated by men and men's ways of looking at the world. That said, there is in all academic work the danger that people will lose touch with the diversity of social disadvantage; and this, for sociologists, male and female alike, is intellectual death. Gloria Steinem specifically criticized academic language (jargon), stating that it obscured feminist thought. All sociologists, whatever their types and origins, must be aware of the limitations imposed on them by their social location and gendered socialization.

intersectionality a theoretical approach that examines the interconnection of social categories—especially, social disadvantages—related to ethnicity, class, and gender that creates more complex, interdependent systems of oppression and disadvantage.

Dashboard
Interactive activtiy

TABLE 7.1 Examples of Feminist Icons

Name (year of birth) Nationality	Key contributions
bell hooks (1952) American	A prominent feminist scholar and prolific author on women's issues, intersectionality, capitalism, art, and mass media. She obtained her doctoral degree in literature from the University of California–Santa Cruz in 1983. Recognizing a lack of diverse voices in feminist thought, she authored *Feminist Theory: From Margin to Center* in 1984, which urges people to think about feminism from the perspective of racialized groups and class.
Gloria Steinem (1934) American	A feminist journalist and political activist, especially during the 1960s and 1970s, and still active today (Shafy, 2016). She rose to fame as an American feminist leader after the publication of an article entitled, "After Black Power, Women's Liberation" in *New York Magazine*. She campaigned for the Equal Rights Amendment of the United States Constitution and co-founded *Ms. Magazine* in 1970 to produce non-male-controlled media for women. She criticized the use of academic language (jargon) in feminist theory because she believed it created barriers to the understanding of feminist positions.
Malala Yousafzai (1997) Pakistani	Began her activism in the Taliban-occupied Swat District in Pakistan where the Taliban had forbidden girls from attending school. She currently is an advocate for human rights and female education, and published her autobiography *I Am Malala* in 2013. In the 2009 documentary *Class Dismissed*, she expressed a desire to become a politician to help solve the crises of the world, and in 2014 she was awarded a Nobel Peace Prize, making her the youngest ever laureate at age 17.
Buffy Sainte-Marie (1941) Canadian (Indigenous)	A famous singer-songwriter and social activist. She belongs to Plains Cree First Nation in Saskatchewan, Canada. Her music features social activist themes, such as the anti-war ballad "Universal Soldier" (1964) and Indigenous issues such as in the song "Starwalker" (1976). She is also a philanthropist and has developed the Cradleboard Teaching Project, which aims to provide education about Indigenous culture and values to mainstream audiences to correct misperceptions of Indigenous culture.
Naomi Klein (1970) Canadian	A Canadian author, journalist, and activist. She criticizes globalization, consumerism, and corporatism and supports feminism and environmentalism. She is the author of *No Logo* (2000), *The Shock Doctrine* (2007), and *This Changes Everything* (2014).

Source: Author-generated

TABLE 7.2 Theoretical Approaches to Gender Inequality

Theory	Main points
Conflict Theory	• Gender inequality results from struggle for economic, political, and social power. • Capitalism benefits from gender inequality. • Gender inequality leads women to support the workforce without pay.
Structural Functionalism	• Gender roles and the division of labour support an efficient society. • Women are well positioned to take care of children and the home, while men work to provide for the family. • Gender inequality stems from what was at one time an effective household arrangement, which has failed to develop with the times.
Symbolic Interactionism	• Socialization and labelling shape gender identities. • Most variations between men and women are cultural and learned. • Media depictions and language help maintain gender differences.
Feminist Theory	• Elements and inequalities in society intersect. • Gender differences reflect variations in performativity. • Inequality is a result of patriarchal values, also prevalent in social institutions.

Source: Author-generated

Gender at Home, at Work, and at School

Within the household, we usually find a gendered division of labour. Some jobs are stereotypically done exclusively by women, other jobs exclusively by men, and some jobs are shared or rotated between them. These roles have changed over time in Canada. Gendered divisions of labour also varied by Indigenous nation and settlement area before contact with European colonizers, though in most cases there was no hierarchy of work (men's and women's work was valued equally), and approximately one-third of the Indigenous communities in North America had a concept of two-spirit as a third category of gender, people who played unique roles in their societies (Roscoe, 1998). The first settlers to Canada from Europe were exclusively men; it is important to note, though, that the first "pioneer" women took on significant labour and farming roles. As the Industrial Revolution changed the way households functioned, more of the goods that were made at home became readily available for purchase, requiring more of a cash income from men and reducing dependence on the labour of women for survival. By the late nineteenth century in Canada, men as the income earners or "breadwinners" had more control of the household's finances, while housework was considered primarily the domain of women and was considered lesser work.

The changes in organization of family life and paid work occurring during the twentieth century have had particular impact on women today. Women have entered the labour force in large numbers. In Canada the proportion of dual-income families has risen from 36 per cent in 1976 to 69 per cent in 2015 (Statistics Canada, 2016). The proportion of dual-income families with men working full time and women working part time also declined from 32 per cent to 22 per cent in the same period, suggesting that women increased both their labour market participation and their work intensity during that period. Despite these changes to the labour market, studies of domestic labour have found that on average women still spend significantly more time than men on domestic work, as well as more time caring for their children and aging relatives, than men (Milan, Keown, & Urquijo, 2015). Many Canadian women are employed full time and still do most of the housework and caretaking—work that is often referred to as women's "**second shift**." One result is that female partners typically have less free time than their male counterpart and often feel overburdened (Hochschild, 2012). In comparison, same-sex families are more likely to have an equal distribution of domestic labour and report greater satisfaction with their labour domestic arrangements than heterosexual couples (Foster, 2005). This suggests that many men have not made the parallel shift to assuming an equal responsibility for domestic work, while women have made their way into paid labour. While there has been a reduction in the gender gap between hours spent on housework when comparing generational trends, studies have found that this is because women have reduced the number of hours they spend on housework (while increasing the number of hours they spend on paid work), while the number of hours men spend on domestic work has not changed (Marshall, 2011). Many women rely increasingly on paid domestic and child-care services (daycare, fast food, house cleaners, and so on) to make up the gap in household work hours they can no longer put in.

It is difficult to have a serious career *and* a fulfilling partnership if you are a heterosexual woman, since you are expected to carry a full load in both activities. Today, few women quit their work when they have children, though many interrupt it for a maternity leave. Approximately two out of three mothers of preschoolers and around 80 per cent of mothers whose youngest child is in school (aged 6 to 15) are employed (Ferrao, 2010).

As a result of their extended time away from work after pregnancy and during motherhood, women who carry heavy domestic responsibilities find it hard to compete effectively with men at work. Moreover, employers expect women to be carrying this domestic responsibility and, therefore, see women as less valuable—since less available—employees. In this way, continued gender inequality at home ensures continued gender inequality in the workplace. Similarly, recent scholarship suggests that it is likely that societal and institutional norms and policies (rather than sexist attitudes in individuals themselves) are at fault for continued gender inequality at home and work. Pedulla and Thébaud (2015) found "that persistently gendered workplace norms and policies limit men's and women's ability to create gender egalitarian relationships at home" (p. 116). Using the practice of paternity leaves as a

second shift women's unpaid housework and caretaking in addition to paid work performed in the formal sector.

notable example, there is a perception that not many men take paternity leaves when their wives have children. About a decade ago, the government of Quebec changed its policy regarding paternal leaves, extending the program to more men for a longer time, and keeping the program separate from maternity leave (taking one does not take away from time for the other). As a result, the number of fathers who took paternity leaves skyrocketed from 32 per cent in 2005 to 72 per cent in 2011 (Rehel, 2014). It seems that men take paternity leaves when there is a supportive organizational and managerial environment. Men also take paternity leaves because *other men do*—over time, it becomes the new norm. And when fathers have an opportunity to develop the parenting skills necessary for an egalitarian co-parenting situation (instead of the mother gaining all of these skills when she is privileged with a longer maternity leave), fathers may not view themselves as lacking in parenting skills when their child or children are in need, thus further reducing the need to rely on a gendered division of parenting in the future.

Time to reflect

In what ways did your parents model gender roles for you when you were growing up? Which of your parents did or did not take parental leave? Who did which chores? Were gender roles ever problematized?

Gender Inequality in the Workplace

Does a double standard exist in North America when it comes to hiring, promoting, and paying women? Is there a glass ceiling that keeps women from moving up the ladder as far as similarly qualified men? Do bosses discriminate against women? These are hard questions to answer.

The average wage of women (across all occupations) according to the United Nations is about 72 per cent of what men receive (OECD estimates are higher at 81 per cent). In Canada, for example, women have an educational advantage, but still earn only $0.82 to every $1 earned by men (Catalyst,

Think Globally

7.4 | Labour Participation of Women Worldwide

Worldwide, it is hard to determine precise rates of labour force participation by women because much of women's work is done in the informal economy and so it is not officially counted. Statistics provided by the World Bank show a pattern of gendered participation in the work force. The World Bank reports that from 2011 to 2015, the highest rates of paid economic activity by women were found in nations in the Global South: 80 per cent in Eritrea, 86 per cent in Madagascar, and 80 per cent in Nepal. According to the World Bank, the lowest participation rates from 2011 to 2015 were found in the Middle East: 16 per cent in Afghanistan, 17 per cent in Iran, and 15 per cent in Iraq. Like the domestic division of labour, occupational segregation is universal. In the Global North, women typically work in clerical, service, and sales jobs. In Africa, women typically work in agriculture. According to OECD (2016) estimates, women "provide approximately 70 per cent of agricultural labour and produce about 90 per cent of all food." It is no accident that these "women's" jobs all have low status and are poorly paid.

Time to reflect

Do you remember ever being socialized towards one career or another based on your gender, or other social circumstance? Were your experiences straightforward, or more subtle? Is there a career that you might enjoy but that social stereotypes dictate you not pursue?

2016). The wage differences in Canada are most marked among the 25 to 44-year-olds with at least one child (29% wage difference), while they are much lower (7% wage difference) among those of the same age with no children (OECD, 2012). In Box 7.4 we look at gender differences in labour force participation across various nations.

Let's consider some possible explanations. Some women who work "full-time" do in fact work fewer hours per week, or fewer weeks per year, than men who work "full-time." This is because they take more time off work to attend to family business (e.g., taking sick children to the doctor). That might account for their lower income.

As well, women in a particular occupation may have less experience and seniority than men in the same occupation—perhaps because the women took a maternity leave, losing time that would otherwise count towards experience. Since income is often a function of age, experience, and seniority, women will earn lower incomes than men on average. Feminist economic analyses done by Canadian scholar Pat Armstrong (2007) suggests that the situation is more dire; Armstrong argues that "the wage gap increases with age, in spite of women's education and experience" (p. 15). Armstrong (2007) cites 2006 Canadian census data to reveal that while the wage gap between men and women (aged 18–24) is approximately $10,000 per annum, the gap doubles for those aged 45 to 54 to approximately $20,000.

Geographic locale also plays a factor in determining the economic success of a woman. Economic security varies across different cities in Canada. While 63 per cent of women in St. John's, NL, are employed, only 53 per cent of women are employed in Windsor, ON, with one in four women living below the poverty line (McInturff, 2016). This may be attributed to women holding jobs in worse-paying locales or being forced to get work in small towns or small companies where competition may be less fierce.

While these factors all contribute to disparities in pay equity, they do not fully explain the pay gap between men and women. For instance, with regard to work interruption linked to maternity leaves, differences in pay are not fully explained as Canadian data shows that this disparity holds true also for those who have recently graduated: men and women one year out of university have a 6 to 14 per cent wage gap (Bourdarbat & Connolly, 2013), which tends to increase over time. Hence, inequality in pay is more deeply rooted in social norms.

This pay gap also exists *between* women. For example, racialized women earn approximately 12 per cent less than their white female peers (Conference Board of Canada, 2017b). Those statistics only take into account full-time workers, but racialized women, particularly immigrant women and especially refugee women, are more likely than both racialized, immigrant, and refugee men as well as white and Canadian-born women to be employed in temporary work or to be unemployed (Block & Galabuzi, 2011). And when they do get full-time work, immigrant women earn 23.2 per cent less than their Canadian-born women counterparts (Conference Board of Canada, 2017a). Indigenous women are also paid less than non-Indigenous women in Canada; the hierarchy of pay scale by ethnicity has Indigenous women at the bottom (Lambert, 2010). There is also a sexuality pay scale hierarchy in Canada, with straight men at the top, then gay men, then lesbian women, and then straight women (Waite & Dernier, 2015). In this one case, the marginalized status of lesbian women works in their favour—by being seen as less feminine, the gender biases of the workplace do not work as strongly against them. Similarly, in the case of transgender Canadians, one study found that transgender women found their wages decrease by nearly one-third after transition, while transgender men found their wages increased slightly (Ginter, 2016). In the cases of sexuality and gender identity, gender discrimination seems to be stronger than homophobia and transphobia.

Technology, Gender, and Education

In most societies, men and women have been provided with different educational opportunities. In the European Enlightenment tradition, men were encouraged to go into the trades, to learn an apprenticeship, or to engage in more formal training. By contrast, women's education was restricted to the domain of domestic labour, often consisting of learning how to maintain a household, weaving and sewing, and care for the family, including entertainment. One of the first texts to question these gender stereotypes was *A Vindication of the Rights of Woman* written in 1792 by the British writer Mary

Wollstonecraft. She argued that women need to also obtain a formal education. Her rationale was that education would allow them to be good companions to men and help in building knowledge in society. This text historically represents a first step toward reform and a more egalitarian education system.

Since Wollstonecraft's controversial writings, women have become fully integrated into the primary and secondary education systems in many parts of the world. Indeed, in Canada, women are more likely to graduate from high school and to obtain a bachelor's or master's degree than men (Davies & Guppy, 2013; AUCC, 2011). Despite women's increased enrolment in higher education, a gender gap still continues to exist.

In the Canadian context, gender differences can be observed in high school course enrollment. Men consistently have a higher representation in STEM subjects. The acronym encompasses four disciplines: **s**ciences, **t**echnology, **e**ngineering, and **m**athematics. The primary reason why STEM discrepancies have recently received much attention from scholars and policy makers is that this area is seen as *critical* not only for how well individuals fair in terms of job availability and security, but also for the competitiveness and economic prosperity of entire nations (Gonzalez & Kuenzi, 2012). Individuals specialized in these subjects are also, generally, better paid than those specialized in subjects where women represent the majority, such as literature.

The reasons are not clear as to why girls and boys are not equally represented in STEM courses in high school. Some attribute this to gender preferences, but the majority of research points toward deeper-rooted problems surrounding socialization. Thorne (1993) was among the first to point out how gender construction occurs in schools, leading students toward different social roles and identities. The effect of socialization is evident in how teachers behave toward girls and boys in elementary and secondary schools, often placing different expectations on girls and boys. This is often termed the **hidden curriculum**, as it is not explicit; it is only implicitly perceptible in expectations and approaches (Hafferty, 1998). Efforts are being made to get girls involved in robotics, biology, and technology at younger ages. A YouTube video titled "GoldieBlox and Rube Goldberg 'Princess Machine'" gained notoriety by advocating for more toy choices for girls, beyond the reduction of girl play to dolls and pink toys.

When looking at how these trends unfold in university, it becomes apparent that the gender gap continues and even widens when it comes to STEM. Women have not only caught up with men in terms of obtaining a university degree, but women aged 25 to 34 actually surpassed men in 2011 with 66 per cent of graduates in non-STEM disciplines being women (Hango, 2013). These statistics contrast, however, with the 39 per cent of university graduates with a STEM degree who are women. Figure 7.2 shows the breakdown of women and men in STEM fields based on 2011 data from the Canadian National Household Survey (Hango, 2013). It becomes evident that across all STEM disciplines men outnumber and almost double the rate of enrolment of women. Hango (2013) investigated if women were less likely to pursue STEM degrees because of a lack of background in mathematics. He found that regardless of their mathematical ability, women were always less likely to choose a STEM program. That is, women often have the academic background

STEM Science, Technology, Engineering, and Mathematics; commonly used to refer to education, research, and employment in this sector.

hidden curriculum the implicit lessons in social roles, values, and expectations that are communicated in schools; for example, how students are taught in educational institutions such as high schools demonstrates gender inequalities that are not explicitly communicated, but are implicit in how men and women are treated differently in the classroom.

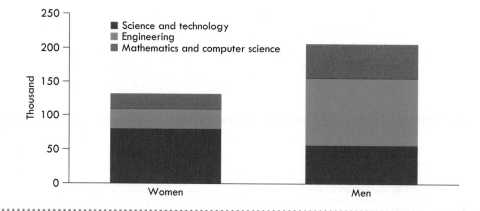

FIGURE 7.2 Number of STEM University Graduates by gender, 2011

Source: Hango, D. (2013). Gender differences in science, technology, engineering, mathematics and computer science (STEM) programs at university (Catalogue no. 75-006-X, Statistics Canada Report). Retrieved from http://www.statcan.gc.ca/pub/75-006-x/2013001/article/11874-eng.pdf

to pursue STEM degrees, but, for other reasons, such as uncertainty about their own abilities and feeling in the minority in male-dominated fields, they end up in non-STEM fields. Statistics Canada data shows that women remain underrepresented in occupations in natural and applied sciences but overrepresented in occupations in elementary and secondary education and health care (Dionne-Simard, Galarneau & LaRochelle-Côté, 2016). In fact, the most common occupation among young women with a university degree is elementary/kindergarten teacher (Ferguson, 2016).

Time to reflect

What did or did not work to interest you in STEM disciplines as a child and young adult? Did your gender play a role in whether or not you were encouraged to pursue a career in STEM? What kinds of approaches do you think would be most effective in schools and universities to promote STEM among all genders, based on your own experiences?

Despite the ratio of men to women in the STEM disciplines, not much work has looked into what kinds of approaches need to be developed to encourage more egalitarian gender representation. As society continues to rely on digital technology and scientific innovation for economic prosperity, it is of paramount importance to educate both boys and girls in STEM-related fields. Box 7.5 showcases two approaches to increasing involvement of girls and women in STEM.

However, there is not as of yet any substantial proof that any current interventions help in seeing more women pursue STEM careers. The Society for Canadian Women in Science and Technology and Canadian Women in Communications and Technology are excellent programs to help girls and women, yet a sensibility for STEM has to be formed early, when gender roles and stereotypes form—as early as kindergarten or elementary school.

Another aspect of the STEM gap is that just over half of all STEM degrees in Canada are held by those who immigrated to Canada—whether newcomers or those who have lived in Canada for many years, which suggests that to gain a better representation of women in STEM fields within Canada, the recruitment to STEM programs may need to be an international, as well as a national effort (Statistics Canada, 2016).

We will have more to say about women at work, in families, and in politics in the respective chapters of this book devoted to these topics.

Digital Divide

7.5 | Initiatives to Promote the STEM Curriculum to Girls

How can we encourage more girls to immerse themselves in the STEM curriculum and for women to pursue STEM degrees and careers? Two programs exist in Canada that attempt to encourage girls to participate in STEM.

The first is the Society for Canadian Women in Science and Technology. Founded in 1981, this non-profit organization works to encourage girls to consider careers in STEM and supports women already working in these fields. The organization has a wide range of programs to help high-school girls understand and navigate the many career possibilities in the STEM fields. They facilitate conferences and workshops, provide opportunities to meet with women working in those fields, offer online mentoring and role modelling programs, and provide volunteer opportunities for girls interested in pursuing a science or technology-related career in the future.

The second is the Canadian Women in Communications and Technology (WCT) organization, which helps women enter the information technology (IT) sector, advance their careers, and start their own businesses. It was founded in 1991, and now has chapters in British Columbia, Edmonton, Greater Toronto Area, Kitchener-Waterloo, and Quebec. The group's mentorship program matches women with years of experience in the IT sector with women just starting out who are seeking advice and support.

Tyler Irving

Professor Angela Schoellig (*right*) demonstrates a flying robot to a future innovator. Professor Schoellig was part of the International Day of Women and Girls in Science panel in Toronto, 2017. Do you think encouraging STEM sensibilities in young girls will lead to more women taking on STEM roles in the future?

Violence against Women

As we saw in the chapter on crime and deviance, women are often the victims of violence at the hands of people they know—family members; former, current, or potential romantic partners; and so on—rather than strangers. The 2014 General Social Survey showed that women maintained a risk of violent victimization at about 20 per cent higher than for men in Canada (Perreault, 2015). Women are also reluctant to report assaults. Data from Statistics Canada (Sinha, 2015) indicate that roughly 88 per cent of women who have been sexually assaulted in the past 12 months do *not* report their assault to the police. This may be because so many reported sexual assaults are dropped as "unfounded" often before any investigation occurs, and a woman's likelihood of being believed is a lottery based on where she lives (Doolittle, 2017). Approximately 19 per cent of sexual assault allegations in Canada from 2010 to 2014 were cleared as unfounded, though this ranged from 32 per cent considered "unfounded" in New Brunswick to 11 per cent in British Columbia (Doolittle, 2017). In areas with higher than average rates of female officers, the rates of "unfounded" cases was lower at 15 per cent (Doolittle, Pereira, Blenkinsop & Agius, 2017).

Increasingly, researchers find the line has blurred between consensual and non-consensual sex, and between violent and non-violent sex. That is because non-physical (e.g., psychological) coercion is hard to measure—and hard to prove in courts of law or sometimes even in victims' minds. According to the research, many young women drift into sexual activities they would prefer to avoid, if they are sufficiently threatened, shamed, or guilt-tripped into doing so (Koss, 1993). To circumvent these conceptual difficulties, more researchers are now talking about "unwanted sex" (Impett & Peplau, 2002; Katz & Schneider, 2015). By definition, all unwanted sex is the result of coercion by some means or another; and the coercion may not be violent. Consent may be reluctantly given, or not given at all, yet compliance will take place (Impett & Peplau, 2002).

Unwanted sex can have dire psychological consequences, such as feelings of shame and guilt, and sometimes even long-term educational or occupational consequences, such as a reluctance or inability to interact with strangers at school or on the job, or even fear of leaving the house (Blythe et al., 2006).

A majority of sexual assaults—81 per cent, according to victims interviewed in Canada's 2004 General Social Survey (the most recent reported statistics)—are classified as Level 1 assaults, involving unwanted sexual touching, but no physical injuries (or only minor injuries). Of these, 94 per cent go unreported to police, typically because the victim considered the incident to be not important enough (58% say this), because the matter was dealt with in another way (54%), and/or because the victim did not want to get involved with the police (41%). The more serious sexual assaults, Levels 2 and 3, are attacks typically involving penetration, threat, injury, and in some cases even a weapon; these are much rarer and more traumatizing. Of these (Levels 2 and 3), 22 per cent are reported to the police. So, as we see, even the most serious forms of sexual assault are likely to go unreported and unpunished. However, most women's far-too-common experiences of sexual victimization are less likely to be violent, and mostly go unreported.

Digital environments have been no exception when it comes to violence against women. Comments against women that would be condemned during in-person interactions are common on YouTube, blogs, and personal web pages. Video games have been at the centre of much attention as discussed in Box 7.6 because women report being the victims of verbal abuse, bullying, and harassment.

Dashboard
Case study

The Process of Intimate Partner Violence and Victimization

One of the most commonly studied forms of victimization is intimate partner violence, which is recognized today as a widespread social problem. Every nine seconds, somewhere in the United States, a woman is abused by someone she knows, and there is no reason to think that the frequencies

Sociology 2.0

7.6 | #Gamergate

In August 2014, video game designer Zoë Quinn was accused by an ex-boyfriend in a blog post of pursuing a romantic relationship with a game review journalist with the aim of obtaining a positive review of her game, *Depression Quest*. This led to a harassment campaign, going as far as threatening her with rape and death, on Twitter, using the hashtag #Gamergate (Todd, 2015). Although the allegation against Quinn was later found to be untrue, supporters of Gamergate argued against the "anti-freedom" movement in video game culture, particularly feminism and the culture of political correctness. Chess and Shaw (2015) interpret that "systemic sexism structures the industry and gaming culture as a whole to the extent that the very idea of integrating elements of feminism into video games is read as actual evidence of a conspiracy" (pp. 208–209).

However, opponents of Gamergate have used this opportunity to bring to light the negative treatment and portrayal of women in video games and the misogynist part of video gaming culture in general. For instance, research suggests that women account for at least 48 per cent of the gaming community (Duggan, 2015) but many female gamers emphasize their skill level and often choose to disguise their true identities or genders by not choosing female characters, not using in-game chats, or lying when asked directly for fear of misogynistic bullying (Gray, Buyukozturk, & Hill, 2017). Opponents of Gamergate also problematize portrayals of women in video games as "submissive, sexualised and victimized characters" (Todd, 2015, p. 65), leading to a misrepresentation of women in general.

Time to reflect

Video games are one example, but gender plays a role in the experience as well as the representation of almost everything we do. Use your sociological imagination, and think about the gender stereotypes, roles, and representations related to what you do for fun. How does your gender interact with your hobbies or after school activities? Are there parallels to the gaming industry?

are lower in Canada, although comparable data are unavailable. Each year, 1.5 to 2 million women in these abusive relationships require immediate medical attention as a result of domestic violence (Roberts, 2007). Such relationships rarely start out being abusive, however.

A battered woman, by definition, is someone who has been repeatedly assaulted emotionally, physically, and/or sexually by her intimate partner. As Stark (2007) points out, physical violence is only one element in an abusive relationship; other aspects of everyday behaviour also cause significant physical and emotional harm. Emotional abuse and controlling behaviour can lead to long-term debilitating effects such as Post-Traumatic Stress Disorder (PTSD), depression, low self-esteem, anxiety, and suicidal ideation (Doherty & Berglund, 2012). Gaslighting, a tactic in which an abuser makes the victim question her or his own reality and sanity, is a common and powerful tactic that can prolong an abusive relationship, and can have long-term effects on the way the victim thinks.

In general, women run more serious risks of intimate partner violence than men. The National Violence Against Women Survey estimates that 25 per cent of women have experienced intimate partner violence at one time or another. As well, women are more likely than men to be abused in a variety of ways: verbally, emotionally, physically, and sexually. For many women, this comes as part of a long history of abuse. According to data from the National Crime Victimization Survey, women who were sexually and physically abused in childhood are more likely to be abused in adulthood as well (Reyns, 2010), with the result that roughly 15 per cent of women experience repeated victimization over the course of their lives (Goodlin & Dunn, 2010).

Why don't these women leave their dangerous, abusive partners? There is no one answer to this question. Often, women do leave. Some women who manage to escape an abusive household end up returning to their batterers or are dragged back against their will. Research has estimated that, on average, women leave and return five times before they permanently cut off all contact with their batterer (Barnett, 2000). If there is only emotional abuse in a relationship, it may be harder for the woman to leave because it is less tangible than physical abuse, therefore harder to use as evidence of the need to escape an abusive partner (Barnett, 2000).

Many women stay in abusive relationships because they cannot imagine leaving and living without their partner. Often abusers encourage this line of thinking to keep the abused partner in the relationship. If a woman has been psychologically abused, she may come to doubt her own judgment and ability to make decisions for herself. This form of self-control entraps women in relationships with their abusers (Sabina & Tindale, 2008).

Many women do not leave after the first assault because they think the situation is temporary and may improve. Feelings of guilt and shame, at least in the early stages of abuse, are mixed with a hope that things will get better. According to Ferraro and Johnson (1983), women use "techniques of neutralization" to rationalize the actions of their abuser as normal, acceptable, or at least justifiable. Often women don't want to believe or admit to themselves or others that they have chosen an abusive person as their partner.

Women may also stay from a realistic fear of the violence that might occur if they were to leave (Roberts, 2007; Sabina & Tindale, 2008). Research shows abused women are most likely to be murdered by their partner when they try to end the relationship (Brown, 1987; Sabina & Tindale, 2008). In some cases, women are driven to killing their abusive partner (Brown, 1987; Sabina & Tindale, 2008). An estimated 500 chronically abused women kill their partners each year in response to terrifying death threats, PTSD, and/or intrusive fears of their own death at the hands of the abuser (Roberts, 2007).

A lack of sufficient resources may also keep some women from leaving abusive relationships. Many stay because they worry that they have nobody to ask for help, or they worry that they will be judged and disbelieved if they go to anyone for help. In addition, some cultures consider divorce a personal failure; it is seldom undertaken without emotional upheaval, and not all families may approve of or support divorce as an option. Often, women who are victims of intimate partner violence suffer from a shortage of resources—social capital, education, and income—that would make leaving easier. Reportedly, most chronically abused women have a low educational attainment—fewer than 20 per cent have a degree higher than a high school diploma. Women with low educational attainment are more likely to stay in a violent relationship because of their financial dependence on their partner. By contrast, victimized women who leave their partner shortly after the violence begins are more likely to come from the middle- or upper-income class and have completed at least some post-secondary schooling (Roberts, 2007).

Having children also makes it difficult for women to leave an abusive relationship. Compared to women who are able to escape from short-term intimate partner violence, women suffering from long-term violence (ranging from 4 to 40 years) are more often mothers of young children (Roberts, 2007). There are far more logistical and resource demands that come from leaving an abusive relationship with one's children than leaving without; and they often put the physical needs of their children over their own safety. They may also be concerned about the safety of their children were they to leave.

To summarize, not leaving an abusive relationship can be a result of social circumstances (including income, emotional supports, and access to safe space such as a shelter), a result of rational fear for one's life, a result of psychological wear from the abuse itself, or more likely some combination of the above.

Time to reflect

Have you ever hesitated to, or even not made, a change because of sociological factors? For example, were you worried about disappointing people around you if you made a change? Did you lack the resources to make a change?

Victimization of Indigenous Women

In Canada, as in the United States and elsewhere, Indigenous people are overrepresented as victims of violence, including intimate partner violence (Brzozowski, Taylor-Butts, & Johnson, 2006). The intersection of inequalities that Indigenous women in Canada experience creates a unique circumstance that accounts for the increased risk of violence that they face. General Social Survey data (Perreault, 2015) from 2014 show a sexual assault rate in Indigenous women of 115 incidents per 1,000 population, much higher than the rate of 35 per 1,000 recorded by their non-Indigenous counterparts (see Box 7.7).

Dashboard

Video: *Survival, Strength, Sisterhood*

Spotlight On

7.7 | #NoMoreStolenSisters: Violence Against Indigenous Women

In the past few years a national conversation has taken Canada by storm. Shocking reports over the number of missing and murdered Indigenous women has outraged communities across the country, prompting a national inquiry after years of resistance from Canadian governments. Research suggests that Indigenous women are five to eight times more likely to be murdered or experience a violent death in Canada than non-Indigenous women (Gilchrist, 2010; Pedersen, Malcoe & Pulkingham, 2013; Daoud et al., 2013). According to a report released by the Royal Canadian Mounted Police (2014), 4.3 per cent of Canada's female population identifies as Indigenous and yet Indigenous women comprise 16 per cent of all female homicides. In other words, Indigenous women are highly overrepresented in female homicide rates. The same can be said for intimate partner violence, assault, and physical abuse during pregnancy (Daoud et al., 2013).

The gravity of these statistics has been known for years, but only recently has there been any national response from the Canadian government. The reason these statistics are so disproportional is varied and complex. To start, Canada has a long history of colonialism, which researchers argue has incurred and encouraged violence toward Indigenous women, first through collective violence and structural discrimination, then through the imposition of Christian and European values, and finally, through colonial Canadian policies (Daoud et al., 2013). Past governments have neglected to take action; former prime minister Harper has gone on record saying that an inquiry into this issue is "not really high on our [the government's] radar" (Mansbridge, 2014; Maloney, 2015).

Mainstream media has not helped the situation either. A 2010 study looked at the coverage in newspapers surrounding three cases of murdered or missing Indigenous

Continued

women and three cases of white women (Gilchrist, 2010). The study showed that, compared to white women, Indigenous women received three and half times less news coverage, and their articles were less likely to be featured on the front page of a newspaper. Other reports have pointed out the disproportionate coverage that positions Indigenous women as sex workers (e.g., *The National*, 2015). While coverage in mainstream news is important, social media and blogs have emerged as alternative spaces for debate. Using hashtags such as #NoMoreStolenSisters, #MMIW, and #ourinquiry, alternative narratives and stories are shared, bringing much needed attention to the issue.

In short, the high rate of homicide experienced by Indigenous women in Canada is easily understood with the help of sociological analysis. Perhaps this is why former prime minister Stephen Harper urged us not to "commit sociology" on the topic of violence against Indigenous women. Since these comments by Stephen Harper, the Liberal Government under Prime Minister Justin Trudeau has initiated an independent inquiry on the missing and murdered Indigenous women which began on 9 December 2015 with an expected final report in November 2018. Sociological analyses can be a powerful ally in bringing to light problems and issues in our society and point to ways of solving them. They can also be helpful in keeping our politicians accountable for their actions or lack of action in regards to social issues.

Conclusions

This chapter examined the concept of gender by going beyond a simple dichotomization that sees an individual as either female or male based on biological sex. Gender is a social construction that takes place in our everyday life and through cultural norms and expectations. Though it is socially constructed, gender has measurable impacts on our lives—from our careers to our safety from certain kinds of violence. As we grow up, we experience gender in different contexts and forms through social interactions with family and peers, media portrayals, and the institutions that we are a part of. Gender is specifically defined in opposition to sex and is a diversity of experiences that cannot easily be placed in "little boxes."

The chapter specifically takes a closer look at how social and technological advances have shaped how we experience and make sense of gender. Advancements in science can provide new opportunities for individuals who wish to transform their bodies to better match their gender identities. Communication technologies allow for individuals with a diversity of gender-related experiences and identities to connect and build communities by broadcasting to a large, dispersed, global audience. As one example, transgender people no longer need to feel as marginalized and alone as they once did. They can read comments by others, like posts on Instagram, and share their own experiences.

Women in many parts of the world have joined the workforce in large numbers. Nonetheless, the evidence continues to show that there is occupational segregation in terms of the types of jobs and positions that women occupy and the wages they obtain. We discussed in the chapter the relevance that is given today to receiving an education in STEM (science, technology, engineering, and mathematics). Despite the many advantages of pursuing a STEM career, women tend to be underrepresented in this field, which places them at a disadvantage in a rapidly growing industry. Yet, it continues to be unclear why women are underrepresented in these fields. However, current initiatives are geared toward increasing women's representation in STEM and advocate for promoting early involvement of girls in science and technology subjects.

Women experience inequality also in the form of violence and abuse, both offline and online. The statistics around sexual assault continue to be shocking and many instances continue to go unreported. These traumatic events have consequences for women's physical and psychological well-being including feelings of depression and PTSD. The online controversy of Gamergate also drew attention to the wide range of anti-feminist activism that takes place in digital environments and the need to counter online harassment, bullying, and abuse against women. We also discussed how in Canada a large proportion of Indigenous women have been the target of violence and domestic abuse, and are now taking to social media to raise awareness and advocate for social change with hashtags such as #idlenomore, #NoMoreStolenSisters, and #MMIW.

Questions for Critical Thought

1. Explain how *gender* is defined in opposition to *sex*. Do you think that a strict gender binary is changing in Canadian culture? Explain your position.
2. Explain how the functionalist approach looks at gender and discuss what unique insights it provides.
3. Why are there fewer women working in STEM jobs? What societal norms, biases, and expectations continue to alienate women from this industry and what changes are needed for the industry to be more inclusive of women?
4. Why do women often remain silent about their experiences of sexual assault? Discuss the reasons why the majority of women who have been sexually assaulted do not report their assault to the police.
5. Why do women stay in abusive relationships and not leave after the first instance of physical or psychological abuse? Focus on both individual level factors as well as structural factors in society.
6. In what way is the vulnerability of Indigenous women in Canada an example of intersectionality? How have social media campaigns helped increase awareness of Indigenous women's struggles?

Take it Further: Recommended Readings

C. Carter, L. Steiner, and L. McLaughlin, eds. *The Routledge Companion to Media and Gender* (New York: Routledge, 2013). This comprehensive volume includes contributions from scholars around the world on the topic of media and gender, including issues of production and policy making, representation, audience engagement, and the place of gender in media studies.

J.M. Cohoon and W. Aspray, *Women and Information Technology: Research on Underrepresentation*, vol. 1 (Cambridge, MA: MIT Press, 2006). The contributors to this report look at reasons for the persistent gender imbalance in computing and explore some strategies intended to reverse the downward trend.

M.E. Kelm and L. Townsend, eds. *In the Days of Our Grandmothers: A Reader in Aboriginal Women's History in Canada* (Toronto: University of Toronto Press, 2006). This collection of essays critically examines 300 years of Indigenous women's experience locating their voice in Canadian society, through the fur trade, law, sexuality, and beyond.

A. Nelson, *Gender in Canada*, 4th ed. (Toronto: Pearson Education Canada, 2009). *Gender in Canada* presents a comprehensive look at the past and present of gender relations in Canada across a broad range of topics.

S. Razack, *Looking White People in the Eye: Gender, Race, and Culture in Courtrooms and Classrooms* (Toronto: University of Toronto Press, 1998). In this book, Razack examines issues of colonialism, race, gender, and disability as experienced by largely non-white women within the legal and educational systems.

Take it Further: Recommended Online Resources

Canadian Women in Communications and Technology (WCT)
www.wct-fct.com/en

Council of Canadian Academies, "Strengthening Canada's Research Capacity: The Gender Dimension"
www.scienceadvice.ca/en/assessments/completed/women-researchers.aspx

GoldieBlox and Rube Goldberg "Princess Machine"
www.youtube.com/watch?v=IIGyVa5Xftw

Canada Learning Code
www.canadalearningcode.ca

Pew Research Center Internet & Technology, Gender Resources
www.pewinternet.org/topics/gender

Society for Canadian Women in Science and Technology
www.scwist.ca

UNESCO, *A Complex Formula: Girls and Women in Science, Technology, Engineering and Mathematics in Asia*
http://unesdoc.unesco.org/images/0023/002315/231519e.pdf

UNESCO, Women and Girls Education
http://en.unesco.org/themes/women-and-girls-education

More resources available on **Dashboard**

8

Racialization and the Construction of Social Marginality

Learning Objectives

In this chapter, you will:

> Consider the cultural and ethnic diversity of Canadian residents

> Learn about some key concepts and practices pertaining to racialization/ethnicity

> Reflect on how racialization/ethnicity can affect people's everyday lives

> Consider different theoretical perspectives for studying racialization, including the influence of digital technologies

Introduction

multiculturalism political and social policy that promotes ethnic tolerance and diversity in communities.

When people think of Canada, they usually think of snow and **multiculturalism**. Indeed, many other nations aim to learn from Canadians about how they have historically managed their incredible diversity and the solutions they seek for the future.

Canada comprises diverse Indigenous groups such as First Nations, Inuit, and Métis; the descendants of early fur traders from diverse cultural backgrounds; and more recent immigrants. Immigrants add to Canada's diversity as they stem from 200 different ethnic and racialized groups speaking over 200 different languages (Statistics Canada, 2013). Roughly one in five living Canadians were born outside the country, and at 21 per cent, Canada has by far the highest foreign-born population of any G8 country (Germany is next at 13 per cent). When immigrants and refugees gain Canadian citizenship, they become Canadian in every sense of the word. In fact, the Charter of Rights and Freedoms—a bill of rights entrenched in the Constitution—establishes equal rights for all Canadians, guaranteeing "equal treatment before and under the law, and equal protection and benefit of the law without discrimination."

discrimination includes distinctions, exclusions, and preferential treatment based on an arbitrary trait (e.g., racialization) that jeopardizes a person's human rights and fundamental freedoms.

The Charter of Rights and Freedoms is an important document, as it allows for legal action to take place if equality is undermined. However, it did not always exist, and historical inequalities have been perpetuated through time. In addition, maintaining Charter rights is more complex than it may first seem, and **discrimination** continues to exist, usually in subtle forms.

As we will learn in this chapter, Canada's self-perception as a safe haven for immigrants and refugees does not match reality. Canada also does not exist in isolation from other nations, and trends and social change occurring globally influence Canadians' perceptions and opinions. On the one hand, globalization and new technology have made the flow of ideas, products, and even people across cultural regions easier than ever. At the same time, they have also allowed for more rapid changes and for external influences that are beyond the scope of any one nation.

Andrew Burton/Getty Images

Pictured is a memorial to reservist guard Cpl. Nathan Cirillo, 24, who was shot by Michael Zehaf-Bibeau in front of the National War Memorial in 2014. In a response, Prime Minister Stephen Harper referred to the events as a "terrorist" attack, thereby associating the events with the 9/11 attacks on the World Trade Center.

Because the United States is its neighbour and largest trading partner, Canada is particularly prone to the influence of events occurring in the United States, such as the recent election of Donald Trump as president. Another example of how events in the United States influence Canada is the terrorist attacks of 2001 on the north and south towers of the World Trade Center complex in New York City, often referred to as September 11 attacks or 9/11, which killed 2996 people and injured over 6000. The loss of life and extent of destruction resulting from the 9/11 attacks created increased insecurity and suspicion against particular racialized people, ethnic groups, and religions. Following 9/11, there was a dramatic increase in anti-Arab and anti-Muslim hate crimes; the FBI reported an increase of hate crimes from 28 in 2000 to 481 in 2001, a 17-fold rise (Human Rights Watch, 2002).

The effects of 9/11 on the Muslim and Arab communities in Canada are still evident today. The event continues to shape how news about terrorist attacks is reported in the media and makes Arab Canadians and Muslim Canadians vulnerable to discrimination. This kind of discrimination has also affected other racialized groups living in Canada. Often, other religious groups, like Sikhs, have been subject to unwarranted aggression and suspicion. Box. 8.1 examines how 9/11 continues to have an effect on how news outlets perceive Arabs and Muslims.

Video: *Secret Trial Five*

Theory in Everyday Life

8.1 | Racialization in the Search for Suspects

News of terrorist attacks flows through digital networks in real time. As soon as a terrorist attack occurs, first images of the event, the extent of the human damage, and the police intervention flood social networking sites, news outlets, and TV screens. Often, first speculations are made as to who is responsible for the attack. These early speculations often show clear biases.

A good example of bias based on ethnicity was apparent during the horrific Parliament Hill shooting in 2014, when Michael Zehaf-Bibeau killed a reservist guard in front of the National War Memorial and then made his way toward Parliament. Reports in the media often portrayed Zehaf-Bibeau as Arab or having Muslim connections. In fact, he was French-Canadian and was raised a Roman Catholic. Further analysis by the Centre for Research on Globalization highlights how Zehaf-Bibeau was described in the media often as "Canadian born," which may suggest that he was perhaps not fully Canadian. The use of specific descriptors often places suspects in predefined boxes and persuades readers to read between the lines as it "strips them of their Canadian identity and otherizes them as a foreigner that does not belong to the collective" (Nazemroaya, 2014).

Another group that suffers from racialized profiling is black Canadians. Black people in Canada experience racial profiling when they are still in secondary school. A survey of black youth aged 13 to 24 in Oakville, Ontario, found that the black youth were more likely perceived to be troublemakers than white youth. As Erikson (1968) suggests, youth are often given specific allowances; when they make a mistake, for example, they are not immediately punished, which lowers their anxiety over engaging in improper actions. This, however, does not equally apply to all youth, with more lenience shown toward white youth than black youth (Brown, 2003). The report on racial profiling in Oakville shows that black youth are often the target of police enforcement and are perceived as instigators of youth misconduct rather than participants. In another study, the Toronto District School Board 2011 Student Census showed that, at 8.6 per cent, the suspension rate for black students was almost double the rate for most other groups, including the 4.1 per cent rate for Middle Eastern youth, 2.9 per cent for white students, and 2.1 per cent for South Asian students (Szekely & Pessian, 2015).

In short, Canadians make assumptions about the motivations and intended actions of individuals based on our perceptions of their ethnicity, and this has everyday consequences for racialized people who live here.

Time to reflect

Have you experienced, observed, or heard of instances of racial profiling in your community? If you are racialized, has your behaviour ever been mistaken for violent or threatening? If you are white, have you ever done something that you think would have gotten you in trouble if you were racialized?

Box 8.1 shows the importance of unpacking racialization and ethnicity and how it intersects with many aspects of everyday life. As mentioned in Chapter 1, C. Wright Mills (1959/2000) stressed how the sociological imagination allows us to understand the intersection of history and biography—that is, the complex relations between the two within society. Much contemporary sociological work has taken this insight into new directions by questioning and examining personal experience in a quest to understand the political and historical context that shapes this experience (Daniels, 2016). For sociologists studying racialization and ethnicity, their concern lies with the effect of racialization or ethnicity on educational attainment, employment opportunities, and health and well-being. They not only uncover patterns of inequality related to racialization and ethnicity in institutions, the labour market, and socialization, but they are also concerned with people as they experience prejudice, racism, and discrimination.

By looking at global events and changes in information and communication technologies, this chapter discusses the pervasive influence of racialization and ethnicity on society. We also highlight some of the unique challenges Canada faces as it continues to take in new immigrants and also comes to terms with its own complex history of colonialism and oppression.

Racialization and Ethnicity

Racialization and ethnicity are central aspects of people's identity and influence many aspects of their daily life. When people talk about who they are, they often describe their cultural or geographic origins, including their ancestors' origins. These serve as markers of belonging to social groups, as well as forms of differentiation.

Racialization and ethnicity are related social constructs, yet different in important ways. The term **racialization** refers to the way that others categorize people by visible characteristics and features such as hair colour, hair type, skin colour, and facial features. The process of racialization describes "the way race is produced and bestowed on people by institutional social actions, and not simply as a condition found in people as their racial category" (Martinot, 2003, p. 13). Martinot (2003) stresses that racialization is something people do to other people, rather than a reflection of what they are. As a result, we create racialized inequality by creating and performing the idea of racialization and racialized difference. By contrast, **ethnicity** refers to the people who share a national or cultural background. **Ethnic groups** are usually characterized in terms of four related dimensions (Pitchford, 2001):

racialization the way that others categorize people by visible characteristics and features such as hair colour, hair type, skin colour, and facial features.

ethnicity belonging to a group or category of people that are bound together by common ties of national tradition, language, or cultural heritage.

ethnic group a group of people who share a common homeland, language, or culture.

- Group members share a homeland or ancestry.
- Group members have a shared history, in which key historical events form a sense of collective memory.
- Ethnicity is based on a sense of belonging to a social group whose members share an identity and have similar traditions, customs, and symbols.
- Perhaps most importantly, people who belong to an ethnic group have self-consciousness, which means that they feel they belong and others see them as belonging (Cornell & Hartmann, 1998).

Ethnicity is also socially constructed, because the boundary lines and histories of nations and cultures are social constructions.

Globalization, through the flow of ideas, products, and people, has created unprecedented diversity in many North American cities. In particular, Canadian metropolitan areas like Vancouver, Toronto, and Montreal are the arrival point for a huge number of immigrants and refugees every year. The resulting ethnic diversity, as we will learn in this chapter, has many positive outcomes for people and communities, but it can also lead to conflict between social groups.

Dashboard
Interactive activity

Biological versus Constructivist Conceptions of Racialization

What determines the way that an individual is racialized? As mentioned above, people are judged by their appearance and are racialized into categories by those around them. But these categories are changeable, socially determined, and make little sense.

Consider four "race" options commonly available to choose from in online surveys: white, black, Hispanic, and Asian. When you break it down, these are non-comparable categories. Some are based on colour (for example, white, brown, or black), some on language roots (for example, Hispanic or French), while others are based on continents of presumed ancestral origin (for example, Asia or Africa).

Yet, despite the arbitrariness of this categorization, the category we are racialized into can have real consequences for job searches, our social connections, and even for the quality and the length of our lives (Pitchford, 2007). The underlying assumption of racialization is that our visible characteristics have a biological basis and therefore some insight into our personality, behaviour, strengths, and weaknesses. In fact, advances in science surrounding the decoding of the human genome, through the Human Genome Project, for instance, have shown that there is little biological basis for racialized distinctions. Racialized features such as skin colour have no demonstrated connection to any social, intellectual, or moral qualities—no connection to intelligence or diligence, for example.

While "race" and racialization are social constructs, that does not make their consequences any less real. **Racism** (the unequal treatment based on these constructed categories) systematically disadvantages segments of the population. It impacts day-to-day life on large and small scales, as well as one's sense of self. Passages Canada, a website that aggregates biographies of becoming Canadian, provides instances of racism. Dave Mornix, originally from Trinidad and Tobago, describes his own experience with racism while with friends at a coffee shop:

> Living in Canada has presented me with many new challenges. The first time I experienced racism was like an out-of-body experience. It was at a coffee shop with six friends . . . it was my turn to buy . . . two trays were left, the older gentleman in the line in front of me picked up both. I asked if he could leave one for me and that's when the racial slurs began. It was the first time I realized I was Black—and what does that mean? (Mornix, 2017)

As a result of racism, people who fall into these socially constructed categories (or are placed there by the way they are treated by others) share common experiences that can create community and self-consciousness around racialization (e.g., "I am black"). This is not to say that individuals have no agency when it comes to how they are racialized. Sometimes, people choose to present themselves in a particular way in order to influence how they are treated and to build community. For example, a study by Litchmore, Safdar, and O'Doherty (2016) found that second-generation Canadian youth of African and Caribbean heritage living in the Greater Toronto Area constructed the category of "black" as a racialized identity using historical, social, and descriptive references. This intentional crafting of a shared identity is an example of how the experience of racialization (being treated a particular way because people associate you with a particular category) can create shared experiences that can form the need for, and basis of, a shared identity. The work of W. E. B. Du Bois (1903/2007), mentioned in Chapter 1, discusses the complexities of racialized identity. He described how African Americans could not develop a true self-consciousness, but rather experienced their identity through a *double-consciousness* because of the oppression experienced in a white-dominated society. Du Bois describes this double-consciousness as

> this sense of always looking at one's self through the eyes of others, of measuring one's soul by the tape of a world that looks on in amused contempt and pity. One ever feels his [her] two-ness,—an American, a Negro; two souls, two thoughts, two unreconciled strivings; two warring ideals in one dark body, whose dogged strength alone keeps it from being torn asunder. (1903/2007, p. 8)

Du Bois describes a complex state of "two-ness," of disparate and competing "thoughts," "goals," and "norms" (Pittman, 2016). We will discuss the creation of shared dual identity further in Box 8.2, where we show how discrimination based on racialization influences a candidate's opportunity to get a job, even when qualifications, credentials, and skills are equal.

racism discrimination, prejudice, or antagonism directed against someone of a different ethnicity or racialized group based on the belief that one's own racialized identity is superior.

Time to reflect

How much of your identity relies on how you interact with other people (e.g. "I'm scary," "I'm charming," "I'm awkward," "I'm shocking," "I'm funny")? Does the "race" that people perceive you to be affect these impressions? Does it affect your sense of identity?

Studying Racialization and Ethnicity

The study of racialization and ethnicity is central to much sociological work. Studies vary in their focus, ranging from approaches that examine the concepts themselves and their historical roots to a growing body of work that focuses on the experiences of different ethnic and racialized groups, often in relation to the dominant group.

Here, as elsewhere in sociology, different methodological approaches yield different kinds of understanding. They also have their shortcomings. While qualitative approaches studying ethnic and racialized groups can make use of complex definitions and understandings of racialization and ethnicity, large-scale quantitative studies need to reduce the meaning of racialization/ethnicity to a limited number of questions.

The aim of survey research generally is to gain understandings of trends and changes over time in terms of the composition and structure of society. For the purpose of describing and understanding population dynamics, researchers often categorize people into pre-defined groupings. The census, as discussed in Chapter 2, represents an important means of data collection about Canadians. The census collects a wide range of data including demographic data such as ethnic roots and place of origin. Figure 8.1 provides a snapshot of the 2016 census, depicting three questions used to group people into cultural, ethnic, and racialized groups.

While collecting data on people's ethnic background is important for policy making around the allocation of resources toward programs such as education and health care, any kind of labelling and grouping can be contested. One problem comes from the way that ancestry is defined. Ancestry is determined in terms of nation-states, but nation-states do not fully capture ancestry.

For instance, Canadians who immigrated from Spain might designate their origin as Basque or Catalan. Also, some nation-states are in upheaval and their borders are constantly redrawn. Another problem resurfaces with questions of identity as seen in the example of Question 18 (Figure 8.1). Such complexities related to identity became evident in a recent historic land claim agreement struck by the group called Algonquins of Ontario with the federal and provincial governments (Tasker, 2016). Figure 8.2 shows the settlement area that the treaty covers. The treaty, which is being heralded as historic and modern, has turned out to be also contentious.

Part of the problem is that the treaty is being negotiated with Algonquins of Ontario, but the chiefs of four Anishinaabe First Nations (the autonym—or name a group uses to refer to themselves—of a group of Indigenous nations including the Ojibwe, Odawa, and Algonquin First Nations) contest the land claim. As part of their argument, Lance Haymond, chief of the Kabaowek First Nation stated, "the vast majority" of the Algonquins of Ontario "are not Algonquin at all," but non-Indigenous people who claim a loose connection to an Algonquin 'root ancestor'" (The Canadian Press, 2016). In short, ethnicity-based categorizations are highly contentious and no one term can fully and accurately be designated to an entire social group.

Question 19 (Figure 8.1) on the census asks if the person belongs to one of several racialized and ethnic groups. Choices include White, South Asian, Chinese, Black, etc. As we've discussed above, this category is complex and problematic to define. Interracial marriages further complicate placing people into clear-cut groupings.

In Canada, colonialization brought about intermarriages between European colonizers and Indigenous groups. For example, the Métis, a group of intermarriage discussed in Chapter 4, are people of mixed European and Indigenous ancestry and one of the three recognized Indigenous peoples in Canada. Since then, mixed unions have been a small but growing segment of Canada

This question collects information on the ancestral origins of the population and provides information about the composition of Canada's diverse population.

17 What were the ethnic or cultural origins of this person's **ancestors?**

An ancestor is usually more distant than a grandparent.

For example, Canadian, English, Chinese, French, East Indian, Italian, German, Scottish, Cree, Mi'kmaq, Salish, Métis, Inuit, Filipino, Irish, Dutch, Ukranian, Polish, Portuguese, Vietnamese, Korean, Jamaican, Greek, Iranian, Lebanese, Mexican, Somali, Columbian, etc.

Specify as many origins as applicable using capital letters.

---

18 Is this person an Aboriginal person, that is, First Nations (North American Indian), Métis or Inuk (Inuit)?

Note: First Nations (North American Indian) includes Status and Non-Status Indians.

If "Yes", mark "⊗" the circle(s) that best describe(s) this person now.

○ No, not an Aboriginal person

→ **Continue with the next question**

○ Yes, First Nations (North American Indian)

○ Yes, Métis

○ Yes, Inuk (Inuit)

→ **Go to question 20**

This question collects information in accordance with the *Employment Equity Act* and its Regulations and Guidelines to support programs that promote equal opportunity for everyone to share in the social, cultural, and economic life of Canada.

19 Is this person:

Mark "⊗" more than one circle, or specify, if applicable.

○ White

○ South Asian (e.g., East Indian, Pakistani, Sri Lankan, etc.)

○ Chinese

○ Black

○ Filipino

○ Latin American

○ Arab

○ Southeast Asian (e.g., Vietnamese, Cambodian, Laotian, Thai, etc.)

○ West Asian (e.g., Iranian, Afghan, etc.)

○ Korean

○ Japanese

Other — specify:

FIGURE 8.1 Census Questions Related to Place of Origin and Ethnic/Cultural Background

Source: Statistics Canada, 2016 Census instrument, p. 12: http://www23.statcan.gc.ca/imdb-bmdi/instrument/3901_Q2_V4-eng.pdf

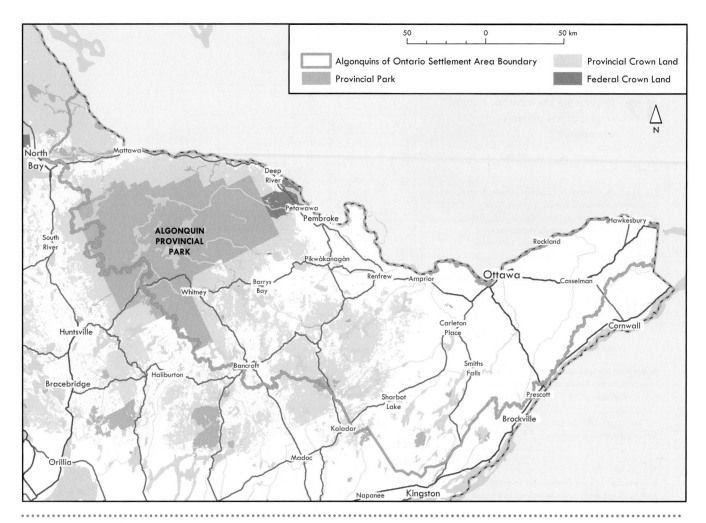

FIGURE 8.2 Settlement Area Involved in the Treaty between the Algonquins of Ontario and the Federal and Provincial Governments

Source: https://files.ontario.ca/maa-algonquins-ontario-settlements-area-boundry.pdf

(see Figure 8.3). The 2011 census reports that 4.6 per cent of couples are in mixed unions, up from 3.1 per cent in 2001 and 2.6 per cent in 1991 (Statistics Canada, 2014). Mixed unions can be either of two different racialized groups or one member being of a racialized group and the other not. Children of these mixed unions may want to select multiple racialized groups to describe their ethnicity and potentially racialization, creating further complexity in any type of categorization.

Qualitative inquiry rejects the use of simple groupings and pre-defined categories and instead aims to gain understandings of meaning and experiences. Often, scholars will use qualitative means of inquiry as those discussed in Chapter 2—for example, ethnography, photovoice, and interviews— to move away from the limitations that survey research imposes on studies of racialization, ethnicity, racism, and inequality. In the Canadian context, much emphasis has been placed on encouraging investigations with a focus on racialized groups.

Particularly, the Social Science and Humanities Research Council of Canada (SSHRC for short), Canada's largest funding agency for research on racialization and ethnicity, has made research with Indigenous groups a priority area of scholarship. On their website, they state, "SSHRC is committed to supporting and promoting research by and with Aboriginal Peoples. This commitment emphasizes the importance of Aboriginal perspectives and knowledge systems to increase and expand our knowledge and understanding about human thought and behaviour in the past and present, as well as the future" (SSHRC, 2015).

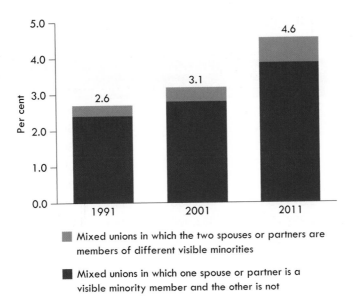

FIGURE 8.3 Proportion of Couples in Mixed Unions, Canada, 1991 to 2011

Source: Statistics Canada. (2014). *Mixed unions in Canada.* Retrieved from www12.statcan.gc.ca/nhs-enm/2011/as-sa/99-010-x/2011003/c-g/c-g3-01-eng.cfm

In these forms of qualitative inquiry, ancestry, racialization, and ethnicity are not pre-defined concepts; rather, they are considered negotiated knowledge systems (Smith, 2012). Being sensitive to issues of colonialism, imperialism, and ways of knowing is critical in any inquiry of Indigenous peoples in Canada. Investigations by and with Indigenous peoples call for careful attention to how racialization and ethnicity are framed, as well as the relations that are built with members of these communities.

To guide this type of research, a set of guidelines has been developed as part of the Tri-Council Policy Statement, discussed in Chapter 2, in collaboration with First Nations, Inuit, and Métis peoples of Canada to establish an ethical space for dialogue on common interests and points of difference between researchers and Indigenous communities engaged in research (Canadian Institutes of Health Research, Natural Sciences and Engineering Research Council of Canada & Social Sciences and Humanities Research Council of Canada, 2014). The shift in funding priorities reflects an increased recognition of the ongoing oppression as well as social and economic disparities of First Nations, Inuit, and Métis peoples, and is consistent with Canada's recent move towards reconciliation (to be discussed further below). Qualitative inquiry provides opportunities to learn about "the intersection of biography and history" through engaging with past and present experiences of Indigenous groups as well as participating in alternative, particularly Indigenous, ways of knowing.

Racialized Minorities and the Dominant Group

Distinguishing between various ethnic groups can teach us a lot about Canada's diversity of customs, values, and beliefs. But to understand issues of racism and ethnic inequality whether related to educational opportunities, jobs, or policing, it is necessary to compare various groups on the basis of racialization and ethnicity.

In Canada, the term *visible minority* was used in the past to refer to people "other than Indigenous persons, who are non-Caucasian in race or non-white in colour" (Statistics Canada, 2013, p. 14). Today, the term is losing acceptance and is slowly being replaced because of two main criticisms. First, it reinforces a problematic belief that whiteness is *not* visible or is the "norm" to which other groups compare themselves. Second, it may promote stigmatization of certain (non-white) groups. Instead, scholars have recently started using the term *racialized group* or **racialized minority**, as these are less discriminatory. Table 8.1 shows Canada's composition in terms of racialized minorities; in 2016 as much as 22 per cent of Canadians identified as belonging to a racialized group, and the large majority are immigrants or children of immigrants. Canadian metropolitan areas vary in

racialized minority those who are treated in a particular way by people around them based on their physical features and the attributes that those features are assumed to signify. Racialization occurs against those who have features distinct from the majority group who hold social power in a society.

TABLE 8.1 Visible Minority Population and Top Three Visible Minority Groups in Selected Census Metropolitan Areas, Canada, 2016

| | Total population | All visible minorities | | Top 3 visible minority groups |
	Number	Number	Percentage	
Canada	34,460,065	7,674,585	22.3	South Asian, Chinese, Black
Toronto	5,862,855	3,011,905	51.4	South Asian, Chinese, Black
Montreal	4,009,790	904,835	22.6	Black, Arab, Latin American
Vancouver	2,426,230	1,185,680	48.9	Chinese, South Asian, Filipino
Ottawa-Gatineau	1,300,730	280,985	21.6	Black, Arab, Chinese
Calgary	1,374,655	463,450	33.7	South Asian, Black, Chinese
Edmonton	1,297,275	363,990	28.1	South Asian, Chinese, Filipino
Winnipeg	761,540	195,370	25.7	Filipino, South Asian, Black
Hamilton	734,880	130,305	17.7	South Asian, Black, Chinese

Source: Adapted from Statistics Canada, 2017. Visible minority (total - population by visible minority), both sexes, age (total), Canada, Newfoundland and Labrador and census metropolitan areas and census agglomerations, 2016 Census — 25% Sample data. http://www12.statcan.gc.ca/census-recensement/2016/dp-pd/hlt-fst/imm/Table.cfm?Lang=E&T=42

Video: *Brooks*

terms of their ethnic composition. For example, the top three racialized minority groups of Montreal are black, Arab, and Latin American, whereas in many other metropolitan areas they are South Asian or Chinese.

Much debate on racialization, ethnicity, inequality, and conflict surrounds the relation between racialized groups and dominant groups. These discussions highlight several trends. First, the dominant group is often unaware of the struggles of racialized minorities in terms of adapting to new cultures or finding a job. For example, to counter discrimination, Canada's Employment Equity Act states that racialized minorities need to be given equal opportunities in the job market. But it is difficult to reinforce the law in hiring practices and prove that racialized discrimination has taken place, as hiring decisions take place behind closed doors, and it is in the best interest of those who benefit from discrimination to remain ignorant of its existence (we'll talk more about this in the section on conflict theory).

Second, tension often results from dominant groups perceiving racialized minorities as threatening their status. A good example of this is the tension and discourse that has been such a strong part of recent policy debates around the added tax on foreign buyers to control the housing crisis in large cities such as Vancouver and Toronto. The Ontario government's 16-point plan for creating more affordable housing specifically targets rich foreign investors, who are identified as a key part of the housing problem in the province. Some analysts, such as Mark McLean, who works in the real estate industry, warn that this policy goes against Canada's open immigration policy, which welcomes people from all over the world (Kupferman, 2017).

ethnic enclaves areas with a high concentration of residents with a particular ethnicity or set of related ethnicities, with a distinct culture and a defined boundary.

Third, critics often think **ethnic enclaves** (areas with a high concentration of residents with a particular ethnicity or set of related ethnicities, with a distinct culture and a defined boundary, such as Vancouver's Chinatown) show a reluctance to integrate into Canadian society, despite the fact that research suggests these ethnic enclaves are socially, politically, and economically integrated with Canadian society. These criticisms also ignore the history of aggressively racist policies in Canada's history, such as the Chinese head tax and Yellow Peril, during which a safe space, often based on geographical delimitations, was vital to survival and a sense of belonging (Li & Li, 2011). Understanding how racialized minorities and dominant groups come together will be important because there is no doubt an increased movement of people within and across nation-states. Though our examples were about racialization as linked to immigration above, First Nations, Inuit, and Métis people are also met with the same lack of awareness, tensions around special treatment, and criticisms around lack of integration. We'll discuss how racialization affects Indigenous groups within Canada later on in the chapter.

Theoretical Approaches to Racialization

Functionalism

Functionalism stresses the organization of society and the institutions through which social order is established and maintained. From this perspective, socially cohesive groups are formed on the basis of shared identities such as those gained through shared experiences of ethnic history or racialization. Members of racialized groups share strong bonds that provide social, emotional, and economic resources.

Sociologist Georg Simmel described the relevance of affiliation in distinct social groups as a key characteristic of the structure of society. Affiliation means belonging to a social group with specified social boundaries and a set of established behavioural expectations. Affiliations in social groups are based on common interests, shared characteristics, and family ties. Simmel was particularly concerned with the status granted to people as a result of belonging, but also with the complexities of navigating loyalties to varied social groups, each with different norms, beliefs, and expectations.

Historically, in early societies, membership was first based on strong household ties, followed by kin ties (or lineage), and then ties to larger associations such as tribes. Similarly to how kin and tribe affiliation worked in the past, in today's global society, ethnic identification provides the grounds for affiliation. In fact, racialized group membership has gained much social relevance and structures many aspects of social life.

When immigrants and refugees arrive in Canada, it can be challenging to feel a sense of belonging to a new place, as many aspects of the new culture are foreign. For these newcomers to Canada, ethnic heritage can serve as a link and means to connect to a cultural past they left behind, and may long for, as well as for developing new connections through their affiliation.

The advantages of connecting to a group of immigrants or refugees who are already established and more familiar with their surroundings are numerous. This has created migration patterns, as recent immigrants tend to resettle in larger metropolitan areas where other members of their ethnic and racialized groups are already settled. Figure 8.4 shows immigrants' place of residence in 2001.

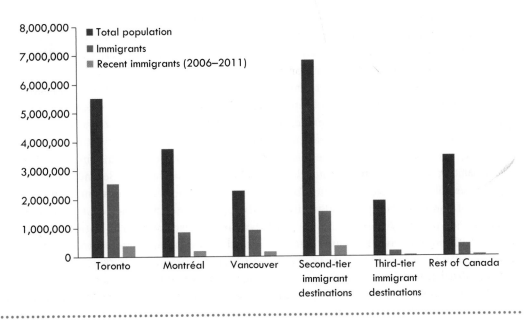

FIGURE 8.4 Immigrants by Period of Immigration—Place of Residence, Canada, 2011

Source: Statistics Canada: www12.statcan.gc.ca/nhs-enm/2011/as-sa/99-010-x/2011001/tbl/tbl1-eng.cfm

Indeed, more than 63 per cent of immigrants live in Canada's three largest cities—Toronto, Montreal, and Vancouver (Chui & Flanders, 2013). Statistics Canada data show Toronto has the greatest share of foreign-born of all three urban centres: 37 per cent of all foreign-born Canadians choose to live in Toronto (Statistics Canada, 2013). Recent migrants choose areas like the Greater Toronto Area or Vancouver because they can find group affiliation and support with finding a job, obtaining information about available services, and building friendship networks.

Functionalists view the ethnic and cultural diversity in large Canadian cities as benefitting society, since it promotes multiplicity in opinions and perspectives as well as exposure to a variety of foods, dress codes, and social practices. The many forms of ethnic solidarity found in large cities increase social cohesion among people of the same ethnic group as well as across ethnic groups. In a multicultural society like Canada, ethnic solidarity also gives newcomers a landing pad and strategies for assimilating. Ethnic identity can facilitate resettlement and provide people with social connectedness in an otherwise individualistic, fragmented society.

As we will discuss next under conflict theory, ethnic affiliation also enforces boundaries, which give groups more cohesion and a sense of identity but can lead to ethnocultural conflict.

Conflict Theory

Conflict theory aims to uncover patterns of inequality based on class, gender, racialization, and ethnicity. More specifically, conflict theory highlights how dominant groups benefit more than racialized groups from differentiation, as differentiation often provides advantages to dominant groups.

stereotypes widely held beliefs about a social group that are overly simplistic and often untrue. Stereotypes can ascribe both positive and negative attributes to members of a group.

Conflict theory seeks to explore, for instance, how economic competition may promote the creation and preservation of ethnic boundaries and racialized **stereotypes**. Majority groups seek to dominate minorities because this can provide advantages. Overt exclusion based on racialization or ethnicity would break with Canadian legal and ethical expectations, but forms of exclusion can be implicit and perhaps not even intentional, while still creating disparities in society and constituting forms of discrimination. Box 8.2 raises legal issues associated with using social networking sites such as LinkedIn and Instagram for personnel selection. Managers must consider the benefits and concerns that using such information presents (Slovensky & Ross, 2012).

Exclusionary decision making of the kind seen in hiring practices is a form of racism. Racialization includes the tendency to introduce racialized distinctions into situations that should be managed without them (Abu-Laban & Bakan, 2008). Examples include hiring and promotion on grounds of "race," matters that should be judged on the basis of job qualifications and experience but that may be determined according to racialized biases, which can be implicit.

critical race theory (CRT) theory that views racialization as a performance and social construction, rather than a reflection of innate, biological qualities.

Perhaps the boldest movement towards identifying the causes and effects of racialization practices, such as hiring biases, has been **critical race theory**, or CRT. CRT views racialization as a performance, rather than an innate, biological quality. Delgado and Stefancic (2017) outline the central ideas of CRT. First, racism has been "normalized" in society; it is a part of how institutions and society function. Because racism is not acknowledged, this invisibility makes it very difficult to address and counter discrimination and disadvantage. Second, the system of "white-over-colour" ascendency legitimizes existing hierarchical structures and reinforces the standing of dominant groups. Finally, differential racialization—the notion that each racialized group has its own origins and history—creates varying policies of discrimination. These often overlap with political and economic interests related to the labour force, as will be discussed below when we examine the head tax applied to Chinese immigrants in 1885. CRT shows how privilege easily blinds people to being able to see racialization and inequality. CRT proposes that only disadvantaged people are in the position to see and assess the lived reality of inequality, as they are the ones who experience it. In relation to this, there is also a growing interest in the study of whiteness as a privileged category in our society that keeps those who are identified and treated as white ignorant of the experiences of everyone else, and who assume that their experiences are universal. We will discuss whiteness later in the chapter.

Digital Divide

8.2 | LinkedIn Profiles as Markers of Identity: To Erase or Not?

Many job applicants today choose to create a profile on LinkedIn, the most popular professional social networking site worldwide. LinkedIn was founded in 2002 and, as of 2016, has 450 million members. The primary goal of LinkedIn is to establish and maintain professional networks and to make available a résumé for potential employers to see. LinkedIn thus allows potential employers to connect with a candidate, carefully scrutinize their credentials and connections, and then make a hiring decision on additional—perhaps more personal and complete—information that may not be available on a standard resumé (Slovensky & Ross, 2012).

Many LinkedIn members, however, are concerned that the networking site may also be indirectly promoting racialized or ethnic discrimination, a phenomenon called implicit bias (Reynolds Lewis, 2014). Researchers have shown that implicit bias frequently comes into play in hiring decisions, disadvantaging racialized groups (Bertrand & Mullainathan, 2004).

A Canadian study showed patterns of discrimination based on applicants' names and foreign education and work experience (Oreopoulos, 2009). Oreopoulus, the author of the study, sent out fictitious resumés to job advertisements via email and found that callback rates were more than three times higher for English-named applicants than for foreign-named applicants. On the basis of his findings, Oreopoulus (2009) concludes, "employers discriminate substantially by name" (p. 168). Many studies of this kind, in Canada and elsewhere, have revealed clear patterns of discrimination against non-white minorities in the selection of job candidates and even applicants for apartment rentals. Based on the evidence, members of racialized groups may also be disadvantaged by having a picture of themselves on LinkedIn that would indicate their membership in a racialized group (Reynolds Lewis, 2014).

A recent study shows that applicants are countering the potential discrimination existent in labour markets by engaging in what is referred to as "résumé whitening," the removing of ethnic cues from résumés (Kang, DeCelles, Tilcsik, & Jun, 2016). But removing markers of one's identity from a profile would mean allowing those with racist and discriminatory beliefs to have succeeded in fabricating a success ladder based on illegal, discriminatory practices. Moreover, connections to racialized groups can be advantageous to employers as the applicant may have access to a valuable professional network that can provide access to resources such as information about national and even international business deals. Being aware and countering discriminatory practices is critical digitally and non-digitally to support fair hiring practices based on qualifications and skills.

When making hiring decisions based on information contained on professional networking sites, such as LinkedIn, employers need to take into consideration legal and ethical frameworks that govern those decisions and prevent implicit bias based on racialization, ethnicity, or gender, for example.

Symbolic Interactionism

Symbolic interactionism examines how interactions with others shape our sense of self and also provide the basis for learning symbols and their meanings, including the meaning, implicit and explicit, of language, images, and abstract symbolism. People, objects, and even social situations acquire meaning that is learned in the context of social interaction.

Symbolic interactionism is used to study how **racialized (or ethnic) socialization** contributes to the formation of identities and conflicts between racialized and ethnic groups. Racialized

racialized (or ethnic) socialization the process by which we learn to perceive and evaluate people (including ourselves) according to presumed racialized or ethnic differences.

socialization is a process that, through interaction, exposes people to the beliefs, values, history, language, and social realities of their own and other people's racialization or ethnic groups. Through racialized socialization an individual becomes a group member by learning what it means, socially and culturally, to be Chinese, Ukrainian, German, and so on. There exists much variability in the process of racialized socialization across regions, subgroups, and even families. Thus, there is no one accurate way to depict any particular group and their beliefs, values, and so on—there is no centralized, universal racialized socialization process for any given group, in the same way that there is no one centralized "Canadian" socialization process. The information is transmitted and learned socially—often in family or peer groups, and sometimes in schools and in the media.

Signalling group boundaries is critical to racialized socialization, as it stresses how groups are different from one another. The sense of belonging experienced by members of an ethnic group is termed **ethnic solidarity** and is often expressed through rituals, ritual objects, and symbols. Racialized and ethnic groups have a shared identity, language, and colloquial expressions (slang) that one can use to share a sense of camaraderie and belonging.

Third culture kids (TCK) are described as children who have been socialized in a culture different than the one that their parents were socialized into (Pollock & Van Reken, 2009) and applies to many Canadian children of immigrant or refugee parents. These children, while able to establish relationships easily with people from diverse cultures due to their cultural flexibility, often report not feeling fully a part of any one culture. TCK have great facility to adapt to new cultures because they have learned to **code-switch**, depending on the context of interaction they are embedded in. They adjust their body language, expressions, and even parts of their self to fit with the cultural context.

It is not only TCK who engage in code-switching, however; most people do it to some extent. For example, think of your own behaviours in various social contexts: you may speak differently when you're with your friends than when you're interacting with your parents or grandparents. Code-switching is most evident when it takes on a racialized or ethnic subtext; in some cases code-switching is an important signifier of ethnic affiliation in socialization practices, and in some instances it can also serve to avoid racism by adjusting one's behaviour to fit with the mainstream (De Fina, 2007). Code-switching occurs a lot online, where people adjust their forms of interaction to various social networking sites, expressing different elements of the self on Facebook, LinkedIn, and Instagram, where each presentation of self is curated to the needs of the social network (Hogan, 2010).

Cultural objects that define ethnic groups can have different meanings, providing a basis for group distinction. Consider the rich and diverse symbolism that exists in Indigenous communities. These symbols reflect past history, values, and beliefs, but many Canadians have an ambivalent relationship with the symbolism. They often have limited knowledge and understandings of the history of the many Indigenous populations in Canada and their customs and symbols, but they readily embrace this symbolism when it comes to representing Canada on the world stage. For example, during the 2010 Vancouver Winter Olympic Games much Indigenous symbolism was used to signal Canada's roots, despite the fact that many controversies continue to surround the rights of Indigenous groups in Canada. The integration of Indigenous symbols, such as the inukshuk as the main logo of the Games, provided an opportunity to not only showcase "Indigenous culture" (admittedly as a homogenous single entity rather than as hundreds of unique nations each with different cultures), but to include Indigenous peoples from the host country as official partners of the Olympic Games for the first time in history (CBC News, 2010). Simultaneously, through the transmission and representation of Indigenous symbols, such as the inukshuk, on television, social media, and websites, the symbols were decontextualized and re-appropriated by global audiences (Quan-Haase & Martin, 2013). Millions witnessing the Olympic Games via television, YouTube, or images on social media admired the symbolic beauty without recognizing or understanding the meaning or importance of these symbols. The use of Indigenous symbolism and partnership with Indigenous communities in Canada for the 2010 Olympic Games is an example of **tokenism**—making a symbolic effort towards equality without enacting real social change.

ethnic solidarity a process in which members of self-conscious communities interact with each other to achieve common purposes.

code-switch a situation in which a speaker effortlessly switches to a different language, dialect, class, and often culture.

Case study

tokenism the policy or practice of making only a token or symbolic effort toward equality and integration without any real change.

Cameron Spencer/Getty Images

During a performance by the Four Host First Nations during the 2010 Games, Indigenous populations' symbolism was showcased to a global audience. The Olympics were possible because the Four Host First Nations shared their land and culture during the Games.

Feminism

Feminist scholars focus much of their work on raising awareness around inequalities and advocating for equal rights for women and other marginalized groups, including those of racialized and ethnic minority groups. This interest stems in part from Simone de Beauvoir's (1949/2011) conceptualization of "the other," which she applied to women to highlight inequalities in society. De Beauvoir was a highly influential social theorist and foundational figure in the development of feminist theory. She argued that men are treated as the standard, and women are defined in opposition to men—as "other" than men—and this defining is usually done *by* men. Parallels can be drawn as to how racialized groups are often portrayed as the "other"—as inherently different and distant from the normalized (typically white, male) group. For feminist scholars, many different kinds of relations, such as colonial relations, involve people who are perceived and treated as "others."

The study of the "other" and "otherness" also has roots with Edward Said, a postcolonial theorist whose analysis of Western perceptions of non-Western peoples has been very influential. He argued that much of the Western "understanding" of the East was a result of projection and imagination that also served important economic and geopolitical interests (Said, 1978). In short, ignorance encouraged Westerners to imagine that Easterners were socially and morally (as well as technologically) underdeveloped, and this point of view served important colonial goals.

The practice of **Orientalism** consists of "orientalizing" a population by assigning them attributes that are undesirable, even shameful, and worthy of repudiation. In this respect, the viewer is imagining a community that deserves dominating. Said's work reminds us of the relativity of perceptions in the social world. He also reminds us that insiders and outsiders will, invariably, have different views of themselves and others, especially when these people compete or conflict with one another.

Earlier in the chapter we discussed ways in which 9/11 has created false images of Muslims and Arabs and the negative impact this has had on these communities. Through Said's work, we

Orientalism emphasizes, exaggerates, and distorts characteristics, features, and cultures of people and cultures from Asia, North Africa, and the Middle East and compares their characteristics to that of Europeans.

can see how this is in part a continuation of Orientalism, as we continue to stereotype and "other" those from the Middle East. This shows that the concept of Orientalism has practical implications for politics and policies of interethnic conflict. The term can also serve to further interrogate interethnic relations in a country like Canada with a history of racist immigration policies, internments (politically motivated inprisonments), and racialized segregation. Examples of discrimination in Canada include the Yellow Peril in the early twentieth century, including the Chinese head tax; black segregation, particularly in Nova Scotia and Ontario; restrictions on pay for South Asians; the policy to refuse immigrants from South Asia, particularly Sikhs, as encapsulated in the Komagata Maru incident of 1914; Ukranian internment during the First World War; Japanese internment during the Second World War; and more recent policies such as the Zero Tolerance for Barbaric Cultural Practices Act and the Strengthening Canadian Citizenship Act—not to mention the atrocities committed against people belonging to the First Nations by early colonizers and against all Indigenous people (more on this below). Some policies were less inherently racist but were designed to target specific groups, one example being the Continuous Journey Regulation of 1908, which required a prospective immigrant's trip to have been a direct route from his or her country of origin to Canada. On paper this is not overtly racist, but in practice it targeted primarily Japanese and Indian immigrants, whose countries offered no direct route to Canada (Canadian Museum of Immigration at Pier 21, n.d.).

Feminist scholars have developed the concept of intersectionality to create awareness around how different dimensions of inequality such as gender, class, racialization, and ethnicity influence experiences of inequality and discrimination jointly, rather than as independent factors. In other words, oppression, subordination, and victimization are a result of the *interaction* (or intersection) of multiple dimensions simultaneously (Crenshaw, 1989). This means we cannot simply sum up a person's status; rather, disadvantages are also conditional, in the sense that a woman will suffer different forms of inequality depending on her racialization, class, age, disability, and other features associated with vulnerability.

Box. 8.3 highlights how ethnicity and other dimensions of inequality such as gender cannot be ignored as these dimensions interact with one another.

Spotlight On

8.3 | Indigenous Youth and Suicide

Indigenous people of Canada confront a unique set of challenges today; among them, mental health is one of the most pressing. Suicidal thoughts—a significant predictor of suicide—were found to be two times more prevalent amongst Indigenous youth than amongst non-Indigenous youth (Khan, 2008; Statistics Canada, 2016). Suicide rates in Indigenous youth are five to six times greater than the national average when compared to non-Indigenous youth (First Nations Centre, 2005). These numbers are even worse in Northern communities, as suicides among Inuit youth are among the highest in the world (Statistics Canada, 2014; Kral, 2012). This has had a devastating impact on families and communities. After the suicide of a sixth girl in northern Saskatchewan, the Federation of Sovereign Indigenous Nations vice-chief Kimberly

Jonathan said, "They're not just statistics. Our little girls are dying" (CBC News, 2016).

Durkheim was the first sociologist to study suicide and argued that suicide can help explain how people relate to society and see their role/value within a social system. His overall conclusion, based on a comparison of different groups in society, was that people who were most integrated and best regulated by their communities were least likely to commit suicide. While Durkheim's methods have since been criticized, his treatment of suicide as a sociological phenomenon is still considered valid today.

From this standpoint, we need to understand the exceptionally high rates of Indigenous youth suicide as a consequence of the loss of integration and regulation. Generations of cultural genocide, not least due to the residential

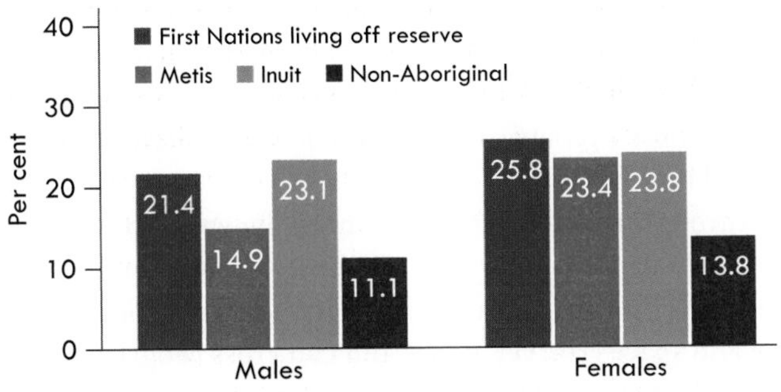

FIGURE 8.5 Prevalence of Lifetime Suicidal Thoughts by Gender and Ethnicity, 2012

Source: Statistics Canada. URL: www.statcan.gc.ca/pub/89-653-x/89-653-x2016008-eng.htm

school system discussed in earlier chapters, and economic deprivation have undermined the integration and regulation that is so critical for Indigenous survival and well-being.

In an attempt to provide needed integration and regulation, communities are currently providing increased support to their youth and mobilizing resources to prevent any further loss of life. A report on mental health in Canada emphasized that the concept of the healthy person prevalent in many Indigenous cultures stresses social relations and connections to others (Public Health Agency of Canada, 2011). People are part of complex webs of affiliations not only within their nuclear families but also within entire communities. These webs of affiliation extend to ancestors, who may be present in memory, stories, and ceremonial practices.

TABLE 8.2 Theoretical Approaches to Racialization

Theory	Main points
Functionalism	• Ethnic identity provides social connectedness in an individualistic society. • Ethnocultural conflict enforces boundaries, which give groups more cohesion and a sense of identity. • Ethnocultural diversity provides a wide range of opinions, perspectives, and values that enrich society.
Conflict Theory	• Dominant groups benefit from excluding and marginalizing minority groups. • Orientalism studies how social groups from the Middle East were assigned negative attributes for purposes of colonialism and domination.
Symbolic Interactionism	• Ethnic differentiation is constructed by a labelling process. • Constant awareness of racialized socialization in daily social interaction increases the likelihood of racialized conflict. • In a networked, global world symbols are easily taken out of context and reappropriated by outsiders for their own interests. • Code-switching facilitates moving between social groups that have different norms and values.
Feminism	• Focuses on how racialized groups are seen as the "other" through comparisons with what is seen as the norm to highlight socially constructed differences. • Examines the intersectionality of racialization with class, sexual orientation, and gender.

Source: Author-generated

Social Distance and Tolerance

Conflict, violence, and economic crises have left 65.6 million people forcibly displaced worldwide (UNHCR, 2017). According to the United Nations, "the world is failing the victims of an 'age of unprecedented mass displacement'" (Jones, 2015).

In addition, many more people have migrated to seek employment elsewhere, contributing to the movement people across borders and regions. We'll discuss reasons for migration and immigration further in Chapter 9. These trends create a pressing need to understand how people from different ethnic and racialized backgrounds get along and appreciate one another's diversity.

Two concepts help in the analysis of diversity and its opportunities and challenges. The first is **social distance**, which refers to racialized and ethnic differences that continue to separate us socially,

social distance the perceived extent to which social groups are isolated from one another, measured by factors such as whether a member of one social class, racialized group, or ethnicity would be welcomed in the meeting place of another social class, racialized group, or ethnicity.

tolerance the idea that people from different ethnic and racialized backgrounds can come together in a single nation-state and show high levels of trust and reciprocity.

homophily a relationship joining actors who have the same or similar attributes or statuses.

culturally, and economically. Conflict often originates from the idea that one ethnic or social group is oppressed by other ethnic or social groups that are seen as holding power and privilege. By contrast, **tolerance** is the idea that people from different ethnic and racialized backgrounds can come together in a single nation-state and show high levels of trust and reciprocity. Often, the dominant group is oblivious to the struggles encountered by minority groups and the ways in which racism and ethnic bias structure access to jobs, education, and health care.

One way to increase tolerance is through contact, which has been shown to be positively associated with tolerance. But how can we expose people to more diverse people in their daily lives? Digital media has often been seen as facilitating contact with diverse sets of people, as communication is not constrained by time and space (Harvey, 1989) and can cross geographical and social boundaries. Recent studies, however, suggest the contrary. As digital media is governed by algorithms and highly personalized for individual preferences, interactions on the web can occur in silos. Box. 8.4 discusses how this kind of echo chamber occurs and its effect on contact with diverse groups.

Sociology 2.0

8.4 | Birds of a Feather Flock Together in Digital Space

Sociologists study the social networks in which people are embedded. A person's social network is a critical source of social support, information, and financial support, and it even influences how we are positioned in society. Social networks can be described in terms of not only how many connections a person has to family and friends, but also how similar people in a person's network are. This measure is usually referred to as **homophily** (McPherson, Smith-Lovin, & Cook, 2001).

Sociologists refer to the phenomenon that we tend to associate with people who are similar to us as "birds of a feather flock together," describing the tendency to seek out those similar to us. Similarity between two people can be assessed in terms of a wide range of characteristics including age, education, and gender. As McPherson et al. (2001) state, racialization and ethnicity are the biggest divide in social networks today, clustering people from similar ethnic and racialized backgrounds into tight-knit networks.

The clustering of similar people based on racialization or their ethnicity is referred to as racial/ethnic homogeneity. People tend to marry, hang out, date, go to school,

and share friendships with others who are from their same ethnic or racialized group. Interestingly, this kind of clustering gets mirrored online, where people's digital connections tend to be to others who are similar to them. Wimmer and Lewis (2010) looked at pictures of Facebook friends among a sample of 736 students. Analyzing the racialized and ethnic backgrounds of those with whom the students were connected, they found that racialized homophily continues to be one of the most important factors leading to the formation and maintenance of social ties (Wimmer & Lewis, 2010).

The greatest level of racialized homogeneity was found among African American students whose Facebook friendship networks were racially homogenous. Wimmer and Lewis (2010) see this pattern associated with past and current practices of discrimination against African Americans in the United States. It seems that the internet, despite its massive collection of information and potential for exposure to diverse perspectives, thoughts, and opinions, tends instead to serve as an echo chamber where similar people come together.

Time to reflect

Take a look at your Facebook friends, Twitter or Instagram followers, or Snapchat network, and reflect upon its racialized or ethnic diversity or homophily. How homophilous is your network?

Tolerance is understood as positive orientation toward (in particular racialized) minorities (Cabrera, Nora, Terenzini, Pascarella, & Hagedorn, 1999; Morley, 2003). Côté and Erickson (2009) distinguish between three core elements:

- Cognitive: thought processes that recognize and reflect upon processes of discrimination
- Evaluative: a sense that minority groups fit into the culture of the host society and if given the opportunity make a positive contribution
- Political: preparedness to welcome additional immigrants and aid them in relocation.

These three core elements determine how a society views minorities and to what extent it will welcome newcomers from minority groups. Between 2006 and 2011, Canada alone has added over one million (1,162,900) foreign-born people to its population (Chui & Flanders, 2013). Canadians often think of themselves as tolerant of minority groups and their cultures.

However, a 2016 poll shows 68 per cent of Canadians indicated that minorities should do more to fit in and 32 per cent thought Canadians should encourage cultural diversity (see Figure 8.6) (Proctor, 2016). In comparison, more Americans were open to cultural diversity and fewer (53%) thought that minorities should do more to fit in (Proctor, 2016). As discussed earlier in the chapter, in Canada as few as 4.6 per cent of couples are in mixed unions, which suggests a preference for partners in the same ethnic or racialized group rather than an embrace of diversity. These statistics suggest that Canada may not be as tolerant as we like to assume.

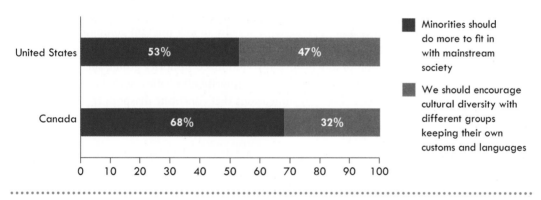

Dashboard
Interactive activity

FIGURE 8.6 Opinions on Cultural Diversity in Canada and the United States

Source: Adapted from: www.cbc.ca/news/canada/british-columbia/poll-canadians-multiculturalism-immigrants-1.3784194

Diasporas

Every day, new people from around the world arrive in Canadian cities to resettle. For many migrants, core elements of their identity are based in their homeland, but because they no longer reside there, they need to establish new identity linkages.

We discussed above that part of this process of resettlement includes building new ties to racialized and ethnic groups of people who are already resettled to obtain help and support and learn from others' personal histories. **Diaspora** consists of ethnic enclaves outside the homeland that provide connections back to one's roots. These communities, however, do not exist in isolation and are not unique to the Canadian context. Immigrant groups such as the Arabs of Montreal or the Sikhs of Edmonton are often members of much larger transnational networks—the global Arab or Sikh community, for example.

diaspora the dispersal of any group of people; originally, the term referred specifically to the tribes of Israel dispersed around the world.

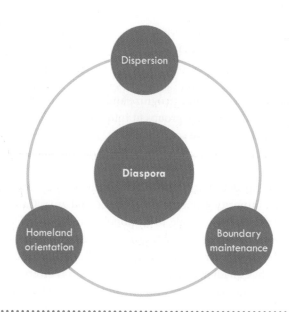

FIGURE 8.7 Key Dimensions of Diaspora

Source: Author-generated

Diaspora was first used to describe the scattering of the tribes of Israel and, following the Nazi genocide of Jews in Europe, was applied to Jewish communities around the world. The term *diaspora* has changed its meaning and is now applied more broadly to any migrant community, including those migrants who are assimilated to their new homeland (Brubaker, 2005). The term is also used to describe the global dispersion of any historically victimized minority group, such as Tamils or Armenians, or racialized and potentially victimized minority ethnicities, such as Arabs in Africa and Chinese people in Indonesia. Three key dimensions that constitute diaspora are as follows (see Figure 8.7) (Brubaker, 2005):

- Dispersion: Diasporas are communities that are dispersed and divided by national borders.
- Homeland orientation: Diasporas are oriented toward an either real or imagined homeland, which they are committed to and to which ideally they would one day return to.
- Boundary maintenance: Members of the diaspora are connected through tightly knit networks of solidarity based on their roots in the homeland.

These three dimensions explain how diasporas are formed and their significance for migrants in maintaining their own cultural and ethnic identity as they simultaneously establish new ties and integrate into a new homeland.

Diasporas need to be understood in the context of both a colonial past and current hegemonic global structures. In other words, most migration today is not simply a willingness of people to re-settle with the goal of experiencing novel locations and cultures. Rather, the flow of people is closely linked to colonial relations established in the contexts of the British Empire and the colonization of the Americas as well as to economic interests and forces of globalization. These colonial relations define identities and influence transnational flows.

Manuel Castells (1997), a sociologist who has written about the networked society, explains how people are always positioned between forces of globalization and the formation of unique, locally rooted identities. Digital media facilitate and reinforce transnational connections, which support the formation of community in digital diasporas (Daniels, 2012).

In Canada, we see the creation of diasporas not only by examining ethnic groups that have come from other countries. We also see people moving across provinces to seek new economic opportunities, often related to employment. In the 2000s, Alberta presented a unique case, as it saw a stronger wage growth than other provinces, which prompted young people to relocate to that province. The average annual wages and salaries earned by unmarried men aged 17 to 34 grew faster in Alberta than in other provinces between 2001 and 2006 (Statistics Canada, 2013b). In 2008 the interprovincial workforce in Alberta was about 128,000 people (Statistics Canada, 2013b).

Diasporas are networks that transcend boundaries, and digital media have largely transformed how diasporas operate. Diasporas benefit from digital technology greatly, as it not only allows them to connect to family back home but also to continue to stay connected with their home culture. This allows those who are far from home to maintain a sense of belonging with their place of origin.

Technology also contributes to people's willingness to relocate. Migrants know they can stay connected with family and friends, and air travel facilitates in-person visits. Smart phones facilitate hyperconnectivity, allowing for frequent communication and strengthening communicative ties through the exchange of pictures, texts, voice, and video (Quan-Haase & Wellman, 2004). Technology also allows migrants to research their new area of residence, which aids integration into their new community. Box 8.5 discusses the relevance of digital networks to the creation of diaspora and the ability of migrant workers to stay rooted to their homeland, even when they are far away.

Box 8.5 shows that digital media not only support transnational diasporas, but also function as an important means of connecting diasporas within national borders as in the case of Newfoundlanders who migrate (Daniels, 2012). The use of information and communication technologies has greatly benefitted diaspora communities around the globe.

The result is a global network of ethnic diasporas—of Chinese communities in Toronto, Sydney, Singapore, Paris, and Buenos Aires, for example. Whether it is through a search for a recipe, or reading the news, diaspora seek racialized identity and community online (Daniels, 2012). Nakamura and Chow-White (2012) document how migrants go to digital media to both create and reaffirm their racialized identities. The result is a network of worldwide cities all connected to one another through intercommunity linkages.

Think Globally

8.5 | Diaspora Communities Build and Sustain Social Ties Online

With many Canadians moving from their province of origin to other provinces with the aim of seeking employment, the question of how they adjust to a new place becomes critical. Digital technologies are particularly well suited in supporting diaspora both across provinces and borders. Many young people move away from home to go to university or college in another province or to take jobs in another country. Migrants can keep in contact via Skype, FaceTime, and other online communication tools that facilitate contact with family and close friends. By contrast, Facebook, Instagram, and Snapchat enable contact with weaker ties, social groups, and community.

Hiller and Franz (2004) studied the use of the internet in supporting diasporic ties. They focused on the experience of migrants from Newfoundland who relied on digital media to establish and maintain ties with both their homeland and others in diaspora. In their study, three types of online relationships were identified: building new ties, nourishing old ties, and rediscovering lost ties. The study shows that digital technologies are closely interlinked with migration processes by both facilitating the formation of new ties based on diaspora identity, as well as maintaining existing ties to communities in the homeland.

Table 8.3 shows how search engines, email, and chat were used to support migrants prior to their migration (pre-migrant), migrants as they settled in a new place (post-migrant), and also those migrants who have already settled (settled migrants). The use of digital media helped migrants throughout the process and provided important source of information, advice, and social support. Migrating can be challenging and having a social network to rely on and share the experience can be a critical asset.

Continued

TABLE 8.3 Role of Digital Media in Different Phases of Migration

	Pre-migrant	Post-migrant	Settled migrant
Online information seeking	Activity: Information seeking related to place of relocation.	Activity: Targeted information seeking to adjust to new home. Stay connected with homeland via news.	Activity: Search engines are used in complex ways to stay connected with homeland.
	Function: Learning about new place to ease migration.	Function: Learning about new community and maintain old ties to homeland.	Function: Maintaining homeland identity in diaspora.
Email	Activity: Email contact with weak and strong ties to initiate relocation.	Activity: Stay in touch with networks at home and establish contact with other migrants in new place.	Activity: Stay in touch with people from home to share experiences.
	Function: Making contacts regarding migration prospects.	Function: Maintaining old ties to homeland. Building ties among migrants.	Function: Maintaining ties with family/ community.
Chat	Activity: Seeking advice from earlier migrants to learn from their experience.	Activity: Keeping in touch with networks back home.	Activity: Connecting with other migrants and friends.
	Function: Learning from other migrants and preparing for relocation.	Function: Looking to maintain meaningful relationships at a distance.	Function: Looking for personal relations and social support exchange.

Source: Adapted from Hiller, H. H., & Franz, T. M. (2004). New ties, old ties, and lost ties: The use of the internet in diaspora. *New Media and Society*, 6(6), 731–752. http://doi.org/10.1177/146144804044327

JONATHAN NACKSTRAND/AFP/Getty Images

Migrant workers connecting via social media to maintain intimate ties with family back home. What are the benefits of maintaining online diaspora communities that provide links to family, friends, and citizens from one's origin country? What kinds of resources are exchanged in diaspora communities?

Racialization Practices

Racialized differences, as we learned earlier in the chapter, are not biologically determined. They are socially constructed. Racism takes the idea of ethnocentrism, which was discussed in Chapter 3, a step further by not only seeing the world from one's own ethnic viewpoint but by favouring this viewpoint above all others and considering viewpoints of others inferior.

For conflict theorists, reviewed above in this chapter, the ambition for power and economic advantage drives unequal racialized and ethnic relations. The dominant group, made up of people in positions of power, holds on to its power by controlling and subjugating less powerful groups.

TABLE 8.4 Key Concepts in the Study of Racialization

Concept	Definition
Institutional racism	Forms of discrimination that rely on formal institutional rules and common practices
Expressed racism	Discriminatory practices based on projected fears onto particular ethnic and racialized minorities
Internalized racism	The acceptance, by those who are racialized, of stereotypes or beliefs existent in society about the racialized group to which they belong as inferior and worthless
Prejudice	A negative or hostile attitude towards members of a particular group simply because they belong to that group, based on untested assumptions about their characteristics
Discrimination	The denial of access to opportunities that would be available to equally qualified people who are part of the dominant group
Microaggressions	Everyday, routine interaction with subtle, indirect, or unintentional forms of discrimination at its root

Source: Author-generated

Racism becomes a convenient tool to justify inequality on the basis of a perceived superiority related to the social construction of "race." In other words, racism can be seen as the result of a group's need to justify the exploitation of another group. Members of the dominant group blame the misfortunes of the subordinate group on an inferior genetic constitution, bad cultural values, or both. Table 8.4 provides definitions of some of the central racialization practices and shows how they are different.

Institutional, Expressed, and Internalized Racism

Institutional racism describes forms of discrimination that adhere to formal rules and are based on common practices. These are often neither conscious nor deliberately malicious, but rather they are based on ingrained practices or biases that are long-standing and implicit. Institutional racism is often invisible unless the institutions are analyzed as a whole.

institutionalized racism a form of racism expressed in the practice of social and political institutions.

Canada's history of institutional racism is evident in the way educational institutions were implemented in Canada for different social groups. A product of the colonial process that rested on racial superiority and Eurocentrism, residential schools were established across Canada by the government to assimilate Indigenous children into Euro-Canadian culture. This goal was founded on the assumption that Indigenous culture was uncivilized and thus inferior to that of Europeans. The government collaborated with Christian religious groups to put these schools in place, with the aim of educating Indigenous children so as "to resemble the white man" (Truth and Reconciliation Committee, 2015b, p. 54).

Residential schools have deeply impacted Indigenous individuals and communities, as children were separated from their families and communities, and forced into abusive and often inhuman circumstances. An estimated 150,000 First Nation, Inuit, and Métis children were forced into residential schools. Students were subjected to physical and sexual abuse, isolation, and experimentation; approximately 6,000 died that we know of as a result of the residential school system. Residential schools robbed these children of the opportunity to understand, experience, and appreciate their own heritage and way of life—an intentional attempt at cultural genocide. Residential schools operated for over 150 years, with the last residential school being closed in 1996. Consequently, the effects of residential schools on Indigenous identity and culture are deeply rooted, and coming to terms with what occurred requires long-term solutions.

The work of the Truth and Reconciliation Committee (TRC) has been significant for Canadian society in providing a new roadmap for inclusion and reconciliation amongst those who lived in Canada first—Indigenous groups—and its colonizers—first Europeans, later from around the world. The TRC works with Indigenous communities and individuals to honour their self-determination and voice, rather than imposing a pre-established framework for reconciliation. The goal was to create opportunities for learning and dialogue where their experiences were honoured and preserved for future generations (TRC, 2015b).

The TRC explains that reconciliation involves coming to terms with past events in such a way as to defeat long-standing conflict and move towards a respectful relationship between Indigenous and non-Indigenous people (TRC, 2015b). This process involves productive action that addresses how the legacy of colonialism continues to wreak havoc on Indigenous communities today in areas such as education, health, and child welfare. A goal must therefore be to "create a more equitable and inclusive society by closing the gaps in social, health, and economic outcomes that exist" (TRC, 2015b, p. 125), a social reality we discussed already in Chapter 6.

The Indian Residential Schools Settlement Agreement in 2007 resulted in the creation of the TRC, a commission dedicated to recognition and restitution through dialogue and action, and also led to a formal public apology by then Prime Minister Stephen Harper in 2008. (A video of the public apology is available on YouTube. Search for "Canadian federal government apology to First Nations.") In 2009, a multi-year process commenced to provide survivors with the opportunity to tell their stories and voice how residential schools impacted them personally. The numerous statements, documents, and related materials helped comprise the National Centre for Truth and Reconciliation (TRC, 2015b).

The TRC has offered an extensive number of recommendations pertaining to the rights, education, and health of Indigenous people. Two examples are calls to the federal government. The first being to create new education legislation through collaboration with Indigenous communities. This would involve a commitment to adequate funding for schools to improve educational outcomes and develop a curriculum that integrates Indigenous cultures. Second, it is recommended that the federal government implement a Canadian Indigenous languages act, with the goal of revitalizing and preserving the numerous languages of different Indigenous groups that have existed for generations. Additionally, it would recognize Indigenous languages as a "fundamental and valued element of Canadian culture and society" (TRC, 2015a, p. 2).

An important piece of the TRC is to mobilize governments, institutions, communities, and individuals to move towards reconciliation. As part of this initiative, the National Centre for Truth and Reconciliation has developed a digital space for community building that allows groups and individuals to record reconciliation-oriented initiatives that are happening across the nation and to reflect on how they are affecting communities. The 2007 Indian Residential Schools Settlement Agreement is one such action; the agreement recognizes the detrimental effects residential schools have had on individuals, families, and entire communities, and has established a multi-billion-dollar settlement fund to support the healing of residential school survivors.

Monetary compensation is not a complete solution, however. The TRC has argued that most Canadians' lack of knowledge about residential schools has negative consequences. Lack of public understanding "reinforces racist attitudes and fuels civic distrust between Aboriginal peoples and other Canadians" (TRC, 2015b, p. 114). In terms of legislation, government officials must be educated so as to make informed policy decisions. Furthermore, the TRC has pushed for the opening of a public discussion on reconciliation of Indigenous and non-Indigenous communities beyond the conflict surrounding residential schools. It is their belief that for Indigenous communities to truly move forward, all Canadians must feel compelled to transform Canadian society into a place where Indigenous people can coexist peacefully and have their culture be respected.

Institutionalized racism has also been documented in Canada's immigration policies. In Canadian history, practices of discrimination have also affected immigration policies as well as institutionalized and informal settlement practices. In the development of immigration policies, racism can become institutionalized as a result of the practices involved in immigrant selection as well as the various challenges and barriers immigrants face upon entering Canada. Bureaucratic requirements such as passports, work permits, medical examinations, and literacy tests can lead to racialized outcomes if the opportunities created for immigrants differ on the basis of nationality or ethnicity (Richmond, 2001). This shows that not all immigrant groups have the same opportunities when arriving in Canada.

In the nineteenth century and first half of the twentieth century, Canadian immigration policy demonstrated an overt preference for European immigrants. Since initial policy was formed with the goal of assimilation in mind, the Canadian government selected immigrants based on what groups they believed were most likely to fit well into Anglo-Canadian culture (Baureiss, 1987). In other words, those who were of European origin were thought to be more capable of blending in. Consequently, overt racism prevailed in immigration policy, with various interventions and barriers being upheld to keep certain ethnic groups from migrating to Canada (Levine-Ravsky, Beaudoin, & St Clair, 2014). "Undesirable" ethnic groups were only permitted to immigrate when sufficient labour could not be obtained from preferential migration countries (Baureiss, 1987). For example, Asian immigrants were particularly vulnerable to this shift, as thousands of Chinese men were brought to Canada between 1880 and 1884 to assist in the completion of the Canadian Pacific Railway. Following this period, however, restrictions were applied to immigrants from China in the form of a head tax to curtail further entrance from these groups. The head tax was a payment demanded from each person of Chinese origin and was introduced when the Canadian parliament passed the Chinese Immigration Act of 1885, its primary goal being to dissuade immigrants of Chinese origin from immigrating to Canada. With the completion of the Canadian Pacific Railway, the government saw no need to promote immigration from China. This shows that preferences for immigrant groups shifted based on economic interests and were reflected in institutionalized racism through immigration policy that discriminated against certain groups. This kind of institutionalized racism also exists in immigration policies in other parts of the world, another example being Australia and its policies toward Chinese immigrants.

Canada's discriminatory immigration policy also affected refugee decisions during the Second World War when, for example, Jewish immigrants from Europe were denied entry. Canada rejected Jewish asylum seekers who came by ship to escape the Nazi persecution. The MS *St Louis* departed Hamburg in 1939 to find asylum for its Jewish passengers (Thomas & Morgan-Witts, 1974). The *St Louis* arrived in Canada in 1939 with 907 Jewish refugees on board. Canada blocked its entry into the country despite the fact that those on board were seeking asylum from Nazi Germany. Though some prominent Canadian figures protested this refusal, Immigration Minister Frederick Blair was adamant in his decision to uphold Canada's race-based immigration policies. Prime Minister William Lyon Mackenzie King suggested that Blair consider the views of the protesters, but he did not exercise his power in vetoing Blair's choice, and thus forced the refugees to sail back to Europe (Bureau, 2013). Following the end of the Second World War, only Jewish individuals with "agricultural experience" or those who were willing to work as servants were considered for immigration (Richmond, 2001). The apathy of the Canadian government towards Jewish refugees demonstrates how discrimination was deeply entrenched in the immigration policies of the period.

Though a new Immigration Act came into effect in 1953, this act continued to discriminate against specific groups, as it identified explicitly "prohibited classes" and allowed for government discretion on the basis of various immigrant characteristics such as ethnic group, occupation, or peculiar customs (Richmond, 2001). Immigration policy became steadily less overtly discriminatory from 1962 on, following the implementation of human rights legislation in Canada. While this meant that explicit discrimination was no longer permitted, differential treatment towards immigrants of different origins did not dissipate completely.

While today it may seem as though Canada has alleviated its Eurocentric bias through the elimination of overtly racist immigration practices, many believe that there is still significant room for improvement (Richmond, 2001). The "problem of diversity" discussed in popular media essentially refers to large numbers of immigrants from non-traditional source countries, who Anglo-Canadian citizens fear will compromise Canada's "national identity" (Li, 2001). This widespread notion impacts immigration policy inadvertently, as the Canadian government attempts to appease the concerns of some Canadians. Recent controversy surrounded the proposition put forward by Kellie Leitch, a member of Parliament for the Conservative Party of Canada, who had also run to become leader of the party. Leitch proposed to screen potential immigrants and refugees for "anti-Canadian values." Her website states, "We must screen for Canadian values. The policy of allowing hundreds of thousands of immigrants and refugees into Canada every year without a face-to-face interview with a trained immigration officer must end" (Leitch, 2017). The idea behind her proposition is that certain groups fit better with Canadian values than others and immigration policies need to identify unwanted newcomers. The proposal drew much media attention and was dismissed for many reasons—namely, because of the simplistic notion that Canadian values can be assessed. More importantly, it is also highly contentious who would determine what those Canadian values are.

Members of Leitch's own party argued that the screening strategy would fail to accurately capture the values of immigrants: "I agree that there are fundamental Western and Canadian values that must be protected such as freedom, democracy, tolerance," stated fellow Conservative leadership candidate Maxime Bernier. "I don't agree however that we should target immigrants with a values test. It is an unworkable way to determine people's beliefs" (Zimonjic, 2016). The imposition of a strict values test implies an intention of assimilating immigrants, an integration strategy that violates Canada's pursuit of a multicultural identity. Instead, Bernier argued, the focus should be placed on providing opportunities for new immigrants to participate in their newfound community and achieve positive outcomes.

Recent immigrants are subjected to "structured inequality" resulting from obstacles such as language barriers and non-recognition of foreign qualifications, along with encountering expressed racism (discussed next). Furthermore, the offices tasked with handling immigration visas do not appear to be equally distributed throughout various countries; more offices exist in the United Kingdom and the United States than in countries in the Global South, for instance (Richmond, 2001). Though Canada prides itself on being a multicultural nation, its "unbiased" immigration policies show forms of institutionalized racism by favouring certain ethnicities over others, leaving many immigrant groups at a disadvantage for attaining success in their new home.

The biases present in hiring practices that we discussed in Box 8.2 are another good example of institutional racism that disadvantages racialized minorities. By contrast **expressed racism** occurs when people project their fears onto particular ethnic and racialized minorities, then act according to these projections, excluding people and denying them jobs or accommodation. They adhere to stereotyping as a way of thinking about the world. The example discussed earlier in the chapter about Dave Mornix's experience is a case of expressed racism.

Internalized racism describes the acceptance by racialized people of the stereotypes or beliefs about the group to which they have been racialized into as being inferior and worthless. Members of racialized minorities internalize negative views about themselves as a result of being exposed to overt racism in day-to-day interaction (Hipolito-Delgado, 2010). Another mechanism that leads to internalized racism comes from being socialized in a racist society. As children grow up and develop a sense of self (see Chapter 4), they incorporate assumptions about who they are into their identity. Internalized racism also has health consequences, leading not only to illness but also depression and high levels of stress (Hipolito-Delgado, 2010).

Prejudice and Discrimination

Often the terms *prejudice* and *discrimination* are used interchangeably, but they are in fact different things. Prejudice is a negative, hostile social attitude toward members of another group. All members of the group—because of their group membership—are assumed to have unsuitable qualities.

An important element in prejudice is the use of stereotypes—fixed mental images that prejudiced people think embody members of a given group. When we make use of stereotypes, we categorize people on the basis of only some characteristics that we exaggerate in importance. Typically, prejudices are negative views based on hidden assumptions about how a person's perceived "race" (i.e., how he or she is racialized) and/or presumed ethnicity is related to intelligence, morality, or other valued qualities. Sometimes these stereotypes are even couched in praise, as in "Jewish accountants know how to juggle the books" or "Black boxers can take a lot of punishment" or "French Canadian women can cook." Stereotypes justify our prejudices against racialized and ethnic minorities, giving them shape and order.

By contrast, discrimination refers to actions carried out against another person because of his or her group membership. In particular, it means denying opportunities that people would grant to equally qualified members of their own group. Discrimination involves favouring some members of society over others based on assumptions about their racialized or ethnic background. When people with the same ability receive different rewards for doing the same work, we can logically claim that discrimination must be present.

The basis of discrimination can be manifold. When people hire others who are "like them," they are practising a form of nepotism, the desire to favour only friends and relatives. This becomes a form of ethnic self-protection or self-advancement: protecting and advancing one's group at the expense

expressed racism explicit discrimination and prejudice towards people based on their racialization or ethnicity.

internalized racism the conscious or unconscious acceptance of racist attitudes, including stereotypes and biases, towards members of one's own ethnic group, including oneself.

of other groups. Such protection or advancement of one's own group can be more about discrimination than prejudice. The continued dominance of the majority is in the best interests of those who belong to the dominant majority, after all. However, often discrimination *is* based on prejudice—as we mentioned above, prejudice functions to excuse discrimination—such as *racial profiling,* which we described earlier. Racialized profiling is the practice of racializing people and using their appearance and assumed background to predict their engagement in criminal activities (Rice, Reitzel, & Piquero, 2005). While we do not have a full picture of racialized profiling across Canada, studies within individual police agencies have shown that racialized profiling is a systemic form of discrimination in Canada (CCLA, 2015). We also discussed racialized discrimination in the overrepresentation of Indigenous people in the criminal justice system in Chapter 5.

Microaggressions

In Canada, many experiences of racism are systemic and invisible. In other words, you may never know you weren't shown a house in a particular neighbourhood or that because of the neighbourhood you grew up in, you ended up at a school with less private funding and so did not get as many opportunities as your peers at wealthier schools. Other experiences of racism are denied or blame is shifted—Indigenous communities without potable water are often described in terms of experiencing a lack of resources, rather than experiencing long-term systemic racism.

Many instances of racism can be considered microaggressions—daily interactions with subtle, indirect, or unintentional discrimination at its root (Baker, 2017). For example, asking someone who looks ethnically diverse where they are "really" from, asking to touch a black woman's hair, or assuming an "Asian"-looking student is good at math are a form of microaggression. These kinds of interactions implicitly communicate to the other person that they are not "one of us," not seen as the unique individual that they are, but rather that they are defined by the way in which they are racialized, and that their rights to personal space and privacy are not important or to be respected. Taken individually, microaggressions may seem relatively harmless, but they can add up cumulatively to be sources of daily stress for those who experience them.

Genocide

We have discussed different types of conflict resulting from tensions between ethnic groups. However, the twentieth century witnessed one of the most horrific, if not the most horrific, ethnic conflicts in history.

The term *genocide* was not introduced until after the Second World War; it describes intentional mass murder. Genocide is not applied to randomized acts of mass murder as in a mass shooting; rather, it describes the systematic, large-scale annihilation of an entire ethnic group, often with the intention of eradicating its people (Lemkin, 1944). The meaning of the word *genocide* can only be understood when one takes into account the actions of the Nazi regime against those of Jewish background living in Europe. During Hitler's regime, 6 million Jewish people, 1.5 million of whom were children, were murdered on their way to or while living in concentration camps. Approximately 60 per cent of the world's Jewish population was killed during the Nazi regime. Many, such as historian Saul Friedländer (2007), view the extent of the horror of the events as next to impossible to put in language.

What also makes it difficult to comprehend is that many nations that view themselves as humanitarian today were also discriminatory against Jewish people. Canada, as discussed above, rejected Jewish refugees who came aboard the MS *St Louis* to escape the Nazi persecution (Thomas & Morgan-Witts, 1974). Canada was not the only country with these discriminatory policies. In fact, none of the countries where the vessel landed granted the passengers asylum, including Cuba, the United States, and Canada. The passengers had to return to Europe after spending over a month at sea. Many of the refugees from the *St Louis* later died in death camps during the Second World War.

In 1948 the United Nations declared the eradication of ethnic groups a crime against humanity and its primary mission became to increase tolerance and understanding and reduce conflict between ethnic groups.

But what is the root of conflict between ethnic groups and how do such conflicts escalate? The psychologist Gordon Allport explains conflicts in terms of perception that ethnic groups are competing for limited resources such as jobs, land, and access to education and health care (Allport & Postman, 1947). As uncertainty increases, people tend to project their fears on other social groups who are perceived as outsiders; these groups become a kind of blank screen. Anti-Semitism was prevalent in Europe since at least the Middle Ages, but it became pronounced as Jewish people were stereotyped as wealthy and blamed for the lack of jobs during financially difficult times. But this characterization of Jewish people has been applied to other ethnic groups as well. Depending on the society, Scots, Arabs, Roma, Turks, Armenians, Asian Indians, Chinese, and Koreans have all historically played this "middle-man" role and been hated, feared, and envied for it.

This kind of prejudice continues today, and the internet can provide yet another platform for these prejudices to be expressed. An example is the case of Ernst Christof Friedrich Zündel, who lived in Canada between 1958 and 2000. Zündel used the internet to deny the Nazi genocide of Jewish people during the Second World War. His website was shut down and he was denied further entry into Canada. The German court ruled that through his website and pamphlets he "denied the fate of destruction for the Jews planned by National Socialist powerholders and justified this by saying that the mass destruction in Auschwitz and Treblinka, among others, were an invention of the Jews and served the repression and extortion of the German people" (*The Jerusalem Post*, 2006) in line with the German criminal code, Section 130, (2). More recently, the increase in refugees from Muslim countries such as Syria has been accompanied by an increase in the rise of Islamophobia (hatred of Islamic people and people from Islamic countries) in Canada. Even as hate crimes have dropped overall, police-reported hate crimes against Muslim Canadians have more than doubled over a three-year period (Paperny, 2016). This shows that laws are still needed to protect racialized and marginalized groups.

Time to reflect

Have you been involved in any social movements combatting islamophobia or racism? Do you think social movements are effective ways of fighting inequality? Keep this question in mind, particularly when you read Chapter 16 on social movements.

Conclusions

As Canadian society becomes more multicultural and multiethnic, it also struggles with understandings of racialization and ethnicity. We learned in this chapter that these are complex terms that shape many aspects of daily life and are central to people's identity. Understandings of racialization and ethnicity not only enrich Canadian cities with food, culture, and a variety of perspectives, but they also create new challenges in terms of helping new migrants and creating equal opportunities, as outlined in the Charter of Rights and Freedoms. We discussed that racialization distinguishes people by visible characteristics, while ethnicity refers to the social groups that share a national or cultural background.

Today, racialized groups continue to suffer from prejudice and discrimination. Both of these are related to the social process that imagines and stereotypes "race" and, as a result, creates racism. Racialization and racism can negatively affect the safety, opportunities, day-to-day life, internal sense of self, and health of racialized individuals.

Digital media have provided new opportunities for racialized groups to create community, voice their opinions, and share personal experiences. Diasporas can retain communication and a sense of community in ways they never could before. At the same time, digital communities can act as silos rather than exposing us to a diversity of cultures and individuals, which has been shown to improve tolerance. Despite the global impression of Canada as a multicultural society, we have significant systemic discriminatory practices that negatively impact racialized Canadians. Sociology is one of the tools that help us see and describe the issues that many Canadians face.

Questions for Critical Thought

1. Explain how racial profiling affects the lives of ethnic minority groups in Canada. What kinds of assumptions come into play when a police officer decides to stop the car of a youth he or she has racialized and searches it?

2. The possibilities for inexpensive and readily available genetic testing have allowed many people to learn more about their ancestry. Discuss to what extent testing for one's genealogy can influence a person's identity. Can this type of genetic testing either increase or decrease tolerance among ethnic or racialized groups?

3. What kinds of insights does conflict theory provide on the politics that led to the election of President Trump in the United States?

4. How are information and communication technologies such Skype, FaceTime, and WhatsApp helping diasporas maintain long-distance intimate social ties?

Take it Further: Recommended Readings

J. Daniels, *Cyber Racism: White Supremacy Online and the New Attack on Civil Rights* (Lanham, MD: Rowman & Littlefield, 2009). *Cyber Racism* documents and problematizes the changing nature of white supremacy on the internet and the role digital media play in civil rights.

F. Henry and C. Tator, *The Colour of Democracy: Racism in Canadian Society*, 4th ed. (Toronto, ON: Thomson Nelson, 2009). This book uncovers how racialized beliefs and practices affect Canadian society and discusses how policies and institutions have failed to effectively address issues of racism.

L. Monchalin, *The Colonial Problem: An Indigenous Perspective on Crime and Injustice in Canada* (Toronto, ON: University of Toronto Press, 2016). Through a detailed and critical examination of the Canadian criminal justice system, Monchalin problematizes the overrepresentation of Indigenous people in jails by looking at social issues linked to colonialism and racism.

L. Nakamura, *Cybertypes: Race, Ethnicity, and Identity on the Internet* (New York: Routledge, 2013). This book shows how race and ethnicity play out online and influence social interactions, often yielding a deeply racialized social space.

V. Satzewich and N. Liodakis, *"Race" and Ethnicity in Canada: A Critical Introduction*, 4th ed. (Don Mills, ON: Oxford University Press, 2017). This volume provides a critical reflection on "race" and ethnicity in Canada, highlighting the complex and often paradoxical issues of "race" and ethnic relations.

Take it Further: Recommended Online Resources

Benetton: A History of Shocking Ad Campaigns
www.ibtimes.co.uk/benetton-history-shocking-ad-campaigns-pictures-252087

The Black Experience Project
www.theblackexperienceproject.ca/

CBC Reporting, Missing & Murdered: The Unsolved Cases of Indigenous Women and Girls
www.cbc.ca/missingandmurdered

Gord Downie, "The Stranger," *The Secret Path* [video]
www.youtube.com/watch?v=za2VzjkwtFc

Paying the Price: The Human Cost of Racial Profiling
http://www.ohrc.on.ca/en/paying-price-human-cost-racial-profiling

Social Science and Humanities Research Council of Canada (SSHRC) Documents for Research Involving the First Nations, Inuit and Métis Peoples of Canada
www.pre.ethics.gc.ca/eng/policy-politique/initiatives/tcps2-eptc2/chapter9-chapitre9

Truth and Reconciliation Commission of Canada, National Centre for Truth and Reconciliation
www.trc.ca/

Elke Winter, discusses "Us, Them and Others: Pluralism and National Identity in Diverse Societies" [video]
www.youtube.com/watch?v=nmOez5Z1Nmo

More resources available on  Dashboard

9

Understanding Global Inequality

Introduction

From a sociological perspective, the systematic study of global inequality goes back only about 250 years. Adam Smith (1776), the founder of economics, was motivated to find an explanation for global inequality when he wrote the first classic work in economics, *The Wealth of Nations*. Why are some nations wealthy and powerful while others are not? Smith concluded the answer was specialization and trade, which allowed educated, trained individuals engaged in economic exchanges to maximize their well-being. Similarly, one of sociology's founders, Émile Durkheim (1892/1933), made a pitch for specialization and cooperation in his classic work *The Division of Labour* just over a century later. A highly specialized workforce that coordinates toward a common goal has an edge: this insight proved central to the functionalist approach in sociology to modernization and global inequality during the last hundred years. Today, a specialized workforce is one that is innovative and highly specialized. Box 9.1 shows the many advantages of technological innovations to health outcomes.

Think Globally

9.1 | Science, Technological Progress, and the Alarming Longevity Gap

Around the world, we see differences in individuals' and social groups' access to health care and advances in medical technology. These variations have profound effects on a person's health and are related to the length of time a newborn baby is expected to live. While a child born in Japan can expect to live for over 80 years (allowing for a slight difference in the life expectancies of males and females), a child born in Malawi can expect to live for about 51 years (WHO, 2016b, 2017). There is no biological or genetic reason for these striking differences in health and life expectancy. These global variations in life expectancy result from social and economic inequalities. When we look at health across the life course, it is shocking to see that many of the health problems and death risks are experienced by children under the age of five. In Canada, similar health risks also exist for specific social groups. For example, Inuit and First Nations children on isolated reserves are at a much higher risk of death before age five than other Canadian children (CIHR, 2008).

Canada is contributing, in various ways, to reducing national and global health inequalities. For example, expertise developed in Canada is shared with other nations to support their health initiatives. The Canadian Institutes for Health Research (CIHR, 2008) has identified global

health research as a priority area and is supporting research that addresses the health challenges of low- and middle-income countries around the world. As well, CIHR is helping to build research capacity in these countries through education and technology transfer, so they are better able to meet their own health challenges.

Thomas Imo/Photothek via Getty Images

The world is vibrating with active, creative people who are using what they have at hand to make their lives better and compete in an unequal global economy.

Time to reflect

In what ways has your own health benefitted from being in Canada? In what ways has the Canadian system let you down?

In this chapter we will also explore other approaches to understanding global inequality in addition to the functionalist approach. For example, we will talk about the role of information flows in facilitating global equality, following the insights of Paul Krugman. Krugman observed that new technological products such as computers and robotic machinery are often developed first in the Global North. This creates an economic advantage linked to technological advancements. For Krugman, the gap closes over time, as these technologies start to spread to countries in the Global South. Yet, what creates further global inequality is the uneven distribution of patents and copyrights obtained by the North through their monopoly on these new products. This means that through constant innovation and diffusion the technological advantages of the Global North can diminish, leading toward a reduction in global inequality, but not eradicating it. We will ask in this chapter, what are the conditions in any society that favour innovation—the discovery and creation of profitable new ideas and practices? We will also ask, what are the conditions in any society that favour the imitation or copying of ideas and practices from other societies?

Under the right conditions, global networking allows developing countries to imitate the most financially and technologically successful nations by importing their knowledge and skills. As we will see, exploiting these opportunities requires government support for the creation of co-operative relationships, with established players in the technology market, for example. For this to happen, government and industry must encourage flexible systems of knowledge production that link science and technology to social and organizational systems. This chapter will discuss that problem.

Finally, in this chapter, we will talk about the ways that nations secure and maintain unequal wealth and power by means of military, political, and economic colonization. Here, the insights of conflict theory are most useful, and we will pay special attention to Gunder Frank's dependency theory (1967) and Wallerstein's "world system theory" (1974). In these theories, the flow of information and ideas is less important than flows of capital and military might. As we will discover, there is no good way to separate these elements of global inequality: information, innovation, capital, and brute force all serve to ensure that certain nations will dominate and, indeed, become ever more dominant. Yet empires that rise also fall, and in the end, we must understand all of the processes that constantly reshape global inequality.

Defining and Measuring Global Inequality

Global inequality generally describes the widely different opportunities or chances people in different societies have for securing a healthy, satisfying life. Around the world, research has found that people want more or less the same things: health, security, a fulfilling family life, a meaningful job, and so forth. But research has also shown that the chances of getting these things vary across countries (and even different parts of the same country). This is what global inequality is all about. These inequalities, as we will see, are evident in widely different levels of per capita income and wealth, standards of living, lifespans and quality of life, chances for a higher education, and opportunities for a fulfilling, secure job.

To start at the most basic level, research has shown that chances for a prosperous life as described above are more favourable in the northern, higher-income countries of the world, which are often referred to as the Global North. The **Global North** includes places such as the United States, Canada, and the countries of Western Europe. Conversely, the term **Global South** is used to describe those countries in the southern hemisphere that are less economically developed. These terms have come to replace terms such as *First World* and *Third World*. Although the term *Global South* is not ideal because it is not limited to countries in the geographical south, scholars find it preferable because it is more empowering and less hierarchical than older terms such as *Third World* or *developing nation* (Hollington, Salverda, Schwarz, & Tappe, 2015). From an economic standpoint, we can gauge the potential for prosperity for a country based on the total income of all the residents of a country divided by its population. This income is called the Gross Domestic Product (GDP) per capita. We can use the mean GDP per capita of the whole world in 2015 (USD$10,004) as an economic equator between the Global North and South demarcating which parts of the world are "lower income" with lower levels of

Dashboard

Case study

Global North the regions of Europe and North America characterized (with some exceptions) as high-income and often politically more stable.

Global South the regions of Latin America, Asia, Africa, and Oceania characterized (with some exceptions) as low-income and often politically or culturally marginalized.

economic productivity and which countries are "higher income" with higher levels of economic productivity (World Bank Group, 2016). Economic inequality is quickly evident when we examine some GDPs per capita in the Global North and South. Representing the Global North, the GDP per capita for the United States is USD$55,836 and Canada's, USD$43,249, while in the Global South, Mexico's GDP per capita measures USD$9,009, and Nigeria's, USD$2,640 (World Bank Group, 2016).

Large differences remain even if we take into account a correction for what economists call "purchasing power parity," which measures the local cost of living. A loaf of bread or a place of residence, for example, will have widely varying costs around the world. Corrected for purchasing power parity, in 2016 the GDP per hour worked was USD$62.90 in the United States, USD$48.90 in Canada, USD$31.80 in South Korea, and USD$23.50 in Russia, for example (OECD.Stat, 2017). This doesn't mean that everyone in lower-income countries is impoverished, unhealthy, or desperate. This system does not factor in, for example, growing your own food or other ways people provide for themselves outside of the formal economy. However, it does mean there is a comparatively low level of material prosperity.

As we see in Figure 9.1, the result is that a majority of the world's millionaires live in a few countries of the world—chiefly in the Global North—while a majority of the world's poorest people live in many countries of the Global South. You will find many more millionaires in some countries (e.g., the United States) than in the rest of the world. A millionaire is also 16 times more likely to reside in the United States than in Canada, only partly due to differences in the population size of the two countries.

We get a somewhat different picture of global inequality and people's well-being if we use measures such as the Human Development Index (HDI) rather than the GDP (UNDP, 2015). The Human Development Index is a statistical tool, developed by the United Nations, to measure and rank countries' levels of social development in addition to their economic development. The HDI combines three important measures of well-being to give a fuller, more contextualized image of people's conditions than solely looking at income (UNDP, 2015):

- Life expectancy: longevity and health measured by life expectancy at birth
- Human capital: formal education and knowledge assessed via adult and youth literacy measures
- Standard of living: as captured by a measure of the gross domestic product (GDP) per capita

Sociologists and economists know that GDP, which measures the average household or individual income by dividing a country's measured productivity by the number of people, can be grossly misleading. In a country that is highly unequal, a few people may monopolize the society's wealth while most people are poor or even destitute. Unlike the GDP, the HDI, which comprises a variety of measures of well-being, is far more likely to capture the experience of the average person. As a result, some countries in the world rank far higher on the HDI than they do on the GDP per capita measure,

Dashboard
Interactive activity

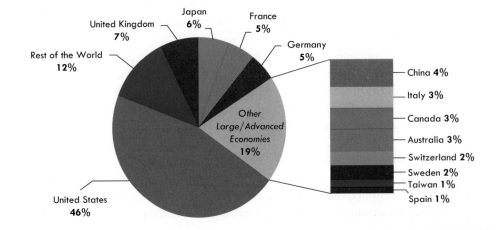

FIGURE 9.1 Percentage of World Millionaires by Country, 2015

Source: http://inequality.org/global-inequality/

TABLE 9.1 Top and Bottom 10 Countries, GDP and HDI

	GDP (per capita) 2014*	HDI 2014
World	$10,755	0.711
Top 10	Luxembourg ($92,400)	Norway (0.944)
	Macau ($88,700)	Australia (0.935)
	Singapore ($81,300)	Switzerland (0.930)
	Monaco ($78,700)	Denmark (0.923)
	Brunei ($77,700)	Netherlands (0.922)
	Kuwait ($71,000)	Germany (0.916)
	Sint Maarten ($66,800)	Ireland (0.916)
	Norway ($65,900)	United States (0.915)
	United Arab Emirates ($65,000)	Canada (0.913)
	Switzerland ($55,200)	New Zealand (0.913)
Bottom 10	Madagascar ($1,400)	Mali (0.419)
	Guinea ($1,300)	Mozambique (0.416)
	Mozambique ($1,100)	Sierra Leone (0.413)
	Niger ($1,000)	Guinea (0.411)
	Liberia ($900)	Burkina Faso (0.402)
	Burundi ($900)	Burundi (0.400)
	Malawi ($800)	Chad (0.392)
	Congo ($700)	Eritrea (0.391)
	Somalia ($600)	Central African Republic (0.350)
	Central African Republic ($600)	Niger (0.348)

Dashboard
Interactive activity

*Note: Countries with uncertain GDPs or those from earlier than 2014 have been skipped

Sources: www.cia.gov/library/publications/the-world-factbook/rankorder/2004rank.html and http://hdr.undp.org/en/composite/HDI

as we see in the Table 9.1. Said another way, there is a fundamental difference between these two measures of global inequality.

Examples of this gap between the HDI and GDP per capita measure are Kuwait and the United Arab Emirates, which have high GDP per capita rankings but do not rank in the top 10 HDI scores. Conversely, Canada and the United States rank in the top HDI scores but do not rank in the top 10 GDP per capita scores. On the other hand, Switzerland and Norway rank in the top 10 on both scales.

But whether we use the flawed GDP per capita measure or the HDI, we find vast and important inequalities in national well-being. In this chapter we will describe some of the factors that create this global inequality and see how different theoretical approaches understand the problem. Let's begin with information flow: we cannot get far understanding global inequality without understanding the importance of inequalities in the global flow of information.

Globalization and Its Relation to Global Inequality

Most people are familiar with the term **globalization**, which was developed to describe the process of corporations operating internationally, and exerting international influence. However, it is a complicated concept, and even academics and diplomats use the term in slightly different ways. So we must ask, what are the defining features of globalization and a "global economy," and how do they relate to global inequality?

This issue is hotly debated, especially when free trade deals, such as NAFTA, are being discussed and renegotiated. Globalization as an economic process is good for Canadian consumers because

globalization the process of increased international influence through economic, ideological, cultural, or technological means, or the results of such a process resulting in a homogeneity of economy, ideology, culture, or technology across the globe.

it makes a wide selection of consumer goods available at lower than usual prices—just look at the prices of TVs, computers, cars, clothes, and other goods today compared to 20 years ago. Some of the price drop is due to better production processes but much is due to lower labour costs abroad. On the other hand, globalization is bad for most unskilled, semi-skilled, and even skilled Canadian workers because it moves manufacturing jobs overseas to regions with lower wages. Since Canadian workers are often unemployed or underemployed as a result, they draw less benefit as consumers of the lower-priced goods than one might expect.

Globalization is partly an economic concept as mentioned above—referring to the increasingly international trade—but it is also partly technological, referring to the role of new technologies in homogenizing world cultures. To some degree, technological innovation has helped significantly to improve co-operation around the world. Consider the role of information technologies like the internet. Today, many people, especially young people, spend more time engaged in communications conducted through cyberspace than in face-to-face interactions. People who may have otherwise never met can find commonalities and form relationships on either side of the world.

Time to reflect

Have you had conversations online with people from other countries who you have never met in person? If so, have those interactions informed your knowledge of and opinions about other countries, or have your knowledge and opinions remained unchanged?

Culture is also a hotly contested area of globalization. We discussed some of these issues in Chapter 3. Is the spread of culture around the world a positive sharing and mixing of experience, history, and aesthetic, or is the globalization of culture simply an Americanizing influence that corrupts and destroys local cultures, undoing region-specific variances that make the world so dynamic and interesting to explore? We'll look at the role of the state in cultural globalization later in the chapter and in Chapter 14.

Globalization affects global inequality in a variety of ways. For example, it helps countries in the Global North build on their existing technological advantages, to increase their wealth and power through access to markets and raw materials in lower income countries. On the other hand, it may lead to conflicting values and aspirations, especially between older and younger generations in lower-income countries.

In the end, is globalization a good thing or a bad thing? In terms of economic globalization, the main beneficiaries of globalization are the global investors, bankers, and multinational corporations that move their resources around the world to maximize their profits, whatever the cost to consumers, workers, and local businesses. They grow ever richer as the rest of Canadian citizens see their incomes and standard of living stagnate or even fall. The result is growing national inequality, as we have seen since the 1970s. Some benefits accrue to the workers in lower-income countries, so global inequality diminishes as a result. However, the dominant investors, bankers, and multinationals, which reside mainly in countries in the Global North, benefit significantly. Global inequality increases because the benefits are not shared by other members of the highest-income countries. The cultural question is more complex—there is no empirical way to judge "good" or "bad" culture, or cultural shifts. The changes to global cultures as a result of globalization will be complex and varied. It may make us more able to relate to one another, but at the same time replacing local and traditional cultures.

To sum up, to understand global inequality, we must understand the ways that information, knowledge, and capital have diffused through the world; and no type of diffusion has been more important than the systematic spread of science and technology. As we have already mentioned, the global spread of information technology has created a global digital divide and new sources of global inequality. Inequalities in the access to new ideas and inventions produce inequalities of wealth and power, as we see in the discussion of diffusion in Box 9.2.

Digital Divide

9.2 | The Study of Innovation and Diffusion

Innovation, in which people devise and adopt new technologies or practices, requires the collection and evaluation of new information. Early research on the adoption of hybrid corn seeds in the 1940s resulted in an important discovery—namely, that learning and experimentation play an important role in the adoption of new innovations (Ryan & Gross, 1943, 1950). Many people are reluctant to take chances with unfamiliar technologies, especially when the consequences of doing so can be disastrous if something were to go wrong. First-hand experience is critical, and for that reason, innovations can also be distinguished between those that involve hands-on learning and those that do not, or at least require less of it (Rogers & Kim, 1985).

Farmers, for example, are not inclined to take wild risks in how they earn their livelihood, so there is no surprise in their tendency to innovate slowly and carefully. In the case of hybrid corn seed, individual farmers, on average, spent five years moving from first awareness to the final adoption of the new seed. During this time, average farmers would test small amounts of the seed on their own farm, under known farming conditions. Farmers were only willing to risk their entire crop—and their survival—after the seed passed this eminently practical test.

As with hybrid corn, we can see a similar "S-shaped" pattern in the adoption of new technologies in business. S-shaped means that it is adopted slowly at first, then sees a rapid uptake and later slows down again. Consider the adoption of computer networking in offices, or robots in factories. As Valente (2010; also Skinner & Staiger, 2005) has shown, we can connect the adoption curve in agriculture to later developments in technology. Gradually, in all cases, new and more advanced technologies become available and replace previous ones. First, mainframe computers replace offices full of filing clerks. Then, stand-alone computers replace mainframe computers. Computer networks are next, and they replace stand-alone computers. Eventually, laptops replace desktops, and tablets and iPads replace laptops. In each case, there is an initial slow adoption, followed by a rapid flood of adoptions and market domination by the new technology. This inevitably ends in declining domination of technologies as yet-newer technologies (both hardware and software) emerge, and a new flood of adoptions takes place creating new S-shape curves of adoption.

Time to reflect

What kinds of innovations are you more likely to adopt without much experimentation and what kinds are you likely to adopt more slowly and cautiously? Are you comfortable with the idea that you may be regularly adopting technological innovations (such as new breeds of corn)?

Technology, Politics, and Global Inequality

Recent influential work by the French historical economist Thomas Piketty (2014) demonstrates that there is a tendency in history toward ever-growing economic inequality and, specifically, ever-increasing wealth among members of the ruling class. Unless interrupted by political forces (whether as legislation or revolution), family fortunes based on rents and investments tend to maintain themselves and grow rapidly.

In the context of likely increases in inequality, one might ask, what is the relationship between technology, politics, and global inequality? Scholars have been debating that question for decades and still have not reached a consensus, though main lines of thinking have emerged.

Nearly 40 years ago, the eminent American economist Paul Krugman (1979) argued that economists wrongly see technology as having the highest priority among the factors influencing global inequality. He noted that while it's true that new technological products such as computers and robotic machinery can be produced at first only in the Global North, in due course, these technologies of

innovation the process by which individuals or corporations devise and adopt new technologies or practices through the process of research and development.

production become available in the Global South too. It is only during the brief and shrinking period of technological lag that imbalanced trade goes on, with the North profitably exporting new products (such as computers) and importing other products (such as raw materials). Patents and copyrights obtained by the North through their monopoly on new products increase global inequality. However, the Global North must continue to innovate to maintain its lead and its income advantage. As we have seen in the cases of South Korea, Singapore, Taiwan, and mainland China, the technological advantages of the Global North can diminish, leading toward a redistribution of global inequality, but not eradicating it. China has become a country that leads globally with technological advances, and its e-commerce site Alibaba resulted in the biggest initial public offering in history.

Smith (1997) built on and updated this argument with specific reference to South Korea, showing how technology plays a role in global commodity chains. In South Korea, planners and policy makers are acutely aware of the need to develop indigenous science and technology capabilities to compete effectively with the higher-income Global North. Drawing on interviews with government officials, academic experts, and corporate engineers, Smith notes that even the seemingly hi-tech South Korean economy is characterized by technological dependence. The game of catch-up that the lower-income societies play with the higher-income societies is seemingly never-ending.

In order to upgrade technologically, sell directly to competitive world markets, and join the ranks of the "advanced" economies, the South Korean state and corporations must continually struggle to break the control of new technology held by interests in the Global North. Multinationals owned by people from the Global North still reap a disproportionate share of global profits, thanks to their advantage in the development and use of new technology. This will not change until more innovation takes place elsewhere.

However, as the South Korean example shows, we cannot discuss technological innovation and competition without talking about the linkages to political (and especially, state) organization. Only the state can deal with the twin problems of poverty and inequality that multinational corporations tend to produce throughout the world. Pieterse (2002) asserts that "within nations poverty is a challenge, while inequality is not; on a world scale, arguably it is the other way round. [However,] the international policy focus on poverty alleviation coexists with neoliberal policies that widen inequality domestically and internationally" (p. 1023).

SeongJoon Cho/Bloomberg via Getty Images

In this photo, visitors to Samsung's promotion booths look at their latest smart phones. The South Korean company was the biggest maker of cellphones in 2016. How much of the company's strategy do you think is influenced, and how much is controlled, by the interests of the Global North?

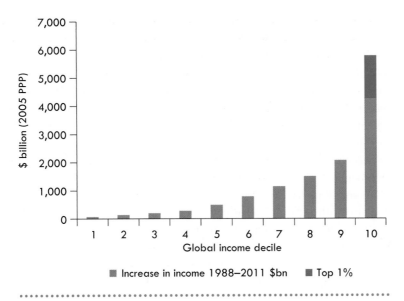

FIGURE 9.2 Global Income Growth that Accrued to Each Decile, 1988–2011

Source: http://policy-practice.oxfam.org.uk/publications/an-economy-for-the-1-how-privilege-and-power-in-the-economy-drive-extreme-inequ-592643

Economists have conventionally assumed that neo-liberal policies and free trade reduce inequality at the same time as they raise average incomes and reduce poverty. However, data show that in periods and places of greatest neo-liberal influence, there has been the steepest increase in inequality. The data show that most of the increase in income benefitted the rich most dramatically. In global terms, this growing inequality maintains domestic privilege and promotes global inequality (see Figure 9.2). It also produces global effects of environmental degradation, mass migration, transnational crime, and terrorism. So we cannot afford to ignore the role of states when explaining economic and social disparities. Without state intervention, globalization increases global inequality, and this inevitably produces marginalization and political turbulence.

Nor can we ignore the role of communications technology in this discussion of global inequality. As Manuel Castells (2008) points out, a **global civil society** is gradually growing in the world. It is an organized expression of the values and interests of society through new forms of communication. The process of globalization is therefore turning debates on inequality taking place in the purely national domain into global discussions about international co-operation and governance. Accordingly, the debate about inequality is gradually shifting from the national to the global, based on global communication networks. In this new context, we see the emergence of new forms of diplomacy that build on shared cultural meanings, and not purely political posturing.

However, this change Castells (2008) notes is still embryonic. Today, as we see with the recent Brexit (a portmanteau of *British* and *exit*) vote and the protectionist agenda under US President Trump, nations continue to compete for advantage over one another, despite the growth of a globalized, technology-intensive society (Inglehart, 2015). Jaumotte, Lall, and Papageorgiou (2013) provide an analysis rooted more deeply in present-day empirical data. These researchers examine the relationship between trade and financial globalization on the one hand and the rise in income inequality on the other hand as observed in the late twentieth century. Using data from 51 countries over a 23-year period from 1981 to 2003, Jaumotte et al. (2013) find technological innovation has a more beneficial impact on reducing global inequality than does a neo-liberal model based on open competition. On the one hand, the expansion of world trade that is based on new technology and higher productivity is associated with a *decrease* in global inequality. On the other hand, financial globalization—and foreign direct investment in particular—that is based on patents and copyrights is associated with an *increase* in global inequality. Said another way, new technology, by increasing productivity, reduces global inequality. However, financial globalization—by giving investors from the Global North more scope for profit making in lower-income societies—has increased global inequality.

global civil society large-scale interconnected groups operating across borders and outside the control of the state.

So, technology transfer comes across as a global benefactor in this analysis. However, we must not forget two main facts. One is that technology is only as socially beneficial as the uses to which we humans put it. The other is that some technology can have and has had a terribly negative effect on the eco-systems of lower income societies (for example, through the pollution of agricultural land or the loss of water supplies), thus increasing global inequality and jeopardizing local lifestyles. Other problems facing lower-income societies as a result of new technology include resource depletion and garbage accumulation. Around the world, people living in poverty, facing ever-harder economic conditions, have plundered natural resources, for example, using wood for cooking until there are no trees left; economists have called this phenomenon the "tragedy of the commons" (Hardin, 1998, p. 682). And of course, as we have discussed throughout the book, global inequality has produced a digital divide in people's access to and use of new communication technology and, as a result, unequal opportunity to secure employment requiring a familiarity with and skill level using new information and communication technologies.

We will discuss many of these facts at length in chapters of this book focused on educational (Chapter 11), environmental issues (Chapter 15), and media (Chapter 14). But we should note, at this time, that disparities in technology have had the effect of impoverishing already poor nations and increasing global inequality.

Theoretical Approaches to Global Inequality

Functional Theory

As we have already noted, theorists have been thinking about global inequality in different ways for well over a century. For example, functional theorists—following Smith (1776) and Durkheim (1892/1933)—have proposed that societies evolve and prosper through increased differentiation and co-operation, and at the centre of these processes are so-called "market forces." These theorists suppose that all societies modernize in more or less the same ways, with the result that, in time, all societies and cultures converge on a single, uniform set of beliefs and activities, assisted by a uniform set of technologies.

Functionalists see the operation of a free, impersonal market as the key to modernization, industrialization, and prosperity. This functionalist belief is currently known as **neo-liberalism**, a term that has been used in a variety of ways, for a variety of purposes; and, indeed, it is used with slightly different emphases in various disciplines (Chomsky, 1999; Jones, 2014; Sewpaul, 2015). Some writers emphasize the economic aspect of neo-liberalism, others the political, philosophical, legal, or cultural aspects, and yet others stress the negative impact it has on societies.

neo-liberalism a social, economic, and political philosophy that favours the deregulation of economic markets to establish the goal of "free markets" wherein the state has limited authority to intervene in the economy; but also refers to the political and philosophical ideologies associated with such a goal.

Whatever their vantage point, people generally agree that neo-liberalism refers to the freeing up of global markets, largely by reducing the state's intervention in the economy. Controls are eased and restrictive tariffs are removed or weakened. Champions of neo-liberalism assume that the markets operate rationally—indeed, optimally—to provide the greatest good for the greatest number of people. When people (supposedly) have the maximum freedom to pursue their private goals, they (supposedly) create the maximum prosperity for everyone. This point of view is most compatible with functionalist approaches to world organization, which emphasize equilibrium, efficiency, modernization, and integration.

In the Global South, neo-liberalism grew up in opposition to the policies of English economist John Maynard Keynes (1883–1946), which revolved around government spending to create jobs and which had dominated the northern hemisphere during the Depression, the Second World War, and the postwar period.

At the national level, the idea of market deregulation was given a strong policy push under the pro-business governments of American president Ronald Reagan and British prime minister Margaret Thatcher. Similar policies were implemented in smaller legislative units at the state and provincial levels. For Canada, a turning point in this process was the beginning of "free trade" with the United States in 1987, which opened Canada to US capital far more effectively than it opened American markets to Canadian manufacturers. Internationally, neo-liberal practices were even more dramatic: countries seeking money from the International Monetary Fund or the World Bank were required, as a condition of borrowing money, to undergo "structural adjustment" by following deregulatory reform plans.

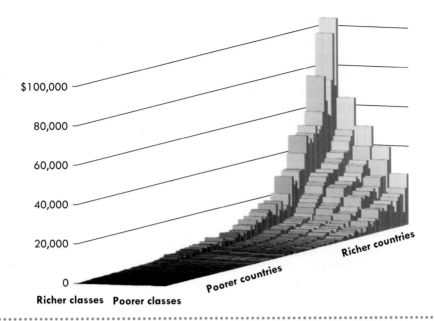

$100,000

80,000

60,000

40,000

20,000

0

Richer classes   Poorer classes

Poorer countries

Richer countries

FIGURE 9.3 The (Unequal) Global Income Distribution (in US Dollars)

Source: https://www.unicef.org/socialpolicy/files/Global_Inequality.pdf.

Time to reflect

Figure 9.3 compares the income of richer and poorer classes in rich versus poor countries. The distribution of wealth is varied both within a country and across one class between countries. What trends can you see in this graph? Pay particular attention to the differences between classes and how that changes depending on the wealth of the entire country.

Some have said that neo-liberal globalization inevitably leads to the decline of the state and the rise of vast multinational corporations. And in fact, there is no question that states become less powerful as multinational organizations become better able to operate freely across borders. Some of the largest multinational corporations have the assets of small to midsize national economies and, by their ability to invest or disinvest in particular countries, exercise a great deal of political influence throughout the world. In a paper by Beck and Grande (2010), the authors note this creates a new form of "modernity which threatens its own foundations" (p. 409), referring to the way in which the modern state allowed for the rise of capitalism, which in turn is now undermining the power of the modern state. But neo-liberals don't necessarily think this change is bad.

In fact, some think it may be time to do away with state-oriented approaches to framing global inequality, as Ulrich Beck (2007) recommends. Instead, we should be focusing on powerful multinational corporations, such as the ones listed in Figure 9.4. Many of the largest multinational organizations are as wealthy as and even more powerful than small and middle-sized countries. No wonder they play a key role in global inequality. The world's financial system has become structurally interlocked due to high-speed, high-stakes international finance, the growing availability of tax havens, and the diversity of free-trade areas. Multinational corporations and international humanitarian organizations have accelerated the process of globalization, as has the global recognition of drug, debt, environmental, and terrorism problems. Throughout the world, multinational corporations' actions and interests shape the flow, form, and location of investment, as well as the conduct of trade and the development of technologies. Today, vast flows of information characterize social life (Hemp, 2009). Social, cultural, and political movements are meaningless without media coverage. Borders, governments, localities, and classes can no longer prevent information flows. As a result, social conflict is no longer conflict between categories or classes of people, as Marx (1973) had claimed. It is between worldwide networks, markets, and other social "identities."

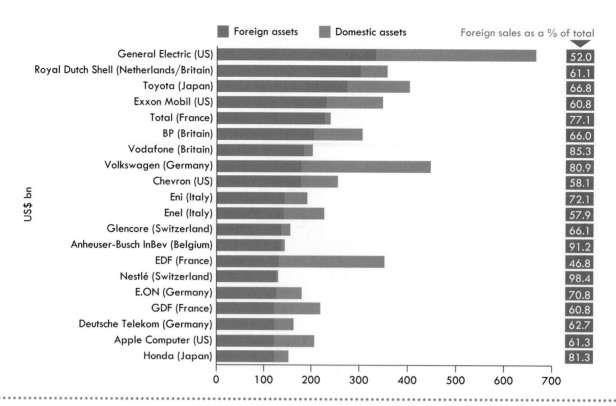

FIGURE 9.4 Multinational Corporations as Key Players in the World Economy (US$ in bn)

Source: http://futurehrtrends.eiu.com/report-2015/driving-forces-behind-a-globalized-workforce/

This has led some to say that the only important actors on the world stage are global entities, not traditional nation-states.

Related to the increased role of multinational corporations in the organization of global inequality is the new international division of labour. An important assumption behind the neo-liberal approach is that the market for labour and goods is politically neutral. Some have even claimed that the decline of **the state** (a nation operating as an organized political unit under a central government) is an inevitable result of globalization and the rise of vast multinational corporations. States necessarily become less powerful as multinational organizations become better able to operate freely across national borders. Some neo-liberals even propose that democracy itself is an irrational force that threatens the rationality and effectiveness (i.e., the freedom) of the market. By this reckoning, neo-liberals argue, democracy must be limited to ensure that economic prosperity is safe from interference from either above (the state) or below (the disadvantaged masses).

Besides focusing on markets, functionalists also focus on the global spread of lifestyles and values prevalent in the Global North, including the desire for democracy and (typically) British and American culture. This global spread of **modernity**, a mix of values, technologies, lifestyles, and political outlooks, brings with it local desires for development and Americanization, including increased contact with American media, consumer items, and life choices. These desires, which encourage and even require the spread of multinational organizations owned in the Global North such as Coke, Kellogg's, and Disney, come unsolicited from citizens in lower-income countries.

In this scenario, no guns or economic threats are needed for modernization to occur. Made aware of the modern consumer abundance, everyone from Guatemala City to Tierra del Fuego, Capetown to Kazakhstan, wants to be "American" or, at least, part of the Global North. Given freedom, free trade, and free markets, Global North culture is predicted to spread everywhere. These desires to modernize readily support the entry of capital from the Global North, which provides jobs and salaries that, however meagre, permit the purchase of mass-market consumer items: Coca Cola and

the state refers to a nation or territory under the control of a single government, or to said government itself.

modernity an era in Western Europe beginning roughly with the end of the medieval age (around 1500) to the present day, associated with the increased influence of rationalism, individualization, secularism, democracy, and capitalism.

Lou-Foto/Alamy Stock Photo

Though it is easy to see influences and products from the Global North in countries around the world, that doesn't mean a standard of living enjoyed in the Global North is available to everyone (even for populations within the Global North), or that it is in the best interest of every country to aim for that standard of living.

Harvard T-shirts for everyone! Functionalists believe that this desire is universal and that modernity is inevitable.

Conflict Theory

To understand global inequality from a conflict perspective, we need to grasp the historical trends that have shaped relations of inequality that exist today. Some of this needed perspective is provided by "dependency theory" (Frank, 1967). Dependency theory proposes that developing states have failed to achieve adequate and sustainable levels of development today because of their neo-colonial (i.e., experienced after the official end of colonialism) dependence on the advanced capitalist world.

Dependency theorists note that from the fifteenth century onwards, **colonialism** was practised by for example Spain, Portugal, Britain, France, and the Netherlands. Colonialism usually brought white populations to settle colonized lands and aid in the exploitation of local economic resources for the colonizer's use. Andre Gunder Frank (1967), a German economist and proponent of dependency theory, popularized the phrase "the development of underdevelopment" (p. 14). Frank proposed that colonialism deformed the economies of the Global South by making these states dependent on the centre, or the more advanced metropolises of the colonial states. In *Capitalism and Underdevelopment in Latin America* (1967), Frank proposed that the Global South was doomed to stagnation, since advanced capitalist countries were using transnational corporations to appropriate the surplus these developing nations produced. From this perspective, Frank argued that nations in the Global South could achieve growth only by cutting ties with capitalist societies and pursuing independent socialist development strategies.

After 1967, when Frank's work was published, the emergence of **newly industrialized countries** (**NICs**) such as South Korea, Singapore, and Taiwan challenged the validity of dependency theory's assumption that development in late capitalism was almost impossible. The NICs have demonstrated that

colonialism the establishment by higher-income countries of formal political control over lower-income areas, usually accompanied by the exploitation of local economic resources and peoples.

newly industrialized countries (NICs) countries whose economies are between those of developed and developing economies.

successful late industrialization *is* possible, despite the commanding lead and power of a few countries in the Global North. Dependency theory's failure to explain these NICs points to the need for a more sophisticated approach to understanding economic development in the countries of the Global South.

Another flaw in dependency theory is its overemphasis on economic factors. It correctly assumes there is a "surplus drain" flowing to capitalist countries thanks to the extraction and appropriation of profits from the Global South—an assumption equivalent to the assumption of Marxist (1973) "exploitation." Recall that Paul Krugman (1979) and others highlighted this in their analyses of the role of technological rents (i.e., patents and copyrights) in creating global inequality. However, a complete analysis of global inequality requires attention to cultural, demographic, and political, as well as economic, factors.

A movement in that direction is signalled by the effort to conceptualize and measure "state fragility" through a "fragile states" index. A "fragile state" is a state whose political or economic system has become so weak that the government is no longer in control (Fund for Peace, 2014). The central driver of fragile states is weak political institutions (Vallings & Moreno-Torres, 2007). Often, this is a result of poorly constructed institutions and forms of governance superimposed onto these states by colonizing countries in the past (Vallings & Moreno-Torres, 2007). This fragility is often marked by widespread and violent social collective action (organized and disorganized), political violence, relatively porous borders and uncontrollable migrations, discriminatory treatment of minority populations, and, most of all, by the absence of a reliable rule of law.

Often, political failure leads to economic failure, and to higher levels of economic inequality. But there is no simple equivalence among these situations. In other words, though most failed states are relatively poor, some are less poor, especially if they have a great deal of valuable oil and minerals to sell. Failed states are found in many parts of the world, though they are overrepresented in Africa. They have quite different histories of connection with colonizing nations, as well as different cultural, demographic, political, and economic histories, compared to the histories of successful NICs. What these states all have in common is a fragile socio-political order that endangers its citizens and other nations.

A second major conflict approach is provided by Saskia Sassen's (1996, 2014) analysis of global cities and their role in the international economy. A critical scholar, Sassen proposes that many or most of the global changes we are noting take place *within* the structure of nation-states. Indeed, she argues for the importance of statehood in a globalizing world. The entire global system of financial capitalism, she proposes, is beyond saving. Moreover, Sassen (2014) suggests that the 2008 financial crisis and the billion-dollar bailouts that accompanied it have shown the error of neo-liberal principles. This fragility of global economics, according to Sassen, is exactly why societies, and particularly societies in the Global North, are ripe for a transformation. More specifically, she says that this is why nation-states—the only reliable bases of financial oversight and regulation—need to be strengthened in a globalizing world. You may note this is in direct contrast to the functionalist argument outlined above, which claims states are fragile and identifies the global financial markets as the stabilizing solution to their fragility.

Global cities, a term Sassen (2001) coined and popularized, are increasingly important in a globalized world. As centres for markets, innovation, and production, they are the social, cultural, and economic bridges to the rest of the world and, as such, have a significant impact on global affairs. As diverse and complex urban environments, these cities are places where new relationships are made. All of this means, in Sassen's view, that the **global city**, not the nation-state or corporate entities, will be the central place of development in the globalized era. In Canada, the influential geographer and public intellectual Richard Florida (2003, 2005) has taken a similar position about the transformational potential of cities. He suggests that some cities in particular are places where there is a concentration of "creative capital"—individuals that possess a high degree of education, skills, and creativity. Members of this "creative class" move to cities because of the potential economic and lifestyle benefits that are afforded to them and not available elsewhere. Cities that possess the "three 'T's"—technology, talent, and tolerance—are particularly successful at attracting members of the creative class (Florida, 2003, 2005). Florida suggests that Canadian cities such as Vancouver, Toronto, and Montreal are examples of such. The new technological innovations and social progress that drive change in society in the Global North (and global society) emanate from these cities inhabited by the

global city a city with significant influence or impact in global affairs deriving from acting as a central locale for economic markets, innovation, production, or diplomacy.

creative class. Florida's (2003, 2005) work suggests that human decisions about where to live are just as important as political or corporate power in shaping our societies.

A third major conflict approach is provided by Wallerstein's (1974/2011) "world system theory." Immanuel Wallerstein's *The Modern World-System* (1974/2011) proposes that since the sixteenth century, an important worldwide social system has developed. The basic linkages are economic, and the system is organized on capitalist principles. The result is a worldwide division of labour and a global system of stratification.

Wallerstein's work draws on the earlier ideas of Marx (1973) and Weber (1905/1930). Like Marx, Wallerstein is building a theory of historical development that is driven by capitalism and relations of inequality. But like Weber, Wallerstein understands the danger of oversimplification; he recognizes that the processes of change from feudalism to capitalism are complex and vary from one locale to another. And, he recognizes that states, armies, civil service bureaucracies, and other political actors are as important as capitalist classes in bringing about this transformation. Wallerstein notes that before the sixteenth century, world economies did exist. World economies were evident in global empires, such as the Greek, Roman, and Spanish empires, which had formal linkages with the colonies they controlled. In the sixteenth century, a new world economy emerged to replace the pre-capitalist system built of empires and colonies. Based on the capitalist mode of production, "The techniques of modern capitalism and the technology of modern science . . . enabled this world-economy to thrive, produce, and expand without the emergence of a unified political structure" (Wallerstein, 1974/2011, p. 13). The capitalist mode of production built and strengthened this emerging world economy, and it persisted as an economic world system, though not a military world system. By the end of the twentieth century, all the major empires remaining—Britain, France, Germany, and Belgium among them—had for the most part removed their military troops and colonial governments from Africa, Asia, and the Americas, but continued to influence the world economically, alongside new powers such as the United States, China, and Russia.

Wallerstein's model consists of three categories of world nations:

- **Core states**: industrialized, wealthy, and powerful,
- **Peripheral states**: lower income and less able to exert political influence internationally, are subject to control or manipulation by core states, and
- **Semi-peripheral states**: as the name suggests, somewhere in between core and peripheral states, but with some political influence

Historically, the differences between core and peripheral states stemmed from the type of labour organization they employed. In essence, the core had the most detailed and "modern" division of labour, while the periphery had the least. It was mainly this modern division of labour that gave the core much of its commercial and manufacturing wealth, even before the Industrial Revolution. In the sixteenth century, Leiss (1977) summarizes, "wage-labor and self-employment were becoming dominant in the core, slavery and feudal relations in the periphery, and sharecropping in the semi-periphery" (pp. 202–203). This differentiation was vital to the world system's operation. As Wallerstein (1974/2011) explains, "the world-economy was based precisely on the assumption that there were in fact these three zones and that they did in fact have different modes of labor control. Were this not so, it would not have been possible to assure the kind of flow of the surplus which enabled the capitalist system to come into existence" (p. 87). As we see in Figure 9.5, over the course of history, territorial units—from tribes to states to empires—grow larger and more complex. What is also evident is that this growth is uneven and unsteady. There are periods of decline mixed with periods of growth and important turning points or take-off points, after which units shoot ahead to a new level of organization.

Think about these ideas as they relate to the triangular trade relations that existed between Europe, Africa, and America from about 1500 to roughly 1850: from Africa to the Americas went slave labourers; from the Americas to Europe went agricultural products (e.g., coffee, sugar, and spices) that these slaves produced; from Europe to the rest of the world—including back to Africa, Asia, and America—went manufactured goods such as textiles and furnishings. This shows that core

core states according to Wallerstein's world systems theory, industrialized, wealthy, and powerful states that control or manipulate semi-peripheral and peripheral states.

peripheral states according to Wallerstein's world systems theory, states that are lower income and less able to exert political influence internationally. They are subject to control or manipulation by core states.

semi-peripheral states according to Wallerstein's world systems theory, middle-income, partially industrialized states that have some power and influence; they are "in between" the classifications of core states and peripheral states.

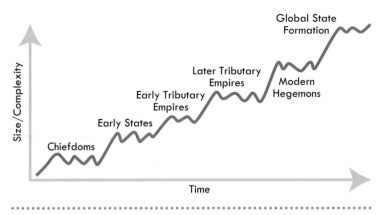

FIGURE 9.5 The Growth of a World Economy

Source: Inoue, Hiroko, Alexis Álvarez, Kirk Lawrence, Anthony Roberts, Eugene N Anderson and Christopher Chase-Dunn 2012 "Polity scale shifts in world-systems since the Bronze Age: A comparative inventory of upsweeps and collapses" International Journal of Comparative Sociology June 53 (3): 210–229 http://cos.sagepub.com/content/53/3/210.full. pdf+html

states, from the beginning, were the source of manufactured goods and the beneficiaries of slave labour taking place in the periphery (Strauss, 2013).

Today, we see similar flows of workers, products, and capital from one part of the world to another. And today too, the core states (like Canada) rely on cheap, poorly compensated labour in the poorest peripheral countries (like Bangladesh) to ensure a high profit margin for manufactured goods.

Another distinguishing feature of the core states was their development of bureaucratic organizations. These bureaucratic organizations allowed the core to control and exploit the periphery more effectively by providing oversight of the flow of goods and control of slaves, local peasants, and indentured workers. Bureaucratic organization also allowed "capitalism to manoeuvre freely because it allowed the economy to operate in an area that was larger than that controlled by any political entity," (pp. 14–15) as Rondo Cameron (1976) explains. Nothing was more efficient at overseeing a colonial empire than the modern army and the modern civil service, both organized bureaucratically (that is, hierarchically and according to written rules). Though bureaucratic organization had been used millennia earlier in the Roman and Byzantine empires, it was nowhere used as thoroughly and efficiently as it was in the late nineteenth and early twentieth centuries in the British and German empires—thanks in part to the invention of technologies such as the telegraph and radio, which allowed for larger organizing bodies to be able to communicate rapidly.

The purpose of capitalist imperial rule is to enrich capitalists in core states at the expense of people living in peripheral states. As noted, the rulers of core states take much of the raw material, cheap labour, and economic surplus from peripheral states, which are unable to resist their efforts due to pre-existing global inequality. They also create enforced trading partners that purchase more than they export. Investors from the core states therefore effectively control the economies of these peripheral states. Profits made in the periphery drain out of the local economy and flow back to the core, perpetuating and exacerbating global inequality. One example where the consequences of inequality becomes visible is in differences between core and periphery in access to health care and how this affects health outcomes. Box. 9.3 compares access to health services across countries and the impact on life expectancy.

The key actors today (i.e., multinational corporations) are not conquering on behalf of a sponsoring country but on their own behalf—and that is something that *is* fairly new and unique to post-1600 empires. The world economy does not give peripheral states an opportunity to improve their situation, but rather exploits their disadvantage (Hall & Chase-Dunn, 2006). *Semi-peripheral states* are sometimes exploited in the same way, and sometimes serve as "middle men" for the core states. But they are somewhat more autonomous—more independent and self-controlling—than peripheral states—and more economically developed.

As is evident from this discussion, conflict theory, like functionalist theory, offers a wide variety of views of present-day global inequality, though most of these views differ only in their emphases on markets and states.

Theory in Everyday Life

9.3 | Access to Health Services

Researchers have predicted that Canadian women and men born in 2030 will live (on average) to about 87 and 84 years, respectively, while life expectancy at birth for 2010 stands at 84 and 79 years for women and men, respectively (CBC News, 2017; Kontis et al., 2017, p. 36). South Korea, on the other hand, is predicted to have a jump from 84 and 77 years in 2010 to 90 and 84 years in 2030 for women and men, respectively. These results are from a study conducted by researchers in the United Kingdom using complex statistical techniques. Among the reasons attributed for this high life expectancy rate in South Korea are massive investments in health promotion and wide availability of medical knowledge, skill, and technology to the population. In Canada inequities between Indigenous and non-Indigenous people have led to differences in their life expectancies. In 2010 Canada had about 2.04 physicians and 9.3 nurses and midwives per 1000 people, while South Korea had 2 physicians and 4.7 nurses and midwives per 1000 people (WHO, 2016a). In 2010 Tanzania had a life expectancy at birth of 59 and 56 years for women and men, respectively. In 2012

the reported number of physicians and nurses or midwives per 1000 people were 0.03 and 0.44, respectively (WHO, 2016a). It is no surprise that in 2010 only 48.9 per cent of child births were attended to by qualified health personnel and under-five mortality rate was 63.4 per 1000 live births. In comparison, Canada had 98.4 per cent of births attended by qualified health personnel in 2011 and under-five mortality rate was 5.6 per 1000 live births in 2010.

Although access to health care alone does not ensure better health, it is an important factor in reducing preventable deaths. Good access to health care includes (but is not limited to) having adequate health personnel distributed evenly throughout the population. It is important to note that access to health care is not just varied between countries; although Canada has universal health care, access is not equitable to all populations within Canada. Indigenous communities living on reserves, for example, generally lack human resources (such as staff), and access to health care facilities is absent in remote locations with small populations (Goraya, 2016; National Collaborating Centre for Aboriginal Health, 2011).

Time to reflect

Reflect back on the global income distribution inequality, as well as your own experiences of health care service within Canada (and, if applicable, around the world). Using your sociological imagination, extrapolate from your personal experience and what you already know about global inequalities, and generate a thesis for how sociological circumstance, including class, might impact health outcomes both within and outside Canada.

Feminist Theory

As we continue to note in this book, feminists are chiefly concerned with the study of marginalized groups—not just women, as feminists recognize that intersectional inequalities make life even more difficult for the majority of women in the world.

Berik and Kongar (2013) note that feminist analyses of global inequality draw important connections between various kinds of inequality. Inequalities based on gender, racialization, ethnicity, and class all undermine people's ability to expand their life chances, and they are all affected in one way or another by policies that affect macroeconomic development. In particular, a faltering macroeconomy limits the achievement of gender equality for women by limiting access to education and jobs; in turn, limits to education, employment, and wage gaps have macro-level impacts on economic development. Thus, policies promoting gender equality are important as both an intrinsic goal and a step toward improving national well-being (and conversely, improving national well-being is an important step towards gender equality).

Sassen (1996) reminds us that economic globalization has influenced properties of the nation-state, and this too has had consequences for gender equality. The most powerful example of this change is the rise of the global city, which operates as a partly denationalized platform for global capitalism. This reconfigures the balance of authority and influence in such a way that the state is obliged to share its power. In that sense, other actors, such as NGOs, minority populations, and international organizations shape and reinforce international laws and policies.

As a result, creating a feminist analysis of the global economy requires us to take these changes into account to fully understand the current economic and social conditions of women and men around the world. A major problems has been that much feminist scholarship has examined gender inequality in the context of the nation-state. But now, in view of the effects of globalization on the state, it becomes important to subject the effects of globalization to critical examination.

The rise of an international human rights regime, and of many varied non-state actors in the global arena is evidence of the growth of an international civil society. Though a contested space, it is "a space where women can gain visibility as individuals and as collective actors, and come out of the invisibility of aggregate membership in a nation-state exclusively represented by the sovereign" (Sassen, 1996, p. 40). In this international context, the actions and claims of varied, non-state actors shapes international human rights and the demands put on firms and markets with global operations. Women operate outside the state, often through NGOs and other non-state groups and networks (Sassen, 1996). As a result, we are now seeing more and more cross-border solidarities with membership rooted in gender, sexuality, and feminism. Questions of class and country status—such as questions of global inequality—cut across all of these membership notions.

Many have pointed to the difficulties besetting this global feminist strategy: for example, the wide differences that separate high-income women in the Global North from women in the Global South. Box 9.4 shows the different realities in which girls grow up and how they experience motherhood at different life stages. Along similar lines, differences potentially divide women in societies that ascribe to gender equality principles versus societies that do not. Should feminists seeking international solidarity insist on the former or accept the "multicultural" alternative—that is, accept non-egalitarian cultures—on an equal footing?

In answer to this question, Volpp (2001) asserts that to frame feminism and multiculturalism as oppositional is to argue by extension that minority women fall victim to their own cultures. In fact, gender subordination is integral only to certain cultures. The claim that cultures from the Global South are universally more subordinating than cultures from the Global North originates in colonialism, the origins of liberalism, and the use of binary logic. Pitting feminism against multiculturalism obscures the many influences that shape cultural practices—and the many forces besides culture that affect women's lives. It also plays down the way women exercise agency within patriarchal societies, and masks the level of subordination, even violence, within cultures in the Global North. With this in mind, we would do well to blur the differences between feminisms in the Global North and the Global South.

Along similar lines, Mohanty (2003) asserts that globalization has colonized women's as well as men's lives, and what is needed to counter these varied means of subjugation is an anti-imperialist, anticapitalist,

Spotlight On

9.4 | The Variety of Adolescent Experiences

Consider two 16-year-old girls, Jenny in Canada and Sula in Bangladesh. Like many of her friends, Sula has had her first baby and is pregnant with a second. Like many of her friends, Jenny is currently finishing high school and won't have her first baby until she is 28. The statistics tell us that about 16 million girls aged 15 to 19 give birth every year. This constitutes more than 10 per cent of all births worldwide. The vast majority of these births to teenage mothers occur in the Global South, in places such as Bangladesh, to mothers like Sula. Sula will have completed only about

eight years of formal education before leaving school to work, then marry, then get pregnant and start her own household with an older husband. Jenny will almost certainly complete some post-secondary education, cohabit with her partner for a few years while working for pay, then start thinking about a family. Both Jenny and Sula will face problems in their adult lives, but their problems will be very different.

Source: Statistics from WHO Fact File on Health Inequities. Accessed at http://www.who.int/sdhconference/background/news/facts/en/

and inclusive feminism. For Mohanty (2003), activists and scholars must also reimagine new forms of collective resistance in which women can take part in their everyday lives to assert their rights. Only this can provide the basis for reimagining a liberatory politics for women in the twenty-first century.

To this end, Mohanty (2003) argues for the need of a *feminist solidarity model or comparative feminist studies model*. This strategy of analysis (and teaching) draws from the idea that local and global forces are not only defined by physical geography or territory, but also exist side-by-side and influence one another. This framework recognizes that "[d]ifferences and commonalities thus exist in relation and tension with each other in all contexts" (p. 242). What we must emphasize in building feminist solidarity, says Mohanty, are relations of mutuality, co-responsibility, and common interests.

This process of consensus-building must begin by rejecting altogether the myths about women in the Global South—indeed, all of the myths about the Global South. Cornwall, Correa, and Jolly (2008) examine the simplistic slogans and myths that cause disillusionment and frustration amongst feminist academics in this area. Common ways of discussing gender have taken the form of popularized, simplistic language that stereotypes women in ways that promote misrepresentations. For example, the authors mention the idea that women are commonly seen as less corrupt than men, more concerned about the environment, and more "inherently peaceful." These misrepresentations can put policy makers on the wrong path towards effective solutions of development problems (Cornwall et al., 2008).

In short, no good can come of believing such myths. As Cornwall and Jolly (2009) point out, communicating honestly about problems, solutions, and policies is an important aspect of policy making. In such a serious matter as development, policies need to be based on facts, not fictions. The remaining question would then be, now that gender has obtained a voice in mainstream development, how should this voice be used?

Elaine Unterhalter (2005) notes that a fundamental debate exists between how **cosmopolitans** and **communitarians** frame discussions around ethics, international relations, and development policy. Cosmopolitans are people who advocate for universal human rights (such as gender equality) that inform policy, while communitarians are those who reject the notion that human rights apply universally to all individuals regardless of their contexts and histories. They think that the norms and processes in a particular community or state should shape decision-making over internationally framed formulations. Unterhalter writes that "[f]or the cosmopolitans, human rights derive from natural rights and an ability to reason; they are universal, and gender is thus no more salient than race or ethnicity" (p. 115), but considered important. By contrast, communitarians think that individuals have rights and exercise those rights in the context of their communities. Depending on the community, gender equality may or may not be an important consideration; this depends on the community's history and cultural norms.

Cosmopolitanism has come under criticism because it cannot address the complex power imbalances in which most women lead their lives. A mere formal acknowledgment of rights—for example, the equal right to an education—does not oblige a state to provide education of a certain quality or guarantee the ability of poor women and girls to activate their right in court (Chinkin, 1999). Only by considering local rights and constraints as parts of institutional change will gender equality in education develop. Success will require focusing on local institutional conditions, while keeping in mind the fundamental principles of gender equality.

cosmopolitans people working in development who advocate for universal human rights (such as gender equality) that can help orient national and local legislation and policy.

communitarians people who reject the notion that human rights apply universally to all communities regardless of their contexts and histories, and argue instead that human rights are established through membership in specific communities.

Time to reflect

What position do you take in the dispute between cosmopolitan feminists and communitarian feminists? Why do you support this position and not the other?

Symbolic Interactionism

Where it touches on macrosociological issues such as global inequality, symbolic interactionism—the study of social interaction and meaning-making—tends to focus on the social construction of legitimating ideas or structures. For example, sociologist Elke Winter (2007) has been interested in

TABLE 9.2 Theoretical Approaches to Global Inequality

Theory	Main ideas
Structural Functionalism	• Global inequality is largely the result of uneven economic development, with some societies being better able to seize economic and technological opportunities.
Conflict Theory	• Global inequality results mainly from dependency or imperialist economic domination by powerful states and multinational organizations.
Feminist Theory	• Global inequality has important consequences for gender relations, including a gradual growth of family and gender norms prevalent in the Global North. Global inequality also allows for exploitation of people with intersecting marginalizations (e.g., poverty, gender, ethnicity) across national borders.
Symbolic Interactionism	• Global inequality requires the construction of co-operative multinational or globalized entities and promotes some degree of cultural homogenization around shared ideas of geography.

Source: Author-generated

the debates about a distinctive North American identity. Taking Canadian identity as an example, these arguments relate to competing debates about the differences in regional identities within Canada (comparing values in Quebec, the interior of British Columbia, the Maritimes, and northern Alberta, for example.) The difficulty we have finding a shared national identity in the midst of valued cultural, economic, and ecological differences helps us to see how hard it is for people to conceptualize global inequality. It is hard to get a clear picture of "global inequality" if we even have a hard time imagining holding in our minds the shared experiences and differences for everyone living within Canada.

This issue is even more dramatic when we consider the problem of imagining the European Union. Without such an "imagined community," as described by Benedict Anderson (1983/2006), it is hard for Europeans to feel an identification or attachment to this larger unit. Brexit, the planned secession of one national unit (Britain) from the whole, is one possible result of this lack of imagined community. But as de Jager (2009) has noted, people have made many competing attempts to imagine this new entity. Some have compared the European Union to medieval (i.e., pre-national) Europe; some describe it as a fortress or as a porous, ever growing organism. Should it be conceived as something wholly new, something virtual, like the internet, rather than situated firmly in geographic space? These are the kinds of issues symbolic interactionists are likely to consider when thinking about global inequality and the competition of national, regional, and multinational units.

The Role of the State
The Role of the State in Global Inequality

As we have already seen, multinationals and global markets exert a powerful influence over the creation and maintenance of global inequality. Yet states also play an important role through the regulation and control of activities that take place within their borders. They are also able to stimulate and promote certain kinds of innovation through taxation and the redistribution of national revenues. In all of these ways, states contribute to social development and international inequality.

Consider, for example, the role of the state in supporting technical innovation and modernization. States often regulate the development and spread of new technologies. In fact, state policy can have a large impact on the rate at which innovations are adopted. In turn, the adoption of some innovations, especially technological innovations, increases the productivity of a nation's economy. Thus economic productivity levels reflect a nation's ability to innovate and adopt new technology (Garcia & Calantone, 2002; Feldman & Florida, 1994).

The tightening of bonds between nations, whether by economic or political means, increases the spread of new ideas, technologies, and products. Of course, not all innovations from elsewhere are easily adopted: adoption may require infrastructural supports and political will. Evidence from Singapore's electronics industry, for example, suggests that industrial development in electronics involved a gradual and systematic accumulation of industrial, education, and infrastructural capabilities, many of which had been associated with earlier forms of manufacturing (Hobday, 1995). Only through government intervention was Singapore able to "leapfrog" over earlier technological patterns to catch up in the field of electronics.

Under the right conditions, global networking strategies can help countries in the Global South to use and build on the knowledge and skills of the Global North to create strong domestic infrastructure. However, exploiting these opportunities requires government support for training and for the creation of cooperative relationships with established players in the technology market. The use of government subsidies to promote the local development and adoption of new technologies may help or hinder the spread of those same technologies (Wallsten, 2000; King et al., 1994).

By restricting diffusion, some policies can impose substantial costs on society. The scientific community has historically relied on open sharing of scientific information. However, national security and corporate interests increasingly infringe on these norms of openness. The public has an interest in an open scientific establishment, so that it can democratically discuss the values and interests that science is serving and build on and gain from the benefit of any discoveries (as happened with the inventions of penicillin and insulin, for example.) Some people say that patents on intellectual property stifle progress when they occur at early phases of research. However, as we can see in Figure 9.6, history suggests the opposite. In India, Brazil, Singapore and other countries an increase in patents is correlated with a growth in innovation for example in the biotech sector.

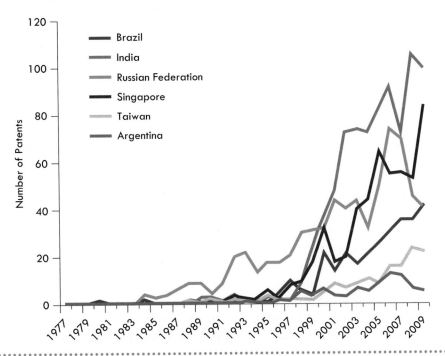

FIGURE 9.6 The Effects of Intellectual Patenting on Innovation

Source: http://blogs.nature.com/news/2012/06/intellectual-property-spurs-innovation.html. Reprinted by permission from Macmillan Publishers Ltd: Nature, 2017; permission conveyed through Copyright Clearance Center, Inc.

The importance of state control is most evident when such control is lacking. Modern states have gone a long way towards "perfecting the market" by controlling it. Most have established reliable currencies, minimized barriers to the entry of goods and services (e.g., low tariffs and trade barriers), minimized transaction costs (e.g., encouraged stock markets with huge numbers of buyers and sellers), enforced laws (e.g., preventing fraud and insider trading), and improved information flow (e.g., through subsidized or protected telephone and cable systems). The financial crisis of 2008 was an extreme example of the potential fallout when these controls fail. The shocks reverberated throughout the world's capital markets.

Time to reflect

If states provide so many useful services to societies and the people who populate them, what is the argument in favour of reducing the power of the state and allowing for freer global markets? Who do state controls benefit, and who do they hinder?

It is only because we can take the market-securing functions of states for granted, and because most states have done a relatively good job in these areas, that globalization is possible. It is paradoxical, then, that globalization largely undermines the functioning of these same states. Globalization itself requires the rule of law, high-quality **human capital**, and certain minimum guarantees of human survival. States that fill these needs will never be actively destroyed by those with a vested interest in globalization. And even within a global framework, states continue to moderate, modify, and censor the actions of large corporate actors. The relationships and power dynamics between states and globalization are complex and continually evolving.

The Role of States in Cultural Globalization

Historically, states have also played—and to some degree, still play—a role in the spread of national cultures and languages. Consider the concept of materialization. **Materialization**, in the form of ceremonies, symbolic objects, monuments, and writing systems, hastens the spread of an ideology and power relations in the larger population. The materialization of an ideology stabilizes power relations within societies that otherwise may fragment into smaller political units. It may also aid in the overpowering of one society by another. Canada, for example, attempted the cultural genocide of Indigenous people through its state-enforced education in residential schools (see Chapter 11).

Thus, to spread British culture and social structures to "the colonies" in earlier centuries was to spread related technologies of control. These included the common law tradition (British legal system) and certain notions about education, social class, and government—all of which took root in the British colonies that would become the United States, Canada, and Australia. By implication, a revolution against the "mother country" would require a reassessment of all these mechanisms of control, and not merely a rejection of the British monarchy.

Likewise, to spread the idea of "progress" as defined in the Global North throughout the world today is to spread a demand for the technologies linked to progress and the relations of production (bureaucracy, capital, and management styles) associated with those technologies. It is also to spread an admiration for the colonizing societies, and their imperial agendas, that are most closely associated with the accomplishment of "progress." Implicit in the factory, the computer, the management expert, the Disney movie is an idea that "the future" is embodied by the capitalism of the Global North (more precisely, at its core, American capitalism). Both states and corporations are involved in these processes.

The highly effective spread of capitalism during the twentieth century can be attributed to the skill with which capitalism has been introduced. The greatest success has come not through transplantation of capitalist values, but by mixing cultures to develop a new cultural logic. This process is called **knowledge translation**, rather than knowledge transfer, as it speaks to the idea of translating bodies of thought and belief to fit local realities—a strategy far more subtle than the mere sharing of indisputable, unchangeable facts. Tacit (or implied) knowledge especially is thought to be dependent on context, and thus on location (Hughes, 2007).

human capital a measure of formal education and learning, including credentials; a skill or skill set, usually including educational attainment or job-related experiences that enhances a worker's value on the job; usually, the result of foregone income and a long-term investment in personal improvement.

materialization the ceremonies, symbolic objects, monuments, and writing systems that hasten the spread of an ideology and power relations in the larger population, in the context of national or global culture.

knowledge translation the process by which the knowledge, values, and cultures of one culture are adapted to fit local thoughts and beliefs rather than transferred directly without any change.

Oleksandr Rupeta/Alamy Stock Photo

Children around the world, like the children pictured above, learn English, often because it is believed this knowledge will help them succeed in the future. Do you think the success of the English language is a kind of colonialism?

It is by changing people's perspectives that ideas spread through the global economy. In spreading its concept of progress through technology and trade, the Global North creates a globalized economy with cosmopolitan and innovative tendencies. As people from transnational companies meet and interact, networks and flows of knowledge—knowledge of capitalism and its underlying concepts and practices—reach all corners of the globe, furthering the diffusion of culture from the Global North (Hughes, 2007). Take as an example the spread of the use of English as the international language of business. Necessity rules: for instance, people today need to learn English because it is the language of international trade, science, and entertainment. Language education can, therefore, play a role in a country's comparative inequality, as countries with better English-language speakers attract business. But, like French, English continues to carry overtones of colonialism and domination throughout the Global South.

The Globalizing Role of Technology

Central to the international spread of culture and ideas is the role of information and communication technologies. Like other technologies, information and communication technologies vastly increase the capacity for more powerful entities to control the direction of information flow, censor information, and place their own desired meanings on the information that is circulating.

The flow of international news between the core and the periphery is also unequal, with countries in the Global North dominating the agenda. This inequality not only means that news from the "core" overwhelms that from countries on the periphery, but it also marginalizes the exchange of news among peripheral countries. The news is told from the perspective of the nation with the loudest voice and greatest reach, and its underlying cultural practices are transmitted across the world. For example, the takeover of the Crimea by Russia-friendly Ukrainian insurgents with the help of Russian troops is told differently in Russia—where it is viewed as a triumph of freedom over tyranny—than it is in the United States (and therefore disseminated internationally), where it is viewed as a type of Russian political meddling or even invasion (see Box 9.5).

Sociology 2.0

9.5 | Different Media Presentations of the Crimean Crisis

In an effort to show different ways of depicting the Crimean Crisis of 2014, Andre Baltz (2014) examined reports in three prominent newspapers: *Frankfurter Allgemeine Zeitung* (Germany), *The New York Times* (United States), and *Pravda* (Russia). He examined stories between 25 February and 30 April in the spring of 2014. He asked, how is Russia's participation in the conflict portrayed in the media and what stylistic elements such as metaphors and binary oppositions are being used to present Russia as "the other" in the conflict? (Baltz, 2014). One image or point of view, mainly pushed forward by Western media, was that of "invasion." By contrast, Eastern media mainly emphasized the idea of "protection." Media in the United States and Europe stressed connections to Russia when they described the activities of military troops in Crimea. Russia at first indicated that it was not involved. Later Russia changed its discourse and argued its role was purely for the purposes of protectionism. Russia is often depicted in the media as aggressive—the "bad other"—in binary opposition to the "good" United States. Finally, the media depictions reflect varied views of democracy where Western nations imply that Ukrainian nationalism is a step towards a free democracy; in opposition Russia views it as a fascist coup against a legitimate government.

Cultural diffusion through the media and otherwise is about capturing hearts and minds; hence, it has emotional as well as cognitive features. This capturing takes place through the flow of information—information as values, ideas, images, practices, and artifacts. Since culture is the sum of all the tools we humans use to think, interact, and manage the non-human environment, cultural diffusion is a redefinition of how we are to live. And since cultural styles typically spread from the Global North to the Global South, following the contours of political and economic power, cultural diffusion not only identifies but also maintains the global power structure.

Time to reflect

Much of the flow of information, cultural content, and capital in the world moves from the Global North to the Global South. Can you think of any exceptions to this rule? What role might states play in this process? What role might new technologies play in this process?

The Role of Migration in Global Inequality

A recent study by Guy Abel and Nikola Sander published in *Science* (28 March 2014) showed that every five years, roughly 0.6 per cent of the world's population moves to another country. From 2005 to 2010, this amounted to no less than 41.5 million people, or an average of 8.1 million people per year. Imagine the entire population of Quebec moving to another country *every* year, with this going on year after year. At that rate, Canada would be emptied of people in roughly four years.

Migration has an important, continuing impact on global inequality, in part because people carry ideas, values, and technologies when they move from one place to another. By leaving and arriving, they change the productive potential of given societies. Also, leaving gives people a chance to use the global inequality to their advantage; they stress how leaving a lesser-off place for a better-off place will allow them to follow their dreams of personal fulfilment and well-being. This in part recreates the notion of the "American Dream" that prevails in the United States, but moves it internationally. Those individuals who work hard and deserve it will be rewarded in their new home.

In general, the most able, ambitious, and adventurous people are the most likely to migrate, unless (like refugees) they are forced to flee. So, for example, Feliciano's (2005) study of 32 US immigrant groups found that nearly all immigrants are more educated than those who remain in their home countries, though immigrants vary substantially in their degree of selectivity, depending upon the origin country and the timing of migration. In general, those coming the longest distance and overcoming the most severe exit hurdles are typically the most educated and motivated. As one might expect, Chiswick (1999) finds that "favorable selectivity for labor-market success can be expected to be less intense for noneconomic migrants, such as refugees, tied movers, and ideological migrants, and for sojourners (short-term migrants) and illegal aliens" (p. 185).

Therefore, migration is largely determined by the availability of information and perception of opportunities. Geographic distance also plays a key role, as influential professor of geography Ernst George Ravenstein showed for the first time in 1885. Of course, geographic distance played a bigger role in the 1880s more than it does today, when air travel reduces travel time in a way that was unimaginable in Ravenstein's day. As well, the risks of moving to a new destination decrease when there are known job opportunities (as Stouffer showed in 1960), and there is an existing community of similar recent migrants (as repeated network analyses of immigration have shown).

Today's world is a world of strangers in motion, and the most dominant societies are the most diverse and cosmopolitan. Some have asserted that Japan's stagnation, for example, had to do with its xenophobia (e.g., see Chiavacci & Hommerich, 2016). Over the past century or so, increasingly easy and rapid migration has increased global diversity and, in large part, also reduced the possibility and extent of conflict. In large part, this is due to the enhanced ease of movement and communication. New migration patterns imply new forms of migrant communities. Migrants can maintain social and economic networks more easily than they could a few decades ago; their scope of action and social relations is transnational, and they constitute transnational non-territorial communities.

With increased ease of migration, we have seen a continued brain drain from the poorest to the richest countries. People leave the Global South, where despite their education and skill they have little opportunity for advancement, for societies in the Global North, where they hope and believe their abilities will be rewarded. States regulate the local social and skill composition of the population by raising or lowering the human capital and solving or creating problems of health, education, welfare, employment, and unemployment. By extension, they influence the supply of educated and skilled labour in other countries. One concern in Canada is the skill outflow, or "brain drain," of students, academics, researchers, and professionals to the United States, though this outflow is far less than witnessed in many other societies (see Figure 9.7).

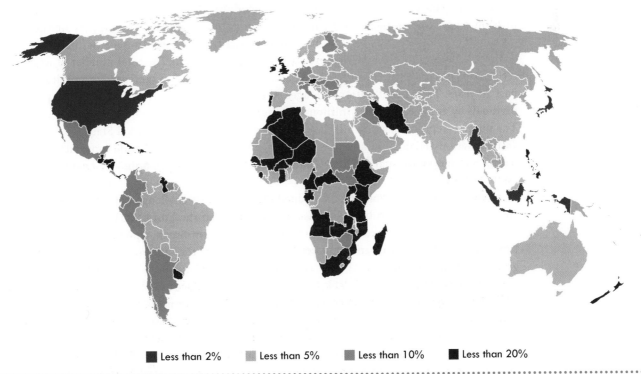

Less than 2%   Less than 5%   Less than 10%   Less than 20%

FIGURE 9.7 International Migration and the "Brain Drain" Phenomenon

Source: OECD, accessed at www.oecd.org/dev/poverty/migrationandthebraindrainphenomenon.htm

Riley Sparks www.sparksriley.com

A group of Syrian refugees walk across a bridge near the Macedonian border in Greece. Do you think the international flow of refugees is a product of globalization and global inequality, or simply a case of difficult local circumstances?

Another source of contention surrounds the global flow of refugees, who are granted admission on grounds other than their social or economic utility. (Instead, they are admitted on compassionate grounds, as victims of human rights violations, or because their admission achieves a political or diplomatic purpose for the government.) The total number of worldwide refugees—also, displaced people and illegal labour migrants—has increased dramatically in the past 20 years. The United Nations Refugee Agency (2016) reports that the total of displaced individuals by 2015 reached 65.3 million—that is, 1 out of every 113 people on Earth is displaced. The number represents a 5.8 million increase on the year before (United States of America for United Nations High Commissioner for Refugees, 2017). The large-scale movement of people within and across national borders will increasingly occupy foreign policy and national security establishments.

Increasingly, population flow has joined the trends that challenge national sovereignty and create global–national institutional tensions—especially in the European Union, where national economic disparities are great. One result has been the recent Brexit, a popular vote in the United Kingdom to exit the European Union so as to better control the inflow of foreign refugees, immigrants, and job-seekers.

Many policy options are available to states that wish to reduce unwanted (im)migration flows by altering the internal conditions generating mass emigration (Cornelius, 2005; Martin, 1994). Such policy options include trade, foreign investment, and development assistance; guest worker policies; refugee return policies; safe havens, both external and internal; exit control policies; political strategies to reduce refugee flows; and if all else fails, military intervention. Thus, international migration and refugee movements are not simple domestic issues but matters of foreign policy. By their law making, foreign policy, and foreign aid, states influence the global flow of workers. Usually, this works to the advantage of more prosperous states.

Pro-Brexit demonstrators in the UK used phrases like the one in the photo above: "We want our country back." What are the implicit assumptions about this slogan? Who is "we" (and who isn't)?

How to Fight Global Inequality

Governments and international NGOs such as the World Health Organization (WHO), International Labour Organization (ILO), and the United Nations Education, Scientific, and Cultural Organization (UNESCO) have been making efforts for decades to fight or reduce global inequality. But what role do global organizations, like the United Nations, play in solving international problems, and how effective are their efforts? On the other hand, how do *seemingly* benevolent and politically neutral organizations play a role in maintaining inequality on a global scale?

Groups have used a variety of mechanisms to reduce global inequality, including most notably foreign aid, debt cancellation, and tariff reduction. Foreign aid has the immediate effect of funnelling money into another country's national coffers; however, funds have often ended up in the hands of corrupt leaders, bringing little benefit to the vast majority of citizens. Or it has taken the form of military spending and/or military equipment, which, once again, has had no positive effect on local or global inequality. Aid also often comes in the form of loans, which can also perpetuate and exacerbate a country's economic difficulties once it begins trying to pay back the loans.

Debt cancellation has often had a more positive benefit, but it is only a short-term solution that helps a country overcome temporary financial difficulties so it can begin to plan for and implement long-term development plans. Tariff reduction can offer a longer-term solution if it opens up markets for foreign goods and, thus, helps countries to improve their balance of trade. However, often, countries in the Global North are only interested in reducing tariffs for raw materials or foodstuffs that are in short supply at home, and less interested in opening their doors to manufactured goods that will compete in price with local manufactured goods. In short, countries often only provide help that will not greatly disrupt the power dynamic between the Global North and the Global South. It is, after all, in the best interest of the Global North that global inequality remains (more on this below).

Social movements, such as Idle No More in Canada, can play an important role in mobilizing people to address problems of global inequality. (See Chapter 16 for a discussion on this topic.) Finally, lower-income countries often develop self-improvement strategies, especially around education, public

Dashboard

Video: *Everyday Rebellion*

health, and industrial development, that will have the long-term effect of improving their position in the world economy. Here, effective and even charismatic leadership—such as that provided by Nelson Mandela in South Africa—may be important. In other instances, anticolonial or revolutionary leaders and ideologies may be important, as they were in China, Cuba, Singapore, North Africa, and elsewhere.

No discussion of global inequality would be complete without some discussion of the violence that results from inequality, and from the attempts made to correct it. In some instances, civil war or revolution is the direct result of foreign provocation, intervention, or meddling by the "great powers." The American Central Intelligence Agency (CIA) is notorious for having intervened numerous times in the politics of Central and South America to ensure a government that was friendly to American interests (see, e.g., Etheredge, 2013). The Soviet Union did likewise in Eastern Europe and the Baltic states, even invading Czechoslovakia (now the Czech Republic and Slovak Republic) and Hungary in the mid-twentieth century. Recent examples include the Russian invasion of the Crimea (Ukraine) and the American invasion of Iraq and Afghanistan, which set in motion the ongoing warfare in Syria and elsewhere in the Middle East.

Acts of political violence—including war crimes—differ from other kinds of violence in that representatives of one political or national group inflict such violence to gain political power (Besley & Persson, 2011). Rationalizations around the "greater good" are commonly devised to "explain away" the extent of violence, its effects, or its lack of fairness.

Finally, the political violence promoted by global inequality can lead to environmental destruction. The wilful destruction of the environment as a strategy of war, as practice for war, or as punishment for the defeated occurred at least as early as Roman times and persists in modern-day society. Roman armies routinely destroyed crops and salted the earth to ruin the land's fertility. A millennium later, the Russians burned their own crops and homes not once but twice to prevent the invading armies of Napoleon and, later, Hitler from making use of them. In a different but no less destructive behaviour, Allied navies during the Second World War routinely used the whales of the North Atlantic for target practice (Mowat, 2012). Environmental disasters are becoming more and more responsible for the degradation of people's quality of life, often exacerbating pre-existing global inequalities. This leads to concerns about the potential number of environmental refugees should climate change continue. See Chapter 15 for more on how climate change is a global inequality issue.

Conclusions

As we have seen, there are many reasons for global inequality but they are related. They involve flows of information, capital, political influence, and sometimes military force. At the core of these processes are the multinational corporation and the nation-state.

As discussed above, when nationalism goes beyond the borders of the state, it creates colonialism: the establishment by higher-income countries of formal political control over lower-income areas, usually accompanied by the exploitation of local economic resources. A history of colonialism is not the only cause of inequality between present-day nations, but it is an important one with lasting effects. **Neo-colonialism** is a related concept: even after political decolonization, societies in the Global North may continue to dominate the production and marketing of goods and culture in former colonies, retaining their economic influence.

neo-colonialism a concept related to colonialism, when, despite political decolonization, the Global North societies that once controlled many parts of the world continue to dominate the production and marketing of goods, culture, and language in their former colonies, thereby retaining their historical influence.

We also discussed Immanuel Wallerstein's analysis of world economic developments, which divides the world's nations into core states, peripheral states, and semi-peripheral states. In the core states, wage labour and self-employment became dominant, and bureaucracies developed to provide rational control. Raw materials, cheap labour, and economic surplus are drained from the periphery and flow back to core states. The goal is always to enrich core states at the expense of the periphery.

We considered the importance of globalization theory as a way of explaining international relations that recognizes the role of ideas. Ultimately, today's global society rests on a global culture, as well as a global economy. From this perspective, humanity is coming to view life in similar ways. Is this just cultural imperialism, the worldwide dominance of American culture and lifestyles enjoyed in the Global North? Supporters of globalization argue against this suggestion, proposing that it mixes cultures and incorporates their best elements. All we can say for certain at this point is that globalization is a new phenomenon, based on a single world market; and it is surely a source of increased economic, political, cultural, technological, and organizational interdependence.

Finally, we briefly considered how global inequality might lead to political violence both within countries and between countries, with consequences for relations between ethnic and tribal groups, and between men and women.

Questions for Critical Thought

1. Explain how capitalism is an expansionist and exploitative system in terms of core and peripheral states. Under what circumstances might the system prevent peripheral states from reaching the core?
2. What do you think Canada's role should be in reducing global inequality? What might get in the way of the best intentions of Canadians?
3. Explain the concept of the creative class as introduced by Richard Florida. What role do you think the creative

class plays in creating diverse and economically and socially successful cities?
4. What are the benefits and drawbacks of international communication tools such as social media, blogs, and YouTube in terms of global inequality and globalization? Do these tools encourage a single culture worldwide, or do they allow for the sharing of different perspectives and values?

Take it Further: Recommended Readings

Francois Bourguignon, *The Globalization of Inequality*, 2nd ed., translated by Thomas Scott-Railton (Princeton, NJ: Princeton University Press, 2017). This book describes recent trends in global inequality and how they affect people's everyday lives. It also discusses the pros and cons of different policies and how well they can ameliorate inequality.

Cati Coe, *The Scattered Family: Parenting, African Migrants, and Global Inequality* (Chicago: University of Chicago Press, 2013). In this book, Coe shows how families have changed because of migration patterns. She shows how family scattering occurs in the context of international migration flows and separation occurs over time and space.

David Held and Ayse Kaya, eds. *Global Inequality: Patterns and Explanations* (Cambridge: Polity, 2007). This edited collection compiles experts' opinions and analysis on global inequality and how it links to globalization and economic development.

Branko Milanovic, *Global Inequality: A New Approach for the Age of Globalization* (Cambridge, MA: Harvard University Press, 2016). This book provides a comprehensive overview of inequality within and among countries. The book goes further and discusses what the future of local and global inequality will look like and how it relates to changes in the global flow of goods and capital.

Timmons J. Roberts and Bradley Parks. *A Climate of Injustice: Global Inequality, North-South Politics, and Climate Policy* (Cambridge, MA: MIT Press, 2006). The authors discuss the complexities of climate change and how they are closely interlinked with economic interests and inequalities. In particular the interests of economically weak countries are contrasted with those of powerful nations and it is shown how these fundamental differences stall meaningful policy development.

Take it Further: Recommended Online Resources

Canadian Council on Social Determinants of Health
http://ccsdh.ca

CIA World Factbook
www.cia.gov/library/publications/the-world-factbook

OECD Inequality Data
www.oecd.org/social/inequality.htm

Institute for Policy Studies, Inequality.org
http://inequality.org/global-inequality

United Nations Human Development Reports
http://hdr.undp.org/en/content/human-development-index-hdi

World Bank Open Data
http://data.worldbank.org

World Health Organization Social Determinants of Health
www.who.int/social_determinants/en/

More resources available on 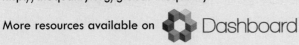 Dashboard

10

Families, Age Groups, and Social Patterns Close to Home

Learning Objectives

In this chapter, you will:

> Learn how different theoretical approaches describe and explain family patterns

> See how gendered inequality in society affects life in different kinds of families

> Understand the forms families can take and the ways family life has changed over time

> See how science and technology have shaped present-day family life in various ways

Introduction

infidelity

a violation of a couple's emotional and/or sexual exclusivity (also referred to as cheating, adultery, or having an affair).

Infidelity and cheating have been considered family problems since ancient times. Now, with the rise of new communication technologies and online dating sites like Ashley Madison (see Chapter 1), cheating is easier and partners more available than they have ever been before. Indeed, with Ashley Madison and other online dating sites promising to organize discrete affairs, people are wondering whether present-day relationships will be able to last. Some fear that the temptation of online dating services, even with the threat of hacking and leaked user names, may prove too great for partners to remain loyal to one another.

While families are one of the most ancient of all social institutions and, in some respects, work the same today as they did a thousand years ago, the above example shows how great an impact science and technology can have. In this chapter, we will discuss families, relationships, and the ways in which both have been affected by new science and technologies. We will discuss, for example, the ways in which various technologies, such as social media, have changed family living, and we will hear both sides of a recent, ongoing debate as to whether technology is dividing or uniting families.

family

any social unit, or set of social relations, that does what families are popularly imagined to do, by whatever means it does so.

In present-day society, norms about what constitutes a "**family**" are changing quickly and are much more open to personal interpretation than ever before. People today hold widely varying ideas about relationships and have different views about divorce, cohabitation, childbearing, and sex outside of marriage. Family units today tend to be much smaller than they were centuries or even mere decades ago. And of course, families are much frailer today than they once were. For example,

Sociology 2.0

10.1 | Online Relationships and the "Virtual" Girlfriend

Information and communication technology (ICT) has increased people's abilities to stay in contact with one another, allowing friends to keep in touch despite the physical barriers posed by distance and enabling couples to remain intimate in long-distance relationships. However, one of the most revolutionary changes brought about by new ICT is the rise of the "virtual" girlfriend industry. This enables all of us to overcome problems of loneliness and disconnection due to "placelessness," especially when travelling (Delistraty, 2014, September 24).

It is common knowledge that new technologies have allowed for the development of "internet relationships"—relationships carried out entirely, or almost entirely, online. Thanks to social media platforms such as Facebook, Twitter, and Instagram, and other forms of ICT, people who have never met in real life can have "virtual" relationships with one another, interacting only in the realm of cyberspace. Today's consumers, however, have taken this to a whole new level by paying for fake internet relationships—in other words, hiring people to play the part of a girlfriend or boyfriend online (Gondelman, 2013; Delistraty, 2014, October 2).

Relationship-for-hire services have been around for centuries. However, in today's society, you can hire someone to play your boyfriend or girlfriend without ever meeting them, going out with them, or speaking to them in person. Some websites allow you to rent the services of an individual who will pretend to be your long-distance partner on social networking sites like Facebook and Twitter, and even on online gaming communities like *World of Warcraft*. Other online websites provide actual fake girlfriends (e.g., GF Rental) who are available for a variety of purposes, including to show off to friends, family, neighbours, and co-workers, but not for sex.

These girlfriend-for-hire sites are not like traditional escort services. In some of these organizations, the interactions between clients and agents take place entirely online; the client and customer never meet in person. Some websites offer services such as texts at pre-arranged times, voicemails to one's family member or boss, and convincingly scripted interactions on social media. One main purpose of these sites is to allow people to convince their friends, family, or employers that they are in a stable long-distance relationship (Dayu, 2014; Goorwich, 2014). What effects these internet relationships will have on the formation and maintenance of families has yet to be seen.

they have much higher rates of divorce and other relationship dissolution than one would have seen 50 years ago or more. That is in part because of new and greater pressures on the family, for economic and other reasons. In larger part, it is due to family legislation that, starting in the late 1960s, liberalized the divorce laws and made marital dissolution much easier than it had ever been.

One great threat to "the family" in Canada was the enforced removal of children from Indigenous communities to attend residential schools from the 1880s to 1996 (see Chapter 11), as well as the Sixties Scoop, during which thousands of Indigenous children were removed from their homes and adopted into white families (Pelley, 2015). Even now, Statistics Canada data shows that almost half (48.1%) of all children aged 14 and under living in foster care in Canada are Indigenous children (Turner, 2016). We will learn, in this chapter, how important family is to socialization—and will conclude that the erosion of the Indigenous family unit resulted in cultural genocide, whether intended or not.

Video: *Journey toward Reconciliation*

Theoretical Approaches to the Family

Conflict Theory

Conflict theory takes a historical approach to families and focuses on political and economic changes that have affected family life, especially changes that cause shifts in power relationships within families. Conflict theory views industrialization as one of the most important of these changes, since it saw the family change from a self-sustaining unit of production (e.g., a farming household) to a unit of consumption (e.g., a dual-income household that purchases shelter, food, clothing, services, and luxuries) in a society marked by consumer capitalism. In doing so, the family became dependent on sources of income outside the household to meet its survival needs. This meant that, in traditional families, working-class men had to sell their labour power to the bourgeoisie in exchange for an income.

Women, for their part, came to have normative responsibility for the home; this included child-rearing, food preparation, and providing emotional support. While families varied immensely two centuries ago, as they do today, there was a gendered division of labour, at least in the minds of middle- and working-class people who lived in towns and cities and did not earn their living from agriculture.

This new family form was far from democratic. Given the large differences in power, strength, age, and social resources among family members, the more powerful members were ideally supposed to protect the less powerful ones. But in practice, this power imbalance made **patriarchy**—control over the family by a dominant male (typically, the father)—a central fact in the history of family life in most known societies. Simply put, men have dominated the family because they owned and controlled the greater share of the resources.

Equally important, the flowering of capitalist economic organization in the last two centuries has led to free, largely unregulated markets in which all goods and services are available at a price. This has meant that the labour force is largely unprotected from sudden economic crises, prolonged unemployment, the decline in unionized labour practices, and monopoly-driven prices. All of these contribute to a need for second and even third earners in families, and to precarious employment for many. In large part, the conflict theory position on families has been continued and enriched by feminist theorists, whom we will discuss shortly.

patriarchy
a social system in which men predominate in roles of political leadership, moral authority, social privilege, and control of property.

Functionalism

Functionalists view the family as a central institution in society—indeed, as a miniature version of society, with individual family members coming together in a unified and productive whole (Lehmann, 1994). For this reason, they expect changes in the family to mirror changes in the larger society.

Talcott Parsons and Robert Bales's (1955) functionalist analysis, following the theories of Émile Durkheim, views the family's division of labour as the key to its success. Ideally, the husband of the household performs an instrumental role as the breadwinner, decision maker, and source of authority and leadership, while the wife fulfills an expressive role as homemaker, nurturer, and emotional centre of the family.

It is through this specialization that the family institution accomplishes several important functions, including the regulation of sexual behaviour and reproduction, the provision for physical (food, shelter) and psychological (nurturing, learning) needs of its members, and the socialization of children. Since the 1950s, however, the roles of the husband and wife have changed, and such specialization may no longer be possible or useful—especially when husbands and wives are both working for pay outside the home. Moreover, the internet is starting to replace the family as the place where **socialization** takes place, and functionalists may need to rework their conception of what, exactly, the family's function is in present-day society.

Symbolic Interactionism

In respect to families, symbolic interactionists study the ways that members of a family interact with one another and the ways they resolve conflicts within the boundaries of their roles in the family. An important part of this process is the creation and revision of myths about family.

Social constructionists, who carry on the symbolic interactionist argument on a societal scale, focus on the development and use of family ideologies such as the "family values" promoted by right-wing religious leaders and conservative politicians. By appealing to people's interest in and concern about their family lives, these moral and political entrepreneurs—people who make considerable efforts to change behaviour in particular directions—channel popular anxieties into hostility against such groups as single mothers, gays and lesbians, and divorced people. The effect of such social constructions is to channel hostility away from exploitive employers and unresponsive governments towards people who are most in need of support and understanding. Thus, traditional ideologies are used to hurt vulnerable families, under the guise of helping to preserve traditional family life (McMullin, 2005).

socialization
the lifelong social learning a person undergoes to become a capable member of society, through social interaction with others, and in response to social pressures.

social constructionists
symbolic interactionist argument on a societal scale; they study how moral entrepreneurs make and enforce claims about reality.

Time to reflect

The term "family values"—concerning issues around marriage, sex, and procreation that stress traditionalism—excludes the reality of a lot of Canadian families. What do you think the impact might be of being told, implicitly, that your family does not count as a "family" by your governing body?

Feminist Theory

Like other theorists, feminist theorists have had a lot to say about the significance of changes to family structure in recent times. Most especially, they have been concerned with the potential that new types of families have offered women for emancipation, free choice, and personal development. Often, contemporary feminist works note the failure of present-day families to accomplish these goals as well as earlier feminists had hoped and call our attention to continuing problems with family violence and the "second shift" and "double ghetto." However, they are also quick to note the much-greater opportunity for women to individualize (or personally tailor) their family lives as well as their work lives through access to more education, better contraception, and more flexible working arrangements.

Feminist analyses of families tend to focus on the link between the present-day nuclear family, the economy, and women's subordination. And we can see how all three topics are connected through the concept of social reproduction. Most generally, social reproduction refers to all the social, economic, ideological, and political processes that preserve the social structure and its component relationships over time.

Dashboard

Video: *In the Name of the Family*

It is easy to see how the family promotes social reproduction in a capitalist society. First, families biologically reproduce the next generation of workers and raise them until they are ready to enter the workforce. Second, families—as key agents of socialization—ideologically reproduce the next generation of workers by teaching them how to function compliantly in a capitalist system. Third, families legally reproduce the next generation of workers, since it is through monogamous patterns of marriage and reproduction that stable patterns of ownership and inheritance are preserved.

Finally, it is through the unpaid and unrewarded—not to mention potentially alienating and often exploitive—practices of motherhood in a patriarchal society that capitalism is able to assume the continued supply of exploitable workers. Thus, from this feminist standpoint, capitalism has a vested interest in preserving both patriarchy and gender inequality—patriarchy because it compels unpaid domestic services from women, and gender inequality because it allows employers to under-pay women when they venture into the paid workforce.

Studies routinely show that wives provide a range of services for their husbands and children at far less than market value (as a classic example, see Meg Luxton's *More Than a Labour of Love*, 1980). The availability of this unpaid domestic work enables capitalists to keep the wages they pay to their workers low. Wives also perform important emotional labour: by absorbing or deflecting the work-related frustrations of their husbands, they help to protect the capitalist system against attack, sometimes even at the cost of physical violence. Finally, under capitalism, housewives make up a large portion of the "reserve army of labour," available for poorly paid part-time or short-term work when extra money is needed at home and work is plentiful. This availability for precarious work increases the flexibility and profitability of capitalism, making it easy to hire and fire workers at will.

National Film Board of Canada. Photothèque/Library and Archives Canada/PA-145667

Mr and Mrs E.J. Way having supper in their kitchen before Mr Way leaves for the night shift at Burrard Shipyard and Engineering Works Ltd., July 1943. Do you take unpaid household work for granted?

TABLE 10.1 Theoretical Approaches to the Family

Theory	Main points
Conflict Theory	• Social reproduction in families supports capitalism. • Women in families maintain the workforce without pay. • Families are no longer self-sustaining economic units, but are consumption units dependent on outside sources of income. • Gender inequality is perpetuated by economic exploitation under capitalism, not the needs of society or even of a given family for *task differentiation based on gender.*
Structural Functionalism	• Families provide nurture and socialization. • A gendered division of domestic labour is functional. • The family is a microcosm of society—individual family members come together in a unified and productive whole. • A gendered familial division of labour is the key to a family's success, • This family form is natural and has evolutionary benefits.
Symbolic Interactionism	• Families involve continued interaction. • They are maintained by shared myths and beliefs. • Their main role is to socialize the next generation. • A married couple builds a shared definition of their family—its goals, identity, and values.
Feminist Theory	• The domestic division of labour is arbitrary and unequal. • Just as factory workers depend on capitalists for a living wage, wives depend on their husbands and are subordinated by them • Partly as a result, women have historically endured political and social inferiority. • The capitalist economy affirms old patriarchal tendencies by providing men differential access to the labour market.

Source: Author-generated

Defining the "Family"

Family structures do vary, making the definition of a family somewhat elusive. Defining a family in a meaningful, practical way, however, is important if we are to ensure that we implement social policies that address the needs and desires of *all* Canadian families, not just the "idealized" ones (i.e., married opposite-sex parents plus one or two children).

Science and technology have played an enormous role in complicating the definition of a family by enabling new variations of family forms. One very important way in which new science has restructured and varied families is through reproductive technologies such as in vitro fertilization (IVF), artificial insemination, surrogacy, and fertility drugs. Assisted reproductive technologies challenge the way biological families are made, as well as the norm that there should only be two opposite-sex parents in a family by allowing single parents, older women, and homosexual families to choose how, with whom, and when to have children.

For heterosexual couples, processes such as in vitro fertilization, artificial insemination, and fertility drug treatments are options to help conceive in the case of infertility (Government of Canada, 2013). Artificial insemination, also known as intrauterine insemination, can also help single mothers, as well as gay and lesbian couples conceive in order to have their own biological children. The process allows sperm to reach the egg in a woman's uterus through the use of a plastic tube called a catheter, and is often used in conjunction with fertility drugs.

In addition to artificial insemination, another method of assisted reproductive technology (ART) is in vitro fertilization, described at length on numerous websites that provide the service, including babycenter.ca. *In vitro* is a Latin term meaning "outside the body," and refers to the process in which a woman's egg is fertilized by a man's sperm in a laboratory dish to produce one or more embryos. The embryo is then transferred into a woman's uterus to achieve pregnancy. IVF can be achieved through a couple's own sperm and eggs, or through donated sperm, eggs, or embryos, and additionally, surrogates may be used to carry the pregnancy.

The family is no longer exclusively for "two opposite sex, married parents with two biological children" (Golding, 2006). The idea of the family has expanded to include single parents, stepfamilies, families with adoptive children, grandchildren, nieces, nephews, foster children, and gay and lesbian families, among many other diverse permutations (Golding, 2006).

Gay and lesbian families are sometimes referred to as "families of choice" because through either adoption or ART, they can choose to be single parents, coupled parents, or co-parents with platonic friends (Ryan & Berkowitz, 2009). Indeed, many of the clients for ART clinics such as sperm banks, IVF clinics, and artificial insemination clinics in urban centres are members of LGBTQ communities, and organizations have developed in those communities to facilitate the process.

In the twenty-first century, more and more women are choosing to use sperm donation and other assisted reproductive technologies, in conjunction with fertility drug treatments, to become single mothers and older mothers (Weissenberg & Landau, 2012). Many women who choose these options must also go through multiple rounds of fertility drug treatments, egg donation, and in vitro fertilization, and will often experience high-risk pregnancies.

Fertility drugs can help ensure a successful pregnancy, but they also increase the chances of having twins, triplets, and other types of multiple births (see Box 10.2). While having twins or triplets can be a blessing for some, women who are pregnant with multiple fetuses will encounter more pregnancy-related problems. Additionally, parents of multiple pregnancies will face an enormous financial burden, as well as a lack of sleep and space (Dickens & Cook, 2008). They will have to face the costs of feeding, clothing, caring for the children, as well as additional costs if any of the children are physically or neurologically disabled; for some, this may be extremely hard to do (Dickens & Cook, 2008). For this reason, multiple birth families are vulnerable to lower quality of life, maternal depression, and increases in social stigma from people who view them as "unnatural" (Ellison et al., 2005).

Assisted reproductive technologies, therefore, have revolutionized the family, complicating family dynamics and relationships. In consequence, the idea of "family" has become rather hard

Spotlight On

10.2 | "Octomom"

Multiple births from in vitro fertilization can be prevented by limiting the number of embryos transferred to the uterus. However, in the case of single mother Nadya Suleman (nicknamed Octomom), her doctor, Michael Kamrava, knowingly endangered her by transferring 12 embryos (conceived through IVF) that could have been expected to yield her eight children (*Time*, 2009). To curb multiple pregnancies, the American Society for Reproductive Medicine recommends no more than two embryos for women of Suleman's age (Stateman, 2009). So, what Dr Kamrava did was ill-advised and even dangerous.

Nonetheless, the birth was successful and Suleman currently holds the world record for longest surviving octuplets. And, though currently healthy, all eight of her octuplets were born nine weeks premature; the smallest of them spent nearly three months in the hospital after birth (Associated Press, 2014). Not surprisingly, like many other mothers who experience a multiple birth pregnancy, Suleman ran into financial trouble and had to apply for public assistance. In 2014, the problem escalated when she was charged with welfare fraud. As well, Suleman had to spend several weeks in a rehab centre for "anxiety, exhaustion and stress" (Associated Press, 2014).

As you can see, abusing fertility drugs and having too many births at once can pose many risks not only for the mother but also for the children. Once again, technology provides new opportunities but also unexpected new dangers.

Think Globally

10.3 | Changes in Marrying Age

Marriage is a social process that, in most societies, forms families. The age at which people marry, however, differs between societies, for many reasons. Statistics Canada researchers report that both men and women are increasingly older when they first marry (Eicher, 2012). In 1980 the average age of first time brides and grooms was 25.9 and 28.5, respectively; while in 2000 first-time brides were on average 31.7 years old while grooms were 34.3. Statistics Canada suggests two reasons for the change: women's improving educational and career opportunities, and a growing number of people living together in common-law relationships, without marrying.

According to UNICEF (2001), brides tend to be much younger outside North America, especially in pre-industrial or early-industrial nations. In sub-Saharan Africa and South Asia, most girls are married young; for example, in Niger, three-quarters of all girls will have married before age 18. A similar pattern, though less extreme, is evident in traditional cultures of the Middle East, North Africa, and other

parts of Asia. Contrast this with Scandinavian and other Western European societies (e.g., Norway, Germany, and France), where the average age of marriage is around 30.

In most pre-industrial, traditional societies, families view the husband as family head, and his wife as guardian. This "guardianship" is especially helpful in in conflict-ridden places such as Northern Uganda, where a girl will be married to a man in the militia to protect her, and often her family as well, from attack.

Throughout the world, the age at which women marry is a function of the amount of formal education they are expected to receive and want to receive—and conversely, the number of children they are expected to bear. These, in turn, are related to the availability of paid work for women and the financial need women have to earn an income to maintain a middle-class lifestyle for the family. They key to all this is fertility: where women's main role is to produce children, education for women is typically curtailed and women marry young.

---

census family
a household that includes two spouses—opposite or same-sex, married or cohabiting (if they have lived together for longer than one year)—with or without never-married children, or a single parent with one or more never-married children.

kin group
a group of people related by blood or marriage.

nuclear family
a group that usually consists of a father, a mother, and their children living in the same dwelling. Such a family comprises no more than three relationships: between spouses, between parents and children, and between siblings.

to define. The **census family** devised by Statistics Canada, however, attempts to offer a practical solution to this problem. Briefly, it defines a family as a married couple (with or without children), a common-law couple (with or without children), or a lone-parent family.

Obviously, this definition tolerates diversity. The couple in a census family may be of opposite sexes or the same sex. Children living only with grandparents with no parents present are considered a census family, though the definition does not apparently include families with larger **kin groups**, including aunts, uncles, or cousins; nor does it attend to the feelings or obligations members of these families have toward each other.

In other words, the Statistics Canada definition focuses on structure or family form, but it is more inclusive than the concept of family *household* used by other agencies of the Canadian government. It does not require marriage, childbearing, opposite-sex partners, blood relation, or sexual relations. This allows for a great deal of diversity.

Changes to Families in the Twenty-First Century
Changes in Family Forms

With new scientific and technological advancements come changes in society, including changes in forms of social institutions like families. For example, if you had to say one important, true thing about changes in family life in the last hundred years, you would likely say that families everywhere have gotten smaller. Indeed, this is the topic of an important sociological study titled *World Revolution and Family Patterns*, written by William Goode back in 1963.

Goode noticed that family patterns everywhere were moving towards the **nuclear family** model and that the family unit of his day was smaller than it once was. These trends still hold true today and, with the widespread increase in contraception use and a decreased birth rate, family size has shrunk almost everywhere.

What is important to understand is the enormous impact that science and technology have had, and continue to have, on this trend. While it is true that some types of birth control, like male condoms, have been around for hundreds of years, present-day science and medicine have made many more effective methods available to the public, helping to keep the family unit small.

The size of families is not the only way in which families have changed over the years (see Table 10.2). Goode noted that role relations within families have also changed and that families have become more flexible. Individual family members, for example, have more freedom today than they did in the past. Parental authority over children has declined—something we will discuss in more detail when we talk about the impact of social media technologies on family relationships below—and with an increase in women's rights, husbands' control over wives has dwindled too. Moreover, since Goode, the family unit has also been extended to homosexual couples, including marriage and adoption as part of the legitimizing of homosexual family units. And with the prevalence of divorce, in vitro fertilization, surrogate pregnancy, and so on, families are now more broadly defined (even as they are smaller).

Goode observed that these changes can be largely attributed to the **industrialization** and **urbanization**—also, the differentiation, commodification, and rationalization—of social life. These trends encourage not only smaller but also more flexible family units because these kinds of units are better able to meet the challenges brought by industrialization. For example, small families can migrate more easily than large families, if one or more income earners see the need to do so.

Additionally, as people have required more formal education to gain a foothold in the workplace, they have tended to delay getting married or, at least, to delay childbearing. This has posed hard problems for highly educated women, who have had to decide whether to have a first child while still in school, immediately after graduating, shortly after starting a new job, or only after having attained some seniority and security in a job.

For the most part, industrialization has produced small, flexible nuclear families throughout the world. Today, this nuclear family type is an idealized family in cultures in the Global North, stemming from 1950s American ideals. However, in some instances, nuclear families have occurred before (even, without) industrialization, and in other instances, extended families have persisted despite industrialization. What is incredible about Goode's work is that many of the trends he

industrialization reorganization of an economy for the purpose of manufacturing, using machinery and inanimate forms of energy, and the social changes that accompany it.

urbanization a population shift from rural to urban areas, resulting in the growth of cities and the development of city lifestyles.

TABLE 10.2 The Variety of Family Forms in Canada Today

Family classification	Type of family	Description of family
Traditional Family Types	Married couple	Two spouses; simplest family type
	Nuclear family	Two spouses and at least one child
	Extended family	Nuclear family (see above) with at least one grandparent
	Joint family	Blood relatives and their spouses and kids staying together
New Modes of Family	Blended family	Either or both partner were previously married, often with children from that previous marriage
	Single-parent family	Only one parent is present with at least one child
	Unmarried family	Couple, unmarried but living together, often with at least one child
	Communal family	A group of families of any type (not necessarily related by blood) living together and sharing responsibilities

Source: Author-generated

identified and the patterns he predicted have turned out to be correct. For example, most Canadian families today are fairly small, just as Goode said they would be. Indeed, even immigrants who come to Canada with non-nuclear, **extended families** tend to adapt to this trend and separate into nuclear units.

extended family
multiple generations of relatives living together, or several adult siblings with their spouses and children who share a dwelling and resources. More than three kinds of relationship may be present.

Additionally, as Goode might have also predicted, marriage rates have been declining in Canada and elsewhere. According to Milan and Bohnert's (2011) *Portrait of Families and Living Arrangements in Canada*, by the end of the new century's new decade the number of unmarried Canadians age 15 and over outnumbered the number of legally married people for the first time ever. Married-couple families accounted for less than 70 per cent of all census families, a significant decrease from the 83 per cent they formed only two decades ago. Indeed, just over half of the population is unmarried—that is, never married, divorced, separated, or widowed. Two decades ago, this number was only 39 per cent (Milan & Bohnert, 2011).

Another fairly recent change when it comes to marriage is the recognition of same-sex married couples. According to the 2016 Census, 0.9 per cent of all couples in Canada are same-sex, and approximately one-third of all same-sex couples in Canada are married (Statistics Canada, 2017). It may not come as a surprise that a majority of these same-sex couples choose to reside in large, metropolitan areas, where untraditional lifestyles are more widely accepted. In 2016, half of the same-sex couples within Canada lived in four of the five largest Census metropolitan areas—Toronto, Montreal, Vancouver, and Ottawa-Gatineau—despite those areas accounting for only 38 per cent of census households (Statistics Canada, 2017).

To date, 20 countries—all of them, modern industrial societies—have legalized same-sex marriages nationwide (Freedom to Marry, n.d.). The Netherlands was the first country to approve homosexual marriages in 2001, followed by Belgium in 2003, and Spain and Canada both in 2005. The United States legalized same-sex marriages in 2015, 10 years after Canada.

THE CANADIAN PRESS/Darren Calabrese

Jen Chang (left) and Inae Lee pose for photos before joining over 100 gay couples in a mass wedding during World Pride 2014 at Casa Loma in Toronto. Why do you think a disproportionately greater percentage of same-sex couples live in Canada's largest metropolitan areas?

In addition to changes regarding same-sex marriages, the number of single-parent families and cohabiting couples has also increased. As William Goode (1918–2003) might have predicted, with the decline in marriage rates over the last few decades, single-parent families have increased from 11 per cent to 16 per cent, and cohabiting couples have increased from 6 per cent to 15 per cent (Milan & Bohnert, 2011). Cohabiting couples are especially common in Quebec, where one-quarter of all common-law families in Canada live.

Families and Housework

Case study

Housework and care work have not always been solely women's responsibility. Naturally, family work, like other kinds of work, has been deeply affected by scientific and technological breakthroughs of the past century.

In the Western pre-industrial family, women were essential to economic production as well as domestic work. In Canada, for example, women's work played an important part in settlement history. Wherever they lived, in the late nineteenth and early twentieth centuries, men went out seeking work but women stayed home, acting as "community builders" and ensuring the survival of the family's farm.

Even non-farm women performed a significant economic role in household food production. The husband may have earned the wages, but female home support—wives and daughters—always made an important contribution to family finances (Armitage, 1985). And not only was the domestic work heavy in these households, it was never-ending. Nearly every chore meant building a fire and hauling water, for example.

The twentieth century saw a surge toward the industrialization of farming, through the incorporation of technology, science, and global markets into agriculture. Even today, agriculture continues to modernize, through the enlargement and intensification of farming operations (Smithers & Johnson, 2004). However, industrialization not only changed the lives of rural families; it also brought an influx of people into urban areas. With the arrival of the urban bourgeois family, people came to think of "home" as a place separate and different from "work." This led to new definitions of women as homemakers and full-time mothers, and a growing industry that catered to home efficiency.

Much of the change in family roles that we associate with present-day life can be traced to the rise of urban, industrial society. New "labour-saving" appliances—the electric iron and the vacuum cleaner, for example—eased women's entry into paid work by making traditional housework less time-consuming. By the 1920s, the urban middle-class had access to many household conveniences that are familiar to us today: hot and cold running water, gas stoves, washing machines, refrigerators, and vacuum cleaners, for example (Mintz, 2006). As mass-produced clothing became available and desirable, fewer women were obliged to sew clothing for their family members. Home sewing moved beyond its purely functional role to become a way of expressing personal tastes (Gordon, 2004).

Ironically, the spread of new household technology did not dramatically reduce the time women spent on housework, even as increased numbers of married women took paid work outside the home (Strasser, 1982). Women were told that high standards of cleanliness would promote health and children's well-being. Concerns about home hygiene and children's health led mothers to assume responsibility for cleaning as part of their duty of health promotion (Fox, 1990).

Increasingly, with the spread of new technology, women were called on to learn and practice home economics—a form of education that many viewed as preparation for social reform (Apple & Coleman, 2003). Women's institutes tried to redefine domestic labour as skilled labour, giving women more status (Morgan, 1996). Indeed, some home economists worked to raise the status of homemakers by promoting the idea that new home technologies needed *skilled* operators.

Time to reflect

How would you explain the fact that, although mechanization of housework reduced the drudgery of many tasks performed in earlier centuries, it did not increase women's leisure time?

It was belatedly in 1974 that British sociologist Ann Oakley published the first truly sociological study on this topic, *The Sociology of Housework*. This classic work drew needed attention to domestic inequality and its relation to other forms of gender inequality. Since men rarely did housework, early sociologists and economists (almost exclusively male) had failed to consider it an important topic and, given its unpaid status, ignored its contribution to the economy. Oakley changed all that.

Oakley based her housework research on a small sample of British working- and middle-class homemakers. Social class, in her sample, made little difference: both classes of women reported similar (negative) attitudes about housework and a similar (high degree of) identification with their homemaker role. All the women in Oakley's sample viewed housework as unpleasant. Despite this dislike, many of the informants viewed the role of homemaker as central to their identity; they felt mainly responsible for tending to the home and children. For this reason, most of these women swallowed their dissatisfaction with the monotony, isolation, and low social status that it provided them. They took it for granted as unavoidable.

Oakley concluded that women are disempowered and imprisoned by their beliefs about the proper role of women, especially, of mothers, in a present-day society. Despite their unhappiness, many housewives feel obliged by their culture to play a basically alienating and frustrating role. They have been socialized by a patriarchal gender ideology into accepting domestic slavery as the natural order of things.

Today, women continue to do more housework than men. However, men are more likely than in the past to see housework as part of their own duties, even when part of a heterosexual couple. In fact, in every country of the world, women do most of the housework. In none of the 20 countries Hook (2006) surveyed did the unpaid work by married men exceed 37 per cent of the domestic total. Because women have the primary responsibility for doing domestic work, many are undertaking a "double day" within a "double ghetto" (Armstrong & Armstrong, 1993) when they enter the labour force—especially if they are mothers. See Chapter 7 for more on the concept of the second shift.

Men contribute to domestic work too, but their contribution is most notably on household maintenance and repairs. Often, they spend less time overall on these kinds of tasks than women spend on day-to-day housework and child care. As well, men can often postpone these sorts of household tasks until time allows: there is no urgency around trimming the hedge or repairing a lamp, for example. This means that men's work at home is less constraining than women's, which often must be done every single day (for example, meal preparation and bathing the children).

TABLE 10.3 The Domestic Division of Labour: Canada, 2010

Working arrangement		Average number of hours per week spent on domestic tasks	
		Women	Men
Respondent was working	Dual earner couples; respondent working full-time	13.9	8.6
	Dual earner couples; respondent working part-time	21.0	11.8
	Single earner couples; respondent working	15.2	8.8
	Singles, respondent working	7.7	6.1
Respondent was not working	Single earner couples; respondent not working	23.4	14.6
	Couples; neither partner working	17.3	10.6
	Singles; respondent not working	10.0	6.3
All Respondents		13.8	8.3

Source: Statistics Canada, General Social Survey, 2010 http://www.statcan.gc.ca/pub/89-503-x/2010001/article/11546/tbl/tbl007-eng.htm

Theory in Everyday Life

10.4 | Technology and the Time Spent on Housework

In today's society, whether or not technology actually reduces the amount of housework women do is hotly debated. On the one hand, recent technological developments—especially in information and communications technology (ICT)—can help women achieve a better work/life balance. On the other hand, studies show that women still perform most of housework, even if they are more active in the workforce (Chung, 2009). Nonetheless, developing technologies may help to further alleviate a woman's workload, thus helping to close the gender gap.

According to the 2014 OECD Better Life Index, Canadian women spend an average of 253.6 minutes each day on unpaid household labour. In contrast, Canadian men spend an average of 159.6 minutes (OECD, 2014). This trend is also reflected in the OECD average, which is based on data from 34 countries (OECD, 2011). Therefore, despite household appliance development in the twentieth century, women still tend to spend more time on housework than men. To explain this persisting trend, sociologists Kan, Sullivan, and Gershuny (2011) posit that Western society is halfway through an 80-year transformation towards an equal sharing of housework (see also Sullivan, 2011).

The role of technology in women's emancipation from unequal housework is significant and should not be dismissed. So, we should look to developing technologies that can further empower women. Here, ICT can play an important role. First, ICT can help women reduce the amount of work they do through more efficient multi-tasking. Innovative mobile applications allow women to perform everyday tasks, such as paying bills, ordering groceries, and organizing their schedules, from their phones.

Second, with the rise of ICT and today's sharing economy, women can increase their peer-to-peer commodity services. For example, TaskRabbit is an online marketplace that allows users to outsource tasks, such as household errands (Raphel, 2014). Thus, women can tackle their to-do list by delegating chores to users willing to work for a fee. This proliferation of peer-to-peer online marketplaces provides a platform for women to gain autonomy. For example, Etsy.com allows users to sell handmade goods. In 2015, 86 per cent of Etsy sellers were women (US Securities and Exchange Commission, 2015). Another potential source of income is creating lifestyle websites; for some women, blogging constitutes a full-time job. Indeed, women can increase their economic self-sufficiency by connecting to an online community.

Finally, ICT allows women to craft an online space for themselves. Social media platforms such as blogs, YouTube, and Facebook give women a platform to voice their experiences, become leaders, and work towards changing the gendered landscape.

As we've seen, technology can both reinforce and disrupt gender roles. If equality is our goal, technology can help to reduce gender disparities. However, as long as women are socialized to care more about the home than men, gender equality will prove elusive. For this reason, developing effective social policy, further developing technology, and involving more women in technological development will help to bridge the gender gap (Knight, 2015; Faisal, 2012; CATA, 2010).

Families and Health

Families provide us with practical and emotional support, and this is especially important when we are ill or infirm. Take marriage itself. Research has shown that marriage is a health-enhancing institution—especially for men—and the social integration associated with it is good for people's health. Generally, family members tend to provide the support that is extremely important for patients' recovery. However, when caregivers work very hard to take care of and support ill family members, the care work itself can have harmful effects on their lives.

After all, family caregivers have to provide practical (instrumental) and emotional help of varied kinds, depending on the illness or disability. Doing so will often use up much leisure time and may eat into hours otherwise used for paid work or sleep. The costs of care may include foregone income, the price of various medicines and treatments, and the cost of hiring people to do household jobs (e.g., cooking, cleaning, shopping, babysitting) that previously were done by the primary caregiver.

Typically, these primary caregivers are women—wives, mothers, and daughters. The research reports a high frequency of depression and burnout among such women, which can have an extremely negative impact on the dynamics of the entire family.

Time to reflect

Does your family have a primary caregiver? Is this caregiver a woman? Does this caregiver get taken for granted (for example, when this person steps up to help family members say something like "oh, that's just how she is"), or is the caregiving role understood by family members to be one that this person takes on by choice and at personal cost?

Many think that technological developments over the past 30 years, such as the internet, have had a positive impact on family health and well-being. Indeed, there is much evidence that, in recent years, family care work has been improved and facilitated by the growth of the internet. The internet is a storehouse of useful information for people facing health challenges. Increasingly, people look to the internet for answers to questions about health.

Due to its ability to connect individuals and disseminate information, the internet also has a role to play in family therapy, especially in treating families that are isolated or whose members are geographically separated. Use of communication technologies allows distant family members to keep in touch with one another, and computer monitoring allows older adults in need of care to live by themselves—a preference of an increasing number of people of all ages (Klinenberg, 2012).

Further, changes in technology that simplify contact among family and friends are likely to contribute to the quality and cohesion of relationships. Present-day technology has made contact less expensive, faster, and easier. As email and internet use spreads, geographic constraints on social relationships continue to lessen (De Souza e Silva & Frith, 2010). Indeed, the spread of easy communication shrinks distances, and we can expect this shrinking of distances to continue, allowing family members at great distances to remain close.

In Pictures Ltd./Corbis via Getty Images

More and more people are dealing with distance and separation by means of Skype and related computer-mediated communication technologies.

The internet can also be a source of help for caregivers and others in need of support. Online chat groups eliminate time and distance barriers and limits on group size; they increase variety and diversity of support, anonymity, pre- and post-group support, opportunity for expression through written communication, and potential training experiences for group leaders (Finn, 1995). More recently, another study evaluated the efficacy of a multimedia support program delivered over the internet to employed family caregivers of persons with dementia. It found that 30 days post-exposure, participants held more positive views about caregiving (Beauchamp, Irvine, Seeley, & Johnson, 2005). The caregivers also showed significant improvements in depression, anxiety, and the level and frequency of stress and caregiver strain.

However, many are also quick to point out the negatives of this new technology. The first and perhaps most obvious downside to the internet and new communication technologies is the fact that, as in the physical world, the virtual world is full of predators, lying in wait to take advantage of unsuspecting internet users. In the virtual world of cyberspace, however, there is a lack of clear and accountable leadership and so there are many opportunities for damaging, destructive interactions (Finn, 1995; Finn & Lavitt, 1994). For example, cyberbullying, cyberstalking, and exploitation (sexual and/or monetary) are just a few of the many types of dangers with forms unique to the virtual world (Kowalski, Limber, Limber, & Agatson, 2012). Misinformation can also be dangerous when it comes to information about one's health.

Families and Socialization

The prevalence of social media has helped to create a generation divide since it has changed the development of young people, who are now growing up in an age of constant connection and communication. The technical skill gap between parents and youth serves to create a disconnect in how they participate online together—indeed, in how they communicate more generally—and this has caused concerns about how the internet is affecting children's socialization and development (O'Keeffe & Clarke-Pearson, 2011).

Parents who find it hard to navigate the web may find themselves excluded from a large portion of the socialization of their children. Moreover, parents may not be able to influence their children to the same degree that online peers or other virtual influences can. There are, however, ways in which parents can try to retain control over their children's internet usage. Time-limiting, filtering and blocking, outgoing content blocking, and monitoring tools are just a few examples of the kinds of strategies parents can use. Time-limiting software allows parents to set limits on how much time a child can use the computer, while filtering and blocking software limits the content that children can access. Outgoing content blocking regulates content leaving the computer to ensure that children do not reveal personal information, and there are also monitoring tools that record addresses of the sites that children visit.

Although these types of software can be effective at blocking sites, not all parents use them. The generation gap contributes to this, since many parents are not tech savvy. Additionally, social media presents youths with positive opportunities for community engagement, enhancement of individual creativity, growth of ideas, and fostering individual identity. In fact, the internet provides the potential for enhanced learning opportunities by allowing children to connect with peers outside of class and find more information quickly. It also allows children to access information anonymously. This way, youths can learn about concerns such as sexually transmitted diseases, depression, and any other health worries they might have—topics they may have felt uncomfortable broaching with their parents.

Some sociologists will say that technologies have not transformed our relations, but only the ways we conduct them. For example, we use new technologies because social life in families has changed so much that, for many, direct communication is not as possible as it once was. Thus, the technological boom itself is created more by the demands of a changing society than by any inherent aspect of the technologies themselves (Brown & Lauder, 2001). Indeed, sociological research finds that technologies and social changes—in gender, for example—are mutually reinforcing (Wajcman, 2010).

If new communication technologies are a response to social needs brought about by changes in families themselves, then it is obvious how these technologies can be seen as not only beneficial but necessary for the present-day family's survival and well-being.

While some fear that online forms of communication are inferior to old-fashioned face-to-face interactions, there are arguments to be made on the other side. Until recently, most social theory assumed that people would form and preserve close relationships mainly through face-to-face interaction (Adams & Alla, 1998; Farrell, VandeVusse, & Ocobock, 2012). Psychologists who studied interpersonal attraction, for example, focused on the importance of visual cues: how physical appearance plays a role in attraction, what gestures and facial expressions people use to show involvement, etc. (see Short, Williams, & Christie, 1976).

In the internet age, however, we need a new inventory of the ways people signal their characteristics, preferences, and qualities. So much of the internet experience is now visual—Skype, uploading photos and videos, video chats—that it enables families and friends to interact in real time (or nearly) as if they were in the same room. Through use of these technologies, members of the "millennial generation" actually report feeling closer during adolescence to their parents than previous generations (Pew Research Center, 2010). This, however, is of course true only in those families where all members are technologically savvy.

Today, any discussion of family relations must consider *virtual communities*, especially close relations that exist in the internet. These relations are characterized by rare face-to-face contact and regular electronic contact. Because of the country's vast geography, Canada's researchers have often been at the forefront of theorizing about long-distance communication technologies. As a nation of vast distances and sparse population, Canada has always relied on transport and communication technology to make social organization possible. Contributing to these networks of communication is the fact that Canada is an immigrant society. Many immigrants retain active connections with relatives and friends in their homelands and in other parts of the world through communication technologies. As such, Canada has been a "connected" nation for many years, with usage rates of basic telephone, internet, and cable services among the highest in the world.

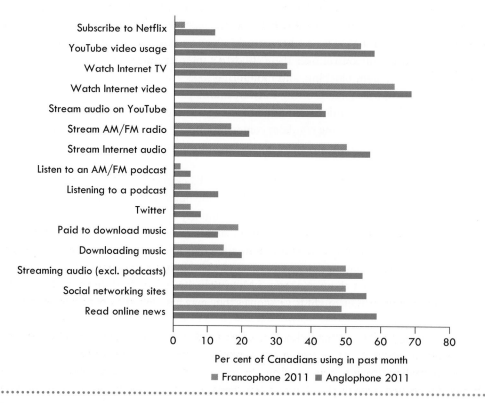

FIGURE 10.1 Popular Internet Activities for Canadian Internet Users, Age 18 and Over

Source: Accessed at http://www.crtc.gc.ca/eng/publications/reports/PolicyMonitoring/2012/cmr4.htm#f455

As a result, ever-speedier delivery of information, goods, and services has become a social fixation. Smart phones, tablets, and laptops connect ever more people, making them continuously available. Since 1999 Canadians have seen an increase from 11.1 per cent to 87 per cent in home internet access, according to the *CIRA Fact Book* (2014). Some propose that this electronic connectedness makes surveillance, censorship, and information management possible on a scale never before imagined. Others, however, propose that connectedness weakens elite control over information and enables ordinary people to air their political, social, and cultural views more freely.

With everything that has been said, the question still remains: What is the overall effect of internet and social media on family relations? On the one hand, the new connectivity may intrude on family life, disturbing family rituals and cohesion. Early research highlighted the tendency of ICT to isolate family members from one another in individual activities, and even produce addictive behaviour. For instance, Nie and Hillygus (2002) found that frequent internet use is associated with less time spent with family and friends, and on social activities in general, as well as increased depression and loneliness. There is also the concern that online communications will replace face-to-face interactions though the former is an inferior method to the latter.

On the other hand, as was mentioned earlier, the internet does provide many positive opportunities for building networks, creating support groups, staying in touch with distant relations, and accessing important information. Moreover, even if one maintains that face-to-face interactions are superior to online ones, there is reason to believe that online communications will not completely replace face-to-face interactions, but will merely add to the variety of communication methods available.

Haythornthwaite, Kazmer, Robins, and Showmaker (2000), for example, have shown that among strongly tied (that is, closely connected) people, easy, cheap technologies such as email or Skype do not replace traditional communication means such as face-to-face meetings or telephone calls. Weakly tied communicators tend not to take advantage of new forms of technology; they rely on one medium and are less motivated to explore new technologies. Accordingly, their relationships remain distant. By contrast, closely related communicators use new as well as old technologies and communicate often.

More frequent and more varied communications serve to strengthen already strong relationships, and so this study seems to suggest that new technologies actually encourage and strengthen interpersonal relationships. Thus, while there are definite cons to the new forms of communication technology that are now available, there are some extremely positive effects as well. Only time will tell whether the effects of new ICTs on families are, overall, for the better or for the worse.

Dashboard

Interactive activity

Digital Divide

10.5 | Can Older Parents Connect with Cyber-Obsessed Kids?

New forms of technology have created new forms of communication. Emojis, memes, and social media platforms provide people with many new ways to express their emotions and vent their frustrations (Johnson, 2014). While this kind of communication allows friends and family to stay in touch over long distances, researchers worry that ICTs are also weakening traditional family bonds (Johnson, 2014).

Cyber-obsessed youths spend a great deal of time online or texting friends, causing them to miss out on family time or skip family activities. For this reason, many parents are finding it harder to connect with their children (Lehman, n.d.). The problem is even worse when children interacting mainly via text and email fail to learn how to communicate verbally or connect emotionally, resulting in a serious lack of emotional intelligence (Johnson, 2014). This shortcoming make it hard for people from older generations (such as parents) to get through to them.

More generally, parents may fail to understand the importance of social media to their child, especially when the social media carry the opinions of peers (Stanescu, 2013).

Continued

This failure may keep parents from fully understanding their child's perspective and from bonding with him or her. Moreover, older parents may see the internet and smart phones as potentially dangerous, since there are so many online predators and inappropriate websites. Some parents may deal with this by installing internet blocks, setting limits on their child's texting or cellphone activities, or tracking their child's online activities. This effort may prove ineffective, however, and may alienate children who want to be more independent (Stanescu, 2013; Lehman, n.d.).

Finally, parents find it hard to connect with their children because of age and generational differences. Forms of communication have changed so much that children may actually be wired to communicate differently than their parents. According to parenting expert and pediatric nurse Denise Daniels, technology can actually "rewrite a child's brain pathways" so that the child develops differently than he or she would normally (Johnson, 2014). The words "I love you" in a text message and the image of a person on a cold, hard computer screen may not convey the same warmth to a parent as to a child, nor as much warmth as a human voice or hug. For this reason, children who spend most of their time interacting with a screen can develop different neural pathways and may end up losing empathy or failing to form deep personal bonds.

Traditionally, face-to-face interactions have been the cornerstones upon which family relationships were built, and some think that replacing them with tech-based interactions may destroy the very foundation of family life. The best way to prevent this from happening may be to use technology only when necessary (i.e., for long-distance communication) but to limit the use of technology so that it does not become the sole method of family communication (Johnson, 2014).

Time to reflect

Can you imagine a time or set of circumstances under which close, long-term relationships between people will be maintained wholly through social media, Skype, or other online technologies? What hypotheses might you draw about the effect this could have on a family?

Families and Work

We have devoted an entire chapter of this book to work and the economy and the ways in which each have changed in the twenty-first century (see Chapter 12). Thus, in this section, we will only briefly discuss some changes that technology has brought about in the workplace and we will focus instead on the impact these work-related changes have had on families.

Information technologies—especially smart phones, social media, tablets, and email—have already changed, and will continue to change, families and family lives. Individuals are now constantly accessible and can take their work with them wherever they go. While this is positive for those wishing to stay in contact or continue unfinished work projects, it can be very stressful for workers who find themselves forced to be on call 24 hours a day.

Indeed, with the rise of information and communications technologies over the past few decades, the conditions under which one can perform paid work have rapidly changed. The internet and email provide workers access to colleagues and work-related information even from home, allowing them to do work while not physically located in the office (i.e., telecommuting).

telecommuting
a work arrangement in which employees do not commute to a central place of work but instead often work at home.

Telecommuting can create a sense of gratification, both professionally and personally, and give individuals a better sense of control with greater levels of autonomy and power as they determine their boundaries. It can, however, also be very challenging to manage to care for families and work in the same space at the same time: "Teleworkers use various cues and rituals to segment their work and home roles and to manage the tension between the flexibility afforded by the telework arrangement and the need to maintain structure in order to accomplish tasks, protect role responsibilities and aid transitions between role domains" (Fonner & Stache, 2012, p. 255). These boundaries do not police themselves, and some people find their lives become more conflictual and stressed as a result of working from home.

Beyond telecommuting, video conferencing allows colleagues to engage with one another in a personal and direct manner despite being far apart. And, finally, cloud-based file sharing tools such

Zivica Kerkez/Shutterstock.com

Have you telecommuted by taking a course online? Are you taking this course online? Do you find it convenient or overwhelming?

as Google Drive and Dropbox make it easier to share documents among team members, thereby encouraging collaboration. These tools also provide remote access to files, which makes it possible to work while out of the office.

On the other hand, many workers have reported experiencing "technology overload," defined as "the point in which a marginal addition of new technology reaches the point of diminishing marginal returns" (Karr-Wisniewski & Lu, 2010, p. 1061), which in turn has been linked to various negative outcomes, such as increased stress, lower productivity, and exhaustion (Harris, Harris, Carlson, & Carlson, 2015).

In fact, in a review of literature on the sociological effects of ICT, Chesley and Johnson (2014) note that that there has been a fair amount of research linking ICT use to more demanding work environments. "There is evidence that ICT use is responsible for 'extending' the work day as many workers report working outside of regular business hours or working more hours as a result of ICT," they say, citing research by Towers, Duxbury, Higgins, and Thomas (2006), and Madden and Jones (2008).

These changes in the workplace, which have been brought about by new communication technologies, seem to threaten the average worker's home and family life. Indeed, many sociologists today are concerned that the line between work and home is becoming increasingly blurred as a result of technological progress. Sociological studies seem to indicate that information and communication technologies have indeed resulted in a more permeable work/home boundary (see, e.g., Gant & Kiesler, 2002; Olson-Buchanan & Boswell, 2006; Nippert-Eng, 2008; Desrochers & Sargent, 2004).

One such study, by Chesley (2005), found a link between persistent communications technology use (e.g., cellphones) among working people and increased distress, decreased family satisfaction, and increased negative work-to-family or family-to-work spillover. Chesley (2005) suggests that her findings underscore the idea that more permeable work/family boundaries appear to favour negative, rather than positive, spillover and are correlated with negative consequences for working people.

Many sociologists fear that ICT is dissolving the boundary between work and home and increasing work/family conflict. Work/family conflict has been linked to various negative outcomes, including increased absenteeism, decreased job satisfaction and performance, and poorer health (Harris et al., 2015). If ICT use does contribute to work/family conflict, this could have extremely negative effects on families and on their members.

While a few studies have explored this issue, the results have been mixed. Wajcman, Bittman, and Brown (2008) found no significant correlation between mobile phone use and negative work/family spillover, while a study conducted by Harris et al. (2015) concluded that technology overload is positively correlated with work/family conflict. Indeed, these researchers found that "as employees experience technology overload, they are likely to have some aspects (e.g., increased communication opportunities 'after-hours' or receiving greater quantities of information to process or think about) of the overload impact their non-work lives" (Harris et al., 2015, p. 415).

Thus, ICT does offer certain benefits for family life, such as allowing family members to stay connected to each other, even when spatially separated; however, it also brings up some potential problems. By allowing people to stay constantly connected to their work no matter where they are or what they are doing, people may find themselves unable to relax, overworked, and disconnected from their families. More empirical evidence, however, must be gathered to determine how much of a threat ICT really poses for family-life (Chesley & Johnson, 2010; also, Chesley, 2014).

Conclusions

It seems that despite the many ways in which families have changed, the institution of the family is likely to continue in quite recognizable ways. Some of the changes we discussed in this chapter included new communication technologies, virtual communities, and the changing role of families in our now "connected society." We noted that new technologies increase the reach of family life, instead of limiting it, as critics had feared. Indeed, we discussed the role of caregivers in families and the ways in which the internet has actually helped give these hardworking individuals additional support and empowering health-related information so that they can provide better care and relieve their own stress. We also noted, at the beginning of the chapter, that the influence of political action, such as the residential school system and the Sixties Scoop, can have lingering and detrimental effects to an entire culture. When the family is under attack, as one of the core means of socialization, an entire culture can be threatened and put at risk of extinction.

The most dramatic future changes to family life are extensions of a change that has been in process for centuries: the individualization of family life. More families are rethinking spousal and parental roles and shifting away from uniform cookie-cutter family structures to a wide variety of non-traditional family structures.

What is important to take away from this chapter is that, as with all aspects of society, even institutions as ancient and traditional as the family can be affected and changed by new science and technology, and by political action. The job of sociologists is to try to understand the ways in which these factors interact, and then make predictions about the future so that we can better prepare ourselves and ensure that society and its institutions are heading in a positive direction.

Questions for Critical Thought

1. Canadian families have become much more diverse in the last few decades. What is the significance of this increased diversity? Do you think new forms of science and technology have contributed to this trend and, if so, how?

2. Traditionally, the family was the place where the socialization of children occurred, and parents controlled the upbringing and values of their offspring. With the rise of the internet, however, children are increasingly being socialized by online peers and are being exposed to

the value systems of many different communities. Do you feel that this change is positive or negative? Explain.

3. What is the key difference between the functionalist and symbolic interactionist perspective on socialization? Do you think that the function of families today is still to socialize children? Why or why not? And how, if at all, do you think that science and technology have changed the function of families in society?

4. In this chapter, we discussed the ongoing debate about whether new science and technologies are uniting or dividing families. What do you think based on your own experience? Does technology unite or divide family members? Can you think of more ways (other than those mentioned in this chapter) in which science and technology can be used to unite families?

5. Considering the invention and diffusion of the home telephone a century ago, do you think that better communication technology makes family members more or less social with one another? What about the more recent invention of the cellphone? What about the internet?

Take it Further: Recommended Readings

Patrizia Albanese, *Children in Canada Today*, 2nd ed. (Toronto: Oxford University Press, 2015). Albanese explores themes of childhood socialization, such as socializing agents and their impact, changes in social policy, and the relation of socialization to family and social problems.

Maureen Baker, *Choices and Constraints in Family Life*, 3rd ed. (Toronto: Oxford University Press, 2014). In this book, the author examines families within a historical and cross-cultural context, including economics, social policies, technology, educational opportunities, and so on. All of these must be examined to understand the changing nature of Canadian families.

Reginald W. Bibby, *Canada's Teens: Today, Yesterday, and Tomorrow* (Toronto: Stoddart, 2001). This book historically explores the experiences of adolescents around topics such as violence, sex, and drugs in relation to teenager beliefs, values, worries, and enjoyments.

Susan A. McDaniel and Lorne Tepperman, *Close Relations: An Introduction to the Sociology of Families*, 4th ed. (Scarborough, ON: Pearson Educational, 2014). This is a Canadian overview of research and social theories about family life, examining topics such as the history of Canadian families, intimate relationships, parenting, stress and violence in the family context, and the future of families.

Take it Further: Recommended Online Resources

Vanier Institute of the Family
www.vanierinstitute.ca/

The National Longitudinal Survey of Children and Youth
www.statcan.gc.ca/imdb-bmdi/4450-eng.htm

Today's Parent
www.todaysparent.com

Canadian Child Care Federation
www.cccf-fcsge.ca

Childcare Research and Resource Unit
www.childcarecanada.org

CBC DocZone, *Angry Parents and Stressed Out Kids* [video]
www.cbc.ca/doczone/episodes/angry-kids-stressed-out-parents

More resources available on  Dashboard

11 Experiences in Schools and Formal Education

◀ Neil Webb/Getty Images

Introduction

Consider one scenario: imagine your name is Joe; you are a young man from a small town in Province X; and you want to get an engineering degree at the nearby University of Y. How much will that cost, and how will you pay it off? Using a "University Cost Calculator" on the website "Get Smarter about Money," Joe learns that the cost of a four-year engineering degree at the University of Y (where tuition is $12,390 per year), plus living expenses for four years, will cost at least $29,000 a year, for a total cost of $116,000 upon graduation.

Now, many students are lucky enough to get financial support from their family; others have saved up some money; and a lucky few may even receive a scholarship or bursary. But suppose that Joe, from a poor family with several other children competing for funds, has none of those resources at his disposal. He will have to work his way through engineering school. But without special job skills or connections, he may have to take a minimum wage job flipping burgers or doing yard work.

Of course, the specific figures will vary from one province to another. But imagine the minimum wage is $11.25 per hour. At this rate, Joe will have to work 10,313 hours to finish his degree out of debt. Now, a 40-hour a week (full-time) job for a year only amounts to a little over 2,000 hours. So even if Joe worked full time for 108 weeks of his 4-year course, he would still be short 2,000 hours worth of money, or roughly $22,000 in debt. And of course, if he worked full time, he would have trouble finding the time to attend classes and do his homework, let alone time for recreation or rest. So, obviously, Joe is going to have to come at the problem a different way.

One alternative is to give up the idea of post-secondary education altogether. Another alternative is to take a two-year community college degree program and look for a better-paying

Sam Dao/Alamy Stock Photo

We like to imagine that schools are places where idealistic and dedicated teachers challenge and nurture young minds.

job; alternatively, he could work for a few years and save as much money as possible before going to university. Still another alternative is to enter a cheaper university program: for example, he might enroll in an undergraduate mathematics or science degree program, rather than a professional engineering program.

But what most students like Joe do, after considering and trying some of these alternatives, is to take a student loan, with the result that, when they graduate, they are tens or hundreds of thousands of dollars in debt. Paying off this student loan, even at a low rate of interest, may take decades. How long it takes Joe will depend on the kind of job he gets after graduating and the amount he is able to put aside after paying taxes, his rent or the mortgage, expenses associated with raising children (if he has any), and everyday living expenses like food, clothes, and gas for the car. Is higher education really worth all this trouble and expense?

Most researchers would say, "Yes, it is." Higher education has proven to be one of the most reliable means of doing well socially and economically (on this, see Pfeffer & Hertel, 2015; Corak, 2013; Blanden, Gregg, & Machin, 2005.) It provides students with the knowledge and educational qualifications they need to gain and keep paid employment. Besides this, **education** provides a kind of pre-job socialization. **Formal education** generally instils concepts such as tolerance, teamwork, and leadership in students. In turn, these ideas help students integrate into the workforce—even, become responsible citizens. Such learning benefits both students and society as a whole. Education also increases people's ability to understand current events and public debates. In the past, education was a privilege reserved only for the wealthy. Today, education—primary and secondary—is considered the right of every child.

This belief is clearly expressed in the United Nations' Millennium Development Goals, which include ensuring children across the globe are able to gain a primary school education (UN, 2009). And increasingly, people are becoming aware that you really need a post-secondary education to understand the world we live in. But, in most of Canada post-secondary education is not yet considered a right, with the result that most students still have to pay tuition. In February 2016 Ontario announced a new plan that will go a long way to solving this problem for its lowest-income residents. As reported in the *Toronto Star*, "the Ontario Student Grant . . . would entirely pay for average college or university tuition for students from families with incomes of $50,000 or less. Half of students from families with incomes of less than $83,000 will qualify for nonrepayable grants for tuition and no student would receive less than they can currently get" (Rushowy, 2016).

However, that is just one province, and even within Ontario, many students (and their families) will have a hard paying all the education-related bills. It is important that we make education more accessible for everyone, because increasingly, people need more education than ever to earn a living in our "information society." As well, unequal access to education has the effect of ensuring that children in high-income families will have more access to better jobs and better incomes than children in low-income families, through their access to higher education. Accordingly, sociologists who study education are interested in questions such as, what are the consequences of education for society? How does schooling influence social relationships between people? What types of inequalities does education create and what kinds, if any, does it eliminate? We will explore these ideas in this chapter.

education a process designed to develop one's capacity for critical thinking, self-understanding, and self-reliance.

formal education education received in accredited schools during formal teaching sessions.

Dashboard

Interactive activity

Time to reflect

Research in Canada has shown that students from families with a household higher income are more likely to attend college or university than students from poorer families. Based on what you've learned so far, do you think this difference would disappear if post-secondary education were made cost-free to all interested students?

Theoretical Perspectives on Education
Conflict Theory

Conflict theorists often focus on the latent functions (see Chapter 1) of education. They have studied the role of schools in keeping young people occupied, especially during times of high unemployment. That is, schools keep young people "off the streets." More, they have studied the *hidden curriculum* in schools that teaches students their "proper" place in society according to their gender and their social class. Some have even proposed that the routine subordination and boredom students suffer in school is good preparation for the routine subordination and boredom they will have to endure at work.

According to conflict theory, the most important (and least discussed) job of schools is to teach students obedience—the essential qualification for most work in our society. As well, schools teach students to hold themselves responsible for success and failure. People who are successful economically are deemed to have deserved success, while people who are not successful are deemed to have deserved failure. This so-called **meritocratic ethic**—the notion that merit rules in our society—suits a free-market capitalist society very well.

Conflict theorists also note that students' experiences of formal education differ according to their socioeconomic class. Schools in poor neighbourhoods are less likely to have an ample supply of computers, laboratories, audio-visual equipment, library books, school supplies, or even teachers. Thus, students from poorer families are likely to have a less well-resourced education than students from wealthier families, as the story in Box 11.1 illustrates.

meritocracy (meritocratic ethic) any system of rule or advancement where the rewards are strictly proportioned to accomplishment, and all people have the same opportunity to win these rewards.

Spotlight On

11.1 | Fundraising and Social Inequality

Fundraising in schools is creating a funding gap between public schools, preserving the already-existing inequalities between children from different class backgrounds. Thanks to pizza lunches and bake sales, schools within a few kilometres of each other may have a funding disparity of over half a million dollars.

A report called *Mind the Gap: Inequality in Ontario Schools* (People for Education, 2013) notes that across Ontario, the top 10 per cent of fundraising schools raise as much as the bottom 75 per cent of fundraising schools combined. This can amount to a difference of hundreds of thousands of dollars between two schools in the same school district.

A 2017 newspaper article titled "Funding Disparities in the Classroom" quotes Chris Ellis, who sits on four Ottawa school councils, as saying that some schools "are dealing with communities that don't have the capacity to raise funds, which is the irony of it, the schools that are most challenged—and you could arguably say have the greatest need for additional resources——are the very schools that find it hard to raise funds." Schools in poorer neighbourhoods need extra funds to supply the school with educational basics, such as books, air conditioning, and breakfast programs. By contrast, schools in wealthier areas may use the funds they raise to buy computers, fund field trips, and offer music and art classes.

As noted, local fundraising increases the inequality between schools, but it also takes the burden off of governments to ensure that schools are receiving the funds they need ("Disparity," 2012). What to do about the inequality fundraising produces? Some say the solution is as simple as banning fundraising altogether. But others would say the schools can't do without the money they raise. Do you see a solution to the problem?

Feminist Approaches

Throughout much of this chapter, we will look at how social class, wealth, and race influence the way students experience formal education. However, as we noted in Chapter 4, on socialization, students' gender also plays a role in how and what they learn in school. In this respect, feminists note that schools socialize boys and girls differently, teaching them to play, dress, behave, and even think in certain ways that have been deemed "appropriate" for their gender. As a result, schools help to establish the different responsibilities and privileges that these children will eventually grow up to enjoy as women and men.

The feminist approach suggests that school-aged children are encouraged to take interest in certain academic subjects depending on their gender. Research supports this suggestion, finding that young girls are often just as interested in science and math as boys are, but that they become much less inclined towards these subjects in high school. Largely, these acquired differences reflect social influences: parents giving their sons more science-related toys, for example, or peers questioning girls' enthusiasm for math, or science teachers providing more encouragement for male students who show an interest in science, technology, engineering, and mathematics (STEM) topics.

These gendered differences are important because they influence the lines of work that children eventually choose to go into as adults. As we saw in Chapter 7, on gender, this means that men will continue to pursue careers in fields such as computer sciences and engineering, while women will continue to choose areas such as social work and teaching. So, because it currently perpetuates gendered stereotypes, the school system ensures that men will continue to do what is traditionally seen as "men's work," while women will do "women's work."

Functionalism

Most functionalists focus on the manifest functions (or intended goals) of education, which are to provide children with basic skills in literacy and numeracy. At the post-secondary level, the liberal arts curriculum supposedly prepares people to be informed citizens, by teaching critical thinking skills (also, literacy and numeracy). The other types of post-secondary education, which are more job-related, supposedly prepare people to be valuable members of the workforce. To a large degree, functionalists are interested in the role of formal education in producing "human capital."

Human capital theory proposes that wage differences in a society reflect differences in the value different workers bring to a job, in terms of skill, education, and work experience. Thus, other things being equal, personal incomes will vary according to the amount of time and effort a person has invested in education and **training**. According to this theory, widespread investment in human capital is a critical basis for the economic growth of a society. Human capital theory, therefore, would suggest that a relative lack of education, qualifications, and/or job experience is the reason that Indigenous people, for example, are underemployed and earn less. Functionalists think that, in a modern society, human capital drives productivity and democratic thinking.

human capital theory the theory that, other things being equal, economic productivity and prosperity grow with the amount of investment in human capital—that is, the education and training undertaken by workers.

training a process designed to identify and practice specific routines that achieve desired results.

Symbolic Interactionism

The symbolic interactionist approach proposes that schools and universities build cultural capital (see Chapter 3), by means of which they preserve the status and privilege of people who are born into higher-income families. For example, schools teach students how to dress and behave in ways that are appropriate to their social roles as girls or boys, middle-class or working-class people. At the higher educational levels, especially in professional schools, schools teach people how to dress and behave for success as lawyers, doctors, accountants, business managers, and so on.

TABLE 11.1 Theoretical Approaches to Education

Theory	Main points
Conflict Theory	• School is a place where people are trained to endure the boredom and subordination of alienating work.
	• Ruling class uses the myth of upward mobility through merit to justify social inequality.
Feminist Theory	• Schools have historically treated boys and girls differently, subtly reinforcing sexism.
	• Today, girls are doing better at every level of schooling and boys are more likely to drop out prematurely.
Structural Functionalism	• The function of school is to give people the skills society needs for economic growth.
	• Schools socialize people for the work world and for citizenship.
Symbolic Interactionism	• Schools help people develop identities and learn to play social roles that they will use in adulthood.
	• Schools are as important for discouraging disadvantaged people as they are for encouraging advantaged people.
	• This was especially true of residential schooling for Indigenous students.

Source: Author-generated

The Academic Revolution

Historically, institutions of higher education were restricted to young men of wealthy or well-off families. Gradually, they opened up to women, and to children from families of more modest means. But for a long time, especially in the liberal arts colleges, they retained some feeling of being a "finishing school" for young people who were being trained to take up positions of influence in their community and society.

However, in the last 50 years, institutions of higher education—especially universities—have become more concerned with research than with undergraduate education. According to Christopher Jencks and David Riesman (1968) in their book *The Academic Revolution*, post-secondary institutions have taken on a special role in modern, post-industrial society. Colleges and universities have been transformed from cohesive, often small, and localized units into a single national system of higher education. In this system, which operates somewhat like a funnel, the top graduate institutions receive and train the best graduates of the best undergraduate colleges. In turn, the top undergraduate institutions receive and train the best graduates of the best secondary schools; and so on, down the line (to pre-kindergarten). More and more, this new kind of university has narrowly specialized curricula, a heavy research agenda, and an all-PhD faculty.

To improve their standing in the eyes of the public and the government, most universities today struggle to increase their research and research funding, decrease their undergraduate teaching, and raise their international profile. Small universities struggle to become larger ones, and polytechnics and community colleges struggle to become universities. The result is a hierarchy of research universities struggling against one another for top faculty, top students, and increased funding from government and key research agencies. The present-day research university is very much like a vast factory that produces "knowledge," in the form of courses, publications, patents, conferences, and other creditable forms of information.

Time to reflect

What are the pros and cons of admitting large numbers of international students to Canadian post-secondary educational institutions, then charging them double the tuition paid by Canadian students? Think about this in the context of Canadian-resident students, international students, Canadian institutions, and international institutions.

In this context, attracting international students is important for two main reasons. First, it helps research universities compete with one another reputationally, especially when they manage to attract top graduating students from other countries. Second, attracting international students, who typically pay higher tuition fees than local students, helps to pay the high salaries and infrastructure costs required to support high research productivity.

Think Globally

11.2 | Why Do Universities Want to Attract International Students?

TABLE 11.2 University Tuition Fees for Full-Time Canadian and Foreign Undergraduate Students (weighted averages, most recent available data, in Canadian dollars)

Field of study grouping	Canadian students (2016–2017)	Foreign students (2013–2014)
Education	$4,580	$14,600
Visual and performing arts, and communications technologies	$5,640	$17,530
Humanities	$5,482	$18,365
Social and behavioural sciences	$5,566	$18,078
Law, legal professions and studies	$11,385	$23,552
Business management and public administration	$6,776	$19,641
Physical and life sciences and technologies	$6,048	$20,039
Mathematics, computer and information sciences	$6,978	$20,699
Engineering	$7,825	$21,819
Architecture and related technologies	$6,581	$18,793
Agriculture, natural resources and conservation	$5,651	$17,558
Dentistry	$21,012	$47,621
Medicine	$13,858	$29,198
Nursing	$5,527	$16,435
Pharmacy	$9,738	$30,479
Veterinary medicine	$7,419	$51,538
Other health, parks, recreation and fitness	$6,135	$17,793

(weighted average tuition fees)

Source: Adapted from www.universitystudy.ca/plan-for-university/what-does-it-cost-to-study-in-canada/; http://www5.statcan.gc.ca/cansim/a26?lang=eng&retrLang=eng&id=4770021&&pattern=&stByVal=1&p1=1&p2=31&tabMode=dataTable&csid=

(TABLE 477-0021)

In this new higher education system, professors become more widely known to their peers through publication, conferences, and grants. Increasingly, these professors—primarily concerned with research and graduate teaching—determine the character of undergraduate education. Universities compete with one another for the best national and international students, basing admission criteria on measured ability (usually, the results of standardized testing), not local residence. In doing so, they determine the allocation of scarce and desirable elite credentials.

Many think that under this system, formal education has *mainly* become a credential machine. Unexpectedly, this **credentialism** has strengthened the link between educational and class position. In the early part of the twentieth century, primary, secondary, and even post-secondary institutions were expected to level the playing field and give everyone, whatever their social origins, a chance to move up the occupational and income ladder. Today, it is evident that children from higher income families are still more likely to get more education and a better education than children from lower income families. Indeed, research by Caro, McDonald, and Willms (2009), using data from Canada's National Longitudinal Survey on Children and Youth, suggests that the effect of socioeconomic status on education even increases as children get older.

In Canada we have seen the growth of highly resourced research universities, the gradual decline of undergraduate teaching, students competing for entry into the top educational programs, and institutions competing for the top faculty and graduate students. Amid this scramble, and because of little growth in public funding for higher education, there has been increased reliance on private endowments and increased pressure to raise tuitions. Currently in Canada, nearly half of a university's operating costs are paid by student tuitions, and the proportion has risen steadily over the past 30 years, with no sign of stopping (see Figure 11.1).

Such developments have given rise to a concern about the growing **corporatization** of the universities. By "corporatization," we mean the often gradual transformation of publically funded but independent organizations into economically dependent organizations that use corporate management techniques of administration and seek to demonstrate their profitability. Increasingly, teaching and research functions are integrated into the profit-making activities of major national and multinational corporations.

Another work that criticizes higher education is Hacker and Dreifus (2010) *Higher Education? How Colleges Are Wasting Our Money and Failing Our Kids—And What We Can Do About It*. A professor emeritus of political science at Queens College in New York, Hacker criticizes the backbreaking tuition fees at top universities, noting that tenure-track professors earn most of the money and benefits, while non-tenure-track adjuncts do most of the teaching. Unnecessarily large graduate

credentialism belief in or reliance on academic or other formal qualifications as the best measure of a person's intelligence or ability to do a particular job.

corporatization the often gradual transformation of publically funded but independent organizations into economically dependent organizations that use corporate management techniques of administration and seek to demonstrate their profitability.

Dashboard

Video: *Generation Jobless*

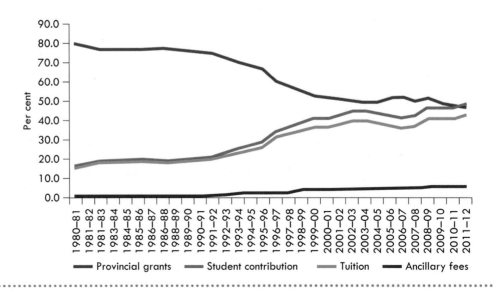

FIGURE 11.1 Student vs. Government Investment in Ontario Universities, 1980–2012

Source: www.ousa.ca/2013/06/27/weve-got-our-wires-crossed-the-slow-changing-story-of-university-operating-funding/

programs continue to pump out new PhDs who can't find suitable jobs, and the main institutional concern is with funding high-status medical, scientific, and business programs.

In short, the humanities departments are starved for funds, so they must increase class sizes, and students are accordingly denied the better learning opportunities found in small classes. Students get an education they don't need and can't use, while putting themselves in debt for the next 10 or so years. This happens because education is being commodified, like every other good and service in our society. But what does this mean?

The Commodification of Education

We need to understand the debates about the "academic revolution" and the "corporatization of education" in terms of a broader framework of commodification. When education is commodified, we lose track of the real relationship between the buyer and seller. According to Schwartzman (2013), a capitalist approach to education treats knowledge as a commodity whose value is measured by comparing the *cost* of acquiring a degree with the *earnings* the degree supposedly provides over a lifetime.

Some of this commodification comes from administrators and non-academic governing bodies who treat professors as though they need managing. Their ultimate objective is to please the consumers, also known as the students and their parents. To do so, they give priority to the most concrete, quantifiable results: degrees awarded, honours earned, jobs obtained, and so on. While university professors are encouraged to spend their time on research projects that sell, the adjuncts left teaching their classes are similarly encouraged to move more students through more quickly, using checklists and standardized measurements that can show quantifiable results. These results are used to sell the institution to customers. This approach frays the traditional fabric of education and feeds into students' desire for grade inflation and easy credentials. This is intensified by the global competition among universities around the world.

Rob Blanchard - Photo UNB

Convocation at the University of New Brunswick. Some educational administrators reimagine the "school" as a place where one comes to buy credentials in the most satisfying possible way, which (some believe) ends up producing robots on an assembly line.

Research universities are now run as corporate entities, whose main objective is to generate income to cover their costs, at the expense of education it should prioritize (Mohamedbhai, 2008). This university model is increasingly based on the "basic economic formula: get the maximum and give the minimum" (Larrasquet & Pilnière, 2012, p. 209). Yet not all learning can be assigned an economic value. An example here is writing: everyone agrees that students need to write better, which requires practice. However, writing instruction is very costly, since it takes a lot of one-on-one time. Moreover, it is hard to show how good writing translates into high incomes after graduation. Since writing quality, writing instruction, and writing evaluation cannot be easily measured, it tends to fall by the wayside.

The strongest argument against purely instrumental, job-related training is that such education has only immediate value for getting a job. It may not, however, continue to have the same value in 10, 20, or more years. Take computer training. Computer technology has changed dramatically in the last 30 or so years. Imagine getting a computer science degree in 1980; how applicable would punch card coding be to today's job market? Our point is that, if students are taught to think critically, to do research, and to ask questions, they are more likely to keep up with (and even predict or be the instigators of) technological changes in their industry of choice. If they're only taught how to use whatever is currently available, their skills could quickly become obsolete.

Much of the recent dismantling of traditional education in North America has been due to neo-liberalism, an ideology that favours reducing the role of government in overseeing and paying for public services (like education and health) and putting the cost on the individual who benefits.

On this, Henry Giroux (2002) notes, "neoliberalism is the most dangerous ideology of the current historical moment . . . Civic discourse has given way to the language of commercialization, privatization, and deregulation . . . Within the language and images of corporate culture, citizenship is portrayed as an utterly privatized affair that produces self-interested individuals" (p. 425). Giroux argues that by emphasizing market relations, individuals are discouraged from participating in the political process.

As Raewyn Connell (2013) similarly points out, ideally education is a "social process of nurturing capacities for practice" (p. 99). Under neo-liberalism, access to education has been continually and increasingly challenged, largely by increasing tuition and, thereby, making higher education harder to attain. Connell notes that capitalist societies require the creation of hierarchies, including education hierarchies. Thus, the goal of formal education is not to ensure everyone has the same education, skills, and credentials, but to ensure that everyone is tested and ranked competitively. In this context, teachers are pressed to make the curriculum narrower: to create insecurity, not intellectual enrichment. Nowhere is this professional insecurity more evident than among the ranks of contract teachers in colleges and universities.

Marta Baltodano (2012) adds that, in this context, neo-liberalism has increased the pressure to speed up teacher preparation programs, to turn out more teachers more quickly and cheaply. With the growing privatization of education (for example, charter schools and for-profit colleges and universities), there is a need for more, low-priced educators to deliver lectures on contract and to grade students in conventional and online courses. The goal, in every instance, is to increase educational profit-making through more student enrolments and lower teaching costs.

Educational Trends and Inequalities

A century ago, schools, from elementary through secondary, provided basic skills: the knowledge, discipline, and social training needed for work. Most people didn't think they needed more than that. Most young people went to work after graduating high school and, in this way, earned enough to support a family. Today, however, it is almost impossible to support a family on the income of a person with no more than high school education, thanks to the development of service industries and professions based on knowledge and specialized skills.

baby boom a period in North America (roughly, 1947 to 1967) when birth rates briefly exploded, declining just as dramatically afterward.

The education explosion was partly ignited by the **baby boom,** which occurred roughly between 1947 and 1967. A temporary marked increase (i.e., "boom") in the birth rate after the Second World War led eventually to a larger-than-average cohort of college-aged students in the 1960s and 1970s. This population growth led to a demand for more schools and more schooling. More young people then acquired higher educational credentials to differentiate themselves from competitors in the increasingly competitive job market. Gradually, people with just a high school diploma became less and less employable, as unskilled, semi-skilled, and skilled (often, unionized) manufacturing jobs were automated or left Canada for lower-wage countries.

The baby boom expansion coincided with a growing contest between the USSR and United States to achieve economic, political, and military superiority. The race to get to the moon was part of this competition, and it fuelled the spending of more and more public money on education, research, and development. The growth of research led to demands for more research scientists for government and industry, in order to develop new technology and produce more patents and copyrights.

The rush to develop new military and non-military technology, set off by the Cold War and then the Hot War (in Vietnam), was imitated in every Western country, including Canada. Fewer and fewer people dropped out of school when they reached the age of 16; more and more went on to graduate high school, then continued on to college or university.

Formal education in Canada and elsewhere correlates highly with employability, employment, and earnings level. People without a high school diploma continue to suffer much higher rates of unemployment than people with some college or a college degree, particularly during fluctuations in the economy. The higher your degree, the less precarious is your employment in relation to the job/economic market. As a result, a growing share of the population—especially, the younger half of the population—acquire a secondary or post-secondary degree, and the fraction of people without a high school diploma has continued to decline in Canada, as in other countries of the industrialized world.

Time to reflect

Did you, or anyone in your family, not obtain a high school diploma? Use your sociological imagination to connect individual circumstances to social forces that might have contributed to this person "dropping out" of school.

Data from the 2011 National Household Survey show that nearly three-quarters of the female Canadian population and two-thirds of the male Canadian population aged 25 to 44 have completed a post-secondary education, compared to under half the male Canadian population ages 65 and over (Statistics Canada, 2016).

As mentioned, more education of every kind means more likelihood of employment; and in this respect, more years of post-secondary education is better than less. As a result, people with a bachelor's degree from a university have lower rates of unemployment than people with a post-secondary diploma or certificate from a college; and people with a post-bachelor's degree do better still, with unemployment rates less than half as high as the population average (see Figure 11.2).

Of course, even with solid educational credentials, graduates suffer in periods of economic decline. When the economy is in recession, with no growth or even a decline in job numbers, the wages of entry-level workers decline and then gradually plateau at a lower-than-usual level. So even though formal education remains a good investment, it pays off most handsomely in periods of economic growth.

In recent decades, there has been a significant rise in women's educational attainment, with girls even outperforming boys at almost every educational level, including the PhD level in certain fields. Roughly 60 per cent of Canadian college students, university students, and university graduates today are women (Intini, 2013). Increasing numbers of women attend and graduate from post-secondary schools, transforming the Canadian society and economy as a consequence. The effects of education on women's lives are enormously important, but their effects are even more dramatic in less developed societies, where increases in education for women produce lower birthrates, higher economic growth, and more moderate, stable political orders. (For information on these and other social effects, see OECD, 2013; Population Reference Bureau, 2011; Kopell, 2013; and Matsui, 2013.)

Yet, despite the promising numbers of women in university, there are still stark contrasts in salary and rank between women and men once they enter the workforce. In part, this is due to a reluctance of women to enter and compete in higher-paid male venues such as jobs in STEM, as discussed in Chapter 7.

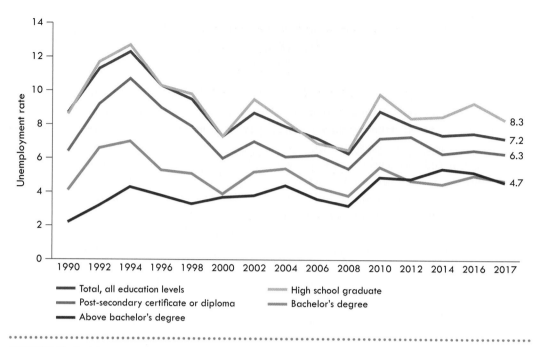

FIGURE 11.2 Educational Attainment and Unemployment Rate

Source: Adapted from CANSIM table (282-0208). Retrieved from www5.statcan.gc.ca/cansim/a47

As well, women who complete the same doctoral programs as men are likely to have careers that are less varied, shorter, and less successful (Wall, 2008). That is largely because women often have more family duties in comparison to men, which can mean the difference between a stellar career and the "mommy track" (The mommy track refers to a path that puts priority on being a mother ahead of priorities to the workplace. It can also refer to work arrangements specifically for women in the workforce, such as flextime, that facilitate motherhood.)

Are these gender disparities the fault of higher education? Some propose that "different structures of opportunities within higher education continue to perpetuate gender inequalities in the labour market" (Andres, Adamuti-Trache, Yoon, Pidgeon, & Thomsen 2007, p. 93). These structures do this in a variety of ways, most especially by steering men in certain directions and women in others, through subtle forms of encouragement and discouragement. Consider, for example, how the harassment of women students at the Dalhousie dentistry school in 2015 may have affected young women all over Canada who were considering a career in dentistry (see Task Force on Misogyny, Sexism and Homophobia, 2015). Many such male-dominated educational spaces are unwelcoming for women and are in serious need of self-evaluation, or perhaps even external control.

Like women, many racialized and ethnic groups in Canada have experienced important increases in educational attainment. In part, these increases have occurred through highly educated immigrants, and not through the advances of native-born racialized groups advancing within the educational system (Zietsma, 2007). Just like women, many racialized groups continue to face obstacles to their educational and occupational advancement. For some, these obstacles include language difficulties and shortage of money for tuition. Moreover, Canadian employers often do not accept foreign credentials and require Canadian working experience before they will hire a job candidate. This often forces educated immigrants to go back to school when they are financially unable to, or to take jobs for which they are highly overqualified.

In a perfectly equal and fair society, we would expect people with the same amount of education to have the same opportunity for good jobs and good incomes. Thus, if we were to analyze data on education and income using a technique called **multiple regression analysis**, a statistical test that shows which out of many variables is the best predictor of outcome, we would expect to find that the

multiple regression analysis a powerful statistical technique used for predicting the unknown value of a dependent variable from the known value of two or more predictor (independent) variables.

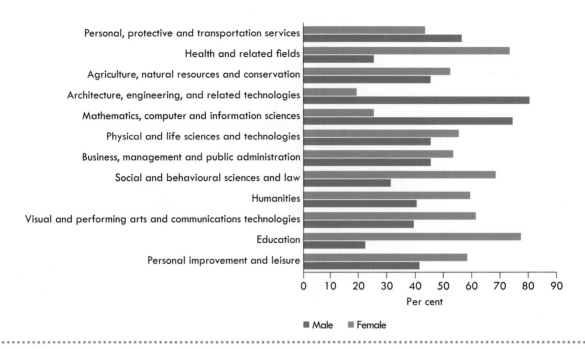

FIGURE 11.3 Gender Distribution of Programs, Canadian Colleges and Universities, 2014–2015

Source: www5.statcan.gc.ca/cansim/a47 adapted from CANSIM table (477-0019)

influence of education on occupational attainment would be very strong—close to 1.0—even if we took into account (or controlled for) other factors such as gender, ethnicity, racialized identity, birthplace, length of time spent in Canada, and so on.

However, we typically find that the measured influence of education is much less than 1.0; moreover, it varies considerably, depending on whether we are looking at men or women, white people or visible minorities, native-born people or immigrants. Typically, advantaged groups—for example, white, Canadian-born men—will gain higher benefits from (or returns on) educational attainment than less advantaged groups.

Sociologists can also use multiple regression analysis to put a direct measure on the advantage or disadvantage (i.e., "cost") of belonging to one group versus another. Peter Li (2001), re-analyzing data from the Census of Canada using regression analysis reports that, compared to the mean annual earnings of all degree holders in the workforce, visible minority men born outside Canada who immigrated at age 25 or over suffer an income penalty (or deficit) of $12,520 and visible minority women who immigrated at age 25 or over, an income penalty of $17,501.

Educational attainment is always important, but it confers the most value when it is attained in Canada. Ferrer and Riddell (2008), again using regression analysis, report that immigrants can make up the disadvantage they face on arrival in the country by getting higher education here, and the income returns to higher education are larger for immigrants than for native-born Canadians. For these reasons, immigrants are far more likely than other Canadians to push their children to get college diplomas and university degrees. In some cases, this may represent an effort to regain a socio-economic status they held in their native country and lost upon coming to Canada.

In contrast, Indigenous groups continue to be underrepresented in Canadian colleges and universities. There is a general recognition that Indigenous education is in crisis (St Germain & Dyck, 2011), with 7 out of 10 Indigenous students not graduating from high school. Less than one-half (48%) of Indigenous people had a post-secondary qualification in 2011. In contrast, almost two-thirds (65%) of the non-Indigenous population in Canada aged 25 to 64 had a post-secondary qualification in 2011, yielding a discrepancy of 17 per cent (Statistics Canada, 2015). However, the situation is improving, as shown by a comparison of generations. Figure 11.4 shows that in 2011, higher proportions of Indigenous people aged 25 to 64 had completed at least high school, compared to 2006.

Dashboard

Cash study

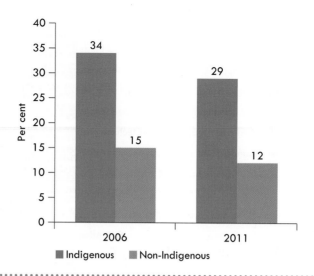

FIGURE 11.4 Per cent of Indigenous and Non-Indigenous Working Age (25–64) Population with Less than High School Educational Attainment, 2006 and 2011

Source: Author-generated from www.aadnc-aandc.gc.ca/eng/1100100016377/1100100016378 and https://www.aadnc-aandc.gc.ca/eng/1376329205785/1376329233875

A 2003 consultation with 128 witnesses and Indigenous service providers from Edmonton, Winnipeg, and Vancouver found that many obstacles to education persisted in Indigenous communities, including racism; lack of parental involvement and guidance; resentment and embarrassment caused by feeling less successful scholastically than other students; instability caused by high rates of residential mobility; feelings of isolation caused by being in environments that are not culturally sensitive; an inability to afford textbooks, sporting equipment, and excursion fees; an unstable home life; and poverty (St. Germain & Dyck, 2011).

A second consultation in 2011 revealed there are no easy solutions to the barriers to education facing Indigenous people. There is a widespread need for better infrastructure, including buildings, resources, technology, and better support systems. Indigenous schools are also perpetually underfunded when compared with their non-Indigenous counterparts (Porter, 2016). Clearly, "federal legislation must enable the development of education systems, rather than prescribing what those systems should look like" (St. Germain & Dyck, 2011, p. 51).

Time to reflect

Use your sociological imagination while thinking about the list of obstacles that Indigenous peoples face. How might those obstacles apply to people you know, who perhaps belong to other marginalized groups in Canada?

Despite these difficulties, a substantial fraction of Indigenous people have post-secondary educational credentials by the age of 35. As we can see from Figure 11.5, in 2011, almost half of Indigenous people aged 35 to 64 had a post-secondary qualification. What's more, according to the 2011 National Household Survey, improvement has been especially dramatic in the last decade or so. Not surprisingly, younger Indigenous people had higher levels of education than older ones. Nonetheless, differences remain between the Indigenous and non-Indigenous populations.

In general, this is related to socioeconomic opportunity. As noted earlier, children from poorer socioeconomic backgrounds are generally less likely to gain a higher education. A study by Macdonald and Shaker (2012) published by the Canadian Centre for Policy Alternatives reports that on average, tuition and compulsory fees for Canadian undergraduate students have tripled between 1993–94 and 2015–16 and will continue to rise over the next four years. As well, rising costs of textbooks, technology (see Box 11.3), and supplies mean many students are unable to continue higher studies.

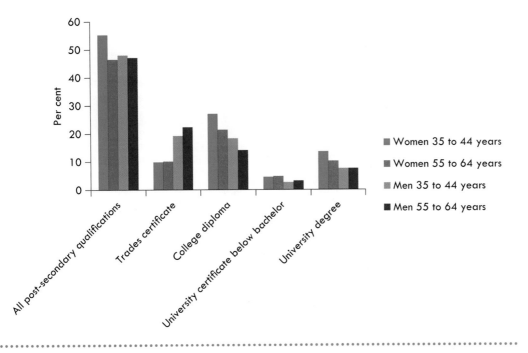

FIGURE 11.5 Post-Secondary Education Levels for Indigenous People, by Age and Sex, 2011

Source: Created from table accessed at: https://www12.statcan.gc.ca/nhs-enm/2011/as-sa/99-012-x/2011003/tbl/tbl1-eng.cfm

Digital Divide

11.3 | Making Technology Accessible

Limited access to computers and other forms of technology is an especially serious problem for low-income students today. In this digital age, technology is incorporated into the classroom because it makes the education process easier. Equally important, educators feel it is necessary for children to develop computer literacy at an early age, to succeed in their education and future careers. Not having access to technology, therefore, presents a serious disadvantage for low-income students who may grow up without the skills needed to succeed academically and secure a good job.

When it comes to accessing and using technology, the gap in today's society is widening. Low-income families are less likely to have information and communication technologies (ICT) for children to use at home, and schools in low-income areas are less able than other schools to provide ICT in the classroom. In this way, inequalities are reinforced and low socioeconomic status is transmitted from one generation to the next. So, providing low-income children with access to technology is extremely important if we are to break this cycle and ensure career success for children from poorer backgrounds.

Many groups and initiatives are already in place to provide equal access to technology and close the digital divide. One such program is the Canadian Computers for Schools program. This program makes refurbished computer equipment available to nonprofit organizations that support low-income Canadians, Canadian seniors, and recent immigrants. The program also pays to refurbish surplus government ICT so that it can be donated to and used in schools. Finally, it provides students with market-relevant skills and training in technology use. Since its inception in 1993, the program has made over 1.2 million computers accessible to Canadian learners (Government of Canada, 2015).

Other organizations focus not on providing access to technology, but on teaching the knowledge and skills associated with it. For example, Code.org is a relatively new nonprofit organization, launched in 2013, and dedicated to expanding access to computer science. It also aims to increase the participation of women and underrepresented students of colour in computer science. Similarly, the Benton Foundation (at Benton.org) is working to increase home access to broadband internet service. Over time, these and other organizations will help to eliminate the digital divide and provide everyone with equal access to technology.

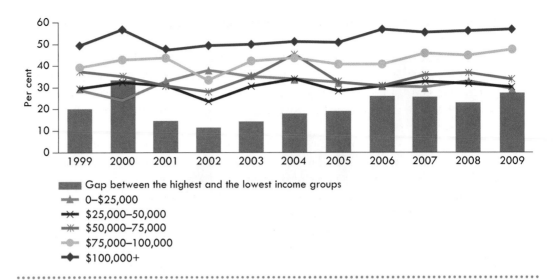

FIGURE 11.6 University Participation among Ontario Youth 18–24 by Income Quartile

Source: p. 18, Figure 4 from Zhao, H. (2012). Post-secondary Education Participation of Under-Represented Groups in Ontario: Evidence from the SLID Data. Toronto: Higher Education Quality Council of Ontario. Accessed at: www.nipissingu.ca/departments/presidents-office/Documents/PSE%20Participation%20of%20Under-Represented%20Groups%20in%20ON%20-%20HEQCO.pdf

Obtaining a higher education is especially difficult for students without parents who can afford to help them. In Canada, as in the United States, children from affluent families are more likely to attend post-secondary educational institutions than poorer ones. That said, the class- or income-effect on education is weaker in Canada than in the United States (Belley, Frenette, & Lochner, 2014). However, data on this are scarce. Figure 11.6 shows full-time university attendance in Ontario, by parental income. The bars represent the gap between the highest and lowest income groups; you can see that the gap increased slightly, particularly between 2002 and 2009.

New Forms of Education

One of the biggest changes to education that has come about as a result of technological development is "e-schooling." Online classes are courses conducted over the internet in a virtual rather than in a physical classroom. This method of instruction has many advantages and has grown in popularity over the years. Accordingly, enrolment in such courses has grown quickly.

A recent report about online instruction in Canada notes "there are no clear, comprehensive, or even apples-to-apples comparators showing participation rates in Canadian online university education. [All that is possible are] . . . rounded, ballpark estimates of for-credit online university registrations gathered from a range of reports and institutional sources" (Canadian Virtual University, 2012, p. 7). By this reckoning, the report's writers estimate 384,000 registrations in online courses; nearly 6000 online courses being offered; and 500 online degrees being granted. Given these numbers, the authors further estimate that online university registrations in Canada about 4 per cent of all registrations (Canadian Virtual University, 2012).

Research on community colleges shows a similar pattern. Clearly, online education has lots of room to grow; and equally clearly, there is an interest in this type of education. One of the reasons students take online courses is the flexibility they offer. Since online learning lets students study when and where they want to, they gain a greater ability to manage busy schedules (Jaggars, Edgecombe, & Stacey, 2013a). Moreover, online courses allow students to learn at their own pace.

In addition to paid-for online courses, many universities, colleges, and companies are now offering massive open online courses (MOOCs). MOOCs are typically free, not for credit, and open to anyone with internet access. Coursera is probably the best-known provider, claiming over 14 million users to date.

Harvard and MIT have teamed up to provide their own range of MOOCs through their jointly created platform edX, launched in the fall of 2012. Although many of the MOOCs being offered are free (including the majority offered by Coursera and edX), certificates of completion require a fee for students who see the course through to its end.

MOOCs are a fairly new concept, but the number of students enrolling in them since their inception has been truly astonishing. One of the first edX courses, an introductory computer science course offered by Harvard, drew 181,410 registrants worldwide. In total, the 17 edX courses offered in the first year of the platform's existence (fall 2012 to summer 2013) drew 841,687 registrations from 597,692 unique users (Zhao & Ho, 2014).

These enrolment figures are impressive, but the percentage of students enrolled who actually completed their courses is troubling. Of the 181,410 registrants in edX's introductory computer science course, for example, only 1 per cent certifiably completed the course. And, of the 841,687 people who enrolled in all 17 of the first edX courses, only 43,196—roughly 5 per cent—earned certificates of completion (Zhao & Ho, 2014).Though some students may have learned all the material without seeking a certificate of completion, there are other reasons for the low completion rate, Despite the many benefits of online courses, students complain that the isolated and unstructured environment of an online class is less conducive to their learning than a physical class (Jaggars, Edgecombe, & Stacey, 2013a).

Many students also feel that online courses lack something hard-to-specify associated with the traditional in-class style of teaching. Indeed, most students taking online courses at a community college say that they would not want to take all of their classes in an online format (Jaggars, Edgecombe, & Stacey 2013a). In particular, they would prefer to take courses they expect to be hard and courses they consider important (such as courses required for their major) in a face-to-face setting (Jaggars, Edgecombe, & Stacey, 2013a). Many students say that teachers of online classes are less accessible than teachers in face-to-face classes.

But do online courses work as well in the long run as in-person courses? To answer this questions, Jaggars, Edgecombe, and Stacey (2013b) investigated the relationship between online classes and general school performance. They found that students in community college who completed online course sections performed more poorly than students who completed face-to-face courses (Jaggars, Edgecombe, & Stacey, 2013b). In fact, online students were 3 to 6 per cent less likely to receive a C or better than their face-to-face counterparts in a similar course. Jaggars, Edgecombe, and Stacey (2013b) also report that withdrawal rates were significantly higher in online courses and online course taking was negatively correlated with college completion.

These results are open to several interpretations. On the one hand, they may show that online courses teach students less well than in-person courses. They may also show that poorer students, or students hampered by non-academic difficulties, are more likely to choose online courses over in-person courses, when they can. The authors write, "Some groups of students had particular difficulty adjusting to online learning, including males, students with lower prior GPAs, and Black students. The performance gaps that existed among these subgroups in face-to-face courses became even more pronounced in online courses. The increases in performance gaps were present in all subject areas . . . [Thus], online courses may exacerbate already persistent achievement gaps between student subgroups" (Jaggars, Edgecombe, & Stacey, 2013b, pp. 4–5).

For online courses to live up to their potential, more will have to be done to engage students, and changes will have to be made to ensure that the quality of education in virtual classrooms is equal to that of physical ones, especially for the weakest students. After improvements, online classes may provide free, high-quality, online education for everyone. However, a survey of online education notes the following barriers to online education and its expansion in Canada:

1. The absence of broadband technologies in large areas of Northern Canada, particularly in Aboriginal communities.
2. The digital divide and the lack of digital knowledge of both some students and the professoriate.
3. The lack of strategic focus on online learning in some post-secondary institutions.
4. The poor design and quality of some early stage online courses and the low level of student engagement these engendered.

Theory in Everyday Life

11.4 | A Feminist Approach to Online Education

Since their development in 2008, massive open online courses (MOOCs) have been touted as an alternative to traditional higher education (DOCC, 2016). Nonetheless, many also criticize MOOCs, for a variety of reasons (Selingo, 2016). As noted above, MOOCs consistently report low completion rates, that the student–teacher relationship is too distant for a student to stay motivated throughout the course, and that the ease of "taking" MOOCs gives students a false sense of retaining information (i.e., easy learning does not translate into retained knowledge) (Catropa, 2013; Reich, 2014; Levinson, 2013; Konnikova, 2014). In an attempt to address certain failures, FemTechNet, a network of feminist academics, created distributed open collaborative courses (DOCCs). According to FemTechNet, MOOCs are hindered by the need to imitate conventional education. FemTechNet contends that the feminist principles upon which DOCCs

were developed provide better learning outcomes than conventional education. DOCCs, based on an egalitarian and decentralized model of instruction, challenge the traditional roles of the instructor and the student. Moreover, rather than following a syllabus, DOCCs are organized around a central theme that is discussed each week, emphasizing experience and collaboration. Finally, DOCCs foster a close and respectful relationship between all class members; therefore, the classes are limited to 40 students (Henderson, 2013).

Nonetheless, these courses have also been criticized. For example, many critics question whether feminist pedagogy really influences DOCCs. Some critics argue that DOCCs are merely anti-MOOC. In response, Anne Balsamo, co-facilitator of DOCCs, asserts that the courses simply adapt the foundation of MOOCs to further innovation of open educational resources (Jaschik, 2013).

5.   The lack of investment by some governments and institutions in instructional design, faculty capacity and infrastructure.
6.   Difficulties in inter-institutional and cross-provincial credit transfer, especially in Ontario. (Online Learning in Canada: At a Tipping Point A Cross-Country Check-Up 2012. Contact North, page 17)

Time to reflect

What are the pros and cons of online instruction? For what kinds of subjects (or disciplines) might it work very well, and for what kinds of subjects would it work less well? Explain your answer.

Areas of Sociological Interest in Primary and Secondary Education

Ability Grouping or "Streaming"

Some schools minimize or control student variation by segregating different "kinds" of students. One common type of segregation is ability grouping, more often spoken of as "tracking" or "streaming."

The advantages of streaming have been known for generations. Streaming allows pupils to advance according to their abilities, adapts instructional techniques to the needs of the group, reduces failures, and helps to preserve interest and incentive. Bright students are not bored by the slower participation of others, and slower pupils engage more when brighter students do not overshadow them. The system also makes teaching easier, since it allows teachers to give individual instruction to small groups with specific abilities. In an age seemingly obsessed with self-esteem, perhaps the most appealing argument is that streaming is less likely to confront students with their individual inadequacies.

Special education is a term applied to both students who are gifted high achievers and to students who struggle to meet basic educational requirements.

However, there are arguments against ability grouping. A stigma attached to low sections or classes in the school can discourage students in these categories. Some students may feel uncomfortable about being placed in a group that is considered "lower" or less demanding. As well, students put in a lower grouping may come to think they aren't smart enough to achieve at a higher level, and they may work down to the teacher's low expectations.

Moreover, there is evidence that streaming or tracking reproduces existing social inequalities. Minority and lower-income students are more likely to end up in the lowest streams because, statistically, they perform worse than children from higher-income families. For example, they are more likely to present a lower school readiness, such as the ability to read and a general desire for learning. Often, students from low socioeconomic backgrounds have not been socialized in the same way and do not have the same resources and experiences as students from higher socioeconomic backgrounds.

Segregation in Schooling

Not all students have the same educational experience, even in primary school. In some cases, this is because some attend unconventional schools. For example, some parents choose to enroll their children in private schools where there is less ethnic or religious variety than public schools.

Parents have various motives for placing their children in these schools. Some think their children will receive a better education than in the public system, or that the private system will better prepare their children to compete for top university and occupational positions. Also, some parents think their children will be taught suitable values and religious dogma as well as academic material.

However, such single-ethnicity (or single-religion or single-race or single-gender, or single-anything) schools minimize contact with students of different demographics. This decreases

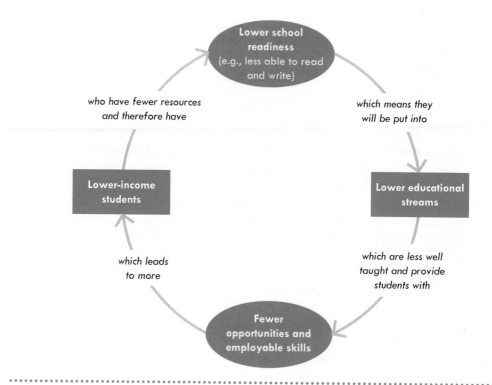

FIGURE 11.7 Streaming Can Reproduce Social Inequality

Source: Author-generated

These kids attend a multi-language public school in Montreal. What are the benefits of integrated vs. segregated schooling?

Spotlight On

11.5 | The Residential School Apology

When Prime Minister Stephen Harper made an historic apology for residential schools on 11 June 2008, Indigenous communities looked forward to change (Government of Canada, 2008). Today, many survivors of the schools are still waiting for adequate reparations. Though the Truth and Reconciliation Commission has worked to raise awareness about residential schools, provide monetary compensation for former residential-school students, and make heard the stories of these people, more than 22,000 general claims and 3000 sexual and physical abuse claims have been rejected due to insufficient evidence, and the process has been painfully slow (Warwick, 2011). A December 2013 report by the chief adjudicator of the Indian Residential School Adjudication Secretariat states that roughly 10 per cent of all claims had been dismissed by that time. The Canadian government had funded residential schools for Indigenous people up until the 1990s. For over a century, these schools had taken children away from their parents, forcing them to speak English and to give up their traditional religion and customs. Some children suffered physical and sexual abuse from teachers and school administrators. Others died of poor nutrition and untreated disease. For many Indigenous people, these educational policies were equivalent to cultural genocide; after all, the schools had aimed to erase the cultural traditions of 150,000 Inuit, Métis, and First Nations attendees. Even today, many Indigenous families have not recovered from the consequences of residential schooling, with high rates of addiction, poverty, family breakdown, and suicide still ravaging Indigenous communities.

Today's Indigenous schools, underfunded and far below the quality of Canadian public schools, are one example of the government's continuing inattention to Indigenous issues. "We're faced with a real moment of reckoning here," Shawn Atleo, national chief of the Assembly of First Nations, said in an interview on the fourth anniversary of the apology. "The rate and pace of change is too slow" (CBC News, 2012).

In addition to monetary compensation, the Truth and Reconciliation Commission has recommended a number of ways to improve the lives of Indigenous people, including more mental health facilities, increased school funding, the creation of parenting programs, and education about residential schools throughout Canada.

---

the familiarity with different groups that students could gain at a mixed school. As well, segregated schools limit public visibility and accountability. At the extreme, this makes children in segregated schools more vulnerable to the harm and neglect associated with total institutions. For example, horrible abuses occurred in the isolated, segregated residential schools designed for Canada's Indigenous children (see Box 11.5).

Time to reflect

How might you design a study to find out whether a same-sex school worked "better" in important educational or social senses? How might you test for socialization?

Dissatisfied with both the public and private school systems, some parents choose to home-school their children. Over the past few decades, **home-schooling** has been increasing in both the United States and Canada. Home-schoolers often see themselves as resisting formal control. Some parents say they want to avoid the socialization that happens at schools; or they may not want their children to become "good" obedient citizens, instead remaining critical of social structures. Other parents choose home-schooling because they do not want their children to be exposed to ideas of

home-schooling the education of children at home by their parents.

multiculturalism and the equality of all peoples, or to secular, scientific ideas that disagree with preferred religious beliefs.

Whatever the benefits of educational segregation—in public schools, private schools, religious schools, same-sex schools, or at home—segregation keeps people apart, which fails to teach young people how to deal with those who are different. Worse, it does this among young students who may already have trouble dealing with differential treatment based on sex, class, and racialized identity.

Education and Mental Health

Families differ in the priority they give to their children's educational attainment. But sometimes parents put too much pressure on their children to excel in school and the results for mental health may be devastating. Sociologist John R. Seeley (along with Alexander Sim, Elizabeth Loosley, and David Riesman) (1956/1963) was one of the first to explore this problem in his classic work *Crestwood Heights*, a study of a Toronto neighbourhood for upwardly mobile immigrants and children of immigrants in the mid-twentieth century. Seeley's goal was to study how children in this high-achievement culture responded to demands at school and at home. In other words, it was a study of education, but also a study of childhood with a goal to understand the culture of the child, his goals in life, and his resulting mental health problems.

Viewed from the standpoint of parents in this community, the child is a problem to be solved. Every parent wants a "trophy child"—a child to be proud of. These parents train their children to be "perfect"—competitive and successful in all their pursuits. For them, though they are likely unconscious of the fact, children are a consumer item—like a car or home—that speaks to the aspirations, wealth, power and "classiness" of the parent.

So, even at a young age, they teach their children to seek success in scout groups, music lessons, hockey teams, and summer camps—of course, also in school! These parents view the school as the authority on raising children and the main place where children can prove their perfection. Today, more than 50 years later, the same patterns of socialization and education are evident in many urban and suburban communities. Many North American middle-class parents socialize their children to be ambitious, independent, and successful above all else. Often, the values schools promote are just an extension of values already promoted by parents, which stress ambition and advancement, especially among families of higher socioeconomic backgrounds (Lareau, 2003).

Pressure for success may lead to health problems. Books such as *College of the Overwhelmed: The Campus Mental Health Crisis and What to Do About It* (Kadison & DiGeronimo, 2004), by two authors who work at the Harvard University Health Service, hammer home the message that parents expect too much of their children, and schools may expect too much of their students. Students might turn to plagiarism, get physically ill, or even commit acts of self-harm.

According to a 2013 study of teenaged students by the Toronto District School Board, some students experience so much school-related pressure that they can't sleep, feel anxious all the time, and have excessively low self-esteem. Strangely enough, these anxiety issues are most marked among the highest achieving students. In large part, this anxiety is the fault of overly demanding families. To some degree, it is also the fault of a society that is preoccupied with educational and occupational success, even at the expense of creativity and critical thinking. Ideally, schools could help to mitigate or reduce stress and anxiety around job success. However, budget cuts, losses of key personnel, and the arrival of at-risk students continually jeopardize this. Schools tasked with producing high scores on standardized tests are unlikely to spend a lot of time thinking about ways to reduce the pressures on students to succeed.

Sociology 2.0

11.6 | Plagiarism and Turnitin.com

Many higher education and corporate professionals see plagiarism as one of the greatest challenges faced by schools and education as a result of new technology (Economic Intelligence Unit, 2008). Though the internet is an invaluable source of information, its easily accessible online databases and huge repositories of texts can be all too tempting for plagiarists.

There is a perception among many in and around higher education that the incidence of plagiarism, in general, has increased since the advent of the internet (Scanlon & Neumann, 2002). This view seems supported by the high prevalence of internet plagiarism within higher education. In a 2002 study by Scanlon and Neumann, 8.3 per cent of students admitted to having sometimes or very frequently used the internet to purchase a paper to hand in. A study of plagiarism by McCabe, Butterfield, and Trevino (2003; see also McCabe, Butterfield, & Trevino, 2004) found that 38 per cent of the business and other undergraduate students surveyed admitted to having committed one or more acts of "cut-and-paste" internet plagiarism within the previous year. Wang (2008), in a survey of education majors, also found high rates of plagiarism among students.

Some have connected the high incidence of plagiarism today with the high levels of stress and pressure to do well experienced by today's students. Some academics, however, believe that students' lax attitudes towards plagiarism offer an explanation as to why the incidence of plagiarism is so high. Almost half of the students in McCabe et al.'s 2003 study regarded the practice of internet "cut-and-paste" style plagiarism as "trivial or not cheating at all" (Rimer, 2003). Many surveyed students do not see copying sentences from online sources as a serious offence (see, for example, Baker, Berry, & Thornton, 2008; Baruchson-Arbib & Yaari, 2004).

Some researchers attribute students' nonchalance about internet plagiarism to a false notion millennials have about the nature of internet content. John Barrie (co-founder of Turnitin.com) and David Presti (2000), for example, suggest that many students see information or media on the internet as free or as public knowledge that does not, therefore, require a citation.

One of the ways educational institutions today combat internet plagiarism is via plagiarism detection software like Turnitin, a web-based service designed to catch plagiarized papers by checking submitted papers against a database of texts, including academic articles, reference books, and previous student submissions.

There is considerable evidence suggesting that the use of Turnitin reduces the rate of plagiarism amongst students (Heckler, Rice, & Bryan, 2013). Turnitin, however, does have its limitations, as there are some forms of plagiarism it cannot detect. For example, it cannot detect the use of custom-written essays that have been purchased through online "paper mills" (Batane, 2010; Jump, 2013). The software may also sometimes return false positives in instances where similar phrasing is coincidental (Batane, 2010).

Time to reflect

Given that not all students are plagiarizing all of the time, what would you hypothesize are the conditions under which students are most likely to commit plagiarism?

Abuse and Violence in Schools

In today's society, bullying is an area of increased concern, especially the use or threat of violence against children at or near school. With the evolution of the internet, bullying has become "virtual," but it is no less real in its consequences.

Bullies terrorize their victims, whether physically, emotionally, or socially. In face-to-face bullying, they may be bigger and stronger than the victim, or belong to a higher status group within the school's social hierarchy. The goal of bullying is to humiliate—to humble—another person, whether through threats, blackmail, gossip, or otherwise.

Research shows that childhood bullies are also likely to display anti-social behaviours in adulthood. So for example, Vaughn, Fu, Bender, DeLisi Beaver, Perron, and Howard (2010) studied bullying with a nationally representative survey sample that conducted structured psychiatric interviews on 43,000 American adults. In this sample, 6 per cent of US adults were found to report a lifetime history of bullying others.

Generally, research has found that the motives for bullying originate at home, where children's behavioural patterns are first established. Bullies tend to have parents who are hostile, neglectful, or in conflict, or who punish their children severely. In some cases, bullies imitate their parents' own social behaviour; that is, they have parents who are bullies. Sometimes, they learn that bullying is acceptable because their parents tolerate fighting in the household among siblings.

Here, the best recent survey of the literature is by Canadian social work scholar Faye Mishna (see Mishna & Van Wert, 2015; also, Mishna, 2012). Researchers regularly report that bullies show aggression toward many people, not just their peers and siblings, but also their parents and teachers. They seek out and enjoy aggressive situations, show little empathy for people they hurt, and feel no remorse for their actions. Many have quick tempers and are hyperactive, disruptive, and impulsive. In particular, male bullies tend to be physically strong and use their strength to threaten and coerce others (see also Baldry & Farrington, 1998).

Like bullies, victims too have certain definable characteristics (see, for example, Haynie et al., 2001; Veenstra et al., 2005; Perren & Alsaker, 2006). Many display anxiety, low self-esteem, and depression, including sadness and withdrawal from activities. These traits are commonly reported among both boys and girls. As they get older, children are less likely to be victims of bullies. But likely, just as bullies will continue to bully in adulthood, victims will continue to display victim-like traits, though perhaps to a reduced extent.

Most childhood bullying happens in the presence of peers. Although five out of six students say they feel uncomfortable when they see someone being bullied, peers often watch or participate in some way, whether by joining in or cheering the bully on (Pepler & Craig, 1997). Peers tend to support the bully, rather than the victim, and this support can help reinforce the bully's power over the victim and his or her own social standing. Bullying by a child considered a friend can be especially upsetting. It can be difficult for the child to recognize that a friend is a bully, and for parents and teachers to identify these interactions as bullying.

Bullying is not merely a psychological pathology: it is embedded in the social norms and values common to a whole community, and especially in the social world of adolescents, who distinguish so clearly between winners and losers. Often only the students themselves—members of this adolescent society—can understand the meanings popularly attached to bullying rumours, gossip, and threats. This is why bullying is possible even in the presence of the teacher, during classes.

Bullying tends to focus on certain culturally supported stereotypes and prejudices. This includes singling out people who are disabled (for example, deaf, blind, obese, people who stutter), unpopular, LGBTQ, or otherwise socially isolated. Bullying often employs homophobic verbal taunts—for example, calling victims "gay" for getting a good grade in English class. These epithets are used even against boys who are not homosexual, the implication being that the victims are outsiders, effeminate or powerless, and worthy of ridicule. Often aggressive, sexist, and heteronormative subcultures support these actions.

Certain hypermasculine activities associated with contact sports such as football also encourage bullying. This tendency occurs due to the values and attitudes that circulate within these male-only (also known as homosocial) contexts and their historical preference for hardiness, solidarity, and stoicism. Tensions and social anxieties around masculinity emerge in schools wherever a hypermasculine sporting identity flourishes (see, for example, Hickey, 2008; Wilson, 2002; Klein, 2006).

Currently, there is a lot of discussion about the dangers of cyberbullying. It takes places in a wide variety of ways, via email, chat rooms, mobile phone cameras, websites, and texting, among others. This is now recognized as a global problem, with research on it taking place throughout the world (Campbell, 2005). In certain respects, it is no different from earlier forms of bullying, and the same types of people are bullying and being bullied as before.

How do students feel about this problem? Researchers (Agatston, Kowalski, & Limber, 2007) interviewed middle and high school students, asking focus groups a set of scripted questions in a same-gender setting. Not surprisingly, they report that "students—particularly females—view cyber bullying as a problem, but one rarely discussed at school, and . . . students do not see the school district personnel as helpful resources when dealing with cyber bullying" (p. S59).

All forms of bullying—direct, indirect, and cyberbullying—have important harmful effects on health that may persist into adulthood. Many children do not tell anyone about their bullying experience or seek help and support. They need to be encouraged to speak out, as peer support programs are an important way to tackle and prevent bullying. These programs build resilience, promote friendship, and challenge negative peer group roles.

Improving Student Learning and Performance

Student achievement and school performance vary widely, even within schools and among students with similar socioeconomic backgrounds. As we have noted, student learning is influenced by many factors, including family resources, school organization, effective school curriculum, as well as teachers' skills, attitudes, and practices.

In the short run, it is difficult for policy makers to influence factors such as family and community background. However, policy makers can improve teacher quality and teaching practices. In fact, many commentators agree that improving teacher quality is the most influential factor in terms of student achievement (Santiago, 2004; Schacter & Thum, 2004). If instruction and teaching quality are improved, student learning and achievement will also improve.

However, improving teaching—especially in low-performing schools—is challenging. Schools must be diligent to ensure that students get on track, stay on track, and receive quality instruction (Quint et al., 2005). Researchers Sanders and Rivers (1996) have estimated that the effects of teacher quality are substantial and cumulative over time. Unequal access to high-quality teachers puts students of low socioeconomic status at a great disadvantage, affecting their ability to receive a proper education. It is hard to reach a consensus on what we mean by "good teaching" and how to measure it (Courneya, Pratt, & Collins, 2008). Yet some efforts to define and measure good teaching have concluded that it does, indeed, make a difference.

Akiba, LeTendre, and Scribner (2007) conducted an analysis that showed that students with high-quality teachers achieved higher mathematical scores than those with lower-quality instructors. Interestingly, there was no significant difference in achievement between students with low and high socioeconomic status. One can therefore conclude that low-performing students benefit more from more effective teachers than other students. So far, Canada does not have a federal education policy, and so any sweeping changes to improve teacher access would be next to impossible.

Conclusions

In this chapter we saw that education is ideally meant to develop a student's general capacity for thinking. It is the process of *learning how to learn*. However, for many people, education is mainly about training—preparing people for employability and employment in particular jobs. People expect education to provide them, and their children, with skills to prepare them for an insecure and uncertain future.

In our society and most other industrial societies, formal education helps the advantaged few gain valuable credentials—entrance tickets into top occupations. Formal education is a seemingly fair way of allocating people to unequal economic positions. However, we know that access to educational credentials is unequal, since people from wealthier, more educated families are more likely to receive support and encouragement for higher education, as well as access to better teachers, which we know is one of the best ways to ensure higher achievement. Therefore, through formal education, class position is passed down from one generation to the next.

Today, most top North American universities are designed to train researchers and produce research findings, with only a small emphasis on undergraduate teaching. As we have seen, there is a strong and troubling tie between the rise of research universities and the commodification of education more generally.

Many middle-class and immigrant families still view higher education as a ticket to social mobility. However, increased pressure on children, teenagers, and young adults takes a toll on students, with high rates of mental illness and unhealthy stress levels among high school and university students. One of the sources of that stress is bullying, which, with the increased use of the internet, has become harder to spot and more difficult to stop.

Questions for Critical Thought

1. In your own words, what is the difference between "education" and "training"?

2. Who benefits most from research universities? As a university student, what do you think are some disadvantages of this type of institution?

3. What are the positive and negative effects of ability grouping (also known as streaming or tracking)?

4. Canada has private, public, faith-based, same-sex, and even home schools. What are the benefits of each? Which do you think is most beneficial for educating Canada's citizens and why?

5. To what degree, and for what reasons, are costs a barrier to higher education, even among people who have the ability and desire to attend?

Take it Further: Recommended Readings

Barbara Coloroso, *The Bully, The Bullied, and the Bystander: From Preschool to High School—How Parents Can Help Break the Cycle of Violence* (New York: Harper Resource, 2003). This text examines bullying in schools, and suggests steps that victims, teachers, and parents can take to end bullying in schools.

Richard Kadison, and Theresa Foy DiGeronimo, *College of the Overwhelmed: The Campus Mental Health Crisis and What To Do About It* (San Francisco: Jossey-Bass, 2004). In this book, the authors examine the troubling increase in serious mental health problems among university students.

Margaret Kernan and Elly Singer, eds., *Peer Relationships in Early Childhood Education and Care* (Oxen: Routledge, 2011). This text is recommended for students interested in early childhood education and the social development of children at the early stages of their lives.

D.W. Livingstone, *The Education–Jobs Gap: Underemployment or Economic Democracy* (Toronto: Garamond, 2004). As the title suggests, this book, by an eminent Canadian sociologist, discusses the gap people experience between the education they receive and the skills and knowledge necessary in their occupation.

Take it Further: Recommended Online Resources

Canadian Council on Learning (CCL)
www.changelearning.ca/canadian-council-learning.html

Flare, **"Female Bullying"**
www.flare.com/celebrity/female-bullying/

Educational Resources Information Center (ERIC)
www.eric.ed.gov

Homeschool Canada
http://homeschoolcanada.ca/

StopBullying
www.stopbullying.gov/

StudyCanada
www.studycanada.ca

More resources available on  Dashboard

12

Work and the Economy in Real Life

Learning Objectives

In this chapter, you will:

> Learn about theories of social class

> Understand the relationship between work, social class, and conflict

> Observe how the organization of work has changed over time

> See how globalization affects the organization of work

> Learn about the ways in which science and technology have changed the workplace

Introduction

Work today is not the same as it was 50, 100, or 1000 years ago. In this chapter, we will learn that modern work is the result of a great many historical forces. One of the most important forces is an advance in technology: there would not be modern-day Canada without industrialization, and there would not be industrialization without the revolutionary invention, application, and spread of new kinds of machinery and new sources of power.

However, technology does not invent or apply itself. To understand modern work we also need to understand the capitalist economic system through which critical investments were made in technology. And we cannot understand present-day capitalist economics without understanding the political system that stimulates and regulates capitalist investment.

We cannot do any of this without understanding the global context. In a world where capital, labour, information, and technology move around almost without boundaries, the lives of Canadian workers are becoming less secure and less comfortable, though the lives of workers in less developed societies may be improving. Technology and science have altered our workplaces in ways for both the better and the worse. Consider the problem outlined in Box 12.1.

Industrialism and the Industrial Revolution

In pre-industrial societies, people worked collectively in mainly agricultural settings. Because of the small size of rural communities and the interconnectedness of people's experiences, work was largely inseparable from family and personal life. People led similar lives and held similar moral, religious, and political beliefs (Durkheim, 1904/2014).

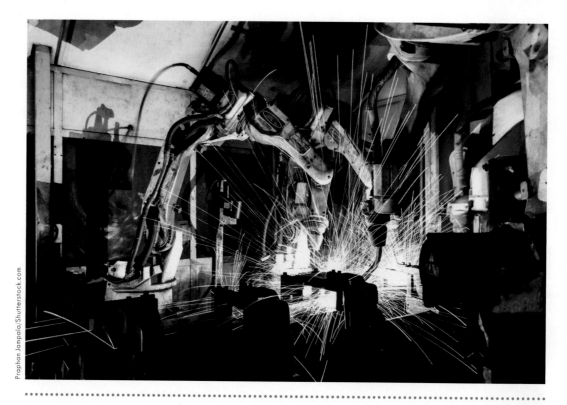

Praphan Jampala/Shutterstock.com

In today's economy, machines do a lot of the work, and some of the most secure, best-paying human work has been outsourced to low-wage countries overseas.

Sociology 2.0

12.1 | Is Facebook the New "Background Check"?

In today's digital society, most people are "plugged in" and have an online social media presence. Though social media are typically meant to facilitate casual, social interactions, many companies also use them to check the backgrounds of potential employees. Companies often look at social media profiles to see whether or not a potential employee behaves professionally and whether or not he or she would fit in well with the company's culture. The realms of socializing and work are, therefore, becoming blurred as your Instagram or Twitter accounts are now, in some sense, a part of your resumé. As a job applicant, therefore, you should probably remove or hide any inappropriate photos or posts from your online profiles. In addition, recruiters might cross-reference the skills posted on your social media profiles with the ones listed in your resumé, so job applicants should also make sure not to put any false or erroneous information in their applications (Wasser, 2013; Waters, 2011).

However, in Canada, using social media as part of an employee background check is somewhat problematic given the many existent privacy laws. Four jurisdictions in Canada (federally regulated employers, employers in Alberta, employers in BC, and employers in Quebec) have specific privacy legislation restricting employers' ability to conduct employee background checks. For example, one restriction states that companies can only gather information that is "necessary for reasonable purposes" (Big Brothers, Big Sisters, 2012). Social media sites give a lot of personal information that employers are not permitted to access legally (e.g., friends, relationship statuses, and comments betraying a political opinion). A great deal of information on social media profiles cannot be used in hiring decisions, and doing so would be discrimination.

For all of these reasons, Canadian companies may be deterred from utilizing social media in employee background checks. However, it can be difficult to prove that a hiring decision was made due to one's social media presence. It is ultimately the company's decision as to whether or not the legal risks are worth the potential rewards.

City of Toronto Archives. Fonds 1548, Series 393, Item 511

This is an image of the railway yards near Union Station in Toronto in 1913. The Industrial Revolution profoundly changed people's lives. In the eyes of many in the nineteenth century, it changed life for the worse, making the world dark, dingy, and dangerous.

Two major economic developments changed this: an agricultural revolution and the Industrial Revolution. By the early eighteenth century, an agricultural revolution that began thousands of years earlier had reached a point where farmers could produce a large surplus of food. This enabled many people to work at enterprises outside of food production, creating a surplus in food and farm workers (Overton, 1996).

Around the same time, new factory systems created a large surplus in manufacturing, such as the textile and steel industries. A combination of this surplus and an influx of workers coming from the countryside created the foundation for an emerging capitalist production system (Wallerstein, 1974), and the modern city. This shift is what we call the Industrial Revolution.

Time to reflect

Using the skills you've gained so far in this course, exercise your sociological imagination. What do you think the impact of the Industrial Revolution was on the working lives of those who lived through it? Keep your hypothesis in mind as you continue to read the chapter, and see whether the evidence supports your hypothesis.

Industrial Society

industrial society a society that uses advanced technology that, when combined with a detailed division of labour, promotes mass production and a high standard of living.

The term **industrial society** refers not only to a society in which industrial (or mass) production prevails, but to a whole packet of associated features we consider basic to contemporary life. In the shift to an industrial society subsistence farming disappears; workers begin to produce goods in large factories that rely on machinery for production; and jobs and workers become highly specialized.

In these respects, societies as different as Canada and China, Russia and Argentina, are all industrial societies. Whatever the political system or economic ideology, industrialization leads a society to develop the features listed above. Sociologists have spent a lot of time identifying these features of industrial society. Generally, industrial societies have a secular culture focused on efficiency, consumerism and a high standard of living; a highly developed state that provides health, education, and welfare benefits to its citizens; and a class structure dominated (numerically) by the urban, middle class.

There are important similarities between industrial societies like Canada and Japan which, a century ago, had almost nothing in common. The growing similarity of industrial societies around the world has lent support to what sociologists call the **convergence thesis**. Supporters of this thesis argue that as societies industrialize, their social patterns converge or become more similar, despite differences that existed before. It is not clear whether industrial societies converge because they must satisfy the same societal needs (e.g., for literacy) or because social practices spread from richer to poorer societies. There is evidence to support both views.

convergence thesis the theory that under conditions of modernization, less-developed societies will start to change more rapidly than more-developed societies, with the result that all societies will eventually reach the same social, cultural, and economic conditions, regardless of their starting points.

Other factors are also important. American sociologist Gerhard Lenski (2015) provided an important modification of materialist theory, the premise that capitalist production is the main driver of social change. He proposed a five-stage evolutionary theory of societal change, in which he defined five kinds of societies, according to their mode of production and level of subsistence. As he points out, these societies are (in turn) shaped by their level of technological development and the natural environment in which they exist.

Some environments, like deserts, do not allow more than subsistence, whatever the level of technology. But many environments allow a variety of societal types, ranging from hunting and gathering societies, which use simple tools to obtain food from wild plants and animals; through horticultural societies, where people use simple tools to raise crops; to pastoral societies, where people raise animals for livestock; to agricultural societies, where people cultivate plants

Dashboard
Interactive activity

Spotlight On

12.2 | Five Famous Women Inventors

Margaret Knight (1838–1914)

Margaret Knight was an exceptionally prolific inventor in the late nineteenth century; journalists occasionally compared her to her better-known male contemporary, Thomas Edison, by nicknaming her "the lady Edison" or "a woman Edison." She was awarded her first patent in 1871, for a machine that cut, folded, and glued flat-bottomed paper shopping bags, thus eliminating the need for workers to assemble them slowly by hand. Knight received 27 patents in her lifetime, for inventions including shoe-manufacturing machines, a "dress shield" to protect garments from perspiration stains, a rotary engine, and an internal combustion engine.

Melitta Bentz (1873–1950)

Melitta Bentz updated coffee brewing for the modern world. At the turn of the twentieth century, the usual method was to tie up the coffee grounds in a small cloth bag and place the bag into a pot of boiling water; the result was a bitter, gritty drink. Bentz came up with a new method. She put a piece of thick, absorbent paper into a brass pot with a few holes punched in it and poured the coffee through this two-part contraption, which trapped the grounds and allowed the filtered liquid to seep through and drip into a waiting cup. Her invention has improved the lives of workers to this day.

Caresse Crosby (1891–1970)

In 1910 Mary Phelps Jacob—later known as Caresse Crosby—feeling frustrated by the bulky and restrictive corset that women customarily wore beneath their clothing, asked her maid to bring her two handkerchiefs, some ribbons, and a few pins. From these items she fashioned a lighter, more flexible undergarment that she called a "backless brassiere." In 1914 she received a patent for her idea and a few years later she founded the Fashion Form Brassière Company to manufacture and sell her invention. She eventually sold her patent to Warner Brothers Corset Company, which began producing bras in large quantities. Women have literally breathed easier ever since, allowing for further participation of women in the labour force.

Katharine Burr Blodgett (1898–1979)

Scientist and inventor Katharine Blodgett was the first woman to receive a PhD in physics at England's Cambridge University and the first woman hired by General Electric. During the Second World War, Blodgett contributed important research to military needs like gas masks, smoke screens, and a new technique for de-icing airplane wings. Her work in chemistry, specifically in surfaces at the molecular level, resulted in her most influential invention: non-reflective glass. Her "invisible" glass was initially used for lenses in cameras and movie projectors; it also had military applications such as wartime submarine periscopes. Today, non-reflective glass is still essential for eyeglasses, car windshields, and computer screens.

Stephanie Kwolek (1923–2014)

Shortly after graduating from Carnegie Mellon University, Stephanie Kwolek began working at the chemical company DuPont. She was assigned to work on formulating new synthetic fibers, and in 1965 she made an especially important discovery. While working with a liquid crystal solution of large molecules called polymers, she created an unusually lightweight and durable new fiber. This material was later developed by DuPont into Kevlar, a tough yet versatile synthetic used in everything from military helmets and bulletproof vests to work gloves, sports equipment, fiber optic cables, and building materials (Murphy, 2015)

Time to reflect

What sociological factors do you think influence which stories become famous, and which do not? Why might an inventor story starring a man resonate with a wider Canadian audience than a story starring a woman? Think about social norms and expectations when trying to answer this question.

or animals on a large scale, using energy resources such as animal-driven ploughs; to industrial societies, in which people produce and manufacture foods using advanced sources of energy and machines.

Key Processes of Industrialization

Specialization and the Division of Labour

Early in the twentieth century, the proliferation of factory and office workers led to the invention of scientific management techniques—a strategy for reorganizing the workplace through the application of "scientific" methods to management and the work process. Scientific management was sometimes called Taylorism in recognition of Frederick Winslow Taylor, who invented this approach and, in this way, helped to revolutionize industrial production. In particular, scientific management introduced time-and-motion research to study and break down the tasks of individual workers into faster, smaller, repetitive steps. The result was a specialized division of labour and more efficient use of time by workers. A task undergoes a **division of labour** when it is broken into many smaller tasks, each carried out by a different person. Then, we say the tasks are "specialized." With **specialization**, people are limited to doing a single task or step in the work process.

Specialization is almost inevitable in a large organization. Breaking up a big job into small, easy-to-perform tasks, and then having different people perform these different tasks repeatedly reduces the time and cost needed to do the job. Consumers benefit because producers sell their goods and services at a lower price, while keeping up a healthy profit margin. But specialization carries costs of its own. Often, it makes jobs repetitive and dull, causing workers to become bored and frustrated. And, as sociologist Harry Braverman (1974/1998) wrote, specialization is also "de-skilling." It takes away skills that people once had, making them less able to perform a variety of jobs and more dependent on their employers.

Émile Durkheim was the first sociologist to see that too much specialization would pose a serious threat to social solidarity. Studying pre-industrial societies, Durkheim noticed that when the division of labour is slight, based mainly on age and gender, most people make a living the same ways. Members of the group feel a sense of unity, or "mechanical solidarity" as Durkheim (1904/2014) called it, based on their common experiences, feelings, values, and beliefs—what Durkheim calls the "common conscience." This "mechanical solidarity" proves to be a powerful form of social cohesion and control.

Now, imagine all these elements gone. In periods of rapid social and economic change, problems of disorganization—or anomie—arise. In general, specialization, mobility, and rapid social change all cut people off from one another. It seemed clear to Durkheim that in industrial society, where people had a greater division of labour and therefore greater differences in daily experiences, a new type of social order, which he named **organic solidarity**, was needed to pull people together.

People need intimacy, emotional attachments, and rules to live by. They also need to find ways of settling disputes with the people and groups they rely on but do not know well. In a community with organic solidarity, there is a sense of interdependence with others. The far-reaching division of labour means no one can live without the contributions made by other people. We may not know all of the people we depend on, but we need them and we know we do. In such a society, people learn to foster a "live and let live" philosophy. Durkheim argues that two factors associated with industrialization were responsible for this growth in "moral density": "social volume" and "material density." A society's social volume is simply the total number of its members. A society's material density is its frequency of social connections and communication, which increases when the spatial distance between individuals is reduced (as in cities) and through advances in communication and transportation.

One result of organic solidarity is greater reliance on non-traditional units of organization (e.g., occupational groups, rather than tribe or kin). Durkheim recognizes that we have yet

division of labour the coordinated assignment of different parts of a task to different people, in order to improve efficiency

specialization a system of production in which different individuals or groups each focus on producing a limited range of products or services to yield greater productive efficiency overall.

organic solidarity social cohesion based on a division of labour that results in people depending on each other; it binds people together in technologically advanced, industrialized societies.

to complete this transition. Even today, a century after Durkheim wrote his influential works, we are still searching for supportive yet flexible sources of social cohesion (see more on this in Chapter 13).

Professions and Professionalization

One process of industrialization that works to combat the problems of social cohesion is found in the growth of professions. In the professions, each person is considered a specialized expert and each has a high degree of control over decision making. Throughout society, professionalization is the main alternative to bureaucratic decision making. Whereas a bureaucracy is impersonal and tends to centralize authority, a profession assigns both high status and autonomy to individuals, bringing back in an organic organization style one would have experienced in feudal societies—holistic, personal, undivided. Think about physicians in an emergency ward: their decision making is necessarily fast-paced and not hindered by multiple levels of bureaucracy.

Professionals like physicians do high-status, high-paying, specialized work that requires a lot of schooling and permits a lot of freedom. The growing importance of professionalization is shown by the fact that, increasingly, access to high-paying jobs in industrial societies requires a "credential." This credential, which is usually an educational degree, shows that a person qualifies for the job. It also prevents non-accredited people from performing the task, which creates a monopoly on the rights to enter the profession.

In future, professional organization may be the basis for most personal services, even for some industrial work. On the other hand, there is evidence that some professions are losing their high status. We may even see a **proletarianization** of lawyers in large law firms, engineers in large manufacturing companies such as Apple, and managers in large merchandisers like Amazon. In every instance,

proletarianization the creation of a subordinate wage–working class among people with professional qualifications.

Professionalism is found in almost every line of work, but we tend to think of "the professions" as types of work that require high education and bestow high rewards.

these highly trained employees are made strongly aware of their obligations to the company and vulnerability of their employment.

The Bureaucratization of Work

Bureaucracies are a defining feature of modern work life, and are associated with (though not directly caused by) industrialization. In contrast to professions, bureaucracies are large, complex organizations that employ specialized workers who work within the context of what Max Weber (2009) called a legal-rational authority structure. Bureaucracies are known for their written rules that govern how people are to perform their jobs.

Historically, industrialization and capitalism favoured the rise of bureaucracies. Bureaucracies control large workforces well—even highly educated and differentiated workforces. It's much harder to plan for, coordinate, and supervise an office of 20 lawyers—each with different specialties and types of clients—and 30 support staff, for example, than it is to plan for, coordinate, and supervise an office of 2 lawyers and 2 support staff. So, often, with the growth in scale of an organization, bureaucratization is implemented.

Below the surface of the ideal or formal structure, which prescribes how a bureaucracy ought to work, there inevitably exists an informal structure (Kramer, 1999). This informal structure develops through communication and trust among co-workers. Trust forms through friendship, acquaintance, and gossip. Employees typically have stronger attachments to their fellow workers than they do to "the organization," an abstract entity.

The McDonaldization of Work

Nowhere is the rationalization, specialization, bureaucratization, and commodification of work more apparent than in what sociologist George Ritzer (1993/2015) calls the "McDonaldization" of work. As Ritzer notes, all of these processes are clearly evident in the fast food industry, epitomized by McDonald's restaurants—hence the term *McDonaldization*.

This process of McDonaldization combines four elements that are already familiar to us individually. Specifically, it includes a concern with efficiency (i.e., minimizing the time to complete a task, such as filling an order); calculability (i.e., getting workers to quantify how much they're delivering, and getting customers to quantify how much they're getting versus how much they're paying); predictability (i.e., standardizing the price, product, and service delivery from one location to another, which requires that all work tasks will be repetitive, routine, easily taught, and easily learned); and control (i.e., achieving maximum control over the work process through standardized employees, meaning an easy replacement of workers by other workers and human workers by technologies) (Ritzer, 1993/2015).

Another related influence on work and the workplace has been the effect of neo-liberalism, an ideology that has implications for government, investment, and workplace management. Neo-liberalism is widely understood to have aided in the globalization of manufacturing, through the shipping of jobs offshore. In this and other ways, neo-liberalism has undermined trade union strength; this, in turn, has undermined the unions' ability to safeguard workers' interests within the labour market, employment relationship, and society (Smith & Morton, 2006).

One effect has been to increase in workplace danger to health and safety. Ellen McEachern (2000), for example, notes "neo-liberal rationalities . . . assume a greater burden on individual responsibility to avoid risk" (p. 315). She studies the way "managers in four Ontario newspaper workplaces understand and respond to workers complaining of repetitive strain injury (RSI)," and finds that managers view "RSI-prone workers as undisciplined and neglectful of their own bodies." This leads them to "reduce workers' claims for compensation through extensive surveillance of 'risky' worker bodies. The worker body emerges as a biopolitical terrain for the working out of tensions between welfarist and neoliberal rationalities as worker health becomes a locus for discourse on where to draw the line between rights and responsibilities and between civilian and the state" (2000, p. 315).

Quinlan, Mayhew, and Bohle (2001; see also Quinlan & Sheldon, 2011) observe that this effect of neo-liberalism on job safety and security is part of a worldwide transition. They note that the increase in contingent (or precarious) work in industrial countries has harmful effects on the health of workers. Of course, harm and danger were common aspects of industrial work in all nineteenth- and early twentieth-century societies, and remain common today in "developing" countries such as Bangladesh. The problem of concern to these authors is that precarious work is becoming common once again in North America and some other Western economies, as less-regulated employers seek to increase their profits at the expense of workers' health. The growth and resurgence of precarious work throughout the world is a concern not only because it drives down wages in the highest-income countries but because it poses serious hazards to the health of workers there and elsewhere.

Class and Status Group Conflict

Another process of industrialization is the creation of new, often more extreme, class inequalities. Recall from Chapter 1 that Karl Marx (see Marx & Engels, 1848/2002) was the first important thinker to write about class inequalities under industrial capitalism. In his theory, capitalists (or bourgeoisie) and workers (or proletariat) were the two key classes in capitalist industrial society.

The essential idea of Marxism is that capitalist society is built on a conflict between the owners of the means of production (the bourgeoisie) and the working class (or proletariat) who must sell their labour for wages, in order to survive (Marx & Engels, 1848/2002). This binary social split between the "haves" and the "have-nots" of society is fundamental to social relations and **class** conflict.

What defines the bourgeoisie is not mainly their wealth or power, but their exploitive control over the proletariat. The bourgeoisie use capital to expand their riches by buying the proletariat's time and labour, and profiting from what the workers produce. Their amount of profit depends mainly on the price of the manufactured product minus the cost of labour and materials—so making a profit depends on keeping prices high and wages (and other costs of production) as low as possible. The proletariat, for their part, must sell their time and labour to the bourgeoisie because they do not have the capital needed to own the means of production. This relationship between bourgeoisie and proletariat is, therefore, paradoxical: they depend on one another and they are in continual opposition.

This oppositional relationship between capitalists and workers reveals the two defining properties of capitalism: exploitation and alienation. *Exploitation* means that the proletariat is paid (much) less than the price of the finished product, so the capitalist is able to take the surplus profit. *Alienation*, as mentioned earlier, means that the exploitative labour process deprives workers of the ownership of their own products and, worse, distances them from the productive process, from themselves, and from others. This alienation or estrangement is a form of dehumanization; thus, capitalism is inherently dehumanizing.

In a present-day post-industrial society, however, Marx's portrayal is too simple for several reasons. First, it is no longer necessary to own a business to control the means of production. Now, it is only necessary to manage the organization and/or serve on its board of directors. Second, the working class today is international because of multinational ownership and global competition. This globalization of work makes it even more difficult for workers to mobilize, because jobs can always be shipped overseas if the workers demand higher wages or more job security (as described in the section below).

Weber, in contrast to Marx, distinguished economic class (or ownership) from two other sources of power in industrial society: *parties* and *status groups*. According to Weber, parties are associations and organizations that give people non-economic power and influence. Meanwhile, status groups are sets of people who share a social position in society from which they derive identity and honour. These status groups organize around factors such as religion, ethnicity, region, or even racialized

class according to Marx, a group of people who share the same relationship to the means of production, or to capital; according to Weber, a group of people who share a common economic situation, based on (among other things) income, property, and authority.

identity. Even professional associations (e.g., of dentists) are status groups. They all practise exclusion to maintain the boundaries between their own group and others. Through their broader understanding of power, Weber's insights improve Marx's understanding of capitalism in the present day.

Economic Turmoil

Interactive activity

According to Marx, capitalism creates economic turmoil, in the form of cyclic (or repetitive) economic crises. Bursts of high productivity lead to overproduction, which in turn drives down prices. With the fall in prices, capitalists stop investing and the economy slows down, which creates the conditions for a recession and loss of jobs. These highs and lows lead to periodic unemployment cycles in the economy. For capitalists, the goal is always to get into a market while the profits are rising and get out before they start falling. However, workers do not have the same flexibility, as they are dependent on their wages. So, they gain less than capitalists when markets are good and suffer more than capitalists when markets are bad. Without organization, they have little security or bargaining power in relation to the ruling capitalists.

The continued risk of unemployment also lets capitalists threaten workers who demand too much. Workers who protest too hard in times of high unemployment find themselves replaced by the unemployed, or by machines, or by workers in lower-wage countries. In this way, capitalists use the unemployed, and the threat of unemployment, to prevent or quash labour unrest (see Box 12.3).

Think Globally

12.3 | Europe's Lost Generation: Youths Out of Work

Europe's record-breaking youth unemployment rate is producing public outcries of anger and frustration in Italy, Spain, Greece, and Britain. One in five people aged 18 to 25 are jobless and, of those youths with jobs, many have only part-time or temporary positions. Greece and Spain are two of the hardest hit countries in Europe, with over 40 per cent of youths out of work (Holodny, 2016). These young people, many of whom are inexperienced and thus uncompetitive on the job market, are among the 16.3 million unemployed people in Europe. Called the lost generation because of its unpromising prospects, the unemployed young people of Europe may have a long struggle ahead of them.

In the long term, mass youth unemployment may have disastrous, far-reaching effects on an individual and national level. A study in Britain suggests that youth unemployment today will severely affect future earnings, with jobless youths incurring a wage "penalty" of up to 21 percent later in life (Bell & Blanchflower, 2011). Additionally, the International Labour Organization warns that mass youth unemployment may lead to "increased crime rates in some countries, increased drug use, moving back home with the parents, [and] depression" (Allen & Ainley, 2012). Other scarring consequences of being unemployed when young include an increased likelihood of smoking and

lower life satisfaction. In addition to many other "scarring effects" of youth unemployment, having fewer skills from a lack of previous job experience also results in lack of confidence (McQuaid, Raeside, Edgell, & Graham, 2016).

Youth unemployment (and underemployment) is one of the biggest problems facing the world today, although it gets far less notice than terrorism and environmental degradation. Perhaps you are already wondering what kind of job you will do when you graduate.

Theoretical Approaches to Work

Conflict Theory

For conflict theorists, class is a very important idea, as we have seen. For Marx, class focuses on the means of production. For Weber, class focuses on power and the market. However, for all sociologists, whether Marxian or Weberian, class is hard to define and measure. For conflict theorists, class consciousness is the particular combination of class, work, and status situations.

We still, a century and a half after Marx put forward this concept, have trouble understanding class consciousness and the conditions that give rise to it. What we do know is that people have to learn class differences before they can understand class interests, and often class differences are hard to see and understand.

In earlier decades, skilled blue-collar (or manual) work was highly visible and often considered more prestigious than farm work. Eventually, skilled white-collar (non-manual) work became more prestigious than skilled blue-collar work. Yet, in recent decades, even skilled white-collar work has lost much of its prestige because of depersonalization, exploitation, and alienation. A key culprit is automation, as is evident in Figure 12.1. Automation, like globalization, displaces workers through unemployment and allows employers to ramp up their pursuit of profit at any cost.

Conflict theorists are also likely to consider the changes that technology has brought to the workforce in the context of how technology has provided new means of surveillance and control over workers (see Box 12.4).

Functionalism

Functionalist sociologists are less likely to look at classes organized around the means of production, and more likely to look at what they call a "stratification system"—a hierarchy of different people with different occupational roles and income levels.

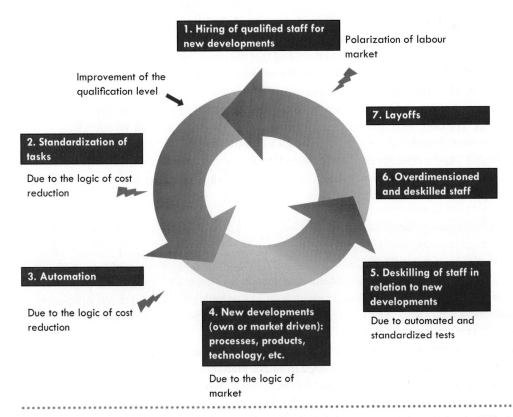

FIGURE 12.1 The Effects of Automation on Hiring and Employment in a Post-Industrial Workplace

Source: Author-generated

Spotlight On

12.4 | Canada Post Clerk Fired for Facebook Posts

An Edmonton woman ("Anne") was one of several discontented older employees who argued with their 24-year-old supervisor, and as a result, received a three-day disciplinary suspension without pay. Shortly after the suspension, Canada Post discovered 30 Facebook postings that made fun of managers and the company. In one posting, Anne mentioned having a voodoo doll of her supervisor, and later posted that, if she had not been drinking, "she would take her out on the driveway and run her over." The posts were visible to more than 50 Facebook "friends," some of whom were Anne's coworkers (Mertl, 2012).

Anne was fired soon after the posts were found. Though the Canadian Union of Postal Workers agreed that the postings were inappropriate, they filed a grievance calling for Anne's reinstatement on the grounds that workplace tensions had driven Anne to vent her frustrations online on a site she had assumed was private. Anne

also blamed her supervisors for creating a hostile environment that left her nowhere to vent her frustrations. She denied that her actions were inappropriate and showed no remorse for her postings. The arbitrator who reviewed the case ultimately decided that, despite her long service, a negative and unrepentant attitude showed that Anne should not be reinstated (Smith, 2012; "Canada Post Clerk," 2012).

So what does this case ultimately show us? First, it shows that people can be alienated even outside capitalist, privately owned workplaces. Second, this example shows that a labour union can play an important role in people's work lives, in this case supporting a worker who might otherwise have had no recourse. Third, we see that, just as new technology provides a new opportunity for communication, it also provides a new opportunity for surveillance, even outside the workplace (Feth & Zurbrigg, 2012).

In this framework, there are no clear-cut classes. However, everyone knows whether they are rich or poor, and everyone wants to get ahead, or at least wants their children to get ahead. In this context, ambition motivates people to work hard and move up the ladder. Jobs at the top of the ladder require much more investment in education and effort, and they therefore carry greater rewards. According to functional theory, the best-paid jobs are also the most socially useful and valued jobs.

Functional theorists assume that people generally agree on the social value of an occupation. And indeed, many surveys around the world have demonstrated a high degree of consensus around job rankings. Typically, jobs that require extensive education and have high incomes (e.g., medicine, law, university teaching) are considered highly desirable and highly prestigious. On the other hand, jobs that require little education and have a low income (e.g., food server, babysitter, unskilled labourer) are considered the opposite. CEOs tend to see human capital as one of the top sources of continued profitability of their businesses.

Time to reflect

Can you think of any jobs in Canadian society that are highly paid but do not require extensive education? How about examples of jobs that require an extensive education but are not highly paid? Can you think of any jobs that are highly paid but are not prestigious or desirable?

Human capital theorists argue that money invested in the well-being (education, health, welfare, and security) of people is money invested in future economic growth. The better educated and healthier that people are, the better they are able to perform all of the duties necessary for society to function. However, investment in human capital is expensive and returns are slow.

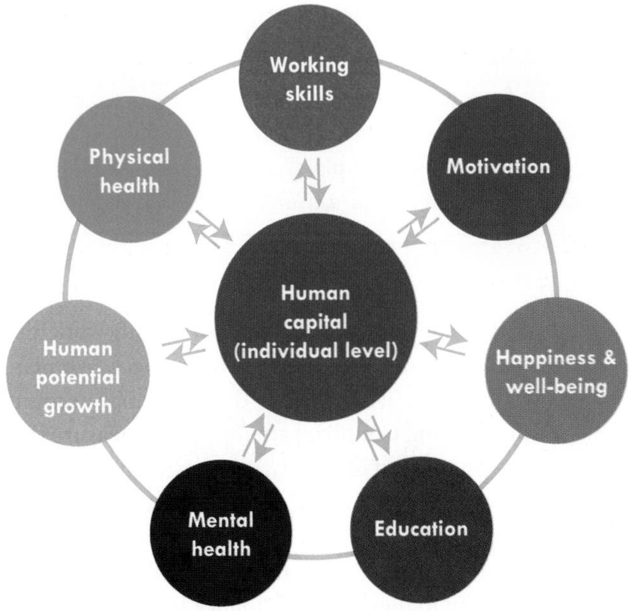

FIGURE 12.2 What Produces Human Capital?

Source: http://buddhajeans.com/sustainable-fashion-design-contents-page/diagram-downloads-library/human-capital-diagram-library/

Given this general agreement about the value of human capital and, therefore, the unequal value of different occupations, inequality is good for society because it brings out excellence and productivity. Consider, as an example, the job of a physician. Doctoring requires a great deal of skill and expertise. A physician needs many years of education to develop his or her skills. After obtaining a medical degree, the physician then faces a highly stressful career filled with long shifts and hard, challenging work. By contrast, consider the job of serving coffee and doughnuts at Tim Hortons. The training required to do this job is minimal; likewise, the job complexity and associated stress and responsibility are perceived to be minimal.

When investments in skill and effort are consistent with compensation, as with doctors and doughnut servers, the functional theory of inequality works well. However, investments and compensations are not always in balance. Consider the inflated salaries of professional athletes, entertainers, and professional criminals, or the much lower salaries of nurses, teachers, and child-care workers. In these cases, the compensations do not obviously suit the social importance of the jobs and their study requirements. Of course, the athletes, entertainers, and criminals may have invested thousands—even tens of thousands—of hours perfecting their "skills," but how valuable are these skills to society? Are they necessary for our survival? And, if not, does this mean that these skills are of lower functional importance or value?

Feminist Theories

Feminist theorists note that women and men have very different experiences at work, even if they belong to the same class. Some of this was discussed in Chapters 6 and 7, so we will summarize and consider other aspects of gender inequality and work here.

Feminists who study class relations tend to take an intersectionalist approach of the kind that was discussed in Chapters 6 and 7. This approach recognizes the fact that different combinations of disadvantage produce different outcomes. Thus, it is impossible to make universal statements about social class or about gender inequality.

Feminists note that many Canadian women still disproportionally work for little or no pay, whatever their class. Domestic work is particularly notable in this respect. Women perform three times more unpaid household labour than men (UNDP, 2015). This work may account for as much as one-third of the world's economic production. Countries attempting to measure the value of unpaid care work estimated that 20 per cent to 60 per cent of their GDP is due to unpaid work, most of it being performed by women—though the way to actually count the value of unpaid work remains controversial (UNDP, 2015). When unpaid agricultural work and housework are considered with wage labour in developing countries, women's work hours are estimated to exceed men's by almost 30 per cent (UN, 2015). Also, men, who usually occupy higher-paid and higher-level jobs than women often profit at the expense of women who work for them. As a result, capitalists profit from the hard work of women even more than they profit from the hard work of men. For women, this results in job dissatisfaction, a lack of job control, and a rising prevalence of depression and other psychosomatic illnesses.

Marx introduced the concept of social reproduction to describe the social structure and norms that recreate social inequality, including gaps in pay over time. Despite the fact that new opportunities, such as access to higher education, have opened up for women in the last few decades, the gender wage gap in Canada has remained stuck since the mid-1990s at one of the highest levels in the industrialized world (Grant, 2016). Women are overrepresented in the lower end of the occupational marketplace, where dead-end and/or part-time work dominates. Low wages and job instability often mean that even full-time workers must live in poverty (Lefroncois, 2015). Racialized women in Canada are even more likely to have lower wages and unstable employment.

Stereotypes persist of women as nurturing and emotional and of men as more dominant and rational. As a result, women are recruited for careers that place them in a caring role—like nursing—and less often encouraged to enter occupations requiring abstract reasoning skills—like engineering. Consider advancements within the information technology industry in Canada. While these advances have led to mass employment opportunities, women seem to be largely underrepresented within this sector of work in Canada (Bogart, 2014).

For these and other reasons, women are still underrepresented in leadership positions, though the share of women in management has been increasing in recent decades. However, there is continued debate about whether this increase is attributable to a greater acceptance of femininity in the workplace, or whether this merely reflects the increasing success of women at showing more masculine character traits (Bailey, 2014). The "glass ceiling" that results in this gender-based earning difference, and other gender-related workplace concerns, such as harassment, were discussed at length in Chapter 7.

People who have alternative gender identities or expressions also face discrimination in the workplace. Transgendered people, whether male, female, or otherwise gendered are more likely than other workers to experience discrimination and harassment in the work place. A survey of findings in the United States showed that a staggering 90 per cent of trans people reported facing some form of harassment at work and 26 per cent were fired for being transgendered (Grant et al., 2011). Trans people are also more likely than people with a normative gender identity and expression to have a lower income.

Symbolic Interactionism

For their part, symbolic interactionists focus on the ways that meanings are attached to social inequality—for example, how the labels "wealthy" and "poor" are constructed through social interaction. More recently, social constructionists have begun to ask how a particular social arrangement emerged. In other words, how did popular beliefs and demands for change lead to the current social situation? In his book *Contested Terrain: The Transformation of the Workplace in the Twentieth Century* (1979), Richard Edwards argues that management practices evolved from simple (or direct) control, to technological control, to what he calls "bureaucratic control." These changes happened alongside other changes in the type of work done and the kind of technology used in the workplace. In addition, they responded to the ways workers tried to stop managerial control. When one control stopped working, another would be invented and taught to new generations of managers. In every instance, they reflect the employer's perception of what it would take to control a particular "kind" of worker.

Time to reflect

What is your perspective on work, and workplace dynamics? Do you recognize your perspective in the described theoretical approaches? Where do you think your perspective came from? Has it been informed by culture, experience, your class and other social locations, or elsewhere?

Similarly, social constructionists are interested in the evolution of popular thinking about work. In the 1950s and 1960s, the main concerns about work were how work in large organizations turns people into machine-like robots. In the 1970s and 1980s, the main concerns changed to the exploitation of workers here and abroad, the possibility of computers replacing humans in the workplace, and the need to secure more leisure. Since then, with the rise of globalization, the main concerns have been job insecurity, job loss (that is, the export of jobs to low-wage countries), and the effects of bad work lives on people's family lives and health.

TABLE 12.1 Theoretical Approaches to Work

Theory	Main points
Conflict Theory	· Capitalists benefit from the current organization of work.
	· Work promotes social inequality.
	· Work is a place of repression and mistreatment.
	· Unemployed people depress wages and provide a **reserve army of labour**.
Structural Functionalism	· Work is a basic human need.
	· Everyone profits when everyone works.
	· Work provides a basis for social interaction, social solidarity, and cohesion.
Feminist Theory	· Women continue to be disadvantaged at work.
	· Patriarchy operates in the workforce.
	· Women are paid less than men for the same jobs and work in lower-paying sectors.
	· Capitalists benefit from the unpaid work of women.
Symbolic Interactionism	· Socialization and labelling shape the content and perception of different jobs.
	· Meanings are found in work and unemployment.
	· Work provides a major part of our identity.

reserve army of labour people who, because they are impoverished and often unemployed, form an easily mobilized, easily disposable workforce at the mercy of employers.

Source: Author-generated

The Organization of Work in Canada Today

The theories of Marx, Weber, and Durkheim are slightly too simplistic in our age of high-tech, multi-national capitalism. Moreover, state institutions exercise much of the power in our society, and state institutions can be as oppressive as capitalists. Most importantly, technological developments like the World Wide Web connect people from around the world. So, the exercise of economic and political power has become increasingly global and multinational, as has the exercise of social cohesion. Therefore, we must ask, how should we think of class conflict in global terms?

In the late twentieth century, industrialism in Western societies evolved into post-industrialism. **Post-industrialism** is the shift from a manufacturing-intensive economy to an economy based on services and information, and we can date the beginnings of this to the period following the Second World War (Myles, 1991; also Myles, Picot, & Wannell, 1993). Some might even date it earlier than this, with the rise of sales forces in the modern economy (here, a key work is *White Collar* [1951] by C. Wright Mills).

With post-industrialism, communication has no boundaries: geography, distance, and national borders are no longer communication barriers. Technology and other factors have increased the flow of information, products, and people (Myles, 1991). Interestingly, social philosopher H.G. Wells foresaw some of the last century's most important changes well before they happened (see Box 12.5).

post-industrialism an economic system based more on knowledge, services, and information than on manufactured goods or primary production.

Theory in Everyday Life

12.5 | H.G. Wells

Over a century ago, world famous historian, philosopher, and novelist H.G. Wells predicted changes in the future of work. In 1901, he attempted to "anticipate" or predict the coming social classes (or "elements") of the twentieth century. He made the following predictions.

1. A new sort of property and proprietor class (i.e., the investor) will emerge, created by the stock market system that is, by its very design, irresponsible, since "property that can be owned at any distance and yields its revenue without thought or care on the part of its proprietor is, indeed, absolutely irresponsible property, a thing that no old world property ever was" (Wells, 1901/1999, p. 72).

2. The apprenticeship system will evolve into a system of continuous education, since workers "must keep on mastering new points, new aspects, they must be intelligent and adaptable, they must get a grasp of that permanent something that lies behind the changing immediate practice. In other words, they will have to be educated rather than

trained after the fashion of the old craftsman" (Wells, 1901/1999, p. 83).

3. More complex power classes, including management and trader classes, will emerge. "A great number of non-productive persons . . . who are engaged in more or less necessary operations of organization, promotion, advertisement, and trade. There are the business managers, public and private, the political organizers, brokers, commission agents, the varying grades of financier down to the mere greedy camp followers of finance, the gamblers pure and simple, and the great body of their dependent clerks, typewriters, and assistants" (Wells, 1901/1999, p. 87).

4. There will be a loss of unskilled labour jobs, which will create a class of unemployable workers: "that broad base of mere toilers now no longer essential, and the great body of their dependent labourers, [that] is, with the development of toil-saving machinery, dwindling and crumbling down bit by bit towards the abyss" (Wells, 1901/1999, p. 99).

Time to reflect

Do you worry about your future job prospects in the context of sociological change? What, if any, plans have you made to help ensure you stay relevant to the job market (Hint: Postsecondary education was a good start!)?

Technological Influence on the Workplace

What is the role of technology and science in this global spread of communication, organization, and trade? As always, technology is amoral and apolitical: it can be used for good or for bad, as its owners require and regulators permit.

Today, as we have noted, much of our work is done with computerized technology. This has led some to imagine that work will become—and is becoming—less arduous, more satisfying, and more humane. Indeed, mechanization might lead workers to expect more leisure time, more job autonomy, fewer repetitive tasks, more opportunity to spend time on interesting work, and generally, a more satisfying work experience.

That said, computer technology has had negative as well as positive effects. For one, technology has increased workplace inequality. This is because computers have replaced people at the bottom of the work hierarchy, or rendered their skills redundant. More and more, organizations have reduced the number of full-time and permanent jobs in order to increase their profitability and flexibility. Though technology is not the sole cause of this trend, it has made many people more readily replaceable. Workers need to constantly upgrade their skills to remain competitive in a continuously changing job market. However, as we see in Box 12.6, many workers are falling behind in this race to upgrade.

Skill upgrading is largely limited to people with the financial and educational means to do so, and those who work in a sector of the economy that wants and promotes such changes. Low-wage positions (e.g., in food service or manual labour) do not need constant skill adaptation, but neither do they offer many opportunities for greater self-improvement and wealth (Acemoglu, 2002; Booth, Francesconi, & Frank, 2002). Instead, the impact of technology on unskilled and semi-skilled workers is that their jobs are being replaced by machines.

Time to reflect

Given what you have learned about the tendency of computer-controlled technology to eliminate low-wage positions, as well as what you've learned about job security more generally, what kind of jobs would likely be most secure against unemployment in the future?

Digital Divide

12.6 | Are New Information and Communication Technologies Creating A "Digital Skills Gap"?

Today's rate of technological development is astounding and new information and community technologies are implemented almost immediately in the workplace. However, the rate at which these new technologies are adopted may be too fast for the majority of employees to keep up, resulting in a growing digital skills divide (Rong & Grover, 2009).

Workers' confusion about new technologies can result in a loss of productivity. In the United States, this confusion has been estimated to cost the economy about US$1 trillion per year (Fernandez, 2001). Many think that it is mostly older workers who cannot keep up with the new technologies, due to the existing generational digital divide. However, studies have shown that even younger, tech-savvy workers are finding it difficult to keep up with the rapid rate of technological development (Presnky, 2007; Kotamraju, 2002).

As the digital skills gap continues to grow, the pool of skilled employees becomes smaller and smaller, and businesses find themselves fighting tooth-and-nail for the few workers capable of using the latest forms of workplace technology.

Niloo/Shutterstock.com

What are the chances that, during your work life, you will be replaced by a smart machine? You may think the chances are small, but think again and plan accordingly. Many workers at Toronto's Pearson Airport may not have done so.

Computer-controlled machinery replacing human workers benefits owners and managers for several reasons. First, it removes human error. Second, high-tech machines can manufacture products with more uniformity and precision than human workers. Third, machines, unlike humans, can run non-stop, and this is very cost-effective in the long run. Fourth, replacement of humans with machines reduces conflict between workers and bosses—computing devices do not demand an income, never go on strike (although they do break down), never become tired or bored by their work (no experience of alienation), and do not take vacation or parental leave. Only a few well-trained employees are needed to program, supervise, and maintain the otherwise robotic workflow (Carlopio, 2011).

No wonder some fear that technology could lead to an unprecedented rise in unemployment. To some extent, this fear has been justified. It's true that, people are still needed to invent, use, maintain, and fix technology in the workplace. However, we need a better match between the skills that people acquire and the skills that jobs require. Some workers without the necessary job skills—whether computer-based or otherwise—have had to accept **non-standard work arrangements**—sometimes called "McJobs." These arrangements usually do not guarantee a career, as most jobs did in the past.

Post-industrial workplaces have also been altered by communication technologies. Telephones, texting, Skype, email, and social media websites such as Facebook, Twitter, and Instagram allow workers separated by great physical distances to remain in real-time contact with one another, either over a wire or in cyberspace. This has resulted in the emergence of virtual work—that is, the completion and performance of work duties away from the traditional office through the use of computer technology (Golden & Veiga, 2005).

non-standard work arrangements dead-end, low-paying, insecure jobs, also known as precarious employment.

Time to reflect

How might the social and cultural aspects of work change in the context of virtual work environments? Hypothesize how a virtual work culture might vary from an in-person work culture.

Virtual work has become commonplace throughout North America. According to a 2010 Statistics Canada report, 11.2 percent of all Canadian workers and one in five university-educated workers worked from their homes (Turcotte, 2010). A growth in the variety and availability of information and communication technologies has reduced the need for geographic proximity, and where face-to-face contact is needed, it can be achieved through the use of Skype. Accordingly, work expectations have changed. Everything and everyone must now be accessible at any time and instantaneously. Among many other things, this changes the way we work, and whether it does so for better or worse is still under study.

Modern Capitalism and Neo-Liberalism

Managers are the new class of people in control of capital. These managers are not Marx's easy-to-identify bourgeois factory owners, who control the fates of workers, investors, pensioners, and their dependents. In fact, these managers are farther away from ownership and the shop floor than Marx could ever have imagined. Still, managers have more power than the bourgeoisie: the 2008 economic downturn was due to the misbehaviour not of owners but of managers of the means of production. Because of mismanagement by directors, executive officers, financiers, speculators, and bankers, the economies of Canada, the United States, and European countries were sent into crisis.

Since Marx's time, other new classes have been identified as having great influence in Canadian society, even though they do not own the means of production or sell their labour to capitalists. Examples of such people include doctors, civil servants, judges, elected officials, and other employees of organizations outside the profit sector (for example, social workers employed by cities). Even sociology professors fall into this category.

Hero Images Inc./Alamy Stock Photo

Managers really didn't have a place in the Marxian theory of social classes, yet the management (or administrative) class is among the most rapidly growing work categories in modern society. How do managers create wealth (if they do)?

Video: *Smoke Traders*

Typically, all of these people have expert knowledge and special skills. They also exercise authority of certain kinds without possessing or controlling wealth. The power of some of these non-capitalists (like cabinet ministers or high court judges, for instance) is sometimes even equal to that of capitalists. So, we can say with certainty that only some inequality in modern Canada is due to exploitation in the form that Marx imagined.

The state also plays a large role in both the creation and reduction of this inequality. First, it regulates (and sometimes deregulates) financial processes that can drastically affect financial stability. Second, it sets the tax rates. Third and equally important, the state provides transfer payments—for example, pensions and social assistance payments—which are of great importance to the most vulnerable members of society. And fourth, the state sets rules and legislation around the use of power, such as discrimination law, voting regulations, bribery and intimidation laws, and rules governing immigration and trade.

The general trend towards a decrease in state intervention is referred to as *neo-liberalism*. No sociological topic connected with inequality under capitalism has created more debate in recent years than neo-liberalism. Under this system, markets are assumed to operate on their own to provide the greatest good for the greatest number of people. People (supposedly) have the maximum freedom to pursue their private goals and, in doing so, they (supposedly) create the maximum prosperity for everyone. This point of view is most compatible with functionalist approaches to world organization, which emphasize equilibrium, efficiency, modernization, and integration.

Underlying neo-liberal thinking is a kind of economic Darwinism that assumes the greatest good comes from an uncontrolled marketplace. In this imaginary economic world, profit "trickles down" to lower-income people, providing opportunity for units on the lowest level to prove themselves. Productive units will struggle for survival and transcendence. The less effective or inefficient units will fail and become obsolete, while the best ones triumph and remain in place because they maximize the economic system's productivity.

However, under neo-liberalism income inequality has increased. Neo-liberal lack of oversight and restriction also helped bring the world economy to near meltdown in the Wall Street collapse of 2008.

> ## Time to reflect
>
> On a day-to-day basis, do you worry more about individual crime (for example, having your wallet stolen) or corporate crime (for example, having your entire savings account become worthless)? What social factors can you point to that have influenced your answer?

Globalization

One factor that has worsened the job situation of unskilled and semi-skilled workers in Canada is neo-liberal-driven globalization. Globalization has outsourced jobs, driven down wages, and increased the demand by employers for non-standard work arrangements. Global cities, such as New York and Toronto, are important financial hubs for multimillion-dollar financial corporations. However, with the decline of manufacturing work, even in these cities that dominated the industrial era, contingent and temporary work has grown.

On the other hand, global cities have expanded commerce, tourism, and the financial sector (Sassen, 1995). In turn, this has created a tiered economy that requires workers in the food, hotel, and cleaning industries. And, as the service sector expands, the demand grows for people to work as restaurant waiters, building janitors, valet car attendants, cab drivers, and street vendors. Immigrants with few social ties, few skills (or unrecognized accreditation), and (often) a lack of documentation are drawn into these jobs. They must seek their labour on a day-to-day basis and live without the comforts of permanent employment.

Non-standard work is the fastest-growing type of employment in high-income countries today. The rise in non-standard work arrangements, such as part-time work, has even affected full-time workers. With fewer full-time jobs, more is expected of full-time workers. Many are forced to work longer hours, often unpaid, to compensate for the shortage of workers on site (Jackson, Baldwin, Robinson, & Wiggins, 2000). So, while some workers today are unemployed or fear unemployment, others are underemployed—working well below their skill and training level—while others still are overemployed. This leads to less solidarity and more inequality among workers.

The "Feminization" of Work

One feature of all non-standard work is that it tends to be "precarious"—uncontrollable and unpredictable. In Canada, 39.1 percent of employed women hold "precarious jobs" (Law Commission of Ontario, 2009). Precarious jobs have one or more of the following features: part-time employment, self-employment, fixed-term work, temporary work, on-call work, homework, and telecommuting. What they have in common is that they are not "standard" types of jobs, typified by full-time work by one particular employer.

A United Way report by Wayne Lewchuk et al. (2015; see also Lewchuk et al., 2016) on precarious employment in the Greater Toronto and Hamilton area, *The Precarity Penalty*, shows that standard employment relationships (i.e., non-precarious employment) have continued to decline in the last few years; and today, men and women are almost equally likely to hold precarious (i.e., non-standard) jobs, at a rate of roughly 50 per cent (see Figure 12.3). According to these same data, non-standard jobs have been increasing even more rapidly for men than for women. The decline in non-standard employment is more rapid for racialized workers than for white workers, and it is particularly marked for racialized men (Lewchuk et al., 2015).

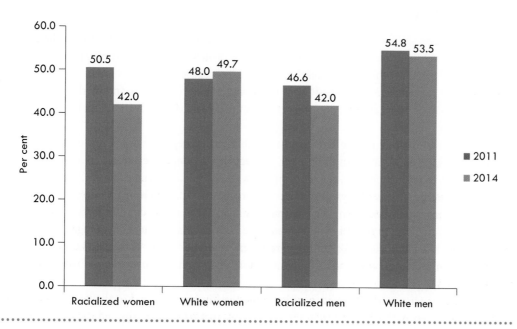

FIGURE 12.3 Percentage of Workers of Each Type employed in "Standard Work Relationship," by Sex and Racialization, GTHA 2011 and 2014

Source: Adapted from www.unitedwaytyr.com/document.doc?id=307 p. 28

"Feminization," in the context of work, refers to not only the increase of women in the workforce but also the increase of precarious work that was previously assigned only to women. This includes a variety of part-time jobs (for example, as a sales clerk in liquor store) and jobs with a high worker turnover (for example, as burger flipper or counter staff at McDonald's). In other words, some of the gender equality that women have achieved in the past few decades has been through the downward mobility of men into similarly precarious jobs.

The End of Class Politics?

Another change, one Marx would not have expected, is the near disappearance of class politics. In many countries, class politics—political competition in which different parties vocally represent different classes—has been replaced by "identity politics." Today, many more people express concerns about racism, sexism, ageism, or religious discrimination than about economic inequality or class-based poverty, although, as Abramson and Inglehart (2009) note, they do stress the value of freedom, self-expression, environmentalism, and identity politics.

Concerns about economic equality are often filtered through these –isms or issues that appeal to particular portions of the working class or middle class—women, visible minorities, gays and lesbians, or the elderly, for example. This change illustrates the importance of Weber's contribution to social theory: that there are many routes to power besides ownership of the means of production, and status groups exercise a strong hold over people's identities.

Time to reflect

Reflect back on this question asked in Chapter 1: Does Marx's emphasis on class as the basis of social conflict resonate with you? Why or why not? Has your answer changed since you were first asked this question?

The Decreasing Role of Unions

An important consequence of neo-liberalism and globalization has been a decline in the power of labour unions. Unions are for the working class what professional associations are for professors, doctors, lawyers, and others in professional fields. For example, both regulate entry into paid jobs. However, unions are concerned with improving pay, job security, and working conditions. Professional associations are more concerned with upholding the reputation and independence of the profession.

Unions give working people strength in numbers: they negotiate wage settlements, set standards for working conditions, and argue for job security, among other measures. As such, unions are important to their members, the working class as a whole, and the economy. And since work is socially structured, it is always negotiable; unions ensure that such negotiations get underway. Union members usually enjoy higher pay than their non-unionized counterparts. They also gain other benefits, such as job security and extended health care plans. These advantages are especially important for low-paying jobs. According to research conducted by the Canadian Labour Congress, in 2015, unionized workers earned $5.28/hour more than non-union workers (Canadian Labour Congress, 2015).

However, as we see in Figure 12.4, union membership has declined in the last 30 years, especially in male-dominated (largely, manufacturing) occupations. This drop reflects dramatic changes in Canada's labour movement, workforce demographics, labour laws, and economic structure. Unionization has decreased among technical health workers (medical, dental, and veterinary technologists), but the statistics also reflect a loss of (traditionally unionized) manufacturing jobs that

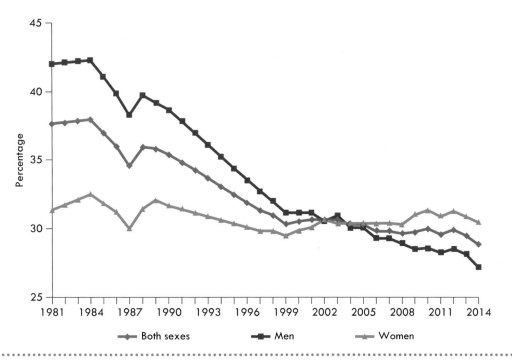

FIGURE 12.4 Percentage of Workers Unionized in Canada, 1981–2014, by Sex

Source: www.statcan.gc.ca/pub/11–630–x/11–630–x2015005-eng.htm

have moved overseas (Hyman, 2002). By contrast, levels of unionization among women—many of whom are in public service jobs—have declined far less in the same period, due at least in part to huge growth of labour participation by women (Hyman, 2002). Happily, we are seeing increased efforts by precarious workers in the hotel, retail, and post-secondary sectors to organize around their interests.

Conclusions

In this chapter, we saw how new technological and scientific advancements affect the workplace, the economy, and society as a whole. We also saw that work and economic relations, especially in markets and workplaces, create social classes. The sociological study of class inequality begins with Karl Marx, who showed that class inequalities are always linked to exploitation. Under capitalism, the bourgeoisie (capitalists) exploit the proletariat (workers). In doing so, they set the stage for class warfare. Ultimately, however, a working-class revolution never occurred in Canada, despite what some would call a continued degradation of quality of work under capitalism.

This is not to say that the issues Marx pointed out are no longer relevant to our current society, however. Consider the evolution of work in Canadian society over the past three centuries and the ways in which technological and scientific developments have influenced this process. Since the 1970s, manufacturing has changed dramatically in Canada due to robotics, new communication technologies, and globalization. As manufacturing has shrunk, the service sector has grown, with an increase in precarious jobs, which are characterized by low pay, little job security, distrust between workers and bosses, close direction and surveillance, and high stress among workers. Marx would have said that the growth of precarious employment has increased the alienation of labour in our society.

Through globalization and new technologies, the ways in which we interact with one another have changed, and the world has become more and more closely connected thanks to new and improved forms of communication and transportation. As is clear, this change has brought new dangers and difficulties, as well as benefits. One result is a global competition for well-paid work.

Questions for Critical Thought

1. Why do you think unionization has declined in Canada and elsewhere? How might the decline be related to the increase in non-standard work?

2. Do you think that modern technology and social media have increased or decreased alienation in contemporary society? Why or why not? Say what you mean by "alienation."

3. What do you think will be the long-term consequences of the shift toward non-standard work? Is a system based on precarious employment sustainable? Why or why not?

4. How have advances in science and technology, like the Industrial Revolution, electricity, and social media changed the work environment? Do you believe that the experience of modern-day workers is better or worse than that of workers who lived before these advances? Explain your answer.

5. If you were designing an education system to prepare young people for the workforce as it exists today, what would you teach and how would you teach it?

Take it Further: Recommended Readings

Wallace Clement and Leah F. Vosko, ed., *Changing Canada: Political Economy as Transformation* (Montreal and Kingston: McGill-Queen's University Press, 2003). This is a wide-ranging collection of papers in which recognized Canadian experts examine a variety of transformations in Canadian society and politics that centre on, and largely originate in, Canada's globalized capitalist economic organization.

Norene Pupo, Ann Duff, and Daniel Glenday, *Crises in Canadian Work: A Critical Sociological Perspective* (Toronto: Oxford University Press, 2016). This textbook provides a clear and provocative overview of issues in the sociology of work, labour markets, and the economic, especially as they are affected by the powerful forces of automation and globalization.

Andrew Ross, *Nice Work If You Can Get It: Life and Labor in Precarious Times* (New York: New York University Press, 2009). The author analyzes the implications of growing precarious work for workers across national, racial, and class lines on a global scale.

Richard Sennett and Jonathan Cobb, *The Hidden Injuries of Social Class* (Cambridge: Cambridge University Press, 1977 [1972]). This book introduced fascinating new theories about the effects of social class on people at the bottom of the class structure, including the effects on those who cannot find ways of improving their situation. For those who think class is a trivial abstraction, this book is an eye-opener.

Leah Vosko, ed., *Precarious Employment: Understanding Labour Market Insecurity in Canada* (Montreal and Kingston: McGill-Queen's University Press, 2006). This book provides a thorough picture of precarious employment in its many forms, and the ways it is maintained or challenged by laws, policies, and labour market institutions, including trade unions.

Take it Further: Recommended Online Resources

Canadian Centre for Occupational Health and Safety (CCOHS)
www.ccohs.ca

Canadian Committee on Labour History
www.cclh.ca

Employment and Social Development Canada
www.canada.ca/en/employment-social-development.html

More resources available on 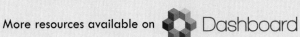 Dashboard

The Future of Work **with Jacob Morgan [podcast]**
https://itunes.apple.com/us/podcast/the-future-of-work-podcast/id907990904?mt=2

International Labour Organization (ILO)
www.ilo.org

UFCW, Facts about Unions
www.ufcw.ca/index.php?option=comcontentandview=articleandid=29andItemid=49andlang=en

13 The Power of Religious Ideas and Institutions

Learning Objectives

In this chapter, you will:

> Define religion as a social phenomenon

> Recognize the role of religion today and the characteristics that define a religion

> Identify the trends of religious participation in Canada today

> Evaluate the contributions of religion to social well-being

> Understand how religion can both include and exclude others in civic relationship

Introduction

At several points in this book, we note that the Enlightenment's emphasis on rational thinking influenced the cultures that came after it—modern cultures largely rejected religious thinking in favour of logic, rationality, and reason. As you can recall from previous chapters, sociologist Max Weber described this shift as the "rationalization" and "disenchantment of the world."

Yet, despite the Enlightenment, religion remains an important force in the modern world. This survival of religion in the modern, industrial, scientific world is something that none of the founders of sociology would have expected. As a result, much of twentieth- and twenty-first-century sociology of religion is taken up with explaining this persistence of religious belief. As we will see, religion continues to have an appeal for people, despite apparent "secularization" in most domains of life.

Examples of the continued fascination with religion surround us. Think about the current fear of Islamic terrorism. Why are so many Canadians concerned that Muslim refugees from Syria will include terrorists? How does terrorism fit into their religion, if at all? You may not have spent much time thinking about these questions—unless, of course, you are Muslim, or have a friend or romantic partner who is Muslim. All of a sudden, religious differences are important again, even in highly secular, highly tolerant Canada.

You may not know much about world religions and may want to know more; unfortunately, limited space prevents us from providing detailed information on specific religious beliefs. We also won't have the space to discuss why monotheism replaced polytheism in the West, or why Christianity replaced paganism in Europe. Religious scholars themselves debate the core values, beliefs, and trajectories of different religions, and it would be risky to venture into these waters without extensive expertise. That said, students interested in comparing religions might start simply, with Google searches for major world religions. There may also be a course on comparative or world religions offered at your college or university.

AP Photo/Ted S. Warren

As we see in this Sikh service, religious people gather to pray to supernatural beings in the company of other religious people, using ritual objects and wearing special clothing. This chapter is about the meaning of that social behaviour.

Defining Religion

Why is **religion** still alive and relevant today? This chapter will try to make sociological sense of this question. But before we can do so, we need to think carefully about what sociologists mean by religion, as compared with common sense definitions of the term. The *Oxford Dictionary of Sociology* defines religion as "a set of beliefs, symbols, and practices (for example rituals), which is based on the idea of the sacred, and which unites believers into a socio-religious community. The sacred is contrasted with the profane because it involves feelings of awe" (Scott, 2014, p. 641).

All of the founders of sociology, including Marx, Durkheim, and Weber, distinguished religion from science. Quoting the *Oxford Dictionary of Social Science*'s definition of religion,

> They were greatly concerned to specify the origins of religion in animism and other concepts of primitive supernatural belief, and to trace religious development through to modern forms of monotheism. Many of these models were organized by a strong Enlightenment sense of religion as an irrational practice, soon to be superseded by scientific or philosophical reason. (Calhoun, 2002)

When people in Canada think about religion, they apply their own common-sense definition. They tend to think about the belief in a Supreme Being: God in Christianity, Allah in Islam, the prevailing spirit in Sikhism, and Yahweh in Judaism. They also think of veneration for particular prophets of the Supreme Being: Jesus in Christianity, Mohammad in Islam, and the still awaited Messiah in Judaism (the Gurus in Sikhism play a slightly different role). Finally, they think of the worship of these supreme beings and their prophets, and how they take place mainly within designated churches, mosques, gurdwaras, or synagogues, following designated rituals and with designated ritual objects. However, these conventional definitions are modelled after Christianity—which at one point in time dominated Canadian society—and do not apply to some of the most popular religions in the world today. Hinduism, for example, has no one single set of rituals that all Hindus adhere to. Buddhism, as another example, includes no creator in its belief system.

As we will see, scientists by and large do not subscribe to religions as defined above. They often do not believe in a Supreme Being, in the sacredness of that Being's prophets, or in the importance of sacred rituals and ritual objects. But that does not mean scientists lack **spirituality**. They are greatly concerned with matters of morality and ethics, with questions about the meaning of life, the reasons for suffering, and a love of humanity. Scientists are spiritual more than they are "religious" in a conventional sense.

So, for example, the great physicist Albert Einstein was born Jewish but never prayed or attended religious services at synagogue. He considered himself a pious man, owing to his profound wonder and admiration at the design of nature. He thought both science and religion were necessary because they fulfilled different needs. As he famously said, "Science without religion is lame; religion without science is blind." So, Einstein was spiritual, even if he wasn't religious in a conventional sense (Jammer, 2011.)

Spirituality and **religiosity** are different in ways we will explore below; the **secularization** of modern societies has reduced people's religiosity, but it may not have reduced their spirituality so much as it has redirected it away from traditional religious practices.

Substantive and Functional Definitions

As we have already seen, religion is a difficult concept to define, since it encompasses many ideas connected to spirituality and faith, and may mean different things to different people. As a first approximation, Peter Berger (1974) discusses the useful but sometimes confusing differentiation between *substantive* and *functional* definitions of religion. Substantive definitions focus on what religion *is*: a religion's core elements, such as the belief in a higher being and supernatural forces. Functional definitions describe what religion *does* for an individual or a social group: how religion connects people to one another, while often also creating conflict between different religious beliefs.

religion any system of beliefs about the supernatural, and the social groups that gather around these beliefs.

spirituality an openness to or search for "sacred" aspects of life, where "the sacred" is broadly defined as that which is set apart from the ordinary (or profane) and worthy of veneration

religiosity the sum of all the various aspects of religious activity, dedication, and belief (religious doctrine) one finds in a group or society.

secularization a steadily dwindling influence of formal (institutional) religion in public life; also, the process whereby, especially in modern industrial societies, religious beliefs, practices, and institutions lose their social significance.

What all religions have in common, from a substantive and functional perspective, is a set of beliefs. All religions lay claim to an almost unquestionable significance and validity. So, you might wonder, what could sociologists possibly bring to the understanding of religion?

The Sociological Approach to Religion

Eighteenth-century Enlightenment thinkers were committed to the idea that humanity was constantly improving which expressed itself in terms of "progress." These thinkers saw previous societies as "primitive" or "less advanced," and judged that European white men and women were the pinnacle of civilized humanity. According to this way of thinking, the natural trajectory of human progress was away from "irrational" ignorance and superstition, including traditional religion, towards rational thinking and planning based on scientific evidence. Early anthropological and sociological analyses of religion were conducted with this belief in mind.

Sociologists today are interested in how people act out their religious beliefs in everyday life, how these beliefs affect their interactions with others and with society, and how, in turn, different aspects of life—work, family, education, and so on—influence religious beliefs. Sociologists are also concerned with how certain beliefs (and not others) are legitimized, and who in society controls this process. From a macro-sociological perspective, they are interested in the rise and fall of religions.

Durkheim and Weber did not fully believe that reason, science, and knowledge would eradicate religion. They understood that religion had a social value that could not be (easily) supplanted by any other social institution. Further, Durkheim and Weber, unlike Marx, did not think that religion was a result of ignorance, delusion, or mental illness. They saw religion as something *beyond* reason—something *non*-rational rather than *ir*rational. However, they still expected religious beliefs to decline in importance over time.

As suggested, this chapter will be concerned with the unexpected survival of religion in a "modern" society, and with the various ways in which new technologies, like computers and the internet, protect and undermine traditional religious values (for example, see Box 13.1).

Creative Touch Imaging Ltd./NurPhoto via Getty Images

Hindu devotees take a selfie (with the idol of the Goddess Durga in the background) during the Durga Puja festival at a pandal (temporary temple) in Mississauga, Ontario.

Think Globally

13.1 | Can the Digital Divide Be Used for Religious Social Control?

In Canada, many people would consider any restriction on our freedom of self-expression a violation of our human rights. However, in some parts of the world, people do not have this freedom guaranteed. Indeed, in some societies, the government legally regulates information and, in this way, regulates the ideas people are and are not allowed to express.

Governments can have all kinds of reasons for engaging in such censorship activities: political, ideological, or religious. Though governments and other powerful bodies (such as churches) have practised censorship for centuries, what is extremely worrying today is the power that technology gives governments when it comes to controlling their citizens (Dahan, 1995).

In Iran, for example, the right of religious censorship has given government the right to limit citizens' access to all kinds of online information. Thus, Iranian law requires all bloggers to register with the Ministry of Art and Culture. By forcing bloggers to register, the government gains control over the ideas Iranians put online. Should any registered blogger express feelings of hostility towards the Mullahs (religious leaders who run Iran) or share negative views about Islam, its doctrines, or religious practices, the government can easily identify that person and take punitive actions (Gohdes, 2015). The authorities harass authors of anti-religious (and anti-government) blog posts and imprison them if they do not cease these activities. In this way, the government maintains religious, social, and political control (Aryan, Aryan, & Halderman, 2013). To bring social change, therefore, citizens will have to overcome censorship and gain awareness of other perspectives. See Chapter 14 for the importance of digital technologies in social movements today.

Time to reflect

Based on your experience of the internet in Canada, does unrestricted internet access guarantee that citizens are exposed to different perspectives and unbiased information? Does internet access, alone, combat misinformation?

Theoretical Approaches to Religion

Conflict Theory

Karl Marx, the earliest figure we can associate with conflict theory, viewed religion as largely a form of social control, and, therefore, as a cause of conflict (Calhoun, 2007). Marx thought that religions, by their nature, tend to support society's dominant ideology—the set of values that benefit only the ruling class and their interests, to the detriment of everyone else. For the working class, religion was a way to cope with reality. Many working-class people believed that their difficult lives on Earth would lead to afterlife in Heaven. So, these people accepted their hardships as a test of their faith, *not* as a result of bourgeoisie oppression. Marx famously characterized religion as the "opiate of the masses" in reference to its ability to make ordinary workers submissive, uncritical, and easy to manipulate.

Marx's discussion of religion was closely tied to the concept of fetishism. By fetishism, we typically mean something that excites irrational awe or excitement. For Marx, religion used the human capacity for irrational excitement to enslave people.

As noted earlier, Marx believed that religion would lose its influence over time. In Marx's ideal socialist society, there would be little place for religion. In this society, workers would identify with, and mobilize around shared societal goals, and religion would cease to be a defining force. So far, Marx's prediction has proven incorrect, as religion continues to be a relevant social phenomenon. Nevertheless, religion continues to cause conflicts between people and societies, and to exert power over them, so Marxism and conflict theory continue to play an important role in the sociology of religion. Additionally, new phenomena such as commodity fetishism, and the "cult of personality" that develops around celebrities and political leaders, can be analyzed in Marxist terms as new forms of religion.

Functionalism

Durkheim (1903/2001) noted that religion exists in every known society. This observation led Durkheim to ask, why is religion universal? And what social functions does religion perform? In contrast with Marx, he concluded that religion has the power to bring people together and keep them together. Durkheim's idea that religion promotes social solidarity places him squarely within the functionalist framework.

In order to answer the questions he posed about religion, Durkheim studied totemism, the use of natural objects and animals as symbols of spirituality. These symbols unite all members of a society under a common belief and thus contribute to social solidarity. Examples of totems include animals and birds, but also crosses, flags, and other symbols of the group. These totemic objects are used in rituals and ceremonies, which also reinforce group solidarity and shared group beliefs.

Durkheim thought that religion divided social life into the sacred and the profane (secular). Symbols, rituals, and ceremonies connect people, and provide an opportunity to escape everyday, "profane" life into a higher, so-called sacred experience. Durkheim hypothesized that this division was functional for people's lives, as people need a portion of life to be sacred. Sometimes, sacred rituals and ceremonies mark annual or periodic events, such as harvests or wars. Oftentimes, they mark important life transitions, such as marriages, births, deaths, and so on. So, rituals and ceremonies give important life events a religious significance.

According to Durkheim, by themselves, ritual or totemic objects and ritual activities are not important or meaningful. However, when used in a religious context, the social cohesion that totems create, maintain, and celebrate makes them important. Religion excites people because it brings them together in out-of-the-ordinary, emotionally moving rituals. Often, these rituals involve strange sounds, smells, and images; strange prayers, dances, songs; even (occasional) drugs and alcohol. In general, drugs and alcohol fall under the profane part of life. However, some religions also use drugs such as peyote or magic mushrooms (for example, traditional religions in Mexico and South America) as sacred tools to help people shift their consciousness to otherworldly concerns.

When people engage in such religious (that is, sacred) practices, they link themselves to each other as social beings. For Durkheim, these shared totemic objects and ritual activities create a collective consciousness—a shared way to understand the world.

Time to reflect

Is the Durkheimian distinction between "sacred" and "profane" activities useful for categorizing the parts of your own life? In other words, are you able to categorize your life into sacred and profane activities?

Durkheim believed that religion would decline as people gradually started to place more value on scientific and technological (rather than religious) thinking (Thompson, 1990). This then led Durkheim to wonder, what would replace religion as a source of social solidarity?

In the end, the survival of organized religion makes sense to functionalists, since nothing has shown itself to be an effective replacement source of social solidarity. Most societies today—even Canadian society—remain religious, and will not become completely secular any time soon. However, there is growing evidence of the secularization Durkheim predicted, and we will discuss it throughout this chapter.

Creative Touch Imaging Ltd./NurPhoto via Getty Images

One of the consequences of secularization is anti-religious sentiment, particularly racialized in the form of Islamophobia. In this photo, Muslim Canadians pray before commencing a massive protest during the National Day of Action against Islamophobia and White Supremacy in downtown Toronto, 2017.

Time to reflect

Is the functionalist argument persuasive to you? Can you think of any other reasons why religion might have persisted for this long?

Symbolic Interactionism

Sociologist Max Weber was interested in religious values and symbols, and how both affected people's behaviour. Weber believed that people have a need to understand the world as "meaningful," and often use religion to find this meaning in the world, or at least, bestow meaning on the world. Without this, they have trouble making sense of, and coping with, the tragedies and injustices we have to endure in life. So, Weber focused on the subjective meaning and personal experience of religion.

Weber was especially interested in the way religious doctrines shape people's world views and behaviours. As you may remember from Chapter 3, in his well-known book, *The Protestant Ethic and the Spirit of Capitalism* (1905/1930), Weber proposed that Protestantism, especially strict Calvinism, supported the rise of capitalism in northwestern Europe. This is because Protestantism and capitalism had an "elective affinity;" they shared several values, such as a strong work ethic, strong character formation, sobriety and thrift, the organization and rationalization of work practices, and the striving towards successful business endeavours. So, when people practised Protestant values, they were also helping capitalism develop. According to Weber, this is the reason why capitalism arose in Protestant Europe and North America, and not in pre-modern India, China, Israel, or Catholic southern Europe.

For symbolic interactionists and other sociologists concerned with the human need for "meaning," the survival of religion makes sense as a way of understanding and coping with life. And as Weber also showed us, religion can play a key role in motivating people to act in new, world-changing ways.

That said, Weber's Protestant ethic thesis has been criticized from a number of quarters. Some have asserted that his characterization of Catholicism was simplistic and largely incorrect, noting that in practice, Catholicism tolerated capital accumulation. Others have noted that his characterization of Calvinism did not apply to most forms of (non-Calvinist) Protestantism. Some have noted that many aspects of "modern" capitalism were to be found in earlier, pre-capitalist and pre-Protestant civilizations where commerce had thrived. Finally, many note that Weber's view that Protestantism and capitalism have an "elective affinity" for one another is, at best, a weak claim and far from a causal assertion.

Feminism

In recent decades, no sociologists have contributed more to our understanding of religion than feminists. In particular, they have focused on the questions of whether traditional religions are misogynistic—that is, show hatred towards women—and whether, therefore, organized religion should be criticized on these grounds.

A number of feminist scholars and others charge that, in most mainstream religions, social processes operating within the religious structures have acted to exclude women from positions of power and decision making, in both doctrine and practice. Although women today have more chance to participate at higher levels of religious organization, these processes remain in operation, to a greater or lesser extent depending on the religion or denomination. In the more "conservative" religions and denominations, exclusionary processes remain in force; and in the more "liberal" religions and denominations, they remain part of the religious structure, though their

Lucas Vallecillos/Alamy Stock Photo

Women occupy a very narrow range of possible roles in most religions. In Judaism, for example (depicted above), women have a limited role in the orthodox synagogue.

operations are masked and contested. Movements such as those for inclusive (i.e., non-sexist) language within religious communication are generally viewed as secondary or "fringe interests" (i.e., not essential).

Mary Daly (1975, 1985), well known as a critic of established Christian churches, shows that the structure, symbolism and language of churches are profoundly anti-woman. Churches promote the concept of hierarchy, with "God" at the apex, followed by men (in some churches, various levels of male priests, then laymen), women, and children. This hierarchy is strengthened and promoted by an overwhelming number of male images. Most often, "God" is still presented as male; images of Jesus abound in many churches; and figures of the (male) apostles appear everywhere.

Often, the only apparent female image is that of Mary, viewed as mother and described in ways that (as many feminist theologians and sociologists point out) make plain that she is set apart from "ordinary" women, and so cannot be truly emulated. Besides, even as mother of "God," she has no power, and she does not form part of the male Trinity. When, in 1987, the world's first female Catholic theology professor, Uta Ranke-Heinemann, challenged the concept of the Virgin Mary as asexual, untainted and pure—an impossible model for women to emulate—the Catholic Church revoked her authority to teach theology.

At its worst, church-driven patriarchy was a matter of life and death for women. The witch craze, culminating in the sixteenth and seventeenth centuries, took the lives of thousands of women and men (see Hester, 1992; Whitney, 1995). About 80 per cent of those accused of witchcraft were women; the men were most often those associated with the women condemned as witches—their fathers, sons, or husbands, or men who tried to defend them. The theology of the times made the witch craze possible. Women were seen as the carriers of evil, susceptible to the advances of the devil, as described in the story of Eve. Even civil judges at the time, under the influence of church doctrine, sought supernatural explanations for phenomena such as the death of animals or sickness of people (see Briggs, 1991; Book, 2002).

It is no coincidence that this was also a period of the growing domestication and restriction of women. At the start of this period, women acted in the public sphere, as farmers, traders, craftspeople, midwives, and folkhealers. By the end of it, a woman's place was as an adjunct to her husband, if she had one. Seen in a broader context, the process of accusation, trial, torture, and execution of thousands of "witches" proved to be one method by which men were able to restrict women's lives in the early 1800s.

Today, most analyses of the witch craze still do not mention the intense misogyny inculcated by Christian doctrines, or the determined extinction of folk-religious practices. Where it is mentioned, the witch craze is seen as something "in the past," irrelevant to modern society. Many feminist scholars, however, point out that the effects of the witch craze period are still with us in popular images of women, and especially the ways we speak of older women, troublesome women, and disobedient women as "witches."

Traditional religions are still misogynistic. Harassment of women attending theological colleges is commonly reported, and the images of divinity presented today within Christianity (as an example) are still overwhelmingly male (Jantzen, 1999). Women disproportionately participate in religious activities, playing a large part in the organization of the everyday life of religions, from bake sales to visiting charity work and vast amounts of committee work; but women remain organizationally invisible. In part because of this, increasing numbers of women are looking for and finding their religion outside traditional ones. Some writers are attempting to construct feminist theologies in which divinity is conceptualized as female, or as both female and male (see, for example, Griffin, 1995). Many other people within North America and Europe

Who were the women who went to their death accused of witchcraft, and what had they done to deserve this distinction?

TABLE 13.1 Theoretical Approaches To Religion

Theory	Main points
Conflict Theory	· Religions discourage questioning and protest.
	· Religious hierarchies tend to support the status quo.
	· Religions try to interfere with all areas of social life.
Structural Functionalism	· Religions create social cohesion through ritual activity.
	· Religions provide a division of life into sacred and profane.
	· Religions create and strengthen social bonds.
Symbolic Interactionism	· Religions give people a sense of meaning.
	· Religions give people an identity and purpose.
	· Religions shape laws and morality in a society.
Feminism	· Religions give women a secondary role.
	· Religions tend to be patriarchal.
	· Religions have punished women for asserting their rights.

Source: Author-generated

are exploring their spiritualties through reconstructed practices. These new religious movements will be discussed further below.

It is too early to tell what kind of challenge these new and reconstructed religions will pose to Christian hegemony within North America. It may be that in a postmodern world, with an atmosphere of more religious tolerance, each religion (however small) will be able to hold its own and empower its adherents.

Trends in Religious Belief
Secularization

Durkheim and Marx thought that, eventually, people would find secular substitutes for religion. They saw secularization, the steadily dwindling influence of religion in public life, as a positive development—Durkheim because it denoted a growth in tolerant diversity, and Marx because it signalled the growth of class consciousness.

Yes, secularization has meant a reduced discrimination for or against people on the basis of their religion. For example, people who lack a current religious affiliation are most likely of all people to marry someone of a different religious background: they simply don't care about the religion of their mate. However, evidence shows religion is still an important part of modern societies. For example, in Canada, most people still marry people of the same religion (see Figure 13.1).

As we have seen, secularism and secularization are not so simple to understand. For one, secularization doesn't just mean a disappearance of organized religion or spirituality. Scholars who have studied secularization within Western industrial societies have found three common features that lead toward, or are associated with, secularization: *social differentiation*, *societalization*, and *rationalization*.

Social differentiation, following Durkheim's notion, is the process by which a society becomes increasingly complex and diverse. In the past in Canada, churches taught children basic skills, supported people in need, cared for the sick, and served as meeting places for social events. In modern Canada, these social roles are split among many separate institutions: schools, hospitals, government agencies, social clubs, and so on.

Societalization refers to the way people increasingly connect to an abstract "society," and not to a concrete community in which every person knows everyone else. In North America and Europe today, most people look to society—a large, shapeless unit made up of organizations run on bureaucratic

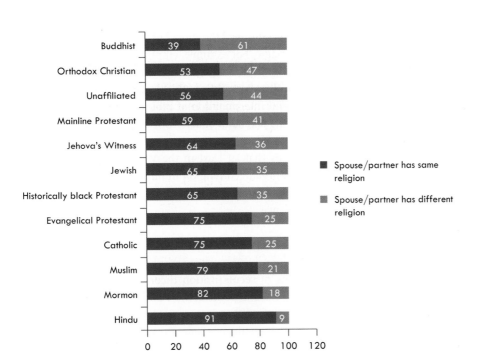

FIGURE 13.1 Patterns in Religiously Mixed Marriages and Partnerships, 2014

Source: www.pewforum.org/2015/05/12/chapter-2-religious-switching-and-intermarriage/pr_15-05-12_rls_chapter2-07/

principles—to provide for their needs. People regularly go to work, read and watch the news, attend school, and vote in elections. All of these activities put them in contact with a society that regulates their activities, often through the state. Interaction with this society leaves little room for religion, which people increasingly view as personal (not societal) and subsequently, a less important part of their everyday lives.

Rationalization, as we have said repeatedly throughout this book, represents an effort, first noted by Weber, to explain the world through the logical interpretation of empirical evidence. Paradoxically,

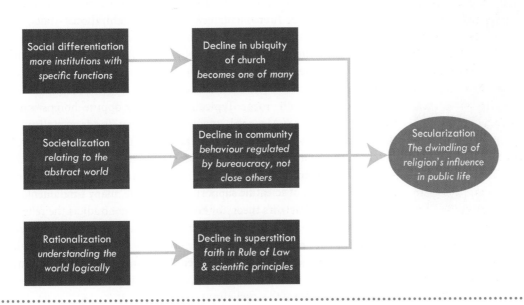

FIGURE 13.2 The Three Main Aspects of Secularization

Source: Author-generated

the Judeo-Christian religions themselves encouraged the spread of rationalization, to reduce people's earlier reliance on superstition and folk magic. For example, emphasis on rationality stressed theology (systematic doctrinal investigation) over mythology (unsystematic leaps of faith). In most Christian denominations, church leadership still stresses philosophical inquiry into the nature of people's link with the divine, as opposed to a literal interpretation of Bible stories. However, secularization largely supplanted the reliance on religious texts and beliefs with a reliance on empirical evidence, scientific thinking, and non-religious "rule of law."

The secularization paradigm proposes that, at least in the West, we can view the Protestant Reformation as the first move away from organized religion in human history. This Reformation is seemingly correlated with a great many features of modern life, including individualism, industrial capitalism, relativism, rationality, and science.

Fundamentalism

fundamentalism the belief that religions should strictly follow the oldest, most traditional, and most basic theological texts, also known as the religion's holy books.

In recent decades, contrary to the claims of secularization theory, religious fundamentalism has played an increasingly important role in social and political life. **Fundamentalism** is the belief that religions should strictly follow the oldest, most traditional, and most basic theological texts, also known as the religion's "holy books." Indeed, fundamentalism is generally understood as a strong attachment and commitment to unchangeable beliefs. As such, it is also viewed in opposition to more modern, "liberal," or morally relativistic versions of a religion. Accordingly, opponents tend to accuse fundamentalism of being conservative or reactionary. At first, the term *fundamentalism* was created to apply to a specific branch of American Protestantism. Today, it can be applied to practitioners of any religion who fit the definition.

Fundamentalists should not be confused with evangelical groups, though the two sometimes overlap. Evangelical groups, more so than fundamentalists, are committed to the recruitment and conversion of new church members. Moreover, unlike fundamentalists, evangelicals are often willing to interact with members of other religious groups who hold different doctrines.

People often identify fundamentalists through ideological characteristics, such as a dualistic world view (i.e., a belief in the split between two things—body and mind, good and evil, etc.) and messianism (i.e., a belief in the coming of a savior such as Judaism's Messiah or Christianity's Christ). People also identify fundamentalism through organizational traits, such as a strong, somewhat exclusionary sense of identity and rigid behavioural requirements (Almond, Sivan, & Appleby, 1995). Research shows that most religious fundamentalists have traditional views of family and gender, and support a patriarchal world view (Antoun, 2001; Apple, 2001; Bartkowski 2001, 2004; Bendroth, 1999). Typically, they also oppose homosexuality (Fulton, Gorsuch, & Maynard, 1999). In this way, fundamentalism can appear to be a battle against modern values, one that is increasingly being fought in the political arena (Emerson & Hartman, 2006).

Opponents criticize fundamentalists for their resistance to empirical evidence and lack of scientific support. For example, many fundamentalists refuse to accept Darwin's theory of evolution, as it contradicts the religious belief that God created human beings. In these, as in other matters, fundamentalists are more concerned with remaining faithful to their original doctrine than in examining new evidence. Ultimately, this makes fundamentalists fierce political competitors, as they are single-minded and unwilling to be talked out of their beliefs.

From this standpoint, fundamentalism may be a reaction against modernity and secularization, so the study of fundamentalism is also the study

n8n photo/Alamy Stock Photo

Some think that traditional religions have no place in a modern society, while others think that religions and religious leaders, such as Buddhism and the Dalai Lama (here visiting Canada), are well-suited to the needs of many people in the modern world.

of modern secularization. However, fundamentalism may also be symptomatic of a continuing and even desperate need for stable, secure meanings in life, for principles to live by and values to embrace in a consumer-oriented world that many find rootless and unhinged.

The Religion/Science Debate: Past and Present

Comparing fundamentalists and secularists can make the differences between science and religions seem rigid and all encompassing. For example, in a 2012 survey by Angus Reid Public Opinion, 61 per cent of Canadians and 69 per cent of Britons said they think human beings evolved from simpler life forms (i.e., they believe in evolution), compared to only 30 per cent of Americans. According to Gallup poll data collected in May 2014 and reported in the *Huffington Post*, "42% of Americans hold the creationist belief that God created humanity as it currently exists a mere 10,000 years ago" (Hafiz, 2014). What these data show is that religious people, especially in religious countries like the United States, are much less inclined than scientifically educated and less religious people to believe in scientific theories like the Darwinian theory of evolution. With contradictory beliefs like these, are science and religion mutually exclusive?

Many are inclined to draw a clear boundary between science and religion, based on several important distinctions. Sociology has historically viewed science and religion as entrenched in a battle over *what we know* and *how we know it*. Sociologically speaking, science is a cultural and social orientation towards the search for *scientific knowledge*, while religion is a search for *divine knowledge*. Science is evidence based, while religion is faith based. Science advances through peer review—a process where expert scholars evaluate the research methods, hypotheses, and findings of other scientists—while religious doctrine is determined hierarchically. That is, those at the top of a religious group make pronouncements that those on the bottom are to follow. Most important of all, science requires organized skepticism, while religion requires loyalty and trust. And unlike science, which is always striving to advance by disproving previous thinking, religion is expected to remain faithful to the traditions that have borne out of its timeless, inflexible truths.

Institutional inflexibility makes it difficult for religions to stay "current." For example, many feel that Catholicism's long-standing views about birth control, abortion, and premarital sex are outdated. Already, Western Catholics—especially, in northwestern Europe, but even in South America—have rejected these Catholic teachings. In contrast, science can and does change the questions it asks in order to remain culturally relevant.

In its worst incarnation, religious inflexibility has resulted in millions of deaths (for example, the witch craze discussed above). But dogmatic science has also led to deaths (recall the section on eugenics in Chapter 3).

With all that said, religion creates social solidarity in a way that science does not. Moreover, the seeming inflexibility and timelessness of religious beliefs may be a feature that attracts adherents looking for deep existential truths—for example, about the meaning of death and suffering—that science has no answer for. So, we find that science and religion are compatible under certain conditions. Perhaps the best example of this is in the religious views of scientists.

Scientists and Religious Belief

Studies about the religiosity of scientists have repeatedly presented science and religion as incompatible ways of thinking, with belief in one undermining belief in the other (Evans & Evans, 2008).

Research on the religious views of scientists, like the scientific views of religious people, goes back a long way. In 1916, the eminent American psychologist James H. Leuba conducted the first study on the religiosity of scientists. This landmark survey found that 58 per cent of 1000 randomly selected US scientists expressed disbelief or doubt in the existence of God. Moreover, this figure rose to near 70 per cent among the 400 so-called "greater" scientists within his sample. Leuba (1916) attributed the higher level of disbelief and doubt among the best scientists to their greater knowledge and understanding.

In 1997 researchers Larson and Witham reported on a repeat of Leuba's 1916 survey. Among American scientists, Larson and Witham found little change from Leuba's original findings: 60.7 per cent of the scientists surveyed still expressed religious disbelief or doubt. In 1998, the same researchers (Larson & Witham, 1998) surveyed so-called "greater" scientists, members of the National Academy of Sciences. Then, they found that only 7 per cent of respondents held any religious beliefs at all—a large decline in religiosity from 1914.

A recent study by the Pew Research Center (Funk & Raine, 2015) has found that these differences between scientists and the lay public continue to hold today, especially when we compare scientists with evangelical Protestants. As we see in Figure 13.3, examining the religious composition of scientists, we find that atheists and agnostics are overrepresented among sampled scientists and evangelical Protestants are underrepresented. Said simply, scientists are unlikely to be drawn from the ranks of evangelical Protestants and much more likely to be drawn from the ranks of atheists, because science and evangelical religion are difficult to reconcile.

Sociologist Elaine Ecklund, who has studied the religion of scientists for years, questions this hard boundary between science and religion—or at least, between science and spirituality. After interviewing tenured and tenure-track faculty in the natural and social sciences at 21 US research universities in 2011, Ecklund and her collaborators, Park and Sorrell, found that only 15 per cent of those surveyed view religion and science as *always* in conflict. Another 15 per cent say the two are *never* in conflict; while the remaining 70 per cent believe religion and science are *sometimes* in conflict. A majority of scientists interviewed by Ecklund and colleagues viewed both religion and science as valid means of deriving broader answers to important questions (Ecklunk, Park, & Sorrell, 2011).

In the same study, Ecklund found that more than two-thirds (68%) of scientists surveyed consider themselves spiritual to some degree. Scientists who view themselves as spiritual/ religious are less likely to see religion and science in conflict; and, under some circumstances, non-religious scientists describe even their most religious peers in positive terms. All of this evidence suggests that the integration of religion and science is not as problematic for scientists as some have imagined.

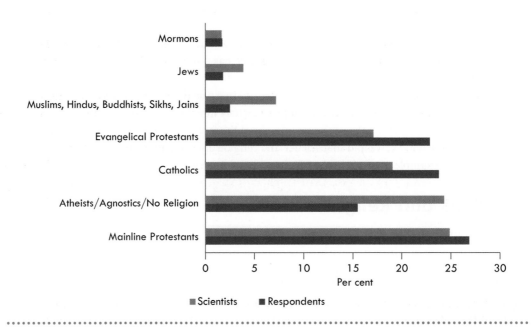

FIGURE 13.3 Scientists Compared to Members of the General US Public ("Respondents")

Source: From Table 5 in Funk & Raine (Pew), 2015

Sociology 2.0

13.2 | Religion? We've Got Apps for That

The development of science and technology in the past two centuries has truly transformed religious practices. In today's busy world, people are less likely to attend religious services and ceremonies and are much more likely to spend their time online or on their smart phones. However, while some see technology as the death knell of religion, others see it as an opportunity to help people maintain and learn more about their particular faith (Campbell, 2012). Just take a look at all of the religion-related applications available for purchase on the App Store. *Hindu Calendar* will let you know when the next Hindu holiday is, *Bible Gateway* allows you to easily search biblical passages, even if you are unsure of the exact verses, *My Digital Menorah* lets you light virtual candles for Jewish holidays even if you are on a plane or at another location where candles and matches are out of reach, and *iPray* reminds Muslims of their prayer times throughout the day.

These and other digital applications let people of all faiths take advantage of the spare time they have available during their hectic days and use this time to maintain or learn more about their faith (Helland, 2005).

Survey findings from the Pew Internet and American Life Project (Madden et al., 2013) show 25 per cent of internet users have received religious or spiritual information online at one time or another. These "Religious Surfers" (a name given by the researchers) report using the internet to look for information about their own faith (67%); to look for information about another faith (50%); to email a prayer request (38%); to download religious music (38%); and to give spiritual guidance via email (37%). They must find this use of the internet efficacious, since a majority of Religious Surfers said they were likely to use the internet for this purpose even more in the future.

Time to reflect

Do you use any kind of religious app, or do "Religious Surfing" on the internet? If so, do you find these digital religious materials different to use than non-digital religious materials? If not, what if any digital technology would engage you in religious thought or discussion?

However, even Ecklund senses a contradiction in the data. In a 2007 thought piece published in the American Sociological Association journal *Contexts*, Ecklund pulls her findings together as follows:

> Scientists come disproportionately from liberal religious and irreligious backgrounds. The question of why scientists come from these backgrounds will need further exploration beyond the findings presented here. One possible explanation is that there may indeed be tension between the religious tenets of some groups . . . and the theories and methods of particular sciences, making members of such religions less likely to pursue scientific careers.

So, in the end, research on scientists shows that people can lead secular, rational lives and still identify themselves as spiritual and sometimes even religious. But scientists—especially, "great" scientists—tend to be less conventionally religious than members of the general public, and they are generally more opposed to religious intrusion into the teaching of science—for example, the teaching of evolution.

Religion in Political Life
The Social Gospel Movement

Despite its sometimes non-rational and disruptive features, religion has sometimes played a positive political role in Canada and elsewhere. In this respect, let's consider the late nineteenth-century Social Gospel movement, an important progressive force in Canadian society between roughly 1880 and 1940.

The Social Gospel movement first made its appearance in Canada during a decade of political corruption and economic distress. The goal of the movement was to use Christian doctrine to help solve problems in modern industrial society—problems like unemployment, poverty, poor housing, family breakdown, and so on. Canadian Evangelical Protestant churches became engaged in the creation of urban settlement houses and missions. One such example is the Fred Victor Mission, founded in Toronto in 1894, which still exists today.

The Social Service Council of Canada and the Women's Christian Temperance Union were two of the most important and long-lasting initiatives created by the Social Gospel movement. The Women's Christian Temperance Union proved to be especially important: it promoted temperance, moral purity, women in public affairs, and the women's suffrage movement. During this period, when most men chose to ignore women's concerns, women's movements found practical and moral support in the Social Gospel movement.

After the end of the First World War, the Social Gospel movement went into decline for several reasons. In part, the decline was due to the failure of certain initiatives such as Prohibition (a nation-wide alcohol ban), which succeeded for some time in the United States but failed to gain adequate support in Canada. Economic depression also undermined the earlier optimism of the movement. Additionally, Canadian secularization and protest politicization shifted the energy towards political action. For example, more radical Social Gospel proponents such as J.S. Woodworth created the Co-operative Commonwealth Federation in 1932. The Social Gospel movement should not be viewed as a failure. It accomplished some of its more practical goals and spawned political offspring such as the Co-operative Commonwealth Federation (which later become the party known as the NDP), which continues its work today.

Civil Religion

civil religion an organized secular practice that serves many of the same social functions as traditional religion: bringing people together, giving people direction, explaining how the world works, and so on.

Civil religion—an idea developed by sociologist Robert Bellah (1967)—represents an interesting mid-point between secular and sacred approaches to political life. From one standpoint, civil religion is a celebration of the state. Because civil religion is a way of celebrating the state, it implicitly reinforces the politics of the state. But it also has all the trappings of a religion: rites, rituals, shared values, sacred occasions, totemic objects, martyrs, etc.

The importance of civil religion as a concept is that it resolves the debate about secularization and whether industrial societies were more secular than pre-industrial societies. In effect, the "discovery" of civil religion in industrial societies showed that sacred rites, rituals, and objects were just as important today as in the past; but today, they centre on the state or civil society, not on distinctive religious institutions.

To the extent that civil religion focuses on the state, the most important and widespread version of civil religion today is nationalism. Since the nineteenth century, nationalism has provided many people in the Global North with a sense of meaning and purpose. In especially patriotic countries such as the United States, nationalism and patriotism continue to be powerful forces, much more so than in Canada. In the United States and elsewhere, nationalistic principles were often linked to certain beliefs—to a belief in American exceptionalism and the sense that America was God's beacon to humanity, for example.

Let's consider one important enactment of the American civil religion: the Super Bowl. The Super Bowl celebration contains many rituals: the ritual of cheering for your favourite team alongside thousands of fans, special commercial advertisements, special foods, and lavish halftime shows. According to Bellah (1967), this kind of event brings people together for a celebration—the main function of religion—though it is not affiliated with a particular religious denomination.

The value of the concept of civil religion is that it allows us to analyze modern societies with the tools we use to study religions, even though their rituals are cloaked in secularism. From this perspective, modern people have not become less religious; rather, religion has become a commercial or commodified cultural product. It is perhaps in resistance to this commodification of religion that we have seen the resurgence of fundamentalist religions in modern societies discussed earlier.

New Religious Movements

New religious movements (NRMs), of which the present-day Wiccans—followers of a modern pagan, witchcraft religion—are one example, exist all over the world and have been gaining popularity.

As discussed earlier in the chapter, some explore their spirituality through practices based in the folk religions of Africa, America, and Europe. In Canada and elsewhere, a variety of groups, looking to their own ancestral backgrounds, focus on African religious traditions and beliefs, or on European Celtic and Nordic folklore and mythology (Hiebert & Shaw, 2000). Others share an idea of the earth (Gaia) as the mother of all beings, and become promoters of environmental awareness. From this standpoint, environmentalism represents, for some, an effort to satisfy spiritual needs (Carmody, 1983). Similarly, Indigenous groups are working to re-establish Indigenous religions. Recall from Chapter 11 that these religious traditions were ruthlessly suppressed during the period of residential schools, when it was believed that Indigenous children should be forced to embrace Christianity and forget their traditional ways.

Some efforts to revive ancestral religions, or create new ones, suffer ridicule by the mass media, and are depicted contemptuously as "cults." You have likely heard of some such groups being accused of "brainwashing" and exploiting their followers. The term *cult*, or the preferred term *new religious movement* (NRM), lacks a precise, scientific meaning. Perhaps that is because there are so many different kinds of NRMs, with such varying rituals and memberships.

You can find many lists of famous (or infamous) NRMs online. Scientology, the Unification Church, the Fundamentalist Church of Jesus Christ of Latter-Day Saints, Order of the Solar Temple, the Carny Cult, and the Santa Muerte Cult are just a few examples. The stance of sociology is that NRMs, like religions, are just like any social phenomena, and are a product of social life that plays an important role in society's functioning.

Field research by sociologists has shown that some new religious movements are mainly groups of people who share similar views about the world and should not be dismissed as "lesser" than the mainstream religions. To an outsider, many of their practices and beliefs may seem strange. However, members of these groups likely feel the same way about mainstream religious practices, and have therefore found an alternative religious path to fulfill their spiritual needs. Today, most researchers report that new religious movements, though unfamiliar, are not necessarily harmful.

In Canada, for example, Susan Palmer (2004) studied Raelians, a Quebec-based NRM that believes in divine extraterrestrial beings and claims that they have successfully cloned a human being. After years of fieldwork with the group, Palmer reported that the Raelians challenged many of the stereotypes commonly associated with NRMs. For example, fears of brainwashing are unwarranted: group members make no effort to force their children into the faith, as they believe in the importance of personal choice. For this reason, baptism in this group does not occur until at least the age of 15.

By now, we know what Durkheim would say: the Raelians have merely substituted UFOs for other totemic or holy objects in their practice of religion. In this sense Raelian beliefs perform the same functions—and are no more bizarre or dangerous—as any mainstream religion.

new religious movements (NRMs) groups and institutions that share similar religious or spiritual views about the world, but are not part of mainstream religious institutions.

THE CANADIAN PRESS/Andre Forget

The movies have given us ghoulish images of cult rituals, but in fact, most NRMs are no more ghoulish or bizarre than other religions and social movements. Depicted is Raelian leader Claude Vorilhon.

Religion in Canada Today

In Canada more and more people are likely to say that they "have no religious affiliation" (see Figure 13.4). However, this can be misleading. According to a study by Statistics Canada (Clark & Schellenberg, 2006), religion plays a more important role in the lives of Canadians than many think. Only about one-third of adult Canadians go to church at least once a month, but more than half conduct their own private religious activities every month. For example, these private activities may include praying, meditating, worshipping, or reading sacred texts. Clearly, then, religion is still important to many Canadians. Canadian sociologist Reginald W. Bibby touches on this and related themes in his study of religion in modern-day Canada, as described in Box 13.3.

As we read above, church attendance on its own is not an accurate measure of religiosity in Canada. Statistics Canada (2002) uses a more useful indicator: the religiosity index. This index includes four dimensions of religiosity: affiliation, attendance, personal practices, and (stated) importance of religion. This index recognizes, and corrects, the limitations of just using attendance at a place of worship to measure religiosity. The value of this measure is that it reminds us that different religions of the world encourage people to experience and express their religious sentiments in different ways.

According to this religiosity measure, 40 per cent of Canadians have a low degree of religiosity, 31 per cent a moderate degree, and 29 per cent have a high degree of religiosity (Statistics Canada, 2002). Religiosity varies demographically: it is highest among older people, women, and people from religious families, especially families in which both parents had the same or a similar religious background (for example, where both parents were raised as Catholics). It also varies with the religious denomination of the person.

The Canadian decline in religiosity has been most marked in Quebec. Historically, Quebec was the *most* religious part of Canada, as it was controlled culturally by the Roman Catholic Church. For three centuries (from roughly 1650 to 1950), the Church influenced almost every aspect of life, providing its parishioners with education, work, assistance, and opportunities for communication between parishes. Starting in the 1960s, however, church participation dropped dramatically. This marked the beginning of Quebec's Quiet Revolution, which removed Church control over the education system and provincial politics.

People had begun to see the Church as anti-modern, oppressive, and pro-establishment. They felt it had prevented French Canadians from gaining the education they needed to succeed economically and socially, allowing English industries to gain influence and success (Gauvreau & Gossage, 2001). As Quebecois urbanized and gained more education, they turned against the Church. Since the Quiet Revolution of the 1960s, Quebec has been consistently less religious than the rest of Canada—to the point where some are concerned that Quebec has swung too far the other way (see Box 13.4)

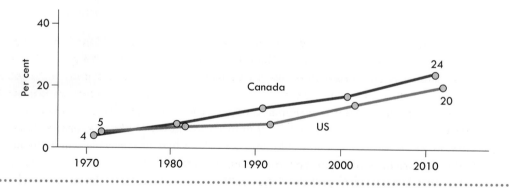

FIGURE 13.4 Growth of the Religiously Unaffiliated in Canada and the US

Source: www.ohrc.on.ca/vi/book/export/html/10923

Theory in Everyday Life

13.3 | Reginald Bibby

Since the 1970s, Canadian sociologist Reginald W. Bibby has been studying, analyzing, and interpreting social trends in Canada, using national surveys of teens and adults. In his book *A New Day: The Resilience and Restructuring of Religion in Canada* (2012), Bibby proposes that the rumoured demise of religion in Canada is misguided and misleading. He proposes that the face of Canadian religion is merely changing, adapting to a more complex, globalized future.

Repeatedly, Bibby (2011) has concluded that religion still has a strong foothold in society. Both Islam and Christianity are experiencing huge revivals of interest in different parts of the world, including places like Russia and China, which had previously suppressed religious practice. In Canada, religious interest and practice is stimulated by the continued arrival of immigrants from countries where secularization has been weaker. For these and other reasons, Bibby denies that the decline in religious service attendance in Canada supports the claim that Canadians have rejected religion. Rather, he proposes that Canadians are merely celebrating their spirituality in different, and more private, ways today.

This does not mean that unorganized or personalized spirituality is replacing organized religion, but that Canadians are willing to become involved in institutional religion only to the extent that their involvement visibly benefits them. Consequently, denominational religiosity will continue to decline, and the preference for a more personal spirituality will continue to increase, he warns, unless organized religious groups find new ways to meet Canadians' spiritual and personal needs.

Based on these observations, Bibby and Grenville (2016) offer three conclusions. First, religion has far from outlived its usefulness in Canadian society. Second, there are still many Canadians who are open to religion, if it appeals to them in the right way. Third, religious groups will have to work together if they want to see organized religion continue in Canada's future. What is striking is his use of language that frames religious participants as though they were customers, which arguably does reflect how they are coming to see themselves: as consumers of spiritual services. Religious service attendance has, for the most part, been on a steady decline in Canada.

Time to reflect

Exercise your sociological imagination. What social factors might influence whether a religious person regularly attends religious service?

Spotlight On

13.4 | Should Governments Try to Enforce Secularism?

The dangers to freedom implicit in a commitment to strict secularism came to the forefront in a Quebec debate about banning symbols of religion—though only certain non-Christian symbols—in public places.

Quebec's human rights commission made this statement:

> The Quebec government's plan to ban public servants from wearing symbols of their faith at work violates Quebec's Charter of Rights

and will fail if it is subjected to a legal challenge. The proposition to ban religious signs shows a poor understanding of freedom of religion such as is protected in the Charter (of rights) as well as in international law. This obligation applies to institutions of the state, but not its agents (Woods, 2013).

In 2014 the proposal to ban teachers, bureaucrats, police officers, nurses, doctors, and others whose salary

Continued

is paid by tax dollars from wearing turbans, kippas, hijabs, crucifixes, and other religious symbols resulted in sharp divisions in Quebec. Sovereigntists splintered in protest, feminists were pitted against one another, and more homogeneous rural areas of Quebec clashed with multicultural Montreal.

But Premier Pauline Marois's government vowed to forge ahead with the proposal in order to ensure the religious neutrality of the state and to bolster the principle of gender equality. The human rights commission said the proposed changes were unnecessary. Equality of the sexes

is already protected in Quebec's human rights legislation, a 1975 precursor to the federal charter. So, the new law would only result in denying work to people of particular religious beliefs. That would be both an attack on freedom of expression and the right to work.

Quebec seems split on the matter of secularism. On the one hand, cities have been dropping Christian prayers before meetings of municipal councils. However, the National Assembly in Quebec City has opted to retain a large Christian cross hanging over the seat of the Speaker (Authier, 2015).

Time to reflect

The Quebec secularism example illustrates how a policy written to be impartial can have a more damaging impact on particular groups. Can you think of other examples within Canada where an ostensibly impartial policy has had a greater impact on some groups more than others? Think, for example, about some of the policies outlined in Chapter 8, as a place to start.

As the example of Quebec suggests, each case of secularization is slightly different, each with its own starting and ending point, and rate of change. Is it conceivable that more recent declines in religion have been associated with growing internet usage? That possibility is considered in Box 13.5.

Interactive activity

Religion continues to survive in North America, especially among non-European immigrants. In part, this is because religious institutions provide immigrants with supports. For example, religious organizations help immigrants learn English and prepare for citizenship exams (Ebaugh & Chafetz, 2000). More research is needed to examine how religious participation changes over generations (Cadge & Ecklund, 2007). For example, we need more research about second-generation immigrants who leave immigrant religious organizations (known as the "silent-exodus" within Asian studies [Chai, 1998]). We also need to explore how these departures affect identity formation, community interaction, and civic participation. Obviously, more people are getting along without a religious affiliation but one wonders whether they have substituted something in its place.

Digital Divide

13.5 | Internet Usage and the Decline of Religion

Are internet usage and the decline of religion related? Allen Downey (2014), a computer scientist at the Olin College of Engineering, thinks so, asserting that the rise of internet usage in the past two decades is a major factor behind the recent decline of religious observance.

Downey's conclusions come from his analysis of data from the NORC (University of Chicago) General Social

Survey—a survey that has sampled the demographics and attitudes of Americans since 1972.

The data show that individuals brought up in households that have continuously participated in religious events/rituals are more likely to remain religious themselves as adults. However, the number of these religion-practising households has dropped significantly since 1990. One contributing cause is a growth in the number of people who receive a post-secondary education. However, this correlation, Downey explains, could only account for roughly 5 per cent of the total drop in religious affiliation. The question remains, what is the main factor behind the drop in religious affiliation?

As you may have guessed, Downey's answer is the internet. From 1980 to 2010, internet usage increased from 0 per cent of the population to roughly 53 per cent, with more than half of the population spending at least two hours a week online and 25 per cent spending more than seven hours online per week. Downey notes that this increase in internet use correlates directly to the decline in religious affiliation, and that a causal link would make sense. The internet exposes people in somewhat enclosed communities to people in other communities, allowing people from different religions and backgrounds to communicate differing opinions. Though Downey's conclusions are debatable, many find his argument quite compelling. Look at Figure 13.5—do you see a correlation between digital access and religious importance? Does this correlation convince you that internet use is reducing the strength of religious commitment?

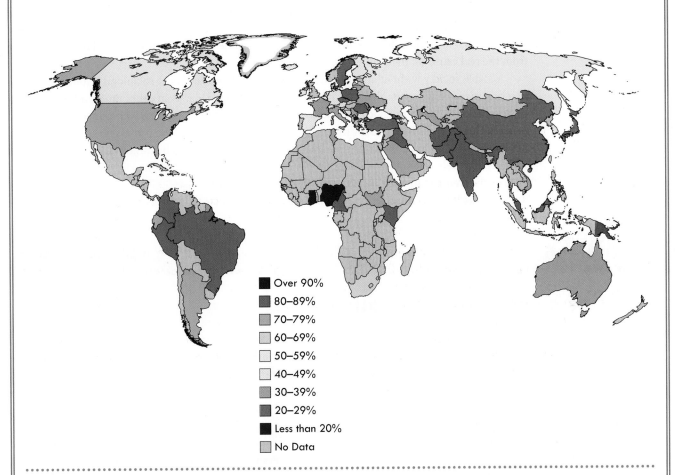

Legend:
- Over 90%
- 80–89%
- 70–79%
- 60–69%
- 50–59%
- 40–49%
- 30–39%
- 20–29%
- Less than 20%
- No Data

FIGURE 13.5 Per cent Reporting that Religion is Important to Them (Gallup Poll, 2007–08)

Source: http://www.nextbigfuture.com/2013/07/prediction-religious-will-be-global.html

Time to reflect

As Figure 13.5 shows, the most religiously devout people are found in South America, Africa, the Middle East, and South Asia. Which (if any) of the theoretical approaches to religion outlined in this chapter does this finding support, and which (if any) does it contradict?

Source of box: Adapted from "How the internet is taking away America's religion" (2014), Pew Research Centre (2010)

Conclusions

There are many reasons people appear to need religion: to address feelings of disappointment and fear, to answer existential doubts, to interpret social and political events, and to give their lives meaning beyond everyday survival. Most important, religions give people a sense of community. With all these important functions, it is no wonder that religion is a universal aspect of culture: there are no known human societies without a religious life. That said, sociologists have had some difficulty defining "religion."

Some sociologists focus on a substantive definition (what a religion is), while others focus on a functional definition (what a religion does for people), but most consider both. In his functional definition of religion, Durkheim stressed the importance of religion for social cohesion. In his substantive definition of religion, Durkheim stressed that religion divides the world into the "sacred" and the "profane," which creates a division between religious escape and everyday life. According to Marx, religion was a form of false consciousness that justifies the elites' right to rule and distracts people from the real causes of their suffering.

A stable society without any religion is hard to imagine, and most sociologists today recognize that organized religion has changed, not disappeared. In Canada, as in other modern industrial societies, participation in religious ceremonies has fallen over the years. However, Canadians' reported belief in God has not changed very much. The number of Canadians who profess no religion whatever has increased slightly. At the same time, these rates are being affected by immigration from countries with higher levels of religiosity. Along similar lines, Bellah called attention to the present day importance of civil religion in what are often called secular societies.

Taking all of this into account, are we more or less secular than we were before?

Questions for Critical Thought

1. Canada is a very multicultural country. What are some potential benefits and conflicts to have people of so many different religious affiliations live and work together?

2. Canada allows freedom of religious practice and expression. To what extent is our society secular? Should all societies be secular? To what extent? Why?

3. How do new religious movements further complicate the definition of religion? What makes something a religious movement and not just a new club, hobby, or extracurricular activity?

4. Do you think science and religion are compatible? On a global level, which do you think will prevail? Or will a new relationship between them emerge? Why or why not?

5. Do you think it is possible to find an equal substitute for religion? Are there any functions of religion that are unique to religious experience?

6. In your opinion, do religions bring people together or keep them apart? Explain why you think so.

Take it Further: Recommended Readings

Lori G. Beaman and Peter Beyer, eds., *Religion and Diversity in Canada* (Boston: Brill, 2008). The essays that make up this book explore the many different religions in Canada today and the different ways people have adopted a variety of religious practices into their everyday lives.

Ronald Beiner, *Civil Religion: A Dialogue in the History of Political Philosophy* (New York: Cambridge University Press, 2011). This text critically examines the issue of religion in contemporary society from four important traditions in the history of political thought, with commentary from 20 influential thinkers.

Lorne L. Dawson, *Comprehending Cults: The Sociology of New Religious Movements*, 2nd ed. (Don Mills, ON: Oxford University Press, 2006). This is a comprehensive introduction to new religious movements, including major theories of cult formation, the type of people that are most likely to join cults, and various issues surrounding cults.

Murray R. Thomas, *Religion in Schools: Controversies around the World* (Westport, Conn.: Greenwood Publishing Group, 2006). The text analyzes religious conflicts in schools, using case studies of all major religions from 12 countries, and addresses the causes of the conflict, the approaches used and the consequences.

Take it Further: Recommended Online Resources

CBC Archives on Religion and Spirituality
www.cbc.ca/archives/categories/society/religion-spirituality/religion-spirituality.html

Centre for Studies in Religion and Society
http://csrs.uvic.ca

Religion and Diversity Project
www.religionanddiversity.ca

Religion and Society Research Programme
www.religionandsociety.org.uk

Religion and Violence e-learning (RAVe)
www.theraveproject.com/index.php

Statistics Canada, Information about Religion
www.statcan.gc.ca/search-recherche/bb/info/3000017-eng.htm

"What Canadians Really Believe," by Aaron Hutchins
www.macleans.ca/society/life/what-canadians-really-believe/

More resources available on 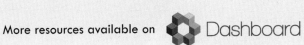 Dashboard

14

Mass and Social Media in a Global Age

Introduction

mass media a collection of media organizations that mass communicate information through a variety of media technologies.

Mass communication is defined as the creation, repackaging, and distribution of content on a large scale through the **mass media** including print, cinema, photography, recordings, advertising, radio and television broadcasting. Content is mass distributed on a global scale and centrally produced by media conglomerates such as Disney, 21st Century Fox, and Time Warner in the United States, and Astral Media, Shaw Media, and Quebecor in Canada. For example, Disney exerts considerable influence on children globally with its movies, shows, dedicated TV channel, and toys. Framed around notions of innocence, Disney offers children a sense of fun, fantasy, and a world of imagination, also teaching them ways of making sense of the world (Giroux & Pollock, 2010). Disney films in particular often portray gender roles and national and racial identities in antiquated ways, influencing how children understand cultural values. The Walt Disney Company also ingrains values of consumption in children, eliciting them to be good consumers from an early age by wanting the most popular toys, trips to Disneyland, and viewing the latest Disney movies. For example, Disney's blockbuster *Star Wars: Episode VII* in 2015 made $250 million in North America alone and $517 million worldwide in its first week, setting a new record in ticket sales (Reuters, 2015).

new media media characterized by a decentralized process of content creation and distribution.

With the massive popularity of **new media**, traditional definitions of the mass media have expanded to include these decentralized forms of content production and distribution by a networked, global user base. New media comprise a wide range of tools and applications such as websites, social media, and mobile technology. This has not only created different types of mass communication

paulette kaylor/Shutterstock.com

The mass media of today are accessed on the go from anywhere, anytime through multiple personalized devices. This creates a fragmented, networked, and global audience that accesses customized information sources from around the globe relevant to their own lives, cultures, and needs and wants.

but has also provided traditional media with distinct forms of production, distribution, and engagement with a fragmented, networked, and global audience. For instance, the *Globe and Mail*, one of Canada's largest and earliest newspapers, founded in 1844, today has a digital presence that includes a website, blog, Facebook page, and Twitter account (@globeandmail).

In this digital, networked environment, we do not learn about the news from a single source; rather, information is delivered to our myriad devices through multiple applications and in real time. We can follow events as they unfold in remote places across the globe, creating much greater global integration of information. Without our devices, we feel disconnected not only from friends and family but also from the larger circulation of visual culture, the immediate news cycle, and events unfolding around the world. This immersion into vast amounts of data from multiple sources, apps, and social networks allows us to stay well informed about the weather, celebrity news, and local and global events.

One important source of news for young Canadians is Facebook. As of June 2017, Facebook had 2 billion monthly active users (*Fortune*, 2017), who every 60 seconds provided 293,000 status updates, posted 510 comments, and uploaded 136,000 photos (Zephoria, 2017). Canadians are one of the largest adopters of Facebook, with 18.6 million active users in 2017 (Statista, 2017). There has also been a large increase in mobile Facebook use, with 10 million Canadians accessing the site daily via a mobile device in 2014, which puts Canada at the forefront of mobile Facebook adoption (Oliveira, 2014). This move toward social media use is also having an effect on how Canadians access the news, search for information, and share stories and events.

Let's imagine a friend updates her news feed on Facebook and in her post there is an amazing image of a city landscape with two full moons shining in the background. The caption under the image reads, "Mars is so close to Earth that it will appear like a second Moon in the sky." Your friend has shared the story because she loves nature and this is clearly a once-in-a-lifetime event. You choose the appropriate **emoji** to like the post and forward the story to your grandfather, who is a science aficionado and loves chatting about the galaxy. Through social networks **misinformation** can easily circulate online without users even realizing that the information they are interacting with is falsified. It turns out that the "two moon landscape" is one of 2015's 10 biggest scientific hoaxes (O'Callaghan, 2015). There are many other hoaxes circulating on the internet; our fast-paced, information-rich environment makes it difficult to evaluate the accuracy of stories. Misinformation is false information spread either intentionally or unintentionally. "Fake news" became a key concern in the lead up to and aftermath of the 2016 presidential election in the United States (Allcot & Gentzkow, 2017). The traditional mass media had greater control over the quality of information they disseminated because it was centrally produced and distributed, and the publishing cycles were slower, allowing for more careful fact-checking.

Dashboard

Case study

emojis small digital icons or images used in digital communication to express an emotion, idea, or reaction.

misinformation false information spread intentionally or unintentionally.

Time to reflect

Can you think of an example of a hoax that you have encountered while online? What strategies can users of social media sites employ to identify and debunk misleading information and hoaxes?

New technologies have transformed the mass media by creating a networked audience with global reach, for example. In this chapter, we will examine key technologies that have shaped the dissemination of content in the past and also look at how content is produced, disseminated, and circulated in the context of new media on a global scale. Processes of globalization, already discussed in Chapter 9, are also discussed throughout this chapter to demonstrate their relevance to and impact on many domains in sociology. We will examine both the positive effects that decentralized content production has on citizens and new challenges that arise from these possibilities. New media affect all social groups in society and have created a shift in who the key players are—those who control messages and therefore hold power.

There is probably no domain in society where technological change has been more influential than in the realm of the mass media. The mass media of today have changed in many ways compared to the mass media of only a decade ago. Canadians in the 1990s and 2000s consumed their news primarily through local and national print newspapers delivered daily to their front doors (Quan-Haase, Martin, & Schreurs, 2016). Today, many local newspapers have had to close their print operations and even influential national papers like the *Globe and Mail* and *National Post* have seen their readership and influence dwindle.

> ## Time to reflect
>
> Where do you get your daily news from? Do you pay attention to the source of your news when you read, watch, or listen to it? Do you use the same news sources as your parents? Your grandparents?

Theoretical Approaches to the Study of Mass Media

Conflict Theory

dominant ideology refers to the ideas, values, and norms shared by the majority in a given society; thus it often denotes the beliefs of the dominant class.

Conflict theory examines the struggles among social groups over resources with the aim of obtaining and maintaining positions of power and privilege. Holding on to power is closely linked with being able to control messages and the information they carry. The greater the control over messages, the more power an individual can hold. In the introductory chapter, we discussed Marx's (1867/1996) seminal work, in which he argued that the capitalist economic system is associated with a specific way of thinking, which he termed **dominant ideology**. Dominant ideology is critical for maintaining the status quo and justifying capitalist means of production through a neo-liberal consumer culture. Conflict theory helps us understand how the mass media disseminate and influence the dominant ideology. Western nations represent the dominant ideology, as they hold on to power through economic domination, military superiority, and control over mass media. **Political economy** is the study of power relations at the intersection of media, economics, and politics (Greenberg & Elliott, 2013). Mass media play an important role in informing the public, shaping public opinion, and keeping governments and other institutions in check.

political economy the study of power relations at the intersection of media, economics, and politics particularly related to economic value and its relationship to law and government.

The power inherent in the mass media and the messages they disseminate has led to much conflict and struggle over controlling and accessing the mass media. In many countries this control over the mass media is pervasive, particularly in the context of dictatorships, where newspapers, radio outlets, and even the internet have no independent voice and function as the propaganda arm of those in power.

elites those in positions of power who control the means of production and dissemination of mass content.

Concerns about how the media are manipulated extend to democratic nations such as Canada. The media are considered one of the most critical resources for maintaining the status quo and reinforcing the elites' ideology. Within mass media scholarship the **elites** are those in power who control both the content of messages and the mechanisms of diffusion. Elites include not only those who own the mass media as one may assume, but also those who are given a voice by the mass media to craft messages and voice their opinions. The term *middle elites* describes those whose views are also represented in the mass media, but who do not directly own the mass media. These include experts and opinion leaders, who have high social status through their credentials. Table 14.1 describes the three tiers of influence by access, representation, and use of the media. The elites have the greatest control and power, while the bottom holds little power and is primarily a receptor of messages.

TABLE 14.1 Three Tiers to Media Access, Use, and Representation

	Elites	Middle elites	Bottom
Access	Have the most power as they own and control the mass media.	Well-known opinion leaders including doctors, professors, opinion leaders, and politicians.	Exposed to mass media without critical understanding. Often skeptical of mass media, but still continue to consume the content.
Representation	Comprised of leaders in the political, military, and business domains.	Comprised of experts, government officials, and interest groups.	Comprised of average citizens who are often unorganized.
Use	The mass media typically represent their interests and voice the dominant ideology.	Given a voice in mass media as experts.	Entertainment as the key source for content consumption within mass media.

Source: Author-generated

The mass media hold control over which individuals they deem worthy listening to and which voices remain silent. In their book, *Manufacturing Consent*, Edward Herman and Noam Chomsky (1988) discuss the ways in which media content serves as a means to control people's opinions and reinforce the dominant ideology. Table 14.2 describes five mechanisms that the authors have identified as asserting the dominant ideology put forth by the elites.

TABLE 14.2 Mechanisms of Control Exerted by the Mass Media

Mechanism	Description
1. Elites own or control the media	Media ownership is concentrated in the hands of a few powerful and wealthy people—the elites. The media present the elites' views of society in subtle ways, primarily through conservative views that reinforce the status quo and suggest how society should function.
2. Consumer culture	Media to a large extent depend on revenues from advertisers; this motivates the media to broadcast simple and light-hearted topics of broad appeal that elicit a consumer mood in audiences and entices them to purchase goods and services.
3. Voice of the experts	The media rely on experts for commentary and opinion; they are also likely to be members of the elite themselves and represent to a large extent the elites' viewpoint on key issues.
4. Flak & disciplinary action	The elites make use of various forms of discipline or "flak" to keep the media in line and continually establish the elites' viewpoint on central issues.
5. Polarization	An important aspect of maintaining the dominant ideology is to encourage the development of strong ideologies or viewpoints in people's minds. This is often achieved by identifying critical enemies or alliances that aid in the justification of the elites' strategy. These ideologies create polarization among citizens, forcing them to take a stance.

Source: Author-generated. Based on the work of E. S. Herman and N. Chomsky, *Manufacturing consent: The political economy of the mass media* (New York: Pantheon Books, 1998).

citizen journalism original reporting and news coverage by ordinary people, who commonly use the internet, blogs, and social media to voice their opinions and to counter the "messaging" present in the dominant ideology.

These five mechanisms help identify the key players in the production and control of messages, and in what ways average citizens are elicited to maintain the dominant ideology. Until recently, it has been difficult to challenge the mass media and their control over information. Average citizens, and in particular marginalized social groups, had few means of voicing their opinions and challenging assumptions and messages communicated by the mass media, even when these were wrong. The rise of social media has been a game changer. Now average citizens with internet access have various means at their disposal to voice their opinions and to counter the "messaging" present in the dominant ideology. Social media provide excellent means to engage with content, as users can comment on posts, retweet posts, or even disprove points with alternative perspectives. This has transformed how many young people access the news and stay informed. Box 14.1 describes a new form of journalism, **citizen journalism**, which undermines the position of power held by the elites and the mass media.

The rise of citizen journalism has made room for more voices and alternative players to join in the struggle of overcoming dominant ideologies and institutions in a move toward equality. Developments in digital media have contributed to putting these citizens in contact with one another for the amateur expression of opinions and the debate of people from all walks of life (Shirky, 2008). Despite its many advantages, citizen journalism has also received much criticism (Mejias & Vokuev, 2017). While it accomplishes its primary purpose of undermining the role of traditional gatekeepers, citizen journalism also brings with it new challenges for journalism more generally (Lindner, 2016). The first is that it is difficult to verify the information provided and to identify the potential hidden agenda behind citizen journalists' accounts (Mejias & Vokuev, 2017). Second, all narratives have biases, including narratives from the ground. While these narratives may be more authentic, they may not be able to convey the full story and may leave out critical information. Finally, citizen journalists are not trained in the journalistic practice and hence may not cover a story comprehensively or over long periods of time. Rather, they provide a snapshot of an event without proper follow-up on its development. Journalists undergo rigorous training in journalism schools, are bound by ethical standards of news production, and are committed to writing balanced stories that show multiple angles of a single event.

Video: *Freedom of Press Under Attack in Montreal*

Think Globally

14.1 | Social Media as Citizen Journalism

The role of the mass media as gatekeepers of information has radically transformed with the widespread diffusion of social media. The mass media no longer control messages and cannot ignore multiple voices on a single issue. This became apparent in 2003 during the Iraq War (branded in the media as "Operation Iraqi Freedom"), when the US government tried to control the message to its citizens via the mass media. The only footage of the war that could be published had to be preapproved by the Pentagon. The footage released was closely controlled. Footage that displayed casualties of military personnel or of Iraqi citizens, including women, children, elderly, and the sick, for example, was immediately censored to prevent a change in public opinion toward the deployment. The US government under George W. Bush was aware of the potential loss of public support for the war if images of casualties or destruction were made public. For the Bush administration, social media proved unexpected and difficult to control, broadcasting alternative stories of the events. Salam Pax became one of the most well known bloggers during and after the 2003 invasion of Iraq. His book, *The Baghdad Blog*, compiles many of the blog posts circulated online and provides a behind-the-scenes view of what it was like to be in Baghdad during the intense bombing and aftermath of the war. Blogs like Pax's have transformed our understanding of real-time news and the power of citizen journalism. Twitter posts have also been used by citizens and can serve as a reliable source of information that can provide insights into events as they develop on the ground. Both blogs and posts on social media sites like Twitter highlight the power of personal narratives in comparison to framed stories by the mass media, which are heavily edited and censored.

Feminist Theory

The media we consume play a central role in how we make sense of the world. While our interpersonal communities are important to forming our world view, we learn a great deal about what it means to be a man or a woman based on the representations put forth by dominant media institutions such as the film, television, advertising, and recording industries.

It is important to remember that these media representations are not simple reflections of reality, but that they are *constructs* produced by real people with values, politics, and experiences that shape how they see and represent the world (Richardson & Wearing, 2014). For that reason, sociologists continue to pay close attention to how men and women are portrayed in our shared cultural texts. For example, the documentary *Miss Representation* (2011), which includes Jean Kilbourne, an author and film maker who critically examines the reprentation of women in advertisement, as one of the interviewees, directly challenges media representations that put forward the idea that women should strive to be beautiful, sexy, and caring instead of aiming to be the innovators, thinkers, and leaders of tomorrow. Understanding this can tell us a great deal about how we come to see ourselves and biases that exist in representations of various social groups. In this way, gender and media representation scholarship aims to deconstruct how inequitable power relations are perpetuated within these important cultural spaces.

As part of a larger international study, Plan Canada surveyed 1000 Canadian youth between the ages of 12 and 17 (CTV News, 2011). The study's findings showed that many Canadian youth continue to hold on to stereotyped roles for women and men. As much as 31 per cent of the boys felt a woman's most significant role is to take care of her home and prepare meals for the family. In the study, about half of Canadian youth agreed that "to be a man you need to be tough," which is certainly a stereotype reinforced by the media and depicted in many Hollywood blockbusters. In fact, about half of the respondents reported that pressure to conform to these stereotypes came from the media.

Time to reflect

What role do the media play in perpetuating and challenging traditional gender roles? What types of media do you hypothesize are more influential in creating these stereotyped roles for youth: traditional media such as movies, magazines, and books, or new media such as blogs, Instagram, Twitter, and Facebook? How might you design a study to test your hypothesis?

The role of the media in perpetuating traditional gender roles and opening discussions for new gender roles is rather complex. On her blog *Dykes to Watch Out For*, Alison Bechdel first introduced what has come to be known as the Bechdel Test. The test asks if a film adheres to three simple criteria and is often applied to demonstrate the lack of meaningful roles given to women in film. To pass the test, the film or show must meet the following criteria:

1. It includes at least two women,
2. who have at least one conversation,
3. about something other than a man or men. (Bechdel, n.d.)

You might be surprised about how many widely popular films fail this simple test. Some examples include *Shrek, District 9, Tomb Raider, The Dark Knight, Up, Braveheart, Toy Story, Gladiator,* and *X-Men*. To further underscore this point, a 2015 study from the Media Diversity and Social Change Initiative examined 700 films from 2007 to 2014 and found that only 30 per cent of speaking characters were women and only 11 per cent had a gender-balanced cast (Smith et al., 2015). The invisibility of women of colour is even more prominent. The same study found that in 2014, only 13 per cent of speaking characters were black and only about one-third of those characters were black women. What this means is that women are often cast in roles that give them only a secondary role or present them as supporting the main (usually white) male character. Understanding depictions of women in the mass media is not only about determining the ratio of men to women. It is also about understanding how these women are presented.

Feminist media scholarship has long worked to call attention to the way that dominant media institutions represent women as objects for consumption rather than active human subjects. Much analysis has focused on Hollywood's depiction of women and the kinds of viewing that are promoted, in which women on screen function as the object of erotic viewing pleasure. Within the convention of Hollywood, women connote a "to-be-looked-at-ness" (Mulvey, 1975), while men bestow the gaze. Men are positioned as the active desiring subject; women operate as the more passive object of their desire. This is exemplified in Michael Bay's *Transformers* (2007), where the camera slowly passes over Megan Fox's body while Shia Lebeouf (and the audience) are invited to gaze upon it. Note that Fox herself does not return the gaze of either Lebeouf or the audience. In fact, she is largely unconcerned with the attention at all. She performs the role of object of viewing pleasure, and not that of subject who views, or in Laura Mulvey's (1975) terminology, Fox performs the social role of "to-be-looked-at-ness."

Clearly, when scrutinizing the mass media's depiction of women, women have little in the way of meaningful representation to draw upon to inform their sense of self. Visibility in these dominant cultural texts matters because seeing yourself reflected back is crucial for feeling counted as part of the larger community. The invisibility of women in mainstream media is also linked to the fact that male producers, managers, and content creators often dominate the industry. Until more gender equity exists in the production of content, few changes can be expected in how women are depicted in the mass media.

vipflash/Shutterstock.com

Actress Megan Fox during a photo op for a special screening of *Transformers* with director Michael Bay (right) performs the role of "to-be-looked-at-ness."

Structural Functionalism

Functionalism emphasizes order and looks at the role of institutions in maintaining a stable and functional society. Without institutions, societies could quickly enter into a state of chaos. Within this framework, the media provide members of society with information of personal and social importance on socio-political and cultural events at both the local and global levels. The mass media also function as watchdogs over governments. As arms-length institutions from governments, media follow parliamentary debates from the **press gallery**, where journalists follow federal and provincial debates, and report back to citizens on decisions made by parliament. The Parliamentary Press Gallery in Canada has an important function and consists of journalists who have direct access to parliamentary proceedings. The press also conducts audits of government spending and often scrutinizes government decisions. These are all central tasks of the mass media in a democratic society and keep citizens informed of important political, governmental, and policy developments. In societies where the mass media are weakened and controlled by the government, democratic debate is jeopardized. This demonstrates the critical role of the mass media as institutions that provide many services to citizens ranging from entertainment to the news to eliciting political debate.

press gallery an area in a parliamentary building where members of the press can observe and report on parliamentary proceedings.

Symbolic Interactionism

Symbolic interactionism concerns itself with the study of social interaction, which can take place in-person or via mediated communication. Of particular interest to scholars of symbolic interactionism is the use of symbols to convey meaning to others and signal one's social status, group membership, or emotional state. This becomes particularly relevant in the context of the mass media, as symbols are used to give credibility to a news source. Symbols can be diverse and include gestures, words, street signs, and even emojis as used in digital communication to provide context to a message. In news stories, several strategies are employed to signal credibility (Pavlik & McIntosh, 2016):

- Often pictures, video clips, or quotes are used to provide veracity to the story.
- Expert sources are cited to demonstrate the truth underlying the story. Often these are experts in a specific domain such as lawyers, lawmakers, scientists, professors, and medical doctors.
- Language is used to emphasize the accuracy of a story. Stories are told not as personal narratives, but as factual statements.
- Professional settings are chosen to emphasize the credibility of the news reporting.

From a symbolic interactionism perspective, it is relevant to understand how symbols help convey stories and support or question the credibility of a source. Young people today tend to also seek information on Instagram, Facebook, and Twitter because they see hashtags and retweets as new ways of learning about the news, devoid of the symbols present in traditional media (Bode, 2016).

TABLE 14.3 Theoretical Approaches to Mass Media

Theory	Main points
Conflict Theory	• Social groups fight to maintain control over the mass media.
	• The mass media help maintain the dominant ideology.
	• Elites constitute the social groups that maintain power over the mass media.
Feminist Theory	• Gender inequality results from struggles for economic and social power.
	• The mass media perpetuate gender stereotypes and patriarchal values.
Structural Functionalism	• The mass media are part of an important institution in society, one that keeps citizens informed.
	• The mass media serve as a watchdog over governments.
Symbolic Interactionism	• Meaning is conveyed through the symbols depicted in the mass media.
	• Symbols embedded in the mass media convey authority and give the mass media credibility.

Source: Author-generated

Consumer Culture and Convergence

Much of society today revolves around consumption—that is, the exchange of goods and services, including digital services made available via apps. Indeed, much of consumer culture has moved online, and e-commerce has grown rapidly. In 2016 Amazon alone made USD$136 billion in sales, which represents 27 per cent growth from the previous year (González, 2017). What is interesting about developments in consumer culture is not only that e-commerce facilitates the exchange of digital services, but people shop online for material goods, such as vacuum cleaners, books, and furniture, as well.

The notion of a mass society that consumes goods and services on a large scale formed and influenced by the mass media only emerged in the mid-twentieth century in the writings of sociologists working at the Frankfurt School, which was part of the Institute for Social Research at the University of Frankfurt (Henning, 2017). Max Horkheimer, Theodor Adorno, and Herbert Marcuse based their writings on Karl Marx's (1867/1996) analysis of the exploitation of workers through capitalist means of production. As part of this analysis, they were the first to critically investigate the impact of the mass production of cultural goods on cultural life. For them, mass-produced cultural goods led to standardization and uniformity in content, destroying individuality and multiplicity of choice. Exposure to standardized cultural goods (e.g., movies produced in Hollywood) caused members of society to become a homogenous, uncritical, and passive mass with little willpower to resist the appeal and influence of the mass media. Although today's conception of the *mass audience* and the effects of mass media on the audience have changed dramatically since the early writings of the Frankfurt School, their notion of the mass audience remains a key concept in sociological studies of mass communication and consumption.

Zygmunt Bauman's (2007) book, *Consuming Life*, critically examines how consumption has become a prevalent part of society through what he calls the "society of consumers." For Bauman, the dominance of consumptive practices in daily life has created a situation where people are valued for being a "good consumer," thereby reducing social relations to economic transactions. The mass media, by encoding messages about the acceptable consumption practices, reinforced the sense that these behaviours are normalized and expected. Even for Valentine's Day, a day where love is celebrated, consumption patterns—flowers, gifts, and chocolates—dominate social relations.

The last 50 years have seen many structural differences in production and consumption, particularly the move toward Web 2.0, which coincided with the rise in **participatory culture**: consumers can purchase products, services, and information as easily as they can produce them. In 2006 Don Tapscott and Anthony Williams talked about a new means of consumption, which they termed **prosumption** by combining the words *production* and *consumption*. In prosumption, customers play a central role in the design, development, and use of the end product (Tapscott & Williams, 2006). An example would be Instagram, a social media site where the corporation makes the infrastructure available but the consumer creates the product—pictures, comments, and likes. Prosumers become co-producers because they drive the creation of the product, and, moreover, there would be no product without their active engagement. Box 14.2 explores a moment in popular culture that challenged the traditional funding dynamics for products and even further blurred the line between producer and consumer.

participatory culture a culture where consumers can purchase products, services, and information as easily as they can produce them.

prosumption a combination of *production* and *consumption*, this term describes the process of customers playing a central role in the design, development, and use of the end product.

crowdsourcing an alternative funding model that looks to consumers and audiences to make contributions and provide resources to help make products, start services, and support ideas.

Spotlight On

14.2 | Crowdsourcing

The changes in production and distribution models have opened up new avenues for consumers to request what they want in a product and to take part in the production process. One popular form of doing so is through **crowdsourcing** (Howe, 2008). Crowdsourcing is an alternative funding model that looks to consumers and

Continued

audiences to make contributions and provide resources to help make products, start services, and support ideas. Take, for example, the film version of *Veronica Mars*. *Veronica Mars* was a television show with three seasons that ran from 2004 to 2007. The show followed a teenage detective in high school, played by actress Kristen Bell (Hills, 2015). Despite its short life the show accrued a large and strong fan base. When its third season ended and was not renewed, fans and critics alike were disappointed. Years later, in 2013, after continued support from fans, the original writer and producer, Rob Thomas, began a Kickstarter campaign to raise money

for a *Veronica Mars* film (Hills, 2015). In the first 12 hours the campaign reached its goal of $2 million (Rappaport, 2014). By the end of the campaign, fans collectively had raised $5.7 million (Rappaport, 2014). What makes this so different from the normal financing process is that a single person initiated the campaign and the money came from fans instead of the usual studio-based funding and support (such as Warner Bros, MGM, or Disney). This kind of funding model is called "fan-ancing" (instead of financing) because it relies on "fandom as a source of production capital and extracted surplus value" (Hills, 2015, p. 184).

Time to reflect

How might crowdsourcing interfere with the gatekeeping function of traditional mass media? Can you think of downsides to crowdsourcing as a funding model?

Media Ownership

Media ownership is a central topic because of the relevance the mass media have in society and in the production of culture: they not only shape how we see the world but also what we see and consider relevant. These industries are so important to sociological inquiry and in particular to theories of symbolic interactionism, as discussed above, because "such industries are directly involved in the production of social meaning" (Hesmondhalgh, 2013, p. 16). Understanding who owns the media provides important insights into both the distribution of power in society and the processes underlying meaning making. When governments directly or indirectly control the mass media, media messages will no longer serve the public interest. This is often the case in dictatorships, where the mass media are closely aligned with and their operations dictated by those who rule. Similarly, when the mass media are in the hands of a small number of corporations or individuals, this can jeopardize the ability of the media to serve the public by limiting the perspectives and voices represented.

Canada faces unique challenges when it comes to media ownership. Despite its large geographic size, the low population density of many regions creates enormous economic pressures. Few media corporations see real market value in investing in geographic areas sparsely populated. As a result, some regions have little to no locally produced media, and overall a few key players dominate the media market. This leads to few choices for consumers and increases prices of services dramatically. Another unique Canadian challenge is linked to cultural production. Canada shares borders with the United States, which is one of the largest producers of content in the world, with a total audience of over 320 million consumers. This makes it difficult for Canada to keep its independent voice and produce its own content, reflecting uniquely Canadian values, opinions, and views of the world. We will discuss below how regulatory bodies play an important role in helping Canadian content remain relevant in the mass media.

In Canada two distinct models of media ownership are prevalent: public and private. **Public media ownership** represents media that are owned by the government, while at the same time operating at arm's-length from the government. Public ownership serves several purposes: it represents the public's interest; uniquely represents Canadian values and content; provides content and services in both official languages; serves as watchdog over governmental decision making and operations; provides free access to services and content; follows educational, cultural, and social goals in content provision; and is present for citizens in remote regions, where other profit-based services are usually not available.

public media ownership media that are owned by—while at the same time operating at arm's-length from—the government.

CBC-Radio Canada has radio programming available in both English and French. Similarly, CBC-Radio Canada has a strong internet presence, making news of Canadian interest available in both official languages. The fact that the CBC is a public broadcaster and serves the interests of Canadians does not mean that it does not also fall under "corporate interest." CBC Radio is ad free, but CBC TV obtains part of its revenue through advertisement and hence needs to balance the interests and needs of Canadian citizens with the interests of corporations. For instance, the CBC made about $225-million in annual advertising revenue from selling ads during *Hockey Night in Canada*. Since the rights to air *Hockey Night in Canada* were lost to Rogers Communications, the company had to let go about 600 employees and cut its operations in half (Shoalts, 2014). This model has received much criticism, as some Canadians feel public media ownership should be devoid of corporate interests.

The second model is **private media ownership**. As discussed above, the Canadian context is fairly unique because a small number of corporations own the majority of the media. There are four key national players: Bell Canada, Corus Entertainment, Rogers Communications, and Quebecor. In contrast to publicly owned media, privately owned media follow a profit-maximization model, where decisions are made based on the likelihood of increasing revenue. Private media have several sources of income, including, for example, revenues from sales of magazines, daily newspapers, and tickets to movies, but a large proportion of revenues also come from advertisements. This links the media very closely to the interest of corporations that are willing to pay large sums for product placement.

Private media in Canada, as well as globally, are often owned and controlled by a small number of wealthy and influential individuals and families. Canada in particular has a fairly small and highly concentrated market. In 2012 Canada ranked second in cross-media ownership out of 32 countries studied by the International Media Concentration Research Project (Winseck, 2012). The high concentration of media ownership restricts the public's sources of information and types of content available. For example, Rogers, a privately owned media enterprise in Canada, has stakes in television,

private media ownership when media are owned by corporations and follow a profit-maximization model, where decisions are made based on the likelihood of increasing revenue.

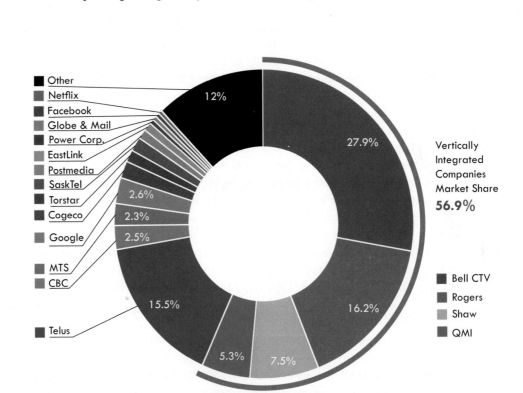

FIGURE 14. 1 Media Ownership and Concentration in Canada, 2013

Source: www.cmcrp.org/media-and-internet-concentration-1984–2013/

radio, and magazines. This gives Rogers the opportunity to manipulate or suppress any news that negatively impacts the company's activities across those media (Babe & Potter, 2015). Figure 14.1 shows the high degree of **media concentration** that exists in Canada. Telus, Google, CBC, and MTS have 15.5 per cent, 2.6 per cent, 2.5 per cent, and 2.3 per cent of the market share, respectively, making them the key players (Winseck, 2014). What is even more telling is the right side of Figure 14.1: four companies in Canada—Bell CTV, Rogers, Shaw, and QMI—have 56.9 per cent of the market share and thereby control most of the media and their messages.

> **media concentration** the ownership of many industries, products, or content by one company or organization.

Time to reflect

Take a moment to exercise your sociological imagination. How has the concentration of media ownership in Canada impacted your life? Consider variables such as the kinds of stories that get perpetuated, the cost of media access, as well as the media that you do and do not consume.

Regulatory Bodies

The economic and structural changes occurring in mass media organizations are closely influenced by regulations introduced and reinforced by governments. Because of the great importance of the mass media as a core institution in society, new regulatory bodies have been put in place to help regulate how the mass media operate and how they take into account citizens' interests. Most countries have regulatory bodies in place that will regulate different aspects of the mass media ranging from who can own the mass media to what the nature of content is presented in different types of media.

GP Images/Getty Images

(left to right) General Manager of Programming at CBC Sally Catto, Executive Producer Miranda de Pencier, Writer/Showrunner Moira Walley-Beckett, and Actress Amybeth McNulty attend the CBC World Premiere of *Anne* in 2017. The show is one of many media properties based on the 1908 novel *Anne of Green Gables*. Are remakes exciting reimaginings of good content, or a safe way to meet can-con requirements?

Canadian Radio-television and Telecommunications Commission (CRTC) an independent governing body funded by the Canadian government with the goal of fulfilling the media needs and representing the media interests of Canadian citizens.

Canadian content ("can-con") governmental policy of quotas to guarantee that media by Canadian artists, producers, and companies are sufficiently represented in the mass media.

The institutionalization and regulation of the mass media are critical, however, as considerations come into play beyond profit maximization.

The regulatory body charged with the regulation of broadcasting and telecommunications in Canada is the **Canadian Radio-television and Telecommunications Commission**, most commonly known as the CRTC, its abbreviation. The CRTC is an independent governing body funded by the Canadian government with the goal of fulfilling the media needs and representing the media interests of Canadian citizens. In Canada, for instance, the CRTC regulates the proportion of Canadian content that is included in programming. Given the prevalence of influential media originating from the United States, **Canadian content** (also referred to as **"can-con"**) quotas guarantee that media by Canadian artists, producers, and companies are sufficiently represented in the mass media. For example, radio stations need to guarantee that Canadian musicians are given sufficient airplay. These regulations, however, can also create a burden to mass media corporations, as they need to constantly monitor their content and be accountable to the CRTC for their broadcasting decisions. What complicates the work of the CRTC is that it also needs to take industry concerns into account and work with various interest and advocacy groups. One of the CRTC's greatest challenges has been to regulate digital content. As new forms of content production and dissemination emerge online, the CRTC is constantly being challenged to rethink traditional models of regulation. Box 14.3 discusses today's remix culture as an example of the challenges presented to the CRTC.

Sociology 2.0

14.3 | Participating in Remix Culture

Today we can see reappropriation of otherwise copyrighted material in remixes, mash-ups, memes, and GIFs. **Copyright** is understood as the legal right of authors to print, publish, perform, film, or record their materials, and to give authorization to others. To some extent, remixing and mash-ups have become part of our digital culture. In large part, this has to do with the compressible and homogenous format of digital content, which makes remixing easy. The 2008 documentary *RIP! A Remix Manifesto* sheds light on the changing environment of copyright and content creation. The film focuses on renowned mash-up artists, such as Girl Talk, on the changing relationship between producers and consumers, and on important questions about content creation and originality. The aims of the documentary are to challenge the idea of ownership, to leave behind stringent holds on a person's creation, and to adopt a free-flowing, **Creative Commons (CC)** approach to creative work. This is a divisive topic with support on both sides of the debate. An interesting example of support in favour of loosening traditional copyright laws and strengthening new copyright models, like creative commons, happened in 2004 when Danger Mouse, a hip-hop producer, mashed elements of The Beatles' self-titled "White Album" together with Jay-Z's *The Black Album*, releasing the project commercially as *The Grey Album* (Miller, 2011). The Beatles' copyright holder, EMI, sent Danger Mouse a cease and desist order to halt production and to destroy all existing copies of the album (Miller, 2011). In response to music giant EMI's hard copyright stance, over 170 websites took part in an online protest known as "Grey Tuesday" by hosting the album for free distribution. This resulted in over one million downloads (Miller, 2011). This example shows how mash-ups, remixes, and reappropriation further complicate ideas of ownership, authorship, and originality, and create a need for new forms of regulation online.

Time to reflect

What are your views on copyright? Do think that authors, such as Danger Mouse, should be allowed to remix content and disseminate it online?

Media Convergence and Monopoly

When examining private media ownership, we realize that much has changed since the 1980s in terms of how private media companies operate. Prior to these changes media companies that published newspapers or books, for example, would exclusively operate in this niche market (Jenkins, 2006). Digitization and media concentration, however, are two important factors that have contributed to moving away from this ownership model. Companies now tend to produce a range of cultural products and operate in multiple and diverse industries, often combining movie production, book publishing, and digital content creation. Hesmondhalgh (2013) identified four waves of change in media ownership that help explain how our current model was established.

The first wave of change was sparked by changes in communications policy in the United States throughout the 1980s. In 1934 the Federal Communications Commission was established by the Communications Act, which included media, broadcast, and telecommunications regulations, to ensure that mass media operated with the public interest in mind. In the 1980s corporations challenged the ability of the US government to regulate telecommunications and this lead to the **marketization** and **deregulation** of media industries. Deregulation is the removal of regulation in an industry where regulation exists and signals neo-liberalism, with a market- and profit-driven approach to cultural production.

The second wave began in the mid-1980s and involved other industrialized countries in Western Europe, Australasia, and Canada. In these countries telecommunications and broadcasting had previously followed mostly a public service broadcast model, whereby industries would be accountable to the public, provide universal (country-wide) service, and audiences would be considered citizens rather then consumers. Although elements of a public service broadcast model remain in the United States and Canada, there is consensus between industry and governments that a "vigorous private sector with some kind of corrective provided by a public service broadcaster" is a beneficial model for all (Hesmondhalgh, 2013, p. 146). For instance, in Canada, the Trudeau government has allocated CAN$675 million over five years to fund various operations of the CBC, thereby signalling the importance given to publicly funded mass media (Abma, 2016).

The third wave saw transitional and mixed societies initiate policies of marketization starting around 1989. Although neo-liberalism was a major influence, political and bureaucratic changes in various countries such as India, China, and South Korea opened up pathways for outside cultural markets. This created new markets, made up of millions of potential consumers, to which companies could dissemination cultural goods, but who could also participate in its production. An example is the multibillion-dollar industry of Bollywood, which extends worldwide.

The fourth wave begins in the late 1990s with the expansion of the internet, but has roots that go back to technological developments in the 1970s in telecommunications and computing. The rise of digital media has made it apparent that digitalization allows for **convergence** between technologies and industries. The fourth wave that Hesmondhalgh identified is particularly important because it stresses convergence, which is understood as a powerful force, as it "alters the relationship between existing technologies, industries, markets, genres, and audiences" (Jenkins, 2006, pp. 15–16). For Jenkins, it completely changes the logic by which media industries operate and by which media consumers process news and entertainment. The notion of convergence has been around for a long time, yet in recent years it has taken on new meaning as it has grown to focus on the new and complex ways that old and new media interact and the social implications of those interactions (Jenkins, 2006; Miller, 2011).

Earlier in this chapter we discussed structural functionalism as a key theoretical approach for understanding how societies are organized. Convergence represents a new organizational structure that directly impacts many aspects of society, including economics, social relations, cultural production, and dissemination. Convergence describes the fusion of at least four elements:

- developments and advances in computing, which facilitate the production of cultural goods such as video games like *Clash of Clans* or animation films like *Minions*;

copyright a form of intellectual property that ensures work created by a particular person or company cannot be used freely and without consent of the creator/owner.

Creative Commons (CC) an organization that assists people with protecting their creations while also making those creations accessible.

deregulation/ marketization the removal of regulation and changes to policy that serve neo-liberal and free-market agendas.

convergence the combination and intersection of otherwise different and dispersed regulations and laws, industries, or technologies.

regulatory convergence the systemic undoing, relaxing, and merging of laws, policies, and other regulations that leads to media industries that are virtually indistinguishable from one another.

industry convergence the horizontal or vertical integration of different media industries.

horizontal integration the expansion of one type of industry into other types of industries, enabling control of companies across industry boundaries.

vertical integration expanded control of the production process (such as raw materials, packaging, distribution, marketing, and final sales).

Interactive Activity

- sophisticated telecommunications infrastructure that provide access to high-speed broadband connectivity;
- the digital transformation of cultural goods, as most content is either born digital or, if created in analog, digitized (an example is the sitcom *Full House*, which first aired on ABC in the 1980s and has had a revival by streaming via Netflix); and
- the expansion of the entertainment industry into daily life through 24/7 streaming of content, often on demand (via YouTube, for example).

Convergence emerged as a result of reforms in the 1980s and 1990s in laws and policies regulating the media industry (Hesmondhalgh, 2013). Governments had put in place laws to keep media industries separate and thereby both control their audience reach and minimize their influence on public opinion and politics. For example, newspapers were considered a print industry and could not merge with television broadcasters, as broadcasters were seen as part of a distinct industry. This change would protect industries from hostile takeovers, thereby allowing for a multiplicity of views. And, it would also protect people from media concentration and monopolies (Miller, 2011; Schiller, 1971).

Media convergence can occur at different levels; we will discuss three next. First, the systemic undoing, relaxing, and merging of laws, policies, and other regulations is an example of deregulation, which leads to **regulatory convergence**. Regulatory reforms altered the environment in which media, telecommunications, and computing companies operate as they began to integrate and form transnational and multimedia conglomerates (Miller, 2011). Second, media industries are now virtually indistinguishable from one another. For example, Apple may still be known as a computer company, but it has highly competitive products in telecommunications (e.g., the iPhone), music (e.g., iTunes, Apple Music, and the iPod), and streaming services (e.g., AppleTV). This integration of different media industries is known as **industry convergence** and consists of two kinds of cross-sector integration: **horizontal integration**, and **vertical integration**. Horizontal integration is the expansion of one type of industry into other types of industries as discussed in the Apple example, where Apple moved from producing hardware to producing software and now streaming content. Vertical integration describes the expanded control of the production process. Miller (2011) explains that vertical integration enables corporations to control the entire production process (such as raw materials, packaging, distribution, marketing, and final sales) whereas horizontal integration enables them to have control of companies across industry boundaries. Typically, vertical integration occurs within one industry while horizontal integration spans across different industries. Box 14.4 on the Irving Oil Company describes an example of vertical and horizontal integration.

Spotlight On

14.4 | Vertical and Horizontal Integration and the Irving Oil Company

The importance of vertical and horizontal integration for building media empires can be seen in the case study of K.C. Irving, one of the world's leading industrialists. In the early 1900s, K.C. Irving, then a young entrepreneur, turned his father's convenience store into a gas and service station (Poitras, 2014). Over the span of the twentieth century, Irving worked to expand that business into large and more diverse companies such as oil refineries, pulp mills, and newspapers (Poitras, 2014). Today, these companies are collectively known as "the Irving Companies" and remain owned and operated by K.C. Irving's sons and grandsons. The Irving family, through its ownership of refineries like the Irving Oil refinery, pulp and mill factories like Irving Pulp & Paper, and convenience stores around the province, basically control the entire cycle of news production in New Brunswick, including newspaper publishing company Brunswick News. In 2012, Brunswick News owned 29 daily, weekly, and other newspaper publications in the province, thereby holding a significant print media monopoly in New Brunswick. Horizontal and vertical integration provides greater control over the production and dissemination of information: raw materials (paper mills and oil refineries), the information (newspapers), and distribution or points of sale (convenience stores).

To survive in a highly competitive market, media corporations often rely on industry convergence by either owning the entire production cycle (vertical convergence) or owning many different news sources (horizontal convergence). This type of ownership structure is primarily driven by economics, but has implications for how and what information citizens obtain. As Miller (2011) points out, there can be "threats to democracy and accountability that follow when media and the public sphere become owned by a small number of large corporations" (p. 79).

> ### Time to reflect
>
> What problems might arise for the residents of a province when, for example, an oil and lumber company owns the majority of newspapers and radio stations in the province where the company is located?

Lastly, **technological convergence** is "the movement of almost all media and information to digital electronic formats, storage, and transfer: the digitisation of all media, communications, texts, sounds, images and even currency into a common digital format or language" (Miller, 2011, p. 73). This has created a system of information exchange that enables text, sound, image, and video to be consumable by the same device (Miller, 2011). In other words, digital devices such as smart phones, tablets, and computers have become the "electronic equivalent of a Swiss army knife" (Jenkins, 2006, p. 5), being able to produce, edit, upload, distribute, and interact with content. Box 14.3 describes this technological converging using the remix culture as an example.

> **technological convergence** the trend toward providing media and information in digital formats, creating a system of information exchange that enables text, sound, image, and video to be consumable by the same device.

Globalization and the Media

Global Audiences

Early theories of mass communication did not consider the nuanced way different kinds of audiences engage with cultural products and were unaware that different people make meaning of content in different ways. Sociologists Elihu Katz and Paul Lazarsfeld (1955), pioneers of **uses and gratifications** theory, argue that more attention needs to be devoted to what people do with the media rather than the influence or impact of the media on the individual. The theory asks two questions: First, how do people use a specific medium and how does it fit into their everyday routines, practices, and habits? And second, what gratifications does the medium provide? From this perspective, the audience is characterized as active, discerning, and motivated in their media use (Quan-Haase & Brown, 2013). In addition to the growth of interest communities and easy access to audiences, online social networking has also created a new social space for **interactive audiences** to emerge. Interactive audiences not only consume content; they also produce content for a global audience by adding content, sharing content, and providing feedback to content creators. Marshall McLuhan and Powers (1989) introduced the notion of the **global village** to describe how electronic media compress time and allow individuals who are geographically and socially removed to have similar experiences by interacting with the same content. Today, we can receive updates about political unrests in other parts of the world in real time, as we discuss in Chapter 16 in the examination of the M-15 movement in Spain.

The shift toward global audiences is linked to several transformations in the media industry. The first important transformation links to the four waves of marketization we discussed above (Hesmondhalgh, 2013). These have created the right conditions for the establishment of conglomerates that cross national and international boundaries. For example, Disney's release of *Star Wars: Episode VII* in 2015 was a global event, with the movie being released almost simultaneously in many continents and creating buzz online in the form of news stories, tweets, blog posts, videos, and images. Global media outlets like Disney benefit from their international presence because a single product (the movie) is sold and resold to a global audience of millions, leading toward unprecedented wealth creation for the company. Its international box-office haul is

> **uses and gratifications** a media theory founded on the idea that more attention needs to be devoted to what people do with the media.
>
> **interactive audiences** media users who not only consume content but also produce content for a global audience, by creating content, sharing content, and providing feedback to content creators.
>
> **global village** the notion that electronic media compress time and allow individuals who are geographically and socially removed to have similar experiences by interacting with the same content.

Newzulu/Alamy Stock Photo

Attendees pose with a lightsaber at the *Star Wars: The Force Awakens* premiere in Saudi Arabia.

estimated at $1.75 billion, with domestic receipts of $815 million in the United States; worldwide it will make $1.2 to $1.4 billion in revenues (McClintock, 2016). These revenues do not include the range of products associated with the film including toys, DVDs, promotional materials, and other derivatives. Media conglomerates, like Disney, greatly benefit from their global operations and continue to grow their brand internationally, appealing to audiences in diverse cultures.

Globalization

The interconnection in markets and communication and the reliance and relationships between societies and cultures that emerge from these operations is referred to as globalization. Globalization "signals the growing *interdependence* and *interpenetration* of human relations alongside the increasing *integration* of the world's socio-economic life" (Webster, 2014, p. 77, italics in original). Although globalization is typically thought about as an economic force that unites countries, markets, and companies around the globe, it is also a dominant social, cultural, and political condition (Webster, 2014). Globalization allows for the easy flow of goods and services across borders, facilitating commerce and bringing nations closer together. At the same time, globalization raises many concerns in terms of media production and dissemination. We discuss three central concerns next and look at how they influence Canada's ability to produce and disseminate Canadian content.

Diversification

Although no one company dominates an entire industry, which would be called a monopoly, a small number of companies may dominate together, and this is called an oligopoly (Campbell, Martin, & Fabos, 2011). Since there is more than one company in the market, there might be the illusion of diversification, but in reality it is very difficult for other, smaller companies to gain access and compete (Campbell, Martin, & Fabos, 2011).

Cultural Imperialism

The increased chatter between nations and the increasingly connected global marketplace introduces products and services to new parts of the world where they had not previously been. These products and services also impart cultural values and beliefs. The imposition of those values and beliefs on another culture that was not previously tied or influenced to that culture is called cultural imperialism (Hesmondhalgh, 2013). One fear of cultural imperialism is that it will overshadow, erase, or erode the values, beliefs, and cultures unique to some parts of the world.

Accountability

Transnational corporations obscure what is owned by any given nation. While a company like this may be given a "national label," so much of the company takes place in various countries that it becomes difficult to know their connections to one country (Webster, 2014). The important question to ask is, who are these transnational corporations and global media companies responsible to? To whom are they accountable?

Media Literacy

Understanding the media and being able to consume media requires **media literacy** skills. Media literacy and digital literacy are prevailing concepts that focus on a critical approach towards media messages (Koltay, 2011). Media literacy is often understood as the ability to find, access, analyze, evaluate, and communicate messages in a wide range of formats including print, audio, video, and digital (Hobbs, 1998). Media literacy skills have been central to the education system since the mid-1970s but have gained greater relevance recently with the move toward a digital society. The education system currently faces two challenges. First, it is important to not only have the skills to access and evaluate digital resources but also to contribute content in the form of YouTube videos, blog posts, Instagram updates, and Facebook pages. The skills required to navigate the increased digital information landscape are referred to as **digital skills** or digital literacy. Digital literacy is more than just the ability to use software or operate a digital device; it includes a variety of "complex cognitive, motor, sociological, and emotional skills, which users need in order to function effectively in digital environments" (Eshet-Alkalai, 2004, p. 93). Second, a central challenge for the educational system is to prepare students with the right skillset to take on twenty-first-century jobs. One problem is that teachers in the elementary and secondary school systems are often themselves lacking digital skills. As discussed in Chapter 1, having the right kinds of skills has become increasingly critical in a competitive society where many of those seeking employment will be similar in terms of the degrees they have. The importance of developing and updating digital skills stems from the notion that it helps people take full advantage of the resources available online for finding information, getting a job, and connecting with friends and family. In Box 14.5 we show how sociologists are developing approaches for understanding and measuring digital skills.

> **media literacy** the ability to find, access, analyze, evaluate, and communicate messages in a wide range of formats including print, audio, video, and digital.

> **digital skills** ability to access, understand, and utilize a wide range of digital services including but not limited to email, social media, search engines, and devices such as laptops, tablets, and smart phones.

Time to reflect

What kinds of digital skills do you think need to be taught to youth in Canada today? Do you feel sufficiently trained in digital skills by your high school or post-secondary courses for the jobs of the future?

Theory in Everyday Life

14.5 | Understanding and Measuring Digital Literacy

Digital skills have only recently become relevant to policy makers and educators. Much early attention was drawn toward access to the internet and the development of policies that could help individuals get online. Being online, however, is just the first step, as individuals need to learn to navigate a complex digital environment (Quan-Haase, 2016). This drew attention toward inequalities in digital skills and the effect that these may have on how individuals navigate and make use of the internet.

One approach to measuring digital skills is to focus on people's knowledge about digital tools, applications, and concepts. That is, rather than using attitudinal questions measuring a person's subjective perception of expertise, which may be biased, this approach suggests using more robust means. Hargittai and Hsieh (2012) have developed an approach that asks individuals their level of understanding of various internet-related terms and concepts such as Rich Site Summary (RSS), JPEG, tagging, and malware.

To measure your own level of digital literacy, indicate for each of the terms in Table 14.4 your level of understanding: 1 = "no understanding"; 2 = "little understanding"; and 3 = "full understanding." Then count the number of times you chose option 3 (full understanding) to determine your level of digital literacy.

TABLE 14.4 Measuring Your Digital Literacy

Term	1	2	3
Reload			
Advanced search			
Favourites			
Bookmark			
Spyware			
Preference setting			
Blog			
Firewall			
PDF			
JPEG			
Tagging			
Weblog			
Newsgroup			
Tabbed browsing			
Frames			
Podcasting			
Web feeds			
Torrent			
BCC (on email)			
Bookmarklet			
Wiki			
Cache			
Widget			
Phishing			
Malware			
Social bookmarking			
RSS			
Total = (sum of option 3 answers)	of 27	of 27	of 27

Source: Republished with permission of Sage Publishing, from Succint Survey Measures of Web-Use Skills, E. Hargittai and Y.P. Hsieh, Social Science Computer Review 30(1), 2012; permission conveyed through Copyright Clearance Center, Inc.

digital immigrants people who have learned how to use digital technologies later in life and have been generally slow and apprehensive in adopting novel forms of communication.

digital natives people who have grown up with digital technologies and did not know a time without the internet.

The terms **digital immigrants** and **digital natives** are used to describe varying levels of skill and comfort using digital media (Prensky, 2001). Digital immigrants learned how to use digital technologies later in life and have been generally slow and apprehensive in adopting novel forms of communication. Canadian adults 65 and older are still the slowest to adopt the internet as a communication tool; they are particularly slow in the adoption of social media (Haight, Quan-Haase, & Corbett, 2014). By contrast, digital natives have grown up with digital technologies and did not know a time without the internet. Digital literacy and media literacy in general are critical in our digital society. Individuals who do not have the skills to evaluate information and its trustworthiness can fall prey to all kinds of misinformation (see Box 14.6).

Children around the ages of 9–11 have difficulty differentiating between real and fake information online.

fake news hoaxes or the deliberate use of misinformation in the traditional news media or social media.

Digital Divide

14.6 | Fake News and Kids' Vulnerability

One example of mass reaction to fake news occurred in New Brunswick when the fake newspaper, the *Manatee*, announced that Halloween had been cancelled. The Fredericton police were bombarded with angry calls from parents. This is clearly a benign example, but inaccurate information around health care, diets, and product information abound online. Since the 2016 US presidential election, much debate has also surfaced around the term **fake news**. In a digital environment, it is difficult for citizens to evaluate what news is fake (Chazan, 2017). Often vulnerable populations are the ones most affected by a lack of digital skills, and they can easily fall into phishing attempts or scams that can cost thousands of dollars. One population that is particularly vulnerable in digital environments are children. Instances of cyberbullying and online harassment (Mascheroni, Ponte, Garmendia, Garitaonandia, & Murru, 2010)

demonstrate how challenging it is for kids to navigate digital spaces, where users can be anonymous, post under false pseudonyms, and engage in hurtful behaviours. An important part of social media literacy is for children to realize that not all portrayals online are necessarily "real" accounts of the world and as such need to be critically examined for their validity and intention (Livingstone, 2014). Livingstone interviewed 9- to 11-year-olds and learned that this age group finds it difficult to unmask fakery. The kids reported that they themselves often falsify information online successfully; for example, they falsify their real age to create a profile. This vulnerability in various populations makes it particularly important to understand how inequalities affect the acquisition of media literacy skills and what programs and policies can be put in place to support those who fall behind.

Conclusions

The mass media constitute an important institution in democratic societies, as they keep the public informed, serve as a watchdog for governments, and through cultural production and dissemination allow for the creation of meaning in society. The mass media have undergone massive transformations as a result of technological developments, in particular in the realm of digital technologies. Digitization has not only transformed who can generate and circulate content but has also had an impact on where people acquire the news. Traditional news sources have seen their influence dwindle as young Canadians go to Facebook, Instagram, and alternative news sources to learn about current events, stay tuned to cultural trends, and even keep up with local events. This has largely changed who the key players are in content production and how messages disseminate, as peer networks have emerged as a central source for information.

The changing nature of the mass media has also largely changed our understanding of audiences and their roles. Audiences today are no longer passive recipients of information, sitting on a couch. They have transformed into active participants and content producers, engaging with television shows via Twitter and directly engaging with celebrities on Instagram. Within news production, citizen journalism has emerged as a new form of reporting and disseminating the news, where citizens themselves, often in real time and from the ground, report on events around the world using their smart phones. This loosens the tight grip on the control of messages previously held by private owners of media and creates a new plurality of opinions and views. At the same time, it also introduces new biases and makes it more difficult to identify misinformation in a fast-paced environment that is overflowing with myriad messages.

Questions for Critical Thought

1. The morning newspaper used to be a ritual for many Canadians. How have new media influenced the way you and your friends access news? What kinds of rituals do you take part in on a daily, weekly, or monthly basis? Do you still use traditional, large media organizations? If so, how do you engage with them?

2. Is misinformation a problem for social media websites, news organizations, or for the individual reader? Who should be responsible for information accuracy? How can people protect themselves from misinformation?

3. Technological convergence has allowed us to reduce the amount of devices we need by packaging cameras, scheduling software, messaging, and email—to name but a few—into a smart phone. This makes our phone an incredibly important device, with our personal, financial, and social details available at the click of a button. What unintended consequences have arisen as a result of this technologically converged device?

4. How has technological convergence influenced citizen journalism? For example, smart phones are a tool for easy photo and video journalism and allow people to post from virtually anywhere. Is yielding a smart phone with the ability to speak to the world (in theory) a democratic tool?

5. Does media concentration influence popular thought? Explain your position. If so, how can we overcome this influence?

Take it Further: Recommended Readings

Z. Bauman, *Consuming Life* (Cambridge, UK: Polity Press, 2007). Bauman analyzes some of the changes to consumer practices and habits in the late twentieth and early twenty-first centuries. Drawing on a variety of theoretical resources, he highlights the pitfalls and anomalies in, what he calls, the transformation of a "society of producers" into a "society of consumers."

A. Briggs and P. Burke, *A Social History of the Media: From Gutenberg to the Internet* (Cambridge, UK: Polity Press,

2009). Briggs and Burke focus on the social significance of communication technologies and media cultures. With an emphasis on major changes, they trace the adaptation, circulation, and evolution of media throughout history.

H. Giroux and G. Pollock, *The Mouse that Roared: Disney and the End of the Innocence*, 2nd ed. (Lanham, MD: Rowman & Littlefield, 2010). Giroux and Pollock explore how Disney has a profound and global influence on children, shaping their media consumption and how they see the world.

D. Hesmondhalgh, *The Cultural Industries*, 3rd ed. (London: Sage, 2013). Hesmondhalgh draws attention to the changing landscape of the cultural industries. He pays particular attention to threads of continuity and draws on the creative, commercial, and political facets of the cultural industries to demonstrate his arguments.

H. Jenkins, *Convergence Culture: Where Old and New Media Collide* (New York: New York University Press, 2006). Jenkins looks at the new ways information flows across media industries and media technologies. He examines the collision of regulation, technology, and culture through empirical examples of contemporary popular media.

J. Pavlik and S. McIntosh, *Converging Media: An Introduction to Mass Communication*, 5th ed. (New York: Oxford University Press, 2016). This introductory text provides a comprehensive overview of the traditional and new media and the challenges that arise through the introduction of digital media.

Take it Further: Recommended Online Resources

Access Copyright
www.accesscopyright.ca

Creative Commons
www.creativecommons.org

Globalization101.org
www.globalization101.org

***The Grey Album*, by Danger Mouse**
https://archive.org/details/DjDangerMouse-TheGreyAlbum

Internet World Stats
www.internetworldstats.com/links10.htm

Kickstarter
www.kickstarter.com

MediaSmarts
http://mediasmarts.ca

"Newspapers," in *The Canadian Encyclopedia*
www.thecanadianencyclopedia.ca/en/article/newspapers

More resources available on Dashboard

15

The Social Impact on Populations and the Environment

Learning Objectives

In this chapter, you will:

> Learn the effects of population size and urbanization on life experiences

> Consider the interrelationship between the natural and built environments we live in

> Recognize the problematic relationship between population and environment

◀ Neil Webb/Getty Images

Introduction

The single most important, least debatable fact about societies is that they are made up of collections of human beings. But human beings are flesh and blood; they need food and they occupy space. In every important sense, people possess materiality—they are embodied in ways we can perceive with our senses—so we need to spend some time talking about the social and sociological implications of this fact.

Many of the issues we discuss in this chapter are especially urgent. In the past 50 years, Canada's population has more than doubled. More important, the population of the world has continued to increase exponentially over much of the past two centuries, leading to great concern about **overpopulation** and its effects on the environment.

Can humanity survive another century like the twentieth century? Today, it is hard to ignore the environmental destruction that our growing population has caused. Climate change has become an important social and political issue, especially in the last few decades. It has forced us to think more critically about humanity's impact on the environment, as well as the effects humanity will have to endure if we continue to destroy our **natural resources**—the air, water, minerals, plants, and other species on which we depend for survival.

Theoretical Approaches to Population
Conflict Theory

Sociologists are agreed that rapid population growth is a social as well as environmental problem, because it produces social upheaval and poverty. However, conflict theorists explain excessive population growth and its consequences in a different way. Conflict theorists propose that the problems poor countries face

overpopulation a condition wherein the number of humans (or other animals) exceeds the relevant resources such as the water and essential nutrients they need to survive.

natural resources materials or substances such as minerals, forests, water, and fertile land that occur in nature and can be used for economic gain.

The Ionce family of Abbotsford, BC, photographed with 13 of their 18 children.

today result not from overpopulation but from an unfair and harmful distribution of the world's wealth. By this reasoning, recent famines that have plagued various less-developed parts of the world—such as Africa, Central and South America, and South Asia—are a result of improper land use, civil wars, and other social and political factors, such as protectionist tariffs established by more-developed countries to keep out goods and agricultural products from the Global South. Less-developed countries accordingly have trouble producing the food they need to eat or gaining the capital they need to industrialize.

So, according to conflict theorists, we cannot take famine, in itself, as proof of overpopulation. After all, to keep food prices in balance, many developed nations pay their farmers *not* to grow crops, even if this causes shortages elsewhere in the world. Furthermore, historical records and computer simulations used to study the effects of famine on human history suggest that famine has not historically been a significant "positive check" on population size. Nor can we assume plagues or epidemics are **positive checks** that result from overpopulation. In fact, they may indicate economic development is taking place (albeit perhaps unevenly).

Poverty and inequality often cause problems that are similar to those caused by (or apparently caused by) overpopulation and may also contribute to overpopulation. For example, peasants often produce large numbers of children to do the farm work and care for them in their old age. With economic development, health care accessibility improves but people continue to have lots of children, and so the population explodes, at least in the short term. Only gradually does population growth slow down. With lower death rates, people have less need for many children, especially once old-age security benefits become available in their society. A large family—a benefit in farm work—is a liability in urban industrial societies, especially where children are expected to attend school for an extended period, becoming consumers and not producers of family well-being.

Time to reflect

What, in your view, are the pros and cons of having children? How might those pros and cons change if your social circumstances were to change?

In poorer nations, then, the problem is not merely too many people; it is also a shortage of capital for industrialization, and a lack of markets for agricultural products. In this context, a large, rapidly growing population merely compounds the problems of poverty, dependency, plague, and famine. Faced with a rapidly growing population, some have come to advocate **zero population growth** (ZPG) as the solution. ZPG occurs when births are exactly balanced by deaths. Then, the size of the population remains constant over time—in a state of **equilibrium**. ZPG is a global strategy of survival, not merely a national one.

positive checks according to Malthus, forces that limit the population by raising the death rate due to disease and starvation.

zero population growth (ZPG) the maintenance of a population at a constant level by limiting the number of live births to only what is needed to replace the existing population; an absence of any increase (or decrease) in a population over a period of time.

equilibrium a balance, in this case between population numbers and potential for feeding these numbers.

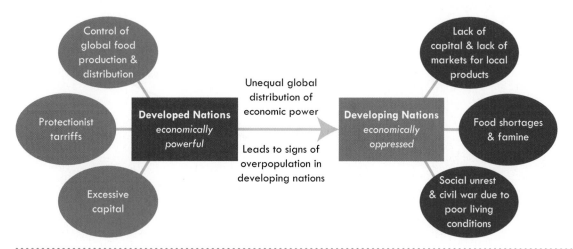

FIGURE 15.1 Conflict Theorist Perspective on Overpopulation

Source: Author generated

That said, it is clear that more than sheer numbers are at issue. Location is also a concern: a great many people are located in places that are poorly suited to feed, house, and employ them. City life solves many of the problems of rural life—for example, the risk of starvation and epidemic is prevented through public health and welfare measures; unemployment is prevented through the offer of new kinds of employment and economies of scale in the provision of needed services. But urbanization also brings new problems in its wake, which will be discussed below.

Feminism

Feminists point out that the birth rate required in order to maintain the population size (2.2) is the rate that women naturally fluctuate to in societies where they are given education, birth control methods, and choices around consent (Caldwell, Phillips, & Barkat-e-Khuda, 2002; Morgan & Taylor, 2006 Campbell, 2007). Their argument is that gender equality (particularly equal rights and equal education for women) would result in natural decline in population growth. Historically, this has proved to be the case in every part of the world, over the past century.

This points to a more general phenomenon—namely, the widespread link between higher education and lower birth rates. At least in our society over the past half-century or more, women who attained more education tended to marry later, bear children later, and bear fewer children in total. This is true of all modern societies, so that societies in which women have received the most education are societies that typically have the lowest birth rates among native-born women.

It should be noted, however, that the great (and never reversed) decline in childbearing that began in Western Europe and North America around 1870 as part of the so-called demographic transition was *not* mainly a result of higher education for women, since it began before most women received much schooling. It was a result of urbanization, industrialization, the growth of middle classes (and middle-class aspirations), and new opportunities for upward mobility in (non-farming) occupations that did not require large numbers of children.

Functionalism

Thomas Malthus proposed that, while the Earth's available food increases additively (or arithmetically), population increases exponentially (or geometrically). A population increasing exponentially at a constant rate is adding more people every year than it did the year before, while an arithmetical increase in food supply adds the same amount of food each year. In the end, arithmetic growth is always outstripped by geometric growth, no matter the starting points or rates of growth in each.

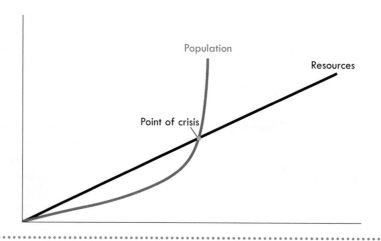

FIGURE 15.2 Malthus's Basic Theory: The Changes in Population and Resources Over Time

Source: http://study.com/academy/lesson/malthusian-theory-of-population-growth-definition-lesson-quiz.html

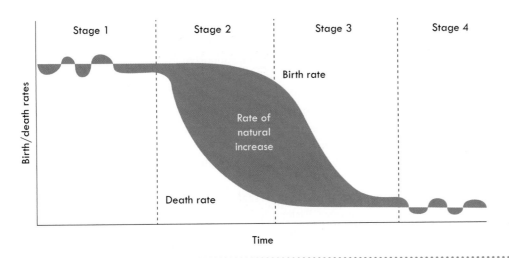

FIGURE 15.3 Demographic Transition Theory

Source: Lorne Tepperman, *Starting Points*, 2e. © Oxford University Press Canada 2011. Reprinted by permission of the publisher.

Malthus concluded that population would always outgrow its food supply, as depicted in Figure 15.2 on the previous page. There would, inevitably, be a "point of crisis" where population would start to die off in large numbers, whether through famine, disease, war, or otherwise.

This massive catastrophe could threaten the survival of the national population. Moreover, this disaster would occur even if a society, moved by generosity or religion, shared out all of society's wealth equally. According to Malthus, if poor people were suddenly enriched by the equalization of wealth, they would marry and start producing babies as quickly as nature allowed. Soon, food would be in short supply again and inequality would reassert itself, with those who had produced the fewest babies again being in the best economic position.

Though Malthus disapproved of many preventive checks, especially abortion and contraception, he preferred preventive checks to positive checks. Accordingly, he urged people to use preventive checks so that they would not have to suffer the horrible consequences of positive checks. Mainly, he proposed this could be best accomplished through sexual abstinence.

Malthus's argument is recognizably a piece of functional analysis. Like other functional analysis, it is concerned with the conditions that maintain social equilibrium and the dangers associated with losing equilibrium (e.g., war, famine, and epidemic).

However, the "demographic transition theory," developed in the mid–twentieth century by sociologist Kingsley Davis (1945) and others (see Figure 15.3), suggests that perhaps Malthus was wrong, because he had failed to take into account other ways that equilibrium might be restored. Demographic transition theory, based on the analysis of European population history, proposes that following a decline in the death rates, societies tend to lower their birth rates within one or two generations. In doing so, they re-establish something like zero population growth at low, rather than high, levels of mortality and fertility. In this way, increasingly prosperous societies avoid Malthusian disaster.

Time to reflect

Do you, or any of your friends, have children? If so, what were the reactions of those around you to you or your friend having a child? If not, can you identify any social forces in your life that have encouraged you not to have children?

What happened between the time of Thomas Malthus (1766–1834) and that of Kingsley Davis (1908–1997) is precisely the Industrial Revolution—a change to human history that vastly increased the food supply, moved people into cities and factories, and reduced the need for large families.

carrying capacity the number of people, other living organisms, or crops that a region can support without environmental degradation.

Still, population pressures remain a problem in certain parts of the world, especially those where industrialization has not taken hold. It is hard to put meaningful numbers on the world's **carrying capacity**—that is, the number of people who can be supported by the available resources at a given level of technology. (It depends a lot on the quality of social and political organization.) And, as the technology improves—for example, the technology associated with food production—a society's carrying capacity increases, so more people can be fed.

So, it is hard to say decisively whether Malthus was wrong. On the one hand, there is evidence to suggest he was wrong. After all, here we are, two centuries later, with a world population that is about four times the size it was in Malthus's time—7.2 billion now compared with 1.8 billion then. We haven't all died off yet.

One fact Malthus didn't take into account is that population size and population growth are not spread evenly over the world's surface. Faster rates of growth, whether through natural causes or immigration, may be more tolerable in some parts of the world than in others, depending on the current population size and the region's carrying capacity. So, for example, in Canada, the provinces of Ontario, British Columbia, and Alberta are economically more capable of supporting a larger population than certain other provinces with less fertile land, a harsher climate, and fewer natural resources. So, population growth in those "more favoured" provinces poses less of a problem.

That said, in Canada population growth is currently highest in all three territories (the Northwest Territories, Nunavut, and the Yukon), and population pressure is aggravating poverty problems there. On the other hand, we can see rapid population growth in these areas as illustrating the healing and rebuilding of Indigenous cultures that were damaged and in some cases, even destroyed, by white settlement and colonialism.

Many demographers currently estimate that world population will peak around 2070 at 9 billion people, and then slowly decrease to 8.4 billion by 2100. However, in Figure 15.4, we can see a range of estimates, reflecting different assumptions about the rate of fertility decline in different parts of the world.

When the human population became very large in the last few hundred years, it also became mainly urban. Urban communities, housed vertically in tall buildings, can hold many more people

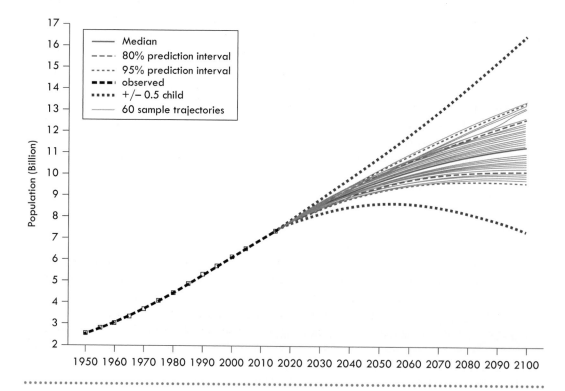

FIGURE 15.4 World Population Growth, 1950 to 2100 (Projected)

Source: United Nations, Department of Economic and Social Affairs, Population Division (2017). World Population Prospects: The 2017 Revision. Http://esa.un.org/unpd/wpp/

"A day at the beach" takes on a new meaning when hundreds of thousands of people get the same idea at the same time.

than rural communities. Urban life is a very different experience than rural life, as we have already noted; but it is part of a long transition from transience to settlement. Starting from the dawn of time, as humanity grew in number, people changed from transient hunter-gatherers, to settled agriculturalists, then to urban industrialists and post-industrialists. Population growth was both a cause and consequence of these economic and geographic changes.

Growth promotes complexity and invention: large, dense populations tend to invent new social and economic roles, dividing the labour of society in specialized ways. Productive tasks are broken into smaller, detailed tasks that require training. Increasingly, social roles are distinguished not only by age and sex but also by characteristics associated with skill, aptitude, and interest. What's more, population growth tends to keep a population young. A slower-growing, older population is costlier to maintain and often consumes more than it produces. So growth can be a good thing.

An older, longer-living society relies more on immigration to provide needed population renewal through new skills and human capital, which the older community is unable to provide for itself. In Canada, demographically an aged and aging society, this turnover is especially important, since many immigrants are the young parents of young families—so they are changing the age distribution of Canada even as they are changing the cultural distribution.

Symbolic Interactionism

Symbolic interactionists are interested in the meanings people attach to their own and other people's behaviour. For example, they note that people in low-income nations are coming to deal differently with childbearing and its meaning in a postmodern society. Araujo et al. (2014) note the current widespread concern with "correcting" infertility and its relationship to a woman's body and identity. The authors wonder whether the yearning to have children in newly developed countries is rooted in traditional notions of family life or in more up-to-date notions about the fulfillment of personal desire in a consumerist culture. Gradually, people in low-fertility modern societies come to view childbearing as a conscious choice, not a social given.

Symbolic interactionists are also interested in the ways people in a given population—for example, residents in the same city—structure and interpret their lives there. Herbert Gans (1962), for example, has focused on how the meaning of city life varies among groups and subcultures.

We all learn how to live effectively in cities, using urban etiquette. For example, we use civil inattention, defined by Erving Goffman (2008) as avoiding eye contact or seeming to stare at others in public places. However, within the urban culture, we find a variety of urban subcultures. An urban *subculture* is a group of people who share some cultural traits of the larger society but who, as a group, also have their own distinctive traditions, values, norms, style of dress, and behaviour. Urban subcultures allow individuals who are otherwise isolated within an impersonal city to form connections with other neighbours. The mere existence of urban subcultures reminds us that city dwellers use ingenuity in finding small-scale local solutions to problems like anonymity.

Interactive activity

When examining population and environmental problems from a symbolic interactionist perspective, researchers ask why and how certain issues enter the public consciousness—what kinds of social "claims" make the greatest impact, and under what circumstances? Our ideas about population and the environment determine our receptiveness to calls for behaviour change (e.g., conservation or birth control). No one wants to pay the cost of overpopulation or environmental degradation, but everyone wants to see the problems solved. At the same time, we should recognize that different observers, with different amounts of power, are struggling to define whether population growth and rapid industrialization are global problems. While these may seem to be "problems" from the standpoint of affluent industrialized Western societies, with low population growth, they may not seem to be problems of the same magnitude to people living in low-income, less industrialized, countries whose people Westerners tend to racialize.

Here is the difficulty: solving the problem of overpopulation means solving the problem of good social and political organization. As population expert Joel Cohen (1995) points out in his article "How Many People Can the Earth Support?," the earth can support many more people than currently live on it, but it will support them with more or less ease under different conditions. For example, Earth can support many more people than it does today if steps are taken to equalize global resources,

TABLE 15.1 Theoretical Approaches to Population

Theory	Main points
Conflict Theory	• Overpopulation is a myth, and the problem is an unequal distribution of wealth. • High rates of population growth produce conflicts over scarce territory and resources. • Cities contain neighbourhoods of greater and lesser comfort, as well as homeless people.
Feminism	• Gender equality would result in a natural decline in population growth.
Structural Functionalism	• Malthus proposed that excess population would lead to human disasters (e.g., war, plague, and starvation) that would reduce the excess. • Demographic transition theory proposes that high fertility rates decline to establish a new level of population equilibrium. • Too-rapid urban growth produces disorganization, crowding, and stress.
Symbolic Interactionism	• Our ideas about population and the environment determine our receptiveness to calls for behaviour change (e.g., conservation or birth control). • We all learn how to live effectively in cities, using urban etiquette (e.g., civil inattention). • No one wants to pay the cost of population and environmental issues, but everyone wants to see the problems solved.

Source: Author-generated

provide honest and effective government everywhere, build safer and more productive workplaces, and tolerate more risk of environmental disaster. This means that, to solve the earth's population problem, we need to debate and reach agreement about a variety of social, economic, and political issues that have so far eluded agreement. In the end, humanity's population problem is a social and cultural problem of belief, meaning, and expectation.

World Population

In studying the population history of humanity, American demographer Ansley Coale (1974) divided human history into two parts. The first part covers the beginning of humanity's existence over a million years ago (the Stone Age) to around 1750 CE. This period was characterized by slow population growth—little growth at all for thousands of years—with the number of people being born more or less staying consistently equal to the number dying. From 1750 to the present, however, the population grew exponentially, meaning an increasingly larger number of people were added each year.

Through slow growth, the human population reached its first billion around 1800. Then, with more rapid growth, each successive billion has arrived more quickly than the previous one: the second billion arrived in 1927, the third in 1961, the fourth in 1974, the fifth in 1987, and the sixth in 1999 (Bongaarts, 2009; see also Coale, 1974).

Note, however, that despite all this growth, the world population is not growing as quickly today as it was a hundred years ago (see Figure 15.4). This is due to a worldwide fertility decline that took hold in the past few decades. If fertility levels continue to fall in the economically developing, as well as in the developed, countries, the United Nations predicts world population will reach about 9.6 billion in 2050, then start to level off (UN Department of Economic and Social Affairs, 2015)

Changes in childbearing are the key to this change: currently, women around the world are having fewer babies than their mothers and grandmothers. Globally, total fertility is projected by the

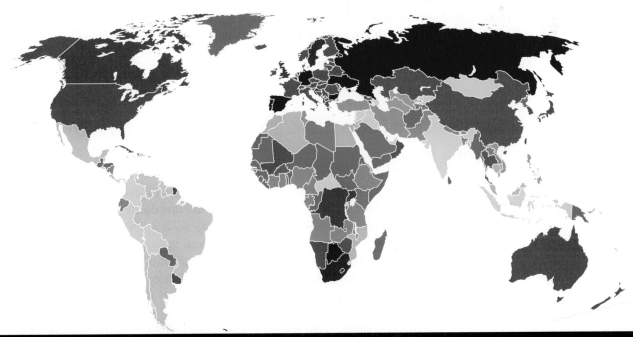

FIGURE 15.5 World Fertility: Number of Live Births per Year, per 1000 Population

Ranges from <-6.0 to 34.0>

Source: Adapted from https://www.cia.gov/library/publications/the-world-factbook/rankorder/2127rank.html. Based on data from the CIA, World Factbook.

United Nations to decrease from 2.56 children per woman to only 2.02 children per woman 40 years from now (UN Department of Economic and Social Affairs, 2009). The decline of one-half child over 40 years may not sound like much until you consider that billions of women are expected to follow this same pattern. This means billions of fewer babies being born. During your lifetime, then, the world's population will continue to grow, but much more slowly than in the recent past.

Owing to different rates of population change, the fraction of humanity living in less-developed countries today is greater than in the past. This proportion will increase by 2050—as will the numbers in rapidly growing societies like Brazil, Nigeria, and Indonesia, all demographic giants of the future. At the same time, the proportion of people living in more-developed countries will *drop* from 18 per cent in 2008 to less than 14 per cent in 2050 (UN Department of Social and Economic Affairs, 2015). This will predictably be accompanied by major shifts in the balance of world power, largely through changed patterns of production, buying, and selling.

Ironically, some of the countries with relatively low fertility rates will experience the highest population increases in the next few decades. Here, China is a prime example. It is one of 76 countries with below-replacement fertility at present, yet it is projected to be the world's second-most populous country in 2050. Though few children are being born per woman, there is already a huge Chinese population. Thus, even though China's population growth is expected to slow down over the second half of the twenty-first century, it will continue rising in the first half (UN Department of Economic and Social Affairs, 2015).

More than half of the world's population currently lives in countries with sub-replacement fertility (Wilson & Pison, 2004) (see Figure 15.5). Based on current trends, demographers estimate that global population will stop increasing shortly after the middle of this century (Bongaarts & Bulatao, 2000). This end to population growth will help us achieve a more sustainable global population. Over the long term, however, zero population growth will have negative consequences as well, producing rapidly aging populations and a shrinking workforce around the world (Borsch-Supan, 2003; Anderson & Hussey, 2000). We already see the effects of this in Canada, and have already discussed the effects of population aging in Chapter 10.

One significant concern related to population growth is **environmental degradation,** since an increasing population means more consumption and intensified pressure on the natural surroundings. Westerners are only starting to appreciate the importance of achieving a sustainable level of development. By contrast, sustainability has been a core concern of many Indigenous peoples (of Canada and elsewhere) for millennia.

environmental degradation any change or disturbance to the environment that is deleterious or undesirable.

Theoretical Approaches to the Environment
Conflict Theory

Where the environment is concerned, conflict theorists will emphasize that when environmental problems arise, they hurt the poor more often and more severely than they do the rich. And, in a great many cases, environmental problems are a direct result of the negligence or profit-motive of the powerful.

Consider what are often thought of as "natural" disasters: Between 1991 and 2011, 33 per cent of natural disasters happened in low- and lower-middle-income countries, but 81 per cent of deaths occurred in these countries (UNDP, 2014). In other words, less-developed countries suffer the biggest and harshest impacts. So, for example, the Royal Geographic Society (n.d.) points out that

> natural disasters frequently occur across the world, affecting both developed and developing countries. However . . . the vast majority of lives both lost and affected by natural disasters come from developing countries, underlining the link between poverty and vulnerability to disaster . . . Simply put, people in wealthier countries have better access to the kinds of resources that help both prevent natural disasters becoming crises and to cope with them when they do occur.

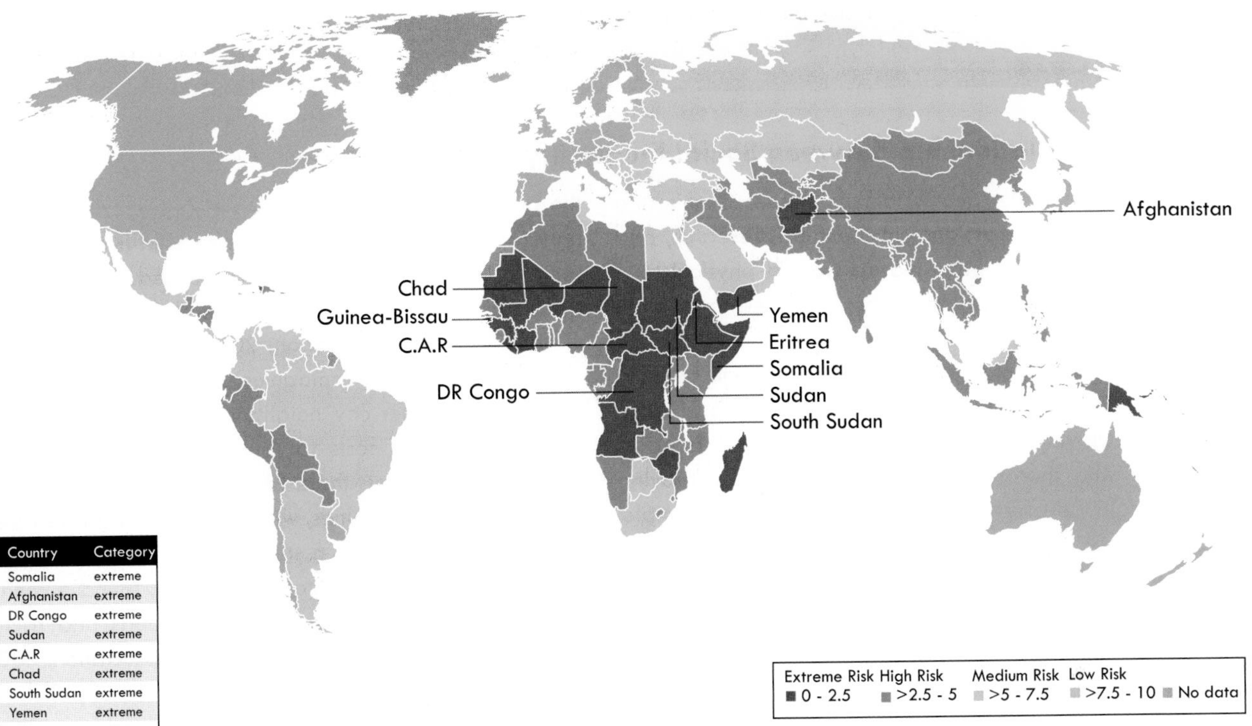

Rank	Country	Category
1	Somalia	extreme
2	Afghanistan	extreme
3	DR Congo	extreme
4	Sudan	extreme
5	C.A.R	extreme
6	Chad	extreme
7	South Sudan	extreme
8	Yemen	extreme
9	Eritrea	extreme
10	Guinea-Bissau	extreme

FIGURE 15.6 Socioeconomic Resilience Index, 2013 Exposure to, and Ability to Recover from, Natural Hazards

Source: http://reliefweb.int/map/world/world-socio-economic-resilience-index-2013

That is not to say that developed nations are unscathed, however. In the same 20-year period, upper-middle and high-income countries experienced 72 per cent of disaster-related economic damage (UNDP, 2014), since there is more property to lose in developed societies. An agricultural drought in Canada's prairies would result in reduced crops and farm bankruptcies, though few deaths.

These "natural" disasters have social consequences because they have social causes as well as natural ones. Research shows that disasters result more often from reckless industrial practices driven by capitalism than from the unpredictable effects of geophysical events. Accordingly, possible solutions will involve redistributing wealth and power in society, not merely seeking technological solutions to the problem (Smith, 2013). Even the destruction caused by the South Asian tsunami of December 2004, for example, would have been greatly lessened had the region's protective coastal mangrove forests not been significantly destroyed earlier to make room for aquaculture farms and upscale tourist resorts, and had the coral reefs not been slowly decimated by years of unsustainable fishing methods. Likewise, the damage and loss of life in poor Puerto Rico, as a result of tropic storms in 2017, was far worse than was suffered in more prosperous Florida and Texas the same year.

Feminist Theory

The feminist perspective opposes the exploitation of marginalized groups and the degradation of nature that occurs in service to the prevailing capitalist celebration of unceasing growth, unlimited resources, and unregulated commerce. Françoise d'Eaubonne coined the term *ecofeminism* "to identify theoretical work on the potential for women to bring about an ecological revolution and to ensure the survival of the planet" (Humphrey, Lewis, & Buttel, 2002). Ecofeminism, then, is a value system, a social movement, and a theoretical practice. It encourages political analysis that explores the links between androcentrism—a preoccupation with male interests and perspectives—and environmental destruction (Rynbrandt & Deegan,—2002). Ecofeminists adopt a "feminine" way of engaging with environmental social problems that is said to be nurturing, co-operative, and communal.

Theory in Everyday Life

15.1 | The Relationship Between Social Inequality and Pollution

In our digital society, access to the internet is almost a necessity. Homework assignments, lectures, research, and even job applications have moved from a physical to a digital medium, and to access them you need to be able to get online. But if job opportunities rely on access to the internet, anyone who does not have access will be at a disadvantage. Unfortunately, it is usually people who are already disadvantaged who cannot afford internet packages and who, therefore, find their chances of improving economically severely limited. In Canada, for example, about 42 per cent of family households making less than $30,000 have no access to the internet (Statistics Canada, 2013). Thus, the digital divide in our society serves to reinforce and further disadvantage any already disadvantaged social groups.

The relationship between the digital divide and social inequality can perhaps best be seen with an example. Low incomes typically lead to poor living conditions, and these poor living conditions may lead to limited internet access. If you look around any major city, chances are that you will find the people without access to the internet living in the most polluted parts of the city. Indeed, it is often the case that the same individuals without access to new information and communication technologies are the ones living in impoverished areas and breathing in

the pollution created by our society's factories. Thus, not only are they unable to access the benefits of our digital society, but they are also being harmed by the concentration of industrial factories around them (Canadian Environmental Law Association, 2008).

Many industrial companies set up their factories in impoverished inner-city neighbourhoods or impoverished suburbs, since the costs for building there are relatively cheap. The pollutants these factories release is inhaled by impoverished communities, with extremely negative effects on their health. Indeed, a study focused on factory pollution and poverty in Toronto, Ontario, has found a connection between impoverished neighbourhoods and factory pollution (Canadian Environmental Law Association, 2008). Other scientific studies have linked the intake of pollution to a higher frequency of diseases and debilitating conditions (Brook et al., 2004). Thus, there are many impoverished communities that do not have access to the benefits of our digital society but who still suffer the costs of such a society by inhaling the pollution caused by our society's factories.

The digital divide, therefore, has an obvious correlation to other forms of social inequality. Therefore, bridging the digital divide may involve remedying income-related forms of inequality (including housing and pollution) that exist in our society (Brook et al., 2004).

A central argument by ecofeminists is that the domination of men over women, leading to gender inequality, is analogous to human domination over nature that leads to environmental destruction. Some ecofeminists explicitly link the exploitation of women and the "rape of the wild" (Rynbrant & Deegan, 2002). In short, according to Gaard (1993) the environment as a social problem is a feminist issue.

Functionalism

Functionalists, for their part, recognize that everyone is implicated in the pollution of the environment, though some perhaps more than others. In an individualistic consumer society like ours, most of us seem willing to do anything to increase our immediate pleasure. So, functionalists are not surprised that modern people's activities have contributed to the pollution of their natural surroundings and the overharvesting of resources.

Several cultural ideologies support these ecologically harmful practices. One example is the cornucopia view of nature. This way of thinking views nature as a storehouse of resources that exists only for the use of humans—especially, those humans currently living. Another environmentally unfriendly belief is the growth ethic, especially popular in North America. This view, linked closely with materialism, celebrates the (imagined) ability of technology to easily solve all the problems in the world, including those that technology itself has caused. It promotes the belief that things will always get better and therefore encourages us to discard just about everything in favour of the production and consumption of new items.

Finally, the Western notion of individualism, which privileges personal goals and desires over collective interests, is the driving force behind the so-called "tragedy of the commons." This term, coined by environmentalist Garrett Hardin in 1968, refers to the unwelcome result of actions by many self-interested individuals, acting independently, that taken together deplete a shared resource, even though none intended to have this effect. Each actor believes that his or her small action will have no effect on the collective well-being, when in fact, all the actions taken together have an enormous effect.

Case study

Symbolic Interactionism

Sociologists who approach environmental problems from the symbolic interactionist perspective ask why and how certain environmental problems enter the public consciousness: What kinds of social "claims" make the greatest impact, and under what circumstances? The symbolic interactionist perspective also offers insights into how environmental polluters manipulate symbols to protect themselves from criticism. Many companies and businesses, increasingly sensitive to greater public awareness over their impact on the environment, have attempted to boost their image and profits by using a public relations strategy known as greenwashing. This technique involves redesigning and repackaging their products as "environmentally friendly" or "green," playing to (some) consumers' wish to help solve the environmental problem by purchasing ecologically friendly items.

Paul & Paveena Mckenzie/Getty Images

The land, the skies, the oceans, and even the stomachs of animals have become repositories for the world's trash, and, with more people and more consumption, the pollution is mounting.

TABLE 15.2 Theoretical Perspectives on the Environment

Theory	Main points
Conflict Theory	• Environmental problems negatively affect the poor more often and more severely than the rich. • The solution to environmental problems is through redistribution of wealth. • Collective action by underclass is needed to gain political attention to their needs.
Feminist Theory	• Ecofeminism links destruction of the environment and the male-centric political and corporate worlds. • The domination over women and nature ultimately leads to gender inequality and environmental degradation. • Humans' relationship with nature should be more nurturing and co-operative.
Structural Functionalism	• Environmental problems result naturally from population growth, density, and specialization. • Cultural ideologies support ecologically harmful practices (e.g., materialism and the growth ethic emphasize the triumph of progress and ingenuity, and encourage the discarding of the old in favour of innovations).
Symbolic Interactionism	• How are environmental issues imbued with meaning? • The focus is on the lived experience of humans. • How are environmental issues constructed as problems? • Environmental polluters manipulate symbols to protect themselves from criticism.

Source: Author-generated

The Natural Environment

Today, compared to a generation or two ago, we are all much more aware of the natural environment. This is due in large part to the rise of the environmental movement as expressed in the important work of environmental and climate scientists, as well as campaigning scientists, such as Rachel Carson, David Suzuki, and Ulrich Beck. Equally, organizations such as Greenpeace have raised our awareness of deeply problematic issues, from Alberta's oil sands to the accumulation of plastic in our oceans.

By **natural environment**, we mean all of those natural processes that affect us as animals having survival needs similar to those of other animals. Take for example the processes that affect the fertility of the land: the availability of soil nutrients, water, sunlight, and so on. All humans need food and water; concerns about the food supply and clean water are essential. This is why Thomas Malthus was interested in the relationship between food supply and population growth.

Humans compete with other species for survival. For the most part, we have developed tools and strategies that give us an advantage over these species. For example, we have invented weapons to hunt some animals for food and keep predators at bay. We have learned how to domesticate and harvest animals for food, and constantly improve our efficiency at doing so. We are still struggling to keep up with the rapid and sometimes fatal mutation of viruses and bacteria. It is unlikely we could ever fully destroy our smaller competitors (and, given the complexity of the biosphere, it would be unwise to try). So, we usually keep them under control; but now and then, an epidemic like SARS, swine or avian flu, or HIV/AIDS reminds us that even our best efforts can fail.

natural environment the territory in which human action occurs, which is itself modified by human agency; all living and non-living things occurring naturally on Earth, excluding the human component.

Time to reflect

Do you feel in control of the natural environment around you? How might your answer change as your social circumstances change? For example, might you feel more or less in control of the natural environment if you were a refugee from the southern hemisphere? What about if you were the child of a billionaire living in a major city?

To this end, we have learned to understand and control many biochemical interactions, through the creation of pesticides, herbicides, fungicides, and antibiotics and other medicines. We are increasingly able to manage our relationships with problematic species—from bacteria to protozoa, mosquitoes to cockroaches, invasive plants to cereal rusts.

To survive in the natural environment—to produce enough food and shelter, for example—and develop the tools we need for protection against other species, we need to harvest and process natural resources. Modern medicine depends on modern pharmaceuticals, but these rely, in turn, on natural minerals and plants. The same is true of modern agriculture, which relies on mineral fertilizers. To heat our homes and transport our food we depend on petroleum-based fuels. The plastics we use for food transport and storage also rely on petroleum. To build our homes we need wood from trees; granite, limestone, and sand for concrete and bricks; iron ore and bauxite for steel; and other materials.

And, of course, we crave luxuries too, from televisions to mobile phones to cars to home furnishings. These too are all derived from natural resources, and require energy to manufacture. Finally, the resource extraction and manufacturing processes usually take large amounts of water. Water is an especially valuable resource, and its rapid depletion by (mainly) high-income nations will increasingly make water conservation even more important. A report by the United Nations World Water Assessment Programme (n.d.) points out, "As demand for water increases across the globe, the availability of fresh water in many regions is likely to decrease because of climate change . . . These pressures will exacerbate economic disparities between certain countries, as well as between sectors or regions within countries. Much of the burden . . . is likely to fall on the poor" (n.p.). Thus, as the global population continues to grow, and the demand for food continues to grow, the demand for water will grow accordingly.

Global water consumption has been made possible by the building of dams and reservoirs, which affect over 50 per cent of the river basins in the world. However, the water available to humanity is not equally distributed. Currently, 2.3 billion people live in areas that lack an adequate water supply, and by 2050, 3.5 billion people will be in this situation (UNESCO, 2015).

Like water, most of the natural resources we need are non-renewable: there is only so much petroleum, aluminum, iron, and wood on (or in) the Earth. Once we have used it all . . . well, no one knows how to finish that sentence yet. One preventative strategy is recycling. Another is to invent alternatives (for example, nuclear energy) or find natural alternatives (for example, wind or solar power). A third strategy is to find another planet to inhabit, or perhaps to look for new resources in currently inaccessible places (for instance, under the sea or at the centre of the Earth). A fourth is to reduce the rate at which we use these resources; however, this is only a short-term answer—it only slows down their inevitable disappearance.

Spotlight On

15.2 | The Development of Renewable/Sustainable Energy

Some societies have begun moving towards renewable and sustainable energy sources by harnessing the power of solar, wind, geothermal, and ocean resources. These energy sources are naturally replenished; just as important, they emit none of the greenhouse gases that are often cited as the causes of climate change. About 63 per cent of Canada's energy

Continued

comes from renewable resources, with hydroelectricity—the energy that is harnessed from falling water sources such as Niagara Falls—making up most of the contribution at 60 per cent (Energy and Mines Ministers' Conference, 2013). This percentage is expected to continue increasing as the capacity of these energy sources, and the efficiency of technology at extracting energy from them, increases.

These renewable energy sources are good not only for the environment's health, but also for human health since they give off less toxic and pollutant fumes. A report by over 70 Canadian scientists, economists, and engineers states that Canada could move entirely to renewable energy as its source of electricity by 2035 so long as there is a strong political will to transfer from fossil fuels (McCarthy & Semeniuk, 2015).

Yet, despite their benefits, renewable energy sources are not without faults. For instance, solar and wind power depend on environmental factors that are uncontrollable, which makes them less reliable than fossil fuels. Renewable energy sources also produce energy less efficiently than fossil fuels, because fossil fuel energy technology has been under development since the Industrial Revolution while renewable energies have only been developed fairly recently. Another problem with renewable energy sources is that the initial cost of creating the infrastructure to harness renewable energy sources—i.e., the cost of solar panels, wind turbines, and hydroelectric dams—is extremely high and, is, therefore, out of the reach of many developing nations (Maronese, 2014).

The Role of Science

Can science solve or prevent environmental problems? Not necessarily. Scientific advancement often brings new risks and unforeseen dangers. Increasingly, people in modern societies are beginning to doubt the infallibility of science. After all, "science" is nothing more than a human community of scientists, behaving according to its social norms. And like all human communities, the scientific community is liable to make mistakes. Today, as we saw in the chapter on culture, much of modern science—commercial or industrial science—departs from traditional, socially responsible norms. Commercial research of the kind described in Chapter 3 by John Ziman (2000) tends to support (rather than trying to reject) conventional ways of thinking. And many scientific researchers compete with one another for fame and fortune—that is, they are not communalistic.

As well, science and technology operate within a political and commercial framework, with other goals to satisfy. That is why, as sociologist Charles Perrow shows in his classic study, *Normal Accidents: Living with High-Risk Technologies* (1984/2011), science is great but technological advances are not infallible. In fact, accidents are to be expected. The more complex technologies get, the more likely they are to break down, the worse are the consequences, and the harder they are to fix. Consider, for example, the Fukushima nuclear disaster of 2011. We still have no idea of the long-term effects of this disaster, and since its radiation has apparently hit the Pacific North American coast, it is directly relevant to Canada, though originating many thousands of miles away.

There have been many discussions of how to best solve our environmental problems. However, as we see in Box 15.3, for political and economic reasons, some high-income nations as well as some of the lower-income nations, are unwilling to make environmental commitments that will risk their position in the economic competition with other nations. Canada, unfortunately, is among the laggards.

Think Globally

15.3 | Rio+20

Marking 20 years since the first Earth Summit, the 2012 Rio+20 summit brought together 130 countries in Rio de Janeiro to create a global plan to protect the environment. The summit took place amidst a flurry of demonstrations, celebrity appearances, cultural celebrations, and riot police.

Though outwardly the summit exploded with attention-grabbing activity, media reports expressed dissatisfaction with the world leaders' lack of action. The summit agreement, a 53-page statement signed by those present, promises that governments will eventually define long-term objectives for sustainable development and the eradication of poverty, making few new commitments and not specifying particular goals or timelines (Scoffield, 2012).

The Rio+20 summit differed vastly in attitude and outcome from the 1992 Earth Summit. In 1992, the summit resulted in detailed treaties aiming to combat global warming and to prevent the extermination of endangered animal and plant species. The treaties laid out dozens of specific goals.

Reporters suggest several possible reasons for the less ambitious goals and reduced popularity of the 2012 summit, pointing particularly to disillusionment with the summits themselves. Enthusiasm infused the first summit, pressuring politicians to make bold commitments. However, the pledges went mostly unfulfilled. The first summit's global action plan, known as *Agenda 21*, provided blueprints for comprehensive environmental protection. A recent United Nations follow-up study of *Agenda 21* found that only four goals (out of the 90 that the UN tracked) had seen some improvement (Walkom, 2012). The areas of improvement were in reducing ozone depletion, removing lead from gasoline, improving water access, and boosting research for marine pollution. Other target areas had actually gotten worse, such as the destruction of coral reefs. At Rio+20, leaders may have been more aware of the difficulty of keeping commitments to the environment, hoping to avoid broken pledges by not setting any definite goals (Waldie, 2012).

Urbanization

Because of the advantages—especially, the economies of scale—that urban centres provide, many more people now live in cities than ever before. In fact, according to the Population Reference Bureau, 2008 was a landmark year. It marked the first time ever that the world's population was divided more or less equally between urban and rural areas (PRB, 2008).

This fact is significant, considering that in 1950, less than 30 per cent of the world's people lived in urban areas. Countries in the Global South such as Nigeria and India had the fewest urban dwellers then, but today these countries are urbanizing rapidly.

ariyo olasunkanmi/Shutterstock.com

Lagos, Nigeria, has gone through extensive development and urbanization since the 1950s. This is part of the Lagos skyline in 2015.

Another surprising feature of modern life is the continued distinctiveness of rural and urban life, especially in developing nations. While most developed nations have urban centres spread all around the country, developing nations tend to have only a few, massively populated urban areas that act as magnets for the rest of the national population. Consider India for instance, which is widely known for its megacities, including Mumbai (earlier known as Bombay), Kolkata (earlier known as Calcutta), and Delhi. Even though these megacities are huge by Canadian standards, their populations taken together make up only 30 per cent of all the people living in India. Even today, a majority of Indians continue to live in rural villages or small towns (Kavitha & Gavathri, 2017).

This urbanizing trend is far from over, and by 2050, the percentage of humans living in urban areas is expected to rise to about 70 per cent (Kavitha & Gavathri, 2017). Of course, estimates and predictions are uncertain. Moreover, around the world, people use somewhat different definitions of *urban* and *rural*. In Peru, for example, an urban area may contain only 100 people, while in Japan, an urban area will always contain over 50,000 people. Clearly, other factors besides size enter into these varying definitions, including population density, the presence of governmental authority and policies, and economic activity (Cohen, 2006; Bocquier, 2005).

Paradoxically, although 54 per cent of the world's population currently lives in urban areas (UN, 2014), most of today's urban growth is occurring in towns, villages, and smaller cities with 500,000 citizens or fewer, rather than in megacities of 10 million or more (UN, 2014). Indeed, only 12 per cent of the world's population lives in megacities (UN, 2014). In the next few decades, most of the world's population will live in these smaller cities, especially in developing nations where the rate of urbanization is accelerating, as in Latin America, Asia, and Africa (UN, 2014; UN Department of Economic and Social Affairs, 2014; Galea, Freudenberg, & Vlahov, 2005).

The UN predicts that, of an estimated 2 billion people who will join the world's population by 2050, as many as 1.9 billion will live in smaller-sized cities in developing nations (Galea, Freudenberg, & Vlahov, 2005; UN Department of Economic and Social Affairs, 2014). By 2050 Africa's urban population alone is expected to triple, and in North America, 90 per cent of the population is expected to live in or near cities (UN Department of Economic and Social Affairs, 2014).

Digital Divide

15.4 | Technology and Housing

In many parts of the world, technology has made housing much more comfortable. However, new household technologies are expensive. Thus, though we have the technology to dramatically improve people's housing, this technology is sometimes only available to the very wealthy, resulting in a technology divide.

The contrast can be made clearer through an example. In 2011 researchers found that 42 per cent of houses on Indigenous reserves needed major repairs, while only 7 per cent on non-Indigenous homes needed them (Stastna, 2014). Many Indigenous populations have to live with mould, inadequate plumbing, and overcrowding, while more affluent non-Indigenous people live with heated floors and toilet seats. While the technology to improve Indigenous people's housing exists, the cost of getting this technology to isolated Indigenous communities is too expensive for many of them to afford (Puxley, 2015). Though some Indigenous communities experience such dire housing problems, Canada's Indigenous population is known to benefit least from the technological development of housing in Canada.

As well, many Indigenous homes also lack an internet connection that would allow them to order products and/or materials online, if they could afford them. Indigenous people living in poverty may find themselves isolated not only because of their physical location, but also because of their limited or non-existent access to the internet.

Another group of Canadians who are cut off digitally and cannot benefit from technological housing developments are people who live in community housing. Their homes are often in dire need of repair and maintenance. Toronto has tried to improve housing technology for people in community housing. Toronto's Connected for Success program, for example, brings internet access, computers, and software to eligible youth in community housing (Toronto Community Housing, 2015). However, only youth benefit from this program; many other disadvantaged people have gone without the benefits of modern digital technology.

Fortunately, the Ontario Energy Board has started a program to help low-income households. Low-income customers of electric utilities may qualify for a reduction in their electricity bill—a reduction based on the number of people living in the home and the combined income of those individuals. Initiatives like this one may help to ensure that, in future, all members of society have access to basic and essential technologies.

In Canada and other developed nations, many greater metropolitan area residents live in surrounding communities—some call them bedroom suburbs—and commute downtown to work every day. The term *bedroom suburb* implies that adult family members use their home mainly as a place to sleep, with little time between working and the long daily commute to do much else. The rise of bedroom suburbs, and the commuter revolution of the past century, was made possible by the building of high-speed roads for automobiles and of tracks for trains and subways. Thus, over the last few centuries, suburban development has relied on innovations in transportation technology and construction.

Time to reflect

Exercise your sociological imagination. How much do you rely on transportation technology and infrastructure in your everyday life? Remember not just to consider your regular commute, but to also consider the sources and infrastructure supporting your food, clothes, communication technology, and hobbies.

Sociologists continue to debate the social consequences of this urban spread: for example, they ask whether suburbanization reduces people's social lives, undermines civil society, and makes people lonely and alienated. Debates about the fragmentation and loneliness of urban life started early in the twentieth century, revived in the 1950s with discussions of suburbanization, and revived again with the publication of Robert Putnam's (2001) classic book, *Bowling Alone*. Putnam alleged that, since the 1960s, there has been a steady increase in cocooning, and a steady decline in people's willingness to participate in social life outside their homes.

Sociologists today tend to think that Putnam exaggerated the problem, and that, in fact, many people conduct active social lives, but many of them do so by telephone or online—that is to say, outside the vision of social observers. Nonetheless, many continue to believe that we are less connected and less committed to one another today than we were in the past.

Built Environments

Cities today continue to develop, relying on varied forms of new technology. In our human efforts to improve and enlarge the built environment, innovations of many kinds have been necessary. Take tall buildings as an example. The use of any tall building demands elevators as well as stairs, reliable heating and cooling systems, complex electrical wiring, and developed communication technology—telephones, computers, fax machines, and so on—so people on the thirtieth floor of one building can contact people on the fiftieth floor of a building 10 or more kilometres away. (This seems obvious, but we need to say it because—except for the occasional times when a city's electrical system goes down and most human activity is paralyzed—we all tend to take it for granted.) Therefore, technological innovation in the past few centuries has largely been driven by the needs associated with living and working in a vertical urban environment.

The built environment, and our reliance on it, has put a huge pressure on the natural environment, well beyond what one might expect from the number of humans alone. North Americans use a disproportionate share of the entire world's energy and mineral resources, much more than would be predicted based on the size of its population. This imbalance comes about because our quality of life—or standard of living—relies on the built environment we have created through technological ingenuity.

During the 1970s and 1980s, large protest movements led to the creation of government agencies responsible for environmental regulation, and eventually, to environmental reforms. The mobilization of this group has changed the environmental movement in recent years, by creating a group known as **green consumers**. These green consumers comprise a large number of environmentally concerned citizens who have a growing influence on capitalism.

green consumers consumers who have examined the effect of goods production and consumption and reflect environmental consciousness in their purchasing behaviour.

Sociology 2.0

15.5 | Technotrash

These days, technology is advancing at unprecedented rates. New digital devices hit the market many times a year, all boasting to be slimmer, faster, and more powerful than their predecessors. Both companies and consumers who want to stay up to date with technology find themselves constantly upgrading to the latest gadgets.

But what happens to our old phones, computers, and television screens when we decide to replace them with the newest versions? Every year, millions of used electronic goods, such as computers and televisions, end up improperly dumped in landfills (Sullivan, 2014; Kang & Schoenung, 2005).

The improper disposal of this e-waste or technotrash has harmful repercussions for both the environment and human health. In the last decade, more than 80 per cent of e-waste was dumped in landfill sites. These electronics are not biodegradable, and what's more, they contain toxic chemicals and heavy metals such as arsenic, cadmium, cobalt, chromium, mercury, and zinc that end up leaching out of these landfill sites up and contaminating ground water that is used both for human consumption and the irrigation of food crops (Umesi & Onyia, 2008; Hargroves, Stasinopolous, Desha, & Smith, 2007).

The good news is that many Canadian companies are takings steps to implement more responsible and sustainable operating practices, and initiatives are being put in place that help deal with the problem of e-waste. Buy-back programs have sprung up, which allow users to sell back their old electronics, provided they're still in working condition. Take-back programs, on the other hand, generally won't give you any money for your old equipment, but provide an easy way of getting rid of old electronics by returning them back to the manufacturer. There are also recycling companies that specialize in recycling old electronics, though they may charge a small fee for the service.

These changes are partially encouraged by new regulations; over the last few years, a growing number of waste diversion or recycling regulatory programs have been put into place by provincial governments in Canada (Mortillaro, 2015). The basis behind these Extended Producer Responsibility regulations is that producers of products in Canada should assume responsibility of managing the waste of their products. Businesses that import or sell electronic goods in a Canadian province must be registered in an e-waste Extended Producer Responsibility or stewardship program and either take back the goods for recycling or pay prescribed fees to have them recycled. While these regulations vary from province to province and a more comprehensive federal strategy is needed, they certainly are a step in the right direction towards more sustainable practices (Fishlock, 2012).

David Paul Morris/Bloomberg via Getty Images

An employee assembles a refurbished Apple iPhone at a recycling facility. Facilities like this one ensure gadgets are repurposed or recycled into component parts. Unfortunately, only a percentage of technotrash makes it to facilities like this one.

Today, social movements and NGOs regularly enlist the aid of green consumers in media campaigns to challenge environmentally unfriendly corporations (Gereffi, Humphrey, & Sturgeon, 2005; Newell, 2001), and some of these efforts are successful. This greening of major corporations goes back nearly three decades. For example, in the 1980s, McDonald's partnered with the Environmental Defense Fund to reduce polystyrene and other harmful materials in its food packaging. Not only did this save McDonald's from a damaging ad campaign; it also made McDonald's one of the first Fortune 500 companies to actively work with environmental groups (Bartley, 2007).

Increasingly, public attention to environmental threats has led many people to change their behaviour, but sometimes their efforts backfire. Szasz (2007) notes that many affluent families today try to reduce their health risks by purchasing high-end products such as bottled spring water and organic foods. These expensive alternatives are not a realistic option for less-affluent people, however. Moreover, this self-protective consumption by affluent members of society has tended to undermine efforts to get new environmental policies that would protect people with less money to spend (Szasz, 2007).

The "organics movement" has aimed at shifting green consumers away from the products of large agribusinesses that use genetically modified seeds and chemical additives, to the products of smaller, owner-run organic farms. However, this effort has had little success: many of the larger agricultural enterprises have made minor changes to their production practices to qualify for the "organic" label (Guthman, 2004). In addition, the spread of organic food has caused new, unforeseen problems. For example, organic milk tends to sit on the grocery shelf much longer than mass-market milk because there is a small market for it. Also, organic milk has to be pasteurized in special plants that are often at a considerable distance, meaning that organic milk incurs a higher environmental cost than regular milk (Diamond, 2009).

Environmental reforms have led to the use of "cleaner" technologies that use fewer natural resources per unit of production—a good thing, environmentally speaking. However, a consequence of "green" technologies is that these natural resources become less expensive than they used to be and this leads to greater public consumption. For example, as cars become more efficient users of fuel, and

Dashboard

Video: *How to Change the World*

China's rapid expansion has meant a steady and noticeable decline in air quality in major metropolitan areas. The smog visible in this photo has meant significant health problems and quality of life concerns for city residents.

the price of gasoline falls, more people can afford to buy and drive cars. This unexpected outcome is referred to as the Jevons paradox (York, 2006), and is seen in rapidly developing countries.

China, for example, is undergoing a large expansion in the production of everything; and even though cleaner technologies are being implemented, personal consumption is growing rapidly. The result is that China is now the world's largest greenhouse gas emitter, with levels doubling from 2001 to 2009 (Int. Energy Agency, 2009). With the continued industrialization of other low-wage countries, increases in energy consumption and greenhouse gas emissions will pose a serious threat to the environment.

Only a generation ago, population growth was at the forefront of social activist concerns. The classic work *The Limits to Growth* (1972) inflamed a widespread concern with overpopulation. Meadows, Meadows, Randers, and Behrens warned that human population growth was outstripping the ability of science to increase (or replace) the needed natural resources. Today, population growth is no longer a central concern. Attention has shifted to environmentalism and the various social and cultural factors that undermine the environment.

Conclusions

demography the study of human populations—their growth and decline through births, deaths, and migration.

This chapter has focused on matters of life and death—specifically, on issues related to **demography**, the natural environment, and cities. Under current conditions, world population will continue to rise in coming decades, but it will rise more slowly than before, thanks to birth control, increased gender equality, and family planning programs. Most future population increase will be in low-income countries, accompanying (or even causing) major shifts in the balance of world power.

In Canada there will be a continuing need for immigrants to maintain the workforce and support an aging population. Population aging will have large implications for health care, the economy, and government spending; so, population issues are key to understanding other social issues. For example, increased spending on health care means decreased or static spending on education.

Fulfillment of our most basic needs depends on natural resources, and most of these resources are non-renewable. *The Limits to Growth* (1972) concluded that if population, industrial output, pollution, food production, and resource depletion continued to grow at the current rate, humanity would reach "the limit to growth" on this planet sometime in the next 100 years. In short, the problem of sustainability—achieving a balance between population and the environment—is critical. On this problem, rests the survival of humanity.

Not only has increased population growth taken a large toll on the environment, it has also affected how and where we live. As people increasingly migrate to urban areas, this changes how we relate to each other and how we relate to our natural environment. Technology will never solve all our problems. Often, it (briefly) solves our present problems and then creates new problems, which we try to solve with new technology, and so on, ad infinitum.

Questions for Critical Thought

1. The number of megacities in the world is increasing. What consequences will this have for the environment? The economy? Lifestyles and culture? Is one city of 20 million people better than 10 cities of 2 million people?

2. Natural resources are being rapidly depleted. Once they are fully depleted, what consequences will this have for life on this planet? Is it possible that the gloomy forecast by Meadows et al. was wrong?

3. Developing nations have high birth rates and fast growing populations. How might this promote or hinder the development of these very nations?

4. In a modern world defined by urbanization, globalization, technological progress, and mass communication, how much do you think location still affects lifestyle?

5. What is the connection between population growth and environmental degradation? Do more people simply make more mess?

6. What kinds of technology, if any, can save us from our current problems with population growth and environmental degradation?

Take it Further: Recommended Readings

Riley Dunlap, Frederick Buttel, Peter Dickens, and August Gijswijt, eds., *Sociological Theory and the Environment: Classical Foundations, Contemporary Insights* (Lanham, MD: Rowaman and Littlefield, 2002). This is an overview of sociological theories of the environment, both classic and modern.

Michael T. Klare, *The Race for What's Left: The Global Scramble for the World's Last Resources* (New York: Macmillan, 2012). This text discusses the specific natural resources being depleted, the response of governments and corporations, and the long-term consequences for the globe.

P.H. Liotta and James F. Miskel, *The Real Population Bomb: Megacities, Global Security and the Map of the Future* (Washington, DC: Potomac Books, 2012). This book focuses

on the effect of megacities on international stability, human security, and environmental degradation.

James M. Rubenstein, *The Cultural Landscape: An Introduction to Human Geography* (Upper Saddle River, NJ: Pearson, 2014). The text aims to show the importance of geography to human problems and the influence of geography on cultures, lifestyles, etc.

Frank Trovato, *Canada's Population in a Global Context: An Introduction to Social Demography*, 2nd ed. (Toronto: Oxford University Press, 2015). This book shows how Canadian population trends vary from or conform to patterns elsewhere in the world.

Take it Further: Recommended Online Resources

Canadian Solar Energy
www.cansia.ca/resources.html

Environment Canada
www.ec.gc.ca

The Life and Legacy of Rachel Carson
www.rachelcarson.org

Thomas Malthus on Population
http://evolution.berkeley.edu/evolibrary/article/history_07

The David Suzuki Foundation
www.davidsuzuki.org

Water Conservation
www.wateruseitwisely.com

Worldometers
www.worldometers.info/world-population

United Nations Population Division
www.un.org/en/development/desa/population/

More resources available on  Dashboard

16

Social Movements and Collective Action

◀ Neil Webb/Getty Images

Introduction

Social movements are central to how citizens express their dissatisfaction with existing power structures and elites, and advocate for social change through forms of collective action such as riots, protests, and postcard writing. Elites can also use social action to consolidate and increase their power. Social movements have a long history and are constantly undergoing change. Recent developments in information and communication technologies (ICTs) have provided activists with new tools for spreading information at low cost to far-reaching audiences. Many social movements have taken advantage of the new possibilities afforded by ICTs and have integrated them into their mobilization and communication strategies (Poell, 2013).

Even though thousands of activists can engage in a campaign from a distance and help spread the message via social media, this type of online participation has received considerable criticism and has been dismissively termed **slacktivism** or **clicktivism** (Schomerus, Allen, & Vlassenroot, 2012). The term *slacktivism* derives its meaning from the laissez-faire attitude and simplistic actions required by online activists to show support for a campaign. The key criticism is that forms of online participation like retweeting a message on Twitter or liking a post on Facebook barely deserve to be included as social activism. The controversy around slacktivism arises from the fact that individuals feel they are social activists or they have contributed to a social cause by simply sharing, retweeting, or posting about a social issue on social media, rather than participating in more direct forms of collective action.

slacktivism (or clicktivism) derives its meaning through the laissez-faire attitude and simplistic motions (clicking a "like" button, for example) required to show support for a social movement in comparison to past forms of activism.

Dashboard

Case study

Time to reflect

Do your peers and family members support, encourage, discourage, or actively prevent you from participating in activism? Have their opinions and social sanctions impacted your behaviour?

One example that demonstrates the myriad problems underlying digital activism is the Kony 2012 campaign. In the spring of 2012, the nonprofit organization Invisible Children released a video that centred on the atrocities taking place in Central Africa, mainly in Uganda, by the Lord's Resistance Army (LRA), a rebel group that had existed since the 1980s (Invisible Children, 2014). The campaign concentrated on one man, Joseph Kony, leader of the rebel group. The campaign advocated for the arrest of Kony, who has held thousands of children hostage as child soldiers and sex slaves. At the centre of the campaign was a video, which begins with the personal story of one child soldier, Jacob, and his personal experience of losing his brother and adapting to life following his traumatic LRA experience. Briefly focusing on the conflict in Central Africa and the plight of thousands of families, the video then switches toward outlining the importance of spreading awareness of this injustice. At one point, the narrator explains, "It's obvious that Kony should be stopped. The problem is 99 per cent of the planet doesn't know who he is. If they knew, Kony would have been stopped long ago" (Invisible Children, 2012, March 5). The remainder of the video is spent encouraging donations, the acquisition of bracelets, and above all, sharing the movie online.

By the end of March 2012 most news organizations in North America had provided some coverage of the Kony 2012 campaign and the video had received over 100 million views on YouTube within one week (Green, 2015). According to the organization's website (Invisible Children, 2012, July 9), the money raised helped build schools in war-torn towns, created jobs for the people in those towns, and built an early warning radio network. Despite the overwhelming online reaction consisting not only of social media engagement, but also of monetary donations, people living in LRA-affected zones have criticized the Kony 2012 campaign as being "simplistic and naïve"; Ugandan politics are more complicated than one "bad guy" (Schomerus, Allen, & Vlassenroot, 2012). Although the motivations behind the creation of the video were well intentioned, the goals of the campaign were not achieved (Green, 2015). First, it has not been possible to locate and arrest Kony. Second, a large proportion of the donated money went toward funding the campaign itself instead of helping those affected in the war zone. Third, it has been argued that this kind of activism feeds the idea that Western nations need to "save" developing nations in what is referred to as the "white-savior industrial complex" (Cole, 2012). Finally, those who clicked,

Paul Brown/Alamy Stock Photo

Promotional poster for the short film *Kony 2012* produced by the non-profit organization Invisible Children to raise awareness of the injustices caused by Joseph Kony. This photo was taken during the "Cover the Night" campaign, an evening to raise awareness of the video through postering and demonstration, in London, UK.

shared, and liked content still know little about the political landscape and the complexity of the history of Central Africa. Thus, it can be argued that their social engagement was rather limited and short-lived.

The Kony 2012 example shows that online participation does not necessarily translate into real social activism. By sharing information with their personal or professional social networks via social media, individuals may feel they have contributed to a social movement through their online engagement. This gives online participation a bad reputation for being a "feel good" measure, rather than eliciting more meaningful and long-term forms of engagement. Examining what motivates individuals to participate in social activism, how they participate, and their trajectory of participation are all important themes in better understanding the nature of modern social movements and their intersection with ICTs.

This chapter examines how ICTs are changing the nature and scope of social movements, by facilitating citizen involvement, the flow of information across boundaries, and the mobilization of resources. It also takes a critical view of the effects by investigating the unexpected and sometimes negative ways in which ICTs are changing social movement involvement, as in the case of slacktivism. In addition, the chapter provides an overview of different types of social movements and compares theoretical approaches that inform our understanding of how social movements operate and unfold. We present examples of Canadian and global social movements to demonstrate how social movement strategies and tactics are used and executed, as well as the role social movements have played throughout history in leading toward social change.

What Are Social Movements?

A key problem with defining the term **social movements** is that many different types exist. Some social movements are small in scale and contained to a single geographical region (e.g., SlutWalk in Toronto), while others garner worldwide attention (e.g., the environmental movement). Social movements also vary in terms of their focus. Though they are called "social" movements, they might focus not only on social issues, but also on political, environmental, or religious ones.

social movements organized efforts by groups in society to promote or resist social change through various types of engagement ranging from pacific protests to armed rebellions.

collective behaviour (or group action) the mobilization and actions of members of a social movement toward a unifying goal.

WUNC an acronym to describe social movement actors as worthy, unified, numerous, and committed.

social movement organization (SMO) describes specific social movements instead of social movements in general.

Sociologists have identified some key characteristics that are unique to social movements. First, social movements are often characterized by **group action** or **collective behaviour**. For group action to take place, groups of individuals need to be involved in achieving a common goal. Central to social movements, then, is that they have a shared goal that guides their endeavour. Second, while the focus can be on social, economic, or political issues, the ultimate goal is to advocate for social change; this can mean altering people's attitudes as well as bringing about more fundamental changes in the social structure of society. Third, those participating in the social movement, referred to as movement actors, are perceived as worthy, unified, numerous, and committed (Tilly & Wood, 2016), which is often summarized under the acronym **WUNC**. These characteristics of movement actors give the movement momentum, entice others to join, and allow the movement to garner attention from the media, the public, and governments. Fourth, social movements have an underlying organizational structure that helps mobilize resources, coordinate members, organize events, and share messages with the media and the public. Even social movements that have decentralized structures still have ways to facilitate communication and to help members coordinate (Castells, 2015). These four characteristics allow us to identify social movements and also help us describe their scope and purpose.

Social movements can be structured into social movement industries, each industry having as its focus a different kind of concern. Examples of distinct industries include animal rights, food, the environment, and human rights. Within a single social movement industry, different **social movement organizations** (SMOs) with relatively similar objectives can operate and compete with one another. McCarthy and Zald (1977) define a SMO as a "complex, or formal, organization which identifies its goals with the preferences of a social movement or a countermovement and attempts to implement those goals" (p. 1218). For instance, in the environmental movement industry, several different SMOs can be identified, including Greenpeace, the World Wildlife Fund, and the Sierra Club. This means

©Ken Cedeno/Greenpeace

In January 2017 activists from Greenpeace hung this 70-foot banner from a 300-foot-high crane near the White House to protest newly inaugurated President Donald Trump's first executive orders. Does the visual created by this protest contribute to the strength of its message?

that not only are industries competing for attention and resources, but also single SMOs in the same industry compete against each other (see Chapter 15 for more on environmental movements).

When we examine the history of social movements, it becomes evident that their main function is to provide a vehicle for ordinary individuals to participate in public life and take a political stance on critical issues. Social movements usually emerge as a result of injustice, inequality, conflict, and oppression, and a perception that there is an opportunity to effect social change (Castells, 2015). While we may think that only individuals with a radical stance or incredible sense of justice may get involved in activism, this is not the case. Most Americans and Canadians will at some point in their life be part of a social movement (Corrigall-Brown, 2012). For example, on 21 January 2017, the Women's March on Washington and its sister events, including the Canadian Women's March, drew millions of total protestors around the world and can be seen as part of the broader women's rights and human rights movements (CBC, 2017).

Time to reflect

Have you ever been given the opportunity (i.e., been invited) to join a social movement? If so, what choice did you make around whether or not to participate, and why? If not, what aspects of your social networks do you think might be restricting (for good or ill) your invitations?

How can we best understand a person's engagement in social activism? Several studies have attempted to uncover what factors best predict someone's engagement in social activism. Schussman and Soule (2005) found that being asked to get involved was the single most important predictor of individual participation in protests. Additionally, the authors found "that younger, better educated individuals who are interested in politics and enjoy political debate and discussion are more likely to be asked to protest, as are students" (Schussman & Soule, 2005, pp. 1097–1098). This highlights the relevance of social networks—friends, colleagues, and family—in motivating citizens to participate and join social movements.

Schussman and Soule's (2005) research also shows that there is a group of individuals who become involved in social activism without ever being asked by their social networks. This group consists of politically liberal individuals who have high levels of civic skills and are interested in and knowledgeable of politics. Civic skills include the capability to organize small and large events and communicate effectively with various stakeholders including members, the public, and the mass media. Those involved in social movements require civic skills to effectively communicate a movement's messages and motivate others to join.

Not all individuals are equally involved in social movements throughout their life course. Table 16.1 presents four typical trajectories of participation and shows how people vary in terms of their level of engagement, which also helps explain the demise of large social movements, for example the women's movement (Corrigall-Brown, 2012), which only recently has seen a revival (CBC, 2017).

TABLE 16.1 Four Trajectories of Participation in Social Movements

1. Persistence	Individuals remain in their initial SMO and/or continue participating in protest activities over time.
2. Transfer	Individuals disengage from their SMO or protest activities and become active in another cause. These individuals disengage from the original movement organization but not from contentious political participation.
3. Individual abeyance	Individuals disengage from their SMO or protest activities and then return to participation in either that same cause or another later in life.
4. Disengagement	Individuals permanently disengage from their SMO and from participation altogether. These individuals both leave their SMO and stop participating in collective action.

Source: Adapted from Corrigall-Brown, C. (2012). *Patterns of protest: Trajectories of participation in social movements.* Stanford, CA: Stanford University Press.

Protesters gather on the streets of Toronto to object to the full construction of the Spadina Expressway in 1970.

Source: heritageutarms1.59:48, heritageutarms1:77, default:10087, 701157-34-h.jpg https://collections.library.utoronto.ca/islandora/object/heritageutarms1.59%3A48

Origins and Historical Background of Social Movements

Many kinds of protests and unrest have been documented throughout history, but social movements as we know them today are a recent phenomenon (Staggenborg, 2015). As conflict theory highlights, the emergence of social movements is closely linked to the amount of frustration and dissatisfaction experienced by individuals (Castells, 2015; McAdam, 1999; Smelser, 1962). American sociologist Charles Tilly (1986) has investigated early forms of social movements in the European context and describes how protests taking place in seventeenth-century France were small in scale, localized in nature, had little to no organizational structure, and effected minimal social change. Looking at these earlier forms of social movements suggests that movements have become more complex, resourceful, and sophisticated over time, learning from past tactics and approaches as well as from mistakes (Rheingold, 2002).

These early forms of activism would not be considered social movements because they were short-lived, limited in scope, and focused on concerns of a local nature. Tilly (1986) describes the behaviours, tactics, and patterns of engagement of these activists as the **repertoires of collective action**, which he defines as sets of skills or behaviours. For him, the repertoires evolve over time through small changes and variations that activists make to practices imitated from previous movements. Thus, learning occurs only slowly and incrementally, as various tactics and approaches are tested on the ground. Innovations are constantly being introduced into the repertoires of collective action, and it is through imitation and learning by trial and error that activists continuously modify and improve their tactics. Hence, it is critical for political sociologists to look at the historical trajectory of social movements, the evolution of the repertoires of collective action, and how various events served as

repertoires of collective action the specific behaviours, tactics, and patterns of engagement of activists.

both a model and precedent. This is particularly true with the transformations that have taken place in the twenty-first century with repertoires of collective action becoming closely aligned with developments in ICTs (Castells, 2015).

Hobsbawm (1959) discusses early types of social engagement, including bandits, mafias, and city mobs, to show why they are ineffective. He explains that these early forms of protest were insufficient because of their inability to organize in a decidedly swift, methodical, and executable way. They often lacked a plan and organizational structure. We can conclude that what differentiates earlier types of social movements from more modern ones is their size, persistence, scalability, reliance on technology, and elements of planning and organizational structure.

New social movements tend to learn from past experiences and build on key convictions and mobilization strategies. Historically, the following five social movements provided critical lessons and continue to shape SMOs today.

Machine Breaking (Eighteenth and Nineteenth Centuries)

The Industrial Revolution (1760–1840) brought about many changes in workers' daily lives. Large machinery was introduced into the textile and agricultural industries; as a result, employers could hire non-skilled workers at lower wages, which led to an increase in unemployment among highly skilled craftspeople (Berg, 1994). The term **machine breaking** was introduced to describe workers' actions against machinery and the social changes resulting from industrialization (Hobsbawm, 1952). The English weavers and textile workers who participated in these actions were known as Luddites.

machine breaking workers' actions against machinery and the social changes resulting from industrialization.

Women's Suffrage (Nineteenth and Twentieth Centuries)

Gaining the right for women to vote was the main objective of the **women's suffrage** movement, along with the right for women to run for and to hold elected offices in government. In Canada, the majority of women—with the exception of women of Asian or Indigenous descent, as well as some foreign-born women—obtained the right to vote in 1918 (Strong-Boag, 2016), two years prior to their American counterparts. For decades, women fought to gain equal voting rights to men in Canada. Mary Ann Shadd, for example, used her editorial position at *The Provincial Freeman* paper to draw attention to women's rights and upcoming suffrage meetings in both Canada and the United States that impacted women of colour during the mid-nineteenth century (Strong-Boag, 2016). Others, such as Dr Emily Howard Stowe, Violet McNaughton, and Thérèse Casgrain, were important suffragists who fought for women's rights and enfranchisement through political activism, which ultimately led to Canada-wide voting privileges for women by the mid-twentieth century. It is important to note, though, that women's suffrage in Canada was not initially inclusive of all women and did not occur at a single point in history (Paxton, 2000). For example, in 1916, women in Manitoba, Saskatchewan, and Alberta received the right to vote in provincial elections; yet, it was not until 1940, when women in Quebec were enfranchised at the provincial level, that women's voting rights were protected in law in all provinces (Tremblay & Trimble, 2003). These rights, however, were largely extended only to white and Métis women, and voting rights for other marginalized groups, including Asian, Inuit, and First Nations women, were finally granted between 1948 and 1960.

women's suffrage the right of women to vote in political elections and the movement formed to achieve this right.

Indigenous women faced particular voting challenges, however, and were largely disconnected from the suffrage movement because they were viewed as a "dying race" (Strong-Boag, 2016). This was complicated further by the Indian Act's (1873) gendered language that politically benefitted men and disempowered women (Huhndorf & Suzack, 2010). Many First Nations women lost their Indigenous rights, including status and treaty rights, when they acquired federal voting rights (Leddy, 2016). The particular struggles that First Nations women faced reflected the colonial elements of women's suffrage in Canada, aspects that distinguished their struggle from the majority of white women of European descent.

Commemoration of the Famous Five, five Alberta women who established the rights of women to hold public office in Canada in 1929.

Source: https://en.wikipedia.org/wiki/Feminism_in_Canada

American Civil Rights Movement (1950s–1970s)

Multiple factors facilitated the emergence of the civil rights movement in the United States, including the decline of the cotton industry in the South of the United States; migration of southern blacks to metropolitan cities; pressures from the international community, in particular the UN Commission on Human Rights; and advocates within the federal government in support of equal rights for all Americans. The movement fought for equal rights for black citizens with regards to their freedom, and the ability to participate in civil and political life without discrimination or repression. The civil rights movement was critical for the development of SMOs because it provided a basis for the development of effective organizational structures, tactics, collective action frames, and best practices that then were transferred to other social movements in the United States and countries around the world (Staggenborg, 2015). Effective strategies that were developed include test case litigation, direct action, mass action, non-violent protest, sit-ins, and voting organization, to name a few.

Anti-Apartheid Movement (1959–1994)

South African apartheid was a system of government, based on racism and colonial oppression, that violated human rights by forcibly separating people based on race and ethnicity (Gruney, 2000). The Anti-Apartheid Movement (AAM) opposed the division of South Africa's people. The segregation was based on colonial notions of power, with white Europeans seeking to maintain their rule over South Africa. Many people were forced into isolated and poor living conditions, prohibited from voting,

Pool BOUVET/DE KEERLE/Gamma-Rapho via Getty Images

Nelson Mandela was liberated on 11 February 1990 from Victor Verster Prison in South Africa, after being incarcerated for 27 years.

excluded from owning land, and forbidden from marrying whites. These segregationist policies were met with resistance from many people who demanded civic rights through non-violent protest as a means to oppose and to attempt to change the system of apartheid.

Many local forms of resistance began to develop, albeit with a considerable loss of human life. For example, the 1960 Sharpeville massacre and the 1976 Soweto student uprising resulted in the deaths and injuries of hundreds of peaceful protestors. Following these demonstrations many other protestors and activists were arrested and imprisoned, including high profile activists such as Nelson Mandela and Steve Biko. In addition to these community and student demonstrations, the 1980s witnessed the involvement of the United Democratic Front and the Confederation of South African Trade Unions, which organized boycotts and strikes.

The AAM is now considered one of the most important social movements in history (Thörn, 2012). It gained international governmental and popular support from countries such as the United States, Britain, and France, accompanied by the divestment of South African assets by institutions such as Chase Manhattan Bank. In addition, supporters of the AAM boycotted South African universities, scholars that supported apartheid were boycotted, and South African sports clubs were banned from participating in the World Cup and the Olympics. The AAM is considered socially relevant because it impacted both national and international political culture. The AAM carefully followed events in the United States and learned some of its tactics from the civil rights movement, while at the same time the Anti-Apartheid Movement served as motivation and inspiration for the civil rights movement.

Environmental Movements (1980s to Today)

The *environmental movement*, often also called the ecology movement, is a broad term used to refer to many related movements and SMOs, rather than a single unified movement. Many of these SMOs aim to draw attention to important issues such as air, water, and soil pollution, deforestation, waste disposal as a result of overconsumption, and decreasing biodiversity in areas such as the oceans' coral reefs. In addition to these environmental issues, other movements have intensified their focus on sustainable energy sources and their relation to other environmental concerns, such as climate change. Environmental movements are committed to non-violent, creative confrontation as a means to eliminate environmental problems.

Energy is one of industrialized society's most basic needs. In Canada fossil fuels are the most widely used source of energy, yet they are environmentally demanding and damaging because of how they are extracted from the earth and used in everyday life (Tester, Drake, Driscoll, Golay, & Peters, 2012). To create greater awareness and change around fossil fuel usage, environmental movements, such as the New Energy Movement, have emerged with the intent of studying and promoting alternative sources of energy through international conferences, outreach, and funding programs for alternative energy (New Energy Movement, n.d.). Greenpeace, a group founded in Vancouver as part of the environmental movement of the 1960s, has adapted and is now also an actor in the modern climate change movement (Maslin, 2014).

Resistance to fossil fuels has been prominent in many Indigenous communities in Canada, as part of broader Indigenous rights movements. Communities are often impacted by free market capitalism and government policy, which have resulted in long-standing land rights disputes and many social and economic challenges. Some Indigenous groups have successfully resisted big oil companies' fossil fuel and coal extraction, the expansion of tar sands, and fracking practices (Klein, 2014). While resistance movements have proven to be beneficial for some Indigenous groups, others have been coerced into doing business with big oil companies as a means to meet their basic human needs (Klein, 2014). Chapter 15 shows how the environmental movement and its causes have become commodified in what is referred to as greenwashing, with the marketing of eco-friendly products to consumers who are increasingly aware of problems of environmental degradation.

Types of Social Movements and Engagement

Social movements can be distinguished by the extent of social change they want to accomplish and the strategies and tactics they employ to accomplish their goals. Anthropologist and sociologist David Aberle (1966) proposed four different types:

Arab Spring the collective action in which citizens engaged during 2010 and 2011 in several Middle Eastern and North African countries to resist government rule, protest social and economic inequality, and advocate for social change.

- *Transformative*: These movements aim to change an established order by focusing on supra-individual systems (Aberle, 1966). During the **Arab Spring**, the uprisings were transformative in their desires to remove the current leaders and enact a more democratic structure to their governments.
- *Reformative*: This type of movement works to enact partial change within larger systems. They focus less on changing the whole system and instead work to have groups' rights better represented within it (Aberle, 1966). Examples include the women's suffrage movement in Canada and the civil rights movement in the United States.
- *Redemptive*: These social movements look to change the whole individual (Aberle, 1966). This is common among religious movements, whereby constituents reach out to others and offer the chance at radical personal transformation by virtue of joining and working alongside adherents of a particular religion.
- *Alternative*: The aim is to create partial change to a specific aspect of people's behaviour (Aberle, 1966). For example, *Truth* is a national anti-tobacco campaign aimed at stopping people from smoking. Using pithy slogans like "Don't get played while they get paid," this campaign aims at stopping the practice of smoking tobacco altogether (The Truth, 2017).

The four categories proposed by Aberle (1966) are meant to be informative and as such should not be seen as completely distinct—the lines can be blurred, and social change can occur at multiple levels.

When people mobilize in a collective fashion toward a particular goal or objective, things can get chaotic. During the G20 protests in Toronto in June 2010, many social activists were arrested, police were on the streets demanding order, and protesters felt that their right to voice dissent was not respected (Poell, 2013). Despite this apparent chaos, social actors have indeed formulated effective methods to approach collective action; new social movements learn from past approaches and strategies. To demonstrate how varied different types of social movements are and the different methods of engagement they rely upon, we now discuss six of the most important ones.

Petition

This form of activism is highly popular and consists of a formal written statement typically addressed to an authority figure, for example a prime minister, president of an organization, or member of parliament, regarding a particular cause. Petitions are signed and signatories counted, thereby presenting an effective way to demonstrate the extent of support behind a cause. Online petitions are highly visible and often garner thousands of signatures within a short time frame. For example, environmentalists in Canada began a petition in support of legislation that would ban microbeads from being added to beauty products. Microbeads are plastic particles less than 5 millimeters in size that do not easily break down and can cause tremendous damage to the environment by polluting rivers, lakes, and oceans. The petition accrued more than 50,000 signatures, leading to Environment and Climate Change Canada's announcement that it would ban microbeads from all beauty products as of August 2015 (Change.org, 2017).

Protest

This form of public action takes place with the intent of expressing disapproval or discontent. Protests generally revolve around a gathering of people and can vary in size and format. Some protests feature signs and megaphones, while other protests are silent in nature. Noteworthy Canadian examples include the G20 Toronto summit protests in 2010 and the Quebec student protests in 2012. Protests need to be distinguished from **riots**, which are chaotic collective protests that are undirected, emotional, and often turn violent. The term *riot* is often applied by the media or dominant groups to discredit a protest and its members by associating them with unpredictable and disordered collective behaviour that is potentially threatening to civil order.

riots chaotic collective protests that are undirected, emotional, and often violent.

Rebellion

This is an act of defiance to authority with the goal of demonstrating the need for social change; it usually involves the use of arms and force. The term has been contentious, as the difference between a **rebellion** and a **revolution** is often determined by the winning side. One example from the early days of Confederation was the Red River Rebellion, a Métis movement under the leadership of Louis Riel, which resulted in the formation of the province of Manitoba in 1870.

rebellions armed opposition to an established government or authority by a social group.

revolutions aim to overthrow those in power to establish a new social order that is more egalitarian and places new elites into positions of power.

Letters and Postcards

This type of social movement is a tried and true method of confronting different leaders and authority figures. This is similar to a petition, whereby mass interest encourages leaders to take concerns seriously. For example, the province of New Brunswick had laws that put restrictions on access to safe abortion. A campaign that aimed at repealing those laws included a postcard blitz to the Conservative premier of the time, David Alward. Postcards from across the province were sent to the premier's office to show support for safe abortion measures and demand social change.

Blockade

A blockade is the act of obstructing entry into a specific place or area. Blockades are usually made up of people or vehicles and take place in areas that are meaningful to the cause. For example, in 2013 people gathered on a main access highway near the Mi'kmaq community in Elsipogtog, New

Brunswick, to block vehicles from entering (APTN National News, 2013). These vehicles were there to begin hydraulic fracturing (often called fracking) near First Nations land.

Hacktivism

As information and communication technologies (ICTs) continue to develop, new types of activism are emerging. Hacktivism is part of a larger branch of cyber-activism, which manipulates and deploys ICTs for a particular cause. It consists of hacking a computer network to obtain information or impede the regular functioning of ICTs for a socially or politically motivated purpose (see Box 16.1).

Time to reflect

Does hacktivism excite you with its possibilities, or does it make you worried for the future? How much of your life could be disrupted through hacktivism? How might your answer change along with changes to your social location and circumstances?   Have the messages about hacktivism that you've seen been positive, or negative?

Social movements can be long-term or short-term in duration, collaborative or group-oriented, localized or global in scale; there is extensive variability. As Box 16.1 shows, they can also rely solely on ICTs for their strategies, without a single person ever having to go on the street. However, many of

Sociology 2.0

16.1 | Hacktivism: Anonymous in Action

Hacktivists range from single individuals acting alone, to loosely coupled networks who gather around a target, to tightly organized groups who coordinate their activities (Friedman & Singer, 2014). One such group is Anonymous, which operates as a decentralized network that does not follow directives from any one leader, but comes together to accomplish specific goals (Friedman & Singer, 2014). The main goal of Anonymous is to create mass awareness of injustices and to draw attention to those responsible, while maintaining anonymity. The strategies and tactics employed by the group are sophisticated, so only in rare instances have those behind cyber-attacks been identified. Through its numerous and high-profile interventions, Anonymous has become a key player in the social activism realm. On 16 June 2015, Anonymous orchestrated a massive cyber-attack on the Canadian federal government to protest against a controversial anti-terror bill. On YouTube the group stated, "Today, Anons around the world took a stand for your rights. We now ask that you follow suit. Stand for your rights, take to the streets in protest this 20th of June 2015. Disregard these laws which are unjust, even illegal" (Minsky, 2015). The attack was confirmed by the government,

which used Twitter to refer the public to its phone line (Figure 16.1).

As part of the attack, the group crashed federal government websites and stopped all email communication through a distributed denial of service (DDoS) attack (Chase, 2015). In a DDoS attack, hackers flood a website with multiple requests, leaving the system unable to deal with the increased traffic and needing to shut down. Government workers were directly affected as they could not exchange emails and all web-related work came to a sudden halt. These kinds of cyber-attacks are effective strategies in garnering media attention and getting Anonymous's message to a larger audience.

FIGURE 16.1 Tony Clement Tweet

Source: https://twitter.com/tonyclementcpc/status/611231622843789312

the types of engagement and the end goals of social movements overlap and draw from each other. In many cases, a single social movement will utilize a combination of types, for instance starting with a petition and then moving toward a protest.

Controversial Movement Strategies

Movement strategies have also received attention because of their potential risks to society, including damage to private and public property and harm to individuals. We discuss in this section several strategies that have come under scrutiny. Civil disobedience is a public and non-violent form of protest that is used to communicate opinions in opposition to governmental law and policy (Smith, 2013). Civil disobedience can include silent protests, marching, or hunger strikes. Sit-ins can also be a powerful form of civil disobedience, which, for example, were used during the #blacklivesmatter movement in Toronto in 2016. Social movements use civil disobedience to draw awareness to governmental injustice and aim to bring about change at local, national, or international levels (Smith, 2013). Most commonly, civil disobedience is criticized for being a disruptive form of protest that involves willingly and knowingly breaking the law, which can provoke others to react confrontationally and create further unrest (Smith, 2013).

Both sabotage and property damage are forms of "material destruction" that can be considered non-institutional armed resistance (Dudouet, 2015). They are employed with the intent to damage property rather than directly injure people. Sabotage and property damage have been used when other forms of unarmed resistance, such as litigation, fail (Dudouet, 2015). These two forms of protest differ in terms of their execution. Property damage is exercised with the intent to destroy public or private property. By contrast, sabotage is intended to deliberately obstruct the functioning of society for specific purposes. As protest strategies go, sabotage and property damage highlight the strength of protesters' beliefs and opinions, and they often attract a lot of media attention. They are considered controversial because they risk escalating beyond their intended goals due to heightened "emotional behaviours" (Bosi, Demetriou, & Malthaner, 2014) and because of the risks they pose to human life.

An example of how controversial movement strategies can draw media attention is the Wiebo Ludwig case. In the 1990s a Christian fundamentalist named Wiebo Ludwig and his commune in Trickle Creek, Hythe, Alberta, were the focus of national media attention in relation to a number of gas and oil pipeline bombings. Ludwig had determined that members in his commune and their livestock were becoming ill and dying as a result of leaked "sour gas" from an oil-drilling site near his property. A former lobbyist against big oil companies in Canada (Nikiforuk, 2001), Ludwig was accused of vandalizing, causing property damage, and sabotaging oil pipelines after letters to politicians and official bureaucrats failed. Some deemed Wiebo's actions to be domestic terrorism, while others sympathized with him yet condemned his practices (York, 2011). His strategies were largely controversial because of the danger they posed to the lives of innocent people.

Theoretical Approaches to Social Movements
Conflict Theory

At the centre of conflict theory is the notion that most social movements result from power imbalances and a need to re-establish a new social system that is more egalitarian for all social groups. Consider the Arab Spring, which unfolded in Middle Eastern and North African countries in 2011. Its main arguments concerned the equalization of power and the poor quality of life of many citizens faced with regards to employment, food, and the ability to freely express their ideas. Those in power at the time were not willing to engage with the population, give up their positions of power, or reconsider the current unjust social system. It is difficult for participants of social movements to create social change as "coercion and intimidation, based on the state's monopoly of the capacity to exercise violence, are essential mechanisms for imposing the will of those in control of the institutions of society" (Castells, 2015, p. 5). Box 16.2 demonstrates how conflict often occurs and spreads, leading toward a social movement.

Digital Divide

16.2 | The Arab Spring of 2011: A Twitter Revolution

The Arab Spring is often termed a digital or Twitter revolution because of the heavy reliance that organizers had on social media to provide information and mobilize citizens to join the protest. Social activists tweeted events in real time for a global audience to follow, they posted important topics on Facebook so others could discuss and comment, and they organized in a loosely connected network via text messages on mobile phones. As the tension on the streets of Cairo increased, the Egyptian government realized the central role that digital technologies and mobile phones were playing in coordinating the social movement. The government fought back by shutting down the internet in an attempt to cut off communication between social activists. This is termed the **internet kill switch**; the Arab Spring was its first use (Quan-Haase, 2016). However, the use of the internet kill switch was not successful in Egypt. On the contrary, citizens went to the streets to express their anger about what they felt was an abuse of power on the part of their government. The event infused a social movement with renewed strength and focus. The Egyptian example shows how internet connectivity and mobile phones represent a central means for social movements to communicate, coordinate, and mobilize. The United Nations has made internet connectivity a human right since and advocates against such overuse of governmental power.

The 2011 protest in Tahrir Square, Cairo, Egypt.

Source: https://twitter.com/tonyclementcpc/status/611231622843789312

---

internet kill switch when a government shuts down the internet in an attempt to cut off communication between social activists.

comparative historical analysis comparing countries to derive insight into how their political systems developed and what economic, social, and historical factors lead to differences.

bourgeois revolution describes how social change could come about from incremental economic, technological, and social changes in society.

Class conflict is at the centre of Marx's and Lenin's ideas around the proletarian revolution. The aim of the proletarian revolution is to give more power to the working class by overthrowing the bourgeoisie (those who control the means of production). A proletarian revolution would allow for the working class to take control over production processes, sharing a greater part of the wealth created through production. Marx and Lenin predicted that proletarian revolutions were inevitable in capitalist societies, because of the inherent conflict between the classes in the capitalist system.

Moore (1993) agreed with Marx and Lenin, seeing social class as a critical element in studying conflicts between groups and the formation of social movements. For him, it was important, though, to compare and contrast societies that differ along key dimensions—their level of industrialization, advances in science and technology, and social structures. He did not shy away from this complex and challenging enterprise; in his book *Social Origins of Dictatorship and Democracy*, he compares such different countries as England, India, and Germany to derive insight into how their political systems developed and what factors could explain differences across nations. This approach has led to what is today called **comparative historical analysis** in the social sciences and has become a prevalent and highly regarded method. He also stressed the relevance of examining social movements in their historical context instead of only focusing on current events in isolation. For him, it is a set of social and political factors and inequalities that over time lead to the development of a social movement. He also criticized one of the central propositions of Marx and Lenin, arguing that a revolution of the working class was not needed to produce social change. At the centre of Moore's theory was the notion of the **bourgeois revolution**, which described how social change could come about from incremental, rather than revolutionary, social, economic, and technological changes in society.

Feminism

While feminism is a movement that has existed since the beginnings of the Industrial Revolution, and while women have participated actively in other social movements, women came to realize that their participation was limited and that they faced numerous barriers in fully integrating into social and political life. Three periods are particularly relevant for understanding how the rights of women and the feminist movement itself have evolved over time:

- *First-wave feminism:* This wave came about from social changes resulting from industrialization in many Western countries. As women's social roles in the home changed, they advocated for greater rights and inclusion. Central issues for which women fought in first wave feminism include a right to education, property and custody rights, and reforms in the political system—in particular, the right to vote.
- *Second-wave feminism:* The height of second wave feminism was in the 1960s, where the women's movement expanded its objective to include issues related to reproductive rights, recognition of housework as labour, equal pay, and violence against women.
- *Third-wave feminism:* The failings of white middle-class feminists to recognize issues of race, sexuality, and class gave way to third-wave feminism, where intersectionality is given central importance. Intersectionality, already discussed in Chapters 1 and 7, is the study of how different systems of oppression are related. This way of thinking has led to the emergence of contemporary movements for trans and queer rights, and a recognition of unique ways that women of colour and disabled women experience gender inequality. In Canada, Indigenous feminism has emerged as a counter voice to mainstream feminism, raising concerns about issues such as colonialism and cultural discrimination (Dhruvarajan & Vickers, 2002).

Movements that adopt a feminist approach tackle many different issues and inequalities. Despite making progress on a variety of fronts, many feminists continue to advocate for equal rights for women. These struggles are closely interwoven with advances in ICTs, such as mobile phones (for an example, see Box 16.3).

Spotlight On

16.3 | Hollaback!

In 2005 a group of young women and men began a project to raise awareness and help combat street harassment in New York City, after the story of Thoa Nguyen, a woman who was riding a subway in New York City when a man began masturbating in front of her, made headlines. Though terrified, intimidated, and above all disgusted, Nguyen had the forethought to use her cellphone to snap a photo of her harasser. The police were unable to help Nguyen, so she decided to upload the photo to Flickr, a popular photo-sharing site, in hopes of finding out more about the incident and perhaps bring some justice to the situation (Krieg, 2011).

Inspired by this story, Hollaback began as an initiative to address street harassment more directly by harnessing the popularity of mobile technology as a way to track street harassment and make it more visible. Encounters with street harassment can be reported and catalogued through a dedicated mobile app called *Hollaback!,* and support and awareness can be raised through their website, Facebook, Twitter, and YouTube. According to their website,

> The real motive of street harassment is intimidation. To make its target scared or uncomfortable, and to make the harasser feel powerful. But what if there was a simple way to take that power away by exposing it? You can now use your smartphone to do just that by documenting, mapping, and sharing incidents of street harassment. Join an entire community ready to Hollaback!

Although street harassment is a widespread concern and remains present on streets around the world, it is often hidden and in general remains largely undiscussed. Encouraging individuals to report incidences of street harassment to a community that extends beyond city limits gives a stronger voice to the victims and the social actors working to stamp out such actions.

In particular, Twitter and Instagram have served as spaces for bringing forward issues of gender and race inequality. Despite the potential for these digital spaces to provide a forum for open debate and engagement, often offensive language and harassment will be used online to silence voices that are already marginalized in society, including women's voices. Thus, social media provides new spaces for women and other marginalized groups to advocate for their rights, but not without new challenges and barriers to overcome. The opportunities and challenges provided to women and LGBTQ groups by social media are discussed in Chapter 7.

Network Theory

From the standpoint of network theory, social movements are made up of individuals connected to one another via social networks; i.e., social connections based on interpersonal relations and interactions. It is these networks that facilitate the flow of information among members and allow for the mobilization of resources toward collective action. The move away from looking at social movements as closely knit groups toward examining the connections not only among movement members, but also across movements is critical (Zhuo, Wellman, & Yu, 2011). While networks have been an important means for social movements to organize, ICTs have allowed for these networks to increase in relevance, scale, and range; information travels easily and quickly. Manuel Castells (2015) describes how **network social movements** represent a new type of social movement that was not possible prior to the wide diffusion of digital technologies in society and brings with it its own repertoire of collective action. Key characteristics of these types of networked social movements include the speed and distance to which information can be disseminated to interested parties, the number of people reached, and the diverse means of mobilization including via Twitter, Facebook, and place-based protests on city streets.

A key goal of network theory is to better understand the nature of the social networks that facilitate the mobilization of resources within social movements. We describe two types of network structures here (for a summary of the strengths and limitations of each, see Table 16.2).

network social movements new types of social movements that are decentralized and heavily rely on ICTs to share information, mobilize resources, and engage social activists.

Centralized Networks

Early social movements believed that centralization was key for the success of a social movement. In particular, social movements stressed the need for gatekeepers, opinion leaders, and some form of hierarchical or vertical organization to give the movement direction and help coordinate action. However, centralized forms of collective action have several limitations. First, messages are only mobilized slowly and may take a long time and lead to high costs to reach the needed critical mass. Second, centralized movements are vulnerable, as they can cease to exist when the key organizers dismantle, join a new movement, or simply lose interest.

Decentralized Networks

An emerging body of sociological research argues that the low cost, speed, scale, and degree of connectivity of digital media may reduce the need for formal, centralized organization of collective action (Bennett & Segerberg, 2012). These forms of organizing are described as **horizontal forms of organizing** and rely on a network spread across space and time. Box 16.4 describes the case of M-15, a decentralized network that heavily relied on digital, participatory media to make its message available, reach a large audience, and scale up to thousands of activists spread over an entire country. Moreover, there was worldwide support for the movement, with many activist groups connecting and making meaningful contributions to the digital presence as well as the physical engagement on the ground.

horizontal forms of organizing the organization or structure of a group, whereby every member of the group is considered as equal—no superiors or subordinates. Instead of hierarchies, it emphasizes teamwork and equal collaboration among group members.

Think Globally

16.4 | M-15 or Los Indignados: Networked Mobilization

What is M-15 all about? The Spanish movement *los indignados* (the indignant ones) is also known as M-15, after the date the first mass mobilization took place in the streets of around 60 Spanish cities (15 May 2011). The main aim of M-15 was to protest the economic crisis unfolding in Spain that affected ordinary citizens the most, in particular young people who were unable to obtain employment (Burgen, 2015). Key slogans included: "¡Democracia real YA! No somos mercancía en manos de políticos y banqueros" ("Real democracy NOW! We are not merchandise in the hands of politicians and bankers"). One unique characteristic about the M-15 movement is that it successfully separated itself from large organizations, unions, and political parties (Bennett & Segerberg, 2012), thereby remaining a movement organized and led by ordinary citizens. Because of the loose affiliation of members, the lack of a centralized organizing committee, and the sheer scale of the movement, many assumed that it would be short-lived. However, the movement managed not only to mobilize effectively, but it also served as a case study for future movements like Occupy. So what made the movement so effective despite its lack of centralized networks? M-15's primary means of mobilization consisted of a web page entitled "¡Democracia real YA!," updates via Twitter, YouTube videos, TED Talks, and commentary and discussion via Facebook.

What did we learn from the M-15 movement about the new forms of repertoires of collective action developed in networked social movements? Bennett and Segerberg (2012) identify two broad organizational forms that support these decentralized networks. First, "they cast a broader public engagement net using interactive digital media and easy-to-personalize action themes, often deploying batteries of social technologies to help citizens spread the word over their personal networks" (p. 742). Second, "technology platforms and applications tak[e] the role of established political organizations. In this network mode, political demands and grievances are often shared in very personalized accounts that travel over social networking platforms, email lists, and online coordinating platforms" (p. 742).

Despite its many merits, the decentralized network structure also has some limitations that need to be considered. First, it is almost impossible to control the message, the nature of the movement, or its core activities. This can lead to a movement that seems disparate and without a clear mandate. For example, the Occupy movement was often criticized for lacking a clear cause at its core. Second, the time activists invest may be moderate to minimal. Members may feel highly invested in the movement at first, but then their interest may dwindle and their commitment fade. This was discussed in the Kony 2012 campaign Invisible Children, where initial interest was immense, but then faded quickly. Finally, the long-term effects may be minimal, if no clear goals have been specified that would indicate when the movement has achieved its ends. Still, many social movements have become decentralized with the prevalence of social media, cellphones, and digital technologies to facilitate the exchange of messages and the mobilization of resources.

TABLE 16.2 Network Typologies: Strengths and Limitations

Centralized network structure		Decentralized network structure	
Strengths	**Limitations**	**Strengths**	**Limitations**
Central coordination	Slow diffusion of information	Speed	Control low
Control high	Vulnerability	Scale	Time investment moderate
Long-term	Slow mobilization	Range	Long-term effects unclear
Commitment	High cost	Low cost	
		Commitment	

Source: author-generated

New Social Movement Theory

The political climate of the post-industrial economy has experienced several key changes in relation to how people engage in politics, including downturns in voter turnout, growing disinterest in memberships of mainstream political parties, and the professionalization and media-driven nature of politics (Miller, 2011). In response to such trends new types of political and social engagement have emerged, particularly among young people, commonly referred to as new social movements (NSMs).

Some examples of SMOs that fall under the NSM perspective include the anti-nuclear movement, the animal rights movement, the LGBTQ movement, and the free software movement. Furthermore, the concerns of those involved in NSMs differ from those voiced in traditional social movements. NSMs are concerned with addressing the ever-invasive nature of capitalism, institutionalization, and industrialization on the **lifeworld**. The lifeworld encompasses the subjective meaning we give to everyday life practices, understandings, and routines. Habermas (1984) argues that our lifeworld is in danger of being taken over by post-industrial forces that populate every domain of life including the private sphere, leisure time, and social interactions. NSMs are thus concerned with creating awareness around the domination of capitalist, post-industrial forces and aim to regain control over the subjectivity of the lifeworld. The study of NSMs is called **new social movement (NSM) theory**. Although NSMs are relatively new, elements of the NSM perspective have been around since the 1960s (Buechler, 1999). NSMs differ from traditional social movements in three fundamental ways (Staggenborg, 2015):

- NSMs have different organizational structures, often operating in a decentralized network rather than in a centralized fashion.
- The types of members are more varied, often crossing across social class, education level, and political parties.
- The underlying ideology and focus is different: Instead of focusing on labour issues exclusively as did the labour movement, NSMs tend to focus on issues of everyday life including quality of life, the environment, and inequality. Hence, the focus of the social movement is not necessarily based on any particular ideology, but instead on a single issue. As a result of the emphasis on a single key issue, some have called it single-issue politics.

A central contribution of NSM theory is its focus on the role of culture and identity in the formation and functioning of social movements. It is important to examine how activists who are part of a social movement form a collective identity and how this identity shapes their participation over time. Although the formation of a collective identity during collective action is not a new occurrence, what is new is the centrality of that identity (Porta & Diani, 2006, p. 62). In other words, for NSMs identity is key (Tilly & Wood, 2016).

lifeworld describes how the world is experienced or lived; all the activities and contacts that make up the world of an individual or group.

new social movement (NSM) theory explains how modern social movements come to form and mobilize.

Time to reflect

Exercise your sociological imagination. How might a person's identity and social location play a role in his or her participation (or lack thereof) in social movements?

Alberto Melucci (1988) adds that collective identities are formed by the opinions of small groups or cliques and are constantly changing because they are embedded in the everyday life experiences of the SMO members. What this means is that as SMO members interact with key stakeholders including other members, members of other SMOs, and the public, their perceptions of themselves change. As a result, Melucci (1988) argues that collective identities are fluid and embedded in complex and changing social networks. Hence, when these small groups can no longer agree on a common collective identity and its core tenets, they lose solidarity and the social movement starts declining.

Collective identity has been identified in much sociological work as a key feature in social movements. Though this is true, there is an emerging approach to understanding identity that opposes notions of collectivity. Joshua Gamson (1995) writes about this in relation to sexual identities, explaining that the compulsion to form a single collective identity runs contrary to a common logic often contained in queer activism that seeks to dismantle identity categories. He argues that fixed or rigid identity categories serve the purpose of social control, and so moving beyond and breaking down stable identities has a liberating potential. Further, Gamson (1995) challenges us to consider the implications these opposing tendencies have on social movements. On one hand, collective identity can help bring solidarity to collective action, but on the other, it has the potential to oversimplify complex internal differences and leave unchallenged the very processes at which many social movements

TABLE 16.3 Theoretical Approaches to Social Movements

Theory	Main points
Conflict Theory	• Social movements result from power imbalances and injustices. • The aim of social movements is to create a new social order.
Feminism	• The social movements analyze and critique the sources of gender inequality and male dominance. • The movements make a call for the equal treatment of all individuals in society regardless of race, gender, and age. • Intersectionality stresses the relevance of looking at inequality from multiple perspectives simultaneously.
Network Theory	• Social and digital networks facilitate social movements. • ICTs allow for decentralized networks to emerge through which information and resources mobilize effectively.
New Social Movement Theory	• NSMs often operate in a decentralized network rather than in a centralized fashion. • The types of members participating are more varied. • NSMs focus on issues of everyday life including quality of life, the environment, and inequality. • NSMs call attention to identity formation as key to the movement.

Source: Author-generated

take aim. This shows that even concepts like collective identity need to be carefully looked at and their role in social movements questioned.

Sociologists in addition to critically examining the concept of collective identity have also scrutinized the value of NSM theory in general. Sociologist Nelson Pichardo (1997) has been critical of NSM theory for three reasons. First, he questions whether NSM theory has anything new and unique to offer that has not already been a part of previous sociological theories. Second, the argument that NSMs are a direct result of post-industrial society and its social injustices is not well supported. Rather, issues of identity and culture have always been a part of social movements. Finally, Pichardo criticizes NSM theorists for focusing primarily on left-wing movements, ignoring the revival of right-wing movements (one recent example, since the time of this writing, is the rise of the Tea Party movement in the United States). For Pichardo, all social movements regardless of political affiliation need to be a part of sociological scrutiny. Pichardo (1997) does acknowledge that NSM theory has made a contribution to sociological inquiry by calling attention to previously overlooked aspects of social movements, such as identity and culture.

Processes of Social Movements

Understanding social movements as a dynamic process instead of a stable phenomenon is critical. Not only do social movements constantly redefine themselves in their tactics, aims, and available technologies, but they also change in terms of the availability of resources. We describe next two important components of the dynamics of social movements: resource mobilization theory and the life cycle of social movements.

Video: *Angry Inuk*

Resource Mobilization Theory

Central to understanding how social movements evolve is **resource mobilization theory**, as no social movement can succeed without adequate resources. For McCarthy and Zald (1977), it "deals with the dynamics and tactics of social movement growth, decline, and change" (p. 1213). Resource mobilization theory was developed to counter many of the assumptions present in earlier theories. First, it dismisses the notion that collective action results directly from a feeling of deprivation (McCarthy & Zald, 1977). Second, it questions the need for a generalized belief or ideological justification, as

resource mobilization theory examines how social movements acquire, manage, and mobilize resources.

prior theories had suggested that without a core belief or ideology a social movement could not exist (McCarthy & Zald, 1977). In resource mobilization theory, a range of resources are identified as pivotal to how SMOs function, from their inception, to their ability to recruit new members, to the potential to mobilize and effect social change. Without the necessary resources, a SMO cannot function adequately and will fail. The kinds of resources that are essential include

- tangible assets, such as funding, donations, physical space, and sustainable cash flow;
- intangible assets, including long-term participation of movement actors either through donations or active involvement;
- moral resources that legitimate the cause;
- cultural resources and civic skills, such as repertoires of collective action, strategic know-how, and connections to key players;
- social-organizational resources, including social networks and organizational structures; and human resources, which are all those resources that constitute labour and movement actors' experiences (Staggenborg, 2013).

While not all SMOs will be able to obtain all kinds of resources listed above, some are more essential than others. One central resource that was less prevalent in the past is the technological component. SMOs are drawing heavily on the internet and technical competency to disseminate their message, recruit new members, keep in touch with members, and mobilize members when needed.

The Life Cycle of Social Movements

Sociologist Herbert Blumer (1969) was among the first to describe the life cycle of a social movement, examining how it emerges, grows, and eventually declines. While the terminology has been adapted and modified over time, the key stages described remain somewhat constant and are shown in Figure 16.2. In Box 16.5 we apply Blumer's life cycle of social movements to the Idle No More movement to serve as a case study.

Stage 1. Emergence: In the early stages of a social movement, activists become aware of a cause to which they feel drawn, creating an initial interest in a group that then decides to involve others. The emergence stage can be slow or relatively quick.

Stage 2. Coalescence: This stage is characterized by the movement growing, gaining momentum and making its messages available to others. A central part of coalescence is recruitment; through

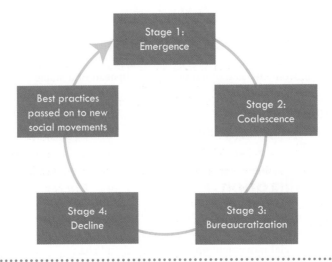

FIGURE 16.2 Life Cycle of Social Movements

Source: Adapted from various authors and based originally on the work of Blumer, H. G. (1969). Collective behavior. In A. M. Lee (Ed.), *Principles of Sociology* (3rd ed., pp. 65–121). New York: Barnes & Noble.

publicizing its core mission and aims, the movement continues to draw further members. Participation is another central aspect of coalescence as new members become active in various movement tasks and through their enthusiasm and commitment further draw new members.

Stage 3. Bureaucratization: In this stage, the movement no longer relies exclusively on grassroots volunteerism. As it becomes a more established SMO, it hires paid staff to support the movement with publicizing its goals and organizing events.

Stage 4. Decline: Like many social processes, social movements have an evolutionary trajectory, and often social movements decline.

Table 16.4 depicts a wide range of reasons why a social movement may decline. Note that decline does not necessarily signal failure, as often movements will cease to exist if they have been successful in reaching their goals and therefore have no need to continue existing.

TABLE 16.4 Decline of Social Movements

1. Success	SMO achieves its goals and as a result dismantles.
2. Organizational failure	SMO fails in getting more people involved in the movement and fades away.
3. Co-optation	Leaders of a SMO abandon the cause because they either change their values or are influenced by opposing views or groups.
4. Repression	Authorities or those in power could use various strategies and mechanisms to undermine the social movement to the extent where it ceases to exist.

Source: Adapted from Miller, F. D. (1999). The end of SDS and the emergence of weatherman: Demise through success. In J. Freeman & V. Johnson (Eds.), *Waves of protest: Social movements since the Sixties* (pp. 303–324). Lanham, MD: Rowman & Littlefield.

Dashboard

Interactive activity

emergence the process of coming into existence and gaining prominence.

coalescence the process of bringing different people together to form a single, unified group.

It is important to note that these stages highlight the general framework of social movements and allow sociologists to understand how social movements affect society, but these stages cannot be applied in a strict or rigid fashion. In fact, not all social movements will experience each stage, or they may experience each stage several times.

Theory in Everyday Life

16.5 | Idle No More

Idle No More began in Saskatchewan, Canada, in October 2012 (Devaney, 2013) as a conversation between four women who were concerned about Bill C-45, which proposed changes that would undermine treaty and Indigenous rights and erode the protection of Canadian land and water (Devaney, 2013; CBC News, 2013). What began as a conversation quickly escalated into a national and international debate. The initial stage of **emergence** was characterized by widespread discontent and social agitation (Hopper, 1950; Porta & Diani, 2006). Idle No More started out as a direct response to proposed legislation, which is an example of social agitation caused by unpopular policies and governmental inefficiencies (Hopper, 1950). In the

emergence stage, the demands and goals of the political and social agitation remain somewhat vague. By contrast, in the **coalescence** stage the sense of discontent becomes more targeted, as it is collective in nature and less about single individuals (Hopper, 1950). In the Idle No More movement, a defining and unifying moment was the 43-day hunger strike of Chief Theresa Spence from the Attawapiskat First Nation community in December 2012 (Devaney, 2013; CBC News, 2013). The movement was also active on Twitter, and the first tweet with the hashtag #IdleNoMore was sent 4 November 2015 by Idle No More co-founder Jessica Gordon [@JessicaPGordon].

Continued

Following the first tweet, the hashtag #IdleNoMore started trending on Twitter. The **bureaucratization** stage of social movements is characterized by higher levels of organization and social actors' roles beginning to formalize as a way to achieve the movement's goals. Idle No More did not see a strong bureaucratization stage and instead remained largely decentralized with broad concerns and open-ended goals. The decline of social movements does not necessarily signal failure. Social movements decline for many reasons as discussed in Table 16.4 (Miller, 1999). The goal of Chief Spence's hunger strike was to force then Prime Minister Stephen Harper to sit down and discuss Bill C-45 with Indigenous and First Nation leaders. After 42 days, Harper agreed to such a meeting. What resulted from that meeting was a 13-point declaration of key points of concern and means of intervention the government would make regarding First Nations and Indigenous communities as well as the environment more generally. While some consider the 13-point declaration a success, others have criticized it as unattainable, idealistic, and a mere summary of larger issues (Woods, 2013). The Idle No More movement continues its advocacy work and posts updates on its website and Twitter.

Conclusions

bureaucratization to manage an organization by adding controls such as adherence to rigid procedures, protocols or set of regulations or an organizational structure.

Social movements have a long history. Early activism relied on simple and short-lived means of collective action. Social movements constantly evolve and change, adopting new strategies and learning from past means of engagement. There is no doubt that the internet, social media, and mobile phones have radically transformed the nature of social movements and have come to play an increasingly important role in how movement actors acquire resources and mobilize. However, new technologies have also been criticized for making engagement too easy and leading toward shallow, "slacktivist" involvement.

We learned in this chapter about the plurality of understandings that exist around what constitutes a social movement and the types of social movements that exist. We looked at six types including petitions, protests, rebellion, letters and postcards, blockades, and hacktivism. Often a single social movement will utilize several of these types over its life cycle. Most Canadians join a social movement in the course of their lifetime, but their trajectories of involvement can vary considerably, with some individuals remaining a member of the same movement throughout their life, while others switch movements. Moreover, we learned that different sociological theories help us to understand how social movements emerge, evolve, and mobilize. Each theory makes a unique contribution by drawing our attention to different aspects of social movements.

This chapter also examined the processes underlying social movements and focused on resource mobilization theory, which helps explain the emergence, evolution, and decline of a social movement. In particular, the availability of technological resources has become critical in the twenty-first century.

Questions for Critical Thought

1. Social activists have often been described as radical and extremist, willing to take risks to achieve social change. What evidence exists to refute this argument? What are alternative ways of describing social activists?

2. What is a protest? Does it have to take place in person, or can protest occur online?

3. How have demographic characteristics such as age, education, and income changed as predictors of involvement in social movements? What do you think will be the best predictor of social movement involvement in the future?

4. In your own words, explain the importance of individual and group identity for both new social movements

(NSMs) and collective action more broadly. How does identity support group action? Are there any limitations to a cohesive group identity? If so, what are those?

5. Four trajectories of individuals' participation in social movements have been described. Why do you think people fall in these trajectories? Could other trajectories also exist?

Take it Further: Recommended Readings

M. Castells, *Networks of Outrage and Hope: Social Movements in the Internet Age*, 2nd ed. (Cambridge, UK: Polity Press, 2015). Castells presents a rich and compelling analysis of diverse social movements, their key players, and motifs, including Occupy Wall Street, Indignados, and the Egyptian Revolution.

C. Corrigall-Brown, *Patterns of Protest: Trajectories of Participation in Social Movements* (Stanford: Stanford University Press, 2012). This book highlights the influence that life experiences and social and cultural contexts have on the way people participate in social movements.

S. Staggenborg, *Social Movements*, 3rd ed. (Don Mills, ON: Oxford University Press, 2015). This book provides a comprehensive overview of social movements and social change. It answers key questions about social movements and their connection to larger currents in society.

J. Goodwin and J.M. Jasper, eds. *The Social Movements Reader: Cases and Concepts* 3rd ed. (West Sussex, UK: Wiley Blackwell, 2015). Using a blend of past and current examples, this book provides the reader with the knowledge to understand where social movements emerge, how they are sustained, and their relevancy to life in an increasingly globalized world.

C. Tilly and L.J. Wood, *Social Movements, 1768–2008*, 3rd ed. (Boulder, CO: Paradigm Publishing). The book presents a historical perspective of the evolution of social movements since 1768 to present, why people get involved in social movements, and the impact of these movements on society.

M. White, *The End of Protest: A New Playbook for Revolution* (Toronto, ON: Knopf Canada, 2016). An insightful book based on lessons gained from the Occupy movement on how social movements have changed over time, the role of technology, and the challenges that lie ahead.

Take it Further: Recommended Online Resources

"12 Hashtags That Changed the World in 2014," *Yes! Magazine*
www.yesmagazine.org/people-power/12-hashtags-that-changed-the-world-in-2014

Canadian Women's March
www.womensmarchcanada.com/

Change.org
www.change.org

¡Democracia Real Ya! (Real Democracy Now)
www.democraciarealya.es/manifiesto-comun/manifesto-english

The Feminist eZine
www.feministezine.com/feminist/historical/Third-Wave-Feminism.html

Hollaback!
www.ihollaback.org

Idle No More
www.idlenomore.ca

Invisible Children
http://invisiblechildren.com

Movements
www.movements.org

"Online Social Change: Easy to Organize, Hard to Win," TED Talk by Zeynep Tufekci
www.ted.com/talks/zeynep_tufekci_how_the_internet_has_made_social_change_easy_to_organize_hard_to_win

"Our Demand Is Simple: Stop Killing Us," by Jay Caspian Kang
www.nytimes.com/2015/05/10/magazine/our-demand-is-simple-stop-killing-us.html?_r=0

More resources available on  Dashboard

Glossary

absolute poverty not having enough income to meet basic survival needs such as water, food, shelter, and access to critical health care.

agents of socialization the individuals, groups, or institutions that form the social situation in which socialization takes place.

androcentric or sexist language language that implies male dominance or exclusivity (and female inferiority or invisibility), as in *postman*, *mankind*, or the *Rights of Man*.

anticipatory socialization the process in which non-group members adopt the values and behaviours of groups that they aspire to join.

Arab Spring the collective action in which citizens engaged during 2010 and 2011 in several Middle Eastern countries to resist government rule, protest social and economic inequality, and advocate for social change.

baby boom a period in North America (roughly 1947 to 1967) when birth rates briefly exploded, declining just as dramatically afterward.

backstage when the actor is off stage and thus freed from social norms and expectations and can therefore cease performing and be his or her "true self."

behavioural model of health an approach to health that considers the lifestyle choices of the individual as the only factors relevant to a person's well-being.

bias any predisposition that prevents neutral consideration of a question or idea. It can influence a researcher's interpretation of participants' responses or the interpretation of the data.

binary anything separated into two distinct and clear-cut categories.

biomedical model of health an approach to health that considers only physiological and genetic factors as relevant to a person's well-being.

biopsychosocial model of health an approach to health that recognizes how a variety of emotional, mental, and physical aspects associated with a person's life contribute to their overall well-being.

bodily discipline according to Michel Foucault, strategies of regulation that use power to reduce social agents to docile bodies, through punishment of various kinds.

bourgeois revolution describes how social change could come about from incremental economic, technological, and social changes in society.

bourgeoisie (or capitalists) the social group that possesses capital and thus also owns and commands the means of production.

bureaucratization to manage an organization by adding controls such as adherence to rigid procedures, protocols, or set of regulations or an organizational structure.

Canadian content ("can-con") governmental policy of quotas to guarantee that media by Canadian artists, producers, and companies are sufficiently represented in the mass media.

Canadian Radio-television and Telecommunications Commission (CRTC) an independent governing body funded by the Canadian government with the goal of fulfilling the media needs and representing the media interests of Canadian citizens.

capital punishment putting people to death as a penalty for criminal behaviour.

carrying capacity the number of people, other living organisms, or crops that a region can support without environmental degradation.

census a recurring and official count of a particular population, used to systematically gather and record information about the members of the population.

census family a household that includes two spouses—opposite or same-sex, married or cohabiting (if they have lived together for longer than one year)—with or without never-married children, or a single parent with one or more never-married children.

citizen journalism original reporting and news coverage by ordinary people, who commonly use the internet, blogs, and social media to voice their opinions and to counter the "messaging" present in the dominant ideology.

civil religion an organized secular practice that serves many of the same social functions as traditional religion: bringing people together, giving people direction, explaining how the world works, and so on.

class the division of people into social groups based on the distribution of material resources and power.

class consciousness a sense of shared identity and common interests that stem from an awareness of similar economic position, particularly relative to the economic position of others.

class system a hierarchical classification system that places individuals in relation to one another based on differences in their command of the means of production, work situations, and life chances.

coalescence the process of bringing different people together to form a single, unified group.

code-switch a situation in which a speaker effortlessly switches to a different language, dialect, class, and often culture.

collective behaviour (or group action) the mobilization and actions of members of a social movement toward a unifying goal.

colonialism the establishment by higher-income countries of formal political control over lower-income areas, usually accompanied by the exploitation of local economic resources and peoples.

communitarians people who reject the notion that human rights apply universally to all communities regardless of their contexts and histories, and argue instead that human rights are established through membership in specific communities.

comparative historical analysis comparing countries to derive insight into how their political systems developed and what economic, social, and historical factors lead to differences.

computational social sciences the academic subdisciplines that apply computational approaches to research.

conspicuous consumption the purchasing of valuable goods for the purpose of expressing class belonging and status.

constraining power the ability of a social institution to control people's behaviour and increase their obedience to social norms.

context collapse the potential that exists on social media for people, information, expectations, and norms from one context to collapse with another, and the problems that may arise.

convergence the combination and intersection of otherwise different and dispersed regulations and laws, industries, or technologies.

convergence thesis the theory that under conditions of modernization, less-developed societies will start to change more rapidly than more-developed societies, with the result that all societies will eventually reach the same social, cultural, and economic conditions, regardless of their starting points.

copyright a form of intellectual property that ensures work created by a particular person or company cannot be used freely and without consent of the creator/owner.

core states according to Wallerstein's world systems theory, industrialized, wealthy, and powerful states that control or manipulate semi-peripheral and peripheral states.

corporatization the often gradual transformation of publicly funded but independent organizations into economically dependent (and potentially commercial) organizations that use corporate management techniques of administration and seek to demonstrate their profitability.

cosmopolitans people working in development who advocate for universal human rights (such as gender equality) that can help orient national and local legislation and policy.

counterculture a subculture that rejects conventional norms and values and adopts alternative ones.

Creative Commons (CC) an organization that assists people with protecting their creations while also making those creations accessible.

credentialism belief in or reliance on academic or other formal qualifications as the best measure of a person's intelligence or ability to do a particular job.

criminality behaviour that violates criminal laws.

critical race theory (CRT) theory that views racialization as a performance and social construction rather than a reflection of innate, biological qualities.

crowdsourcing an alternative funding model that looks to consumers and audiences to make contributions and provide resources to help make products, start services, and support ideas.

cultural capital a body of knowledge, ideas, tastes, preferences, and skills that helps people get ahead socially. Cultural capital often includes learning about and participating in high culture.

cultural integration the process that fits together parts of a culture—for example, ideal culture and real culture—so that they complement one another.

cultural literacy a solid knowledge of what people "need to know" to sound educated and well-read in our society.

cultural relativism the principle that a culture and its beliefs and values should be viewed from the standpoint of that culture itself, not another culture.

cyberbullying a form of bullying or harassment using electronic forms of contact.

cyberspace the virtual environment in which people communicate with one another over computer networks.

data curation the processes and activities involved in managing data so that the data remains available for reuse over time or for future research purposes.

decriminalization reflecting a change in social or moral views, the abolition of criminal penalties for a particular act.

demography the study of human populations—their growth and decline through births, deaths, and migration.

deregulation/marketization the removal of regulation and changes to policy that serve neo-liberal and free-market agendas.

deterrence a legal and criminological concept that reflects the view punishment should prevent (or deter) crime by imposing significant costs on people who commit crimes.

deviance any behaviour that diverges from usual or accepted standards and, in doing so, violates social rules.

diaspora the dispersal of any group of people; originally, the term referred specifically to the tribes of Israel dispersed around the world.

digital immigrants people who have learned how to use digital technologies later in life and have been generally slow and apprehensive in adopting novel forms of communication.

digital natives people who have grown up with digital technologies and did not know a time without the internet.

digital skills ability to access, understand, and utilize a wide range of digital services, including but not limited to email, social media, search engines, and devices such as laptops, tablets, and smart phones.

discrimination distinctions, exclusions, and preferential treatment based on an arbitrary trait (e.g., ethnicity), which jeopardizes a person's human rights and fundamental freedoms.

disruptive technologies technologies that are responsible for transformative social change.

division of labour the coordinated assignment of different parts of a task to different people to improve efficiency.

dominant ideology refers to the ideas, values, and norms shared by the majority in a given society; thus it often denotes the beliefs of the dominant class.

downward mobility vertical social mobility into lower-regarded and paid occupational positions.

dyad a two-person set of people who interact and communicate with each other.

ecological validity the extent to which findings can be generalized to real-life settings.

education a process designed to develop one's capacity for critical thinking, self-understanding, and self-reliance.

elites those in positions of power who control the means of production and dissemination of mass content.

emergence the process of coming into existence and gaining prominence.

emojis small digital icons or images used in digital communication to express an emotion, idea, or reaction.

environmental degradation any change or disturbance to the environment that is deleterious or undesirable.

epistemology the study of the origin of knowledge and the logic of one's beliefs.

equilibrium a balance, in this case between population numbers and the potential for feeding these numbers.

ethnic enclaves areas with a high concentration of residents with a particular ethnicity or set of related ethnicities, with a distinct culture and a defined boundary.

ethnic group a group of people who share a common homeland, language, or culture.

ethnic solidarity a process in which members of self-conscious communities interact with each other to achieve common purposes.

ethnicity belonging to a group or category of people that are bound together by common ties of national tradition, language, or cultural heritage.

ethnocentrism the tendency to use one's own culture as a basis for evaluating other cultures; also, the view that your culture is superior to other cultures.

exchange mobility movement within an occupational hierarchy that can only occur when an existing position becomes vacant.

expressed racism explicit discrimination and prejudice towards people based on their racialization or ethnicity.

extended family multiple generations of relatives living together, or several adult siblings with their spouses and children who share a dwelling and resources. More than three kinds of relationship may be present.

fake news hoaxes or the deliberate use of misinformation in traditional news media or social media.

family any social unit, or set of social relations, that does what families are popularly imagined to do, by whatever means it does so.

femininity a social construction of gender and includes stereotypical behaviours and attitudes such as being emotional, caring, and nurturing.

formal education education received in accredited schools during formal teaching sessions.

frontstage the performance of a role in relation to those around us, the audience, that follows specific social norms and expectations.

fundamentalism the belief that religions should strictly follow the oldest, most traditional, and most basic theological texts, also known as holy books.

gender the social construction of what men and women should be like in terms of appearance, behaviours, preferences, and social roles and expectations.

gender identity a sense, usually beginning in infancy, of belonging to a particular gender.

gender inequality differences that exist in education, income, and other opportunities based on a person's gender or sexual orientation.

gender roles the behaviours, attitudes, and markers ascribed to men and women by society.

genderfluid describes a person who has a gender (or genders) that changes over time and contexts.

genderqueer describes a person who resists gender norms, but does not seek to change their sex.

Gini coefficient a measure of the inequality in the distribution of income among households within a country, as compared to a theoretical country of similar attributes but where everyone has the same income (where the coefficient would be 0), or where there is perfect inequality (where the coefficient would be 1).

global city a city with significant influence or impact in global affairs deriving from acting as a central locale for economic markets, innovation, production, or diplomacy.

global civil society large-scale interconnected groups operating across borders and outside the control of the state.

Global North the regions of Europe and North America characterized (with some exceptions) as high-income and often politically more stable.

Global South the regions of Latin America, Asia, Africa, and Oceania characterized (with some exceptions) as low-income and often politically or culturally marginalized.

global village the notion that electronic media compress time and allow individuals who are geographically and socially removed to have similar experiences by interacting with the same content.

globalization the process of increased international influence through economic, ideological, cultural, or technological means, or the results of such a process resulting in a homogeneity of economy, ideology, culture, or technology across the globe.

governmentality coined by Michel Foucault, the way in which the state exercises control over, or governs, its citizenry.

green consumers consumers who have examined the effect of goods production and consumption and reflect environmental consciousness in their purchasing behaviour.

hidden curriculum the implicit lessons in social roles, values, and expectations that are communicated in schools; for example, how students are taught in educational institutions such as high schools demonstrates gender inequalities that are not explicitly communicated, but are implicit in how men and women are treated differently in the classroom.

hidden homeless people without homes who stay with friends or family temporarily rather than in shelters or in public spaces.

high culture high-status group preferences, tastes, and norms. Examples include fine arts, classical music, ballet, and other "highbrow" concerns.

home-schooling the education of children at home by their parents.

homophily a relationship joining actors who have the same or similar attributes or statuses.

horizontal forms of organizing the organization or structure of a group, whereby every member of the group is considered equal—no superiors or subordinates. Instead of hierarchies, it emphasizes teamwork and equal collaboration among group members.

horizontal integration the expansion of one type of industry into other types of industries, enabling control of companies across industry boundaries.

hot spots areas in a city where the risks of crime are especially high, usually because the area draws many vulnerable victims and policing is relatively light.

human capital a measure of formal education and learning, including credentials; a skill or skill set, usually including educational attainment or job-related experiences that enhances a worker's value on the job; usually, the result of foregone income and a long-term investment in personal improvement.

human capital theory the theory that, other things being equal, economic productivity and prosperity grow with the amount of investment in human capital—that is, the education and training undertaken by workers.

identity the unique combination of traits, values, and expressions that make people who they are.

impression management a conscious or subconscious process in which a person works to shape other peoples' perceptions of his or her self.

industrial society a society that uses advanced technology that, when combined with a detailed division of labour, promotes mass production and a high standard of living.

industrialization reorganization of an economy for the purpose of manufacturing, using machinery and inanimate forms of energy, and the social changes that accompany it.

industry convergence the horizontal or vertical integration of different media industries.

infidelity a violation of a couple's emotional and/or sexual exclusivity (also referred to as cheating, adultery, or having an affair).

informed consent a process for getting permission before involving a participant in a research endeavour.

innovation the process by which individuals or corporations devise and adopt new technologies or practices through the process of research and development.

institutionalized racism a form of racism expressed in the practice of social and political institutions.

interaction a pattern exchange of information, support, and/or emotions between at least two people in a social setting.

interactive audiences media users who not only consume content but also produce content for a global audience by creating content, sharing content, and providing feedback to content creators.

intergenerational mobility the movement of people into positions that are higher or lower than the positions held by their parents.

internalized racism the conscious or unconscious acceptance of racist attitudes, including stereotypes and biases, towards members of one's own ethnic group, including oneself.

internet kill switch when a government shuts down the internet in an attempt to cut off communication between social activists.

intersectionality a theoretical approach that examines the interconnection of social categories—especially, social disadvantages—related to ethnicity, class, and gender that creates more complex, interdependent systems of oppression and disadvantage.

intragenerational (career) mobility social mobility into positions that are higher or lower within a person's lifespan.

kin group a group of people related by blood or marriage.

knowledge translation the process by which the knowledge, values, and cultures of one culture are adapted to fit local thoughts and beliefs rather than transferred directly without any change.

lifeworld describes how the world is experienced or lived; all the activities and contacts that make up the world of an individual or group.

looking-glass self a social psychological concept coined by Charles Horton Cooley, which states that a person's self develops from interpersonal interactions in society and observations of others.

low income cut-off (LICO) the method used to measure low income in Canada that identifies income thresholds below which a family will likely spend a larger proportion of its income on necessities than an average family of a similar size.

low income measure (LIM) the method used to measure low income in Canada that calculates the low income threshold of a household as one half of the median income of a household of the same size in a community of a similar size.

machine breaking workers' actions against machinery and the social changes resulting from industrialization.

market basket measure (MBM) the method used to measure low income in Canada that calculates how much income a household requires to meet its needs, including subsistence needs (such as basic food and shelter) and the needs to satisfy community norms.

marketization/deregulation the removal of regulation and changes to policy that serve neo-liberal and free-market agendas.

masculinity a social construction of gender and includes such stereotypical male behaviours and attitudes such as being strong, brave, and rational.

mass media a collection of media organizations that mass communicate information through a variety of media technologies.

material culture the physical and technological aspects of people's lives—in short, all the physical objects that members of a culture create and use.

materialization the ceremonies, symbolic objects, monuments, and writing systems that hasten the spread of an ideology and power relations in the larger population, in the context of national or global culture.

media concentration the ownership of many industries, products, or content by one company or organization.

media literacy the ability to find, access, analyze, evaluate, and communicate messages in a wide range of formats including print, audio, video, and digital.

meritocracy (meritocratic ethic) any system of rule or advancement where the rewards are strictly proportioned to accomplishment, and all people have the same opportunity to win these rewards.

misinformation false information spread intentionally or unintentionally.

modernity an era in Western Europe beginning roughly with the end of the medieval age (around 1500) to the present day, associated with the increased influence of rationalism, individualization, secularism, democracy, and capitalism.

moral entrepreneurs promoters of "morality" who use their resources as rule-makers, campaigners, and enforcers to shape public policy.

moral panic a condition resulting from social concern over an issue that provokes intense feelings and fears; usually the work of moral entrepreneurs, this is often an overreaction to certain deviant or unfamiliar behaviours.

multiculturalism political and social policy that promotes ethnic tolerance and diversity in communities.

multiple regression analysis a powerful statistical technique used for predicting the unknown value of a dependent variable from the known value of two or more predictor (independent) variables.

natural environment the territory in which human action occurs, which is itself modified by human agency; all living and non-living things occurring naturally on Earth, excluding the human component.

natural resources materials or substances such as minerals, forests, water, and fertile land that occur in nature and can be used for economic gain.

negotiation a type of interaction whose goal is to define the expectations or boundaries of a relationship.

neo-colonialism a concept related to colonialism, when, despite political decolonization, the Global North societies that once controlled many parts of the world continue to dominate the production and marketing of goods, culture, and language in their former colonies, thereby retaining their historical influence.

neo-liberalism a social, economic, and political philosophy that favours the deregulation of economic markets to establish the goal of "free markets" wherein the state has limited authority to intervene in the economy; also refers to the political and philosophical ideologies associated with such a goal.

network social movements new types of social movements that are decentralized and heavily rely on ICTs to share information, mobile resources, and engage social activists.

new media media characterized by a decentralized process of content creation and distribution.

new religious movements (NRMs) groups and institutions that share similar religious or spiritual views about the world, but are not part of mainstream religious institutions.

new social movement (NSM) theory explains how modern social movements come to form and mobilize.

newly industrialized countries (NICs) countries whose economies are between those of developed and developing economies.

non-standard work arrangements dead-end, low-paying, insecure jobs, also known as precarious employment.

norms the rules or expectations of behaviour people consider acceptable in their group or society. People who do not follow these norms may be shunned, punished, or ridiculed. Norms, like values, vary from one society to another and change over time.

nuclear family a group that usually consists of a father, a mother, and their children living in the same dwelling. Such a family comprises no more than three relationships: between spouses, between parents and children, and between siblings.

open-source software computer software with its source code made available to users, meaning that they are given the rights to examine, modify, and share the software with anyone and for any purpose.

organic solidarity social cohesion based on a division of labour that results in people depending on each other; it binds people together in technologically advanced, industrialized societies.

organizational culture the values, norms, and patterns of action that characterize social relationships within a formal organization; also, the way an organization deals with its environment. It includes norms and values that are culturally specific to the organization.

Orientalism emphasizes, exaggerates, and distorts characteristics, features, and cultures of people and cultures from Asia, North Africa, and the Middle East and compares their characteristics to that of Europeans.

overpopulation a condition wherein the number of humans (or other animals) exceeds the relevant resources such as the water and essential nutrients they need to survive.

Panopticon a type of institutional building designed by the English philosopher Jeremy Bentham that allows all inmates to be observed by a single watchman without the inmates knowing if they are being watched. In modern societies, the metaphor for universal, unseen surveillance.

parole the release of a prisoner before the completion of a sentence, on the promise of good behaviour.

participatory culture a culture where consumers can purchase products, services, and information as easily as they can produce them.

patriarchy a social system in which men predominate in roles of political leadership, moral authority, social privilege, and control of property.

performativity the idea that certain social factors, such as gender, are socially constructed and then acted out using words and behaviours that have come to be associated with what it means to be, say, male or female.

peripheral states according to Wallerstein's world systems theory, states that are lower income and less able to exert political influence internationally. They are subject to control or manipulation by core states.

political economy the study of power relations at the intersection of media, economics, and politics particularly related to economic value and its relationship to law and government.

popular (or mass) culture the culture of ordinary people; the objects, preferences, and tastes that are widespread in a society.

population the complete group of units to which the results are to be generalized. Units can be anything from individuals, animals, or objects to businesses or trips.

positive checks according to Malthus, forces that limit the population by raising the death rate, due to disease and starvation.

post-industrialism an economic system based more on services and information than on manufactured goods or primary production.

postmodern(ism) a style of thinking or school of thought in social science and humanities that denies the validity of universal, sweeping statements about the world or groups of people within the world, and analyzes the motives behind such statements and the consequences of people's believing them.

poverty line an agreed upon income at which a standard of living that is considered "acceptable" should be affordable. What is considered acceptable is not static, but varies considerably within societies, across societies, and over time.

press gallery an area in a parliamentary building where members of the press can observe and report on parliamentary proceedings.

prestige A person's reputation in a social group, which commands honour and respect, often irrespective of income, authority, or class position.

primary labour market industries that provide jobs with high wages, good opportunities for advancement, and job security.

primary socialization the first stage in the socialization process, during which children develop basic values and norms as well as ideas of the self.

prisonization (theory) the degradation of prisoners, their socialization into prison life, and their subsequent inability to function effectively outside these prison environments.

private media ownership when media are owned by corporations and follow a profit-maximization model, where decisions are made based on the likelihood of increasing revenue.

proletarianization the creation of a subordinate wage-working class among people with professional qualifications.

proletariat (or working class) the social group that exchanges their labour for wages. As they do not own the means of production, they are at the mercy of the bourgeoisie (or capitalists) who own the means of production and prescribe work conditions.

prosumption a combination of *production* and *consumption*, this term describes the process of customers playing a central role in the design, development, and use of the end product.

public media ownership media that are owned by—while at the same time operating at arm's-length from—the government.

racialization the way that others categorize people by visible characteristics and features such as hair colour, hair type, skin colour, and facial features.

racialized (or ethnic) socialization the process by which we learn to perceive and evaluate people (including ourselves) according to presumed racial or ethnic differences.

racialized minority those who are treated in a particular way by people around them based on their physical features and the attributes that those features are assumed to signify. Racialization occurs against those who have features distinct from the majority group who hold social power in a society.

racism discrimination, prejudice, or antagonism directed against someone of a different ethnicity or racialized group based on the belief that one's own racialized identity is superior.

reactivity when people who are being observed change their usual or typical behaviour because they know that they are being observed.

rebellions armed opposition to an established government or authority by a social group.

recidivism refers to prisoners who re-offend, often multiple times.

reciprocal process when both the parent and children socialize each other through their interactions; children socialize parents just as parents socialize children.

regulation the process of controlling people through the creation and enforcement of social rules.

regulatory convergence the systemic undoing, relaxing, and merging of laws, policies, and other regulations that leads to media industries that are virtually indistinguishable from one another.

rehabilitation the idea that punishment should reform criminals and help them become law-abiding members of society.

relative poverty having enough to meet basic survival needs, but living well below the general standard of living of a community, social group, or society.

reliability the degree to which the work can be replicated. In qualitative work, reliability is often expressed in terms of trustworthiness and authenticity.

religion any system of beliefs about the supernatural, and the social groups that gather around these beliefs.

religiosity the sum of all the various aspects of religious activity, dedication, and belief (religious doctrine) one finds in a group or society.

repertoires of collective action the specific behaviours, tactics, and patterns of engagement of activists.

research design the blueprint of the study. It defines the study type, research question, hypotheses, variables, data collection methods, and a statistical analysis plan.

reserve army of labour people who, because they are impoverished and often unemployed, form an easily mobilized, easily disposable workforce at the mercy of employers.

resocialization a process that involves a replacement of an individual's values, beliefs, and sense of self.

resource mobilization theory examines how social movements acquire, manage, and mobilize resources.

restorative justice a set of approaches to criminal punishment aimed to ensure that the criminal takes responsibility for his or her actions and that the victim, the criminal, and the community are all restored to a healthy state.

reverse socialization the process by which children influence parents and help them learn or acquire some social skills; in reverse socialization, parents learn from their children.

revolutions aim to overthrow those in power to establish a new social order that is more egalitarian and places new elites into positions of power.

riots chaotic collective protests that are undirected, emotional, and often violent.

role a set of connected behaviours, rights, obligations, beliefs, and norms as conceptualized by people in a social situation.

role conflict when a person is obligated to fulfill two different positions that have clashing requirements.

role theory a viewpoint that considers that an individual's behavior is guided by expectations held both by the individual and other people, which is guided by socially defined categories (e.g., mother, teacher, doctor), social learning, and experience.

routine activity theory the theory that victimization results when a vulnerable person (or "suitable target") is regularly in a dangerous place without the presence of a trusted guardian.

safety net the public and private services provided to individuals with low incomes or no incomes to prevent them from falling into poverty.

sample a subset of the population of interest in a study, reducing the number of participants to a manageable size.

saturation a method used to confirm that sufficient and valuable data are collected to support the study.

science the systematic study of the structure and behaviour of the physical and natural world through observation and experiment. Science, from a sociological standpoint, is a communal system of organized doubt and skepticism that aims to refine theories through the collection and use of empirical data.

second shift women's unpaid housework and caretaking in addition to paid work performed in the formal sector.

secondary (or marginal) labour market sectors in the economy that offer low-paying jobs characterized by fewer opportunities for advancement and insecurity.

secondary socialization the acquisition of the knowledge and skills needed to participate in society beyond the context of the family.

secularization a steadily dwindling influence of formal (institutional) religion in public life; also, the process whereby, especially in modern industrial societies, religious beliefs, practices, and institutions lose their social significance

self a stable understanding of one's identity: who we are in relation to others.

semi-peripheral states according to Wallerstein's world systems theory, middle-income, partially industrialized states that have some power and influence; they are "in between" the classifications of core states and peripheral states.

sexual deviance any behaviour that involves individuals seeking erotic gratification through means a community (or its most influential citizens) considers odd, different, or unacceptable.

sexual orientation the direction of an individual's erotic impulses in terms of the gender to which they are most attracted.

signs gestures, artifacts, or words that express or meaningfully represent something other than themselves.

slacktivism (or clicktivism) derives its meaning through the laissez-faire attitude and simplistic motions (clicking a "like" button, for example) required to show support for a social movement in comparison to past forms of activism.

social assistance a program that provides money to the lowest earning and some vulnerable groups in society to enable them to meet their basic needs.

social cohesion the existence of bonds of trust that bind people together in a community or society, enabling co-operation and interdependence.

social constructionists symbolic interactionist argument on a societal scale; they study how moral entrepreneurs make and enforce claims about reality.

social determinants of health (SDOH) the numerous social factors such as income, education, and employment security that affect a person's health and well-being.

social distance the perceived extent to which social groups are isolated from one another, measured by factors such as whether a member of one social class, racialized group, or ethnicity would be welcomed in the meeting place of another social class, racialized group, or ethnicity.

social exclusion the inability to participate in commonly accepted activities in a given society.

social institution one kind of social structure governed by established or standardizing patterns of rule-governed behaviour. Social institutions include the family, education, religious, economic and political structures.

social mobility a change in social status where individuals or families move from one strata to another. Movement may be vertical or horizontal, across generations or within a generation.

social movement organization (SMO) describes specific social movements instead of social movements in general.

social movements organized efforts by groups in society to promote or resist social change through various types of engagement ranging from pacific protests to armed rebellions.

social norms rules, whether written or unwritten, that people are expected to follow as members of a particular group, community, or society.

social relationship a pattern of ongoing contact and communication between two or more people that follows an expected pattern.

social roles a set of behaviours, responsibilities, and norms associated with a particular status in society.

social stratification a system of hierarchy that integrates class, status, and domination with other forms of differentiation, such as gender and ethnicity, to describe societal inequality.

social structure any enduring, predictable pattern of social relations among people in society that constrains and shapes people's behaviour.

socialization the lifelong social learning a person undergoes to become a capable member of society, through social interaction with others, and in response to social pressures.

society a group of people who occupy a particular territorial area, feel themselves to constitute (or are viewed as) a unified and distinct entity, and in many respects, share a common set of assumptions about reality.

socioeconomic status a method of ranking people that combines measures of wealth, authority (or power), and prestige (reputation that commands honour and respect, often irrespective of income, authority, or class position).

sociological imagination the ability to perceive the underlying societal causes of individual experiences and issues; and to think outside the accepted wisdom and common routines of daily life.

specialization a system of production in which different individuals or groups each focus on producing a limited range of products or services to yield greater productive efficiency overall.

spirituality an openness to or search for "sacred" aspects of life, where "the sacred" is broadly defined as that which is set apart from the ordinary (or profane) and worthy of veneration.

standpoint theory individuals view society from different social locations depending on their class, gender, and status.

the state refers to a nation or territory under the control of a single government, or to said government itself.

statistics a branch of mathematics that concerns itself with the collection, analysis, interpretation, and representation of numerical data.

status the relative rank that an individual holds, with attendant rights, duties, and lifestyle, in a social hierarchy based upon honour or prestige.

STEM Science, Technology, Engineering, and Mathematics; commonly used to refer to education, research, and employment in this sector.

stereotypes widely held beliefs about a social group that are overly simplistic and often untrue. Stereotypes can ascribe both positive and negative attributes to members of a group.

stigma disgrace and marginalization because of life circumstances or physical or social characteristics of a person that prevent that person from being fully socially accepted.

strain theory (anomie theory) rooted in Émile Durkheim's notion of anomie and elaborated by Robert K. Merton in his typology of modes of adaptation, this theory proposes that deviant behaviour results from unequal opportunities and is a function of the gap between norms of success and access to the legitimate means of achieving them.

street crime crimes associated with the public and individual offenders working alone or in small groups rather than large crime structures, such as shoplifting, vandalism, break and enter, car theft, assault, and homicide.

structural mobility movement within an occupational hierarchy that can occur as a result of structural growth through the creation of new jobs or positions, and that is commonly associated with organizational or economic growth.

subculture a group that shares the cultural elements of the larger society but also has its own distinctive values, beliefs, norms, style of dress, and behaviour patterns.

subculture theory the theory that certain groups or subcultures in society have values and attitudes that are conducive to deviance, crime, or violence.

substance abuse excessive use of, or dependence on, an addictive substance, especially alcohol or drugs.

suitable target a person distinguished by particular characteristics that are likely to invite or incite victimization.

surveillance close observation, especially of a suspected criminal.

symbol a sign whose relationship with something else also expresses a value or evokes an emotion.

technological convergence the trend toward providing media and information in digital formats, creating a system of information exchange that enables text, sound, image, and video to be consumable by the same device.

technology objects developed to serve a particular (e.g., social, political, cultural, or personal) purpose.

telecommuting a work arrangement in which employees do not commute to a central place of work but instead often work at home.

tokenism the policy or practice of making only a token or symbolic effort toward equality and integration without any real change.

tolerance the idea that people from different ethnic and racialized backgrounds can come together in a single nation-state and show high levels of trust and reciprocity.

total institution a concept developed by Erving Goffman, defined as an isolated, confined social system whose main objective is to control most aspects of its participants' lives.

training a process designed to identify and practise specific routines that achieve desired results.

transformative power the tendency of social institutions and social experiences to radically change people's routine behaviour.

transgender describes a discrepancy between the gender that individuals identify with and the biological sex they were identified as at birth.

triangulation a technique used by researchers to determine validity in their studies by gathering data from multiple sources. Different research methods are used with the aim of arriving at consistency across results.

underemployment employment in a job that requires far less expertise, skill, or ability than the job-holder has to offer.

upward social mobility vertical social mobility into more highly regarded and higher-paying occupational positions.

urbanization a population shift from rural to urban areas, resulting in the growth of cities and the development of city lifestyles.

uses and gratifications a media theory founded on the idea that more attention needs to be devoted to what people do with the media rather than the influence or impact of the media on the individual.

validity the extent to which findings are an accurate reflection of the social world.

values shared understanding of what a group or society deems good, right, and desirable; a way of viewing the world and attaching positive or negative sentiments.

vertical integration expanded control of the production process (such as raw materials, packaging, distribution, marketing, and final sales).

victim precipitation theory a theory that analyzes how a victim's characteristics or interactions with an offender may contribute to the crime being committed.

white privilege the advantages and immunities that are unequally and unfairly experienced by people who are perceived and treated as "white," beyond what people racialized as "non-white" experience under similar social, political, or economic circumstances.

white-collar crime comprises the illegal acts and misdeeds of middle-class members of the business world.

women's suffrage the right of women to vote in political elections and the movement formed to achieve this right.

WUNC an acronym to describe social movement actors as worthy, unified, numerous, and committed.

zero population growth (ZPG) the maintenance of a population at a constant level by limiting the number of live births to only what is needed to replace the existing population; an absence of any increase (or decrease) in a population over a period of time.

References

Chapter 1

Albanese, P., Tepperman, L., & Alexander, E. (Eds.). (2017). *Reading sociology: Canadian perspectives* (3rd ed.). Don Mills, ON: Oxford University Press.

Amato, P. R. (2000). The consequences of divorce for adults and children. *Journal of Marriage and Family, 62*(4), 1269–1287.

Beijing institutes Queuing Day. (2007, February 8). *China Daily*. Retrieved from www.chinadaily.com.cn/2008/2007-02/08/content_804734.htm.

Berger, P. L., & Luckmann, T. (1966). *The social construction of reality: A treatise in the sociology of knowledge*. Garden City, NY: First Anchor.

Blumer, H. (1986). *Symbolic interactionism: Perspective and method*. Berkeley: University of California Press.

Bruckman, A. (1992). *Identity workshops: Emergent social and psychological phenomena in text-based virtual reality*. (Unpublished doctoral dissertation). MIT, Cambridge, MA.

Clement, W. (1975). *Canadian corporate elite: Analysis of economic power*. Montreal, QC & Kingston, ON: McGill-Queen's University Press.

Collins, R. (1974). *Conflict sociology*. New York: Academic Press.

Collins, S. T. (2014, October 17). Anita Sarkeesian on GamerGate: "We have a problem and we're going to fix this." *Rolling Stone*. Retrieved from www.rollingstone.com/culture/features/anita-sarkeesian-gamergate-interview-20141017

D'Anastasio, C. (2015, April 15). Avatar IRL. *Motherboard/Vice*. Retrieved from https://motherboard.vice.com/read/avatar-irl.

Darden, J. T. (2004). *The significance of white supremacy in the Canadian metropolis of Toronto*. Lewiston, NY: E. Mellen Press.

Durkheim, É. (1951). *Suicide: A study in sociology* (J. A. Spaulding & G. Simpson, Trans.). Glencoe, IL: Free Press. (Original work published 1897)

Durkheim, É. (1964). *The division of labor in society*. (G. Simpson, Trans.). New York: Macmillan. (Original work published 1933)

Elias, N. (1978). *The history of manners. The civilizing process* (Vol. 1). New York: Pantheon.

Goffman, E. (1959). *The presentation of self in everyday life*. Garden City, NY: Doubleday.

Hamlin, J. (2016). *Harriet Martineau: Morals and manners*. Unpublished manuscript. Retrieved from www.d.umn.edu/cla/faculty/jhamlin/4111/Martineau/Martineau.pdf

Hathaway, J. (2014, October 10). What is Gamergate, and why? An explainer for non-geeks. *Gawker*. Retrieved from http://gawker.com/what-is-gamergate-and-why-an-explainer-for-non-geeks-1642909080

Helmes-Hayes, R. C. (1998). *The vertical mosaic revisited*. Toronto, ON: University of Toronto Press.

MacKinnon, M. (2009, August 11). China's citizens in a shove-hate relationship. *The Globe and Mail*. Retrieved from www.theglobeandmail.com/news/world/chinas-citizens-in-a-shove-hate-relationship/article4283456/

Marmot, M. (1993). Epidemiological approach to the explanation of social differentiation in mortality: The Whitehall studies. *Sozial-und Präventivmedizin/Social and Preventive Medicine, 38*(5), 271–279.

Marmot, M. (2005). Social determinants of health inequalities. *The Lancet, 365*(9464), 1099–1104.

Marmot, M., Feeney, A., Shipley, M., North, F., & Syme, S. L. (1995). Sickness absence as a measure of health status and functioning: From the UK Whitehall II study. *Journal of Epidemiology & Community Health, 49*(2), 124–130.

Marmot, M. G., Stansfeld, S., Patel, C., North, F., Head, J., White, I., . . . & Smith, G. D. (1991). Health inequalities among British civil servants: The Whitehall II study. *The Lancet, 337*(8754), 1387–1393.

Marx, K., & Engels, F. (2002). *The communist manifesto*. New York: Penguin. (Original work published 1848)

Mead, G. H. (1934). *Mind, self and society*. Chicago, IL: University of Chicago Press.

Merton, R. K. (1957). *Social theory and social structure*. New York: Simon & Schuster.

Miller, C. (2015, October 16). Why what you learned in preschool is crucial at work. *The New York Times*. Retrieved from www.nytimes.com/2015/10/18/upshot/how-the-modern-workplace-has-become-more-like-preschool.html

Mills, C. W. (1959). *The sociological imagination*. New York: Oxford University Press.

Nakamura, L. (1995). Race in/for cyberspace: Identity tourism and racial passing on the Internet. *Works and Days, 25*(26). Retrieved from http://mysite.du.edu/~lavita/edpx_3770_13s/_docs/nakamura_race_in_cyberspace.pdf

Nisbet, R. (1993). *The sociological tradition*. New Brunswick, NJ: Transaction Publishers.

Nisbet, R. (2014). *The quest for community*. New York: Open Road Media.

Olsen, D. (1980). *The state elite*. Toronto, ON: McClelland & Stewart.

Parsons, T. (1937). *The structure of social action*. New York: Free Press.

Parsons, T. (1951). *The social system*. New York: Free Press.

Porter, J. (2015). *Vertical mosaic: An analysis of social class and power in Canada*. Toronto, ON: University of Toronto Press. (Original work published 1965)

Raphael, D. (2009). *Social determinants of health: Canadian perspectives.* Toronto, ON: Canadian Scholars' Press.

Reynolds, J. (2008, July 11). Queuing day. *BBC.* Retrieved from www.bbc.co.uk/blogs/thereporters/jamesreynolds/2008/07/queuing_day.html

Stuart, K. (2013, July 31). Gamer communities: The positive side. *The Guardian.* Retrieved from www.theguardian.com/technology/gamesblog/2013/jul/31/gamer-communities-positive-side-twitter

Stuart, K. (2014, December 3). Zoe Quinn: "All Gamergate has done is ruin people's lives." *The Guardian.* Retrieved from www.theguardian.com/technology/2014/dec/03/zoe-quinn-gamergate-interview

Wallerstein, J. S., & Blakeslee, S. (2004). *Second chances: Men, women, and children a decade after divorce.* New York: Houghton Mifflin Harcourt.

Wilkinson, R. G., & Marmot, M. (Eds.). (2003). *Social determinants of health: The solid facts* (2nd ed.). Copenhagen: World Health Organization.

Yee, N., & Bailenson, J. (2007). The Proteus effect: The effect of transformed self-representation on behavior. *Human Communication Research, 33*(3), 271–290.

Chapter 2

Agger, B. (2007). *Public sociology: From social facts to literary acts* (2nd ed.). Lanham, MD: Rowman & Littlefield Publishers.

Allen, R. (2017, February 6). *What happens online in 60 seconds?* Retrieved from www.smartinsights.com/internet-marketing-statistics/happens-online-60-seconds/

Altheide, D. L., & Schneider, C. (2013). *Qualitative media analysis* (2nd ed.). Thousand Oaks, CA: Sage.

Babor, T., Caetano, R., Casswell, S., Edwards, G., Giesbrecht, N., Grube, J., . . . & Rossow, I. (2010). *Alcohol: No ordinary commodity: Research and public policy* (Rev. ed.). Oxford: Oxford University Press.

Baker, S. C., Watson, B. M., Baker, S. C., & Watson, B. M. (2015). How patients perceive their doctors' communication. *Journal of Language and Social Psychology, 34*(6), 621–639. http://doi.org/10.1177/0261927X15587015

BC Interior Health Authority. (2017). *Research ethics board.* Retrieved from www.interiorhealth.ca/AboutUs/ResearchandEthics/Pages/REB.aspx

Beaujot, R. P., & Kerr, D. (2004). *Population change in Canada* (2nd ed.). Don Mills, ON: Oxford University Press.

Beaujot, R., & Kerr, D. (2007). Emerging youth transition patterns in Canada: Opportunities and risks. *PSC Discussion Paper Series, 21*(5), 1–40.

Berg, B. L., & Lune, H. (2014). *Qualitative research methods for the social sciences* (8th ed.). Boston, MA: Pearson.

Bernard, R. H. (2013). *Social research methods: Qualitative and quantitative approaches* (2nd ed.). Thousand Oaks, CA: Sage Publications.

Brown, L., & Strega, S. (2005). Transgressive possibilities. In L. Brown & S. Strega, *Research as resistance: Critical, Indigenous, and anti-oppressive approaches* (pp. 1–18). Toronto, ON: Canadian Scholars' Press.

Brydon-Miller, M. (2001). Research and action: Theory and methods of participatory action research. In D. L. Tolman & M. Brydon-Miller (Eds.), *From subjects to subjectivities: A handbook of interpretive and participatory methods* (pp. 76–89). New York: New York University Press.

Buffam, B. (2011). Can't hold us back! Hip-hop and the racial motility of aboriginal bodies in urban spaces. *Social Identities, 17*(3), 337–350. http://doi.org/10.1080/13504630.2011.570973

Campbell, M., & Gregor, F. (2004). *Mapping social relations: A primer in doing institutional ethnography.* Walnut Creek, CA: AltaMira Press.

Charmaz, K. (2014). *Constructing grounded theory* (2nd ed.). Thousand Oaks, CA: Sage.

Clavel, P., Fox, K., Leo, C., Quan-Haase, A., Saitta, D., & LaDale, W. (2015). Blogging the city: Research, collaboration, and engagement in urban e-planning. Critical notes from a conference. *International Journal of E-Planning Research, 4*(1). http://doi.org/10.4018/ijepr.2015010104

Collins, R. (1998). *The sociology of philosophies: A global theory of intellectual change.* Cambridge, MA: Harvard University Press.

Corbin, J. M., & Strauss, A. L. (2014). *Basics of qualitative research: Techniques and procedures for developing grounded theory* (4th ed.). Thousand Oaks, CA: Sage.

Couper, M. P. (2000). Web surveys: A review of issues and approaches. *Public Opinion Quarterly, 64,* 464–494.

Creswell, J. W. (2013). Steps in conducting a scholarly mixed methods study. *DBER Speaker Series,* paper 48. Retrieved from http://digitalcommons.unl.edu/cgi/viewcontent.cgi?article=1047&context=dberspeakers

Davis, R. E., Couper, M. P., Janz, N. K., Caldwell, C. H., & Resnicow, K. (2010). Interviewer effects in public health surveys. *Health Education Research, 25*(1), 14–26.

Dillman, D. A. (2000). *Mail and Internet surveys: The tailored design method* (2nd ed.). New York: John Wiley.

Dillman, D. A., Smyth, J. D., & Christian, L. M. (2014). *Internet, phone, mail, and mixed-mode surveys: The tailored design method* (4th ed.). Hoboken, NJ: Wiley.

European Court of Justice. (2014). Case No. C-131/12 – Google Spain and Google.

Foucault, M. (1995). *Discipline and punish: The birth of the prison.* (A. Sheridan, Trans.). New York: Vintage Books.

Fortune. (2017, June 27). Mark Zuckerberg: Facebook now has 2 billion users worldwide. Retrieved from http://fortune.com/2017/06/27/mark-zuckerberg-facebook-userbase/

Gans, H. J. (1989). Sociology in America: The discipline and the public American Sociological Association, 1988 presidential address. *American Sociological Review, 54*(1), 1–16.

Garfinkel, H. (1967). *Studies in ethnomethodology.* Englewood Cliffs, NJ: Prentice-Hall.

Geertz, C. (1973). *The interpretation of cultures: Selected essays.* New York: Basic Books.

Giesbrecht, N., Wettlaufer, A., April, N., Asbridge, M., Cukier, S., Mann, R., . . . & Stockwell, T. (2013). *Strategies to reduce alcohol-related harms and costs in Canada: A comparison of provincial policies.* Toronto, ON: Centre for Addictions &

Mental Health. Retrieved from https://dspace.library.uvic.ca/bitstream/handle/1828/4798/Strategies%20to%20Reduce%20Alcohol%20Related%20Harms%20and%20Costs%202013.pdf?sequence=1

Given, L. M. (2008). *The Sage encyclopedia of qualitative research methods*. London: Sage Publications.

Gladwell, M. (2000). *The tipping point: How little things can make a big difference*. Boston: Little, Brown and Company.

Glaser, B. G., & Strauss, A. L. (1967). *The discovery of grounded theory: Strategies for qualitative research*. Chicago, IL: Aldine Publishing Company.

Goel, V. (2014, August 12). As data overflows online, researchers grapple with ethics. *New York Times*. Retrieved from www.nytimes.com/2014/08/13/technology/the-boon-of-online-data-puts-social-science-in-a-quandary.html?_r=0

Goffman, A. (2014). *On the run: Fugitive life in an American city*. Chicago, IL: University of Chicago Press.

Government of Canada, Panel on Research Ethics. (2015). *Research involving the First Nations, Inuit and Métis Peoples of Canada*. In *Tri-Council policy statement: Ethical conduct for research involving humans (TCPS 2)*. Retrieved from www.pre.ethics.gc.ca/eng/policy-politique/initiatives/tcps2-eptc2/chapter9-chapitre9/

Guppy, N., & Gray, G. (2008). *Successful surveys: Research methods and practice* (4th ed.). Toronto, ON: Thomson Nelson.

Ilieva, J., Baron, S., & Healey, N. M. (2006). On-line surveys in international marketing research: Pros and cons. *International Journal of Market Research*, 44(3), 361–376.

Johnson, R. B., Onwuegbuzie, A. J., & Turner, L. A. (2007). Toward a definition of mixed methods research. *Journal of Mixed Methods Research*, 1(2), 112–133. http://doi.org/10.1177/1558689806298224

Kemmis, S., & McTaggart, R. (2008). Participatory action research: Communicative action and the public sphere. In N. K. Denzin & Y. S. Lincoln (Eds.), *Strategies of qualitative inquiry* (pp. 271–330). Thousand Oaks, CA: Sage.

Klockars, C. B. (1988). Rhetoric of community policing. In J. R. Green & S. D. Mastrofski (Eds.), *Community policing: Rhetoric or reality* (pp. 239–258). Westport, CT: Praeger.

Kramer, A. D. I., Guillory, J. E., & Hancock, J. T. (2014). Experimental evidence of massive-scale emotional contagion through social networks. *Proceedings of the National Academy of Sciences of the United States of America*, 111(24), 8788–8790. doi: 10.1073/pnas.1320040111

LeCompte, M. D. (1995). Some notes on power, agenda, and voice: A researcher's personal evolution. In P. L. McLaren & J. M. Giarelli (Eds.), *Critical theory and educational research* (pp. 91–111). Albany, NY: SUNY Press.

Leedy, P. D., & Ormrod, J. E. (2015). *Practical research: Planning and design* (11th ed.). Upper Saddle River, NJ: Pearson.

Lewis-Kraus, G. (2016, January 12). The trials of Alice Goffman. *New York Times Magazine*. Retrieved from www.nytimes.com/2016/01/17/magazine/the-trials-of-alice-goffman.html?_r=1

Lincoln, Y. S., & Guba, E. G. (1985). *Naturalistic inquiry*. Newbury Park, CA: Sage.

Logan, J., & Murdie, R. (2016). Home in Canada? The settlement experiences of Tibetans in Parkdale, Toronto. *Journal of International Migration and Integration*, 17(1), 95–113. http://doi.org/10.1007/s12134-014-0382-0

Lubet, S. (2015, May 26). Ethics on the run. *The New Rambler Review*. Retrieved from https://ssrn.com/abstract=2611742

Luker, K. (2008). *Salsa dancing into the social sciences*. Cambridge, MA: Harvard University Press.

Marx, K. (1938). A workers' inquiry. *The New International*, 4(12), 379–381. Retrieved from www.marxists.org/history/etol/newspape/ni/vol04/no12/marx.htm

Maynard, D. (1991). The diversity of ethnomethodology. *Annual Review of Sociology*, 17(1), 385–418. http://doi.org/10.1146/annurev.soc.17.1.385

Meier, P., Purshouse, R. & Brennan, A. (2009). Policy options for alcohol price regulation: The importance of modeling population heterogeneity. *Addiction*, 105(3), 383–393.

Milgram, S. (1963). Behavioral study of obedience. *The Journal of Abnormal and Social Psychology*, 67(4), 371–378.

Mitra, R., Siva, H., & Kehler, M. (2015). Walk-friendly suburbs for older adults? Exploring the enablers and barriers to walking in a large suburban municipality in Canada. *Journal of Aging Studies*, 35, 10–19. http://doi.org/http://dx.doi.org/10.1016/j.jaging.2015.07.002

Mowat, D., Pullman, D., Mahleka, D., Reading, J., Frank, J., Routledge, M., . . . Stockwell, T. (2015). *The Chief Public Health Officer's report on the state of public health in Canada: 2015*. Ottawa, ON: Public Health Agency of Canada. Retrieved from www.canada.ca/en/public-health/services/publications/chief-public-health-officer-reports-state-public-health-canada/2015-alcohol-consumption-canada.html

Nichols, N. (2014). *Youth work: An institutional ethnography of youth homelessness*. Toronto, ON: University of Toronto Press.

Orr, D., Rimini, M., & van Damme, D. (2015). *Open educational resources: A catalyst for innovation*. Paris: OECD Publishing. Retrieved from http://dx.doi.org/10.1787/9789264247543-en

Palys, T., & Atchinson, C. (2014). *Research decisions: Quantitative, qualitative and mixed-method approaches* (5th ed.). New York: Nelson.

Quan-Haase, A., & Sloan, L. (2017). Introduction to the handbook of social media research methods: Goals, challenges and innovations. In L. Sloan & A. Quan-Haase (Eds.), *The Sage handbook of social media research methods* (pp. 1–9). London: Sage.

Rasmussen Neal, D. (2012). *Social media for academics*. Sawston, UK: Chandos.

Reason, P., & Bradbury, H. (Eds.). (2008). *The Sage handbook of action research: Participative inquiry and practice* (2nd ed.). Thousand Oaks, CA: Sage.

Rose, G. (2008). Using photographs as illustrations in human geography. *Journal of Geography in Higher Education*, 32(1), 151–160.

Schneider, C. J. (2016). Police presentational strategies on Twitter in Canada. *Policing and Society*, 26(2), 129–147. http://doi.org/10.1080/10439463.2014.922085

Sloan, L., & Quan-Haase, A. (Eds.). (2017). *The Sage handbook of social media research methods*. London: Sage.

Smart, R.G. & Mann, R.E. (2000). The impact of programs for high-risk drinkers on population levels of alcohol problems. *Addiction*, 95(1), 37–52.

Smith, D. (1990). *Texts, facts and femininity: Exploring the relations of ruling.* London: Routledge.

Sørnes, J.-O., Hybertsen, I. D., & Browning, L. (2014). Identity challenges in field research: Three stories. *Journal of Applied Communication Research, 43*(1), 136–140. http://doi.org/10.1080/00909882.2014.983141

Social Sciences and Humanities Research Council of Canada (SSHRC). (2016, August 19). Definitions of terms, Aboriginal research. Retrieved from www.sshrc-crsh.gc.ca/funding-financement/programs-programmes/definitions-eng.aspx#a0

Statista. (2017, March 2). Number of Facebook users 2018. Retrieved from www.statista.com/statistics/282364/number-of-facebook-users-in-canada/

Statistics Canada. (2015). *Aboriginal peoples: Fact sheet for Canada.* Retrieved from www.statcan.gc.ca/pub/89-656-x/89-656-x2015001-eng.htm

Statistics Canada. (2017, January 27). Census program. Retrieved from www12.statcan.gc.ca/census-recensement/index-eng.cfm

Steers, M.-L. N., Wickham, R. E., & Acitelli, L. K. (2014). Seeing everyone else's highlight reels: How Facebook usage is linked to depressive symptoms. *Journal of Social and Clinical Psychology, 33*(8), 701–731.

Stockwell, T., Auld, C., Zhao, J., & Martin, G. (2012). Does minimum pricing reduce alcohol consumption? The experience of a Canadian province. *Addiction, 107*(5), 912–920.

Sullivan, L. (2009). Participant observation. In L. Sullivan (Ed.), *The Sage glossary of the social and behavioral sciences* (p. 372). Thousand Oaks, CA: Sage.

UNESCO. (2002). *Forum on the impact of open courseware for higher education in developing countries.* Paris, France. Retrieved from http://unesdoc.unesco.org/images/0012/001285/128515e.pdf

Vitak, J. (2017). Facebook. In L. Sloan & A. Quan-Haase (Eds.), *The Sage handbook of social media research methods* (pp. 627–644). London: Sage.

Wang, C., Burris, M. A., & Ping, X. Y. (1996). Chinese village women as visual anthropologists: A participatory approach to reaching policymakers. *Social Science and Medicine, 42*(10), 1391–1400. http://doi.org/10.1016/0277-9536(95)00287-1

Wellman, B. (1998). Doing it ourselves: The SPSS manual as sociology's most influential recent book. In D. Clawson (Ed.), *Required reading: Sociology's most influential books* (pp. 71–78). Amherst: MA: University of Massachusetts Press.

Wiebe, S. M. (2016). Guardians of the environment in Canada's Chemical Valley. *Citizenship Studies, 20*(1), 18–33.

Yang, S., Quan-Haase, A., & Rannenberg, K. (2016). The changing public sphere on Twitter: Network structure, elites, and topics of the #righttobeforgotten. *New Media & Society.* http://doi.org/1461444816651409

Chapter 3

Anderson, E. (1999). *Code of the street: Decency, violence, and the moral life of the inner city.* New York: W. W. Norton.

Antonio, A., & Tuffley, D. (2014). The gender digital divide in developing countries. *Future Internet, 6*(4), 673–687.

Atkinson, M. (2009). Parkour, anarcho-environmentalism, and poiesis. *Journal of Sport and Social Issues, 33*(2), 169–194.

Baker, S., Waycott, J., Pedell, S., Hoang, T., & Ozanne, E. (2016, October). Older people and social participation: From touchscreens to virtual realities. In *Proceedings of the International Symposium on Interactive Technology and Ageing Populations* (pp. 34–43). doi:10.1145/2996267.2996271

Berger, J. (1972). *Ways of seeing.* Harmondsworth, UK: Penguin.

Bourdieu, P. (1984). *Distinction: A social critique of the judgement of taste.* Cambridge, MA: Harvard University Press.

Bourdieu, P. (2011). The forms of capital. In I. Szeman & T. Kaposy (Eds.), *Cultural theory: An anthology* (pp. 81–93). Toronto, ON: John Wiley & Sons. (Original work published 1986)

Brown, A. (1999). *The Darwin wars: How stupid genes became selfish gods.* New York: Simon & Schuster.

Brown, R. (1976). Reference in memorial tribute to Eric Lenneberg. *Cognition, 4*(2), 125–153.

The Canadian Press. (2010, June 2). 16 million Canadians on Facebook: Report. *The Globe and Mail.* Retrieved from www.theglobeandmail.com/technology/16-million-canadians-on-facebook-report/article1372008/

Delgado, R., & Stefancic, J. (2012). *Critical race theory: An introduction* (2nd ed.). New York: New York University Press.

Doolittle, R. (2017, February 3). Unfounded: Why police dismiss 1 in 5 sexual assault claims as baseless. *The Globe and Mail.* Retrieved from www.theglobeandmail.com/news/investigations/unfounded-sexual-assault-canada-main/article33891309/

Engerman, S. L. (2000). Review of *The Protestant ethic and the spirit of capitalism* by Max Weber. *EH Net Economic History Services.* Retrieved from https://eh.net/book_reviews/the-protestant-ethic-and-the-spirit-of-capitalism/

Gentilcore, D. (2010). *Pomodoro!: A history of the tomato in Italy.* New York: Columbia University Press.

Haight, M., & Quan-Haase, A. (2015). Digital inclusion project: Findings and implications from a Canadian perspective. Benton Foundation [Report]. Retrieved from www.benton.org/initiatives/digital-inclusion-project

Harvey, D. (2009). The art of rent: Globalisation, monopoly and the commodification of culture. *Socialist Register, 38,* 93–110.

Hird, M. (2011). *Sociology of science: A critical Canadian introduction.* Toronto, ON: Oxford University Press.

Hirsch, E. D., Jr. (1988). *Cultural literacy: What every American needs to know.* New York: Vintage.

Kemp, S. (2014, August 8). Global social media users pass 2 billion. *We Are Social* [Blog post]. Retrieved from https://wearesocial.com/uk/blog/2014/08/global-social-media-users-pass-2-billion

Kemp, S. (2015, January 22). Global digital & social media stats: 2015. *Social Media Today.* Retrieved from www.socialmediatoday.com/content/global-digital-social-media-stats-2015

Kubrin, C. E. (2005). Gangstas, thugs, and hustlas: Identity and the code of the street in rap music. *Social Problems, 52*(3), 360–378.

Larson, B. (2006). The social resonance of competitive and progressive evolutionary metaphors. *AIBS Bulletin, 56*(12): 997–1004.

Larson, B. J., & Brauer, F. (Eds.). (2009). *The art of evolution: Darwin, Darwinisms, and visual culture.* Lebanon, NJ: University Press of New England.

McIntosh, P. (1989, July/August). White privilege: Unpacking the invisible knapsack. *Peace and Freedom Magazine,* 10–12. Retrieved from www.soaw.org/resources/anti-opp-resources/108-race/696

Merton, R. K. (1973). The normative structure of science. In Merton, R. K., *The sociology of science: Theoretical and empirical investigations* (pp. 267–278). Chicago, IL: University of Chicago Press. (Original work published 1942)

Murdock, George P. (1945). The common denominator of culture. In R. Linton (Ed.), *The science of man in the world crisis* (pp. 123–142). New York: Columbia University Press.

Oxford English Dictionary. (2016). New words list December 2016. Retrieved from http://public.oed.com/the-oed-to-day/recent-updates-to-the-oed/december-2016-update/new-words-list-december-2016/#new_words

Paul, D. (2003). Darwin, social Darwinism and eugenics. In M. J. S. Hodge & G. Radick (Eds.), *The Cambridge Companion to Darwin* (pp. 214–239). Cambridge: Cambridge University Press.

Quan-Haase, A., & Wellman, B. (2006). Hyperconnected network: Computer-mediated community in a high-tech organization. In C. Heckscher & P. Adler (Eds.), *The firm as a collaborative community: Reconstructing trust in the knowledge economy* (pp. 281–333). London: Oxford University Press.

Quan-Haase, A., Martin, K., & Schreurs, K. (2014). Not all on the same page: E-book adoption and technology exploration by seniors. *Information Research, 19*(2). Retrieved from www.informationr.net/ir/19-2/paper622.html#

Quan-Haase, A., Martin, K., & Schreurs, K. (2016). Interviews with digital seniors: Challenges and opportunities of everyday ICT use in the third age. *Information, Communication & Society.*

Rogers, E. M. (1999). Georg Simmel's concept of the stranger and intercultural communication research. *Communication Theory, 9*(1), 58–74.

Ruse, M. (2000). Darwin and the philosophers. In R. Creath & J. Maienschein (Eds.), *Biology and epistemology* (pp. 3–26). Cambridge: Cambridge University Press.

Shapin, S. (1995). Here and everywhere: Sociology of scientific knowledge. *Annual Review of Sociology, 21*, 289–321. Retrieved from www.jstor.org/stable/2083413

Simmel, G. (1921). The sociological significance of the stranger. In R. E. Park & E. W. Burgess (Eds.), *Introduction to the science of sociology* (pp. 322–327). Chicago, IL: University of Chicago Press.

Simmel, G. (1950). *The sociology of Georg Simmel.* (K. Wolff, Ed. and Trans.). New York: Free Press.

Statista. (2017a). *Distribution of internet users in Canada from 2014 to 2019, by gender.* Retrieved from www.statista.com/statistics/482438/canada-online-user-distribution-gender/

Statista. (2017b). *Internet usage rate worldwide in 2015, by gender and region.* Retrieved from www.statista.com/statistics/491387/gender-distribution-of-internet-users-region/

Statistics Canada. (2013). Canadian Internet use survey, Internet use, by age group, Internet activity, sex, level of education and household income, occasional. CANSIM 358-0153 [Table]. Retrieved from www5.statcan.gc.ca/cansim/pick-choisir?lang=eng&p2=33&id=3580153.

Stebbins, R. A. (1996). *The barbershop singer: Inside the social world of a musical hobby.* Toronto, ON: University of Toronto Press.

Weber, M. (1930). *The Protestant ethic and the spirit of capitalism.* (T. Parsons, Trans.) New York: Penguin. (Original work published 1905)

Ziman, J. (2000). Postacademic science: Constructing knowledge with networks and norms. In U. Segerstråle (Ed.), *Beyond the science wars: The missing discourse about science and society* (pp. 135–154). Albany: State University of New York Press.

Chapter 4

Anthis, K. S. (2002). On the calamity theory of growth: The relationship between stressful life events and changes in identity over time. *Identity: An International Journal of Theory and Research, 2*(3), 229–240.

Bailey, J. R., & Yost, J. H. (2001). Role theory: Foundations, extensions, and application. In E. F. Borgatta, & R. J. V. Montgomery (Eds.), *Encyclopaedia of Sociology* (2nd ed., pp. 2420–2425). New York: Macmillan Reference USA.

BBC. (2016, February 6). Cosmetic surgery ops on the rise. Retrieved from www.bbc.com/news/health-35501487

Bierman, K. L., Domitrovich, C. E., Nix, R. L., Gest, S. D., Welsh, J. A., Greenberg, M. T., . . . Gill, S. (2008). Promoting academic and social-emotional school readiness: The Head Start REDI program. *Child Development, 79*(6), 1802–1817.

Bourdieu, P. (1973). Cultural reproduction and social reproduction. In R. K. Brown (Ed.), *Knowledge, education, and cultural change: Papers in the sociology of education* (pp. 56–68). London: Tavistock Publications Ltd.

boyd, danah. (2006). Friends, Friendsters, and top 8: Writing community into being on social network sites. *First Monday: Peer-Reviewed Journal on the Internet, 11*(12). Retrieved from http://firstmonday.org/htbin/cgiwrap/bin/ojs/index.php/fm/article/view/1418/1336

CBC Digital Archives. (2008). A long-awaited apology for residential schools [Broadcast]. Retrieved from www.cbc.ca/archives/entry/a-long-awaited-apology-for-residential-schools

Cooley, C. H. (1964). *Human nature and the social order.* New York: Schocken Books. Originally published 1902.

Corsaro, W. A., & Eder, D. (1990). Children's peer cultures. *Annual Review of Sociology, 16*(1), 197–220. doi: 10.1146/annurev.so.16.080190.001213

Coser, R. L. (1975). The complexity of roles as a seedbed of individual autonomy. In L. A. Coser (Ed.), *The idea of social structure: Papers in honor of Robert K. Merton* (pp. 237–262). New York: Harcourt Brace Jovanovich.

Crawford, C., & Greaves, E. (2015). *Ethnic minorities substantially more likely to go to university than their White British peers.* London: Institute for Fiscal Studies. Retrieved from www.ifs.org.uk/publications/8042

Davies, S., & Guppy, N. (2006). *The schooled society: An introduction to the sociology of education.* Don Mills, ON: Oxford University Press.

DeGroot, J. M., & Vik, T. A. (2017). "We were not prepared to tell people yet": Confidentiality breaches and boundary turbulence on Facebook. *Computers in Human Behavior, 70*, 351–359. https://doi.org/10.1016/j.chb.2017.01.016

Dews, C. L. B., & Law, C. L. (1995). *This fine place so far from home: Voices of academics from the working class.* Philadelphia: Temple University Press.

Ditchburn, J. (2015). *"Because it's 2015": Trudeau forms Canada's 1st gender-balanced cabinet.* Retrieved www.cbc.ca/news/politics/canada-trudeau-liberal-government-cabinet-1.3304590

Duxbury, L., & Higgins, C. (2012). *Revisiting work-life issues in Canada: The 2012 national study on balancing work and caregiving in Canada [report one].* Ottawa, ON: Sprott School of Business, Carleton University.

Entertainment Software Association of Canada. (2015). *Essential facts about the Canadian video game industry.* Retrieved from http://theesa.ca/wp-content/uploads/2015/11/ESAC_2015_Booklet_Version02_14_Digital.pdf

Gecas, V. (2001). Socialization. In E. F. Borgatta & R. J. V. Montgomery, *Encyclopedia of Sociology* (2nd ed., pp. 2855–2864). New York: Macmillan Reference USA.

Giddens, A. (1991). *Modernity and self-identity: Self and society in the late modern age.* Stanford, CA: Stanford University Press.

Goffman, E. (1959). *The presentation of self in everyday life.* Garden City, NY: Doubleday.

Goffman, E. (1961). *Asylums: Essays on the social situation of mental patients and other inmates.* Garden City, NY: Anchor Books.

Government of Canada. (2016, April 20). Hours of work. Retrieved from www.esdc.gc.ca/en/reports/labour_standards/hours_work.page

Gurdus, E. (2017). Hiring slows in February as workers flock from the Rust Belt: LinkedIn. Retrieved March 9, 2017, from www.cnbc.com/2017/03/08/hiring-slows-in-february-as-workers-flock-from-the-rust-belt-linkedin.html

Hand, M. (2017). Visuality in social media: Researching images, circulations and practices. In L. Sloan & A. Quan-Haase (Eds.), *Handbook of social media research methods* (pp. 215–231). London: Sage.

Herring, S. C., & Kapidzic, S. (2015). Teens, gender, and self-presentation in social media. In J. D. Wright, (Ed.), *International Encyclopedia of the Social & Behavioral Sciences* (2nd ed., pp. 146–152). Oxford: Elsevier. http://doi.org/10.1016/B978-0-08-097086-8.64108-9

Higgins, E. T. (1987). Self-discrepancy: A theory relating self and affect. *Psychological Review, 94*(3), 319–340.

Hogan, B. (2010). The presentation of self in the age of social media: Distinguishing performances and exhibitions online. *Bulletin of Science, Technology & Society, 30*(6), 377–386.

Klassen, T. R., & Dwyer, J. A. (2016). *How to succeed at university (and get a great job!).* Vancouver, BC: UBC Press.

Lareau, A. (2000). *Home advantage: Social class and parental intervention in elementary education* (2nd ed.). Lanham, MD: Rowman & Littlefield Publishers.

Lehmann, W. (2014). Habitus transformation and hidden injuries: Successful working-class university students. *Sociology of Education, 87*(1), 1–15.

Levine, K. J., & Hoffner, C. A. (2006). Adolescents' conceptions of work: What is learned from different sources during anticipatory socialization? *Journal of Adolescent Research, 21*(6), 647–669. doi:10.1177/0743558406293963

Logan, T. (2015). Settler colonialism in Canada and the Métis. *Journal of Genocide Research, 17*(4), 433–452.

Lubbers, M., Jaspers, E., & Ultee, W. (2009). Primary and secondary socialization impacts on support for same-sex marriage after legalization in the Netherlands. *Journal of Family Issues, 30*(12), 1714–1745. http://doi.org/10.1177/0192513X09334267

Manyika, J., Chui, M., Bughin, J., Dobbs, R., Bisson, P., & Marrs. (2013). *Disruptive technologies: Advances that will transform life, business, and the global economy.* McKinsey Global Institute. Retrieved from www.mckinsey.com/business-functions/digital-mckinsey/our-insights/disruptive- technologies

Marcia, J. E. (1966). Development and validation of ego-identity status. *Journal of Personality and Social Psychology, 3*(5), 551–558.

Marwick, A. E., & boyd, d. (2011a). "I tweet honestly, I tweet passionately": Twitter users, context collapse, and the imagined audience. *New Media & Society, 13*(1), 114–133. doi:10.1177/1461444810365313

Marwick, A., & boyd, d. (2011b). To see and be seen: Celebrity practice on twitter. *Convergence, 17*(2), 139–158. doi:10.1177/1354856510394539

McCrae, R. R., & Costa, P. T. (1990). *Personality in adulthood.* New York: Guilford Press.

McKinsey & Company. (2014). *Offline and falling behind: Barriers to Internet adoption.* Retrieved from www.mckinsey.com/~/media/McKinsey/dotcom/client_service/HighTech/PDFs/Offline_and_falling_behind_Barriers_to_Internet_adoption.ashx

Michael, J. (2015). It's really not hip to be a hipster: Negotiating trends and authenticity in the cultural field. *Journal of Consumer Culture, 15*(2), 163–182. http://doi.org/10.1177/1469540513493206

Miller, J. R. (2012). Residential schools. In *The Canadian Encyclopedia.* Retrieved from www.thecanadianencyclopedia.ca/en/article/residential-schools/

Parsons, T. (2007). The American family: Its relations to personality and the social structure. In T. Parsons & R. F. Bales (Eds.), *Family socialization and interaction processes* (pp. 3–34). Oxon: Routledge.

Parsons, T., & Bales, R. F. (2007). *Family socialization and interaction processes.* Oxon: Routledge.

Pater, J. A, Miller, A. D., & Mynatt, E. D. (2015). This digital life: A neighborhood-based study of adolescents' lives online. *Proceedings of the ACM CHI'15 Conference on Human Factors in Computing Systems, 1,* 2305–2314. http://doi.org/10.1145/2702123.2702534

Primack, B. A., Shensa, A., Sidani, J. E., Whaite, E. O., Lin, L. y, Colditz, J. B., Radovic, A., & Miller, E. (2017). Social media use and perceived social isolation among young adults in the U.S. *American Journal of Preventive Medicine, 4,* 1–8.

Rainie, L., & Wellman, B. (2012). *Future of the networked.* London: Reed Business Information UK.

The Renfrew Center Foundation. (2016). *"Barefaced & beautiful presents: Reflections on being real" campaign encourages everyone to share make-up free photos.* Retrieved from http://renfrewcenter.com/news/%E2%80%98barefaced-beautiful-presents-reflections-being-real%E2%80%99-campaign-encourages-everyone-share-make-f

Saltz, J. (2014, January 26). Art at arm's length: A history of the selfie. *Vulture*. Retrieved from www.vulture.com/2014/01/history-of-the-selfie.html

Saskatchewan Archives Board. (n.d.). *Letter to J. H. McKechnie, Deputy Minister of Education from E. J. Brandt, Superintendent of Schools.*

Schmidt, E., & Rosenberg, J. (2014). *How Google works.* New York: Grand Central Publishing.

Sedikides, C., & Spencer, S. (2007). *The self.* New York: Psychology Press.

Stryker, S. (2001). Identity theory. In E. F. Borgatta & R. J. V. Montgomery (Eds.), *Encyclopedia of sociology* (2nd ed., pp. 1253–1258). New York: Macmillan Reference USA.

Sullivan, O., & Katz-Gerro, T. (2007). The omnivore thesis revisited: Voracious cultural consumers. *European Sociological Review, 23*(2), 123–137.

Tepperman, L., & Upenieks, L. (2016). *Social control.* Don Mills, ON: Oxford University Press.

Turkle, S. (2011). *Alone together: Why we expect more from technology and less from each other.* New York: Basic Books.

The UN Refugee Agency. (2017). *Syria regional refugee response.* Geneva. Retrieved from http://data.unhcr.org/syrianrefugees/regional.php

Utz, S. (2016). Is LinkedIn making you more successful? The informational benefits derived from public social media. *New Media & Society, 18*(11), 2685–2702.

Wachter, A. (2016, March 7). Do you hate your body? *Huff Post The Blog.* Retrieved from www.huffingtonpost.com/andrea-wachter/do-you-hate-your-body_1_b_9384854.html

Vitak, J., Lampe, C., Gray, R., & Ellison, N. (2012). Why won't you be my Facebook friend? Strategies for managing context collapse in the workplace. *Proceedings of the 2012 iConference* (pp. 555–557). *New York:* ACM. doi:10.1145/2132176.2132286

Chapter 5

Abramovich, E. (2005). Childhood sexual abuse as a risk factor for subsequent involvement in sex work: A review of empirical findings. *Journal of Psychology & Human Sexuality, 17*(1/2), 131–146.

Allen, M. (2016, July 20). *Police-reported crime statistics, 2015.* Retrieved from www.statcan.gc.ca/pub/85-002-x/2016001/article/14642-eng.htm

Associated Press. (2015, October 5). Toronto's Trump hotel hit by credit card hackers. *The Star (Toronto).* Retrieved from www.thestar.com/business/2015/10/05/torontos-trump-hotel-hit-by-credit-card-hackers.html

Bahadur, N. (2015, January 15). On actress Caitlin Stasey's Herself.com, women pose nude to reclaim their bodies. *The Huffington Post.* Retrieved from www.huffingtonpost.ca/entry/herself-empowering-women-caitlin-stasey_n_6478836

Bamgbose, O. (2002). Teenage prostitution and the future of the female adolescent in Nigeria. *International Journal of Offender Therapy and Comparative Criminology, 46*(5), 569–585.

Beran, T., Mishna, F., McInroy, L. B., & Shariff, S. (2015). Children's experiences of cyberbullying: A Canadian national study. *Children & Schools, 37*(4), 207–214.

Bernstein, E. (2007). Sex work for the middle classes. *Sexualities, 10*(4), 473–488.

Boyce, J. (2015, July 22). *Police-reported crime statistics in Canada, 2014* (Statistics Canada, catalogue no. 85-002-x). Retrieved from www.statcan.gc.ca/pub/85-002-x/2015001/article/14211-eng.htm

Brandon, J. (2014, January). Why your business might be a perfect target for hackers. *Inc.* Retrieved from www.inc.com/magazine/201312/john-brandon/hackers-target-small-business.html

Brennan, S. (2011). *Violent victimization of Aboriginal women in the Canadian provinces, 2009* (Statistics Canada, catalogue no. 85-002-x). Retrieved from www.statcan.gc.ca/pub/85-002-x/2011001/article/11439-eng.pdf

Brzozowski, J-A., Taylor-Butts, A. & Johnson, S. (2006). Victimization and offending among the Aboriginal population in Canada. *Juristat: Canadian Centre for Justice Statistics, 26*(3) (Statistics Canada, catalogue no.85-002-XIE). Retrieved from www.statcan.gc.ca/pub/85-002-x/85-002-x2006003-eng.pdf

Carlen, P. (1990). *Alternatives to women's imprisonment.* Milton Keynes, UK: Open University Press.

Cass, A. I. (2007). Routine activities and sexual assault: An analysis of individual- and school-level factors. *Violence and Victims, 22*(3), 350–366.

Clemmer, D. (1940). *The prison community.* New York: Holt, Rinehart, & Winston.

Cohen, S. (1972). *Folk devils and moral panics: The creation of the mods and rockers.* London: MacGibbon & Kee .

Davis, K. (1937). The sociology of prostitution. *American Sociological Review, 2*(5), 744–755.

Decker, M. R., Pearson, E., Illangasekare, S. L., Clark, E., & Sherman, S. G. (2013). Violence against women in sex work and HIV risk implications differ qualitatively by perpetrator. *BMC Public Health, 13*(1), 876. doi:10.1186/1471-2458-13-876

Divon, J. (2015, February 2). Cyberattacks an ongoing threat to Canadian small businesses. *The Globe and Mail.* Retrieved from www.theglobeandmail.com/report-on-business/small-business/sb-managing/cyberattacks-an-ongoing-threat-to-canadian-small-businesses/article22653793/

Elias, N. (1978). *The history of manners: The civilizing process* (Vol. 1). New York: Pantheon.

Foucault, M. (2012). *Discipline and punish: The birth of the prison.* (A. Sheridan, Trans.). New York: Vintage. (Original work published 1977)

Gannon, M., & Mihorean, K. (2005). *Criminal victimization in Canada, 2004.* Ottawa, ON: Canadian Centre for Justice Statistics.

Government of Canada. (2015, March 3). Shopping online. *Get cyber safe.* Retrieved from www.getcybersafe.gc.ca/cnt/rsks/nln-ctvts/shppng-nln-en.aspx

Government of Canada, Office of the Correctional Investigator. (2013). *Backgrounder: Aboriginal offenders: A critical situation.* Retrieved from www.oci-bec.gc.ca/cnt/rpt/oth-aut/oth-aut20121022info-eng.aspx

Grimes, G. A., Hough, M. G., Mazur, E., & Signorella, M. L. (2010). Older adults' knowledge of internet hazards. *Educational Gerontology, 36*(3) 173–192.

Heath, Nicole M., Lynch, S. M., Fritch, A. M., & Wong, M. M. (2013). Rape myth acceptance impacts the reporting of rape to the police: A study of incarcerated women. *Violence against Women, 19*(9), 1065–1078.

Herron, J. (n.d.). *5 ways thieves steal credit card data.* Retrieved from www.bankrate.com/finance/credit-cards/5-ways-thieves-steal-credit-card-data-1.aspx.

Hirschi, T. (2002). *Causes of delinquency.* New Brunswick, NJ: Transaction Publishers. (Original work published 1969)

Holfeld, B., & Leadbeater, B. J. (2015). The nature and frequency of cyber bullying behaviors and victimization experiences in young Canadian children. *Canadian Journal of School Psychology, 30*(2), 116–135.

Jamshed, Z. (2016, January 8). From "cow" to cover girl, model Winnie Harlow is changing beauty standards. *CNN.* Retrieved from www.cnn.com/2016/01/06/fashion/winnie-harlow-interview-model-qa/index.html

Jennings, W. G., Higgins, G. E., Tewksbury, R., Gover, A. R., & Piquero, A. R. (2010). A longitudinal assessment of the victim–offender overlap. *Journal of Interpersonal Violence, 25*(12), 2147–2174.

Jessica's Law Now blog. (2011). *About predators and treating sexual abusers.* Retrieved from https://jessicaslawnow.wordpress.com/about-predators-and-treating-sexual-abusers/

Lind, D., & Lopez, G. (2015, May 20). 16 theories for why crime plummeted in the US. *Vox.* Retrieved from www.vox.com/2015/2/13/8032231/crime-drop

Litwiller, B. J., & Brausch, A. M. (2013). Cyber bullying and physical bullying in adolescent suicide: The role of violent behavior and substance use. *Journal of Youth and Adolescence, 42*(5), 675–684.

Mahony, T. H. (2011). *Women in Canada: A gender-based statistical report* (Statistics Canada, catalogue no. 89-503-x). Retrieved from www.statcan.gc.ca/pub/89-503-x/89-503-x2010001-eng.pdf

Makin, K. (2013, October 5). How Canada's sex-assault laws violate rape victims. *The Globe and Mail.* Retrieved from www.theglobeandmail.com/news/national/how-canadas-sex-assault-laws-violate-rape-victims/article14705289/?page=all

McClanahan, S. F., McClelland, G. M., Abram, K. M., & Teplin, L. A. (1999). Pathways into prostitution among female jail detainees and their implications for mental health services. *Psychiatric services, 50*(12), 1606–1613.

McKnight, Z. (2015, July 31). The real reason crime is falling so fast. *Maclean's.* Retrieved from www.macleans.ca/society/the-real-reason-crime-is-falling-so-fast/

Messmer, E. (2014, May 28). 10 IT security risks that small businesses can't afford to ignore. *Network World.* Retrieved from www.networkworld.com/article/2358151/network-security/10-it-security-risks-that-small-businesses-can-t-afford-to-ignore.html

Mulvey, L. (1975, August). Visual pleasure and narrative cinema. *Screen, 16*(3), 6–18.

Mustaine, E. E., & Tewksbury, R. (2000). Comparing the lifestyles of victims, offenders, and victim-offenders: A routine activity theory assessment of similarities and differences for criminal incident participants. *Sociological Focus, 33*(3), 339–362.

Myhill, A., & Allen, J. (2002). *Rape and sexual assault of women: The extent and nature of the problem.* London: Home Office.

Pepler, D., Jiang, D, Craig, W., & Connolly, J. (2008). Developmental trajectories of bullying and associated factors. *Child Development, 79*(2), 325–338.

Pérez, M. Z. (2014, August 7). Fat activists take body acceptance to the beach. *Colorlines.* Retrieved from www.colorlines.com/articles/fat-activists-take-body-acceptance-beach

Perreault, S. (2015, November). *Criminal victimization in Canada, 2014* (Statistics Canada, catalogue no. 85-002-x). Retrieved from www.statcan.gc.ca/pub/85-002-x/2015001/article/14241-eng.htm

Perreault, S., & Brennan, S. (2010). *Criminal victimization in Canada, 2009* (Statistics Canada, catalogue no. 85-002-x). Retrieved from www.statcan.gc.ca/pub/85-002-x/2010002/article/11340-eng.htm

Pinker, S. (2011). *The better angels of our nature: The decline of violence in history and its causes.* London: Penguin UK.

Porteus, F. L. (2015, February 5). A digital beauty revolution: How the internet has bred a culture of women defining attractiveness on their own terms. *Bustle.* Retrieved from www.bustle.com/articles/62409-a-digital-beauty-revolution-how-the-internet-has-bred-a-culture-of-women-defining-attractiveness-on

Schur, E. M. (1965). *Crimes without victims: Deviant behaviour and public policy: Abortion, homosexuality, drug addiction.* Englewood Cliffs, NJ: Prentice Hall.

Sinha, M. (Ed.). (2013). *Measuring violence against women: Statistical trends* (Statistics Canada, catalogue no. 85-002-x). Retrieved from www.statcan.gc.ca/pub/85-002-x/2013001/article/11766-eng.pdf

Smart, C. (1991). *Feminism and the power of law.* New York: Routledge.

Southard Ospina, M. (n.d.). *Redefining fat* [Video]. Retrieved from http://stylelikeu.com/the-whats-underneath-project-2/marie-southard-ospina/

Statistics Canada. (2017, March 3). Canada's crime rate: Two decades of decline. *The Daily.* Retrieved from www.statcan.gc.ca/pub/11-630-x/11-630-x2015001-eng.htm

StyleLikeU. (n.d.). *True style is self-acceptance* [Media kit]. Retrieved from http://stylelikeu.com/wp-content/uploads/2016/02/slu-media-kit.pdf?x11311

Sutherland, E. H. (1939). *Principles of criminology.* Philadelphia: Lippincott.

Taylor, T. J., Peterson, D., Esbensen, F. A., & Freng, A. (2007). Gang membership as a risk factor for adolescent violent victimization. *Journal of Research in Crime and Delinquency, 44*(4), 351–380.

Toby, J. (1957). Social disorganization and stake in conformity: Complementary factors in the predatory behavior of hoodlums. *Journal of Criminal Law, Criminology and Police Science, 48*(1), 12–17.

United Nations Office on Drugs and Crime. (1998). *Financial havens, banking secrecy and money laundering.* Retrieved from www.imolin.org/imolin/finhaeng.html

Viuker, S. (2015, January 21). Cybercrime and hacking are even bigger worries for small business owners. *The Guardian.* Retrieved from www.theguardian.com/business/2015/jan/21/cyber security-small-business-thwarting-hackers-obama-cameron

Chapter 6

Association of Universities & Colleges of Canada. (2011). *Trends in higher education: Volume 1—Enrolment.* Ottawa, ON: The Association of Universities and Colleges of Canada.

Atler, D. A., Stikel, T., Chong, A., & Henry, D. (2011). Lesson from Canada's universal care: Socially disadvantaged patients use more health services, still have poorer health. *Health Affairs, 30*(2), 274–283.

Balakrishnan, A. (2016, December 5). *Amazon just revealed a new plan for revolutionizing how people buy groceries.* Retrieved from www.cnbc.com/2016/12/05/no-waiting-at-the-register-new-amazon-go-store-bills-everything-to-your-amazon-account.html

Baranowski, T., Cullen, K. W., Nicklas, T., Thompson, D., & Baranowski, J. (2003). Are current health behavioral change models helpful in guiding prevention of weight gain efforts? *Obesity Research, 11*(S10), 23S–43S.

Benoit, K. (2017). *Federal budget 2017: What Indigenous groups are looking for.* Retrieved from www.cbc.ca/news/indigenous/federal-budget-2017-indigenous-expectations-1.4034867

Berg, M. (1994). *The age of manufactures, 1700–1820: Industry, innovation and work in Britain* (2nd ed.). London: Routledge.

Booske, B, Athens, J., Kindig, D., Park, H., & Remington, P. (2010). *Different perspectives for assigning weights to determinants of health.* County Health Rankings Working Paper. Retrieved from www.countyhealthrankings.org/sites/default/files/differentPerspectivesForAssigningWeightsToDeterminantsOfHealth.pdf

Boudreau, D. J., Cassell, E.J., & Fuks, A. (2007). A healing curriculum. *Medical Education, 41*, 1193–1201.

Bourdieu, P. (1986). The forms of capital. In J. Richardson (Ed.), *Handbook of theory and research for the sociology of education* (pp. 241–258). New York: Greenwood.

Brayne, S., & Newman, K. (2013). Downward mobility. In V. Smith (Ed.), *Sociology of work: An encyclopedia* (pp. 195–198). Thousand Oaks, CA: Sage Reference.

Breen, R. (2005). Foundations of a neo-Weberian class analysis. In E. O. Wright (Ed.), *Approaches to class analysis* (pp. 31–50). Cambridge, UK: Cambridge University Press.

Brickman, L. (2017, March 22). *Three commandments for online activism.* Retrieved from www.forbes.com/sites/laurabrickman/2017/03/22/three-commandments-for-online-activism/

Bushnik, T. (2016). *The health of girls and women in Canada: Table 1.* Statistics Canada. Retrieved from www.statcan.gc.ca/pub/89-503-x/2015001/article/14324-eng.htm

Canadian Council on Social Development. (2001, October). *Defining and re-defining poverty: A CCSD perspective.* Retrieved from www.ccsd.ca/index.php?option=com_content&view=article&id=112&Itemid=170&lang=en

Canadian Education Statistics Council. (2010). *Education indicators in Canada: An international perspective, 2010* (Statistics Canada, catalogue no. 81-604-X). Retrieved from www.statcan.gc.ca/pub/81-604-x/81-604-x2010001-eng.pdf

The Canadian Press. (2017, March 18). *Ottawa warned about job losses that could stem from automation.* Retrieved from www.cbc.ca/news/business/job-automation-federal-government-1.4031206

CBC News. (2016, November 15). *Food bank use on the rise in Canada, with "drastic" surges in Nova Scotia, territories.* Retrieved from www.cbc.ca/news/canada/food-bank-report-2016-1.3850897

CBC News. (2017, March 22). *Federal budget 2017: Highlights of Bill Morneau's 2nd budget.* Retrieved from www.cbc.ca/news/politics/federal-budget-highlights-2017-1.4032898

Centre for Addiction and Mental Health (CAMH). (2016, December 7). *Nearly one in five young Ontario adults shows problematic use of electronic devices.* Retrieved from www.camh.ca/en/hospital/about_camh/newsroom/news_releases_media_advisories_and_backgrounders/current_year/Pages/Nearly-one-in-five-young-Ontario-adults-shows-problematic-use-of-electronic-devices.aspx

Centre for the Study of Living Standards. (2012). *Aboriginal labour market performance in Canada: 2007–2011.* Retrieved from www.csls.ca/reports/csls2012-04.pdf.

Charlebois, S., Tapon, F., von Massow, M., van Duren, E., Pinto, W., & Moraghan, R. (2012, December). *Food price index 2013: University of Guelph economic brief.* Retrieved from www.uoguelph.ca/cpa/Food-Index-2013.pdf

Chen, W., Boase, J., & Wellman, B. (2002). The global villagers: Comparing Internet users and uses around the world. In B. Wellman & C. Haythornthwaite (Eds.), *The Internet in everyday life* (pp. 74–113). Oxford: Blackwell.

Davis, K., & Moore, W. E. (1945). Some principles of stratification. *American Sociological Review, 10*(2), 242–249.

Ferrao, V. (2010). Paid work. In Statistics Canada, *Women in Canada: A gender-based statistical report* (6th ed., Statistics Canada, catalogue no. 89-503-X). Retrieved from www.statcan.gc.ca/pub/89-503-x/2010001/article/11387-eng.pdf

First Mile. (n.d.). *First Mile developments.* Retrieved from http://firstmile.ca/

Food Banks Canada. (2016). *HungerCount 2016: A comprehensive report on hunger and food bank use in Canada, and recommendations for change.* Toronto, ON: Food Banks Canada.

Gaetz, S., Donaldson, J., Richter, T., & Gulliver, T. (2013). *The state of homelessness in Canada 2013.* Toronto, ON: Canadian Homelessness Research Network.

Gatchel, R. J., Peng, Y. B., Peters, M. L., Fuchs, P. N., & Turk, D. C. (2007). The biopsychosocial approach to chronic pain: Scientific advances and future directions. *Psychological Bulletin, 133*(4), 581–624.

Gensler, L. (2016). *The world's largest retailers 2016: Wal-Mart dominates but Amazon is catching up.* Retrieved from www.forbes.com/sites/laurengensler/2016/05/27/global-2000-worlds-largest-retailers/

Goffman, E. (1959). *The presentation of self in everyday life.* Garden City, NY: Doubleday.

Gore, D., & Kothari, A. (2012). Social determinants of health in Canada: Are healthy living initiatives there yet? A policy analysis. *International Journal for Equity in Health, 11*(41), 1–14.

Hastings, G., & Domegan, C. (2013). *Social marketing: From tunes to symphonies.* New York: Routledge.

Hatfield, M., Pyper, W., & Gustajtis, B. (2010). *First comprehensive review of the Market Basket Measure of low income* (Catalogue no. SP-953-06-10E). Gatineau, QC: Human Resources and Skills Development Canada.

Huizink, A. C., Robles de Medina, P. G., Mulder, E. J., Visser, G. H., & Buitelaar, J. K. (2003). Stress during pregnancy is associated with developmental outcome in infancy. *Journal of Child Psychology and Psychiatry, 44*(6), 810–818.

Hwang, S. W., Kirst, M. J., Chiu, S., Tolomiczenko, G., Kiss, A., Cowan, L., & Levinson, W. (2009). Multidimensional social support and the health of homeless individuals. *Journal of Urban Health, 86*(5), 791–803.

Inglehart, R. F., & Norris, P. (2016). *Trump, Brexit, and the rise of populism: Economic have-nots and cultural backlash.* John F. Kennedy School of Government, Working Paper Boston, MA. Retrieved from https://research.hks.harvard.edu/publications/getFile.aspx?Id=1401

Jeffrey, D. (2015, January 30). N.S. gender wage gap second in nation, despite job numbers: Study. *The Chronicle Herald.* Retrieved from http://thechronicleherald.ca/novascotia/1266412-n.s.-gender-wage-gap-second-in-nation-despite-job-numbers-study

King, M., Smith, A., & Gracey, M. (2009). Indigenous health part 2: The underlying causes of the health gap. *The Lancet, 374*(9683), 76–85.

Korp, P. (2008). The symbolic power of "healthy lifestyles." *Health Sociology Review, 17*(1), 18–26.

Lammam, C., MacIntyre, H., Veldhuis, N., & Palacios, M. (2016). *Measuring income mobility in Canada, 2016.* Retrieved from www.fraserinstitute.org/sites/default/files/measuring-income-mobility-in-canada-2016.pdf

MacLeod, M. (2016, November 25). *Canada will have 563,000 more millionaires by 2021: Report.* Retrieved from www.ctvnews.ca/canada/563-000-more-canadian-millionaires-by-2021-report-1.3177035

Macnaughton, E., Stefancic, A., Nelson, G., Caplan, R., Townley, G., Aubry, T., … Vallée, C. (2015). Implementing Housing First across sites and over time: Later fidelity and implementation evaluation of a pan-Canadian multi-site Housing First program for homeless people with mental illness. *American Journal of Community Psychology, 55*(3/4), 279–291.

Marx, K. (1973). *Grundrisse.* New York: Vintage. (Original work published 1939)

Marx, K., & Engels, F. (1955). *Ausgewählte Schriften* (Vol. 1). Berlin: Dietz. (Original work published 1948)

McMahon, R. (2014). From digital divides to the First Mile: Indigenous peoples and the network society in Canada. *International Journal of Communication, 8,* 2002–2026.

McMahon, R., O'Donnell, S., Smith, R., Walmark, B., & Beaton, B. (2011). Digital divides and the "First Mile": Framing First Nations broadband development in Canada. *The International Indigenous Policy Journal, 2*(2).

McMullin, J. A. (2004). *Understanding social inequality: Intersections of class, age, gender, ethnicity, and race in Canada.* Don Mills, ON: Oxford University Press.

Mikkonen, J., & Raphael. D. (2010). *Social determinants of health: The Canadian facts.* Toronto, ON: York University, School of Health Policy and Management.

Minkler, M. (1999). Personal responsibility for health? A review of the arguments and the evidence at century's end. *Health Education & Behavior, 26*(1), 121–141.

Minotti, M. (2016, April 21). *Video games will become a $99.6B industry this year as mobile overtakes consoles and PCs.* Retrieved from http://venturebeat.com/2016/04/21/video-games-will-become-a-99-6b-industry-this-year-as-mobile-overtakes-consoles-and-pcs/

Mulé, N., Ross, L., Deeprose, B., Jackson, B., Daley, A., Travers, A., & Moore, D. (2009, May 15). Promoting LGBT health and wellbeing through inclusive policy development. *International Journal for Equity in Health.* Retrieved from www.ncbi.nlm.nih.gov/pmc/articles/PMC2698868/pdf/1475-9276-8-18.pdf

Murphy, B., Zhang, X., & Dionne, C. (2012). *Low income in Canada: A multi-line and multi-index perspective* (Statistics Canada, catalogue no. 75F0002M). Retrieved from www.statcan.gc.ca/pub/75f0002m/75f0002m2012001-eng.htm

Nova Scotia, Poverty Reduction Working Group. (2008). *Report of the Poverty Reduction Working Group.* Retrieved from www.novascotia.ca/coms/specials/poverty/documents/Poverty_Reduction_Working_Group_Report.pdf.

The Occupy Solidarity Network. (n.d.). *About.* Retrieved from http://occupywallst.org/about/

OECD. (2014). *Gender wage gap.* Retrieved from www.oecd.org/gender/data/genderwagegap.htm

Office of the High Commissioner for Human Rights (OHCHR). (2016). *OHCHR report 2015.* Retrieved from www2.ohchr.org/english/OHCHRreport2015/index.html

One Laptop per Child (OLPC). (2010). *Vision.* Retrieved from http://laptop.org/en/vision/index.shtml

Pahl, R. E. (1989). Is the emperor naked? Some questions on the adequacy of sociological theory in urban and regional research. *International Journal of Urban and Regional Research, 13*(4), 709–720.

Piketty, T. (2003). Income inequality in France, 1901–1998. *Quarterly Journal of Economics, 111*(5), 1004–1042.

Piketty, T., & Saez, E. (2003). Income Inequality in the United States, 1913–1918. *The Quarterly Journal of Economics, 118*(1), 1–39.

Porter, J. (2016, March 14). *First Nations students get 30 per cent less funding than other children, economist says.* Retrieved from www.cbc.ca/news/canada/thunder-bay/first-nations-education-funding-gap-1.3487822

Prus, S. G. (2011). Comparing social determinants of self-rated health across the United States and Canada. *Social Science & Medicine, 73*(1), 50–59.

Quan-Haase, A. (2016). *Technology and society: Social networks, work, and inequality* (2nd ed.). Don Mills, ON: Oxford University Press.

Québec, Ministère des Finances. (2016). *Daily daycare costs.* Retrieved from www.budget.finances.gouv.qc.ca/budget/outils/garde_en.asp

Rafalow, M. H. (2014). The digital divide in classroom technology use: A comparison of three schools. *International Journal of Sociology of Education, 3*(1), 67–100.

Raphael, D. (2006). Social determinants of health: Present status, unanswered questions, and future directions. *International Journal of Health Services, 36*(4), 651–677.

Riches, G. (2011). Thinking and acting outside the charitable food box: Hunger and the right to food in rich societies. *Development in Practice, 21*(4/5), 768–775.

Riches, G., & Silvasti, T. (2014). Canada: Thirty years of food charity and public policy neglect. In G. Riches & T. Silvasti (Eds.), *First world hunger revisited* (2nd ed., pp. 42–56). New York: Palgrave Macmillan.

Richmond, R. (2015, March 9). Tough talk over funding cut. *The London Free Press.* Retrieved from www.lfpress.com/2015/03/09/tough-talk-over-funding-cut

Robinson, L., Cotten, S. R., Ono, H., Quan-Haase, A., Mesch, G., Chen, W., Schultz, J., Hale, T., & Stern, M. J. (2015). Digital inequalities and why they matter. *Information, Communication & Society, 18*(5), 569–582.

Rogers, E. M. (2003). *Diffusion of innovations* (5th ed.). New York: Free Press.

Rotenberg, S. (2016). *Social determinants of health for the off-reserve First Nations Population, 15 years of age and older, 2012. Aboriginal People's Survey, 2012.* Retrieved from www.statcan.gc.ca/pub/89-653-x/89-653-x2016010-eng.htm

Rutty, C., & Sullivan, S. C. (2010). *This is public health: A Canadian history.* Retrieved from www.cpha.ca/uploads/history/book/history-book-print_all_e.pdf

Sarlo, C. (2007). Measuring poverty—What happened to Copenhagen? *Economic Affairs, 27*(3), 6–14.

Sharone, O. (2013). *Flawed system/flawed self: Job searching and unemployment experiences.* Chicago, IL: University of Chicago Press.

Statistics Canada. (2013, 27 June). Persons in low income after tax. *The Daily.* Retrieved from www.statcan.gc.ca/tables-tableaux/sum-som/l01/cst01/famil19a-eng.htm?sdi=low%20income

Statistics Canada. (2014). *CANSIM Table 206-0003, Canadian Income Survey (CIS), persons in low income, Canada and provinces.* Retrieved from www.statcan.gc.ca/

Statistics Canada. (2015a). *Aboriginal peoples: Fact sheet for Canada* (Catalogue no. 89-656-X). Retrieved from www.statcan.gc.ca/pub/89-656-x/89-656-x2015001-eng.htm

Statistics Canada. (2015b). *Education indicators in Canada: An international perspective 2014* (Catalogue no. 81-604-X). Retrieved from www.statcan.gc.ca/pub/81-604-x/81-604-x2014001-eng.htm

Statistics Canada. (2015c). Income. In *Aboriginal statistics at a glance: 2nd edition* (Catalogue no. 89-645-X). Retrieved from www.statcan.gc.ca/pub/89-645-x/2015001/income-revenu-eng.htm

Statistics Canada, Income Statistics Division. (2016). *Low income lines: What they are and how they are created.* Retrieved from www.statcan.gc.ca/pub/75f0002m/75f0002m2016002-eng.htm

Statistics Canada (2017). *Household income in Canada: Key results from the 2016 Census.* Retrieved from https://www.statcan.gc.ca/daily-quotidien/170913/dq170913a-eng.htm

Stefanovich, O. (2016, September 10). *"How can people afford this?": James Bay communities struggle to eat healthily.* Retrieved from www.cbc.ca/news/canada/sudbury/james-bay-coast-high-food-prices-study-1.3756824

St Germain, G., & Dyck, L. E. (2011). *Reforming First Nations education: From crisis to hope* (Catalogue no. YC28-0/411-3E). Ottawa, ON: Standing Senate Committee on Aboriginal Peoples.

Stone, G. P. (2009). Appearance and the self: A slightly revised version. In D. Brissett & C. Edgley (Eds.), *Life as theater: A dramaturgical sourcebook* (2nd ed., pp. 141–162). New Brunswick, NJ: Aldine Transaction. Originally published 1975.

Strumberg, J. P., & Martin, C. M. (2009). Complexity and health—Yesterday's traditions, tomorrow's future. *Journal of Evaluation in Clinical Practice, 15,* 543–548.

Trypuc, B., & Robinson, J. (2009). *Homeless in Canada.* Retrieved from www.charityintelligence.ca/images/Ci-Homeless-in-Canada.pdf

Turcotte, M. (2011). Intergenerational education mobility: University completion in relation to parents' education level. *Canadian Social Trends, 92* (Statistics Canada, catalogue no. 11-008-X), 37–43.

United Nations Development Programme (UNDP). (2015). *Human development report 2015: Work for human development.* Retrieved from http://hdr.undp.org/sites/default/files/2015_human_development_report.pdf

United Nations Office of the High Commission for Human Rights. (2015). Concluding observations on the sixth periodic report of Canada. Retrieved from http://tbinternet.ohchr.org/_layouts/treatybodyexternal/Download.aspx?symbolno=CCPR%2FC%2FCAN%2FCO%2F6&Lang=en

van Deursen, A. J. A. M., & Helsper, E. J. (2015). The third-level digital divide: Who benefits most from being online? In L. Robinson, S. R. Cotten, J. Schulz, T. M. Hale, & A. Williams (Eds.), *Communication and information technologies annual: Digital distinctions and inequalities* (pp. 29–52). Bingley, UK: Emerald Group.

Veblen, T. (2009). *The theory of the leisure class.* M. Banta (Ed.). Oxford: Oxford University Press. (Original work published 1899)

Villemez, W. J. (2001). Poverty. In E. F. Borgatta & R. J. V. Montgomery (Eds.), *Encyclopedia of sociology* (2nd ed., pp. 2209–2217). New York: Macmillan Reference USA.

Vosko, L. F. (2006). *Precarious employment: Understanding labour market insecurity in Canada.* Montreal, QC & Kingston, ON: McGill-Queen's University Press.

Wajcman, J. (2017). Automation: Is it really different this time? *The British Journal of Sociology, 68*(1), 119–127.

Weber, M. (1978). *Economy and society: An outline of interpretative sociology* (Vols. 1–2). G. Roth & C. Wittich (Eds.). Berkeley: University of California Press.

Wilkinson, R., & Pickett, K. (2009). Income inequality and social dysfunction. *Annual Review of Sociology, 35*(1), 493–511.

Wilkinson, R., & Pickett, K. (2010). *The spirit level: Why equality is better for everyone* (2nd ed.). London: Penguin.

Witte, J. C., & Mannon, S. E. (2010). *The internet and social inequalities.* New York: Routledge.

Woolley, E. (2014, October 24). *How can homeless people afford cell phones?* [Web log comment]. Retrieved from http://homelesshub.ca/blog/how-can-homeless-people-afford-cel

The World Bank. (2014). *World development indicators: Distribution of income or consumption.* Retrieved from http://wdi.worldbank.org/table/2.9

Yip, W., Subramanian, S. V., Mitchell, A. D., Lee, D. T. S., Wang, J., & Kawachi, I. (2007). Does social capital enhance health and well-being? Evidence from rural China. *Social Science & Medicine, 64,* 35–49.

Chapter 7

Armstrong, P. (2007). Back to basics: Pay equity for women today. *Labour and Industry, 18*(2), 11–32.

Association of Universities and Colleges of Canada (AUCC). (2011). *Trends in higher education volume 1—enrolment.* Retrieved from www.cais.ca/uploaded/trends-2011-vol1-enrolment-e.pdf

Baldick, C. (2008). Performative. In *The Oxford dictionary of literary terms* (3rd ed.) Oxford: Oxford University Press.

Barnett, O. W. (2000). Why battered women do not leave, Part 1: External inhibiting factors within society. *Trauma, Violence, & Abuse, 1*(4), 343–372.

Bauer, G., & Scheim, A. (2015). *Transgender people in Ontario, Canada: Statistics to inform human rights policy.* Retrieved from http://transpulseproject.ca/wp-content/uploads/2015/06/Trans-PULSE-Statistics-Relevant-for-Human-Rights-Policy-June-2015.pdf

Bill C-279: An Act to amend the Canadian Human Rights Act and the Criminal Code (gender identity). Referral to committee June 5, 2016, 41st Parliament, 2nd Session. Retrieved from the Parliament of Canada website: www.parl.gc.ca/legisinfo/BillDetails.aspx?billId=6251806&Language=E&Mode=1

Block, S., & Galabuzi, G-E. (2011). *Canada's colour coded labour market.* Retrieved from www.policyalternatives.ca/sites/default/files/uploads/publications/National%20Office/2011/03/Colour%20Coded%20Labour%20Market.pdf

Blythe, M. J., Fortenberry, D., Temkit, M., Tu, W., & Orr, D. P. (2006). Incidence and correlates of unwanted sex in relationships of middle and late adolescent women. *Archives of Pediatric and Adolescent Medicine, 160*(6), 591–595.

Bourdarbat, B., & Connolly, M. (2013). The gender wage gap among recent post-secondary graduates in Canada: A distributional approach. *Canadian Journal of Economics, 46*(3), 1037–1065.

Browne, A. (1987). *When battered women kill.* New York: Free Press.

Brill, S., & Kenney, L. (2016). *The transgender teen.* Jersey City, NJ: Simon & Schuster.

Brzozowski, J.-A., Taylor-Butts, A., & Johnson, S. (2006). *Victimization and offending among the Aboriginal population in Canada.* Ottawa, ON: Canadian Centre for Justice Statistics.

Buchanan, I. (2016). Socialist feminism. In *A dictionary of critical theory (Online version).* Oxford: Oxford University Press.

Butler, J. (1990). *Gender trouble: Feminism and the subversion of identity.* New York: Routledge.

Campbell, J. C., & Soeken, K. (1999). Forced sex and intimate partner violence: Effects on women's health. *Violence Against Women, 5,* 1017–1035.

Cameron, M. (2005). Two-spirited Aboriginal people: Continuing cultural appropriation by non-Aboriginal society. *Canadian Woman Studies, 24*(2/3), 123–127.

Catalyst. (2016). *Women's earnings and income.* Retrieved from www.catalyst.org/knowledge/womens-earnings-and-income

Chess, S., & Shaw, A. (2015). A conspiracy of fishes, or, how we learned to stop worrying about# GamerGate and embrace hegemonic masculinity. *Journal of Broadcasting & Electronic Media, 59*(1), 208–220.

Conference Board of Canada. (2017a). *Immigrant wage gap.* Retrieved from www.conferenceboard.ca/hcp/provincial/society/immigrant-gap.aspx

Conference Board of Canada. (2017b). *Racial wage gap.* Retrieved from www.conferenceboard.ca/hcp/provincial/society/racial-gap.aspx

Cossman, B., & Katri, I. (2017, June 15). Today, trans Canadians celebrate Bill C-16: Tomorrow, the work begins for us all. *The Globe and Mail.* Retrieved from www.theglobeandmail.com/opinion/today-trans-canadians-celebrate-bill-c-16-tomorrow-the-work-begins-for-us-all/article35324961/

Crenshaw, K. (1989). Demarginalizing the intersection of race and sex: A Black feminist critique of antidiscrimination doctrine, feminist theory and antiracist politics. *University of Chicago Legal Forum, 1989*(1), article 8.

Crispell, D. (1992). The brave new world of men. *American Demographics, 14,* 38.

Daoud, N., Smylie, J., Urquia, M., Allan, B., & O'Campo, P. (2013). The contribution of socio-economic position to the excesses of violence and intimate partner violence among Aboriginal versus non-Aboriginal women in Canada. *Canadian Journal of Public Health, 104*(4), e278–e283.

Davies, S., & Guppy, N. (2013). *The schooled society: An introduction to the sociology of education* (3rd ed.). Don Mills, ON: Oxford University Press.

Dines, G. (2010). *Pornland: How porn had hijacked our sexuality.* Boston, MA: Beacon Press.

Dionne-Simard, D., Galarneau, D., & LaRochelle-Côté, S. (2016). Women in scientific occupations in Canada. *Insights on Canadian Society* (Statistics Canada, Catalogue no. 75-006-X). Retrieved from www.statcan.gc.ca/pub/75-006-x/2016001/article/14643-eng.htm

Dobson, A. S. (2016). *Postfeminist digital cultures: Femininity, social media, and self-representation.* New York: Palgrave Macmillan.

Doherty, D., & Berglund, D. (2012). *Psychological abuse: A discussion paper.* Public Health Agency of Canada. Retrieved from www.phac-aspc.gc.ca/sfv-avf/sources/fv/fv-psych-abus/index-eng.php

Doolittle, R. (2017, February 3). Unfounded: Why police dismiss 1 in 5 sexual assault claims as baseless. *The Globe and Mail.* Retrieved from www.theglobeandmail.com/news/investigations/unfounded-sexual-assault-canada-main/article33891309/

Doolittle, R., Pereira, M., Blenkinsop, L., & Agius, J. (2017, February 3). Will the police believe you? *The Globe and Mail.* Retrieved from www.theglobeandmail.com/news/investigations/compare-unfounded-sex-assault-rates-across-canada/article33855643/

Duggan, M. (2015). *Gaming and gamers.* Washington, DC: Pew Research Center. Retrieved from www.pewinternet.org/2015/12/15/gaming-and-gamers/

Ecklund, E. H., Damaske, S., Lincoln, A. E., & White, V. J. (2017). Strategies men use to negotiate family and science. *Socius, 3,* 2378023116684516.

Fardouly, J., Pinkus, R. T., & Vartanian, L. R. (2017). The impact of appearance comparisons made through social media, traditional media, and in person in women's everyday lives. *Body Image, 20*, 31–39.

Ferguson, S. J. (2016). Women and education: Qualifications, skills and technology. In Statistics Canada, *Women in Canada: A gender-based statistical report*. Retrieved from www.statcan.gc.ca/pub/89-503-x/2015001/article/14640-eng.htm

Ferrao, V. (2010). *Paid work*. Statistics Canada. Retrieved from www.statcan.gc.ca/pub/89-503-x/2010001/article/11387-eng.htm

Ferraro, K. J., & Johnson, J. M. (1983). How women experience battering: The process of victimization. *Social Problems, 30*(3), 325–339.

Foster, D. (2005). Why do children do so well in lesbian households? Research on lesbian parenting. *Canadian Women's Studies, 24*(2/3), 51–56.

Gigi Gorgeous. (2013, December 16). *I am transgender* [Video file]. Retrieved from www.youtube.com/watch?v=srOsrIC9Gj8

Gilchrist, K. (2010). "Newsworthy" victims? Exploring differences in Canadian local press coverage of missing/murdered Aboriginal and White women. *Feminist Media Studies, 10*(4), 373–390.

Ginter, F. (2016, May). Examining the wage gap: Who you are could have an impact on how much you make. *Outwords*. Retrieved from http://outwords.ca/2016/issue-may-2016/examining-the-wage-gap/

Gonzalez, H. B., & Kuenzi, J. J. (2012). *Science, technology, engineering, and mathematics (STEM) education: A primer*. Congressional Research Service, Library of Congress.

Goodlin, W., & Dunn, C. (2010). Three patterns of domestic violence in households: Single victimization, repeat victimization, and co-occurring victimization. *Journal of Family Violence, 25*(2), 107–122.

Grant, J. M., Mottet, L. A., Tanis, J., Harrison, J., Herman, J.L., & Keisling, M. (2012). *Injustice at every turn: A report of the National Transgender Discrimination Survey*. Retrieved from www.thetaskforce.org/static_html/downloads/reports/reports/ntds_full.pdf

Gray, K. L., Buyukozturk, B., & Hill, Z. G. (2017). Blurring the boundaries: Using Gamergate to examine "real" and symbolic violence against women in contemporary gaming culture. *Sociology Compass, 11*(3). doi: 10.1111/soc4.12458

Hafferty, F. W. (1998). Beyond curriculum reform: Confronting medicine's hidden curriculum. *Academic Medicine, 73*(4), 403–407.

Hango, D. (2013). Gender differences in science, technology, engineering, mathematics and computer science (STEM) programs at university. *Insights on Canadian Society* (Statistics Canada, catalogue no. 75-006-X). Retrieved from www.statcan.gc.ca/pub/75-006-x/2013001/article/11874-eng.pdf

Hardy, S. (2008). The pornography of reality. *Sexualities, 11*(1/2), 60–64.

Hochschild, A. (2012). *The second shift: Working parents and the revolution at home* (3rd ed.). New York: Viking.

hooks, b. (1984). *Feminist theory from margin to center*. Boston, MA: South End Press.

Horley, J. & Clarke, J. (2016). *Experience, meaning, and identity in sexuality: A psychosocial theory of sexual stability and change*. London: Palgrave Macmillan.

Impett, E. A., & Peplau, L. A. (2002). Why some women consent to unwanted sex with a dating partner: Insights from attachment theory. *Psychology of Women Quarterly, 26*(4), 360–370.

Katz, J., & Schneider, M. E. (2015). (Hetero) sexual compliance with unwanted casual sex: Associations with feelings about first sex and sexual self-perceptions. *Sex Roles, 72*(9/10), 451–461.

Klein, N. (2000). *No logo: Taking aim at the brand bullies*. Toronto, ON: Knopf.

Klein, N. (2007). *The shock doctrine: The rise of disaster capitalism*. Toronto, ON: Knopf.

Klein, N. (2014). *This changes everything: Capitalism vs. the climate*. Toronto, ON: Knopf.

Knudson-Martin, C., & Mahoney, A. R. (2009). *Couples, gender, and power: Creating change in intimate relationships*. New York: Springer Publishing Company.

Koss, M. P. (1993). Detecting the scope of rape: A review of prevalence research methods. *Journal of Interpersonal Violence, 8*, 198–222.

Lambert, L. (2010). Wage gap even more pronounced for Aboriginal women. *Pimatsiwin: A Journal of Aboriginal and Indigenous Community Health, 8*(2). Retrieved from www.pimatisiwin.com/online/?page_id=757

Lane III, F.S. (2001). *Obscene profits: The entrepreneurs of pornography in the cyber age*. New York: Routledge.

Lundberg, S., & Pollak, R. A. (1996). Bargaining and distribution in marriage. *The Journal of Economic Perspectives, 10*(4), 139–158.

MacKinnon, C. (1987). *Feminism unmodified*. Cambridge, MA: Harvard University Press.

MacKinnon, C. (1993). *Only words*. Cambridge, MA: Harvard University Press.

Maloney, R. (2015, September 14). Harper reportedly denies saying MMIW inquiry wasn't high on "radar." *The Huffington Post Canada*. Retrieved from www.huffingtonpost.ca/2015/09/14/harper-missing-murdered-indigenous-women_n_8136604.html?

Mansbridge, P. (2014, December 17). *Exclusive: Full text of Peter Mansbridge's interview with Stephen Harper*. Retrieved from www.cbc.ca/news/politics/full-text-of-peter-mansbridge-s-interview-with-stephen-harper-1.2876934

Marshall, K. (2011). Generational change in paid and unpaid work. *Canadian Social Trends, 92* (Catalogue no.11-008-X, Statistics Canada). Retrieved from www.statcan.gc.ca/pub/11-008-x/2011002/article/11520-eng.htm

Marx, K. (1987). *Capital: A critical analysis of capitalist production*. F. Engels (Ed.). New York: International Publishers. (Original work published 1904)

McInturff, K. (2016). *The best and worst places to be a woman in Canada 2016: The gender gap in Canada's 25 biggest cities*. Retrieved from www.policyalternatives.ca/sites/default/files/uploads/publications/National%20Office/2016/10/Best_and_Worst_Places_to_Be_a_Woman2016.pdf

Milan, A., Keown, L., & Urquijo, C. (2015). *Families, living arrangements, and work*. Statistics Canada. Retrieved from www.statcan.gc.ca/pub/89-503-x/2010001/article/11546-eng.htm#a15

Miller, B., & Behm-Morawitz, E. (2016). Exploring social television, opinion leaders, and Twitter audience reactions to Diane Sawyer's coming out interview with Caitlyn Jenner. *International Journal of Transgenderism*, 18(2), 1–14. http://doi.org/10.1080/15532739.2016.1260513

Mitchell, J. (1971). *Woman's estate*. Harmondsworth, UK: Penguin.

The National. (2015, April 8). *Canada's murdered and missing indigenous women* [Video]. Retrieved from www.youtube.com/watch?v=vqpsoEuQEjU

Nayak, A., & Kehily, M.J. (2006). Gender undone: Subversion, regulation and embodiment in the work of Judith Butler. *British Journal of Sociology of Education*, 27(4), 459–472.

Oakley, A. (2005). *The Ann Oakley reader: Gender, women and social science*. Bristol: Policy Press.

Organisation for Economic Co-operation and Development (OECD). (2012). *Closing the gender gap: Act now*. Retrieved from www.oecd.org/gender/closingthegap.htm

Organisation for Economic Co-operation and Development (OECD). (2016). *Women in Africa*. Retrieved from www.oecd.org/dev/poverty/womeninafrica.htm

Parsons, T., & Bales, R. F. (1955). *Family, socialization and interaction process*. Glencoe, IL: Free Press.

Pederson J. S., Malcoe L. H., & Pulkingham J. (2013). Explaining Aboriginal/non-Aboriginal inequalities in post separation violence against Canadian women: Application of a structural violence approach. *Violence Against Women*, 19(8), 1034–1058. doi:10.1177/1077801213499245

Pedulla, D. S., & Thébaud, S. (2015). Can we finish the revolution? Gender, work–family ideals, and institutional restraint. *American Sociological Review*, 80(1), 116–139.

Perreault, S. (2015, November 30). *Criminal victimization in Canada, 2014*. Retrieved from www.statcan.gc.ca/pub/85-002-x/2015001/article/14241-eng.htm

Rehel, E. M. (2014). When dad stays home too: Paternity leave, gender, and parenting. *Gender & Society*, 28(1), 110–132.

Reyns, B. W. (2010). A situational crime prevention approach to cyberstalking victimization: Preventive tactics for Internet users and online place managers. *Crime Prevention & Community Safety*, 12, 99–118.

Roberts, A. R. (2007). Overview and new directions for intervening on behalf of battered women. In A. R. Roberts (Ed.), *Battered women and their families: Intervention strategies and treatment programs* (3rd ed., pp. 3–32). New York: Springer.

Roscoe, W. (1998). *The changing ones: Third and fourth genders in Native North America*. New York: Palgrave Macmillan.

Royal Canadian Mounted Police (RCMP). (2014). *Missing and murdered Aboriginal women: A national operation overview*. Retrieved from: www.rcmp-grc.gc.ca/en/missing-and-murdered-aboriginal-women-national-operational-overview

Ryan, J. R. (2009). *Reel gender: Examining the politics of trans images in film and media* (Unpublished doctoral dissertation). Bowling Green State University, Bowling Green, OH.

Sabina, C., & Tindale, R. S. (2008). Abuse characteristics and coping resources as predictors of problem-focused coping strategies among battered women. *Violence Against Women*, 14(4), 437–456.

Scott, J. (2014). Sociology of gender. In J. Scott (Ed.), *A dictionary of sociology* (4th ed., pp. 274–275). Oxford: Oxford University Press.

Shafy, S. (2016, July 6). Gloria Steinem's life-long fight for women's rights. *Der Spiegel Online*. Retrieved from www.spiegel.de/international/world/gloria-steinem-and-the-possibility-of-a-clinton-presidency-a-1101464-2.html

Sinha, M. (2015). *Trends in reporting criminal victimization to police, 1999 to 2009*. Retrieved from www.statcan.gc.ca/pub/85-002-x/2015001/article/14198-eng.htm

Stark, E. (2007). *Coercive control: How men entrap women in personal life*. Oxford: Oxford University Press.

Statistics Canada. (2006). *CANSIM Table 202-0101, Income in Canada: Distribution of earnings, by sex, 2006 constant dollars, annual*. Retrieved from: www.statcan.gc.ca/pub/75-202-x/2006000/5203567-eng.htm

Statistics Canada. (2016). *Education in Canada: Attainment, field of study, and location*. Retrieved from www12.statcan.gc.ca/nhs-enm/2011/as-sa/99-012-x/99-012-x2011001-eng.cfm#a4

Steinem, G. (1969, April 4). After Black power, women's liberation. *New York Magazine*. Retrieved from http://nymag.com/news/politics/46802/

Ste. Marie, B. (1964). Universal solidier. On *It's my way!* [Musical recording]. New York: Vanguard.

Ste. Marie, B. (1974). Starwalker. On *Buffy*. [Musical recording]. Toronto, ON: MCA.

Stormhoj, C. (2003). Den politiserede tokønnethed [The politicized two-sex model]. *GRUS*, 69(24), 118–137.

Straus, M. A., Gelles, R. J., & Steinmetz, S. K. (1980). *Behind closed doors: Violence in the American family*. New York: Anchor/Doubleday.

Stryker, S. (2008). *Transgender history*. Berkeley, CA: Seal Press.

Sun, C., Bridges, A., Johnson, J.A. & Ezzell, M. B. (2016). Pornography and the male sexual script: An analysis. *Archives of Sexual Behavior*, 45, 983. doi:10.1007/s10508-014-0391

Thorne, B. (1993). *Gender play: Girls and boys in school*. New Brunswick, NJ: Rutgers University Press.

Tichenor, V. J. (1999). Status and income as gendered resources: The case of marital power. *Journal of Marriage and Family*, 61(3), 638–650.

Todd, C. (2015). GamerGate and resistance to the diversification of gaming culture. *Women's Studies Journal*, 29(1), 64–67.

Yousafzai, M. (2013). *I am Malala: The girl who stood up for education and was shot by the Taliban*. New York: Little, Brown, & Company.

Waite, S., & Denier, N. (2015). Gay pay for straight work: Mechanisms generating disadvantage. *Gender and Society*, 29(4). Retrieved from http://journals.sagepub.com/doi/pdf/10.1177/0891243215584761

Walters, J. (2015, September 10). Stitching together Cid's manhood: In the operating room for a female-to-male surgery. *The Guardian*. Retrieved from www.theguardian.com/society/2015/sep/10/sitching-together-cids-manhood-inside-the-operating-room-for-a-female-to-male-surgery

Willis, E. (2012). *No more nice girls: Countercultural essays*. Minneapolis: University of Minnesota Press.

Zaslow, E. (2009). *Feminism, Inc.: Coming of age in girl power media culture*. New York: Palgrave Macmillan.

Chapter 8

Abu-Laban, Y., & Bakan, A. B. (2008). The racial contract: Israel/Palestine and Canada. *Social Identities, 14*(5), 637–660. doi:10.1080/13504630802343481

Allport, G. W., & Postman, L. J. (1947). *The psychology of rumor.* New York: H. Holt and Company.

Arnott, K. (2003, June 6). Black youths feel alienated in Oakville. *Oakville Beaver,* pp. 1, 4. Retrieved from http://images.oakville.halinet.on.ca/1544946/data

Baker, K. J. (2017). FSU College of Medicine hosts inaugural Racism Awareness Week. *Women in Higher Education, 26*(3), 1–2. doi:10.1002/whe.20409

Baureiss, G. (1987). Chinese immigration, Chinese stereotypes, and Chinese labour. *Canadian Ethnic Studies/Études Ethniques au Canada, 19*(3), 15–34.

De Beauvoir, S. (2011). *The second sex.* New York: Vintage Books. (Original work published 1949)

Bertrand, M., & Mullainathan, S. (2004). Are Emily and Greg more employable than Lakisha and Jamal? A field experiment on labor market discrimination. *The American Economic Review, 94*(4), 991–1013. doi:10.1257/0002828042002561

Boyden, J. (2016). *Wenjack.* Toronto, ON: Penguin Random House Canada.

Brown, M. (2003). *Growing up black in Oakville: The impact of community on black youth identity formation and civic participation.* Retrieved from www.cdhalton.ca/pdf/Growing_Up_Black_in_Oakville_Final.pdf

Brubaker, R. (2005). The "diaspora" diaspora. *Ethnic and Racial Studies, 28*(1), 1–19. doi:10.1080/0141987042000289997

Bureau, A. T. B. (2013). Canada turned away Jewish refugees. *The Chronicle Herald,* December 15. Retrieved from http://thechronicleherald.ca/novascotia/1174272-canada-turned-away-jewish-refugees

Cabrera, A. F., Nora, A., Terenzini, P. T., Pascarella, E., & Hagedorn, L. S. (1999). Campus racial climate and the adjustment of students to college: A comparison between white students and African-American students. *The Journal of Higher Education, 70*(2), 134–160.

Canadian Civil Liberties Association (CCLA). (2015, May 18). A recent history of racial profiling and policing. Retrieved from https://ccla.org/a-recent-history-of-racial-profiling-and-policing/

Canadian Institutes of Health Research, Natural Sciences and Engineering Research Council of Canada, & Social Sciences and Humanities Research Council of Canada. (2014). Research involving the First Nations, Inuit and Métis Peoples of Canada. In *Tri-Council policy statement: Ethical conduct for research involving humans (TCPS2)* (pp. 109–136). Ottawa, ON: Government of Canada. Retrieved from www.pre.ethics.gc.ca/eng/policy-politique/initiatives/TCPS2-EPTC2/Default/

Canadian Museum of Immigration at Pier 21. (n.d.). *Continuous journey regulation, 1908.* Retrieved July 21, 2017, from www.pier21.ca/research/immigration-history/continuous-journey-regulation-1908

Canadian Press. (2016, March 3). Chiefs say proposed Algonquin land claim deal illegal, fraudulent. Retrieved from www.cbc.ca/news/indigenous/algonquin-land-deal-illegal-1.3475359

Castells, M. (1997). *The power of identity.* Cambridge, MA: Blackwell.

CBC News. (2010, February 14). *Aboriginal involvement in Games makes history.* Retrieved from www.cbc.ca/news/canada/british-columbia/aboriginal-involvement-in-games-makes-history-1.945693

CBC News. (2016, November 2). *Parents on edge after northern Saskatchewan suicides.* Retrieved from www.cbc.ca/news/canada/saskatoon/community-response-northern-saskatchewan-suicides-1.3831863

Chui, T., & Flanders, J. (2013). *Immigration and ethnocultural diversity in Canada* (National Household Survey, 2011, catalogue no. 99-010-X2011001). Retrieved from www12.statcan.gc.ca/nhs-enm/2011/as-sa/99-010-x/99-010-x2011001-eng.cfm

Cornell, S. E., & Hartmann, D. (1998). *Ethnicity and race: Making identities in a changing world.* Thousand Oaks, CA: Pine Forge Press.

Côté, R. R., & Erickson, B. H. (2009). Untangling the roots of tolerance: How forms of social capital shape attitudes toward ethnic minorities and immigrants. *American Behavioral Scientist, 52*(12), 1664–1689. http://doi.org/10.1177/0002764209331532

Crenshaw, K. (1989). Demarginalizing the intersection of race and sex: A black feminist critique of antidiscrimination doctrine, feminist theory and antiracist policies. *The University of Chicago Legal Forum, 1989*(1), 139–167.

Daniels, J. (2012). Race and racism in Internet studies: A review and critique. *New Media & Society, 15*(5), 695–719. http://doi.org/10.1177/1461444812462849

Daniels, J. (2016). *White lies: Race, class, gender and sexuality in white supremacist discourse.* New York: Routledge.

De Fina, A. (2007). Code-switching and the construction of ethnic identity in a community of practice. *Language in Society, 36*(3), 371–392. doi:10.1017/S0047404507070182

Delgado, R., & Stefancic, J. (2017). *Critical race theory* (3rd ed.). New York: New York University Press.

Du Bois, W. E. B. (2007). *The souls of black folk.* New York: Oxford University Press. (Original work published 1903)

Erikson, G. H. (1968). *Identity, youth and crisis.* New York: Norton.

First Nations Information Governance Committee. (2005). *First Nations Regional Longitudinal Health Survey (RHS) 2002/03: Results for adults, youth and children living in First Nations communities.* Ottawa, ON: First Nations Centre. Retrieved from http://fnigc.ca/sites/default/files/ENpdf/RHS_2002/rhs2002-03-technical_report.pdf

Friedländer, S. (2007). *Nazi Germany and the Jews: The years of extermination, 1939–1945* (Vol. 2). New York: HarperCollins.

German criminal code in the version promulgated on 13 November 1998, Federal Law Gazette [Bundesgesetzblatt], p. 3322, last amended by Article 1 of the Law of 24 September 2013, Federal Law Gazette, p. 3671 and with the text of Article 6(18) of the Law of 10 October 2013, Federal Law Gazette, p. 3799., § 130(2) (2016) (M. Bohlander, Trans.). Retrieved from www.gesetze-im-internet.de/englisch_stgb/englisch_stgb.html

Government of Canada. (2015). *Research involving the First Nations, Inuit and Métis Peoples of Canada.* In Ottawa, ON. Retrieved from www.pre.ethics.gc.ca/eng/policy-politique/initiatives/tcps2-eptc2/chapter9-chapitre9/

Harvey, D. (1989). *The condition of postmodernity: An enquiry into the origins of cultural change.* Oxford: Blackwell.

Hiller, H. H., & Franz, T. M. (2004). New ties, old ties, and lost ties: The use of the Internet in diaspora. *New Media and Society, 6*(6), 731–752. http://doi.org/10.1177/146144804044327

Hipolito-Delgado, C. P. (2010). Exploring the etiology of ethnic self-hatred: Internalized racism in Chicana/o and Latina/o college students. *Journal of College Student Development, 51*(3), 319–331.

Hogan, B. (2010). The presentation of self in the age of social media: Distinguishing performances and exhibitions online. *Bulletin of Science, Technology & Society, 30*(6), 377–386. doi:10.1177/0270467610385893

Human Rights Watch. (2002, November). *"We are not the enemy:" Hate crimes against Arabs, Muslims, and those perceived to be Arab or Muslim after September 11.* Washington, DC: Human Rights Watch. Retrieved from www.hrw.org/reports/2002/usahate/usa1102-04.htm

The Jerusalem Post. (2006, February 9). German Holocaust denier's trial resumes. Retrieved from www.jpost.com/Jewish-World/Jewish-News/German-Holocaust-deniers-trial-resumes

Jones, S. (2015, June 18). One in every 122 people is displaced by war, violence and persecution, says UN. *The Guardian.* Retrieved from www.theguardian.com/global-development/2015/jun/18/59m-people-displaced-war-violence-persecution-says-un

Kang, S. K., DeCelles, K. A., Tilcsik, A., & Jun, S. (2016). Whitened résumés: Race and self-presentation in the labor market. *Administrative Science Quarterly, 61*(3), 469–502.

Khan, S. (2008). Aboriginal mental health: The statistical reality. *Visions Journal, 5*(1), 6–7. Retrieved from www.heretohelp.bc.ca/sites/default/files/visions_aboriginal_people.pdf

Kral, M. J. (2012). Postcolonial suicide among Inuit in arctic Canada. *Culture, Medicine, and Psychiatry, 36*(2), 306–325.

Kumar, M. B., & Nahwegahbow, A. (2016). *Past-year suicidal thoughts among off-reserve First Nations, Metis and Inuit adults aged 18 to 25* (Statistics Canada, catalogue no. 89-653-X). Retrieved from www.statcan.gc.ca/pub/89-653-x/89-653-x2016011-eng.htm

Kupferman, S. (2017, May 11). A real estate broker and a housing researcher face off over Ontario's tax on foreign buyers. *Toronto Life.* Retrieved from http://torontolife.com/real-estate/real-estate-broker-housing-researcher-face-off-ontarios-tax-foreign-buyers/

Leitch, K. (2017). *Home – Kellie Leitch.* Retrieved June 15, 2017, from https://kellieworks.ca/

Lemkin, R. (1944). *Axis rule in occupied Europe: Laws of occupation, analysis of government, proposals for redress.* Washington, DC: Carnegie Endowment for International Peace, Division of International Law.

Levine-Rasky, C., Beaudoin, J., & St Clair, P. (2014). The exclusion of Roma claimants in Canadian refugee policy. *Patterns of Prejudice, 48*(1), 67–93. http://dx.doi.org/10.1080/0031322X.2013.857477

Li, P. S. (2001). The racial subtext in Canada's immigration discourse. *Journal of International Migration and Integration, 2*(1), 77–97.

Li, P. S., & Li, E. X. (2011). Vancouver Chinatown in transition. *Journal of Chinese Overseas, 7*(1), 7–23.

Litchmore, R. V. H., Safdar, S., & O'Doherty, K. (2016). Ethnic and racial self-identifications of second-generation Canadians of African and Caribbean heritage: An analysis of discourse. *Journal of Black Psychology, 42*(3), 259–292. doi:10.1177/0095798414568454

Martinot, S. (2003). *The rule of racialization: Class, identity, governance.* Philadelphia, PA: Temple University Press.

McPherson, M., Smith-Lovin, L., & Cook, J. M. (2001). Birds of a feather: Homophily in social networks. *Annual Review of Sociology, 27*(1), 415–444. doi:10.1146/annurev.soc.27.1.415

Mills, C. W. (2000). *The sociological imagination.* Oxford: Oxford University Press. (Original first published 1949).

Morley, K. M. (2003). Fitting in by race/ethnicity: The social and academic integration of diverse students at a large predominantly white university. *Journal of College Student Retention, 5*(2), 147–174. doi:10.2190/K1KF-RTLW-1DPW-T4CC

Mornix, D. (2017). *Passages Canada: Story profile.* Retrieved from http://passagestocanada.com/story-profile/?story=1442

Nakamura, L., & Chow-White, P. (Eds.). (2012). *Race after the Internet.* New York: Routledge.

Nazemroaya, M. D. (2014). *Canada and the war on terror: The Ottawa shootings, what really happened?* Retrieved from www.globalresearch.ca/ottawa-attack-isi/5409706

Oreopoulos, P. (2009). Why do skilled immigrants struggle in the labor market? A field experiment with six thousand resumes. *American Economic Journal: Economic Policy, 3*(4), 148–171.

Paperny, A. (2016, April 13). Hate crimes against Muslim-Canadians more than doubled in 3 years. *Global News.* Retrieved from http://globalnews.ca/news/2634032/hate-crimes-against-muslim-canadians-more-than-doubled-in-3-years/

Pitchford, S. (2001). Race. In E. F. Borgatta, & R. J. V. Montgomery (Eds.), *Encyclopedia of sociology* (2nd ed., pp. 2329–2335). New York: Macmillan Reference USA.

Pittman, J. (2016). Double-consciousness. *Stanford encyclopedia of philosophy.* Retrieved from Retrieved from https://plato.stanford.edu/entries/double-consciousness/#UsesExteConc

Pollock, D., & Van Reken, R. (2009). *Third culture kids: Growing up among worlds.* Boston, MA: Nicholas Brealey Publishing.

Porter, J. (2016). New Gord Downie work devoted to First Nations boy who died running away from residential school. *CBC News.* Retrieved from www.cbc.ca/news/canada/thunder-bay/gord-downie-chanie-wenjack-1.3753823

Proctor, J. (2016). CBC-Angus Reid Institute poll: Canadians want minorities to do more to "fit in." *CBC News.* Retrieved from www.cbc.ca/news/canada/british-columbia/poll-canadians-multiculturalism-immigrants-1.3784194

Public Health Agency of Canada, Government of Canada. (2011). *The human face of mental health and mental illness in Canada 2006.* Ottawa, ON: Government of Canada. Retrieved from www.phac-aspc.gc.ca/publicat/human-humain06/15-eng.php

Quan-Haase, A., & Martin, K. E. (2013). Digital curation and the networked audience of urban events: Expanding La Fiesta de Santo Tomás from the physical to the virtual environment. *International Communication Gazette, 75,* 521–537. http://doi.org/10.1177/1748048513491910

Quan-Haase, A., & Wellman, B. (2004). Networks of distance and media: A case study of a high-tech firm. *Analyse und Kritik, 28*, 241–257.

Reynolds Lewis, K. (2014, October 7). Hiding your race or gender on a job application: Is it ever worth it? Retrieved from http://fortune.com/2014/10/07/race-gender-sexual-orientation-job-applications/

Rice, S. K., Reitzel, J. D., & Piquero, A. R. (2005). Shades of brown: Perception of racial profiling and the intra-ethnic differential. *Journal of Ethnicity in Criminal Justice, 3*(1/2), 47–70.

Richmond, A. H. (2001). Refugees and racism in Canada. *Refuge: Canada's Periodical on Refugees, 19*(6), 12–20.

Said, E. (1978). *Orientalism*. New York: Pantheon Books.

Slovensky, R., & Ross, W. H. (2012). Should human resource managers use social media to screen job applicants? Managerial and legal issues in the USA. *Info, 14*(1), 55–69. http://doi.org/http://dx.doi.org/10.1108/14636691211196941

Smith, L. T. (2012). Decolonizing methodologies: Research and indigenous peoples. New York: Palgrave Macmillan.

Social Sciences and Humanities Research Council (SSHRC). (2015, May 3). *Aboriginal research statement of principles*. Retrieved from www.sshrc-crsh.gc.ca/about-au_sujet/policies-politiques/statements-enonces/aboriginal_research-recherche_autochtone-eng.aspx

Statistics Canada. (2013). *Immigration and ethnocultural diversity in Canada: National Household Survey, 2011*. Retrieved from www12.statcan.gc.ca/nhs-enm/2011/as-sa/99-010-x/99-010-x2011001-eng.pdf

Statistics Canada. (2013b, September 4). Inter-provincial employees in Alberta, 2004 to 2009. *The Daily*. Retrieved from www.statcan.gc.ca/daily-quotidien/130904/dq130904b-eng.htm

Statistics Canada. (2014). *Mixed unions in Canada*. Retrieved from www12.statcan.gc.ca/nhs-enm/2011/as-sa/99-010-x/99-010-x2011003_3-eng.pdf

Statistics Canada. (2016). *Lifetime suicidal thoughts among First Nations living off reserve, Métis and Inuit aged 26 to 59: Prevalence and associated characteristics*. Retrieved July 9, 2017, from www.statcan.gc.ca/pub/89-653-x/89-653-x2016008-eng.htm

Szekely, R., & Pessian, P. (2015, August 6). Parents warn black youth are being racially profiled in Durham schools. *Durham Region*. Retrieved from www.durhamregion.com/news-story/5787027-parents-warn-black-youth-are-being-racially-profiled-in-durham-schools/

Tasker, J. P. (2016, October 18). Historic land deal with Algonquin peoples signed by federal, Ontario governments. Retrieved from www.cbc.ca/news/politics/ottawa-ontario-algonquin-agreement-in-principle-1.3809876

Thomas, G., & Morgan-Witts, M. (1974). *Voyage of the damned: A shocking true story of hope, betrayal, and Nazi terror*. New York: Stein and Day.

Truth and Reconciliation Commission of Canada (TRC). (2015a). *Truth and Reconciliation Commission of Canada: Calls to action*. Retrieved from http://nctr.ca/assets/reports/Calls_to_Action_English2.pdf

Truth and Reconciliation Commission of Canada. (2015b). *What we have learned: Principles of truth and reconciliation*. Retrieved from http://nctr.ca/assets/reports/Final%20Reports/Principles_English_Web.pdf

UNHCR (United Nations Refugee Agency). (2017, June 19). *Figures at a glance*. Retrieved from www.unhcr.org/figures-at-a-glance.html

Wimmer, A., & Lewis, K. (2010). Beyond and below racial homophily: ERG models of a friendship network documented on Facebook. *American Journal of Sociology, 116*(2), 583–642.

Zimonjic, P. (2016, September 6). "Anti-Canadian values" test for immigrants rejected by Tory leadership candidates, PM. *CBC News*. Retrieved from www.cbc.ca/news/politics/anti-canadian-values-bernier-1.3750217

Chapter 9

Abel, G. J., & Sander, N. (2014). Quantifying global international migration flows. *Science, 343*(6178), 1520–1522.

Anderson, B. (2006). *Imagined communities: Reflections on the origin and spread of nationalism*. London, United Kingdom: Verso. (Original work published 1983)

Baltz, A. (2014). *Through a media lens—The Crimean crisis: A discourse analysis of media perspectives on the new Crimean crisis*. (Unpublished master's thesis). Umeå University, Umeå, Sweden.

Beck, U. (2007). Beyond class and nation: Reframing social inequalities in a globalizing world. *The British Journal of Sociology, 58*(4), 679–705.

Beck, U., & Grande, E. (2010). Varieties of second modernity: The cosmopolitan turn in social and political theory and research. *The British Journal of Sociology, 61*(3), 409–443.

Berik, G., & Kongar, E. (2013). Time allocation of married mothers and fathers in hard times: The 2007–09 US recession. *Feminist Economics, 19*(3), 208–237.

Besley, T., & Persson, T. (2011). The logic of political violence. *The Quarterly Journal of Economics, 126*(3), 1411–1445.

Cameron, R. (1976). Economic history, pure and applied. *The Journal of Economic History, 36*(1), 3–27.

Canadian Institutes of Health Research (CIHR). (2008). *Global health: Healthy Canadians in a healthy world*. Retrieved from www.cihr-irsc.gc.ca/e/documents/ghb_healthy_canadians_e.pdf

Castells, M. (2008). The new public sphere: Global civil society, communication networks, and global governance. *The ANNALS of the American Academy of Political and Social Science, 616*(1), 78–93.

CBC News. (2017, February 22). *Why life expectancy in Canada, other countries is reaching "breathtaking" levels*. Retrieved from www.cbc.ca/news/health/life-expectancy-lancet-1.3993213

Chase-Dunn, C. & Inoue, H. (2011). *Explanations of scale changes in settlement and polity sizes*. IROWS Working Paper #67. Retrieved from http://irows.ucr.edu/papers/irows67/irows67.htm

Chiavacci, D., & Hommerich, C. (2016). *Social inequality in post-growth Japan: Transformation during economic and demographic stagnation*. London: Routledge.

Chinkin, C. (1999). Gender inequality and international human rights law. In A. Hurrell & N. Woods (Eds.), *Inequality, globalization, and world politics* (pp. 95–121). Oxford: Oxford University Press.

Chiswick, B. R. (1999). Are immigrants favorably self-selected? *The American Economic Review, 89*(2), 181–185.

Chomsky, N. (1999). *Profit over people: Neoliberalism and global order*. New York: Seven Stories Press.

Central Intelligence Agency. (2016). *The World factbook, country comparison, GDP per capita (PPP)*. Retrieved from www.cia.gov/library/publications/the-world-factbook/rankorder/2004rank.html

Cornelius, W. A. (2005). Controlling "unwanted" immigration: Lessons from the United States, 1993–2004. *Journal of Ethnic and Migration Studies, 31*(4), 775–794.

Cornwall, A., & Jolly, S. (2009). Guest editorial: Sexuality and the development industry. *Development, 52*(1), 5.

Cornwall, A., Correa, S., & Jolly, S. (2008). Development with a body: Making the connections between sexuality, human rights and development. In A. Cornwall, S. Correa & S. Jolly (Eds.), *Development with a body: Sexuality, human rights & development* (pp. 1–21). London: Zed Books.

de Jager, T. T. (2009). *Imagining the European Union: A geo-historical overview of dominant metaphors on the EU's political geography* (Unpublished master's thesis). Radboud University, Nijmegen, the Netherlands.

Durkheim, É. (1933). *The division of labor in society.* (G. Simpson, Trans.). New York: Macmillan. (Original work published 1892)

Economist Intelligence Unit. (2015). *Driving forces behind a globalized workforce*. Retrieved from http://futurehrtrends.eiu.com/report-2015/driving-forces-behind-a-globalized-workforce/

Etheredge, L. S. (2013). *Can governments learn? American foreign policy and Central American revolutions*. New York: Pergamon.

Feldman, M. P., & Florida, R. (1994). The geographic sources of innovation: Technological infrastructure and product innovation in the United States. *Annals of the Association of American Geographers, 84*(2), 210–229.

Feliciano, C. (2005). Does selective migration matter? Explaining ethnic disparities in educational attainment among immigrants' children. *International Migration Review, 39*(4), 841–871.

Florida, R. (2003). Cities and the creative class. *City and Community, 2*(1), 3–19.

Florida, R. (2005). *Cities and the creative class*. New York: Routledge.

Frank, A. G. (1967). *Capitalism and underdevelopment in Latin America: Historical studies of Chile and Brazil*. New York: Monthly Review Press.

Fund for Peace. (2014, May 28). *Renaming the failed states index*. Retrieved from http://library.fundforpeace.org/blog-20140528-fsirenamed

Garcia, R., & Calantone, R. (2002). A critical look at technological innovation typology and innovativeness terminology: A literature review. *Journal of Product Innovation Management, 19*(2), 110–132.

Goraya, J. (2016, April 6). Access to health care on Aboriginal reserves. *The Public Policy & Governance Review*. Retrieved from https://ppgreview.ca/2016/04/06/access-to-health-care-on-aboriginal-reserves-2/

Hall, T. D., & Chase-Dunn, C. (2006). Global social change in the long run. In C. Chase-Dunn & S. J. Babones (Eds.), *Global social change: Historical and comparative perspectives* (pp. 33–58). Baltimore, MD: Johns Hopkins University Press.

Hardin, G. (1998). Extensions of "the tragedy of the commons." *Science, 280*(5364), 682–683.

Hemp, P. (2009). Death by information overload. *Harvard Business Review, 87*(9), 82–89.

Hobday, M. (1995). East Asian latecomer firms: Learning the technology of electronics. *World Development, 23*(7), 1171–1193.

Hollington, A., Salverda, T., Schwarz, T., & Tappe, O. (2015). *Concepts of the global south*. Retrieved from http://kups.ub.uni-koeln.de/6399/

Hughes, A. (2007). Geographies of exchange and circulation: Flows and networks of knowledgeable capitalism. *Progress in Human Geography, 31*(4), 527–535.

Inglehart, R. (2015). *The silent revolution: Changing values and political styles among Western publics*. Princeton, NJ: Princeton University Press.

Jaumotte, F., Lall, S., & Papageorgiou, C. (2013). Rising income inequality: Technology, or trade and financial globalization? *IMF Economic Review, 61*(2), 271–309.

Jones, D. S. (2014). *Masters of the universe: Hayek, Friedman, and the birth of neoliberal politics*. Princeton, NJ: Princeton University Press.

King, J. L., Gurbaxani, V., Kraemer, K. L., McFarlan, F. W., Raman, K. S., & Yap, C. S. (1994). Institutional factors in information technology innovation. *Information Systems Research, 5*(2), 139–169.

Kontis, V., Bennett, J. E., Mathers, C. D., Li, G., Foreman, K., & Ezzati, M. (2017). Future life expectancy in 35 industrialised countries: Projections with a Bayesian model ensemble. *The Lancet, 36*. https://doi.org/http://dx.doi.org/10.1016/S0140-6736(16)32381-9

Krugman, P. (1979). A model of innovation, technology transfer, and the world distribution of income. *Journal of Political Economy, 87*(2), 253–266.

Leiss, W. (1977). Review: The modern world-system: Capitalist agriculture and the origins of the European world-economy in the sixteenth century by Immanuel Wallerstein. [Review of *The modern world-system: Capitalist agriculture and the origins of the European world-economy in the sixteenth century* by I. Wallerstein]. *Canadian Journal of Political Science, 10*(1), 202–203.

Martin, P. (1994). Germany: Reluctant land of immigration. In W. A. Cornelius, P. L. Martin, & J. F. Hollifield (Eds.), *Controlling immigration: A global perspective* (pp. 189–226). Stanford, CA: Stanford University Press.

Marx, K. (1973). *Grundrisse*. New York: Vintage. (Original work published 1939)

Mohanty, C. T. (2003). *Feminism without borders: Decolonizing theory, practicing solidarity*. Durham, NC: Duke University Press.

Mowat, F. (2012). *Sea of slaughter*. Vancouver, BC: Douglas & McIntyre.

National Collaborating Centre for Aboriginal Health. (2011). *Access to health services as a social determinant of First Nations, Inuit and Métis health*. Prince George, BC: National Collaborating Centre for Aboriginal Health, University of British Columbia. Retrieved from www.nccah-ccnsa.ca/docs/fact%20sheets/social%20determinates/Access%20to%20Health%20Services_Eng%202010.pdf

OECD. (2016). *Migration and the brain drain phenomenon*. Retrieved from www.oecd.org/dev/poverty/migrationandthebraindrainphenomenon.htm

OECD.Stat. (2017, March 1). *Level of GDP per capita and productivity*. Retrieved from https://stats.oecd.org/Index.aspx?DataSetCode=PDB_LV.

Pieterse, J. N. (2002). Global inequality: Bringing politics back in. *Third World Quarterly, 23*(6), 1023–1046.

Piketty, T. (2014). *Capital in the 21st century*. (A. Goldhammer, Trans.). Cambridge, MA: Harvard University Press.

Ravenstein, E. G. (1885). The laws of migration. *Journal of the Statistical Society of London, 48*(2), 167–235.

Rogers, E. M., & Kim, J. I. (1985). Diffusion of innovations in public organizations. In R. Merritt & A. J. Merrit (Eds.), *Innovation in the public sector* (pp. 85–108). Beverly Hills, CA: Sage.

Ryan, B., & Gross, N. C. (1943). The diffusion of hybrid seed corn in two Iowa communities. *Rural Sociology, 8*(1), 15–24.

Ryan, B., & Gross, N. C. (1950). Acceptance and diffusion of hybrid corn seed in two Iowa communities. *Research Bulletin (Iowa Agriculture and Home Economics Experiment Station), 29*(372), 663–708. Retrieved from http://lib.dr.iastate.edu/researchbulletin/vol29/iss372/1/

Sassen, S. (1996). Cities and communities in the global economy: Rethinking our concepts. *American Behavioral Scientist, 39*(5), 629–639.

Sassen, S. (2001). *The global city: New York, London, Tokyo*. Princeton, NJ: Princeton University Press.

Sassen, S. (2014). *Expulsions: Brutality and complexity in the global economy*. Cambridge, MA: Harvard University Press.

Sewpaul, V. (2015). Neoliberalism. In J. D. Wright (Ed.), *International encyclopedia of the social & behavioural sciences* (2nd ed., pp. 462–468). Oxford: Elsevier.

Skinner, J., & Staiger, D. (2005). *Technology adoption from hybrid corn to beta blockers*. National Bureau of Economic Research Working Paper Series w11251. Retrieved from http://ssrn.com/abstract=697176

Smith, A. (1776). *An inquiry into the nature and causes of the wealth of nations*. London: George Routledge and Sons.

Smith, D. A. (1997). Technology, commodity chains and global inequality: South Korea in the 1990s. *Review of International Political Economy, 4*(4), 734–762.

Smith, K. E., & Light, M. (2001). *Ethics and foreign policy*. Cambridge, UK: Cambridge University Press.

Stouffer, S. A. (1960). Intervening opportunities and competing migrants. *Journal of Regional Science, 2*(1), 1–26.

Strauss, M. (2013, April 24). Canada's Joe Fresh among brands made in collapsed Bangladesh building. *The Globe and Mail*. Retrieved from www.theglobeandmail.com/news/world/canadas-joe-fresh-among-brands-made-in-collapsed-bangladesh-building/article11540359/

Tarde, G. (1903). *The laws of imitation*. New York: Henry Holt and Company.

United Nations Development Program (UNDP). (2015). *Table 1: Human development index and its components*. Retrieved from http://hdr.undp.org/en/composite/HDI.

United Nations Refugee Agency. (2016). *With 1 human in every 113 affected, forced displacement hits record high*. Retrieved from www.unhcr.org/afr/news/press/2016/6/5763ace54/1-human-113-affected-forced-displacement-hits-record-high.html

United States of America for United Nations High Commissioner for Refugees. (2017). Home page. Retrieved from www.unrefugees.org

Unterhalter, E. (2005). Global inequality, capabilities, social justice: The millennium development goal for gender equality in education. *International Journal of Educational Development, 25*(2), 111–122.

Valente, T. W. (2010). *Social networks and health: Models, methods, and applications*. Oxford: Oxford University Press.

Vallings, C. & Moreno-Torres, M. (2007). Drivers of fragility: What makes states fragile? PRDE Working Paper no. 7. Department for International Development, UK. Retrieved from http://ageconsearch.umn.edu/bitstream/12824/1/pr050007.pdf

Volpp, L. (2001). Feminism versus multiculturalism. *Columbia Law Review, 101*(5), 1181–1218.

Wallerstein, I. (2011). *The modern world-system: Capitalist agriculture and the origins of the European world-economy in the sixteenth centenary*. Berkeley: University of California Press. (Original work published 1974)

Wallsten, S. J. (2000). The effects of government-industry R&D programs on private R&D: The case of the Small Business Innovation Research program. *Rand Journal of Economics, 31*(1), 82100.

Weber, M. (1930). *The Protestant ethic and the spirit of capitalism*. (T. Parsons, Trans.) New York: Penguin. (Original work published 1905)

Winter, E. (2007). Neither "America" nor "Québec": Constructing the Canadian multicultural nation. *Nations and Nationalism, 13*(3), 481–503.

World Bank Group. (2016). *GDP per capita, PPP (current international $)*. Retrieved from http://data.worldbank.org/indicator/NY.GDP.PCAP.PP.CD.

World Health Organization (WHO). (n.d.). Fact file on health inequalities. Retrieved from www.who.int/sdhconference/background/news/facts/en/.

World Health Organization (WHO). (2016a). *Global Health Observatory (GHO) data*. Retrieved from www.who.int/gho/en/

World Health Organization (WHO). (2016b). *World health statistics 2016: Monitoring health for the SDGs, sustainable development goals*. Retrieved from www.who.int/gho/publications/world_health_statistics/2016/Annex_B/en/

Chapter 10

Adams, R. G., & Allan, G. (Eds.). (1998). *Placing friendship in context*. Cambridge: Cambridge University Press.

Anderssen, E. (2014, January 14). Dirty work: How household chores push families to the brink. *The Globe and Mail*. Retrieved from www.theglobeandmail.com/life/relationships/dirty-work-how-household-chores-push-families-to-the-brink/article12300024/?page=all

Apple, R. D., & Coleman, J. (2003). "As members of the social whole": A history of social reform as a focus of home economics, 1895–1940. *Family and Consumer Sciences Research Journal, 32*(2), 104–126.

Armitage, S. (1985). Women and men in western history: A stereotypical vision. *The Western Historical Quarterly, 16*(4), 381–395.

Armstrong, P., & Armstrong, H. (1993). *The double ghetto: Canadian women and their segregated work*. Toronto, ON: McClelland & Stewart.

Associated Press. (2014, January 13). "Octomom" Nadya Suleman charged with welfare fraud. *The Star (Toronto)*. Retrieved from www.thestar.com/news/world/2014/01/13/octomom_nadya_suleman_charged_with_welfare_fraud.html

Beauchamp, N., Irvine, B., Seeley, J., & Johnson, B. (2005). Worksite-based internet multimedia program for family caregivers of persons with dementia. *The Gerontologist, 45*(6), 793–801.

Brown, P., & Lauder, H. (2001). *Capitalism and social progress: The future of society in a global economy*. London: Palgrave Macmillan.

CATA Women in Technology Forum. (2010, July 12). *Addressing the shortage of women in ICT*. Digital Canada 150, Government of Canada. Retrieved from www.ic.gc.ca/eic/site/028.nsf/eng/00362.html

Chesley, N. (2005). Blurring boundaries? Linking technology use, spillover, individual distress, and family satisfaction. *Journal of Marriage and Family, 67*(5), 1237–1248.

Chesley, N. (2014). Information and communication technology use, work intensification and employee strain and distress. *Work, Employment and Society, 28*(4), 589–610.

Chesley, N., & Johnson, B. (2010). Information and communication technology, work, and family. In S. Sweet & J. Casey (Eds.), *Work and family encyclopaedia*. Boston, MA: Sloan Work and Family Research Network Chestnut Hill.

Chesley, N., & Johnson, B. E. (2014). Information and communication technology use and social connectedness over the life course. *Sociology Compass, 8*(6), 589–602.

Chung, A. (2009, April 5). The link between appliances and feminism. *The Star (Toronto)*. Retrieved from www.thestar.com/news/insight/2009/04/05/the_link_between_appliances_and_feminism.html.

CIRA Fact Book, 2014. (2014). Retrieved from https://cira.ca/factbook/2014/

Dayu, Z. (2014, October 14). My 24 hours with a virtual girlfriend in China. *CNN*. Retrieved from www.cnn.com/2014/10/14/world/asia/china-virtual-girlfriend/index.html

Delistraty, C. (2014, September 24). The eroticism of placelessness [Blog post]. Retrieved from https://delistraty.com/2014/09/29/the-eroticism-of-placelessness/

Delistraty, C. (2014, October 2). Online relationships are real. *The Atlantic*. Retrieved from www.theatlantic.com/health/archive/2014/10/online-relationships-are-real/380304/.

De Souza e Silva, A., & Frith, J. (2010). Locative mobile social networks: Mapping communication and location in urban spaces. *Mobilities, 5*(4), 485–505.

Desrochers, S., & Sargent, L. D. (2004). Boundary/border theory and work-family integration. *Organization Management Journal, 1*(1), 40–48.

Dickens, B. M., & Cook, R. J. (2008). Multiple pregnancy: Legal and ethical issues. *International Journal of Gynecology & Obstetrics, 103*(3), 270–274.

Eicher, M. (2012, May 2). Marriage in Canada. In *The Canadian Encyclopedia*. Retrieved from www.thecanadianencyclopedia.ca/en/article/marriage-and-divorce/

Ellison, M. A., Hotamisligil, S., Lee, H., Rich-Edwards, J. W., Pang, S. C., & Hall, J. E. (2005). Psychosocial risks associated with multiple births resulting from assisted reproduction. *Fertility and Sterility, 83*(5), 1422–1428.

Faisal, S. (2012, October 10). *Encouraging outlook for women in ICT sector leadership roles*. Retrieved from www.ictc-ctic.ca/encouraging-outlook-for-women-in-ict-sector-leadership-roles/

Farrell, B., VandeVusse, A., & Ocobock, A. (2012). Family change and the state of family sociology. *Current Sociology, 60*(3), 283–301.

Finn, J. (1995). Computer-based self-help groups: A new resource to supplement support groups. *Social Work with Groups, 18*(1), 109–117.

Finn, J., & Lavitt, M. (1994). Computer-based self-help groups for sexual abuse survivors. *Social Work with Groups, 17*(1/2), 21–46.

Fonner, K. L., & Stache, L. (2012). All in a day's work, at home: Teleworkers' management of micro role transitions and the work–home boundary. *New Technology, Work and Employment, 27*(3), 242–257.

Fox, B. J. (1990). Selling the mechanized household: 70 years of ads in *Ladies Home Journal*. *Gender & Society, 4*(1), 25–40.

Freedom to marry website. (n.d.). Retrieved from www.freedomtomarry.org

Gant, D., & Kiesler. S. (2002). Blurring the boundaries: Cell phones, mobility, and the line between work and personal life. In B. Brown, N. Green, & R. Harper (Eds.), *Wireless world: Social and international aspects of the mobile world* (pp. 121–131). London: Springer.

Golding, C. A. (2006). Redefining the nuclear family: An exploration of resiliency in lesbian parents. *Journal of Feminist Family Therapy, 18*(1/2), 35–65.

Gondelman, J. (2013, January 24). I bought three fake girlfriends on the internet. *The Cut*. Retrieved from http://nymag.com/thecut/2013/01/i-bought-three-fake-girlfriends-on-the-internet.html.

Goode, W. J. (1963). *World revolution and family patterns*. New York: The Free Press.

Goorwich, S. (2014, September 17). New website offers invisible boyfriends and girlfriends for those who are unlucky in love. *Metro*. Retrieved from http://metro.co.uk/2014/09/17/new-website-offers-invisible-boyfriends-and-girlfriends-for-those-who-are-unlucky-in-love-4872358/

Gordon, S. A. (2004). "Boundless possibilities": Home sewing and the meanings of women's domestic work in the United States, 1890–1930. *Journal of Women's History, 16*(2), 68–91.

Government of Canada. (2013, February 4). *Fertility*. Retrieved from www.canada.ca/en/public-health/services/fertility/fertility.html

Harris, K. J., Harris, R. B., Carlson, J. R., & Carlson, D. S. (2015). Resource loss from technology overload and its impact on work-family conflict: Can leaders help? *Computers in Human Behavior, 50*, 411–417.

Haythornthwaite, C., Kazmer, M. M., Robins, J., & Shoemaker, S. (2000). Community development among distance learners: Temporal and technological dimensions. *Journal of Computer-Mediated Communication, 6*(1). doi:10.1111/j.1083-6101.2000.tb00114.x

Hook, J. L. (2006). Care in context: Men's unpaid work in 20 countries, 1965–2003. *American Sociological Review, 71*(4), 639–660.

Johnson, C. (2014, August 29). Face time vs. screen time: The technological impact on communication. *Deseret News.* Retrieved from http://national.deseretnews.com/article/2235/face-time-vs-screen-time-the-technological-impact-on-communication.html

Kan, M. Y., Sullivan, O. & Gershuny, J. (2011). Gender convergence in domestic work: Discerning the effects of interactional and institutional barriers from large-scale data. *Sociology, 45*(2), 234–251.

Karr-Wisniewski, P., & Lu, Y. (2010). When more is too much: Operationalizing technology overload and exploring its impact on knowledge worker productivity. *Computers in Human Behavior, 26*(5), 1061–1072.

Klinenberg, E. (2012). *Going solo: The extraordinary rise and surprising appeal of living alone.* New York: Penguin.

Knight, W. (2015, July 24). Personal Robots: Artificial friends with limited benefits. *MIT Technology Review.* Retrieved from www.technologyreview.com/news/539356/personal-robots-artificial-friends-with-limited-benefits

Kowalski, R. M., Limber, S. P., Limber, S., & Agatston, P. W. (2012). *Cyberbullying: Bullying in the digital age* (2nd ed.). Malden, MA: John Wiley & Sons.

Lehman, J. (n.d.). Texting: The new way for kids to be rude. *Empowering Parents.* Retrieved from www.empoweringparents.com/My-Teen-is-Addicted-to-Texting.php

Lehmann, J. M. (1994). *Durkheim and women.* Lincoln: University of Nebraska Press.

Luxton, M. (1980). *More than a labour of love: Three generations of women's work in the home* (Vol. 2). Toronto, ON: Canadian Scholars' Press.

Madden, M., & Jones, S. (2008). *Networked workers.* Retrieved from www.pewinternet.org/2008/09/24/networked-workers/

McMullin, J. A. (2005). Patterns of paid and unpaid work: The influence of power, social context, and family background. *Canadian Journal on Aging/La Revue canadienne du vieillissement, 24*(3), 225–236.

Milan, A., & Bohnert, N. (2011). *Portrait of families and living arrangements in Canada. Families, households and marital status, 2011 Census of Population* (Statistics Canada, catalogue no. 98-312-X2011001). Retrieved from www12.statcan.gc.ca/census-recensement/2011/as-sa/98-312-x/98-312-x2011001-eng.pdf

Mintz, S. (2006). From patriarchy to androgyny and other myths. In S. M. Ross (Ed.), *American families past and present: Social perspectives on transformations* (pp. 11–33). New Brunswick, NJ: Rutgers University Press.

Morgan, M. (1996). Jam making, Cuthbert Rabbit and cakes: Redefining domestic labour in the Women's Institute, 1915–60. *Rural History, 7*(2), 207–219.

Nie, N. H., & Hillygus, D. S. (2002). The impact of Internet use on sociability: Time-diary findings. *IT & Society, 1*(1), 1–20.

Nippert-Eng, C. E. (2008). *Home and work: Negotiating boundaries through everyday life.* Chicago, IL: University of Chicago Press.

O'Keeffe, G. S., & Clarke-Pearson, K. (2011). The impact of social media on children, adolescents, and families. *Pediatrics, 127*(4), 800–804.

Oakley, A. (1974). *The sociology of housework.* Oxford: Basil Blackwell.

OECD. (2011). *Closing the gender gap.* Retrieved from www.oecd.org/canada/Closing The Gender Gap - Canada FINAL.pdf

OECD.stat. (2014). *Employment: Time spent in paid and unpaid work, by sex.* Retrieved from http://stats.oecd.org/index.aspx?queryid=54757

Olson-Buchanan, J. B., & Boswell. W. R. (2006). Blurring boundaries: Correlates of integration and segmentation between work and nonwork. *Journal of Vocational Behavior, 68*(3), 432–445.

Parsons, T., & Bales, R.F. (1955). *Socialization, family, and interaction process.* New York: The Free Press.

Pelley, L. (2015, November 2). Indigenous children removed from homes in the 1960s begin to heal. *The Star (Toronto).* Retrieved from www.thestar.com/news/canada/2015/11/02/indigenous-children-removed-from-homes-in-the-1960s-just-now-beginning-to-heal.html

Pew Research Center. (2010). *Millennials: Portrait of the next generation.* Retrieved from www.pewsocialtrends.org/files/2010/10/millennials-confident-connected-open-to-change.pdf

Raphel, A. (2014, July 22). TaskRabbit redux. *The New Yorker.* Retrieved from www.newyorker.com/business/currency/taskrabbit-redux

Ryan, M., & Berkowitz, D. (2009). Constructing gay and lesbian parent families "beyond the closet." *Qualitative Sociology, 32*(2), 153–172.

Short, J., Williams, E., & Christie, B. (1976). *The social psychology of telecommunications.* Hoboken, NJ: John Wiley & Sons.

Smithers, J., & Johnson, P. (2004). The dynamics of family farming in North Huron county, Ontario. Part I. Development trajectories. *The Canadian Geographer/Le Géographe Canadien, 48*(2), 191–208.

Stanescu, B. (2013, July 4). Five barriers to parent-child communication: Bridging gaps with parental control. *Hot for Security.* Retrieved from www.hotforsecurity.com/blog/five-barriers-to-parent-child-communication-bridging-gaps-with-parental-control-6558.html

Stateman, A. (2009, March 7). The fertility doctor behind "Octomom." *Time.* Retrieved from http://content.time.com/time/nation/article/0,8599,1883663,00.html

Statistics Canada. (2017, August 2). *Census in Brief: Same-sex couples in Canada in 2016.* Retrieved from http://www12.statcan.gc.ca/census-recensement/2016/as-sa/98-200-x/2016007/98-200-X2016007-eng.cfm

Strasser, S. (1982). *Never done: A history of American housework.* New York: Pantheon.

Sullivan, O. (2011). An end to gender display through the performance of housework? A review and reassessment of the quantitative literature using insights from the qualitative literature. *Journal of Family Theory & Review, 3*(1), 1–13.

Towers, I., Duxbury, L., Higgins, C., & Thomas, J. (2006). Time thieves and space invaders: Technology, work and the organization. *Journal of Organizational Change Management, 19*(5), 593–618.

Turner, A. (2016, April 13). Living arrangements of Aboriginal children aged 14 and under. *The Daily*. Retrieved from www.statcan.gc.ca/pub/75-006-x/2016001/article/14547-eng.htm

UNICEF. (2001, March). *Early marriage child spouses.* Retrieved from www.unicef.org/childrenandislam/downloads/early_marriage_eng.pdf

United States Securities and Exchange Commission. (2015, March 4). *Form S-1 registration statement under the Securities Act of 1933.* Retrieved from www.sec.gov/Archives/edgar/data/1370637/000119312515077045/d806992ds1.htm

Wajcman, J. (2010). Domestic technology: Labour-saving or enslaving? In C. Hanks (Ed.), *Technology and values: Essential Readings* (pp. 274–288). New York: Wiley-Blackwell.

Wajcman, J., Bittman, M., & Brown, J. E. (2008). Families without borders: Mobile phones, connectedness and work-home divisions. *Sociology, 42*(4), 635–652.

Weissenberg, R., & Landau, R. (2012). Are two a family? Older single mothers assisted by sperm donation and their children revisited. *American Journal of Orthopsychiatry, 82*(4). doi: 10.1111/j.1939-0025.2012.01187.x

Chapter 11

Agatston, P. W., Kowalski, R., & Limber, S. (2007). Students' perspectives on cyber bullying. *Journal of Adolescent Health, 41*(6), S59–S60.

Akiba, M., LeTendre, G. K., & Scribner, J. P. (2007). Teacher quality, opportunity gap, and national achievement in 46 countries. *Educational Researcher, 36*(7), 369–387.

Andres, L., Adamuti-Trache, M., Yoon, E. S., Pidgeon, M., & Thomsen, J. P. (2007). Educational expectations, parental social class, gender, and postsecondary attainment a 10-year perspective. *Youth & Society, 39*(2), 135–163.

Baker, R. K., Berry, P., & Thornton, B. (2008). Student attitudes on academic integrity violations. *Journal of College Teaching and Learning, 5*(1), 5–14.

Baldry, A. C., & Farrington, D. P. (1998). Parenting influences on bullying and victimization. *Legal and Criminological Psychology, 3*(2), 237–254.

Baltodano, M. (2012). Neoliberalism and the demise of public education: The corporatization of schools of education. *International Journal of Qualitative Studies in Education, 25*(4), 487–507.

Barrie, J. M., & Presti, D. E. (2000). Digital plagiarism: The web giveth and the web shall taketh. *Journal of Medical Internet Research, 2*(1). Retrieved from www.jmir.org/2000/1/e6/

Baruchson-Arbib, S., & Yaari, E. (2004). Printed versus internet plagiarism: A study of students' perception. *International Journal of Information Ethics, 1*, 1–7.

Batane, T. (2010). Turning to Turnitin to fight plagiarism among university students. *Educational Technology & Society, 13*(2), 1–12.

Belley, P., Frenette, M., & Lochner, L. (2014). Post-secondary attendance by parental income in the U.S. and Canada: Do financial aid policies explain the differences? *Canadian Journal of Economics, 47*(2), 664–696.

Blanden, J., Gregg, P. & Machin, S. (2005). Educational inequality and intergenerational mobility. In S. Machin & A. Vignoles

(Eds.), *What's the good of education?* (pp. 99–114). Princeton, NJ: Princeton University Press.

Campbell, M. A. (2005). Cyber bullying: An old problem in a new guise? *Australian Journal of Guidance and Counselling, 15*(1), 68–76.

Canadian Virtual University. (2012). *Online university education in Canada: Challenges and opportunities.* Retrieved from http://flexed.sfu.ca/wp-content/uploads/2014/10/Online-University-Education-jan17-2012.pdf

Caro, D. H., McDonald, J. T., & Willms, J. D. (2009). Socio-economic status and academic achievement trajectories from childhood to adolescence. *Canadian Journal of Education, 32*(3), 558–590.

Catropa, D. (2013, February 24). Big (MOOC) data. *Inside Higher Ed.* Retrieved from www.insidehighered.com/blogs/stratedgy/big-mooc-data

CBC News. (2012, June 11). First Nations kids rally on residential schools anniversary. Retrieved from www.cbc.ca/news/politics/first-nations-kids-rally-on-residential-schools-anniversary-1.1294438

Code.org. (n.d.). *About us.* Retrieved from https://code.org/

Connell, R. (2013). The neoliberal cascade and education: An essay on the market agenda and its consequences. *Critical Studies in Education, 54*(2), 99–112.

Contact North (2012). *Online learning in Canada: At a tipping point, a cross-country check-up 2012.* Retrieved from https://teachonline.ca/sites/default/files/tools-trends/downloads/online_learning_in_canada_at_a_tipping_point_-_a_cross_country_check_up_2012_-_july_18_2012_final.pdf

Corak, M. (2013). Income inequality, equality of opportunity, and intergenerational mobility. *The Journal of Economic Perspectives, 27*(3), 79–102.

Courneya, C-A., Pratt, D. D., & Collins, J. (2008). Through what perspective do we judge the teaching of peers? *Teaching and Teacher Education, 24*(1), 69–79.

Disparity in school fundraising is more than just an academic concern. (2012, June 6). *Waterloo Region Record.* Retrieved from www.therecord.com/news-story/2605207-disparity-in-school-fundraising-is-more-than-just-an-academic-concern/

Economist Intelligence Unit. (2008). *The future of higher education: How technology will shape learning.* Retrieved from www.nmc.org/pdf/Future-of-Higher-Ed-(NMC).pdf

FemTechNet. (n.d.). *DOCC.* Retrieved from http://femtechnet.org/docc

Ferrer, A., & Riddell, C. W. (2008). Education, credentials, and immigrant earnings. *Canadian Journal of Economics/Revue canadienne d'économique, 41*(1), 186–216.

Funding disparities in the classroom. (2017, June 2). *Renfrew Mercury.* Retrieved from www.insideottawavalley.com/news-story/3797358-funding-disparities-in-the-classroom/

Giroux, H. (2002). Neoliberalism, corporate culture, and the promise of higher education: The university as a democratic public sphere. *Harvard Educational Review, 72*(4), 425–464.

Government of Canada, Indigenous and Northern Affairs Canada. (2008, June 11). *Statement of apology to former students of Indian Residential Schools.* Retrieved from www.aadnc-aandc.gc.ca/eng/1100100015644/1100100015649

Government of Canada, Innovation, Science and Economic Development Canada. (2015, May 12). *Computers for Schools Program.* Retrieved from www.ic.gc.ca/eic/site/cfs-ope.nsf/eng/home

Hacker, A., & Dreifus, C. (2010). *Higher education? How colleges are wasting our money and failing our kids—and what we can do about it.* New York: Macmillan.

Hansen, B. (2003). Combating plagiarism. *CQ Researcher, 13*(32), 773–796.

Haynie, D. L., Nansel, T., Eitel, P., Crump, A. D., Saylor, K., Yu, K., & Simons-Morton, B. (2001). Bullies, victims, and bully/victims: Distinct groups of at-risk youth. *The Journal of Early Adolescence, 21*(1), 29–49.

Heckler, N. C., Rice, M., & Bryan, C. H. (2013). Turnitin systems: A deterrent to plagiarism in college classrooms. *Journal of Research on Technology in Education, 45*(3), 229–248.

Henderson, E. (2013, January 15). *Feminist pedagogy.* Retrieved from www.genderandeducation.com/feminist-pedagogy/

Hickey, C. (2008). Physical education, sport and hyper-masculinity in schools. *Sport, Education and Society, 13*(2), 147–161.

Indian Residential School Adjudication Secretariat. (2013, December). *Bringing closure, enabling reconciliation: A plan for resolving the remaining IAP caseload. Chief adjudicator's report to the supervising courts.* Retrieved from www.iap-pei.ca/media/information/publication/pdf/pub/com-2013-12-10-eng.pdf

Intini, J. (2013, December 15). Female university enrolment exceeds male. In *The Canadian Encyclopedia.* Retrieved from www.thecanadianencyclopedia.ca/en/article/female-university-enrolment-exceeds-male/

Jaggars, S. S., Edgecombe, N., & Stacey, G. W. (2013a). *Creating an effective online instructor presence* (Community College Research Center, Columbia University). Retrieved from https://ccrc.tc.columbia.edu/media/k2/attachments/effective-online-instructor-presence.pdf

Jaggars, S. S., Edgecombe, N., & Stacey, G. W. (2013b). *What we know about online course outcomes: Research overview* (Community College Research Center, Columbia University). Retrieved from https://ccrc.tc.columbia.edu/media/k2/attachments/what-we-know-about-online-course-outcomes.pdf

Jaschik, S. (2013, August 19). Feminist professors create an alternative to MOOCs. *Inside Higher Ed.* Retrieved from www.insidehighered.com/news/2013/08/19/feminist-professors-create-alternative-moocs

Jencks, C., & Riesman, D. (1968). *The academic revolution.* New York: Doubleday.

Jump, P. (2013, April 4). Turnitin is turning up fewer cases of plagiarism. *Times Higher Education.* Retrieved from www.timeshighereducation.co.uk/news/turnitin-is-turning-up-fewer-cases-of-plagiarism/2002939.article

Kadison, R., & DiGeronimo, T. F. (2004). *College of the overwhelmed: The campus mental health crisis and what to do about it.* San Franciso: Jossey-Bass.

Klein, J. (2006). Cultural capital and high school bullies how social inequality impacts school violence. *Men and Masculinities, 9*(1), 53–75.

Konnikova, M. (2014, November 7). Why MOOCs are failing the people they're supposed to help. *The New Yorker.* Retrieved from www.newyorker.com/science/maria-konnikova/moocs-failure-solutions

Kopell, C. (2013, April 18). Educate girls, develop nations [Blog post]. Retrieved from https://blog.usaid.gov/2013/04/educate-girls-develop-nations/

Lareau, A. (2003). *Unequal childhoods: Race, class and family life.* Berkeley: University of California Press.

Larrasquet, J.-M., & Pilnière, V. (2012). Seeking a sustainable future: The role of university. *International Journal of Technology Management & Sustainable Development, 11*(3), 207–215.

Levinson, M. (2013, February 8). Where MOOCs miss the mark: The student–teacher relationship [Blog post]. *Edutopia.* Retrieved from www.edutopia.org/blog/where-MOOCs-miss-the-mark-matt-levinson

Li, P. S. (2001). The market worth of immigrants' educational credentials. *Canadian Public Policy/Analyse de Politiques, 27*(1), 23–38.

Macdonald, D., & Shaker, E. (2012). *Eduflation and the high cost of learning.* Ottawa, ON: Canadian Centre for Policy Alternatives. Retrieved from www.policyalternatives.ca/sites/default/files/uploads/publications/National%20Office/2012/09/Eduflation%20and%20High%20Cost%20Learning.pdf

Matsui, K. (2013, March 7). The economic benefits of educating women. *Bloomberg.* Retrieved from www.bloomberg.com/news/articles/2013-03-07/the-economic-benefits-of-educating-women

McCabe, D. L., Butterfield, K. D., Klebe Trevino, L. (2004). Academic integrity: How widespread is cheating and plagiarism? In D. Karp & T. Allena (Eds.), *Restorative justice on the college campus: Promoting student growth and responsibility, and reawakening the spirit of campus community* (pp. 124–135). Springfield, IL: Charles C. Thomas Publisher Ltd.

McCabe, D. L., Butterfield, K. D., Klebe Trevino, L. (2006). Academic dishonesty in graduate business programs: Prevalence, causes, and proposed action. *Academy of Management Learning & Education, 5*(3), 294–305.

Mishna, F. (2012). *Bullying: A guide to research, intervention, and prevention.* New York: Oxford University Press.

Mishna, F., & Van Wert, M. (2015). *Bullying in Canada.* Don Mills, ON: Oxford University Press.

Mohamedbhai, G. (2008, March 31–April 2). The contribution of higher education to the Millennium Development Goals. Paper presented at the 4th International Barcelona Conference on Higher Education, New Challenges and Emerging Roles for Human and Social Development, Barcelona.

Monahan, R. (2014, December 12). What happens when kids don't have internet at home? *The Atlantic.* Retrieved from www.theatlantic.com/education/archive/2014/12/what-happens-when-kids-dont-have-internet-at-home/383680

OECD. (2013, January). What are the social effects of education? *Education Indicators in Focus.* Retrieved from www.oecd.org/education/skills-beyond-school/EDIF%202013--N%C2%B010%20(eng)--v9%20FINAL%20bis.pdf

People for Education. (2013). *Mind the gap: Inequality in Ontario's public schools. People for Education annual report on Ontario's publicly funded schools 2013.* Toronto, ON: People for Education. Retrieved from www.peopleforeducation.ca/wp-content/uploads/2013/05/annual-report-2013-WEB.pdf

Pepler, D., & Craig, W. (1997). Bullying: Research and interventions. *Youth Update, 15*(1), 1–15.

Perren, S., & Alsaker, F. D. (2006). Social behavior and peer relationships of victims, bully-victims, and bullies in kindergarten. *Journal of Child Psychology and Psychiatry, 47*(1), 45–57.

Pfeffer, F. T., & Hertel, F. R. (2015). How has educational expansion shaped social mobility trends in the United States? *Social Forces; A Scientific Medium of Social Study and Interpretation, 94*(1), 143–180.

Population Reference Bureau (PRB). (2011). *The effects of girls' education on health outcomes: Fact sheet.* Retrieved from www.prb.org/Publications/Media-Guides/2011/girls-education-fact-sheet.aspx

Porter, J. (2016, March 14). *First Nations students get 30 per cent less funding than other children, economist says.* Retrieved from www.cbc.ca/news/canada/thunder-bay/first-nations-education-funding-gap-1.3487822

Quint, J., Bloom, H. S., Black, A. R., Stephens, L., & Akey, T. M. (2005). *The challenge of educational reform: Findings and lessons from First Things First. Final report.* Retrieved from www.mdrc.org/sites/default/files/full_531.pdf

Reich, J. (2014, December 8). MOOC completion and retention in the context of student intent. *Educause Review.* Retrieved from http://er.educause.edu/articles/2014/12/mooc-completion-and-retention-in-the-context-of-student-intent

Rimer, S. (2003, September 3). A campus fad that's being copied: Internet plagiarism seems on the rise. *The New York Times.* Retrieved from www.nytimes.com/2003/09/03/nyregion/a-campus-fad-that-s-being-copied-internet-plagiarism-seems-on-the-rise.html

Rushowy, K. (2016, February 25). Free tuition for college or university promised to students from low-income families. *The Star (Toronto).* Retrieved from www.thestar.com/news/queenspark/2016/02/25/free-tuition-for-college-or-university-promised-to-students-from-low-income-families.html

Sanders, W. L., & Rivers, J. C. (1996). *Cumulative and residual effects of teachers on future student academic achievement.* Knoxville: University of Tennessee.

Santiago, P. (2004). The labour market for teachers. In G. Johnes & J. Johnes (Eds.), *International Handbook on the economics of education* (pp. 522–579). Cheltenham, UK: Edward Elgar Publishing Ltd.

Scanlon, P. M., & Neumann, D. R. (2002). Internet plagiarism among college students. *Journal of College Student Development, 43*(3), 374–385.

Schacter, J., & Thum, Y. M. (2004). Paying for high- and low-quality teaching. *Economics of Education Review, 23*(4), 411–430.

Schwartzman, R. (2013). Consequences of commodifying education. *Academic Exchange Quarterly, 17*(3), 1096–1463.

Seeley, J. R., Sim, R. A., Loosley, E. W., & Riesman, D. (1963). *Crestwood Heights: A study of the culture of suburban life.* New York: J. Wiley. (Original work published 1956)

Selingo, J. J. (2014, October 1). Demystifying the MOOC. *The New York Times.* Retrieved from www.nytimes.com/2014/11/02/education/edlife/demystifying-the-mooc.html

Statistics Canada. (2015). *Education: Highest certificate, diploma, or degree.* Retrieved from www.statcan.gc.ca/pub/89-645-x/2015001/education-eng.htm

Statistics Canada. (2016). *Education in Canada: Attainment, field of study, and location.* Retrieved from www12.statcan.gc.ca/nhs-enm/2011/as-sa/99-012-x/99-012-x2011001-eng.cfm#a4

St Germain, G., & Dyck, L. E. (2011). *Reforming First Nations education: From crisis to hope* (Catalogue no. YC28-0/411-3E). Ottawa, ON: Standing Senate Committee on Aboriginal Peoples.

Sun, C.-Y., & Benton, D. (2008). The socioeconomic disparity in technology use and its impact on academic performance. In K. McFerrin, R. Weber, R. Carlsen & D. Willis (Eds.), *Proceedings of Society for Information Technology & Teacher Education International Conference 2008* (pp. 1025–1028). Chesapeake, VA: Association for the Advancement of Computing in Education.

Task Force on Misogyny, Sexism and Homophobia in Dalhousie University Faculty of Dentistry. (2015, June 26). *Report on the Task Force on Misogyny, Sexism and Homophobia in Dalhousie University Faculty of Dentistry.* Retrieved from www.dal.ca/content/dam/dalhousie/pdf/cultureofrespect/DalhousieDentistry-TaskForceReport-June2015.pdf

United Nations. (2009). *The Millennium Development Goals report 2009.* Retrieved from www.un.org/millenniumgoals/pdf/MDG_Report_2009_ENG.pdf

Vaughn, M. G., Fu, Q., Bender, K., DeLisi, M., Beaver, K. M., Perron, B. E., & Howard, M. O. (2010). Psychiatric correlates of bullying in the United States: Findings from a national sample. *Psychiatric Quarterly, 81*(3), 183–195.

Veenstra, R., Lindenberg, S., Oldehinkel, A. J., De Winter, A. F., Verhulst, F. C., & Ormel, J. (2005). Bullying and victimization in elementary schools: A comparison of bullies, victims, bully/victims, and uninvolved preadolescents. *Developmental Psychology, 41*(4), 672–682.

Wall, S. (2008). Of heads and hearts: Women in doctoral education at a Canadian university. *Women's Studies International Forum, 31*(3), 219–228.

Wang, Y.-M. (2008). University student online plagiarism. *International Journal on E-Learning, 7*(4), 743–757.

Warwick, J. (2011, December 17). Residential school payments unable to compensate for "genocidal practices": Survivor. *The National Post.* Retrieved from http://news.nationalpost.com/news/canada/residential-school-payments-unable-to-compensate-for-genocidal-practices-survivor

Wilson, B. (2002). The "anti-jock" movement: Reconsidering youth resistance, masculinity, and sport culture in the age of the Internet. *Sociology of Sport Journal, 19*(2), 206–233.

Zhao, Y., & Ho, A. D. (2014). *Evaluating the flipped classroom in an undergraduate history course* (HarvardX Research Memo). Retrieved from http://harvardx.harvard.edu/files/harvardx/files/evaluating_the_flipped_classroom_-_zhao_and_ho.pdf

Zietsma, D. (2007). *The Canadian immigrant labour market in 2006: First results from Canada's labour force survey* (Statistics Canada). Retrieved from www.statcan.gc.ca/pub/71-606-x/71-606-x2007001-eng.htm

Chapter 12

Abramson, P., & Inglehart, R. F. (2009). *Value change in global perspective.* Ann Arbor: University of Michigan Press.

Acemoglu, D. (2002). Technical change, inequality, and the labor market. *Journal of economic literature, 40*(1), 7–72.

Allen, M., & Ainley, P. (2012). Why young people can't get the jobs they want and what can be done about it. *Soundings 51*, 54–65.

Bailey, S. (2014). Who makes a better leader: A man or a woman? Forbes. Retrieved from www.forbes.com/sites/sebastianbailey/2014/07/23/who-makes-a-better-leader-a-man-or-a-woman/#2dcbb9b21260

Bell, D., & Blanchflower, D. (2011). Youth underemployment in the UK in the Great Recession. *National Institute Economic Review, 215*(1): R23–R33.

Big Brothers, Big Sisters of Ajax-Pickering. (2012). *Service delivery manual.* Retrieved from www.bigbrothersbigsisters.ca/site-bbbs/media/ajaxpickering2012/Service%20Delivery%20Manual%20Updated%202012.pdf

Bogart, N. (2014). What it's like for Canadian women working in tech. *Global News.* Retrieved from http://globalnews.ca/news/1698272/what-its-like-for-canadian-women-working-in-tech/

Booth, A. L., Francesconi, M., & Frank, J. (2002). Temporary jobs: Stepping stones or dead ends? *The Economic Journal, 112* (480), 189–213.

Braverman, H. (1998). *Labor and monopoly capital: The degradation of work in the twentieth century.* New York: New York University Press. (Original work published 1974)

Canada Post clerk fired for nasty Facebook posts. (2012, May 10). *The Star (Toronto).* Retrieved from www.thestar.com/business/personal_finance/2012/05/10/canada_post_clerk_fired_for_nasty_facebook_posts.html

Canadian Labour Congress. (2015). *Why unions?* Retrieved from http://canadianlabour.ca/why-unions

Carlopio, J. (2011). Development strategy by design: The future of strategy. *World Future Review, 3*(2), 11–16.

Durkheim, É. (2014). *The division of labor in society.* New York: Simon & Schuster. (Original work published 1904)

Edwards, R. C. (1979). *Contested terrain: The transformation of the workplace in the twentieth century.* New York: Basic Books.

Fernandez, J. (2014, July 7). How the "digital skills gap" bleeds $1.3 trillion a year from US businesses. *Entrepreneur.* Retrieved from www.entrepreneur.com/article/235366

Fernandez, R. M. (2001). Skill-biased technological change and wage inequality: Evidence from a plant retooling. *American Journal of Sociology, 107*(2), 273–320.

Feth & Zurbrigg. (2012, March 29) Another Brick in the wall: Arbitrator upholds discharge for offensive Facebook posting, workwise: Current employment and labour law issues. *Work Wise: Current Employment and Labour Law Issues.* Retrieved from www.slideshare.net/kempedmonds/another-brick-in-the-wall-12662091

Fisher, M. (2012, July 3). Why are so many Greek youth snubbing work? *The National Post.* Retrieved from http://news.nationalpost.com/2012/07/03/why-are-so-many-greek-youth-snubbing-work

Golden, T. D., & Veiga, J. F. (2005). The impact of extent of telecommuting on job satisfaction: Resolving inconsistent findings. *Journal of Management, 31*(2), 301–318.

Govan, F. (2012, January 27). Spain's lost generation: Youth unemployment surges above 50 per cent." *The Telegraph.* Retrieved from www.telegraph.co.uk/news/worldnews/europe/spain/9044897/Spains-lost-generation-youth-unemployment-surges-above-50-per-cent.html

Goyette, J. (2015, April 18). Why we can't forget transgender people when talking about the pay gap. *Public Radio International.* Retrieved from www.pri.org/stories/2015-04-18/why-we-cant-forget-transgender-people-when-talking-about-the-pay-gap

Grant, J., Mottet, L., Tanis, J., Harrison, J., Herman, J., & Keisling, M. (2011). *Injustice at every turn: A report of the National Transgender Discrimination Survey.* Washington, DC: National Center for Transgender Equality and National Gay and Lesbian Task Force.

Grant, T. (2016, March 7). Women still earning less money than men despite gains in education: Study. *The Globe and Mail.* Retrieved from www.theglobeandmail.com/news/national/women-still-earning-less-money-than-men-despite-gains-in-education-study/article29044130/

Holodny, E. (2016, July 9). This chart highlights one of Europe's biggest problems. *Business Insider.* Retrieved from www.businessinsider.com/youth-unemployment-in-europe-2016-7

Hoskyns, C., & Rai, S. M. (2007). Recasting the global political economy: Counting women's unpaid work. *New Political Economy, 12*(3), 297–317.

HR Insights Blog. (2015, January 14). Should you be performing Facebook background checks? [Blog post]. Retrieved from www.yourerc.com/blog/post/Should-You-Be-Performing-Facebook-Background-Checks.aspx

Hyman, R. (2002). The future of unions. *Just Labour, 1*, 7–15.

Jackson, A., Baldwin, B., Robinson, D., & Wiggins, C. (2000). *Falling behind: The state of working Canada, 2000.* Ottawa, ON: Canadian Centre for Policy Alternatives.

Kotamraju, N. P. (2002). Keeping up: Web design skill and the reinvented worker. *Information, Communication & Society, 5*(1), 1–26.

Kramer, R. M. (1999). Trust and distrust in organizations: Emerging perspectives, enduring questions. *Annual Review of Psychology, 50*(1), 569–598.

Law Commission of Ontario. (2009). *Who are workers in precarious jobs?* Retrieved from www.lco-cdo.org/en/vulnerable-workers-call-for-papers-noack-vosko-sectionVI

Lefroncois, A. (2015, November 5). Canada's working poor and precarious employment. Retrieved from www.livingwagecanada.ca/index.php/blog/canadas-working-poor-and-precarious-employment/

Lenski, G. (2015). *Ecological-evolutionary theory: Principles and applications.* New York: Routledge.

Lewchuk, W., et al. (2015). *The precarity penalty: The impact of employment precarity on individuals, households and communities—and what to do about it.* Retrieved from www.unitedwaytyr.com/document.doc?id=307

Lewchuk, W., et al. (2016). The precarity penalty: How insecure employment disadvantages workers and their families. *Alternate Routes: A Journal of Critical Social Research, 27.* Retrieved from www.alternateroutes.ca/index.php/ar/article/view/22394/18176

Kotamraju, N. P. (2002). Keeping up: Web design skill and the reinvented worker. *Information, Communication & Society, 5*(1), 1–26.

MacEachen, E. (2000). The mundane administration of worker bodies: From welfarism to neoliberalism. *Health, Risk & Society, 2*(3), 315–327.

Marowits, R. (2016, May 23). More employees working from home in shift to "telecommuting." *The Star (Toronto)*. Retrieved from www.thestar.com/business/2016/05/23/more-employees-working-from-home-in-shift-to-telecommuting.html

Marx, K., & Engels, F. (2002). *The communist manifesto.* New York: Penguin. (Original work published 1848)

McQuaid, R. (2014, July 28). Youth unemployment produces multiple scarring effects [Blog post]. *British Politics & Policy.* Retrieved from http://blogs.lse.ac.uk/politicsandpolicy/multiple-scarring-effects-of-youth-unemployment/

McQuaid, R., Raeside, R., Egdell, V., & Graham, H. (2016). *Multiple scarring effects of youth unemployment in the UK.* Retrieved from http://unisalzburg.at/fileadmin/multimedia/SOWI/ documents/VWL/FOSEM/FOSEM_SS_2014/mcquaid_paper.pdf

Mertl, S. (2012, May 13). Canada Post mail sorter who went postal on Facebook loses job. *Yahoo News.* Retrieved from http://ca.news.yahoo.com/blogs/dailybrew/canada-post-mail-sorter-went-postal-facebook-loses-225236845.html

Mills, C. W. (1951). *White collar: The American middle classes.* New York: Oxford University Press.

Murphy, J. (2015, March 11). 5 female inventors who changed life as we know it. *Biography.* Retrieved from www.biography.com/news/famous-women-inventors-biography

Myles, J. (1991). Post-industrialism and the Service Economy. In D. Drache & M. Gertler (Eds.), *The new era of global competition, state policy and market power* (pp. 351–366). Montreal, QC & Kingston, ON: McGill–Queen's University Press.

Myles, J., Picot, G., & Wannell, T. (1993). Does post-industrialism matter? The Canadian experience. In G. Esping-Andersen. *Changing classes: Stratification and mobility in post-industrial societies* (pp. 171–194). London: Sage.

Overton, M. (1996). *Agricultural revolution in England: The transformation of the agrarian economy 1500–1850.* Cambridge: Cambridge University Press.

Powell, N. (2011, November 7). Europe's lost generation: No jobs or hope for the young. *The Globe and Mail.* Retrieved from www.theglobeandmail.com/report-on-business/international-business/european-business/europes-lost-generation-no-jobs-or-hope-for-the-young/article4250416/

Prensky, M. (2007). How to teach with technology: Keeping both teachers and students comfortable in an era of exponential change. *Emerging Technologies for Learning, 2*(4), 40–46.

Quinlan, M., & Sheldon, P. (2011). The enforcement of minimum labour standards in an era of neo-liberal globalisation: An overview. *The Economic and Labour Relations Review, 22*(2) 5–31. https://doi.org/10.1177/103530461102200202

Quinlan, M., Mayhew, C., & Bohle, P. (2001). The global expansion of precarious employment, work disorganization, and consequences for occupational health: A review of recent research. *International Journal of Health Services, 31*(2), 335–414.

Ritzer, G. (2015). *The McDonaldization of society* (8th ed.). Thousand Oaks, CA: Sage. (Original work published in 1993)

Rong, G, & Grover, V. (2009). Keeping up-to-date with information technology: Testing a model of technological knowledge renewal effectiveness for IT professionals. *Information & Management, 46*(7), 376–387.

Salazar, D. (2012, January 28). Europe's lost generation: How it feels to be young and struggling in the EU. *The Guardian.* Retrieved from www.guardian.co.uk/world/2012/jan/28/europes-lost-generation-young-eu

Sassen, S. (1995). On concentration and centrality in the global city. In P. Knox & P. Taylor (Eds.), *World cities in a world system* (pp. 63–78). Cambridge: Cambridge University Press.

Scott, S. (n.d.). Importance of technology in the workplace. *Chron.* Retrieved from http://smallbusiness.chron.com/importance-technology-workplace-10607.html

Smith, J. (2012, May 15). Taking workplace battles online. *Canadian HR Reporter.* Retrieved from www.hrreporter.com/blog/employment-law/archive/2012/05/15/taking-workplace-battles-online

Smith, P., & Morton, G. (2006). Nine years of new labour: Neoliberalism and workers' rights. *British Journal of Industrial Relations, 44*(3), 401–420.

Turcotte, M. (2010). Working at home: An update. *Canadian Social Trends, 91,* 3–11.

UNDP. (2015). *Human development report 2015: Work for human development.* Retrieved from https://issuu.com/unpublications/docs/2015_human_development_rpt

Vosko, L. F., Zukewich, N., & Cranford, C. (2003). Precarious jobs: A new typology of employment. *Perspectives on labour and income, 15*(4). Retrieved from http://www.amillionreasons.ca/Precariousjobs.pdf

Wallerstein, I. (1974). The rise and future demise of the world capitalist system: Concepts for comparative analysis. *Comparative Studies in Society and History, 16*(4), 387–415.

Wasser, L. A. (2013, April). Social media background checks in Canada: Do the risks outweigh the rewards? *Employment and Labour Bulletin.* Retrieved from www.mcmillan.ca/social-media-background-checks-in-Canada-do-the-risks-outweigh-the-rewards

Waters, J. (2011, July 25). Could you pass a Facebook background check? *Market Watch.* Retrieved from www.marketwatch.com/story/could-you-pass-a-facebook-background-check-2011-07-25

Weber, M. (2009). *From Max Weber: Essays in sociology.* New York: Routledge.

Wells, H. G. (1999). *Anticipations of the reaction of mechanical and scientific progress upon human life and thought.* North Clemsford, MA: Courier Corporation. (Original work published 1901)

Chapter 13

Almond, G. A., Sivan, E., & Appleby, R. S. (1995). Fundamentalism: Genus and species. In M. E. Marty & R. S. Appleby (Eds.), *Fundamentalisms comprehended* (pp. 190–233). Chicago, IL: University of Chicago Press.

Angus Reid Public Opinion. (2012, September 5). *Britons and Canadians more likely to endorse evolution than Americans* [News release]. Retrieved from http://angusreidglobal.com/wp-content/uploads/2012/09/2012.09.05_CreEvo.pdf

Antoun, R. T. (2001). *Understanding fundamentalism: Christian, Islamic, and Jewish movements.* Walnut Creek, CA: AltaMira.

Apple, M. W. (2001). Bringing the world to God: Education and the politics of authoritarian religious populism. *Discourse, 22,* 149–172.

Aryan, S., Aryan, H., & Halderman, J. A. (2013). Internet censorship in Iran: A first look [Paper presentation]. Retrieved from www.usenix.org/system/files/conference/foci13/foci13-aryan.pdf

Authier, P. (2015, April 15). Cities dropping prayers, but politicians in Quebec City stick to crucifix in legislature. *Montreal Gazette.* Retrieved from http://montrealgazette.com/news/cities-dropping-prayers-but-politicians-in-quebec-city-stick-to-crucifix-in-legislature

Bartkowski, J. P. (2001). *Remaking the godly marriage: Gender negotiation in evangelical families.* New Brunswick, NJ: Rutgers University Press.

Bartkowski, J. P. (2004). *The Promise Keepers: Servants, soldiers, and godly men.* New Brunswick, NJ: Rutgers University Press.

Bellah, R. N. (1967). Civil religion in America. *Daedalus, 1,* 1–21.

Bendroth, M. L. (1999). Fundamentalism and the family: Gender, culture, and the American profamily movement. *Journal of Women's History, 10,* 35–54.

Berger, P. (1974). Some second thoughts on substantive versus functional definitions of religion. *Journal for the Scientific Study of Religion, 13,* 125–133.

Bibby, R. W. (1990). *Fragmented gods: The poverty and potential of religion in Canada.* Toronto, ON: Stoddart.

Bibby, R. W. (2011). *Beyond the Gods & back: Religion's demise and rise and why it matters.* Lethbridge, AB: Project Canada Books.

Bibby, R. W. (2012). *A new day: The resilience and restructuring of religion in Canada.* Project Canada Books.

Bibby, R. W., & Grenville, A. (2016). What the polls do show: Toward enhanced survey readings of religion in Canada. *Canadian Review of Sociology/Revue canadienne de sociologie, 53*(1), 123–136.

Book, G. (2002). *Women in European history.* Oxford: Blackwell.

Briggs, R. (1991). Women as victims? Witches, judges, and the community. *French History, 5*(4), 438–450.

Cadge, W., & Ecklund, E. H. (2007). Immigration and religion. *Annual Review of Sociology, 33,* 359–379.

Calhoun, C. (2007). *Nations matter: Culture, history and the cosmopolitan dream.* New York: Routledge.

Calhoun, C. (Ed.). (2002). *Dictionary of the social sciences.* Oxford University Press on Demand.

Campbell, H. A. (2012). Understanding the relationship between religion online and offline in a networked society. *Journal of the American Academy of Religion, 80*(1), 64–93.

Carmody, J. (1983). *Ecology and religion: Toward a new Christian theology of nature.* New York: Paulist Press.

Chai, K. J. (1998). Competing for the second generation: English-language ministry at a Korean Protestant church. In R. S. Warner and J. G. Wittner (Eds.). *Gatherings in diaspora: Religious communities and the new immigration* (pp. 295–331). Philadelphia, PA: Temple University Press.

Clark, W., & Schellenberg, G. (2006). Who's religious? *Canadian Social Trends, 81,* 2–9.

Dahan, M. (1995). The Internet and government censorship: The case of the Israeli secret service. In *Proceedings of the International online information meeting* (pp. 41–48). New York.

Daly, M. (1975). The qualitative leap beyond patriarchal religion. *Quest, 1*(4), 20–40.

Daly, M. (1985). *Beyond God the father: Toward a philosophy of women's liberation.* Boston, MA: Beacon Press.

Downey, A. B. (2014). *Religious affiliation, education and internet use.* Retrieved from https://arxiv.org/abs/1403.5534

Durkheim, É. (2001). *The elementary forms of religious life.* New York: Oxford University Press. (Original work published 1903)

Ebaugh, H. R., & Chafetz, J. S. (2000). Structural adaptations in immigrant congregations. *Sociology of Religion, 61*(2), 135–153.

Ecklund, E. H. (2007). Religion and spirituality among university scientists. *Contexts, 7*(1). Retrieved from http://religion.ssrc.org/reforum/Ecklund.pdf

Ecklund, E. H., Park, J. Z., & Sorrell, K. L. (2011). Scientists negotiate boundaries between religion and science. *Journal for the Scientific Study of Religion, 50*(3), 552–569.

Emerson, M. O., & Hartman, D. (2006). The rise of religious fundamentalism. *Annual Review of Sociology, 32,* 127–144.

Evans, J. H., & Evans, M. S. (2008). Religion and science: Beyond the epistemological conflict narrative. *Annual Review of Sociology, 34,* 87–105.

Fulton, A. S., Gorsuch, R. L., & Maynard, E. A. (1999). Religious orientation, antihomosexual sentiment, and fundamentalism among Christians. *Journal for the Scientific Study of Religion, 38,* 14–22.

Funk, C., & Raine, L. (2015, January 29). *Public and scientists' views on science and society.* Retrieved from www.pewinternet.org/2015/01/29/public-and-scientists-views-on-science-and-society/

Gauvreau, D., & Gossage, P. (2001). Canadian fertility transitions: Quebec and Ontario at the turn of the twentieth century. *Journal of Family History, 26*(2), 162–188.

Gohdes, A. R. (2015). Pulling the plug: Network disruptions and violence in civil conflict. *Journal of Peace Research, 52*(3), 352–367.

Griffin, W. (1995). The embodied goddess: Feminist witchcraft and female divinity. *Sociology of Religion, 56*(1), 35–48.

Hafiz, Y. (2014, June 3). Over 40 percent of Americans believe in creationism, survey says. *The Huffington Post.* Retrieved from www.huffingtonpost.ca/entry/creationism-america-survey_n_5434107

Helland, C. (2005). Online religion as lived religion: Methodological issues in the study of religious participation on the internet. *Online-Heidelberg Journal of Religions on the Internet, 1*(1). Retrieved from http://archiv.ub.uni-heidelberg.de/volltextserver/5823/

Hester, M. (1992). The witch-craze in sixteenth-and seventeenth-century England as social control of women. In J. Radford & D. E. H. Russell (Eds.). *Femicide: The politics of woman killing* (pp. 27–39) New York: Twayne.

Hiebert, P. G., & Shaw, R. D. (2000). *Understanding folk religion: A Christian response to popular beliefs and practices.* Grand Rapids, MI: Baker Books.

How the internet is taking away America's religion. (2014, April 4). *MIT Technology Review.* Retrieved from www.technologyreview.com/s/526111/how-the-internet-is-taking-away-americas-religion/

Jammer, M. (2011). *Einstein and religion: Physics and theology.* Princeton, NJ: Princeton University Press.

Jantzen, G. (1999). *Becoming divine: Towards a feminist philosophy of religion.* Bloomington: Indiana University Press.

Larson, E., & Witham, L. (1997). Belief in God and immortality among American scientists: A historical survey revisited. *Nature, 386,* 435–436.

Larson, E. J., & Witham, L. (1998). Leading scientists still reject God. *Nature, 394,* 313.

Leuba, J. H. (1916). *The belief in God and immortality: A psychological, anthropological and statistical study.* Boston: Sherman, French & Co.

Macfarquhar, N. (2007, June 23). Iran cracks down on dissent, parading examples in the streets. *The New York Times.* Retrieved from http://query.nytimes.com/gst/fullpage.html?res=9E04E1D-C1E3FF937A15755C0A9619C8B63&pagewanted=all

Madden, M., Lenhart, A., Duggan, M., Cortesi, S., & Gasser, U. (2013, March 13). *Teens and technology 2013.* Retrieved from www.pewinternet.org/2013/03/13/teens-and-technology-2013/

Manning, J. (1999). *Is the pope Catholic? A woman confronts her church.* Toronto, ON: Malcolm Lester Books.

Orion, L. (1995). *Never again the burning times: Paganism revived.* Long Grove, IL: Waveland Press.

Palmer, S. J. (2004). *Aliens adored: Raël's UFO religion.* New Brunswick, NJ: Rutgers University Press.

Pew Research Center. (2010, February 16). *Religion among the millennials.* Retrieved from www.pewforum.org/2010/02/17/religion-among-the-millennials

Scott, J. (Ed.). (2014). *A dictionary of sociology* (4th ed.). New York: Oxford University Press.

Statistics Canada. (2002). *Religiosity index, Canada, 2002.* Retrieved from www.statcan.gc.ca/pub/11-008-x/2006001/t/4097602-eng.htm

Thompson, K. (1990). Secularization and sacralization. In J. C. Alexander & P. Sztompka (Eds.). *Rethinking progress: Movements, forces, and ideas at the end of the 20th century* (pp. 161–181). London: Unwin Hyman.

Weber, M. (1930). *The Protestant ethic and the spirit of capitalism.* (T. Parsons, Trans.) New York: Penguin. (Original work published 1905)

Whitney, E. (1995). The witch "she"/the historian "he": Gender and the historiography of the European witch-hunts. *Journal of Women's History, 7*(3), 77–101.

Woods, A. (2013, October 17). Quebec's proposed charter violates religious freedom, says rights watchdog. *The Star (Toronto).* Retrieved from www.thestar.com/news/canada/2013/10/17/quebec_charter_violates_religious_freedom_human_rights_watchdog.html

Chapter 14

Abma, S. (2016). *Budget boosts funding to Canada Council.* Retrieved from www.cbc.ca/news/canada/ottawa/arts-federal-budget-canada-council-heritage-1.3501480

Allcot, H., & Gentzkow, M. (2017). Social media and fake news in the 2016 election. *Journal of Economic Perspectives, 31*(2), 211–236.

Aung-Thwin, M. et al. (Producer), & Gaylor, D. (Director). (2008). *RIP! A Remix Manifesto* [Motion Picture]. Canada: EyeSteelFilm.

Babe, R., & Potter, J. (2015). Media ownership. In *The Canadian Encyclopedia.* Retrieved from www.thecanadianencyclopedia.ca/en/article/media-ownership/

Bauman, Z. (2007). *Consuming life.* Cambridge, UK: Polity Press.

Bechdel, A. (n.d.). *Dykes to watch out for.* [Blog]. Retrieved from http://dykestowatchoutfor.com/

Bode, L. (2016). Political news in the news feed: Learning politics from social media. *Mass Communication and Society, 19*(1), 24–48.

Bryce, I., DeSanto, T., di Bonaventura, L., & Murphy, D. (Producer), & Bay, M. (Director). (2017). *Transformers: The last knight.* United States: Paramount Pictures.

Campbell, R., Martin, C. R., & Fabos, B. (2011). *Media and culture: An introduction to mass communication* (7th, 2011 update ed.). Boston, MA: Bedford/St Martin's.

CBC News. (2012, March 22). Media convergence, acquisitions and sales in Canada. Retrieved from www.cbc.ca/news/business/media-convergence-acquisitions-and-sales-in-canada-1.948788

Chazan, G. (2017, March 14). Germany to crack down on social media over fake news. *Financial Times.* Retrieved from www.ft.com/content/c10aa4f8-08a5-11e7-97d1-5e720a26771b

CNN Library. (2017, March 2). Operation Iraqi Freedom and Operation New Dawn fast facts. Retrieved from www.cnn.com/2013/10/30/world/meast/operation-iraqi-freedom-and-operation-new-dawn-fast-facts/

CTV News. (2011). *Gender stereotypes persist among young Canadians.* Retrieved from www.ctvnews.ca/gender-stereotypes-persist-among-young-canadians-1.701258

Eshet-Alkalai, Y. (2004). Digital literacy: A conceptual framework for survival skills in the digital era. *Journal of Educational Multimedia and Hypermedia, 13*(1), 93–106.

Fortune. (2017, June 27). Mark Zuckerberg: Facebook now has 2 billion users worldwide. Retrieved from http://fortune.com/2017/06/27/mark-zuckerberg-facebook-userbase/

Giroux, H., & Pollock, G. (2010). *The mouse that roared Disney and the end of the innocence* (2nd ed.). Lanham, MD: Rowman & Littlefield Publishers.

González, A. (2017, February 2). Amazon sales hit $136B in 2016; dollar hurts overseas business. *The Seattle Times.* Retrieved from www.seattletimes.com/business/amazon/amazon-revenues-hit-by-stronger-dollar-miss-wall-street-expectations/

Greenberg, J. & Elliott, C. (Eds.). (2013). *Communication in question: Competing perspectives on controversial issues in communication studies* (2nd ed.). Toronto, ON: Nelson Education.

Haight, M., Quan-Haase, A., & Corbett, B. (2014). Revisiting the digital divide in Canada: The impact of demographic factors on access to the internet, level of online activity, and social networking site usage. *Information, Communication & Society, 17*(4), 503–519.

Hargittai, E., & Hsieh, Y. P. (2012). Succinct survey measures of web-use skills. *Social Science Computer Review, 30*(1), 95–107. http://doi.org/10.1177/0894439310397146

Henning, C. (2017). Theories of culture in the Frankfurt School of critical theory. In M. J. Thompson (Ed.), *The Palgrave handbook of critical theory* (pp. 255–278). Wayne, NJ: Palgrave Macmillan.

Herman, E. S., & Chomsky, N. (1988). *Manufacturing consent: The political economy of the mass media*. New York: Pantheon Books.

Hesmondhalgh, D. (2013). *The cultural industries* (3rd ed.). London: Sage Publications.

Hills, M. (2015). *Veronica Mars*, fandom, and the "affective economics" of crowdfunding poachers. *New Media & Society, 17*(2), 183–197. doi:10.1177/1461444814558909

Hobbs, R. (1998). The seven great debates in the media literacy movement. *Journal of Communication, 48*(1), 16–32. http://doi.org/10.1093/joc/48.1.16

Howe, J. (2008). *Crowdsourcing: Why the power of the crowd is driving the future of business*. New York: Three Rivers Press.

Jenkins, H. (2006). *Convergence culture: Where old and new media collide*. New York: New York University Press.

Katz, E., & Lazarsfeld, P. (1955). *Personal influence: The part played by people in the flow of mass communications*. New York: The Free Press.

Koltay, T. (2011). The media and the literacies: Media literacy, information literacy, digital literacy. *Media, Culture & Society, 33*(2), 211–221. http://doi.org/10.1177/0163443710393382

Lindner, A. M. (2016). Editorial gatekeeping in citizen journalism. *New Media & Society*. https://doi.org/10.1177/1461444816631506

Livingstone, S. (2014). Developing social media literacy: How children learn to interpret risky opportunities on social network sites. *Communications (Sankt Augustin), 39*(3), 283–303. http://doi.org/10.1515/commun-2014-0113

Mascheroni, G., Ponte, C., Garmendia, M., Garitaonandia, C., & Murru, M. F. (2010). Comparing media coverage of online risks for children in southern European countries: Italy, Portugal and Spain. *International Journal of Media & Cultural Politics, 6*(1), 25–43.

Marshall, K. (2011). Generational change in paid and unpaid work. *Canadian Social Trends, 92* (Statistics Canada, Catalogue no.11-008-X). Retrieved from www.statcan.gc.ca/pub/11-008-x/2011002/article/11520-eng.htm

Marx, K. (1996). *Capital: Critique of political economy* (Vol. I). Washington, DC: Gateway Editions. (Original work published 1867)

Marx, K. (1998). The German ideology. In J. Rivkin & M. Ryan (Eds.), *Literary theory: An anthology* (2nd ed.) Malden, MA: Blackwell.

McClintock, P. (2016, January 13). Box office: "Star Wars" now unlikely to beat "Avatar" global record. *The Hollywood Reporter*. Retrieved from www.hollywoodreporter.com/news/force-awakens-avatar-new-star-855065

McLuhan, M., & Powers, B. (1989). *The global village: Transformations in world life and media in the 21st century*. Oxford: Oxford University Press.

Mejias, U. A., & Vokuev, N. E. (2017). Disinformation and the media: The case of Russia and Ukraine. *Media, Culture & Society*. https://doi.org/10.1177/0163443716686672

Miller, V. (2011). *Understanding digital culture*. London: Sage Publications

Mulvey, L. (1975). Visual pleasure and narrative cinema. *Screen, 16*(3), 6–18. doi:10.1093/screen/16.3.6

Newsom, J. S., & Costanzo, J. (Producers), Newsom, J. S. (Director). (2011, January 22). *Miss Representation* [Documentary]. United States: Girls' Club Entertainment.

O'Callaghan, J. (2015). *Ten biggest scientific hoaxes of 2015*. Retrieved from www.iflscience.com/10-biggest-hoaxes-2015

Oliveira, M. (2014, February 19). 10 million Canadians use Facebook on mobile daily. *The Globe and Mail*. Retrieved from www.theglobeandmail.com/technology/10-million-canadians-use-facebook-on-mobile-daily/article16976434/

Pavlik, J., & McIntosh, S. (2016). *Converging media: An introduction to mass communication* (5th ed.). New York: Oxford University Press.

Pax, S. (2003). *The Baghdad blog*. London: Atlantic.

Poitras, J. (2014). *Irving vs. Irving: Canada's feuding billionaires and the stories they won't tell*. Toronto, ON: Penguin Group.

Prensky, M. (2001). Digital natives, digital immigrants. *On the Horizon*. Retrieved from www.marcprensky.com/writing/Prensky - Digital Natives, Digital Immigrants - Part1.pdf

Quan-Haase, A. (2016). *Technology and society: Social networks, work, and inequality* (2nd ed.). Don Mills, ON: Oxford University Press.

Quan-Haase, A., & Brown, B. (2013). Uses and gratifications. In M. Danesi (Ed.), *Encyclopedia of Media and Communication* (pp. 688–692). Toronto, ON: University of Toronto Press.

Quan-Haase, A., Martin, K., & Schreurs, K. (2016). Interviews with digital seniors: Challenges and opportunities of everyday ICT use in the third age. *Information, Communication & Society*. http://dx.doi.org/10.1080/1369118X.2016.1140217

Rappaport, S. (2014, March 12). *Kickstarter funding brings "Veronica Mars" movie to life*. Retrieved from www.cnbc.com/2014/03/12/kickstarter-funding-brings-veronica-mars-movie-to-life.html

Richardson, N., & Wearing, S. (2014). *Gender in the media*. Houndmills, UK: Palgrave Macmillan.

Reuters. (2015, December 20). "Star Wars" blows past records, hauls in $250 million domestic, $517M global. Retrieved from www.cnbc.com/2015/12/19/star-wars-pulls-in-250-million-globally-on-opening-day-eyes-new-record.html

Schiller, H. I. (1992). *Mass communications and American empire* (2nd ed.) Boulder, CO: Westview Press.

Shirky, C. (2008). *Here comes everybody: The power of organizing without organizations*. New York: Penguin Press.

Shoalts, D. (2014, October 14). Hockey Night in Canada: How CBC lost it all. *The Globe and Mail*. Retrieved from www.theglobeandmail.com/sports/hockey/hockey-night-in-canada-how-cbc-lost-it-all/article21072643/?page=all

Smith, S. L., Choueiti, M., Pieper, K., Gillig, T., Lee, C., & DeLuca, D. (2015). Inequality in 700 popular films: Examining portrayals of character gender, race, & LGBT status from 2007 to 2014.

Media, Diversity, & Social Change Initiative. Retrieved from http://annenberg.usc.edu/pages/~/media/MDSCI/Inequality%20in%20700%20Popular%20Films%208215%20Final%20for%20Posting.ashx

Smythe, D. W. (1982). *Dependency road: Communications, capitalism, consciousness, and Canada*. Norwood, NJ: Ablex Publishing Corporation.

Statista. (2017). *Canada: Number of Facebook users 2018*. Retrieved from www.statista.com/statistics/282364/number-of-facebook-users-in-canada/

Tapscott, D., & Williams, A. D. (2006). *Wikinomics: How mass collaboration changes everything*. New York: Portfolio.

Webster, F. (2014). *Theories of the information society* (4th ed.). New York: Routledge.

Winseck, D. (2012). *Assessing the effects of the Bell-Astral acquisition on media ownership and concentration in Canada*. Ottawa, ON: Carelton University.

Winseck, D. (2014). *Media and internet concentration in Canada, 1984–2013*. Retrieved from www.cmcrp.org/media-and-internet-concentration-1984-2013/

Zephoria. (2017, July 6). *The top 20 valuable Facebook statistics – Updated July 2017*. Retrieved from https://zephoria.com/top-15-valuable-facebook-statistics/

Chapter 15

Anderson, G. F., & Hussey, P. S. (2000). Population aging: A comparison among industrialized countries. *Health Affairs, 19*(3), 191–203.

Araujo, E. S. P., Friedman, R. K., Camacho, L. A. B., Derrico, M., Moreira, R. I., Calvet, G. A., . . . & Grinsztejn, B. (2014). Cascade of access to interventions to prevent HIV mother to child transmission in the metropolitan area of Rio de Janeiro, Brazil. *Brazilian Journal of Infectious Diseases, 18*(3), 252–260.

Badger, E. (2014, April 15). Pollution is segregated, too. *Washington Post*. Retrieved from www.washingtonpost.com/news/wonkblog/wp/2014/04/15/pollution-is-substantially-worse-in-minority-neighborhoods-across-the-u-s/

Bartley, T. (2007). Institutional emergence in an era of globalization: The rise of transnational private regulation of labor and environmental conditions. *American Journal of Sociology, 113*(2), 297–351.

Bocquier, P. (2005). World urbanization prospects: An alternative to the UN model of projection compatible with the mobility transition theory. *Demographic Research, 12*, 197–236.

Bongaarts, J. (2009). Human population growth and the demographic transition. *Philosophical Transactions of the Royal Society B: Biological Sciences, 364* (1532), 2985–2990.

Bongaarts, J., & Bulatao, R. A. (Eds.) (2000). *Beyond six billion: Forecasting the world's population*. Washington, DC: National Academy Press.

Börsch-Supan, A. (2003). Labor market effects of population aging. *Labour, 17*(s1), 5–44.

Brook, R. D., Franklin, B., Cascio, W., Hong, Y., Howard, G., Lipsett, M., . . . & Tager, I. (2004). Air pollution and cardiovascular disease. *Circulation, 109*(21), 2655–2671.

Caldwell, J. C., Phillips, J. F., & Barkat-e-Khuda, T. C. (2002). The future of family planning programs. *Studies in Family Planning, 33*(1), 1–10.

Campbell, M. (2007). Why the silence on population? *Population and Environment, 28*(4/5), 237–246.

Canadian Environmental Law Association. (2008). *Pollution-Watch fact sheet*. Retrieved from www1.toronto.ca/city_of_toronto/social_development_finance__administration/files/pdf/pollutionwatch_toronto_fact_sheet.pdf

Coale, A. J. (1974). The history of the human population. *Scientific American, 231*(3), 40–51.

Cohen, B. (2006). Urbanization in developing countries: Current trends, future projections, and key challenges for sustainability. *Technology in Society, 28*(1), 63–80.

Cohen, J. E. (1995). How many people can the earth support? *The Sciences, 35*(6), 18–23.

Davis, K. (1945). The world demographic transition. *The Annals of the American Academy of Political and Social Science, 237*(1), 1–11.

Diamond, D. (2009). The impact of government incentives for hybrid-electric vehicles: Evidence from US states. *Energy Policy, 37*(3), 972–983.

Dietz, T., Rosa, E. A., & York, R. (2007). Driving the human ecological footprint. *Frontiers in Ecology and the Environment, 5*(1), 13–18.

Energy and Mines Ministers' Conference. (2013). *Canada – A global leader in renewable energy: Enhancing collaboration on renewable energy technologies*. Retrieved from www.nrcan.gc.ca/sites/www.nrcan.gc.ca/files/www/pdf/publications/emmc/renewable_energy_e.pdf

Fishlock, R. (2012). *Canada: Electronic waste regulation in Canada and extended producer responsibility*. Retrieved from www.mondaq.com/canada/x/160982/Waste+Management/Electronic+Waste+Regulation+In+Canada+And+Extended+Prod<>ucer+Responsibility

Gaard, G. (1993). Living interconnections with animals and nature. In G. Gaard, *Ecofeminism: Women, animals, nature* (pp. 1–12). Philadelphia, PA: Temple University Press.

Galea, S., Freudenberg, N., & Vlahov, D. (2005). Cities and population health. *Social Science & Medicine, 60*(5), 1017–1033.

Gans, H. J. (1962). *The urban villagers: Group and class in the life of Italians-Americans*. New York: Free Press of Glencoe.

Gereffi, G., Humphrey, J., & Sturgeon, T. (2005). The governance of global value chains. *Review of International Political Economy, 12*(1), 78–104.

Goffman, E. (2008). *Behavior in public places*. New York: Simon & Schuster.

Guthman, J. (2004). Back to the land: The paradox of organic food standards. *Environment and Planning A, 36*(3), 511–528.

Hardin, G. (1968). The tragedy of the commons. *Science, 162*(3859), 1243–1248.

Hargroves, K., Stasinopoulos, P., Desha, C., & Smith, M. (2007). *Engineering Sustainable Solutions Program: Industry practice portfolio-e-waste education courses*. The Natural Edge Project, Australia. Retrieved from http://www.naturaledgeproject.net/Sustainable_Energy_Solutions_Portfolio.aspx

Hodson, S. (2009, May 11). 3 ways to deal with e-waste. *The Inquisitr News*. Retrieved from www.inquisitr.com/23842/3-ways-to-deal-with-e-waste/human-health-20111001-1l2rr.html

Humphrey, C., Lewis, T., & Buttel, F. (2002). *Environment, energy and society: A new synthesis*. Belmont, CA: Wadsworth Publishing.

Kang, H-Y., & Schoenung, J. M. (2005). Electronic waste recycling: A review of US infrastructure and technology options. *Resources, Conservation and Recycling, 45*(4), 368–400.

Kavitha, B. D., & Gayathri, N. K. (2017). Urbanization in India. *International Journal of Scientific Research and Education, 5*(1). Retrieved from http://ijsae.in/index.php/ijsae/issue/view/4

Malthus, T. R. (1959). *Population: The first essay*. Ann Arbor: University of Michigan Press.

Maronese, N. (2014, November 26). Hyundai offers first Canadian-market hydrogen fuel-cell vehicle—*Autofocus*. Retrieved from www.autofocus.ca/news-events/news/hyundai-offers-first-canadian-market-hydrogen-fuel-cell-vehicle

McCarthy, S., & Semeniuk, I. (2015, March 18). Complete shift to renewable energy within Canada's reach, academics say. *The Globe and Mail*. Retrieved from www.theglobeandmail.com/news/politics/complete-shift-to-renewable-energy-within-canadas-reach-academics-say/article23513579

Meadows, D. H., Meadows, D. H., Randers, J., & Behrens III, W. W. (1972). *The limits to growth: A report to the club of Rome*. New York: Universe Books.

Morgan, S. P. & Taylor, M. G. (2006). Low fertility at the turn of the twenty-first century. *Annual Review of Sociology, 32,* 375–399.

Mortillaro, N. (2015, September 5). Electronic waste is piling up: Here's why you should care. *Global News*. Retrieved from http://globalnews.ca/news/2194391/electronic-waste-is-piling-up-heres-why-you-should-care/

Newell, P. (2001). Managing multinationals: The governance of investment for the environment. *Journal of International Development, 13*(7), 907–919.

O'Brien, N. (2011, October 2). Techno-trash poses dire threat to human health. *The Sydney Morning Herald*. Retrieved from www.smh.com.au/technology/technology-news/technotrash-poses-dire-threat-to-human-health-20111001-1l2rr.html

Perrow, C. (2011). *Normal accidents: Living with high-risk technologies*. Princeton, NJ: Princeton University Press. (Original work published 1984)

Population Reference Bureau (PRB). (2008, August 19). *2008 world population data sheet*. Retrieved from www.prb.org/Publications/Datasheets/2008/2008wpds.aspx

Putnam, R. D. (2001). *Bowling alone: The collapse and revival of American community*. New York: Simon & Schuster.

Puxley, C. (2015, January 29). Grinding poverty faced by Manitoba First Nations worst in country: Aboriginal Affairs documents. *APTN National News*. Retrieved from http://aptn.ca/news/2015/01/29/grinding-poverty-faced-manitoba-first-nations-worst-country-aboriginal-affairs-documents

Royal Geographic Society. (n.d.). *Who are most vulnerable to natural hazards?* Retrieved from http://21stcenturychallenges.org/who-are-most-vulnerable-to-natural-hazards/

Rynbrandt, L. J., & Deegan, M. J. (2002). The ecofeminist pragmatism of Caroline Bartlett Crane, 1896–1935. *The American Sociologist, 33*(3), 58–68.

Scoffield, H. (2012, June 22). Rio 20: Canada exits environmental summit "very happy" with lack of firm commitments for change. *The Huffington Post*. Retrieved from www.huffingtonpost.ca/2012/06/22/rio20-canada-peter-kent-environment-climate_n_1619612.html

Smith, K. (2013). *Environmental hazards: Assessing risk and reducing disaster*. New York: Routledge.

Stastna, K. (2014, April 12). *First Nations housing in dire need of overhaul*. Retrieved from www.cbc.ca/news/canada/first-nations-housing-in-dire-need-of-overhaul-1.981227.

Statistics Canada. (2013, November 26). Canadian internet use survey, 2012. *The Daily*. Retrieved from www.statcan.gc.ca/daily-quotidien/131126/dq131126d-eng.htm

Sullivan, J. (2014). Trash or treasure: Global trade and the accumulation of e-waste in Lagos, Nigeria. *Africa Today, 61*(1), 89–112.

Szasz, A. (2007). *Shopping our way to safety: How we changed from protecting the environment to protecting ourselves*. Minneapolis: University of Minnesota Press.

Toronto Community Housing. (2015). *Connected for success*. Retrieved from www.torontohousing.ca/connected+for+success

Umesi, N. O., & Onyia, S. (2008). Disposal of e-wastes in Nigeria: An appraisal of regulations and current practices. *The International Journal of Sustainable Development & World Ecology, 15*(6), 565–573.

United Nations. (2014, July 10). *World's population increasingly urban with more than half living in urban areas*. Retrieved from www.un.org/en/development/desa/news/population/world-urbanization-prospects-2014.html

UN Department of Economic and Social Affairs. (2009). *World fertility report 2009*. Retrieved from www.un.org/esa/population/publications/WFR2009_Web/Data/WFR2009_Report.pdf

UN Department of Economic and Social Affairs. (2014). *World urbanization prospectus: The 2014 revision highlights*. New York: UN.

UN Department of Economic and Social Affairs. (2015, July 29). *The world population prospects: 2015 revision*. Retrieved from www.un.org/en/development/desa/publications/world-population-prospects-2015-revision.html

UNESCO. (2015). *The United Nations world water development report 2015: Water for a sustainable world*. Retrieved from http://unesdoc.unesco.org/images/0023/002318/231823E.pdf

Waldie, P. (2012, June 19). Environmental summits lose value as past pledges go unmet. *The Globe and Mail*. Retrieved from www.theglobeandmail.com/news/politics/environmental-summits-lose-value-as-past-pledges-go-unmet/article4353692

Walkom, T. (2012, June 22). At Rio 20, Canada furiously backpedals on environment. *The Star (Toronto)*.

Wilson, C, & Pison, G. (2004). More than half of the global population lives where fertility is below replacement level. *Population and societies, 405,* 1–4.

York, R. (2006). Ecological paradoxes: William Stanley Jevons and the paperless office. *Human Ecology Review, 13*(2): 143–147.

Ziman, J. (2000). Postacademic science: Constructing knowledge with networks and norms. In U. Segerstråle (Ed.), *Beyond the science wars: The missing discourse about science and society* (pp. 135–154). Albany: State University of New York Press.

Chapter 16

Aberle, D. (1966). *The peyote religion among the Navaho* (2nd ed.). Chicago, IL: University of Chicago Press.

APTN National News. (2013, November 29). *Rocks, arrests and confrontations on NB highway as fracking fight escalates.* Retrieved from http://aptn.ca/news/2013/11/29/mikmaq-led-fracking-fight-continues-new-brunswick/

Bennett, W. L., & Segerberg, A. (2012). The logic of connective action: Digital media and the personalization of contentious politics. *Information, Communication & Society, 15*(5), 739–768.

Berg, M. (1994). *The age of manufactures, 1700–1820: Industry, innovation and work in Britain* (2nd ed.). London: Routledge.

Blumer, H. G. (1969). Collective behavior. In A. M. Lee (Ed.), *Principles of sociology* (3rd ed., pp. 65–121). New York: Barnes & Noble.

Bosi, L., Demetriou, C., & Malthaner, S. (2014). *Dynamics of political violence: A process-oriented perspective on radicalization and the escalation of political conflict.* Surrey, UK: Ashgate Publishing.

Buechler, S. M. (1999). *Social movements in advanced capitalism.* Oxford: Oxford University Press.

Burgen, S. (2015, March 26). Growth up, joblessness falling—Is Spain's crisis finally over? *The Guardian.* Retrieved from www.theguardian.com/world/2015/mar/26/bank-of-spain-economic-recovery-accelerating

Castells, M. (2015). *Networks of outrage and hope: Social movements in the Internet age* (2nd ed.). Cambridge, UK: Polity Press.

CBC News. (2013, January 5). *9 questions about Idle No More.* Retrieved from www.cbc.ca/news/canada/9-questions-about-idle-no-more-1.1301843

CBC News. (2017, January 21). *Toronto women marched in solidarity with the Women's March on Washington.* Retrieved from www.cbc.ca/news/canada/toronto/womens-march-toronto-1.3944896

Change.org. (2017). Retrieved from www.change.org

Chase, S. (2015, June 17). Cyberattack deals crippling blow to Canadian government websites. *The Globe and Mail.* Retrieved from www.theglobeandmail.com/news/national/canadian-government-websites-appear-to-have-been-attacked/article24997399

Cole, T. (2012, March). The white-savior industrial complex. *The Atlantic.* Retrieved from www.theatlantic.com/international/archive/2012/03/the-white-savior-industrial-complex/254843/

Corrigall-Brown, C. (2012). *Patterns of protest: Trajectories of participation in social movements.* Stanford, CA: Stanford University Press.

Devaney, J. (2013, October 22). Idle no more: Hints of global super-movement. *The Huffington Post.* Retrieved from www.huffingtonpost.com/jacob-devaney/idle-no-more-the-beauty-o_b_2393053.html

Dhruvarajan, V., & Vickers, V. (2002). *Race, gender, and nation: A global perspective.* Toronto, ON: University of Toronto Press.

Dudouet, V. (Ed.). (2015). *Civil resistance and conflict transformation: Transitions from armed to nonviolent struggle.* Oxfordshire, UK: Routledge.

Friedman, A., & Singer, P. W. (2014). *Cybersecurity and cyberwar: What everyone needs to know.* New York: Oxford University Press.

Gamson, J. (1995). Must identity movements self-destruct? A queer dilemma. *Social Problems, 42*(3), 390–407.

Green, A. (2015). *Video killed a star charity: The downfall of Invisible Children.* Retrieved from www.opencanada.org/features/video-killed-star-charity-downfall-invisible-children

Gruney, C. (2000). "A great cause": The origins of the anti-apartheid movement, June 1959–March 1960. *Journal of Southern African Studies, 26*(1), 123–144.

Habermas, J. (1984). *The theory of communicative action: Reason and rationalization of society.* Boston, MA: Beacon Press.

Hobsbawm, E. J. (1952). *Primitive rebels, studies in archaic forms of social movement in the 19th and 20th centuries.* Manchester, UK: Manchester University Press.

Hopper, R. D. (1950). The revolutionary process: A frame of reference for the study of revolutionary movements. *Social Forces, 28*(3), 270–279.

Huhndorf, S. M., & Suzack, C. (2010). Indigenous feminism: Theorizing the issues. In C. Suzack, S. M. Huhndorf, J. Perreault, & J. Barman (Eds.), *Indigenous women and feminism: Politics, activism, culture* (pp. 1–17). Vancouver, BC: UBC Press.

Invisible Children. (2012, March 5). *Kony 2012* [Video file]. Retrieved from www.youtube.com/watch?v=Y4MnpzG5Sqc

Invisible Children. (2012, July 9). *Schools for schools: Building opportunities.* Retrieved from http://invisiblechildren.com/blog/2012/07/09/schools-for-schools-building-opportunities

Invisible Children. (2014, December 23). *Invisible Children programs continuing in 2015.* [Blog post] Retrieved from http://invisiblechildren.com/blog/2014/12/23/invisible-children-programs-continuing-2015

Klein, N. (2014). *This changes everything: Capitalism vs. the climate.* Toronto, ON: Alfred A. Knopf Canada.

Krieg, G. J. (2011, June 29). New York anti-street harassment group asks women to Hollaback! *ABC News.* Retrieved from http://abcnews.go.com/WhatWouldYouDo/construction-workers-harass-woman/story?id=12508548

Leddy, L. C. (2016). Indigenous women and the franchise. In *The Canadian Encyclopedia.* Retrieved from www.thecanadianencyclopedia.ca/en/article/indigenous-women-and-the-franchise/

Maslin, M. (2014). *Climate change: a very short introduction* (3rd ed.). Oxford: Oxford University Press.

McAdam, D. (1999). *Political process and the development of black insurgency, 1930–1970* (2nd ed.). Chicago, IL: University of Chicago Press.

McCarthy, J. D., & Zald, M. N. (1977). Resource mobilization and social movements: A partial theory. *American Journal of Sociology, 82*(6), 1212–1241.

Melucci, A. (1988). Getting involved: Identity and mobilization in social movements. *International Social Movement Research, 1*(26), 329–348.

Miller, F. D. (1999). The end of SDS and the emergence of Weatherman: Demise through success. In J. Freeman & V. Johnson (Eds.), *Waves of protest: Social movements since the sixties* (pp. 303–324). Lanham, MD: Rowman & Littlefield.

Miller, V. (2011). *Understanding digital culture.* London: Sage Publications.

Minsky, A. (2015, June 17). "Anonymous" claims responsibility for cyber attack that shut down government websites. *Global News*. Retrieved from http://globalnews.ca/news/2060036/government-of-canada-servers-suffer-cyber-attack

Moore, B. (1993). *Social origins of dictatorship and democracy: Lord and peasant in the making of the modern world*. Boston, MA: Beacon Press.

New Energy Movement. (n.d.). Retrieved from www.newenergymovement.org

Nikiforuk, A. (2001). *Saboteurs: Wiebo Ludwig's war against big oil*. Toronto, ON: Macfarlane Walter & Ross.

Paxton, P. (2000). Women's suffrage in the measurement on democracy: Problems of operationalization. *Studies in Comparative International Development, 55*, 92–111.

Pichardo, N. A. (1997). New social movements: A critical review. *Annual Review of Sociology, 23*, 411–430.

Poell, T. (2013). Social media and the transformation of activist communication: Exploring the social media ecology of the 2010 Toronto G20 protests. *Information, Communication & Society, 17*(6), 716–731.

Porta, D. D., & Diani, M. (2006). *Social movements: An introduction* (2nd ed.). Maiden, MA: Blackwell.

Quan-Haase, A. (2016). *Technology and society: Social networks, work, and inequality* (2nd ed.). Don Mills, ON: Oxford University Press.

Rheingold, H. (2002). *Smart mobs: the next social revolution*. Cambridge, MA: Perseus Publishing.

Schomerus, M., Allen, T., & Vlassenroot, K. (2012, March 13). Kony 2012 and the prospects for change. *Foreign Affairs*. Retrieved from www.foreignaffairs.com/articles/africa/2012-03-13/kony-2012-and-prospects-change

Schussman, A., & Soule, S. A. (2005). Process and protest: Accounting for individual protest participation. *Social Forces, 84*(2), 1083–1108.

Smelser, N. J. (1962). *Theory of collective behavior*. New York: The Free Press.

Smith, W. (2013). *Civil disobedience and deliberative democracy*. London: Routledge.

Staggenborg, S. (2015). *Social movements* (3rd ed.). Don Mills, ON: Oxford University Press.

Strong-Boag, V. (2016). Women's suffrage in Canada. In *The Canadian Encyclopedia*. Retrieved from www.thecanadianencyclopedia.ca/en/article/suffrage/

Tester, J. W., Drake, E. M., Driscoll, M. J., Golay, M. W., & Peters, W. A. (2012). *Sustainable energy: Choosing among options* (2nd ed.). Cambridge, MA: MIT Press.

Thörn, H. (2012). Anti-apartheid movement. In H. K. Anheier & M. Juergensmeyer (Eds.), *Encyclopedia of global studies* (Vols. 1–4). Thousand Oaks, CA: Sage. Retrieved from http://dx.doi.org/10.4135/9781452218557.n21

Tilly, C. (1986). European violence and collective action since 1700. *Social Research, 53*(1), 159–184.

Tilly, C., & Wood, L. J. (2016). *Social movements 1768–2012* (3rd ed.). New York: Paradigm Publishing.

Tremblay, M., & Trimble, L. (Ed.). (2003). *Women and electoral politics in Canada*. Oxford: Oxford University Press.

The Truth. (2017). *Join the cause: Enlist*. Retrieved from www.thetruth.com

Woods, M. (2013, October 22). Can 13-point Aboriginal declaration serve as real roadmap for Idle No More's demands? *National Post*. Retrieved from http://news.nationalpost.com/news/canada/can-13-point-aboriginal-declaration-serve-as-real-roadmap-for-idle-no-mores-demands

York, D. (Director). (2011). *Wiebo's war* [Documentary]. Canada: National Film Board of Canada.

Zhuo, X., Wellman, B., & Yu, J. (2011). Egypt: The first Internet revolt? *Peace Magazine, 27*(3). Retrieved from http://peacemagazine.org/archive/v27n3p06.htm

Index